PROGRAMMING IN C#

HARSH BHASIN

Assistant Professor
Department of Computer Science
Jamia Hamdard
New Delhi

OXFORD

UNIVERSITY PRESS

Oxford University Press is a department of the University of Oxford.
It furthers the University's objective of excellence in research, scholarship,
and education by publishing worldwide. Oxford is a registered trade mark of
Oxford University Press in the UK and in certain other countries.

Published in India by
Oxford University Press
YMCA Library Building, 1 Jai Singh Road, New Delhi 110001, India

© Oxford University Press 2014

The moral rights of the author/s have been asserted.

First published in 2014

All rights reserved. No part of this publication may be reproduced, stored in
a retrieval system, or transmitted, in any form or by any means, without the
prior permission in writing of Oxford University Press, or as expressly permitted
by law, by licence, or under terms agreed with the appropriate reprographics
rights organization. Enquiries concerning reproduction outside the scope of the
above should be sent to the Rights Department, Oxford University Press, at the
address above.

You must not circulate this work in any other form
and you must impose this same condition on any acquirer.

ISBN-13: 978-0-19-809740-2
ISBN-10: 0-19-809740-9

Typeset in Times New Roman
by Cameo Corporate Services Limited, Chennai
Printed in India by India Binding House, Noida 201301

To
My Mother

Features of the Book

PART ONE
Introduction to C#, .NET, and Procedural Programming

PART TWO
Object Oriented Programming

PART THREE
COM and Advanced Topics

Span of Coverage
The book provides detailed coverage of procedural programming, object oriented programming, and Windows programming—starting from basics to advanced concepts. It entails dedicated chapters on advanced topics such as data connectivity, networking, deployment, and introduction to WPF and WCF.

6 Collections

16 Generics

20 Common Dialogs

In-depth treatment
Topics such as generics and collections, basic and advanced Windows forms, and controls and common dialogs are covered in-depth which will help students develop their own projects.

Program
```
static void Main(string[] args)
{
    char[] name = {'h', 'a', 'r', 's', 'h'};
    String s = new String(name, 1, 3);
    Console.WriteLine(s);
    Console.ReadKey();
}
```
Output
```
ars
```

Program Codes with Output
Numerous program codes along with outputs and description are provided throughout the text to illustrate the implementation of the concepts.

Features of the Book **v**

Projects
The book includes projects on *Finding IP Addresses Entered by a User, Greedy Approach, Notepad, Online Voting System,* and *Genetic Algorithms* to show the implementation of the concepts covered in various chapters of the book.

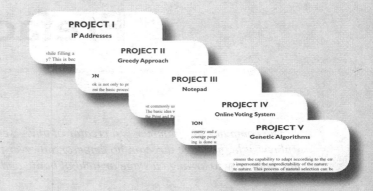

GLOSSARY

Array It is a linear data structure that has elements identified by an index. The elements of an array are of the same type.
Linear search It is the process of searching for an element by examining each and every position of an array.
Jagged array It is an array whose elements are arrays. The elements of a jagged array can be of unequal sizes.

Sorting It is the process of arr order. A sorted array is called $a_i + j$} is such that for every decreasing if {$a_i + j, a_i + (j - 1)$. for every value of $i, a_i + j < a_j$.

Glossary
A glossary of key terms along with definitions is given at the end of each chapter to help readers to quickly memorize important concepts.

POINTS TO REMEMBER

Points to Remember
Points to remember given at the end of each chapter as bulleted points will help readers quickly revise all the important concepts explained in that chapter.

- A form is the basic unit of a C# Windows Application project.
- The look and feel of a form can be changed by changing the settings of its properties.
- The Snap lines give us visual support in locating the controls and in setting their relative alignment.
- The Anchor property sets the distances from the edge of the control.

I. Multiple-choice Questions
1. Which of the following are data types in C#
    (a) Value type (b) Reference typ
    (c) Both (a) and (b) (d) None of these
2. Which of the following is not a type of struc

II. Review Questions
1. Explain the concept of out parameters with the help of an example.
2. Explain the concept of call by reference with the help of

III. Programming Exercises
1. Ask the user to enter a three-digit number and calculate the sum of its digits.
2. Ask the user to enter a three-digit number and reverse the number.

Exercises
Objective type Questions (Multiple Choice and True/False questions with answers given as appendix) provided at the end of each chapter will help readers self-test their understanding and also prepare for competitive examinations.

Numerous review questions test a reader's conceptual knowledge. Programming exercises will help readers apply and implement the learnt concepts thereby enhancing their programming skills.

Preface

The computer programmer is a creator of universes for which he alone is the lawgiver. No playwright, no stage director, no emperor, however powerful, has ever exercised such absolute authority to arrange a stage or field of battle and to command such unswervingly dutiful actors or troops.

Joseph Weizenbaum

Programmers and developers have an important role to play in the IT industry. Becoming an accomplished programmer is a Herculean task as it requires immense hard work and programming acumen. A good programmer should be able to identify problems in the existing programming methodologies and accordingly devise solutions for such problems. Even to become an efficient tester, one must be equipped with a fundamental knowledge of programming. Hence, the knowledge of programming forms the backbone of all the technology development processes in the IT industry. Thus, this book is an effort towards enhancing your core programming skills in C#.

C# is a simple and powerful language developed by Microsoft Inc. It is chiefly used for developing applications in the .NET Framework. It has many features of C and C++, which makes it easier to learn for most of the readers who are already familiar with these languages. Simultaneously, all the deficiencies of these languages have been taken care of by intelligently making use of certain Java language features.

Microsoft spent a lot of resources on the development of C# and .NET Framework and added several new features like operator overloading, thus making it superior to Java. C# has many prefabricated classes which makes it suitable for a variety of applications not limited to scientific nature only. The .NET Framework includes features, such as Mobile Application development, Windows Communication Foundation (WCF), and Windows Presentation Foundation (WPF), which make the framework much superior to its competitors. In the recent times, the .NET Framework is being widely used for applications development in the IT industry. Hence, learning C# will certainly help students in pursuing a professional career in this field.

ABOUT THE BOOK

Programming in C# is designed as a textbook for the undergraduate and postgraduate students of computer science engineering, information technology, and computer applications. The book will also serve as a useful reference for researchers and programmers who intend to pursue a professional career in C# programming. It can also be used by those who do have a prior programming knowledge. The importance of .NET Framework and C# can be gauged by the fact that C# has become the language of choice for Windows and Web development.

This book covers all three segments of programming in C# starting from the language basics, followed by the object oriented programming concepts and finally the component object model (COM). It also covers advanced topics, namely, data connectivity, ASP.NET, networking, deployment, WPF, and WCF. It explains every concept comprehensively and also in an easy-to-understand manner. Moreover, intricate concepts have been explained along with their syntax, programs, and with numerous solved problems.

KEY FEATURES OF THE BOOK

Following are some of the key features of the book:

- Provides comprehensive coverage of all the topics including procedural programming, object oriented concepts, and Windows programming in an easy-to-understand and lucid manner.
- Offers an in-depth treatment of topics such as generics and collections, basic and advanced Windows Forms, and controls and common dialogs.
- Entails dedicated chapters on data connectivity, networking, deployment, and introduction to WPF and WCF.
- Includes projects on *Finding IP Addresses entered by a User, Greedy Approach, Notepad, Online Voting System,* and *Genetic Algorithms* to show the implementation of the concepts covered in various chapters of the book.
- Provides numerous solved programming problems along with their outputs to help students easily assimilate the concepts learnt.
- Provides *points to remember* and a *glossary* with definitions of the key terms at the end of each chapter which will help readers to quickly memorize important concepts.
- Includes a variety of end-chapter exercises in the form of objective type questions (with answers), review questions, and programming exercises to test the understanding of the theory.

ORGANIZATION OF THE BOOK

The book consists of 25 chapters which have been divided into three parts. A chapter-wise scheme of topics in the book is as follows.

Part One of the book examines the .NET Framework and procedural programming. This part lays a foundation for the C# course. Although Visual C# is used for creating most of the projects in the professional arena, knowledge of procedural programming is also considered equally important and forms the very basis of creation of a Visual C# project.

Chapter 1 introduces the .NET Framework. The chapter discusses the basics of Microsoft intermediate language, JIT compiler, and assemblies. It also presents the significance of .NET key components such as CLS, FCL, and CLR. Knowledge of these components is frequently tested in technical interviews and hence the discussion is intended to develop students' confidence to intelligently tackle such interviews. Moreover, the chapter tells how to create a basic project.

Chapter 2 examines the structure of a C# program. Each component of a C# program has been explained in this chapter. This chapter also introduces the concept of compilation. *Chapter 3* explains the concept of data types and their classifications which are required while writing a program. The chapter also throws light on keywords, variables, type conversation, and operators and their classification. All operators and mathematical functions have been explained for better understanding. Topics such as scope of a variable and type casting have also been covered. A brief description of logic gates in the form of an annexure is provided at the end of this chapter.

Chapter 4 discusses the conditional statements. The `if`, `if-else`, nested `if-else` and other conditional statements have been explained and exemplified in the chapter. The chapter also introduces the `switch` case construct. These constructs help in decision making and are essential for any successful project preparation.

The concept of looping has been introduced in *Chapter 5*. This chapter also explains the creation of patterns. Although pattern creation is seldom used in a real project, they give an idea of how to use a particular loop in order to carry out a task. The chapter also examines the `break`, `continue`, and `goto` statements.

Chapter 6 discusses the concept of collections which is not a feature of C and C++ but a special feature of C#. In this chapter, collections have been used to implement important data structures such as stacks, queues, directories, etc. The chapter ends with a project on *IP Addresses*. This project serves as an illustration of concepts discussed till chapter 6. It aims at finding the class of the IP address entered by the user and not for finding the IP address of a computer.

Chapter 7 examines methods. The chapter explains return type, parameters and their types in detail. The chapter introduces two topics: the out parameters and delegates. It is essential to know these topics before starting with a visual project. The concept of recursion has also been explained in this chapter.

Chapter 8 deals with the concept of strings. Each method of a `string` class has been discussed in detail in this chapter. Such methods are commonly used while developing a text processor or a compiler. *Chapter 9* examines arrays. Apart from the essential topics such as 1D, 2D, multi-dimensional and jagged arrays, the chapter also explains use of arrays in linear search and sorting. The chapter ends with a project on greedy approach, a popular algorithmic approach. The concept has been explained by taking examples of job sequencing and knapsack problems.

Chapter 10 is on structures and enumerations. This chapter begins with the description of the importance of structures and its syntax and use. The chapter explains about the concept of properties and nested structures along with its utility. It also exemplifies the concepts of structures through a complex number calculator. The complex number calculator implements the basic functions of complex numbers using structures. It is an important chapter as the concept of structures will also help in understanding Part Two of the book. The chapter also briefly covers the concept of enumerations.

Part Two of the book is devoted to object oriented programming concepts. This part has seven chapters. The aim of this part is not only to explain the creation and usage of a class but also to apply the concept of OOP while developing projects.

Chapter 11 explains the concept of classes and also introduces class diagrams. It is important to think and analyse a problem and then design the class diagrams before writing a program. The chapter also explains the use of each type of constructor. Finally, the chapter introduces various concepts of object oriented programming which are further explained in detail in the subsequent chapters.

Chapter 12 introduces the concept of inheritance. The various types of inheritance have been explained in this chapter. Since C# does not allow multiple inheritance, the important features of multiple inheritance have been retained by including the concept of interfaces. *Chapter 13* explains interfaces and their use.

The developers of Java ignored an essential part of OOP, which is operator overloading. C#, however, has included this important concept in *Chapter 14*. This chapter examines this concept by taking an example of complex numbers. The chapter also explains the different types of operator overloading.

Chapter 15 elucidates the concepts of errors and exceptions. The chapter includes discussion on various types of errors and also exception handling which helps us to make good quality robust software.

Chapter 16 continues with the discussion of collections explained in Chapter 6. This chapter explains generics. The data structures implemented in Chapter 6 have been revisited in this chapter. The knowledge of OOP, discussed in the earlier chapters in Part Two, would help you to deal with the same data structure in a better way.

Mastering the concepts discussed in Chapters 1–16 is perhaps the beginning point of making real software. At this point the knowledge of threads will help in tackling the situations wherein more than one task is to be performed by a single program in such a way that deadlocks are avoided. *Chapter 17* explains the concept of threads in detail. However, it would be better to refresh the basics of operating system before starting the chapter.

Part Three of the book deals with Windows Forms, controls and dialogs, and advanced features. The chapters detailed in this part give an idea of form development in Visual C# and associated complexities. The chapters discussed in this part will be helpful in making a Visual C# project.

Chapter 18, the first chapter of this part, explains the basic concepts of Windows programming such as snap lines, anchor, dock and controls. *Chapter 19* carries forward the discussion and examines some more advanced controls—Panel Control, Tab Control, SplitContainer Control, DateTimePicker Control, MenuStrip Control, ToolStrip Control, Browser Control, etc.

To be able to make applications like a text processor, dialogs, textboxes, etc. are needed. *Chapter 20* introduces dialogs and their usage. A project on creation of notepad is also illustrated in this chapter. Although only basic functionalities have been incorporated in the notepad, the project paves way for the creation of an evolved notepad

Chapter 21 exemplifies data connectivity by web sites and client applications. It introduces ADO.NET. The applications that are developed in Visual C# can be connected to a database using ADO.NET. The chapter illustrates a practical application for creating individual management system.

Chapter 22 introduces ASP.NET. The chapter explains the creation of a Web Form using ASP.NET. Other related concepts such as user control, server control, common HTML tags, creating a user form and creating database in SQL Express have also been dealt with in the chapter. The application of concepts learnt in this chapter is illustrated through a project on *Online Voting System*. This project will also inspire students to create many such websites on their own. *Chapter 23* examines the implementation of clients and servers in C#. The chapter also introduces the concept of remoting which would be detailed further in Chapter 25.

Chapter 24 will help students to create a setup file for the application developed. This is essential for becoming a professional C# client side programmer. *Chapter 25* introduces WCF and WPF and relates these topics with GDI+, remoting, and web services. The chapter ends with a project to create a tool which implements genetic algorithms. The students can generate the initial population, either binary or in hexadecimal, using this tool. The crossover and mutation operations have also been implemented in this project. The project is meant to motivate students to create their own applications based on any of the optimization problems given at the end of this project.

Answers to objective type questions are given in an appendix at the end of the book.

ONLINE RESOURCES

To aid teachers and students, the book is accompanied with online resources which are available at *http://oupinheonline.com/book/bhasin-programming-c/9780198097402*. The content for the online resources are as follows:

For Instructors
- Chapter-wise PowerPoint slides

For Students
- Assignment Questions for each chapter
- Additional Projects (*Hindi–Marathi Converter, Knapsack problem, Web page Similarity, Travelling Salesman problem, and Student management*)
- Source codes of all the programs and projects given in the book

ACKNOWLEDGEMENTS

I have been very fortunate for getting the opportunity to work under the guidance of highly learned seniors. A special thanks to Prof. A. K. Sharma, Former Head, Department of Computer Science and Engineering, YMCA University of Science and Technology, Faridabad for his constant motivation. Without his encouraging words, I may not have successfully completed this book. I would also like to thank esteemed Prof. P. B. Sharma, Vice Chancellor, Delhi Technological University, for showing confidence in me during my formative years in DTU. I am also very grateful to Dr Daya Gupta, Head and Dr Ruchika Malhotra, Assistant Prof., Department of Computer Science and Engineering, DTU for providing their support and encouragement.

I am also very thankful to the editorial team at Oxford University Press for providing valuable assistance.

I would like to express my sincere gratitude to my family, including my pets, Zoe and Xena, and friends for showering their unconditional warmth and support on me.

I would be very glad to receive your comments or suggestions which can be incorporated in the future editions of this book. You can reach me by email at i_harsh_bhasin@yahoo.com.

Harsh Bhasin

Brief Contents

Features of the Book iv

Preface vi

PART ONE Introduction to C#, .NET, and Procedural Programming 1

    1. Introduction to .NET Framework 3
    2. Basics of C# 20
    3. Data Types and Operators 38
    4. Conditional Statements 76
    5. Loops 100
    6. Collections 123
    7. Methods 143
    8. Strings 162
    9. Arrays 178
    10. Structures and Enumerations 212

PART TWO Object Oriented Programming 233

    11. Classes and Objects 235
    12. Inheritance 265
    13. Interfaces 289
    14. Operator Overloading 302
    15. Errors and Exceptions 319
    16. Generics 336
    17. Threads 352

PART THREE Component Object Model and Advanced Topics 367

    18. Windows Forms and Basic Controls 369
    19. Advanced Controls and Menus 398
    20. Common Dialogs 421
    21. Data Connectivity 441
    22. Introduction to ASP.NET 463
    23. Networking 513
    24. Deployment 527
    25. Towards WPF and WCF 543

Answers to Objective Type Questions 586

Index 589

Detailed Contents

Features of the Book iv

Preface vi

PART ONE: INTRODUCTION TO C#, .NET, AND PROCEDURAL PROGRAMMING

1. Introduction to .NET Framework 3

1.1 Introduction 3
1.2 Basics of .NET Framework 4
    1.2.1 Microsoft Intermediate Language 4
    1.2.2 Just-in-Time Compiler 4
    1.2.3 Assemblies 5
    1.2.4 Managed Code 5
    1.2.5 Metadata 5
    1.2.6 Reflection 5
    1.2.7 Garbage Collection 6
1.3 Components of Microsoft .NET 6
    1.3.1 Common Language Specification 6
    1.3.2 Framework Class Library 6
    1.3.3 Common Language Runtime 7
    1.3.4 .NET Tools 7
1.4 Architecture of .NET Framework 7
    1.4.1 ASP.NET 8
    1.4.2 Windows Presentation Foundation 8
    1.4.3 Windows Communication Foundation 8
    1.4.4 Cross-language Interoperability 8
    1.4.5 Runtime Hosts 9
    1.4.6 Security 9
    1.4.7 ADO.NET 9
1.5 Various Languages in .NET Framework 10
    1.5.1 C# 10
    1.5.2 F# 10
    1.5.3 ASP.NET 10
    1.5.4 VB.NET 10
1.6 Introduction to Microsoft Visual Studio 10
    1.6.1 Solution Explorer 11
    1.6.2 Server Explorer 11
    1.6.3 Error List 12
    1.6.4 Toolbox 13
    1.6.5 Properties Window 13
1.7 Developing Projects in Visual Studio 14
    1.7.1 Linking 14
    1.7.2 Types of Applications 14
    1.7.3 Steps for Creating a Windows Application 14
    1.7.4 Steps for Creating a Console Application 15
1.8 Benefits of .NET Framework 16
1.9 C# .NET Framework and C++ 17

2. Basics of C# 20

2.1 Introduction 20
2.2 Writing a Program 21
2.3 Program Structure 22
    2.3.1 Documentation 22
    2.3.2 Methods of Writing Statements 23
    2.3.3 Interface 24
    2.3.4 Class Definition 25
    2.3.5 Namespaces 25
    2.3.6 Output 25
    2.3.7 Input 25
    2.3.8 Main Method 26

2.4	Concept of Main Method	26		3.12	Classification of Operators	51
2.5	Multiple Main Methods in a Program	27			3.12.1 Unary, Binary, and Ternary Operators 51	
2.6	Using Specific Functions	29			3.12.2 Arithmetic Operators 52	
2.7	Comments	30			3.12.3 Relational Operators 52	
	2.7.1 Single-line Comments 31				3.12.4 Logical and Bitwise Operators 54	
	2.7.2 Multiple-line Comments 31				3.12.5 Assignment Operators 57	
2.8	Command Line Arguments	32		3.13	Default Values	58
2.9	Compilation Process	33		3.14	Constant Variables	58

3. Data Types and Operators 38

3.1	Introduction to Data Types	38		3.15	Scope of Variable	59
3.2	Value Types and Their Properties	40		3.16	Type Casting	60
				3.17	Mathematical Functions	61
3.3	Integral Types	40			3.17.1 Abs Function 61	
3.4	Floating Point or Decimal Types	40			3.17.2 Inverse Trigonometric Functions 61	
3.5	String Type	41			3.17.3 Trigonometric and Hyperbolic Functions 62	
3.6	Reference Types	42			3.17.4 Ceiling Function 62	
3.7	Classes and Objects	42			3.17.5 Floor Function 62	
3.8	Keywords	43			3.17.6 DivRem Function 62	
3.9	Variables	43			3.17.7 Max Function 63	
	3.9.1 Rules for Naming Variables 44				3.17.8 Min Function 63	
	3.9.2 Type Conversion 44				3.17.9 Pow Function 63	
	3.9.3 Boxing and Unboxing 45				3.17.10 Round Function 63	
3.10	Operators	45			3.17.11 Sign Function 64	
3.11	Important Operators of C#	46			3.17.12 Truncate Function 64	
	3.11.1 Dot (.) Operator 46				3.17.13 Sqrt Function 64	
	3.11.2 () Operator 47				3.17.14 Constants 64	
	3.11.3 [] Operator 47			3.18	Arithmetic Expressions	65
	3.11.4 ++ Operator 47			3.19	Precedence of Operators	67
	3.11.5 -- Operator 48			*Annexure: logic Gates*		73
	3.11.6 new Operator 48					

4. Conditional Statements 76

	3.11.7 typeof Operator 48			4.1	Introduction	76
	3.11.8 checked Keyword 48			4.2	if Statement	78
	3.11.9 -> Operator 49			4.3	if-else Statement	80
	3.11.10 + Operator 49			4.4	Nested if-else	83
	3.11.11 - Operator 49			4.5	if-else Ladder	85
	3.11.12 ! Operator 49			4.6	Dangling else	88
	3.11.13 ~ Operator 50			4.7	Problem with Floating Point Numbers	88
	3.11.14 & Operator 50			4.8	Use of && and || operators	89
	3.11.15 sizeof Operator 50			4.9	Conditional Statement	91
	3.11.16 * Operator 50			4.10	switch Statement: What Can Be Done and What Cannot Be Done	92
	3.11.17 / Operator 51					
	3.11.18 % Operator 51					

5. Loops — 100

- 5.1 Introduction — 100
- 5.2 `while` Loop — 101
- 5.3 `do` Loop — 102
- 5.4 `for` Loop — 103
- 5.5 `foreach` Loop — 104
- 5.6 Loop within Loop — 105
- 5.7 Patterns — 105
- 5.8 Working in Integrated Development Environment — 109
- 5.9 `break` and `continue` Keywords — 111
- 5.10 `goto` Statement — 113
- 5.11 Comparison of Loops — 116

6. Collections — 123

- 6.1 Introduction — 123
- 6.2 Stack — 124
  - 6.2.1 *Static Implementation of Stack* — 124
  - 6.2.2 `System.Collections.Stack` — 125
- 6.3 Queue — 126
  - 6.3.1 *Static Implementation of Queue* — 126
  - 6.3.2 `System.Collections.Queue` — 127
- 6.4 Directories — 128
  - 6.4.1 *Student Management by Directories* — 128
- 6.5 Lazy type — 131
- 6.6 `HashSet` — 133

Project I: IP Addresses — 136

7. Methods — 143

- 7.1 Introduction — 143
- 7.2 Signature: Parameters, Name, and Modifiers — 144
- 7.3 Syntax — 145
- 7.4 Calling a Method — 146
- 7.5 Return Type of a Method — 147
- 7.6 Parameters — 148
- 7.7 Variable Parameters — 150
- 7.8 Types of Parameters — 151
  - 7.8.1 *Value and Reference Parameters* — 151
  - 7.8.2 *Out Parameters* — 153
- 7.9 Method Overloading — 154
- 7.10 Recursion — 155
- 7.11 Delegates — 158

8. Strings — 162

- 8.1 Introduction — 162
- 8.2 Creating Strings — 163
  - 8.2.1 *Using* `StringBuilder` *Class* — 163
  - 8.2.2 *Using* `String` *Class* — 164
  - 8.2.3 *Verbatim Strings* — 164
- 8.3 Constructors of `String` Class — 165
- 8.4 Operators for `Strings` and `Compare` Method — 166
  - 8.4.1 *!= Operator* — 167
  - 8.4.2 *== Operator* — 167
- 8.5 Common Methods of `String` Class — 168
- 8.6 Manipulation of Array of Strings — 169
- 8.7 Use of `ToCharArray()` — 170
- 8.8 Building Strings Efficiently — 171
- 8.9 Regular Expressions — 172

9. Arrays — 178

- 9.1 Introduction — 178
- 9.2 Linear Search — 184
- 9.3 Sorting — 186
- 9.4 Two-dimensional Arrays — 190
- 9.5 Multidimensional Arrays — 195
- 9.6 Jagged Arrays — 196
- 9.7 `System.Array` Class — 198
- 9.8 `System.Arraylist` Class — 200

Project II: Greedy Approach — 203

10. Structures and Enumerations — 212

- 10.1 Introduction — 212
- 10.2 A Simple Structure — 213
- 10.3 Defining a Structure — 213
- 10.4 Instantiation — 214
- 10.5 Accessing Elements of a Structure — 214
- 10.6 Initialization and Properties — 216
- 10.7 Nested Structures — 217
- 10.8 Methods Inside Structures — 219

10.9	Array of Structures	219	10.11 Complex Number Calculator	222
10.10	Differences between Structures and Classes	221	10.12 Enumerations	226

PART TWO: OBJECT ORIENTED PROGRAMMING

11. Classes and Objects — 235

- 11.1 Introduction — 235
- 11.2 Definition and Design of a Class: Adding Variables and Methods — 236
  - 11.2.1 Syntax — 236
  - 11.2.2 Instantiation — 237
- 11.3 Array of Objects — 241
- 11.4 Constructors — 245
  - 11.4.1 Default Constructor — 245
  - 11.4.2 Parameterized Constructor — 246
  - 11.4.3 Copy Constructor — 247
  - 11.4.4 Constructor Overloading — 249
  - 11.4.5 Private Constructor — 250
  - 11.4.6 Destructor — 251
- 11.5 this Reference — 251
- 11.6 Static Members — 251
- 11.7 Constant Members — 252
- 11.8 Passing Objects to a Function — 252
- 11.9 Basics of Object-oriented Programming — 253
  - 11.9.1 Objects — 253
  - 11.9.2 Classes and Metaclasses — 254
  - 11.9.3 Classes and Interfaces — 254
  - 11.9.4 Aggregation — 254
  - 11.9.5 Specialization and Inheritance — 254
  - 11.9.6 Polymorphism — 255
  - 11.9.7 Overloading — 256
- 11.10 Access Levels — 256
- 11.11 Components of a Class — 258
- 11.12 Properties — 259
- 11.13 Indexers — 260

12. Inheritance — 265

- 12.1 Introduction — 265
- 12.2 Visibility Control — 266
- 12.3 Types of Inheritance — 267
- 12.4 Simple Inheritance: Defining Subclass Methods and Constructors — 268
- 12.5 Multilevel Inheritance — 272
- 12.6 Hierarchical Inheritance — 276
- 12.7 Overriding Methods — 279
- 12.8 Abstract Classes and Methods — 281
- 12.9 Sealed Classes and Methods — 282
- 12.10 Runtime Polymorphism — 283

13. Interfaces — 289

- 13.1 Introduction — 289
- 13.2 Interfaces — 290
  - 13.2.1 Definition and Syntax — 290
  - 13.2.2 Abstract Classes and Interface — 292
- 13.3 Interface Extending an Interface — 293
- 13.4 Explicit Implementation — 295
- 13.5 as Operator — 296

14. Operator Overloading — 302

- 14.1 Introduction — 302
- 14.2 Syntax — 304
- 14.3 Unary Operator Overloading — 305
- 14.4 Overloading Binary Operators — 307
- 14.5 Operators that Cannot Be Overloaded — 309
- 14.6 Miscellaneous Operators — 310
  - 14.6.1 == Operator — 310
  - 14.6.2 >= and <= Operators — 312

15. Errors and Exceptions — 319

- 15.1 Errors are Good — 319
- 15.2 Types of Errors — 319
  - 15.2.1 Compile Time Errors — 320
  - 15.2.2 Runtime Errors and Exceptions — 321
- 15.3 Effective Exception Handling Mechanism — 322

15.4	Nested try–catch	328		17. Threads		352
15.5	Creating User Defined Exceptions	330		17.1	Introduction	352
15.6	finally Statement	331		17.2	Classes in System.threading	353
				17.3	Basic Threads	354
16.	**Generics**	**336**		17.4	Timer Class	355
16.1	Introduction	336		17.5	Thread Priority	358
16.2	Sorted List	337		17.6	Synchronization	359
16.3	Queue	340		17.7	Thread Pool	360
16.4	Stack	343				
16.5	Using Sort Function with a List	346				

PART THREE: COMPONENT OBJECT MODEL AND ADVANCED TOPICS

18. Windows Forms and Basic Controls 369

- 18.1 Introduction 369
- 18.2 How to Add a Form? 370
- 18.3 Basic Properties of a Form 371
- 18.4 Snap Lines 373
- 18.5 Anchor and Dock 373
- 18.6 Controls 374
- 18.7 Some Common Controls 374
  - 18.7.1 Label 374
  - 18.7.2 Linklabel 374
  - 18.7.3 Adding a Button at Design Time 374
  - 18.7.4 Adding a Button at Runtime 377
  - 18.7.5 Adding a Text Box at Design Time 379
  - 18.7.6 Adding a Text Box at Runtime 385
  - 18.7.7 MaskedTextBox 386
  - 18.7.8 ListBox 387
  - 18.7.9 ComboBox 388
  - 18.7.10 NumericUpDown 388

19. Advanced Controls and Menus 398

- 19.1 Introduction 398
- 19.2 Advanced Controls 399
  - 19.2.1 GroupBox Control 399
  - 19.2.2 Panel Control 399
  - 19.2.3 TableLayoutPanel Control 399
  - 19.2.4 TabControl 403
  - 19.2.5 SplitContainer Control 403
  - 19.2.6 CheckedListBox Control 404
  - 19.2.7 ListView Control 406
  - 19.2.8 CheckBox Control 406
  - 19.2.9 RadioButton Control 407
  - 19.2.10 DateTimePicker Control 408
  - 19.2.11 MenuStrip Control 409
  - 19.2.12 ToolStrip Control 412
  - 19.2.13 Browser Control 413

20. Common Dialogs 421

- 20.1 Introduction 421
- 20.2 SaveFileDialog 422
- 20.3 FontDialog 426
- 20.4 ColorDialog 427
- 20.5 OpenFileDialog 430

Project III: Notepad **434**

21. Data Connectivity 441

- 21.1 Introduction 441
- 21.2 Creating Database in Microsoft Access 442
- 21.3 Connection Object 444
- 21.4 Command Object 444
- 21.5 Dataset Object and Datatable Object 445
- 21.6 Creating a Practical Application 447
- 21.7 Insertion of Rows and Updating Records 455

22. Introduction to ASP.NET 463

- 22.1 Introduction 463

22.2	Differences between ASP.NET and ASP	464
22.3	Shortcomings of Traditional ASP	464
22.4	Advantages of ASP.NET	465
22.5	ASP.NET Architecture	465
22.6	Web Forms	466
22.7	Creating ASP Website	466
22.8	File Types in ASP.NET	469
22.9	Adding a New Page to a Project	470
22.10	Opening an Existing Website	471
22.11	Inserting a Table in a Page	472
22.12	User Control	472
22.13	Server Control	474
22.14	Common HTML Tags	474
22.15	Creating a User Form in ASP	476
22.16	Database Creation in SQL Express	481
22.17	Master Page	485

Project IV: Online Voting System   **494**

23. Networking   513

23.1	Introduction	513
	23.1.1 Definition 514	
	23.1.2 How are Computers Connected? 514	
	23.1.3 Types of Networks 515	
23.2	Connecting to the Internet	516
23.3	Transmission Control Protocol and User Datagram Protocol	518
23.4	Server	518
23.5	Client	522
23.6	Remoting	524

24. Deployment   527

24.1	Introduction	527
24.2	Setup Project	528
24.3	ClickOnce Technology	534

25. Towards WPF and WCF   543

25.1	Introduction	543
25.2	Graphics Device Interface Classes: GDI+	544
25.3	Windows Presentation Foundation	546
	25.3.1 WPF Architecture 547	
	25.3.2 Creating a WPF Project 548	
25.4	Web Services	549
25.5	Windows Service	554
	25.5.1 Introduction 554	
	25.5.2 Creating a Windows Service 554	
25.6	Remoting Revisited	558
25.7	Windows Communication Foundation	558
	25.7.1 WCF Architecture 560	
25.8	Messaging	560

Project V: Genetic Algorithms   **565**

Answers to Objective Type Questions   586

Index   589

PART ONE

Introduction to C#, .NET, and Procedural Programming

CHAPTER 1
Introduction to .NET Framework

CHAPTER 2
Basics of C#

CHAPTER 3
Data Types and Operators

CHAPTER 4
Conditional Statements

CHAPTER 5
Loops

CHAPTER 6
Collections
Project I: IP Addresses

CHAPTER 7
Methods

CHAPTER 8
Strings

CHAPTER 9
Arrays
Project II: Greedy Approach

CHAPTER 10
Structures and Enumerations

> "Nevertheless, I consider OOP as an aspect of programming in the large; that is, as an aspect that logically follows programming in the small and requires sound knowledge of procedural programming."
>
> *Niklaus Wirth*

BACKGROUND

The advent of modern programming techniques dates back to 1889. Herman Hollerith was travelling on rail and got a ticket punched. The punching was to roughly describe the physical features of the passenger. In his own words:

I was traveling in the West and I had a ticket with what I think was called a punch photograph. The conductor punched out a description of an individual, as light hair, dark eyes, large nose, etc.

(Source: http://www.historyofinformation.com)

Hollerith used this concept to develop a machine that was used in the 1890 United States Census. The card used in the machine had round holes. It had 12 rows and 24 columns (for detailed information, please refer to Columbia University Computing History website). This machine had all the features that would later help in the development of the first programming language, and therefore, this event is considered as the first step in the development of programming languages.

In the following years, numerical calculations were based on decimal numbers. When it was comprehended, that logic could be represented with numbers, Alonzo Church expressed the lambda calculus in a formulaic way.

This was followed by the turing machines, which set the foundation for storage of programs as data in the von Neumann architecture.

The second half of the 1950s saw the development of the modern programming languages. While John Backus invented *For*mula *Trans*lator (FORTRAN) in 1954, John McCarthy developed *Lis*t *P*rocessor (LISP) in 1958, and *C*ommon *B*usiness *O*riented *L*anguage (COBOL) was developed by the Short Range Committee in 1959.

The concept of algorithm implementation got a boost with the development of ALGol 60. The year 1964 witnessed the invention of BASIC after which the language development took a new turn. BASIC formed the foundation for Visual Basic (VB), which was released by Microsoft in 1987. It was the first visual development tool from Microsoft. After release 3.0, Microsoft Visual Basic became the fastest growing programming language. The development continued until the release of Visual Basic.NET (VB.NET). Alongside, another language, C#, was being developed, which was inspired from Java.

In 1972, Dennis Ritchie of Bell Labs developed a language for system software, called C. C was to structural programming as Martin Luther King was to civil rights. It was followed by C++, which had all the features of C along with object-oriented concepts.

C++ inspired the development of Java. Many of the features of Java were taken from C++. The creation of Java was a consequence of the process of introspection that took place within the computer fraternity. The shortcomings of C++ had to be removed, because it was a period when many projects were initiated, but only a few were completed. Moreover, the absence of exception handling mechanisms and the problems associated with pointers were leading to the debacle of the discipline.

Java was successful in addressing most of these issues. Microsoft was observing the rise of the open source community with dismay. It did what any big company would have done. It stole everything from Java to create a new language called C#. Later, when Sun Microsystems entered the sphere of web applications, it copied most of the features of Active Server Pages (ASP). Many of its other attributes were inspired in a straight line from C#.

1 Introduction to .NET Framework

OBJECTIVES

After completing this chapter, the reader will be able to
- # Appreciate the importance of the .NET Framework
- # Understand the architecture of the .NET Framework
- # Understand the significance of CLS, FCL, and CLR
- # Appreciate the importance of JIT
- # Get an insight into Microsoft Visual Studio
- # Discuss the languages supported by the .NET Framework

1.1 INTRODUCTION

Before proceeding with the discussion of the .NET Framework, it would be better to understand the concept of software framework. Imagine that an inventory control system is to be developed. Will it not be better to focus on the main objective of the project as a first step rather than focusing on the technicalities of the database connection's state management? However, that would be possible only if a more standard working system is provided to the developer, which is what the software framework intends to do.

A software framework provides the developer with standard low-level features. These features result in the reduction of development time but at the same time increase the size of the program. This phenomenon is called *code blot*. However, due to the advancement in technology and reduction in hardware costs, the increase in the size of the program, in spite of being undesirable, is not a big problem nowadays.

Another criticism of a software framework is that it increases the development time instead of decreasing it, as the time required to understand and learn the software framework should also be counted in the project lifecycle. The answer to this is that the software framework is not going to be used for only one project; therefore, the time taken to understand and learn the complexities of the software framework should not be included in only one project but should be divided amongst various projects. The concept is like setting up a unit for manufacturing bolts. The setting up of the unit may require, say, a million dollars; but the cost of the first bolt produced cannot be considered as a million dollars plus the cost of the material required to produce the bolt. The cost of setting up the unit may be divided in the cost of bolts produced in, say, the next 10 years. In the same way, the time taken to learn the framework cannot be included in the cost of one project.

The .NET Framework is a software framework that runs chiefly on Microsoft Windows. It includes a large library and chains several programming languages. This opens the door of language interoperability, a concept that the computer scientists have been trying to achieve for a long time. If a developer writes programs for the .NET Framework, it executes in a software milieu known as the common language runtime (CLR). The .NET Framework contains both the class library and the CLR. Class library is a set of classes that can be used to accomplish many complex tasks. The concept has been explained in Section 1.3.2.

The chapters that follow discuss aspects such as user interface, data access, database connectivity, cryptography, web application development, network communications, and graphics of the .NET Framework along with a few others, which will be discussed throughout the text. Programmers can develop software by combining their own source code with the .NET Framework and other libraries. Microsoft created an integrated development environment (IDE) called Visual Studio for .NET software to facilitate this feature.

However, to understand the .NET Framework, the concepts presented in this chapter must be understood first.

1.2 BASICS OF .NET FRAMEWORK

In order to understand the architecture of .NET Framework it is important to understand the concepts like
- How a program is compiled?
- How it is executed?
- How is the garbage handled?
- In what form is the intermediate code stored and how it is manipulated?

The present section introduces the terms and concepts which would help you understand the above concepts.

1.2.1 Microsoft Intermediate Language

The concept of Microsoft intermediate language (MSIL) is similar to that of the bytecode in Java (Fig. 1.1). When the .NET code is compiled, it gets converted into MSIL, which is not specific to any language. All .NET languages compiled to this language. It helps to attain portability, that is, platform independence.

It is also important to note that .NET supports many languages. Each of these languages when compiled gets converted to the common intermediate language (CIL), which is platform independent. The next step is to convert this into a platform-specific machine-readable code. This task is accomplished by the CLR. The process is shown in Fig. 1.2.

Fig. 1.1 From .NET code to MSIL

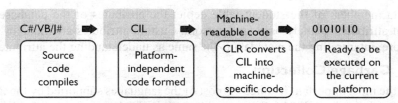

Fig. 1.2 Common language infrastructure

1.2.2 Just-in-Time Compiler

The just-in-time (JIT) compiler compiles MSIL into native code particular to the operating system (OS) and the machine architecture being used. It examines the assembly metadata for any illegal access and suitably handles violations. JIT turns the MSIL into a code directly executable by the CPU. The conversion is performed steadily during the execution of the program. Some of the advantages of JIT compilation are as follows:

1. *Environment-specific optimization*   A software application should use minimum memory and should take minimum time to execute. This is referred to as optimization and is one of the most important goals while designing software. Environment-specific optimization refers to optimal utilization of resources in terms of both time and memory.
2. *Runtime type safety*   C# does not allow all the type conversions supported by C and C++. This is required to prevent spurious type conversion, as illegal conversions can lead to undesirable situations. This reduces the plausibility of runtime errors and thus makes the software more reliable.

1.2.3 Assemblies

When a program is compiled, the MSIL code is stored in an assembly. Assemblies contain both the executable files and libraries. There are two types of assemblies:
1. Process assemblies (EXE)
2. Library assemblies (DLL)

The library assemblies define classes and the process assemblies represent the processes that will use the classes. In spite of the fact that theoretically assemblies can be created using different languages, Visual Studio (IDE for .NET) does not support such assemblies.

1.2.4 Managed Code

If the code is executed to native code, which is the CPU-specific code that runs on the same machine as the JIT compiler, then it is said to be a managed code. A code that does not run under the rule of the CLR is said to be an unmanaged code.

1.2.5 Metadata

As the name suggests, metadata is the data about the data. At times, information of the compiled class needs to be stored to support and find out interfaces, methods, assemblies, and so on. Such information about the data is called metadata.

1.2.6 Reflection

It is important to interpret the metadata in order to understand it. The procedure of interpreting the metadata is called reflection. Metadata is in the form of attributes. For example, if a developer intends to create a student management system, then the details of the students will be stored in a database. However, where will the details of that database be stored?

The data members of the student table depict the attributes of the database. There are two types of attributes, namely basic and custom. Custom attributes are made by extending ones. Therefore, interpreting the metadata is the same as understanding the attributes.

1.2.7 Garbage Collection

One of the most important features of most of the languages supported by the .NET Framework is garbage collection. C# also supports this feature. As the name suggests, it collects garbage, that is, frees or removes the objects that are no longer in use. Therefore, it spares the programmer from the task of explicitly freeing every memory element created. The problem of garbage was prominent in C programs that used pointers. The failure to deallocate memory was an important source of bugs in the software. The garbage collection ability of C# efficiently handles this problem. The value types provided by C# CLR are allocated on runtime stack. They are reclaimed automatically when the code exits.

1.3 COMPONENTS OF MICROSOFT .NET

Microsoft .NET has the following four key components:
1. Common language specification
2. Framework class library
3. Common language runtime
4. .NET tools

Each of the components is briefly discussed in this section.

1.3.1 Common Language Specification

From the foregoing discussion, it must be clear that software developed in the .NET Framework may contain many components developed in different languages. A question that arises in mind is how these objects communicate with one another. The developers of .NET found it better to have a common type system (CTS), which is a set of types common to all the languages of the .NET Framework. In order to communicate with others, the objects expose the features that are common to all the languages of the .NET Framework. This point explains the concept of common language specification (CLS), which is a basic feature for all applications and services made for the .NET Framework. CLS is, in fact, a subset of CTS. An example of the rules that CLS-compliant software must follow is that an array can have elements that are CLS compliant or that enumeration can be of type Int16, Int32, or Int64.

1.3.2 Framework Class Library

In the chapters that follow, we will study file input–output (IO), database handling, exception handling, cryptography, multithreading, and so on in C#, which requires the use of System.IO, System.Text, System.Collections, System.Threading, System.Text, and so on. Here, System is a namespace consisting of many classes. This set of reusable classes is contained in what is called framework class library (FCL). It contains more than 7000 classes, interfaces, and value types. These classes are immensely helpful in IO, gathering information about types, security checks, embodying exceptions, and so on.

These classes can be used directly or derived, as per the needs of the application. However, it may be noted that not all the classes can be derived. .NET Framework types use a dot syntax naming scheme. This technique clusters related types into namespaces, which makes it easy to search the required class. The first part of the full name is the namespace name and the last part is the type name.

For example, `System.Collections.Generic.List` represents a list type that belongs to the `System.Collections` namespace. This naming scheme makes it easy for library developers broadening the .NET Framework to produce hierarchical groups of types and name them in a regular manner.

1.3.3 Common Language Runtime

Common language runtime (CLR) converts common language infrastructure (CLI) into a machine-specific code. As discussed earlier, CLR is defined by CLI and is used by the .NET Framework. It is a stack-based, object-oriented assembly language. Its conversion to native code is the same as that of JAVA. CLR was originally called MSIL; the renaming is attributed to standardization of C# and CLI. Some of the functions performed by CLR are as follows:

1. It manages objects.
2. It enforces code and access security.
3. It handles exceptions.
4. It provides type checking.
5. Many other tasks such as debugging are also attributed to CLR.

1.3.4 .NET Tools

There are some tasks for which the code need not be written from the scratch; the available tools can be used to accomplish the tasks. For example, once a module is developed, the writing of unit test can be greatly simplified by using the NUnit tool. Similarly, documentation can be created using the NDoc tool. CodeSmith helps to generate the code. After going through the book, readers will realize that the creation of a project in Microsoft Visual Studio creates many files. If a developer does not want to create a whole project in Visual Studio and has a small code, then Snippet Compiler will help to create, compile, and run the code. The function of some of the tools has been summarized in Table 1.1.

There are many more tools available in the framework and they will continue to crop up. The important thing is to understand the framework and use the tools as and when required.

It should be noted that it is not a good practice to develop whole projects using tools alone, as it may lead to unlearning of the programming concepts.

More .NET tools have been discussed in the later chapters owing to the fact that the knowledge of the framework is essential before going through the various tools.

Table 1.1 .NET tools

Name of the tool	Function
NUnit	Helps to write unit tests for code
CodeSmith	Helps to generate code
NDoc	Helps to create documentation
Snippet Compiler	Helps to compile and run a small code without making a project in Visual Studio

1.4 ARCHITECTURE OF .NET FRAMEWORK

The .NET Framework is complex, consisting of many components, which are briefly discussed in this section. The knowledge of these components is essential to choose the appropriate components for a project. The architecture of the framework is shown in Fig. 1.4.

1.4.1 ASP.NET

Active Server Pages (ASP) is a web framework for building websites and applications. It supports Java Scripts, CSS, and HTML and can be used to build a web page, web form, and model view controller (MVC). A web page is a simple page. ASP facilitates quick development and easy database connectivity of a web page. A web form refers to the older model of reprocessing controls and integrating data into websites. An MVC has three components: model, view, and controller. The model component is responsible for the data of the application. View is responsible for the interface and the controller is the intermediate between the model and the view. MVC builds on a pattern that cleanly separates the various parts of a web application. All these types will be discussed in the latter chapters. Figure 1.3 depicts the MVC concept.

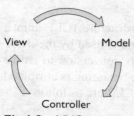

Fig.1.3 MVC concept

1. *ASP.NET web pages* ASP.NET web pages offer a quick and lightweight method to combine server code with HTML to create dynamic web content. They also facilitate connection to databases.
2. *ASP.NET web forms* ASP.NET web forms help in building dynamic websites. They use a drag-and-drop, event-driven programming model.
3. *ASP.NET MVC* MVC is an architecture that separates the implementation from the user interface. ASP.NET MVC provides a pattern-based way to build dynamic websites. It helps in faster development of web pages. The web pages developed use standard components and therefore are less prone to errors. The component-based approach also helps to utilize the advantages of component-oriented model (COM) as well. The main goals of COM are faster development of software, reusability, and significant increase in productivity. If the interface is separated from the data as is done in MVC, it not only helps in the implementation of object-oriented concepts but also helps in reducing bugs and hence increases productivity.

1.4.2 Windows Presentation Foundation

Windows Presentation Foundation (WPF) is a presentation system. It helps in building Windows client applications with visually astounding user experiences. It intends to utilize the modern graphic hardware capabilities, currently not being used by the presentation systems. Its features include two-dimensional and three-dimensional graphics, media, and text. The WPF is a part of the .NET Framework and therefore developers can also include other elements of the framework in their application. The need of using Flash in web pages is thus minimized. It even allows one to create browser-based applications.

1.4.3 Windows Communication Foundation

Windows Communication Foundation (WCF) is a programming model for building service-oriented applications. The website, when it receives a request from a client, provides requisite services. Proper communication between the two is essential for the smooth flow of work. The WCF helps in building secure transacted solutions. Please refer to Chapter 25 for an overview of WPF and WCF.

1.4.4 Cross-language Interoperability

As explained earlier, .NET Framework supports many languages. Hence, it is necessary to have a mechanism for interaction between them. The cross-language interoperability elucidates how managed objects created in diverse programming languages can cooperate with one another.

1.4.5 Runtime Hosts

The runtime hosts, that is, applications that run the web page, supported by the .NET Framework include ASP.NET and Internet Explorer.

1.4.6 Security

The CLR and the .NET Framework offer several services that allow developers to easily write secure code. They also help the system administrators to tailor the permissions settled to the code. The runtime and the .NET Framework provide useful classes and services that facilitate the use of cryptography as well.

1.4.7 ADO.NET

There are many ways to connect to a database, of which ADO.NET is one. As ADO.NET helps us to connect to the databases, it is essential in developing management systems. It is easy to use and is one of the most popular ways of connecting to the data. The concept helps us to isolate data from implementation and has been discussed in detail in Chapter 21.

Figure 1.4 depicts the .NET Framework stack.

Thus, from what we have studied so far, one can conclude that the following are the steps involved in creating a .NET application:

1. Application code is written using a .NET compatible language.
2. The code is compiled into MSIL, which is stored in an assembly.
3. This MSIL code is compiled into the native code using a JIT compiler.
4. The native code is executed in the context of the managed CLR.

These steps are illustrated in Fig. 1.5.

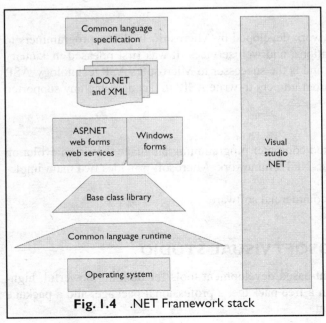

Fig. 1.4 .NET Framework stack

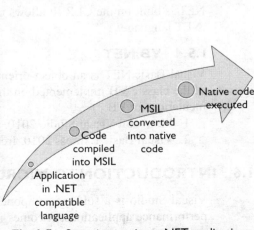

Fig. 1.5 Steps in creating a .NET application

1.5 VARIOUS LANGUAGES IN .NET FRAMEWORK

This section introduces some of the most important languages supported by the .NET Framework.

1.5.1 C#

C# is a language encompassing the following characteristics:
1. Strong typing
2. Object-oriented features
3. Declarative
4. Functional
5. Generic
6. Component-oriented programming disciplines

C# was developed by Microsoft and is one of the programming languages designed for the CLI. It is intended to be a simple, general-purpose, object-oriented programming language. Its development team is led by Anders Hejlsberg. Most of the features of C# seem to be adapted from Java; however, there are some new features in the language as well, thus making it better than Java.

1.5.2 F#

F# is a strongly typed language that uses type inference. It allows explicit data type declaration. It is a CLI-compliant language. The interface, as the name suggests, is essential in order to make the communication between the different components of a project, possibly in different languages, to interact with each other. F# also supports all CLI types and objects but it extends the type system and categorizes types as follows:
1. Immutable types, whose values cannot change during the lifespan of a program
2. Mutable types, whose values can change during the lifespan of a program

The CLI objects classify as mutable types. They are used to provide an object-oriented programming model. Immutable types are chiefly used for functional programming.

1.5.3 ASP.NET

ASP.NET is a web application framework developed by Microsoft. It allows programmers to build dynamic websites, web applications, and web services. It was first released in January 2002 (version 1.0 .NET Framework) and is the successor to Microsoft's ASP technology. ASP.NET is built on the CLR. It allows programmers to write ASP.NET code using any supported .NET language.

1.5.4 VB.NET

Visual Basic.NET is an object-oriented computer programming language that is an evolution of the classic VB implemented on the .NET Framework. Microsoft provides two main implementations of VB:
1. Microsoft Visual Studio 2010, commercial software
2. Visual Basic Express 2010, free

1.6 INTRODUCTION TO MICROSOFT VISUAL STUDIO

Visual Studio is a suite of component-based development tools for building powerful, high-performance applications. It comes in a free package, a professional package, and a package optimized for team-based development.

Microsoft Visual Studio 2010 is an integrated environment that abridges the basic errands of creating, debugging, and deploying applications. One can download Visual Studio from http://www.microsoft.com/download. In order to start a new project, the following steps must be followed:

Go to Start → Programs → Visual Studio. The screen shown in Fig. 1.6 appears.

On the top left is Server Explorer, on the right side is Solution Explorer, and the error list appears on the bottom right. All these components are explained separately in this section. However, it may be noted that the various components can be repositioned in the interface. Figure 1.6 depicts the default settings.

1.6.1 Solution Explorer

Solution Explorer provides an organized view of the projects and their files. It also gives ready access to the commands that relate to them. To enter Solution Explorer, select Solution Explorer on the View menu (Fig. 1.7).

1.6.2 Server Explorer

In order to develop an application such as a management system, a database is needed. In general, a database is created in another application such as MS Access or SQL server; therefore, referring the database repeatedly in the program becomes difficult. Server Explorer comes to the rescue in such a scenario. Server Explorer, as the name suggests, helps connect to the server in which the database is created. It can be used to view the following:

1. Data links
2. Database connections
3. System resources on any server on which network access is available

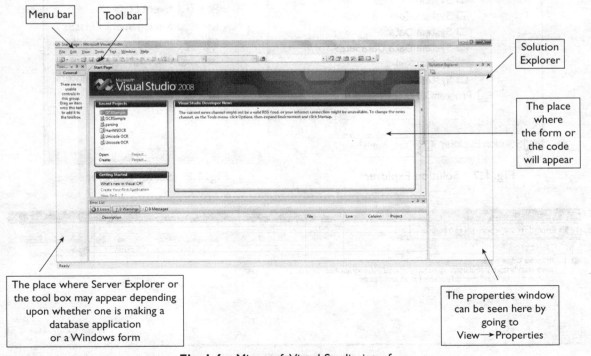

Fig. 1.6 Microsoft Visual Studio interface

Using Server Explorer, one can do the following tasks:
1. Open data connections.
2. Make data connections to either MS Access, SQL Server, Oracle or other databases.
3. Drag nodes from Server Explorer into one's Visual Studio .NET projects. This point will become clear in the third part of the book, in which we will create grid view via this method.

To enter Server Explorer, on the View menu select Server Explorer (Fig. 1.8).

1.6.3 Error List

Error list shows the errors and hence helps to speed up the application development. This window performs the following tasks:
1. Display the errors, warnings, and messages.
2. Find syntax errors using IntelliSense.
3. Find deployment errors.

To display the Error List, on the View menu choose Error List (Fig. 1.9).

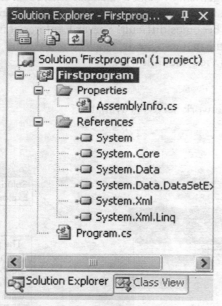

Fig. 1.7 Solution Explorer

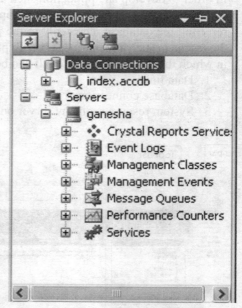

Fig. 1.8 Server Explorer

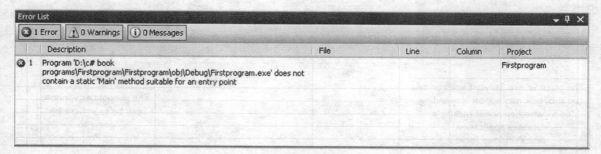

Fig. 1.9 Error list

1.6.4 Toolbox

The toolbox displays icons for items that one can add to Visual Studio projects. It is available in the View menu (Fig. 1.10). The components of the toolbox are discussed in Chapter 18.

1.6.5 Properties Window

The Visual Studio Properties window is a property browser. It supports all Visual Studio products. This window can be opened by selecting properties on the View menu (Fig. 1.11).

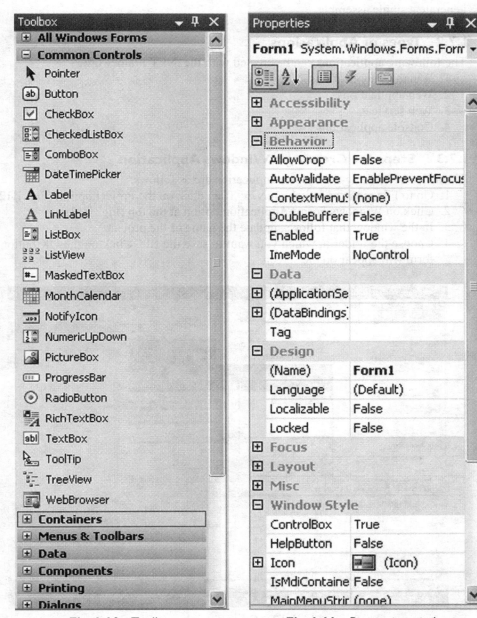

Fig. 1.10 Toolbox   **Fig. 1.11** Properties window

1.7 DEVELOPING PROJECTS IN VISUAL STUDIO

In order to develop a project in Visual Studio, it is essential to understand certain terms. This section briefly discusses the main points.

1.7.1 Linking

If the application has many source files but one wants to create a single assembly, then the concept of linking is used. Linking, as the name suggests, connects the various files in order to generate a single assembly.

1.7.2 Types of Applications

The following applications can be created with the .NET Framework:
1. Windows applications
2. Web applications
3. Web services
4. Console applications

1.7.3 Steps for Creating a Windows Application

The steps for creating a Windows application are as follows:
1. Go to File menu and click on New. Then click on the Project option (Fig. 1.12).
2. Click on Windows Forms Application option at the top (Fig. 1.13).
3. In the window that follows, update the name of the project.
4. Choose the folder in which you want to save the file. Click on the OK button and a new form will appear on the screen.

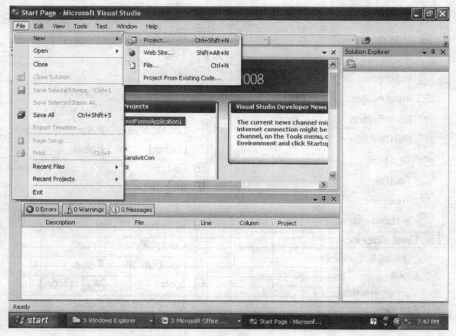

Fig. 1.12 Creating a new project

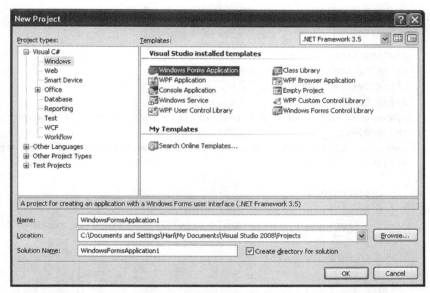

Fig. 1.13 Creating a new Windows Forms Application Project

1.7.4 Steps for Creating a Console Application

The following are the steps to create a Console application:
1. Go to File menu and click on New. Then click on the Project option.
2. Click on Console Application.
3. Update the name of the project (Fig. 1.14).
4. Choose the folder in which you want to save the file.
5. Click on the OK button and a new Console window will appear on the screen.

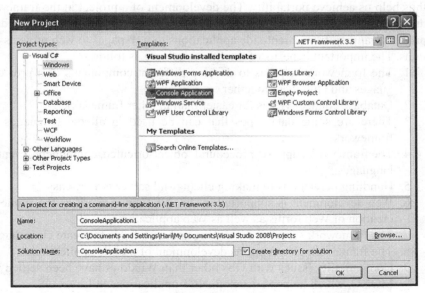

Fig. 1.14 Creating a new Console application

The following is an example code of a simple console application:

```csharp
using System;
    //using directive expained in Chapter 2
    using System.Collections.Generic;
    using System.Linq;
    using System.Text;
    //Whenever you make a new project, the above directives appear automatically in the project
    namespace Chapter1Program1//The name of the namespace is the same as that of the project
    {
        classProgram
        {
            staticvoid Main(string[] args)//Main method is expained in Chapter 2
            {
                . . .
            }
        }
    }
```

In order to execute the program, press F5. An output screen appears, the details of which are explained in Chapter 2.

1.8 BENEFITS OF .NET FRAMEWORK

As explained in this chapter, .NET Framework helps us to create projects in various languages. Moreover, the development of different components in different languages is also possible in this framework. The projects created in the framework are compiled to intermediate code and thus help us achieve portability. The development of a project in the framework is accelerated due to the availability of predefined components. The framework helps one develop all kinds of projects, ranging from client-side applications to web pages to web projects to mobile applications. The important benefits of the framework are as follows:

1. The framework helps us to develop different components of a project in different languages and club them together.
2. Database connectivity is far easier than in other frameworks.
3. There are some data types that can be used in all the languages supported by the framework.
4. The framework supports procedural, object-oriented, component-oriented, and functional languages.
5. Handling network as in making clients and server is very easy.
6. Web development is supported in the .NET Framework as the framework supports the creation of Web forms as well as Web applications.
7. The framework supports versioning and even helps to create class diagrams.
8. The framework also supports development of mobile applications.
9. Compatibility issues with OSs other than Windows have been settled with the advent of MONO, which helps to develop .NET applications in Linux OS.

This book intends to explore each of these points and many more advantages of the framework.

1.9 C# .NET FRAMEWORK AND C++

As already mentioned, .NET is a framework that contains many languages. C# is one such language. The language assumes importance owing to the fact that it can be used in procedural programming, object-oriented programming, and even in component-based project development. C# can be amalgamated with ASP to create web pages with sound foundation. It has many advantages such as provision of garbage collection mechanism and being type safe.

The chapters that follow explore all the major features of C#. The language features are discussed in the first two parts of the book. The third part discusses the COM features and advanced concepts.

C# is considerably better than any of the languages that preceded it. C++ introduced the concept of object-oriented programming. C# also belongs to the same group. However, the differences between the two are many, some of which are stated in the following points:

1. Inheritance in C# is allowed only from one class; moreover, inheritance from an interface is allowed as well. That is, it is not possible to have two base classes of a single class. However, in C++, multiple inheritance is allowed.
2. The way of declaration of arrays is different in C# and C++. In C#, arrays are declared as follows:

    ```
    int[] arr = new int[100];
    ```

    whereas in C++, an array is declared as follows:

    ```
    int arr[100];
    ```

3. In C#, conversion from bool to any other type is not allowed, whereas in C++ it is allowed.
4. In C#, long data type is 64 bits long. In C++, it is 32 bits long.
5. In C#, switch statement fall through is not supported, whereas it is supported in C++. This was the reason for many bugs in software developed in C++. In C#, it is essential to insert a break after every case.
6. In C#, delegate is supported, whereas in C++ the concept is not supported.
7. In C#, the arguments can be of ref or out type, but this is not supported in C++.
8. In C++, main function is outside a class, whereas in C# it is inside a class.
9. In C++, there are just three access specifiers, whereas in C# there are four.
10. C++ is not type safe whereas C# is.
11. In C++, sound garbage collection mechanism is missing, but it is present in C#.

As far as the comparison of C# and Java is concerned, it may be stated here that although C# is highly inspired by Java, there are a few differences as well.

SUMMARY

A software framework can be defined as a standard working system that helps developer create simple console and Window Form applications without worrying too much about the technicalities of the project. The .NET Framework is one such software framework that runs chiefly on Microsoft Windows. It provides a large library and is associated with several programming languages with many features such as JIT, assemblies, managed code, metadata, reflection, and garbage collection. The .NET Framework contains many components such as ASP, WPF, WCF, cross-language interoperability, ADO, and runtime and security features.

There are numerous benefits that .NET provides such as interoperatibility, portability, and managing variety of applications ranging from client-side to web pages and even mobile apps. C# is one among many languages supported by the .NET Framework that is used extensively for creating several such applications. There are many differences between Java and C# and between C++ and C#, which have been explained. However, readers familiar with Java will not miss the similarities as well. The chapter begins the journey towards the destination, which is learning C#; however, it may be stated here that the path that follows is not too easy.

As is obvious from the discussion that the problems in one programming language leads to the development of another. In the same way discovery of problems in C# will pave way for future languages. However, in order to understand the concepts of C#, it is important to get equipped with the basics first and thus components of the .NET framework have been explained first in this chapter.

GLOSSARY

Software framework A software framework provides standard low-level features. These features result in the reduction of development time but at the same time increase the size of the program.

.NET Framework This is a software framework that runs chiefly on Microsoft Windows. It includes a large library and chains several programming languages.

Common type system (CTS) This is a set of types common to all the languages of the .NET Framework.

Common language specification (CLS) This is a basic feature for all applications and services made for .NET Framework. CLS is a subset of CTS.

Framework class library (FCL) This is a set of reusable classes. FCL contains more than 7000 classes.

Just-in-time (JIT) compiler This compiler compiles MSIL into native code particular to the OS and the machine architecture being used.

Assemblies When a program is compiled, the MSIL code is stored in an assembly. Assemblies contain both the executable files and libraries.

Reflection The procedure of interpreting the metadata is called reflection. Metadata is in the form of attributes. Attributes can be custom-made by extending from any other attributes.

Garbage collection This is one of the most important features of C#. As the name suggests, it collects garbage, that is, frees or removes the objects that are no longer in use.

POINTS TO REMEMBER

- Lexical scoping is a concept wherein blocks can have their own variables and functions.
- Simula, not C++, was the first object-oriented programming language.
- B is a programming language that was developed at Bell Labs. It was developed by Ken Thompson.
- Fortran is used in the area of high-performance computing.
- Edger Dijkstra in a letter in 1975 remarked, 'The use of COBOL cripples the mind; its teaching should, therefore, be regarded as a criminal offence.'
- ASP is used for web applications and website development.
- The use of C# is not just restricted to client-side programming; it is also used for mobile and gaming applications.
- F# is a multi-paradigm programming language.

EXERCISES

I. Multiple-choice Questions

1. Visual Studio is used chiefly for running _____ type of application.
   (a) .NET application   (b) Java
   (c) PHP   (d) none of these

2. When we compile a .NET code, it gets converted into _____.
   (a) MSIL   (b) JIT
   (c) CLR   (d) none of these

3. What integrates the code and components from the numerous .NET programs?
   (a) CLS   (b) FCL
   (c) CLR   (d) none of these

4. The collection of classes and data types that allow .NET applications to accomplish many tasks such as reading is _____.
   (a) CLS
   (b) FCL
   (c) CLR
   (d) none of these

5. .Net Framework provides facilities for _____.
   (a) data access
   (b) cryptography
   (c) web development
   (d) network communication
   (e) all of these

6. Formation of machine-readable code in .NET requires the help of CLR. Which of the following statement is correct about CLR?
   (a) CLR forms CIL.
   (b) CLR cuts CIL into machine-readable code.
   (c) Source code goes to CLR.
   (d) CLR is just a specification; it has got nothing to do with compilation of code.

7. Which of the following is not a component of .NET?
   (a) CLS (b) FCL (c) CLR (d) MONO

8. JIT _____.
   (a) converts MSIL into native code
   (b) converts MSIL into CIL
   (c) is a part of FCL
   (d) none of these

9. FCL helps in _____.
   (a) IO
   (b) gathering information about types
   (c) security check
   (d) all of these

10. Assemblies consist of _____.
    (a) EXE
    (b) DLLs
    (c) both (a) and (b)
    (d) none of these

11. The process of interpretation of metadata is called _____.
    (a) reflection
    (b) refraction
    (c) interference
    (d) diffraction

12. The information about a class, if stored, is called _____.
    (a) important data
    (b) metadata
    (c) attributes
    (d) none of these

13. Code that runs under the rule of CLR is called _____.
    (a) managed code
    (b) unmanaged code
    (c) unsafe code
    (d) safe code

14. Which of the following are present in assemblies?
    (a) EXE, DLL
    (b) EXE, Header files
    (c) Header files, Namespaces
    (d) None of these

15. Which of the following examines metadata for illegal entries?
    (a) JLT
    (b) FCL
    (c) CLR
    (d) None of these

16. Which of the following is the repository of classes needed for IO, cryptography, and so on?
    (a) FCL
    (b) CIL
    (c) MSIL
    (d) None of these

17. Which of the following converts CLI into machine-executable code?
    (a) CIL
    (b) MSIL
    (c) Both (a) and (b)
    (d) None of these

18. Java is to bytecode as .NET is to _____.
    (a) MSIL
    (b) JIT
    (c) CIL
    (d) None of these

19. Which of the following is a component of .Net Framework?
    (a) Class library
    (b) Header files
    (c) Both (a) and (b)
    (d) None of these

20. Which is the lowest-level human-readable programming language defined by .NET Framework?
    (a) CLR
    (b) MSIL
    (c) Both (a) and (b)
    (d) None of these
    (c) Garbage collection
    (d) CLS
    (e) Managed code

II. Review Questions

1. What is .NET Framework?
2. What are the various components of the .NET Framework?
3. State various functions of CLR.
4. Explain .NET Framework class library.
5. What do you understand by JIT?
6. Explain the following terms:
   (a) Metadata
   (b) Reflection
7. What is a CTS?
8. Explain the architecture of .NET.
9. What is assembly?
10. What are the various components of Microsoft Visual Studio?

2 Basics of C#

OBJECTIVES

After completing this chapter, the reader will be able to
- Appreciate the importance of programming
- Write a C# program
- Explain the structure of a C# program
- Comprehend the intricacies of the Main method
- Use specific functions
- Appreciate the importance of comments in a program
- Understand the use of command line arguments

2.1 INTRODUCTION

Learning programming is similar to learning how to drive. The more you practice, the better skills you develop. Contrary to the popular belief, programming is not just about coding but is a convoluted art of solving a problem.

In order to become a programmer, one needs to have a good command over algorithm analysis. Learning the syntax is important but not inclusive. The scope of this book is the language features of C# and COM, but utmost care has been taken to explain the other concepts as well. Readers must understand that they will learn programming only by designing as many programs as possible. Numerous errors might be encountered in the programs, but errors teach us how to avoid the error-generating constructs in future. Moreover, while writing a program, the most important factor is to first develop the logic to solve the problem in hand. Thus, the study of algorithms becomes all the more essential.

In the chapters that follow, every attempt has been made to explain the algorithm used to solve the problem in hand. The next step in writing the program is to convert the logic into programming constructs. Hence, developers need to know the syntax and the features of the language they are working in. This is where this book comes to the aid. The final step is to test the program for different sets of input. The importance of software testing cannot, therefore, be undermined. Figure 2.1 depicts the process of designing a program.

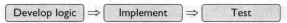

Fig. 2.1 Program design

2.2 WRITING A PROGRAM

This section explains how to write a program and execute it in C#. The steps of building a simple console application have already been explained in Section 1.7.4 of Chapter 1. It is, therefore, advisable to go through Chapter 1 before continuing with the present chapter. However, a brief description of the creation of a simple console application is given as follows:

Step 1 Open Visual Studio and create a new console application. Write the name of the project and start the project. Figure 2.2 shows the screen that appears when you go to File → New → Project

Step 2 The screen shown in Fig. 2.3 appears when you click OK.
In the Main method, write the following code:

```
Console.WriteLine("This moment belongs to me");
```

The statement displays the text 'This moment belongs to me', when you run the program.

Step 3 Run the program either by pressing F5 or by using the menu bar or toolbar.

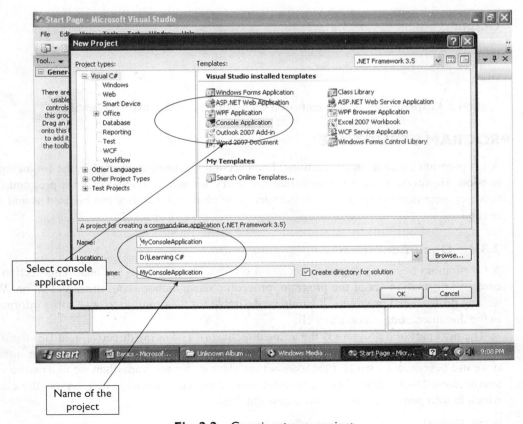

Fig. 2.2 Creating a new project

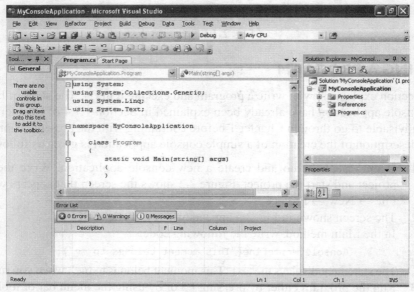

Fig. 2.3 A new project

Output

```
This moment belongs to me
```

Section 2.3 explains the components of a C# program and the involved details.

2.3 PROGRAM STRUCTURE

A C# program contains many sections. Each section has been examined in the following discussion. However, it may be stated that not every section is mandatory in a program. It is, however, necessary to at least know the various sections, so that they can be used as and when needed.

2.3.1 Documentation

A C# program begins with a documentation section. However, it is optional. This section may contain information about the program, procedure used, author, date, time, and so on. When writing professional programs, it would be desirable for the program to have some information in the documentation section as well.

The next part of a program is the using directive(s). The using directive qualifies the use of a namespace so that the namespace need not be written repeatedly in the program. For instance, if we use System.Data.OleDB.OleDbConnection class in our program, then we must write using System.Data.OleDb along with other using directives. The directives help us use the classes, which in turn help us connect to an access database.

```
using System;
using System.Collections.Generic;
using System.Linq;
```

```
using System.Text;        ◄──────  Using directives
using System.Data.OleDb;
namespace BasicProgram1
{
    class Program
    {
        OleDbConnection conn;        ◄──────  We can write OleDBConnection instead of
        static void Main(string[] args)                System.Data.OleDBConnection
        {
            System.Console ...
```

Since we have written "using System.Data.OleDb;", we can use the class System.OleDb. Connection in our program. Had this not been the case, the execution of the program would have resulted in an error.

```
using System;
using System.Collections.Generic;
using System.Linq;
using System.Text;

namespace BasicProgram1
{                                   Using System.OleDB not written
    class Program
    {
        OleDbConnection conn;
        static void Main(string[] args)
        {
```

When this program is executed, the following error appears.

Error

The type or namespace name 'OleDbConnection' could not be found (Are you missing a using directive or an assembly reference?)

So, if you do not want to write the using directive and still want to use the class, then the class needs to be qualified with the name of the namespace to which it belongs. The following snippet exemplifies the situation:

```
using System;
using System.Collections.Generic;
using System.Linq;
using System.Text;
namespace BasicProgram1
{                                   Name of the class is qualified with the name
    class Program                   of the namespace to which it belongs.
    {
        System.Data.OleDb.OleDbConnection conn;
        static void Main(string[] args)
        {
```

2.3.2 Methods of Writing Statements

Writing a statement in a single line or splitting the statement and writing it in multiple lines is the same as far as C# is concerned. Here, listing 1 statement displays: 'Hi there' and so does listing 2.

Listing 1
```
static void Main(string[] args)
{
    System.Console.WriteLine("Hi there");
    Console.ReadKey();
}
```

Output

```
Hi there
```

Listing 2
```
static void Main(string[] args)
{
    System.Console.WriteLine(
    "Hi there"
    );
    Console.ReadKey(
    );
}
```

However, it may be noted that though the style used in listing 2 is allowed, it makes the program unreadable. It is, therefore, not advisable to follow the style of listing 2. The standard style has been used in this book. The premise of allowing the thing might be reinforcing the importance of logic over syntax.

2.3.3 Interface

An interface contains methods but not their definitions. An interface is a blueprint of what is to be done and does not state how it is to be done. Therefore, the behavioural part is not implemented in an interface. It may be stated that an interface may contain more aspects. This concept is explained in detail in Chapter 13.

The methods declared in an interface are defined in the class that implements it. The interface does not define any methods and therefore it cannot be instantiated. The syntax of an interface is as follows:

```
interface <name of the interface>
{
    //Method, properties, index, or events
}
```

For example, if an interface student is to have a method called getdata(), then the following code needs to be written in the editor:

```
interface student
{
    void getdata()
    {
    }
}
```

The interface section of the program contains various interfaces that the programmer wants to use in the program.

2.3.4 Class Definition

The class definition section of the program contains the definition of a class. It may be noted here that there can be multiple classes in a single program. Chapter 11 gives a detailed explanation of classes. A class is a real or conceptual entity, which has importance to problem at hand. For example, in a college there is no person called student, but everyone plays the role of a student; therefore, it is a conceptual entity. An instance of a class is called an object. Consequently, the whole concept of object-oriented programming (OOP) originates from the idea of a class.

2.3.5 Namespaces

As stated in Chapter 1, C# has a lot of predefined classes with functionalities; examples are input–output, data handling, and networking. The classes have been clubbed together as per their role. The grouping together of classes makes organization easy. For example, the evaluation of social status, impact of education, and upliftment of a section of society may be under different departments, but all the departments come under the department of social welfare. In the same way, the input class, the output class, and many such classes that perform similar tasks have been placed under the namespace System. This is why we have been writing System.Console.WriteLine(). Here, System is a namespace; Console is a class in the System namespace, and WriteLine() is a method in the Console class.

2.3.6 Output

The output is essential in a program as it is required both in taking input from the user and displaying the output. In C#, output is displayed by using the Console.WriteLine() method. The WriteLine() method is in the class Console. It takes the string as parameter, which is to be displayed. For example, Console.WriteLine ("Hi"); displays Hi. Console.Write() method can be used if it is not required to display the statement in a new line. Readers familiar with C may find a similarity between the WriteLine() method of C# and the printf() function of C.

2.3.7 Input

In C#, every input is taken as a string. The string, in turn, is converted into the requisite data type. For example, if the user is asked to enter a number, which is to be inserted into an integer variable, then the following statement performs the requisite task:

```
Console.WriteLine("Enter the first number\t:");
number1 = int.Parse(Console.ReadLine());
```

The whole statement, however, needs to be placed in the try block, as the value entered by the user may not be an integer. The concept of try and catch is explained in Chapter 15. At this moment, it is enough to remember that any integer input has to be placed in a try block and with every try block there has to be a catch block, which handles the exceptions.

```
int number1;
try
{
   Console.WriteLine("Enter the first number\t:");
   number1 = int.Parse(Console.ReadLine());
   Console.ReadKey();
}
catch(Exception e)
```

```
    {
        Console.WriteLine("Error" + e.ToString());
        Console.ReadKey();
    }
}
```

In this code, the input statement has been placed in the `try` block. This is done because the input is converted into an integer. If the user does not enter an integer, it will not be possible for the compiler to convert it into an integer. In such a situation, runtime exception will be thrown. This exception will be caught by the `catch` block.

2.3.8 Main Method

Unlike C++, the `Main` method of a program in C# is in a class. The class is contained in a namespace whose name is the same as that of the program. The concept of `Main` method has been explained in Section 2.4.

```
using System;
using System.Collections.Generic;
using System.Linq;
using System.Text;

namespace BasicProgram1
{
    class Program
    {
        static void Main(string[] args)
        {
            System.Console.WriteLine("Hi there");
            Console.ReadKey();
        }
    }
}
```

2.4 CONCEPT OF Main METHOD

When a program is executed, the first method that runs is 'Main'. So, Main needs to be called while running a program. In order to do so, an instance of the class in which Main is called has to be made if the method is not static. Static methods are those methods that have only one copy. They can be called by writing the name of the class followed by the name of the method, thus making things easy for the compiler. The concept of static methods has been explained in detail in Chapter 11.

In general, the return type of Main is void, as it does not return anything. The return type of a method is discussed in detail in Chapter 7. However, in some cases, the Main method can also return a value. For example, assume that the requirement of the project in question is that Main should return 0 on successful completion. For this to happen, the return type of Main should be int.

```
using System;
using System.Collections.Generic;
using System.Linq;
using System.Text;
```

```csharp
namespace MyConsoleApplication
{
    class Program
    {
        static int Main(string[] args)
        {
            int number1;
            try
            {
                Console.WriteLine("Enter the number\t:");
                number1 = int.Parse(Console.ReadLine());
                Console.WriteLine("You have entered" + number1.ToString());
                Console.ReadKey();
            }
            catch(Exception e)
            {
                Console.WriteLine("Error" + e.ToString());
                Console.ReadKey();
            }
            return 0;
        }
    }
}
```

Output

```
Enter the number    :
3
You have entered 3
```

2.5 MULTIPLE Main METHODS IN A PROGRAM

In general, every program contains a single Main method. However, it is possible to have a Main in each class. In such cases, so as to run a particular Main, one needs to make some changes in the properties of the project. For example, in the following program, the Main of Program class runs when the program is executed.

```csharp
using System;
using System.Collections.Generic;
using System.Linq;
using System.Text;
namespace BasicProgram1
{
    class Program
    {
        static void Main(string[] args)
        {
            System.Console.WriteLine("Hi there");
            Console.ReadKey();
        }
```

```
}
...
}
class ABC
{
    static void Main(string[] args)
    {
    System.Console.WriteLine("Hi");
    Console.ReadKey();
    }
}
```

In order to make the Main of class ABC run when the program is executed, the name of the startup object should be changed in the properties of the program. It should be set equal to the name of the class whose Main is required to run. The screenshot shown in Fig. 2.4 shows how this can be done.

The output of this program will now be as follows:

Output

```
Hi
```

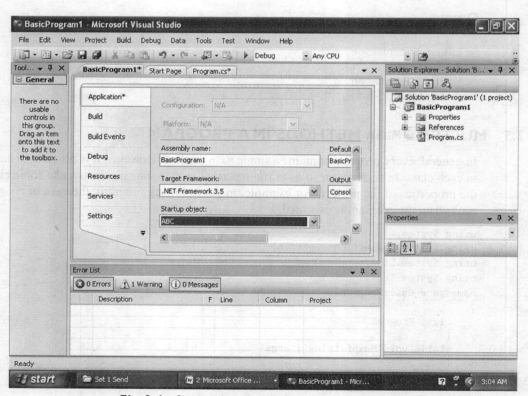

Fig. 2.4 Setting the starting point of the application

2.6 USING SPECIFIC FUNCTIONS

At times, it becomes essential to use mathematical functions or the functions defined in other namespaces. In order to do so, the using directive must be written at the beginning of the program to include the namespace whose function is to be used in the program or the method should be called by qualifying the name of the namespace as well, as explained earlier. For example, the following listing calculates the roots of $y = ax^2 + bx$. Since the solution of the equation is $x = \sqrt{\dfrac{-b}{a}}$, a mathematical function sqrt() is needed. The function is defined in the Math class, which is explained in detail in Chapter 3.

```
using System;
using System.Collections.Generic;
using System.Linq;
using System.Text;

namespace MyConsoleApplication
{
    class Program
    {
    static void Main(string[] args)
    {
        int number1, number2;
        double result;
        try
        {
            Console.WriteLine("Enter the first number\t:");
            number1 = int.Parse(Console.ReadLine());
            Console.WriteLine("Enter the second number\t:");
            number2 = int.Parse(Console.ReadLine());
            result = Math.Sqrt((-1.0 * number2) / number1);
            Console.WriteLine("The result is" + result.ToString());
            Console.ReadKey();
        }
        catch(Exception e)
        {
            Console.WriteLine("Error" + e.ToString());
            Console.ReadKey();
        }
    }
    }
}
```

Output

When the program is executed and two numbers are entered, the requisite result will be shown. If the answer is a double, then the correct answer is displayed.

```
Enter the first number  :
1
Enter the second number :
-2
The result is 1.4142135623731
```

On entering numbers, which give an integer as the output, the decimal places are not shown.

```
Enter the first number  :
1
Enter the second number :
-4
The result is 2
```

Sometimes, the input might result in negative numbers inside the square root. It may be noted that in this case as well the exception part is not executed; rather, NaN is displayed, which means that the result is *not a number*.

```
Enter the first number  :
1
Enter the second number :
2
The result is NaN
```

However, if a string that cannot be converted into an integer is entered, then the exception part is executed.

```
Enter the first number:
harsh
Error System.FormatException: Input string was not in a correct format.
    at System.Number.StringToNumber<String str, NumbrtStyles options,
Number Buffer& number, NumberFormatInfo info, Boolean parseDecimal>
    at System.Number.ParseInt32<String s, NumberStyles style,
NumberFormatInfo info>
    at System.Int32.Parse<String s>
    at MyConsoleApplication.Program.Main<String[] args> in D:\Learning
C#\MyConsoleApplication\MyConsoleApplication\Program.cs:line 17
_
```

2.7 COMMENTS

Comments are the statements that are not executed when the program runs. They are important as far as documentation is concerned and are essential to understand the program. It may be noted that a project is handled not by a single person but by a team. Thus, it is important that a code written by one developer is understood by others as well.

Comments are written in two ways:
1. Single-line comments
2. Multiple-line comments

It may be stated that comments are not considered in software metrics such as lines of code (LOC). However, this does not diminish their importance.

2.7.1 Single-line Comments

Single-line comments are generally preceded by '//', as shown in the following listing:

```csharp
//Using directives
using System;
using System.Collections.Generic;
using System.Linq;
using System.Text;
//namespace
namespace MyConsoleApplication
{
  class Program
  {
//The most important function
    static int Main(string[] args)
    {
        int number1;
        try
        {
          Console.WriteLine("Enter the number\t:");
          number1 = int.Parse(Console.ReadLine());
          Console.WriteLine("You have entered" + number1.ToString());
          Console.ReadKey();
        }
        catch(Exception e)
        {
          Console.WriteLine("Error" + e.ToString());
          Console.ReadKey();
        }
            //Since Main's return type is int
            return 0;
    }
  }
}
```

Annotations point to: *Single-line comments* (//Using directives, //namespace, //The most important function, //Since Main's return type is int)

2.7.2 Multiple-line Comments

At times, the explanation of some of the methods might take more than one line. In such cases, multiple-line comments are needed. The comment is preceded by a '/*' and ends with a '*/'. In the following listing, all the multiple-line comments are preceded by '/*'.

```csharp
using System;
using System.Collections.Generic;
using System.Linq;
using System.Text;
/*namespace
  The name is same as that of the program*/
namespace MyConsoleApplication
{
    class Program
    {
        /*The most important function
        since compiler sees this function first*/
```

Annotations point to: *Multiple-line comments*

```csharp
            static int Main(string[] args)
            {
                int number1;
                try
                {
                    Console.WriteLine("Enter the number\t:");
                    number1 = int.Parse(Console.ReadLine());
                    Console.WriteLine("You have entered" + number1.ToString());
                    Console.ReadKey();
                }
                catch(Exception e)
                {
                    Console.WriteLine("Error" + e.ToString());
                    Console.ReadKey();
                }
                //Since Main's return type is int
                return 0;
            }
        }
    }
```

2.8 COMMAND LINE ARGUMENTS

The arguments given in Main are stored in the array args. When command line arguments are given, these arguments can be handled as normal array elements. It may be stated that a simple for loop is capable of traversing through the array.

```csharp
using System;
using System.Collections.Generic;
using System.Linq;
using System.Text;
namespace MyConsoleApplication
{
    class Program
    {
        static int Main(string[] args)
        {
            for(int i=0;i<args.Length;i++)
            {
                Console.WriteLine("Argument" + args[i]);
            }
            Console.ReadKey();
            return 0;
        }
    }
}
```

The command line arguments can be given in the Debug tab of the properties of the project. In order to do so, right click on the name of the namespace in Solution Explorer and enter the command line arguments in 'Start Options'. Figure 2.5 shows the method to give the command line arguments.

Output

```
Argument Hi
Argument Bye
```

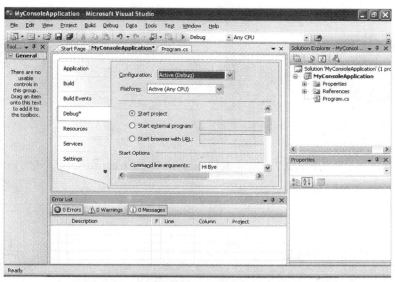

Fig. 2.5 Giving command line arguments

2.9 COMPILATION PROCESS

In order to execute a program, we need to compile it. The process of compilation has five main steps, namely lexical analysis, syntactic analysis, semantic analysis, intermediate code generation, and code generation. The semantic analysis segregates the program into tokens. These tokens are identified by the reduced deterministic finite acceptor. The acceptor, in turn, is made from the non-deterministic finite acceptor. The non-deterministic finite acceptor is shaped from the regular expression of a token.

In order to understand the process, let us consider an example of an identifier, which starts with a letter and is followed by any number of letters or digits; therefore, the regular expression of an identifier will be $l(l + d)*$, where l is a letter and d is a digit. This regular expression is converted into a non-deterministic finite acceptor. In Figs 2.6–2.9, ε represents a null move. It may be noted that in order to understand the diagrams a basic knowledge of the theory of computation is required. The steps to convert the regular expression into a deterministic finite acceptor are as follows:

In the first step, the non-deterministic finite acceptor for $(l + d)$ is made. Here, l and d can be accepted by the automata by two parallel paths. The non-deterministic finite acceptor is depicted in Fig. 2.6.

This is followed by the formation of the non-deterministic finite acceptor for $(l + d)*$. Here, * denotes repetition. From the second symbol onwards, an identifier may have any number of letters or digits; therefore, the initial and the final states of the automata are connected via a null move. That is, one can go from the initial to the final state without giving any input. Moreover, from the final state one can go back to the initial state without giving any input; therefore, the final state is also connected to the initial state via a null move. The non-deterministic finite acceptor is depicted in Fig. 2.7.

This step is followed by the formation of automata $l(l + d)*$. The non-deterministic finite acceptor for $l(l + d)*$ is shown in Fig. 2.8. It may be noted that $\rightarrow \bigcirc$ represents the initial state, whereas $\bigcirc\!\!\!\bigcirc$ represents the final state.

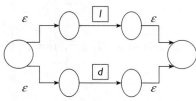

Fig. 2.6 Non-deterministic finite acceptor of $(l + d)$

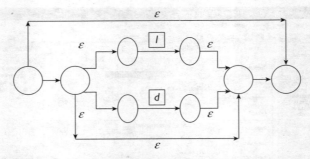

Fig. 2.7 Non-deterministic finite acceptor of $(l + d)^*$

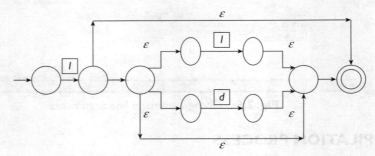

Fig. 2.8 Non-deterministic finite acceptor of $l(l + d)^*$

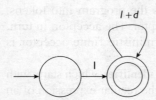

Fig. 2.9 Deterministic finite acceptor of $l(l + d)^*$

In the next step, this automata is converted into a deterministic finite acceptor. The final automaton generated is depicted in Fig. 2.9.

It is an acceptor as it accepts or rejects. It tells us whether the input string is an identifier or not. This process is called lexical analysis. It may be noted that most of the common errors are reported by this phase of the compiler.

This step is followed by the syntactic and semantic analyses. The syntactic analysis checks the syntax, whereas the semantic analysis checks the semantics and interprets the meaning of the construct. The intermediate code generation generates the intermediate code, which is a step towards the final machine level code generation. The error handling mechanism is necessary at every phase of the compilation process. The following are some instances that result in an error:

1. Misspelt Keyword

It is the job of a lexical analyser to check whether a keyword has been spelt correctly. It is done with the help of a deterministic finite acceptor as explained earlier.

2. Syntactic Error

An example of syntactic error is the absence of closing parenthesis in an 'if condition'. The lexical analyser identifies such errors with the help of parse trees.

3. Incompatible Operands to an Operator

The intermediate code generator identifies this type of errors. Such errors become all the more important in C# as it intends to overcome such shortcomings in C and C++.

4. Multiple Declarations of an Identifier

The bookkeeping routine helps identifying such errors.

There can be many more sources of errors. When a program is compiled, the errors will be shown in the error list, as explained in Section 1.6.3. This displays the line number, a brief description of the error, and the error code. The screenshot given in Fig. 2.10 depicts the error in an error pane.

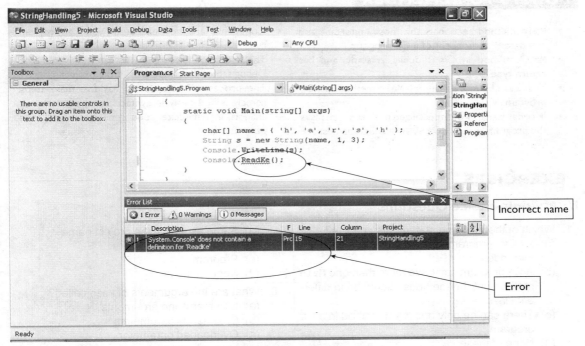

Fig. 2.10 Error in an error pane

SUMMARY

Before proceeding with writing programs in C#, it is imperative for a developer to know the basic input–output functions. The chapter explains the basic input and output functions and the method of writing a program. It is important to understand the correct way of writing a program. If a developer intends to create a big project, or even an organic one, then the code must be clear to the other members of the team as well. This is done using comments. The chapter explains the types of comments. Comments facilitate proper documentation of the program. Moreover, the chapter also exemplifies how a single program can have multiple Main methods and how to set command line arguments. The points explained in this chapter are the bricks of the building that will house the readers' programming acumenship.

GLOSSARY

Interface This contains methods but not their definitions. An interface is a blueprint of what is to be done but does not state how it is to be done.

Command line arguments The arguments given in Main are referred to as command line arguments. These are stored in the array args.

Comments These are the statements that are not executed when the program runs.

Namespace It is an abstract container to hold rational consortium of unique identifiers.

Class It is a real or a conceptual entity, which has importance to problem in hand.

POINTS TO REMEMBER

- Main method section is the most important and mandatory component of a C# program.
- Main method in C# is public, is static, and has return type 'void'.
- There can be more than one Main method in a C# program.
- In order to carry out specialized mathematical tasks, the program should have System.Math namespace.
- Comments are not executed when a program runs.
- The command line arguments can be given in the Debug tab of the properties of the project.
- The process of compilation has five main steps, namely lexical analysis, syntactic analysis, semantic analysis, intermediate code generation, and code generation.

EXERCISES

I. Multiple-choice Questions

1. Which of the following statements are true?
   (a) A C# program can have multiple Main methods.
   (b) A C# program can have more than one Main method but the methods should be in different classes.
   (c) There can be only one Main method in a C# program.
   (d) None of these

2. Which tab in the property window helps you to set the startup object?
   (a) Application   (b) Build
   (c) Build events   (d) None of these

3. Which tab in the property window helps you to give the command line arguments?
   (a) Application   (b) Debug
   (c) Build events   (d) None of these

4. Which of the following is used for writing a multiple-line comment?
   (a) //   (b) /*
   (c) !-   (d) None of these

5. What is the default name of namespace of a project?
   (a) Same as that of the project name
   (b) Main
   (c) Program
   (d) None of these

6. What are the arguments of Main called?
   (a) Command line arguments
   (b) Commands parameters
   (c) Overloaded parameters
   (d) None of these

7. What is the type of command line arguments?
   (a) String[]   (b) Int[]
   (c) Can be anything (d) None of these

8. In C# which is the first method seen by the compiler?
   (a) Main   (b) Program
   (c) Namespace   (d) None of these

9. In C#, Main is _____.
   (a) public   (b) static
   (c) void   (d) all of these

10. In C# which of the following is not used?
    (a) Header file   (b) Using directive
    (c) Both (a) and (b) (d) None of these

II. Review Questions

1. What is meant by command line arguments?
2. Explain the process of setting the startup object in a C# program.
3. What is the importance of comments? Explain how to write single-line and multiple line comments.

4. Write a short note on the art of programming.
5. Explain the steps of writing a basic C# program.
6. Explain the various sections of a C# program.
7. Why is `Main` static in C#?
8. How many `Main` methods can a C# program have?
9. How many classes can a C# program have?
10. What is the importance of documentation section in C#?
11. Explain the process of compilation.
12. What is meant by syntax analysis?
13. What is a namespace?
14. State some of the causes of compile time errors.
15. Explain how to use a function of Math class in a C# program.

III. Programming Exercises

1. Ask the user to enter a three-digit number and calculate the sum of its digits.
2. Ask the user to enter a three-digit number and reverse the number.
3. Ask the user to enter a three-digit number and obtain the number by reversing the order of the digits. Now add the two numbers and obtain the number obtained by reversing the order of the digits of the sum.
4. Ask the user to enter the basic salary and find the HRA, which is 20 per cent of the basic salary; TADA, which is 25 per cent of the basic salary; and the net salary, which is the sum of basic salary, HRA, and TADA.
5. Ask the user to enter temperature in Celsius, C, and convert it into Kelvin, K. The relation between the two is given in the following equation:

$$K = C + 273$$

6. Ask the user to enter two numbers and find the first number to the power of the second number.
7. Ask the user to enter a number and calculate its log to the base 10.
8. Ask the user to enter the concentration of hydrogen ions and calculate the pH. The pH of a solution is given by the following equation:

$$pH = \log_{10} [H^+]$$

9. Ask the user to enter the pH of a solution and find the hydrogen ion concentration.
10. Ask the user to enter the value of concentration of a solution, c, and the value of degree of dissociation, α, and find the value of the dissociation constant, k. The relation between the two is given by the following equation:

$$K = c\alpha^2$$

3 Data Types and Operators

OBJECTIVES

After completing this chapter, the reader will be able to

- Define data types and operators
- Classify data types
- Understand the importance of reference types, type conversion, and type casting
- Describe different operators and classify them
- Comprehend the concept of constant variables
- Appreciate the importance of scope of a variable
- Understand the concept of type casting
- Understand various mathematical functions
- Evaluate expressions

3.1 INTRODUCTION TO DATA TYPES

When a program is designed, data is actually being manipulated. For example, in a program for calculating the sum of two numbers, the user is asked to enter two numbers; then the two numbers are stored in some variables and their sum calculated. The process is depicted in the flowchart given in Fig. 3.1.

In order to accomplish this task, two variables are needed in which the numbers entered by the user can be stored. Let the names of these variables be number1 and number2. Now, number1 and number2 need to store two values, both of which are of integer type. When one writes

```
int number1, number2;
```

one directs the compiler to make two variables capable of storing integer type values. So, the data type of these two variables is `int`. If, in some scenario, two fractional values need to be stored, then two float type variables are required.

Definition

A data type is defined as categorizing one of the various types of data, such as floating point and integer, and the operations that can be done on that type. In this section, we will be discussing the different data types and their properties.

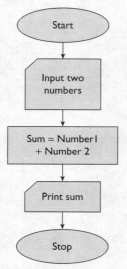

Fig. 3.1 Flowchart for calculating the sum of two numbers

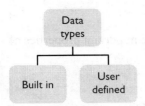

Fig. 3.2 Classification of data types

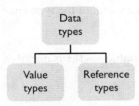

Fig. 3.3 Classification of data types based on type of value being stored

Some data types are predefined and some are defined by the user. The definition of a data type may include the name of the type, range, and constraints. For example, an `int` type can have values ranging from −32,767 to 32,768. On the other hand, a data type can also be defined by a user. On the basis of this premise, a data type can be classified as follows:

1. A built-in data type, for example, `int`, `float`, and `char`
2. A user-defined data type, for example, `class` or `interface`

Figure 3.2 depicts the classification.

Data types can also be segregated on the basis of whether they are capable of storing a value or reference to a value. On the basis of this premise, data types can also be classified as follows:

1. Value types, which store values
2. Reference types, which store references to the actual data

There is another classification called pointer types. However, use of pointers in C# is considered as unsafe programming. So it is advisable to accomplish your tasks with the above two types, as far as possible.

Figure 3.3 depicts this classification.

The value types may further be classified as struct type or enumeration type. The 'struct' type may store a numeric value, a Boolean value, or even a user-defined value. So, on the basis of this premise, the value types consist of two main categories:

1. *Structs* This value type represents a numeric, a Boolean, or a user-defined structure. These are further classified as follows:
   (a) Numeric types:
       (i) Integral types
       (ii) Floating point types
       (iii) Decimal types
   (b) Bool
   (c) User-defined structs
2. *Enumerations* Variables that are based on value types directly contain a value. This differs from the assignment of reference type variables, which copies a reference to the object but not the object itself. All value types are derived from `System.ValueType`. The segregation is depicted in Fig. 3.4. Section 3.2 explains the value types in detail.

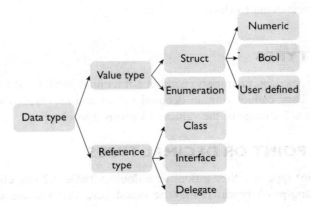

Fig. 3.4 Classification of data types

3.2 VALUE TYPES AND THEIR PROPERTIES

As mentioned earlier, the value types stores the value of a variable. The important properties of value types are as follows:

1. It is not feasible to obtain a new type from a value type.
2. It is not feasible for a value type to hold null value.
3. The 'nullable types' feature allow value types to be assigned to null.
4. Each value type has a default constructor that initializes the default value.
5. Constant expressions are evaluated at compilation time.
6. Simple types can be initialized using literals. For example, 'H' is a literal of the type char and 1979 is a literal of the type int.
7. Local variables in C# must be initialized before being used.

If a local variable is declared without initialization, for example, if a variable numInt is declared as follows:

```
int numInt;
```

then it cannot be used before initialization. The initialization can be done using the following statement:

```
numInt = new int(); // Invoke default constructor for int type
```

which is equivalent to

```
numInt = 0; // Assign an initial value, 0 in this example
```

The concept of initialization can be understood with the help of the following points:

1. It is possible to have the declaration and the initialization of a variable in the same statement. For example,

    ```
    int numInt = 0;
    ```

2. The new operator calls the default constructor and assigns the default value to the variable.
3. The new operator should be used with the user-defined types to invoke the default constructor. The following statement invokes the default constructor of the Point struct:

    ```
    Point p = new Point(); // Invoke default constructor for the struct
    ```

After this call, the struct is considered to be definitely assigned; that is, all its members are initialized to their default values.

3.3 INTEGRAL TYPES

The integral types depict numbers (without a fractional part) in the C# programming language specification. They cannot contain decimal values and are used when the data is a number. Table 3.1 depicts the range of the values of various integer types.

3.4 FLOATING POINT OR DECIMAL TYPES

A floating-point type is either a float or a double. Table 3.2 depicts the range of values for different floating-point types. It may be noted here that the use of a float is depicted in Section 3.9.2.

Table 3.1 Integral types

Type	Size (in bits)	Range
sbyte	8	−128 to 127
byte	8	0 to 255
short	16	−32768 to 32767
ushort	16	0 to 65535
int	32	−2147483648 to 2147483647
uint	32	0 to 4294967295
long	64	−9223372036854775808 to 9223372036854775807
ulong	64	0 to 18446744073709551615
char	16	0 to 65535

Table 3.2 Floating-point types

Type	Size (in bits)	Precision	Range
float	32	7 digits	1.5×10^{-45} to 3.4×10^{38}
double	64	15–16 digits	5.0×10^{-324} to 1.7×10^{308}
decimal	128	28–29 decimal places	1.0×10^{-28} to 7.9×10^{28}

3.5 STRING TYPE

C# provides string data type, which has a lot of methods to help manipulate the data type. The various functions provided by the string class have been discussed in detail in Chapter 8. However, the various literals, which cannot be printed in the normal way, have been depicted in Table 3.3.

Table 3.3 String type

Escape sequence	Meaning
\'	Single quote
\"	Double quote
\\	Backslash
\0	Null, not the same as the C# null value
\a	Bell
\b	Backspace
\f	Form feed
\n	New line
\r	Carriage return
\t	Horizontal tab
\v	Vertical tab

3.6 REFERENCE TYPES

One of the categorization of data types is reference types. Variables of reference types are also referred to as objects. They store references to the actual data. The following keywords are used to declare reference types:

1. Class
2. Interface
3. Delegate

Figure 3.5 depicts the categorization of the various reference types.

Class is a real or conceptual entity having importance to problem at hand. Classes are declared using the keyword `class`. The syntax of a class is given as follows:

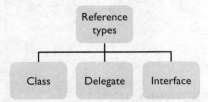

Fig. 3.5 Classification of reference types

Syntax
```
class <Classname>
{
    // Methods, properties, fields, events, delegates
    // Go here
}
```

An interface contains only the signatures of methods, delegates, or events. The implementation of the methods is done in the class that implements the interface, as shown in the following example:

```
public delegate void TestDelegate(string message);
```

The delegate keyword is used to declare a reference type that can be used to encapsulate a name or an anonymous method. Delegates in C# are similar to function pointers in C++.

3.7 CLASSES AND OBJECTS

C# is an object-oriented programming language. The program revolves around an object. An object is an instance of a class. A class may be defined as a real or a conceptual object having importance to the problem at hand. For example, if a developer intends to craft a software application for a college, then student class may be the appropriate one to start with. The class has many components, the most important being attributes and methods. Once a class has been crafted, the next step is to make instances of that class. In the Main method, the functions of the objects can be invoked. There are two types of classes in C#: user-defined classes and the classes that are predefined in the .NET library. The second section of the book, on object-oriented concepts, explains all the concepts related to classes and objects.

It may be noted here that classes can also be defined as generic through the use of type parameters that enable client code to customize the class in a type-safe and efficient manner. A single generic class, for example, System.Collections.Generic.List in the .NET Framework class library can be used by client code to store integers, strings, or any other type of object. Objects, classes, and structs have the following properties:

1. Objects are instances of a given data type. The data type provides a blueprint for the object that is created—or instantiated—when the application is executed.
2. New data types are defined using classes and structs.
3. Classes and structs form the building blocks of C# applications, containing code and data. A C# application will always contain at least one class.

4. A struct can be considered a lightweight class, ideal for creating data types that store small amounts of data, and does not represent a type that might later be extended via inheritance.
5. C# classes support inheritance, meaning they can derive from a previously defined class.

3.8 KEYWORDS

Keywords are predefined reserved identifiers that have special meanings to the compiler. They cannot be used as identifiers in a program unless they include @ as a prefix. For example, @while is a legal identifier but for is not because it is a keyword. Table 3.4 gives the list of keywords in C#.

Table 3.4 Keywords

abstract	event	new	struct
as	explicit	null	switch
base	extern	object	this
bool	false	operator	throw
break	finally	out	true
byte	fixed	override	try
case	float	params	typeof
catch	for	private	uint
char	foreach	protected	ulong
checked	goto	public	unchecked
class	if	readonly	unsafe
const	implicit	ref	ushort
continue	in	return	using
decimal	int	sbyte	virtual
default	interface	sealed	volatile
delegate	internal	short	void
do	is	sizeof	while
double	lock	stackalloc	
else	long	static	
enum	namespace	string	

Table 3.5 Contextual keywords

get	partial	set
value	where	yield

Contextual Keywords

The keywords that are not reserved but are used to provide specific meaning to a code are called contextual keywords. Some of the contextual keywords are given in Table 3.5.

3.9 VARIABLES

Variables represent storage locations. Every variable has a type, which determines what values can be stored in the variable. C# is a type-safe language, and the C# compiler guarantees that values stored in variables are always of the appropriate type. The value of a variable can be changed through assignment or through the use of the ++ and -- operators.

A variable must be assigned before its value can be obtained. However, variables are either initially assigned or initially unassigned. An initially assigned variable has a well-defined initial value and is always considered definitely assigned. A variable that has not been initialized initially has no initial value. Nevertheless, for such variables, assignment is essential before they can be used. The assignment to the variable may occur in any possible execution path leading to that location.

3.9.1 Rules for Naming Variables

While declaring or naming a variable, the following rules must be kept in mind:
1. All variable names must begin with a letter of the alphabet or an underscore (_).
2. Variable names may contain letters and the digits 0 to 9.
3. Spaces or special characters such as ~ and ^ are not allowed.
4. The name can be of any length.
5. Variable names with all uppercase letters are primarily used to identify constant variables.
6. It is not possible to use a keyword for a variable name. For example, for and while cannot be used as a variable.

3.9.2 Type Conversion

A major problem faced with C and C++ was that many conversions that did not make sense were allowed in those languages. Such conversions did not lead to compile time errors but resulted in spurious output. The developers of C# kept this in mind and curtained casting between types. Conversion of data types can be done explicitly using a cast, but in some cases, implicit conversions are allowed. The following is an example:

```
static void TestCasting()
{
    int i = 10;
    float f = 0;
    f = i; // An implicit conversion, no data will be lost.
    f = 0.5F;
    i = (int)f; // An explicit conversion and information will be lost
}
```

A cast explicitly invokes the conversion operator from one type to another. The cast will fail if no such conversion operator is defined. Custom conversion operators can be written to convert between user-defined types. The following program casts a double to an int. The program will not compile without the cast:

```
class Test
{
    static void Main()
    {
        double x = 1266.7;
        int a;
        a = (int)x; // Cast double to int
        System.Console.WriteLine(a);
    }
}
```

Output

```
1266
```

3.9.3 Boxing and Unboxing

Boxing and unboxing facilitates value types to be treated as objects. Boxing means converting a value to an instance of the object reference type. For example, Int is a class and int is a data type. Converting int to Int is an exemplification of boxing, whereas converting Int to int is unboxing. The concept helps in garbage collection. Unboxing, on the other hand, converts object type to value type. In the following example, the integer variable i is *boxed* and assigned to object o.

```
int i = 123;
object o = (object)i;   // Boxing
```

The object o can then be unboxed and assigned to integer variable i.

```
o = 123;
i = (int)o; // Unboxing
```

The advantages of boxing and unboxing will become clear after going through the remaining chapters. However, at this point, it is essential to appreciate that in C#, unlike C++, values can be converted into objects and vice versa.

3.10 OPERATORS

Every programming language supports a set of operators, which operate on operands to give results; so does C#. Common examples of operators are mathematical operations such as '>' for 'greater than'. C# provides a large set of operators. These operators help us to write arithmetic instructions. In addition, many operators can be overloaded by the user, thus changing their meaning when applied to a user-defined type. The list of operators in C# is given in Table 3.6. Some of the important operators are explained in Section 3.11.

Table 3.6 List of operators in C#

Arithmetic	Arithmetic
+	Increment and decrement
–	++
*	––
/	Shift
%	<<
Logical (Boolean and bitwise)	>>
&	Relational
|	==
^	!=
!	<
~	>
&&	<=
||	>=
True	Assignment
False	=
String concatenation	+=

(Contd)

Table 3.6 (Contd)

Arithmetic	Arithmetic
+	-=
*=	+
/=	-
%=	Object creation
&=	new
|=	Type information
^=	as
<<=	is
>>=	sizeof
Member access	typeof
.	Overflow exception control
Indexing	checked
[]	unchecked
Cast	Indirection and address
()	*
Conditional	->
?	[]
Delegate concatenation and removal	&

3.11 IMPORTANT OPERATORS OF C#

Various operators used in C# have been stated in Section 3.10. This section provides an insight into some of these operators. Though the importance and use of the operators are explained here, their actual utility can be fully understood by the developers only after writing numerous programs.

3.11.1 Dot (.) Operator

The dot operator (.) is used for member access. It specifies a member of a type or namespace. This operator is widely used in Chapter 11. In the following example, a class called student has a data member number and a method called getData(). Since both of them are public, they can be accessed from the Main function (classes and access specifiers are explained in Chapter 11). The following example shows how to assign value to a data member and how to call a member function using a dot operator.

Example
```
class Student
{
    public int number;
    public void getData()
    {
    }
}
```

```
Student s = new Student();
s.number = 6;    //Assign to field number
s.getData();     //Invoke member function getData;
```

3.11.2 () Operator

The ( ) operator is used to specify the order of operations in an expression. Parentheses are also used to specify cast, which is the conversion from one type to another. The cast fails if no such conversion operator is defined. This operator cannot be overloaded.

Example 1

```
int a = 1;
int b = 2;
int c = 3;
double x = (a + b) – (a * c);
```

Output

0

Example 2

```
double x = 998.7;
int a;
a = (int)x; // Cast double to int
```

Output

998

3.11.3 [ ] Operator

The [ ] operator is used to access the elements of an array. An array type is a type followed by [ ]. The example that follows gives an idea of how to access the elements of an array using [ ] operator.

Example

Suppose an integer type array is required, then it is declared as follows:

```
int[] arrayNum;
arrayNum = new int[100]; //It is allocated a memory of 100 int types
```

To access an element of an array, the index of the desired element is enclosed in brackets:

```
arrayNum[0] = 1; //The first element of the array is assigned value 1
```

3.11.4 ++ Operator

The ++ operator increments its operand by one. The first form is the prefix increment operation, where the operator is placed before the operand. It increments the operand by one and returns the resulting value.

Example

```
int i = 5;
int b = ++i; //The value of i is first incremented and then b is assigned the value of
i, which is 6 in this case.
```

The second form is the postfix increment operation, where the operator is placed after the operand. It increments the operand by one and returns the value of the operand before it was incremented.

```
int i = 5;
int b = i++; //b is assigned the value of i (5 in this case) and then the value
of i is incremented.
```

In C#, the users can define their own data types. These are called user-defined data types. User-defined types can overload the ++ operator. For example, if a class called complex is created, then addition of two instances of the class can be accomplished using operator overloading.

3.11.5 -- Operator

The -- operator performs a decrement operation. It decrements the operand by one. The first form is the prefix decremented operation. The result of the operation is the value of the operand after it is decremented.

Example

```
int i = 5;
int b = --i; //The value of i is first decremented and then b is assigned the value of
i, which is 4 in this case.
```

The second form is the postfix decremented operation. The result of the operation is the value of the operand before it is decremented.

Example

```
int i = 5;
int b = i--; //b is assigned the value of i (5 in this case )and then the value of i
is decremented.
```

User-defined types can overload the -- operator.

3.11.6 new Operator

The new operator is used to create objects and invoke constructors. For example,

```
Student s = new Student();
```

The new operator is also used to invoke the default constructor for value types. For example,

```
int i = new int();
```

3.11.7 typeof Operator

The typeof operator is used to obtain the System.Type object for a type. A typeof expression is of the following form:

```
int j = 10;
System.Type type = j.GetType();    //Answer will be int
```

3.11.8 checked Keyword

The checked keyword is used to explicitly enable overflow checking for integral-type arithmetic operations and conversions. This keyword can be used to enable checking if it is suppressed globally by compiler options or environment configuration.

3.11.9 -> Operator

The -> operator is used to access the members of a class which are pointers. An expression of the form $a \rightarrow b$ depicts the use of the operator, where a is a pointer of type T^* and b is a member of T. The -> operator can be used only in unmanaged code. It cannot be overloaded. For example, if age is a data member of student class, then $T \rightarrow$ age is used to access the member age of student, where T is a pointer to student.

3.11.10 + Operator

The + operator can function as either a unary or a binary operator. Unary + operators are predefined for all numeric types. The result of a unary + operation on a numeric type is simply the value of the operand.

Example
```
int i = 5;
+i; //i remains 5.
```

Binary + operators are predefined for numeric and string types. For numeric types, + computes the sum of its two operands; when one or both operands are of type string, + concatenates the string representations of the operands.

Example
```
int a, b;
a = 5;
b = 3;
int c = a + b;//c becomes 8.
```

User-defined types can overload the unary + and binary + operators.

3.11.11 - Operator

The - operator can function as either a unary or a binary operator. Unary - operators are predefined for all numeric types. Binary - operators are predefined for numeric types. The - operator computes the difference of its two operands.

Example
```
int a, b;
a = 5;
b = 3;
int c = a - b;//c becomes 2.
```

User-defined types can overload the unary - and binary - operators.

3.11.12 ! Operator

The logical negation operator (!) is a unary operator that negates its operand. It is defined for Bool and returns true if and only if its operand is false.

Example
```
using System;
class MainClass
{
    static void Main()
    {
```

```
            Console.WriteLine(!true);
            Console.WriteLine(!false);
    }
}
```

Output

False
True

3.11.13 ~ Operator

The ~ operator performs a bitwise complement operation on its operand, which has the effect of reversing each bit. Bitwise complement operators are predefined for `int`, `uint`, `long`, and `ulong`.

Example

Consider the following code:

```
static void Main(string[] args)
{
    int a = 5;
    Console.WriteLine("The value of a is" + a);
    Console.WriteLine("Negation" + ~a);
    Console.ReadKey();
}
```

Output

The value of *a* is 5
Negation −6
The value stored in *a* is 5, which is (0)0000000 00000101, in binary. The negation of the number is (1)1111111 11111010 which is −6, since the maximum value that an integer can store is 32,767 after which the next value becomes −32,768.

3.11.14 & Operator

The unary & operator returns the address of its operand. Binary & operator is predefined for the integral types and Bool. For integral types, & computes the logical bitwise AND of its operands. For Bool operands, & computes the logical AND of its operands.

In AND operation, the result is true if and only if both its operands are true. The & operator evaluates both operators regardless of the first one's value. The operator has been explained in the implementation of AND gate.

3.11.15 sizeof Operator

The `sizeof` operator is used to obtain the size in bytes for a value type. For example, the size of the `int` type can be retrieved as follows:

```
int fSize = sizeof(float);//fSize will have value 4
```

3.11.16 * Operator

The multiplication operator (*) computes the product of its operands. It also acts as the dereference operator, allowing reading and writing to a pointer. The * operator is also used to declare pointer types and to dereference pointers. This operator can be used in unsafe contexts. User-defined types can also overload the binary * operator. The following statements depict the use of * operator. The output of the statements is shown after //.

Examples

```
2 * 3;      //6
1.5 * 4;    //6
1.5 * 1.5;  //2.25
```

3.11.17 / Operator

The division operator (/) divides its first operand by its second one. All numeric types have predefined division operators. User-defined types can also overload the / operator. The following statements depict the use of the operator. The output of the statements is shown after //.

Examples

```
4/2;         //2
4/3;         //1
(float)3/4;  //0.75
```

3.11.18 % Operator

The modulus operator (%) computes the remainder after dividing its first operand by its second one. All numeric types have predefined modulus operators. User-defined types can also overload the % operator. The following statements depict the use of modulus operator. The output of the statements is shown after //:

Examples

```
5 % 3;  // 2
5 % 2;  // 1
```

3.12 CLASSIFICATION OF OPERATORS

Most of the operators used in C# have been explained in Section 3.11. This section provides a classification of the operators and explains their usage. It may be noted that this classification is not mutually exclusive.

3.12.1 Unary, Binary, and Ternary Operators

Unary operators are those that operate on one variable, whereas binary operators operate on two variables. The post increment and preincrement operators are examples of unary operators. If the value of a variable *a* is 5, then '*b = a++*' will make the value of *b* equal to 5 and then increment the value of *a*. After the statement is executed, the value of *a* becomes 6 and that of *b* becomes 5.

The post-increment operator, on the other hand, first increments the value of the variable and then places it into the other variable. For example, if the value of *a* is initially 5, the expression '*b = ++a*' will make the value of *a* = 6 and will then make the value of *b* = 6. So, after the statement is executed, the value of *a* becomes 6 and so does the value of *b*. Sections 3.12.4 and 3.12.5 discuss these operators in detail. The following listing depicts the concept of unary operators:

```
using System;
using System.Collections.Generic;
using System.Linq;
using System.Text;
```

```
namespace UnaryOperators
{
    class Program
    {
        static void Main(string[] args)
        {
            int a = 5, b = 3;
            Console.WriteLine("a = " + a + " b = " + b);//Initial values of a and b
            b = a++;
            Console.WriteLine("a = " + a + " b = " + b);//b becomes 5 and a becomes 6
            b = ++a;
            Console.WriteLine("a = " + a + " b = " + b);//Both a and b are now 7
            //b = ++a++; //Invalid
            Console.WriteLine("a = " + a + " b = " + b);//
            Console.ReadKey();
        }
    }
}
```

Output

```
a = 5 b = 3
a = 6 b = 5
a = 7 b = 7
a = 7 b = 7
```

In the statement '$b = ++a++$', the error is that the operand of an increment or decrement operator must be a variable, property, or indexer, which is not the case here. Most of the mathematical operators discussed earlier are, however, binary. For example,

$$y = a + b;$$

adds two variables a and b and places the sum in the variable y. The earlier sections dealt extensively with such operators. There are some operators that operate three variables at a time. These are termed as ternary operators. For example, the conditional operator discussed in Section 4.9 of the next chapter manipulates three variables at a time.

Table 3.7 Arithmetic operators

$a + b$	13
$a - b$	7
$a * b$	30
a/b	3
$a \% b$	1

3.12.2 Arithmetic Operators

The $+$, $-$, $*$, $/$, and $\%$ operators, discussed in Sections 3.11.10, 3.11.11, 3.11.16, 3.11.17, and 3.11.18, qualify as mathematical or arithmetic operators since they accomplish the mathematical tasks of addition, subtraction, multiplication, division and finding out the remainder, respectively. For example, if the value of a variable a is 10 and that of variable b is 3, then Table 3.7 gives the result of the various operators being applied to these two numbers.

3.12.3 Relational Operators

The operators that depict the relation between two variables are called relational operators. The explanation of the various relational operators is as follows:

1. $a > b$ returns true if the value of variable a is greater than that of variable b, otherwise it returns false.
2. $a < b$ returns true if the value of variable a is less than that of variable b, otherwise it returns false.

3. *a* >= *b* returns true if the value of variable *a* is greater than or equal to that of variable *b*, otherwise it returns false.
4. *a* <= *b* returns true if the value of variable *a* is less than or equal to that of variable *b*, otherwise it returns false.
5. *a* != *b* returns true if the value of variable *a* is not equal to that of variable *b*, otherwise it returns false.
6. *a* == *b* returns true if the value of variable *a* is equal to that of variable *b*, otherwise it returns false.

These operators will be used in the conditional statements and therefore have been revisited in Section 4.1. The following program depicts the output in different cases. Try to decode the output on the basis of what we have studied until now:

```csharp
using System;
using System.Collections.Generic;
using System.Linq;
using System.Text;

namespace Relational
{
    class Program
    {
        static void Main(string[] args)
        {
            int a = 10, b = 12;
            Console.WriteLine(a > b);
            Console.WriteLine(a >= b);
            Console.WriteLine(a < b);
            Console.WriteLine(a <= b);
            Console.WriteLine(a == b);
            Console.WriteLine(a != b);
            a = 100;
            b = 12;
            Console.WriteLine(a > b);
            Console.WriteLine(a >= b);
            Console.WriteLine(a < b);
            Console.WriteLine(a <= b);
            Console.WriteLine(a == b);
            Console.WriteLine(a != b);
            a = 10;
            b = 10;
            Console.WriteLine(a > b);
            Console.WriteLine(a >= b);
            Console.WriteLine(a < b);
            Console.WriteLine(a <= b);
            Console.WriteLine(a == b);
            Console.WriteLine(a != b);
            Console.ReadKey();
        }
    }
}
```

Output

```
False
False
True
True
False
True
True
True
False
False
False
True
False
True
False
True
True
False
```

3.12.4 Logical and Bitwise Operators

Logical operators perform the logical tasks. For example, && operator represents 'AND'. The statement 'a && b' is true if a and b are two statements that are individually true. In all other cases, 'a && b' is false.

The || operator depicts 'OR'. The statement 'a || b' is true if either of the two statements is true or if both statements are true. The result is false, however, when both the statements are false. The following program generates the truth tables of AND and OR:

```
using System;
using System.Collections.Generic;
using System.Linq;
using System.Text;
namespace LogicalOperatorsDemo
{
    class Program
    {
        static void Main(string[] args)
        {
        Console.WriteLine("The truth table of AND");
        bool a = true;
        bool b = true;
```

```csharp
            bool c = a && b;
            Console.WriteLine("a\tb\tc");
            Console.WriteLine(a + "\t" + b + "\t" + c);
            a = true;
            b = false;
            c = a && b;
            Console.WriteLine(a + "\t" + b + "\t" + c);
            a = false;
            b = true;
            c = a && b;
            Console.WriteLine(a + "\t" + b + "\t" + c);
            a = false;
            b = false;
            c = a && b;
            Console.WriteLine(a + "\t" + b + "\t" + c);
            Console.WriteLine("The truth table of OR");
            a = true;
            b = true;
            c = a || b;
            Console.WriteLine("a\tb\tc");
            Console.WriteLine(a + "\t" + b + "\t" + c);
            a = true;
            b = false;
            c = a || b;
            Console.WriteLine(a + "\t" + b + "\t" + c);
            a = false;
            b = true;
            c = a || b;
            Console.WriteLine(a + "\t" + b + "\t" + c);
            a = false;
            b = false;
            c = a || b;
            Console.WriteLine(a + "\t" + b + "\t" + c);
            Console.ReadKey();
        }
    }
}
```

Output

```
The truth table of AND
a       b       c
True    True    True
True    False   False
False   True    False
False   False   False
The truth table of OR
a       b       c
True    True    True
True    False   True
False   True    True
False   False   False
```

Table 3.8 Conjunction

a	b	a ^ b
True	True	False
True	False	True
False	True	True
False	False	False

C# also provides & and | operators. These operators behave in the same way as the earlier two operators except for the fact that in & and | both the statements are first individually evaluated and then the operator is applied. In the case of && operator, if the first statement is false the second statement is not evaluated, and the answer evaluates to false. In the same way, in case of ||, if the first statement is true the second statement is not evaluated, and the answer evaluates to true. It may be noted that there will be no difference in the outputs of && and &; the difference is only in the efficiency.

The & and | operators are used as bitwise operators; that is, the operator works even when *a* and *b* are bits. In bitwise operators, the individual statements need not be evaluated. There are some more bitwise operators such as ~, which negates the statement. For example, if *a* is true then ~*a* is false and vice versa.

The ^ operator in C# represents bitwise XOR. The XOR operator works as per Table 3.8. That is, if both the statements are either true or false, then the output is false. The output is true only when one of the statements is true. The following program generates the truth table of XOR:

```csharp
using System;
using System.Collections.Generic;
using System.Linq;
using System.Text;
namespace Chapter4Program2
{
class Program
    {
static void Main(string[] args)
        {
            Console.WriteLine("The truth table of XOR gate");
            bool a = true;
            bool b = true;
            bool c = a ^ b;
            Console.WriteLine("a\tb\tc");
            Console.WriteLine(a + "\t" + b + "\t" + c);
            a = true;
            b = false;
            c = a ^ b;
            Console.WriteLine(a + "\t" + b + "\t" + c);
            a = false;
            b = true;
            c = a ^ b;
            Console.WriteLine(a + "\t" + b + "\t" + c);
            a = false;
            b = false;
            c = a ^ b;
            Console.WriteLine(a + "\t" + b + "\t" + c);
            Console.ReadKey();
        }
    }
}
```

Output

```
The truth table of XOR gate
a       b       c
True    True    False
True    False   True
False   True    True
False   False   False
```

3.12.5 Assignment Operators

The assignment operators can be considered as a replacement of the simple addition, subtraction, division, multiplication, and modulo operators. The only advantage of these operators is the ease of use. Table 3.9 gives the meaning of these operators.
The following program shows the use of these operators.

Table 3.9 Assignment operators

$a\mathrel{+}= b$	$a = a + b$
$a\mathrel{-}= b$	$a = a - b$
$a\mathrel{*}= b$	$a = a * b$
$a\mathrel{/}= b$	$a = a / b$
$a\mathrel{\%}= b$	$a = a \% b$

```
using System;
using System.Collections.Generic;
using System.Linq;
using System.Text;
namespace Chapter4Program5
{
    class Program
    {
        static void Main(string[] args)
        {
            int a = 90, b = 10;
            a += b;
            Console.WriteLine("a= " + a + " b= " + b);
            //a becomes a + b, b remains same
            a = 10;
            b = 3;
            a -= b;
            Console.WriteLine("a= " + a + " b= " + b);
            //a becomes a - b, b remains same
            a = 10;
            b = 3;
            a %= b;
                Console.WriteLine("a= " + a + " b= " + b);
            //a becomes a % b, b remains same
            a = 10;
            b = 2;
            a *= b;
            Console.WriteLine("a= " + a + " b= " + b);
            //a becomes a * b, b remains same
            a = 9;
            b = 3;
            a /= b;
            Console.WriteLine("a= " + a + " b= " + b);
```

```
            //a becomes a / b, b remains same
        Console.ReadKey();
    }
  }
}
```

Output

```
a= 100 b= 10
a= 7 b= 3
a= 1 b= 3
a= 20 b= 2
a= 3 b= 3
```

Table 3.10 Default values

Data type	Default value
Byte	0
Sbyte	0
Char	'\0'
Bool	False
Enum	(E)0
Short	0
Int	0
Uint	0
Long	0L
Ulong	0
float	0.0F
Double	0.0D
Decimal	0.0M

3.13 DEFAULT VALUES

One of the major problems encountered while using C and C++ is that if a variable is defined and not initialized then it uses results in cropping up of garbage values. These spurious values may lead to erroneous output of the program. So, it would be better to initialize the variables to their default values when defined. As stated earlier, a variable cannot be used before it is initialized. However, if a data type is initiated, the variable gets the default value. For example, if one writes

```
bool b = new bool();
```

and prints its value, then 'false' will be displayed. It is the same as writing

```
bool b = false;
```

The default values of various data types are shown in Table 3.10.

3.14 CONSTANT VARIABLES

At times, there will be a requirement for some variables whose value remains constant throughout the program. For example, in a module that calculates the area of two-dimensional figures, the value of pi must remain constant. In such situations, constant variables can be used. A constant variable is one whose value cannot be changed in the program. The variables are preceded by the keyword const. It may be noted here that an access specifier may be used along with the variable at the time of declaration. The syntax of the declaration is as follows:

```
<modifier> <type><name of the variable>
```

Example

```
const int a = 5;
```

If one tries to change the value of a const variable, an error will be displayed. For example, in the following program the value of *a* is changed. The program on compilation will result in an error.

```
static void Main(string[] args)
{
    const int a = 5;
    Console.WriteLine(a);
    a = 7;
    Console.WriteLine(a);
    Console.ReadKey();
}
```

Output

Error:
The left-hand side of an assignment must be a variable, a property, or an indexer.

3.15 SCOPE OF VARIABLE

The scope of a variable is the area within which the variable has its life. There are some variables whose lifespan is until the end of Main. Static variables and instance variables are two such variables. A variable defined in a particular block or function retains its value in that particular block. Once the block ends, a variable with the same name can be declared. In the following program, the variable *a* is declared in the method abc(). However, another variable having the same name is declared in Main as well, which is completely acceptable as it is in a separate method. The scope of the variable *a* declared in the method abc() has ended, and therefore it can be reinitialized.

```
using System;
using System.Collections.Generic;
using System.Linq;
using System.Text;
namespace Chapter3Prog1
{
    class Program
    {
        public void abc()
        {
            int a = 7;
            Console.WriteLine(a);
        }
        static void Main(string[] args)
        {
            int a = 5;
            Console.WriteLine(a);
            Program p = new Program();
            p.abc();
            Console.WriteLine(a);
            Console.ReadKey();
        }
    }
}
```

Output

```
5
7
5
```

A variable in a particular block is called a local variable. It may be noted here that within a block it is not possible to have a variable of the same name as that in the outer block. The following code will, therefore, result in an error:

```
static void Main(string[] args)
{
    int a = 5;
    Console.WriteLine(a);
    {
        int a = 7;
        Console.WriteLine(a);
    }
    Console.WriteLine(a);
    Console.ReadKey();
}
```

(Variable of the same name is declared in the outer block.)

Output
Error:
Different meaning to 'a', which is already used in a 'parent or current' scope to denote something else

3.16 TYPE CASTING

At times, it is required to convert a value in one data type to another data type. For example, if the user is asked to enter two numbers and the program is required to calculate the result of their division, then conversion of at least one of the numbers to a 'float' or a 'decimal' is required. This is because the result of division of two integers is an integer. In such situations, type casting helps us to achieve the target. Type casting refers to the conversion of a data type into another data type. There can be other reasons for type casting as well. For example, when trying to assign value 3.14 to a float variable pi, the following statement might be used:

```
float pi = 3.14;
```

However, this will result in the following error:
Error:
Literal of type double cannot be implicitly converted to type 'float'; use an 'F' suffix to create a literal of this type.

So, the double '3.14' needs to be explicitly converted into a float, which can be done by type casting. Type casting is done by preceding the value with the required data type in parentheses. However, in order to do this, conversion must be allowed. In the given example, the value '3.14' needs to be preceded by the data type float in parentheses.

```
float pi = (float)3.14;
```

In this type of type casting, the variable to be converted is suffixed by the data type in which it is to be converted in parentheses. It may be noted here that C# also has the ability of implicit type casting, if required. Table 3.11 gives the data types that can be implicitly converted.

Table 3.11 Implicit type casting

Byte	Decimal
Unit	double
Ushort	long

The following program depicts implicit type casting. A unit type variable is converted into double in the following snippet:

```
class Program
{
    static void Main(string[] args)
    {
        uint x = 5;
        double d = x;
        Console.WriteLine(d);
        Console.ReadKey();
    }
}
```

Output

```
5
```

3.17 MATHEMATICAL FUNCTIONS

After learning C#, readers would probably create software applications for various clients. Most of the applications require at least a few mathematical operations. It will be difficult to perform those complex calculations without some predefined methods. C# provides the Math class, which has many such functions. Some of the important functions are described in this section.

3.17.1 Abs Function

The Abs function returns the absolute value of the number entered. It may be noted here that the function is overloaded. It can take float, double, decimal, long, sbyte, and short type variable as its argument and returns the corresponding positive value. The various declarations of this method in the Math class are given as follows.

```
public static decimal Abs(decimal value);
public static double Abs(double value);
public static float Abs(float value);
public static long Abs(long value);
public static sbyte Abs(sbyte value);
public static short Abs(short value);
```

3.17.2 Inverse Trigonometric Functions

The inverse sine, inverse cosine, and inverse tan of an angle, in radians, can be found by the Asin, Acos, and Atan methods defined in the Math class. However, for some strange reason, the

Math class also provides atan2 method, which calculates the inverse of '*y/x*', *y* and *x* being two variables of the type double. Overloads of inverse trigonometric functions are shown as follows:

```
public static double Acos(double d);
public static double Asin(double d);
public static double Atan(double d);
public static double Atan2(double y, double x);
```

3.17.3 Trigonometric and Hyperbolic Functions

The sine and hyperbolic sine of an angle in radian may be evaluated with the help of sine and sinh methods. The tanh function calculates the hyperbolic tan of a number. The hyperbolic cos is calculated by the cosh function. The signatures of the various functions are given as follows:

```
public static double cos(double a);
public static double sin(double a);
public static double sinh(double value);
public static double cosh(double value);
public static double tan(double a);
public static double tanh(double value);
```

3.17.4 Ceiling Function

The Ceiling function results in a number greater than or equal to the given number. For example, if the number is 1.78, then its Ceiling will be 2. Again, this function is also overloaded. There are two overloads of the function: one returns a decimal, the other a double. The signatures of the functions are stated as follows:

```
public static decimal Ceiling(decimal d);
public static double Ceiling(double a);
```

3.17.5 Floor Function

The overloaded Floor functions return the greatest integer less than or equal to that number. The signatures of the functions alongside.

```
public static decimal Floor(decimal d);
public static double Floor(double d);
```

3.17.6 DivRem Function

The DivRem function returns the quotient and also gives the remainder as the output parameter. The function is, therefore, different from the division operator, which does not return both quotient and reminder at the same time. The signatures of the functions are given below.

```
public static int DivRem(int a, int b, out int result);
public static long DivRem(long a, long b, out long result);
```

3.17.7 Max Function

The `Math` class provides a `Max` function, which returns the maximum of the two numbers entered by the user. There are eleven overloads of this function, one each for the data types given below.

```
public static byte Max(byte val1, byte val2);
public static decimal Max(decimal val1, decimal val2);
public static double Max(double val1, double val2);
public static float Max(float val1, float val2);
public static int Max(int val1, int val2);
public static long Max(long val1, long val2);
public static long Max(long val1, long val2);
public static short Max(short val1, short val2);
public static uint Max(uint val1, uint val2);
public static ulong Max(ulong val1, ulong val2);
public static ushort Max(ushort val1, ushort val2);
```

3.17.8 Min Function

The `Min` function used for calculating the minimum of two numbers. There are eleven overloads of this function, one each for the data types given as follows:

```
public static byte Min(byte val1, byte val2);
public static decimal Min(decimal val1, decimal val2);
public static double Min(double val1, double val2);
public static float Min(float val1, float val2);
public static int Min(int val1, int val2);
public static long Min(long val1, long val2);
public static sbyte Min(sbyte val1, sbyte val2);
public static short Min(short val1, short val2);
public static uint Min(uint val1, uint val2);
public static ulong Min(ulong val1, ulong val2);
public static ushort Min(ushort val1, ushort val2);
```

3.17.9 Pow Function

The power function returns *a* to the power of *b*, *a* and *b* being the double type variables, which this function takes as an input. The signature of the function is as follows:

`public static double Pow(double x, double y);`

3.17.10 Round Function

The `Round` function generally rounds a decimal value to the nearest integer. There are many overloads of the function. For example, the third overload rounds a decimal value to the nearest integer. 'A parameter specifies how to round the value if it is midway between two other numbers,' as per the definition provided by Microsoft. The various overloads of this function are depicted below.

```
public static decimal Round(decimal d);
public static double Round(double a);
public static decimal Round(decimal d, int decimals);
public static decimal Round(decimal d, int decimals);
public static double Round(double value, int digits);
public static double Round(double value, MidpointRounding mode);
public static decimal Round(decimal d, int decimals, MidpointRounding mode);
public static double Round(double value, int digits, MidpointRounding mode);
```

3.17.11 Sign Function

The Sign function gives the sign of the number. 0 indicates that the number entered is 0, −1 indicates that the number is less than 0, and +1 indicates that the number is greater than 0. There are seven overloads of this function, depicted here.

```
public static int Sign(decimal value);
public static int Sign(double value);
public static int Sign(float value);
public static int Sign(int value);
public static int Sign(long value);
public static int Sign(sbyte value);
public static int Sign(short value);
```

3.17.12 Truncate Function

The Truncate function calculates the integral part of a specific double precision. There are two overloads of the function, which are stated alongside.

```
public static decimal Truncate(decimal d);
public static double Truncate(double d);
```

3.17.13 Sqrt Function

The square root of a number is calculated by the Sqrt function. The signature of the function is given as follows:

```
public static double Sqrt(double d);
```

3.17.14 Constants

The Math class also contains two constants PI and E. PI is the ratio of circumference of a circle to its diameter, and E indicates the base of natural logarithm. The values of these constants are given alongside.

```
public const double E = 2.71828;
public const double PI = 3.14159;
```

3.18 ARITHMETIC EXPRESSIONS

An arithmetic expression is an expression that accomplishes a mathematical task. It may be noted here that an arithmetic expression in C#, as in C, has a single variable on the left-hand side, which gets its value as a result of evaluation of the right-hand side. It may also be noted that the evaluated value of the left-hand side must be the same as, or can be implicitly converted into, the data type of the left-hand side. For example, the area (A) of a circle is given by the following formula:

$$A = \pi r^2$$

where r is the radius of the circle.

In C#, the formula can be written as follows:

```
A = 22 * r * r / 7; //If both r and A are of the type 'double'
```

If the data type of r is double, then the correct result will be displayed. However, if the data type of r is an integer, then the left-hand side will have to be converted into a double, so as to get the correct result. In such cases, type casting is required as depicted in the following statement:

```
A = (double)(22 * r * r / 7); //If r is an integer and A is of the type 'double'
```

The following example helps to understand the basics of an arithmetic expression. The program asks the user to enter two numbers and then calculates their sum, difference, product, and result of division.

```csharp
using System;
using System.Collections.Generic;
using System.Linq;
using System.Text;

namespace FirstConsoleApplication
{
    class Program
    {
        static void Main(string[] args)
        {
            int number1, number2, result1;
            double result2;
            try
            {
                Console.WriteLine("Enter the first number ");
                number1 = int.Parse(Console.ReadLine());
                Console.WriteLine("Enter the second number ");
                number2 = int.Parse(Console.ReadLine());
                //Sum of the numbers
                result1 = number1 + number2;
                Console.WriteLine("The sum is " + result1);
                //Differnce of the numbers
                result1 = number1 - number2;
                Console.WriteLine("The differnce is " + result1);
                //Product of the numbers
                result1 = number1 * number2;
                Console.WriteLine("The product is " + result1);
```

```
            //Division
            result2 = (double)number1 / number2;
            Console.WriteLine("The result is " + result2);
            Console.ReadKey();
        }
        catch(Exception e)
        {
            Console.WriteLine("Exception " + e.ToString());
        }
    }
}
```

Output

```
Enter the first number
23
Enter the second number
412
The sum is 435
The difference is -389
The Product is 9476
The result is 0.0558252427184466
```

The following example is a little more complex. It evaluates the following expression:

$$y = \sqrt{a^2 + b^2}$$

where a and b are entered by the user. The program requires the use of Math.sqrt() function, which calculates the square root of the number given as its argument.

```
using System;
using System.Collections.Generic;
using System.Linq;
using System.Text;

namespace ConsoleApplicationProgram2
{
    class Program
    {
        static void Main(string[] args)
        {
            int a,b;
            double result;
            try
            {
                Console.WriteLine("Enter the first number");
                a = int.Parse(Console.ReadLine());
                Console.WriteLine("Enter the second number");
                a = int.Parse(Console.ReadLine());
                //Sum of the numbers
                result = Math.Sqrt(a * a + b * b);
                Console.WriteLine("The result is" + result);
                Console.ReadKey();
            }
```

```
        catch(Exception e)
        {
            Console.WriteLine("Exception " + e.ToString());
        }
      }
    }
}
```

Output

When the program is executed, the user will be asked to enter two numbers and the square root of the sum of the squares of the numbers will be displayed.

```
Enter the first number
3
Enter the second number
4
The result is 5
```

3.19 PRECEDENCE OF OPERATORS

The understanding of evaluation of an expression is essential as it is the basis of the whole program. An incorrect evaluation may lead to bugs, which are hard to detect. The knowledge of precedence of operators is vital so as to avoid incorrect evaluation. In C#, any arithmetic expression is evaluated from left to right. However, the priority of *, /, and % operators is higher than that of + and − operators. The program code given below gives an idea of the evaluation of an expression. Consider the expression

Step 1 • 2 + 3 * 4/2 − 1

Step 2 • 2 + 12/2 − 1

Step 3 • 2 + 6 − 1

Step 4 • 8 − 1

Step 5 • 7

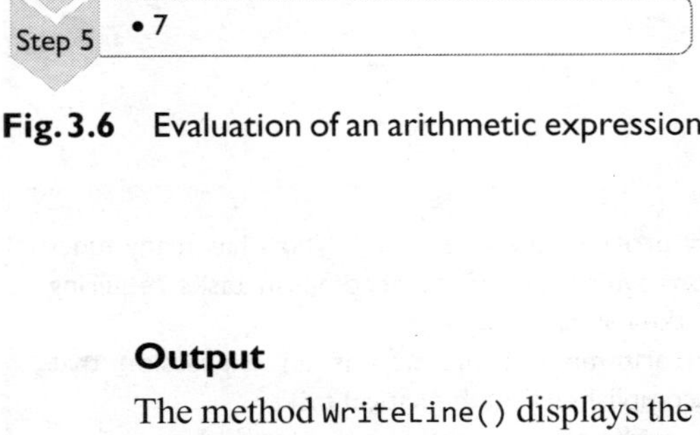

Fig. 3.6 Evaluation of an arithmetic expression

y = 2 + 3 * 4 / 2 − 1;

During evaluation, this expression is seen from left to right by the compiler. First, the * operator is processed. So 3 * 4 becomes 12. This is followed by division, that is, 12/2 is evaluated to 6. Now, 2 + 6 − 1 remains. This expression becomes 8 − 1 in the next pass. The final answer, therefore, evaluates to 7. The process is depicted in Fig. 3.6. The Main method follows the figure:

```
static void Main(string[] args)
{
    int x = 2 + 3 * 4 / 2 − 1;
    Console.WriteLine(x);
    Console.ReadKey();
}
```

Output

The method WriteLine() displays the value of x and ReadKey() expects a key input from the user.

```
7
```

SUMMARY

Some of the types used in a program need explicit conversion such as from float to int. The need of conversion will become clear as developers write numerous programs. The chapter outlines the various data types and operators in C#. The understanding of this topic is essential to write programs. The chapter is a prerequisite to all the three sections of the book. In order to create a program in any language, developers must be familiar with the data types and their use. Data types are like the unit lattices in a crystal. The chapter also introduces the concept of expressions. It is important to fully understand the operators before proceeding with the procedural concepts such as loops and functions. Moreover, one must remember that it is not essential to learn each and every overload of every function. These will become clear as the developer writes various programs. The chapter will also act as a reference point for all the Math functions, which are essential in making any financial software. The functions have deliberately been included in this chapter and not in the appendix of the book so that their purpose and use may become clear. There is a common misconception that C# can be learned only by making visual projects. The idea is misleading and primarily propagated by those who do not understand the intricacies of the language.

GLOSSARY

Boxing and unboxing These facilitate value types to be treated as objects. Boxing means converting a value to an instance of the object reference type. Unboxing refers to converting a data type into an Object.

Value types and reference types Variables of the value types store data. The reference types store references to the actual data. Reference types are also referred to as objects.

Class This may be defined as a real or a conceptual object having importance to the problem at hand.

Keywords Keywords are predefined reserved identifiers that have special meanings to the compiler.

Unary and binary operators The unary operators are those that operate on one variable. The binary operators operate on two variables.

Arithmetic and relational operators The operators that perform arithmetic tasks are referred to as arithmetic operators, whereas the operators that depict the relation between two variables are called relational operators.

Constant variables This is a variable whose value cannot be changed in the program. These variables are preceded by the keyword const.

Scope of a variable This is the area within which the variable has its life.

Type casting This refers to the conversion of a data type into another data type.

POINTS TO REMEMBER

- Value types stores the value of a variable.
- An interface contains only the signatures of methods, delegates, or events.
- The dot operator specifies a member of a type or namespace.
- Parentheses are also used to specify cast, which is the conversion from one type to another.
- The relational operators are used in the conditional statements.
- C# provides the Math class, which has many functions which help us to accomplish tasks requiring mathematical calculations.
- An arithmetic expression is an expression that accomplishes a mathematical task.
- An arithmetic expression is evaluated from left to right. However, the priority of *, /, and % operators is higher than that of + and − operators.

EXERCISES

I. Multiple-choice Questions

1. Which of the following are data types in C#?
   (a) Value type
   (b) Reference type
   (c) Both (a) and (b)
   (d) None of these

2. Which of the following is not a type of struct?
   (a) Integer
   (b) Floating point
   (c) Decimal
   (d) All of these

3. Which of the following is a value type?
   (a) Struct
   (b) Enumeration
   (c) Both (a) and (b)
   (d) None of these

4. Which of the following is a reference type?
   (a) Class
   (b) Interface
   (c) Delegate
   (d) All of these

5. Which of the following is true?
   (a) Each value type has an implicit constructor.
   (b) It is possible for a value type to contain a null value.
   (c) Constant expressions are not evaluated at the compile time.
   (d) All of these

6. Which of the following is not true?
   (a) Simple types can be initialized using literals.
   (b) It is not possible to use a variable before initializing it.
   (c) The new operator calls the default constructor.
   (d) Declaration and initialization cannot be done at the same time.

7. What is the precision of a float in C#?
   (a) 7 digits
   (b) 8 digits
   (c) 15 digits
   (d) 4 digits

8. Which of the following statements is correct?
   (a) \' represents a single quote.
   (b) \\' represents a single quote.
   (c) \\' represents a single quote.
   (d) None of these

9. Which is not a keyword in C#?
   (a) Null
   (b) New
   (c) Struct
   (d) All of these

10. Which of the following statements are true?
    (a) We can use a keyword in C# as an identifier.
    (b) We cannot use a keyword in C# as an identifier.
    (c) We can use a keyword in C# as an identifier by prefixing it with @.
    (d) None of these

11. What will be the output of the following program?
    ```
    static void Main(string[] args)
    {
        const int a = 2;
        Console.WriteLine(a);
        a = 5;
        Console.WriteLine(a);
        Console.ReadKey();
    }
    ```
    (a) 5, 2
    (b) 2, 5
    (c) 5, 5
    (d) None of these

12. What will be the output of the following program?
    ```
    static void Main(string[] args)
    {
        const int a = 2;
        Console.WriteLine(a);
        a = 5;
        Console.ReadKey();
    }
    ```
    (a) 5
    (b) 2
    (c) Either (a) or (b)
    (d) None of these

13. What will be the output of the following program?
    ```
    static void Main(string[] args)
    {
        const int a;
        Console.WriteLine(a);
        Console.ReadKey();
    }
    ```
    (a) 0
    (b) Null
    (c) Either (a) or (b)
    (d) The code will not compile.

14. What will be the output of the following program?
    ```
    static void Main(string[] args)
    {
        int a = 3;
        Console.WriteLine(a);
        {
            int a = 2;
            Console.WriteLine(a);
        }
        Console.WriteLine(a);
    ```

```
        Console.ReadKey();
    }
```
(a) 3, 2   (b) 3, 3
(c) 2, 2   (d) None of these

15. What will be the output of the following program?

    ```
    static void Main(string[] args)
    {
        int a = 3;
        int b = 2;
        Console.WriteLine(a / b);
        Console.WriteLine((float)a / b);
        Console.ReadKey();
    }
    ```
    (a) 0, 1.5   (b) 0, 1
    (c) 1, 1.5   (d) None of these

16. What will be the output of the following?

    ```
    static void Main(string[] args)
    {
        int x = 2 + 12 / 4 * 2 - 1;
        Console.WriteLine(x);
        Console.ReadKey();
    }
    ```
    (a) 7   (b) 5
    (c) 0   (d) None of these

17. What will be the output of the following?

    ```
    static void Main(string[] args)
    {
        int x = 2 * 12 / 4 + 2 - 1;
        Console.WriteLine(x);
        Console.ReadKey();
    }
    ```
    (a) 7   (b) 5
    (c) 0   (d) None of these

18. What will be the output of the following?

    ```
    static void Main(string[] args)
    {
        int x = 2 + 12 - 4 * 2 / 1 - 1;
        Console.WriteLine(x);
        Console.ReadKey();
    }
    ```
    (a) 7   (b) 5
    (c) 0   (d) None of these

19. What will be the output of the following?

    ```
    static void Main(string[] args)
    {
    ```

    ```
        int x = 2 + 12 / 4 * 2 / 1 - 1;
        Console.WriteLine(x);
        Console.ReadKey();
    }
    ```
    (a) 7   (b) 5
    (c) 0   (d) None of these

20. What will be the output of the following?

    ```
    static void Main(string[] args)
    {
        int x = 2 + ++12 / 4-- * 2++ / 1 - 1;
        Console.WriteLine(x);
        Console.ReadKey();
    }
    ```
    (a) 7   (b) 5
    (c) 0   (d) None of these

21. What will be the output of the following?

    ```
    class Program
    {
        static void Main(string[] args)
        {
            int x = 1, y, z;
            y = 2;
            x += y--;
            Console.WriteLine(x+" "+y);
            Console.ReadKey();
        }
    }
    ```
    (a) 1 3   (b) 3 1
    (c) 1 1   (d) 3 3

22. What will be the output of the following?

    ```
    static void Main(string[] args)
    {
        int x = 1, y, z;
        y = 2;
        x += --y;
        Console.WriteLine(x+" "+y);
        Console.ReadKey();
    }
    ```
    (a) 2 1   (b) 1 2
    (c) 2 1   (d) 1 3

23. What will be the output of the following?

    ```
    static void Main(string[] args)
    {
        int x = 1, y, z;
    ```

```
        y = 2;
        z = 3;
        x += --y + z--;
        Console.WriteLine(x+" "+y);
        Console.ReadKey();
    }
```
(a) 5 1 (b) 1 5
(c) 5 5 (d) 1 1

24. What will be the output of the following?
```
    static void Main(string[] args)
    {
        int x = 1, y, z;
        y = 2;
        z = 3;
        x += --y + --z;
        Console.WriteLine(x+" "+y);
        Console.ReadKey();
    }
```
(a) 5 1 (b) 4 1
(c) 1 4 (d) 1 1

25. What will be the output of the following?
```
    static void Main(string[] args)
    {
        int x = 1, y, z;
        y = 2;
        z = 3;
        x += --y+--z++;
        Console.WriteLine(x+" "+y);
        Console.ReadKey();
    }
```
(a) 5 1 (b) 4 1
(c) 1 4 (d) None of these

26. What will be the output of the following?
```
    static void Main(string[] args)
    {
        int x = 1, y, z;
        y = 2;
        z = 3;
        x += y+++++z;
        Console.WriteLine(x+" "+y);
        Console.ReadKey();
    }
```
(a) 5 1 (b) 4 1
(c) 1 4 (d) None of these

27. What will be the output of the following?
```
    static void Main(string[] args)
    {
        int x = 1, y, z;
        y = 2;
        z = 3;
        x += (y++) + (++z);
        Console.WriteLine(x+" "+y);
        Console.ReadKey();
    }
```
(a) 6 3 (b) 7 3
(c) 5 3 (d) None of these

28. What will be the output of the following?
```
    static void Main(string[] args)
    {
        int x = 1, y, z;
        y = 2;
        z = 3;
        x++ += (y++) + (++z);
        Console.WriteLine(x+" "+y);
        Console.ReadKey();
    }
```
(a) 6 3 (b) 7 3
(c) 5 3 (d) None of these

29. What will be the output of the following?
```
    static void Main(string[] args)
    {
        int x = 1, y, z;
        y = 2;
        z = 3;
        (x++) += (y++) + ++z ;
        Console.WriteLine(x+" "+y);
        Console.ReadKey();
    }
```
(a) 6 3 (b) 7 3
(c) 5 3 (d) None of these

30. What will be the output of the following?
```
    static void Main(string[] args)
    {
        int x = 1, y, z;
        y = 2;
        z = 3;
        x += (y++) + (++z)--;
        Console.WriteLine(x+" "+y);
```

```
            Console.ReadKey();
    }
```
(a) 6 3   (b) 7 3
(c) 5 3   (d) None of these

II. Review Questions

1. Explain the following terms:
   (a) Boxing and unboxing
   (b) Classes and objects
   (c) Reference types
   (d) Delegates
   (e) Value types

2. Explain the meaning of the following operators:
   (a) ()   (b) []
   (c) Checked   (d) new
   (e) sizeof

3. What is meant by the scope of a variable? Can a variable in an inner block be defined with the same name as a variable defined in the outer block?

4. What is the importance of constant variables? Can we change the value of such variable after it has been assigned a value?

5. What is meant by user-defined data types? Can all the operators be used for user-defined data types?

6. What are data types? How do you classify data types?

7. Examine the importance of default values in terms of correctness of a program?

8. Explain the importance and use of new operator. Exemplify with the help of a class.

9. What is the importance of checked operator?

10. Which of the operators explained in the chapter cannot be overloaded?

III. Programming Exercises

1. Write a program to generate the truth table of a two-input AND gate*.

2. Write a program to generate the truth table of a three-input AND gate.

3. Write a program to generate the truth table of a two-input OR gate.

4. Write a program to generate the truth table of a three-input OR gate.

5. Write a program to generate the truth table of a NOT gate.

6. Write a program to generate the truth table of a NAND gate.

7. Write a program to generate the truth table of a XNOR gate.

8. Write a program to generate the truth table for the following circuits:

   (a)
   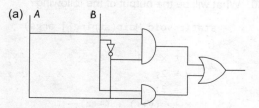

   (b)
   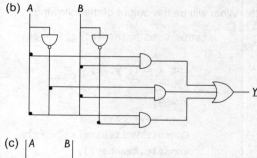

   (c)
   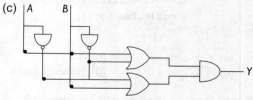

   (d)
   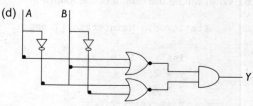

9. Can you find the relation between outputs obtained from parts (c) and (d) of Question 8?

10. Write a program to generate the truth table of a NAND gate.

---

* See Annexure for a brief description on logic gates.

ANNEXURE—LOGIC GATES

A brief background of the logic gates is presented here in order to enable readers to generate the truth tables of various gates. Even if readers are not familiar with the gates, the description provided here will help them in getting started.

Logic gates are the basic building blocks of a digital system. They are called logic gates as they are capable of making decisions. There are three basic logic gates—AND, OR, and NOT. These gates are connected together to realize the required logic and to perform a logic operation; this is known as logic design.

The input of these gates can be either of the following:
1. High (or True or 1)
2. Low (or False or 0)

A table that lists the possible combinations of input variables and the corresponding outputs is called the truth table.

AND Gate

The output of an AND gate is high when all its inputs are high. A two-input AND gate is depicted by the following figure.

Its output, that is, Y, is high only when both A and B are high; in all other cases Y is low. The following is the truth table of a two-input AND gate.

A	B	Y
0	0	0
0	1	0
1	0	0
1	1	1

Three-input AND Gate

The output Y is high only when all A, B, and C are high; in all other cases Y is low. The following is the truth table of a three-input AND gate.

A	B	C	Y
0	0	0	0
0	0	1	0
0	1	0	0
0	1	1	0
1	0	0	0
1	0	1	0
1	1	0	0
1	1	1	1

OR Gate

As in the case of an AND gate, an OR gate can have any number of inputs but it has only one output. The output is high (or '1') when any of the inputs is high. A two-input OR gate is depicted in the following figure.

The output Y will be high if either A or B is high or if both A and B are high. The following is the truth table of an OR gate.

$Y = A + B$

A	B	Y
0	0	0
0	1	0
1	0	1
1	1	1

Three-input OR Gate

$Y = A + B + C$

The output Y is governed by the following rules:
1. A, B, C all are low
2. A high and B, C low
3. B high and A, C low
4. C high and A, B low
5. A, B high and C low
6. A, C high and B low
7. B, C high and A low
8. A, B, C all are high

The following is the truth table of a three-input OR gate.

A	B	C	Y
0	0	0	0
0	0	1	1
0	1	0	1
0	1	1	1
1	0	0	1
1	0	1	1
1	1	0	1
1	1	1	1

NOT Gate

The NOT gate is also called an inverter. It has only one input. Its output is low when the input is high, whereas the output is high when the input is low.

$$Y = \overline{A}$$

The following is the truth table of a NOT gate.

A	Y
0	1
1	0

NAND Gate

NAND means NOT of AND. So, if we attach a NOT gate at the output of an AND gate, we will get a NAND gate.

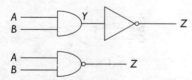

The behaviour of a NAND gate is depicted in the following truth table.

A	B	Z
0	0	1
0	1	1
1	0	1
1	1	0

NOR Gate

NOR means NOT of OR. So, if we connect a NOT gate in front of an OR gate, then we will get a NOR gate.

The following is the truth table of a NOR gate.

A	B	A + B	$Y = \overline{A + B}$
0	0	0	1
0	1	1	0
1	0	1	0
1	1	1	0

Hence, the gate and the truth table can be represented as follows:

$$Y = \overline{A + B}$$

A	B	Y
0	0	1
0	1	0
1	0	0
1	1	0

Note In a NOR gate, the output is true only if both the inputs are low (or '0').

If we connect both the inputs of a NOR gate, we get a NOT gate. If both A and B are 0 the output is 0, and if both are 1 the output is 1.

XOR Gate

The output of a XOR gate is true when the inputs are alternate.

$$Y = A + B$$

This can be explained as follows:
1. When $A = 1$ and $B = 0$, $Y = 1$.
2. When $A = 0$ and $B = 1$, $Y = 1$.

The truth table of a XOR gate is as follows:

A	B	Y
0	0	0
0	1	1
1	0	1
1	1	0

> **Note** XOR gate can also be made from AND, OR, and NOT gates in the following manner.
>
>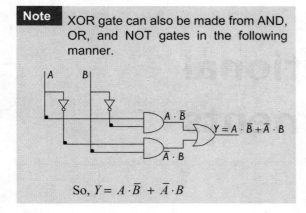
>
> So, $Y = A \cdot \bar{B} + \bar{A} \cdot B$

XNOR Gate

The difference between a XNOR gate and a XOR gate is that in XNOR the output is true iff both the inputs are the same. The gate is depicted in the following figure:

$$\begin{array}{c} A \\ B \end{array} \!\!\!\!\!\!\!\Rightarrow\!\!\!\!\!\!\!\circ\!\!\!-\!\!\!-\!\!\!-\ Y = A + B$$

This is explained as follows:
1. Y is 1 if $A = B = 1$
2. Y is 1 if $A = B = 0$

The truth table is given as follows:

A	B	Y
0	0	1
0	1	0
1	0	0
1	1	1

> **Note** XOR gate can also be made from AND, OR, and NOT gates in the following manner.
>
> So, $Y = A \cdot A + \bar{A} \cdot \bar{B}$

4 Conditional Statements

OBJECTIVES

After completing this chapter, the reader will be able to

\# Apply conditional statements
\# Appreciate the importance of `if-else` construct
\# Use the `if-else` ladder
\# Employ the conditional operator
\# Use && and ||
\# Comprehend the problem associated with floating point numbers
\# Understand dangling `else` condition
\# Handle `switch case` construct

4.1 INTRODUCTION

In a routine scenario, a decision is taken depending on whether a particular condition is true or false. For example, assume that the condition laid down by your father to start a particular business is as follows: 'Start the business only if the earning from the business is greater than 20,000.' If you select a particular business and it seems to satisfy the given condition, then you may start the business, otherwise you will not start it. So the decision depends on the fulfilment of a condition. Similarly, in programming, if the selected statements need to be executed based on the fulfilment of certain conditions, then conditional statements are used. In this chapter, we will discuss the various ways of implementing decision control structures. C#, similar to C or C++, provides two constructs for taking decisions, namely 'if' class and 'switch' statement.

Let us start our discussion with the `if` statement. In programming, 'if(condition)' returns true if the condition is satisfied, otherwise it returns false. The block that follows the `if` statement is executed only if the `if` condition is true and is otherwise skipped.

```
if(condition)
    {
        //Control comes here only if the condition is true
    }
```

Table 4.1 Types of Conditions

To check where a is equal to b	$a == b$
To check whether $a > b$	$a > b$
To check whether $a < b$	$a < b$
To check whether $a \leq b$	$a <= b$
To check whether $a \geq b$	$a >= b$
To check whether a and b are not equal	$a\, != b$
'And'-ing of two conditions (answer is true only if both the conditions are true)	C1 && C2
'Or'-ing of two conditions (answer is true if any of the conditions is true)	C1 || C2

An if can be complemented by a corresponding else. However, it is not mandatory to have else along with if.

```
if(condition)
    {
        //Executed if the condition is true
    }
else
    {
        //Executed if the condition is not true
    }
```

Here, a condition can be any of the conditional statements explained in the previous chapter. Table 4.1 shows how to write a condition, here a and b are two variables (or expressions returning comparable values).

Let us have a look at a popular logic problem given by the American mathematician Raymond Smullyan. The problem relates to an island having two categories of populace—Knights, who always tell the truth, and Knaves, who always lie. In this example, the structure of the construct would be as follows:

```
if(person == Knight)
    {
        He always speaks truth
    }
else
    {
        He always lies
    }
```

The above example only explains the concept of the construct. Now consider more practical example. Programming requires taking decisions. At times, if a particular condition is true then a particular task is performed, otherwise another task is performed. To understand this point, let us take the example of finding the greater of two numbers. The example explains how to implement if condition in programming. Though, it is a simple example, the idea is to make the reader familiar with the syntax and usage of the if statement. However, more intricate example follow in the text. Coming back

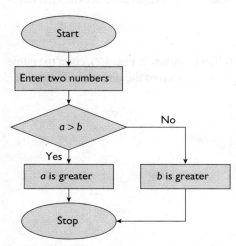

Fig. 4.1 Flowchart depicting determination of greater of two numbers

to the problem, in order to accomplish the given task, we ask the user to enter two numbers, say a and b. If the value of a is greater, we print a, or else b is printed. The concept has been depicted in Fig. 4.1.

In programming, situations of this kind are handled using decision control structures. The following are the ways of implementing the decision control structures:

1. if statement
2. if-else statement
3. if-else if ladder
4. Corditional operators

Let us discuss these decision control structures in detail.

4.2 if STATEMENT

The `if` statement is a conditional statement that is used while making decisions based on a Boolean condition. The block that is executed if the condition is true may be a single statement or a set of statements. If it is a single statement, then the opening and closing braces are optional. However, it may be noted that it is advisable to always use the braces, so that the program is easily comprehensible. The syntax of an `if` statement is as follows:

Syntax

```
if(<condition>)
    {
    }
```

The condition can be any Boolean statement. Since it is a Boolean statement, it returns either true or false. Table 4.1 examines various Boolean statements. To understand this better, let us consider the example given in Problem 4.1. This is a simple one. Harder examples are given in Project I, wherein the class of an IP address is to be determined.

Problem 4.1

Write a program that asks the user to enter two distinct numbers and finds whether the first number is greater than the second one.

Solution

Step 1 Go to File→New→Project. In the window that follows (shown in Fig. 4.2), enter the name of the project (IfElseDemo1 in this case). Change the location of the directory if required.

Step 2 Write the following code:

```
namespace IfElseDemo1
{
    class Program
    {
        static void Main(string[] args)
        {
            int number1, number2, big;
            Console.WriteLine("Enter the first number\t:");
            number1 = Int16.Parse(Console.ReadLine());
            Console.WriteLine("Enter the second number\t:");
```

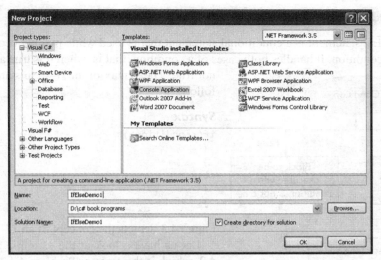

Fig. 4.2 Creating a new project

```
number2 = Int16.Parse(Console.ReadLine());
if(number1 > number2)
{
    big = number1;
    Console.WriteLine("The first number is greater");
}
Console.ReadKey();
        }
    }
}
```

Step 3 On pressing F5, the following screen will be displayed. Enter the two numbers. If the first number is greater than the second one, then the message 'The first number is greater' will be displayed.

```
Enter the first number   :
5
Enter the second number  :
4
The first number is greater
_
```

The problem with this code is that it can tell us whether the first number is greater but there will be no output if the second number is greater. For readers familiar with automata, the problem is similar to that faced in a deterministic finite acceptor with no trap state. The automata works only for the condition for which it is designed and does not work for other conditions. In automata we solve this problem by introducing a trap state. However, in programming, this problem can be solved by using the if-else construct discussed in Section 4.3.

4.3 if-else STATEMENT

The `if-else` statement is a conditional statement that is used while making decisions based on a Boolean condition. It handles both cases of a condition, that is, when it is true and also when it is not true. The syntax of an `if-else` statement is given as follows:

Syntax
```
if(<condition>)
{
}
else
{
}
```

Fig. 4.3 Flowchart depicting the `if-else` statement

Figure 4.3 depicts the concept of an `if-else` condition.

Let us have a look at the example given in Problem 4.2, which is the same as Problem 4.1 except for the fact that it handles both the conditions. It therefore rectifies the problem encountered earlier.

Problem 4.2

Write a program that asks the user to enter two distinct numbers and finds the greater amongst the two.

Solution

Step 1 Go to File→New→Project. In the window that follows, enter the name of the project (IfElseDemo2 in this case). Change the location of the directory if required.

Step 2 Write the following code:

```
namespace IfElseDemo2
{
    class ConditionalOperatorDemo
    {
        public static void Main()
        {
            int number1, number2, big;
            Console.WriteLine("Enter the first number\t:");
            number1 = Int16.Parse(Console.ReadLine());
            Console.WriteLine("Enter the second number\t:");
            number2 = Int16.Parse(Console.ReadLine());
            if(number1 > number2)
            {
                big = number1;
            }
            else
            {
                big = number2;
            }
            Console.WriteLine("The greater number is " + big);
            Console.ReadKey();
        }
    }
}
```

Step 3 Press F5. The following screen will be displayed. Enter the two numbers. The greater of the two numbers is determined and the corresponding number will be displayed after the statement 'The greater number is'.

Output
First Run

```
Enter the first number  :
5
Enter the second number :
6
The greater number is 6
```

Second Run

```
Enter the first number  :
34
Enter the second number :
5
The greater number is 34
_
```

Now let us look at a more complicated example (Problem 4.3) in which we will ask the user to enter the coefficients of a quadratic equation and calculate the roots of the equation.

> **Note**
>
> The quadratic equation $ax^2 + bx + c = 0$ has two roots given by $= \dfrac{-b \pm \sqrt{b^2 - 4ac}}{2a}$.

Problem 4.3

Write a program that asks the user to enter the values of a, b, and c of a quadratic equation $ax^2 + bx + c = 0$ and finds its roots.

Solution

Step 1 Go to File→New→Project. In the window that follows, enter the name of the project (Quadractic in this case). Change the location of the directory (if required). A similar window as shown in the above example appears.

Step 2 Write the following code:

```
namespace Quadractic
{
  class Program
  {
    static void Main(string[] args)
    {
        float a, b, c, d, r1, r2;
```

```csharp
            Console.WriteLine("\nEnter the first number\t:");
            a = float.Parse(Console.ReadLine());
            Console.WriteLine("\nEnter the second number\t:");
            b = float.Parse(Console.ReadLine());
            Console.WriteLine("\nEnter the third number\t:");
            c = float.Parse(Console.ReadLine());
            d = (b * b) - (4 * a * c);
            if(d < 0)
            {
               Console.WriteLine("roots are imaginary");
            }
            else if(d > 0)
            {
               r1 = (float)((-1 * b) + Math.Sqrt(d)) / (2 * a);
               r2 = (float)((-1 * b) - Math.Sqrt(d)) / (2 * a);
               Console.WriteLine("roots are real and distinct\nFirst Root\t:{0}\nSecond
               Root\t:{1}", r1, r2);
            }
            else
            {
               r1 = (-1 * b) / (2 * a);
               r2 = r1;
               Console.WriteLine("roots are real and equal\nRoot(s)\t:{0}", r1);
            }
            Console.ReadKey();
        }
    }
}
```

Step 3 Press F5. The following screen will be displayed. Enter the values of the three coefficients.

◦**Output**

First Run When roots are equal

```
Enter the first number   :
1
Enter the second number  :
2
Enter the third number   :
1
roots are real and equal
Root<s> :-1
```

Second Run When roots are distinct
For example, if the values of a, b, and c are 1, 5, and 6, then the roots will be -2 and -3.

```
Enter the first number    :
1
Enter the second number   :
5
Enter the third number    :
6
roots are real and distinct
First Root      :-2
Second Root     :-3
```

It may be noted that we can have an `if-else` inside an `if`, `else`, or `else-if` block. This is called nested `if-else`. Nested `if-else` helps us make the conditional statement less complex. This concept has been discussed in detail in Section 4.4.

4.4 NESTED if-else

Nested `if-else` refers to having an `if-else` (or more than one `if-else` or `else-if`) within another `if-else`. The syntax of nested `if-else` construct is given as follows:

Syntax
```
if(<condition>)
{
   if(<condition>)
   {
   }
   else
   {
   }
}
else
{
   if(<condition>)
   {
   }
   else
   {
   }
}
```

However, it may be stated that each of the blocks can have any number of `if-else` or `if` blocks. The concept can be better understood with the help of the following example.

You are required to write a program in which the user will enter three numbers and the program will display the greatest of the three numbers.

Now, the concept used in designing the algorithm for this problem is as follows. Let the first number be a, the second be b, and the third be c. If a is greater than b, then check if a is greater than c. If this condition is also true, then a is the greatest number, otherwise c is the greatest one. If a is less than b, then check if b is greater than c; if this condition is also true, then b is the greatest number, otherwise c is the greatest one. This situation is depicted in Fig. 4.4.

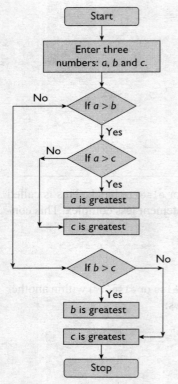

Fig. 4.4 Flowchart depicting the determination of the greatest of three numbers

Such situations are implemented by using the nested `if-else`. The implementation of the solution of this problem is given by the following code:

```
namespace ThreeMax
{
   class Program
   {
      static void Main(string[] args)
      {
         int a, b, c;
         try
         {
            Console.WriteLine("Enter the first number\t:");
            a = int.Parse(Console.ReadLine());
            Console.WriteLine("Enter the second number\t:");
            b = int.Parse(Console.ReadLine());
            Console.WriteLine("Enter the third number\t:");
            c = int.Parse(Console.ReadLine());
            if(a > b)
            {
               if(a > c)
               {
                  Console.WriteLine("a is greatest");
               }
               else
               {
                  Console.WriteLine("c is greatest");
               }
            }
            else
            {
               if(b > c)
               {
                  Console.WriteLine("b is greatest");
               }
               else
               {
                  Console.WriteLine("c is greatest");
               }
            }
            Console.ReadKey();
         }
         catch (Exception e1)
         {
            Console.WriteLine("Error " + e1.ToString());
         }
      }
   }
}
```

Output

Case 1 When the third number is the greatest one:

```
Enter the first number    :
1
Enter the second number   :
2
Enter the third number    :
3
c is greatest
```

Case 2 When the second number is the greatest one:

```
Enter the first number    :
1
Enter the second number   :
3
Enter the third number    :
2
b is greatest
```

Case 3 When the first number is the greatest one:

```
Enter the first number    :
5
Enter the second number   :
2
Enter the third number    :
1
a is greatest
```

This program gives an insight into the use of nested `if-else`. Now, we will consider the situations in which there can be more than two conditions. Section 4.5 explains the 'if-else ladder'.

4.5 if-else LADDER

The next construct we will be discussing is the `if-else` ladder. If there are more than two conditions and if for each condition the task to be performed is different, then the `if-else` ladder is used. The syntax of this construct is as follows:

Syntax
```
if(condition 1)
{
   //Perform the first task
}
else if(condition 2)
{
   //Perform the second task
}
```

```
else if(condition 3)
{
    //Perform the third task
}
else
{
}
```

The flow graph notations for the various constructs are depicted in Fig. 4.5. In the first graph, the first edge depicts the scenario where the condition C is true and the second edge depicts the scenario where the condition is false. In the second graph, conditions C1, C2, C3, and C4 lead to different paths.

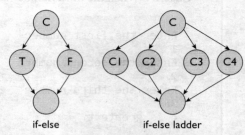

Fig. 4.5 Comparison of the `if-else` and the `if-else-if` ladder

Problem 4.4 demonstrates the use of the `if-else` ladder.

Problem 4.4

The tax slabs of a country are as follows:
Annual Income Tax

Up to 2 lakhs	No tax
2–3 lakhs	10 per cent of the amount exceeding 2 lakhs
3–5 lakhs	10,000 + 20 per cent of the amount exceeding 3 lakhs
>5 lakhs	50,000 + 30 per cent of the amount exceeding 2 lakhs

In addition, there is 20 per cent surcharge on the net tax calculated, as the country happens to be a former colony of the British empire and is strangely proud of the fact. Moreover, the tax is only for those who declare that they earn and therefore the user should be asked to enter the salary.

Solution
```
using System;
using System.Collections.Generic;
using System.Linq;
using System.Text;
Namespace ifElseLadderDemo
{
  class Program
  {
    static void Main(string[] args)
    {
      double monthlySal, annualSal, tax, cwgSurcharge,netTax;
      try
      {
        Console.WriteLine("\nEnter your monthly salary\t:");
        monthlySal = double.Parse(Console.ReadLine());
        annualSal = monthlySal * 12;
        if(annualSal < 200000)
        {
          tax = 0;
        }
        else if((annualSal >= 200000) && (annualSal < 300000))
        {
          tax = (10 * (annualSal - 200000)) / 100;
```

```
            }
            else if ((annualSal >= 300000) && (annualSal < 500000))
            {
                tax = 10000 + ((20 * (annualSal - 300000)) / 100);
            }
            else
            {
                tax = 50000 + ((30 * (annualSal - 200000)) / 100);
            }
            cwgSurcharge = (20 * tax) / 100;
            netTax = tax + cwgSurcharge;
            Console.WriteLine("The net tax is " + netTax.ToString());
            Console.ReadKey();
        }
        catch(Exception e1)
        {
            Console.WriteLine("Exception \t:" + e1.ToString());
        }
    }
  }
}
```

Output
First Run

```
Enter your monthly salary :
15000
The net tax is 0
_
```

In this case, the annual salary is less than 2,00,000; therefore, net tax is zero.

Second Run

```
Enter your monthly salary :
20000
The net tax is 4800
```

In this case, the annual salary is 2,40,000. The tax will be on 40,000, and 10 per cent of 40,000 is 4,000. Surcharge is 20 per cent of 4,000, that is, 800. Therefore, the net tax is 4,800.

Third Run
This pertains to the third condition given in the question.

```
Enter your monthly salary :
30000
The net tax is 26400
```

Fourth Run
If the annual salary exceeds 5,00,000, then the tax is 50,000 + 30 per cent of the amount exceeding 2,00,000. On the net tax, 20 per cent surcharge will be calculated and hence net tax is evaluated.

```
Enter your monthly salary :
50000
The net tax is 204000
```

4.6 DANGLING else

If in a part of code there are one if and two else statements, then the second else is taken along with the nearest if. For example, consider the following snippet:

```
static void Main(string[] args)
{
   int x = 5;
   if(x == 5)
   {
      Console.WriteLine("Hi");
   }
   if(x == 6)
   {
      Console.WriteLine("Bye");
   }
   else
   {
      Console.WriteLine("Hi there");
   }
   Console.ReadKey();
}
```

Output

```
Hi
Hi there
```

Since x is equal to 5, 'Hi' is printed. Moreover is not equal to 6, so the else part of the construct runs giving the output 'Hi there'. Hence, one needs to be extra careful while designing a program using if-else to ensure that the program does not result in an unexpected output.

4.7 PROBLEM WITH FLOATING POINT NUMBERS

Consider the following snippet:

```
static void Main(string[] args)
{
   float x = 2.2347f;
   if(x == 2.2347)
   {
      Console.WriteLine("Hi");
```

```
    }
    else
    {
        Console.WriteLine("Bye");
    }
    Console.ReadKey();
}
```

Output

```
Bye
_
```

This is not the expected output. The value of x in this code is 2.2347; therefore, the statement in the if block should have been displayed. However, it should be noted that a floating point number will be converted into binary before being stored in the memory. Since the memory has only a fixed number of bits, it will not be possible to store the exact number, owing to its translation. For readers familiar with digital signal processing, this situation is similar to the effect of finite word length. It is left to the readers to identify the type of floating point numbers that can be stored in the memory without truncation.

4.8 USE OF && AND || OPERATORS

If a block is to be executed and more than one statements are to be checked, then && or || are used. && is the same as the 'AND' of digital electronics. If a and b are two statements, which are individually either true or false, then a && b is true if both a and b are true. The truth table of a && b is given in Table 4.2.

|| is the same as the 'OR' of digital electronics. If a and b are two statements, which are individually either true or false, then 'a || b' is true if either of a or b is true. The truth table of 'a || b' is given in Table 4.3.

The use of these operators helps to make the program shorter and simpler. As an illustration, consider a program to check whether a triangle is equilateral, scalene, or isosceles. The sides of the triangle are to be provided by the user. A triangle is equilateral if all its sides are equal. If the sides of the triangle in question are represented by a, b, and c, then the triangle is equilateral if $(a = b)$ and $(b = c)$. This can be written as follows:

Table 4.2 The && operator

a	b	a && b
True	True	True
True	False	False
False	True	False
False	False	False

Table 4.3 The || operator

a	b	a || b
True	True	True
True	False	True
False	True	True
False	False	False

```
if((a == b) && (b == c))
{
    //The triangle is equilateral;
}
```

A triangle is isosceles if two of the three sides are equal. If the sides of the triangle in question are represented by a, b, and c, then the triangle is isosceles if $(a = b)$ or $(b = c)$ or $(c = a)$. This can be written as follows:

```
if((a == b) || (b == c) || (c == a))
```

```
      {
         //The triangle is isosceles;
      }
```

The third case, in which none of the sides are equal, would be a scalene triangle.

The snippet of this problem is as follows:

```
class Program
{
   static void Main(string[] args)
   {
      int a, b, c;
      try
      {
         Console.WriteLine("Enter the first side\t:");
         a = int.Parse(Console.ReadLine());
         Console.WriteLine("Enter the second side\t:");
         b = int.Parse(Console.ReadLine());
         Console.WriteLine("Enter the third side\t:");
         c = int.Parse(Console.ReadLine());
         if((a == b) && (b == c))
         {
            Console.WriteLine("The triangle is equilateral");
         }
         else if((a == b) || (b == c) || (a == c))
         {
            Console.WriteLine("The triangle is isosceles");
         }
         else
         {
            Console.WriteLine("The traingle is scalene");
         }
      }
      catch(Exception e1)
      {
         Console.WriteLine("Exception" + e1.ToString());
      }
      Console.ReadKey();
   }
}
```

Output

First Run

The output of this code when all the three sides are equal is as follows:

```
Enter the first side   :
2
Enter the second side  :
2
Enter the third side   :
2
The triangle is equilateral
```

Second Run

When the sides are different, the output is as follows:

```
Enter the first side   :
1
Enter the second side  :
2
Enter the third side   :
3
The triangle is scalene
```

Third Run

The following snapshot depicts the situation wherein two sides are equal.

```
Enter the first side   :
1
Enter the second side  :
2
Enter the third side   :
1
The triangle is isosceles
```

This program has been given with aim of making the use of the 'AND' and 'OR' operators clear. However, one more condition needs to be checked in this program. It is left to the readers to find and implement that condition.

4.9 CONDITIONAL STATEMENT

The conditional operator performs the same task as the `if-else` construct. So, instead of using `if-else`, the conditional operator can also be used. However, there is a disadvantage. It is possible to write only one statement each in the part that depicts the fulfilment of the condition and in the other part. The syntax of the operator is as follows:

Syntax

`<Output variable> = <condition> ? <The result when the condition is true> : <The result when the condition is not true>`

For example, the conditional operator can be used to check which of the two numbers entered by the user is greater.

```
using System;
using System.Collections.Generic;
using System.Linq;
using System.Text;
namespace ConditionalOperator
{
    class Program
```

```csharp
    {
        static void Main(string[] args)
        {
            int a, b, big;
            try
            {
                Console.WriteLine("Enter the first number\t:");
                a = Int16.Parse(Console.ReadLine());
                Console.WriteLine("Enter the second number\t:");
                b = Int16.Parse(Console.ReadLine());
                big = (a > b) ? a : b;
                Console.WriteLine("Bigger\t:" + big.ToString());
                Console.ReadKey();
            }
            catch (Exception e1)
            {
                Console.WriteLine(e1.ToString());
            }
        }
    }
}
```

Output

```
Enter the first number   :
6
Enter the second number  :
7
Bigger :7
```

A more difficult illustration is to determine the greatest of three given numbers. The conditional statement in such a case will be written as follows:

```
big = ((a > b) ? ((a > c) ? a : c) : ((b > c) ? b : c));
```

The rest of the program will be the same as that given earlier except for the fact that instead of two numbers the user will have to enter three numbers.

4.10 SWITCH STATEMENT: WHAT CAN BE DONE AND WHAT CANNOT BE DONE

switch is a construct that is used when there are many conditions and the fulfilment of each leads to a different situation. Each situation is handled by a different code. In such situations, switch case is considered to be a better option than the if-else ladder.

In Problem 4.4, there were four conditions. There might be situations wherein there are many more conditions than just four or five. switch statements can be used in such cases. Thus, switch case is used when there are many conditions and the use of if-else ladder either is not convenient or results in problems such as 'dangling else'. The syntax of switch case is as follows:

Syntax
```
switch(expression)
{
    case value1:
        //Block 1
    break;

    case value2:
        //Block 2
    break;
    ...
    default:
        //Statements
    break;
}
```

Here, the expression results in some value. If the value is value1, then block 1 is executed. If it is value2, block 2 is executed, and so on. If the value of the expression does not match any of the cases, then the statements in the default block are executed.

Problem 4.5 demonstrates the use of switch case.

Problem 4.5

Table 4.4 Relation between marks and grades

Marks	Grade
90	A+
80	A
70	B+
60	B
50	C+
40	C
Less than 40	F

In a class, grades are assigned on the basis of the marks obtained. The policy for assigning the grades is given in Table 4.4.

Moreover, a teacher rewards marks only in multiples of 10 (A student gets 0, 10, 20, 30, ..., 100 marks only). Ask the user to enter the marks and display the grade.

Solution

It is given that the only marks allowed are 10, 20, 30, 40, 50, 60, 70, 80, 90, and 100. Therefore, it will be easy to solve the problem using switch instead of if-else.

```
using System;
using System.Collections.Generic;
using System.Linq;
using System.Text;

namespace SwitchDemo
{
    class Program
    {
        static void Main(string[] args)
        {
            int marks;
            string grade;
            try
            {
                Console.WriteLine("Enter marks");
                marks = Int16.Parse(Console.ReadLine());
                switch(marks)
```

```
                    {
                        case 90:
                            grade = "A+";
                            break;
                        case 80:
                            grade = "A";
                            break;
                        case 70:
                            grade = "B+";
                            break;
                        case 60:
                            grade = "B";
                            break;
                        case 50:
                            grade = "C+";
                            break;
                        case 40:
                            grade = "C";
                            break;
                        default:
                            grade = "F";
                            break;
                    }
                    Console.WriteLine("Grade\t:" + grade);
                    Console.ReadKey();
                }
                catch(Exception e1)
                {
                    Console.WriteLine(e1.ToString());
                }
            }
        }
    }
```

Output
First Run

```
Enter mark
90
Grade :A+
_
```

Second Run

```
Enter mark
80
Grade :A
_
```

The construct is depicted in the flow diagram given in Fig. 4.6.

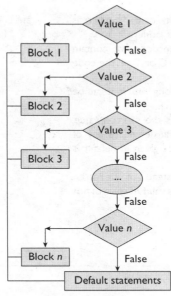

Fig. 4.6 switch construct

Observation

As is done in most of the books, we could have given an integer value to each condition and then used switch case. However, the idea here is to depict the correct use of switch case and not to fit the question in switch case.

SUMMARY

A program is generally written to accomplish a particular task. In order to accomplish any task, decisions are to be made at every step. Decisions are essential to manage the flow of a program. The if, else-if, and switch constructs help us in writing programs for situations wherein different decisions are to be made depending upon the input. This chapter not only discusses these constructs in detail but also explores the problems encountered while using them. The problems of dangling else and floating point numbers have been explained in the chapter. The chapter is the basis of the topics that will be covered in the rest of the book. Moreover, one must not forget that conditional statements will be needed even in client-side and web-based programming, which are discussed in the third section of the book. Even in deterministic finite automata used in compiler design, the implementation is done via conditional statements. So, conditional statements are in the heart of everything you use, from the complier of your language to the word processor in which this chapter is made.

GLOSSARY

if statement This is a conditional statement that is used while making decisions based on a Boolean condition.

if-else ladder This is used when there are more than two conditions and for each condition the task performed is different.

if-else statement This statement handles both cases of a condition, that is, when it is true and also when it is not true.

Nested if-else This is used when the decision-making involves an if-else (or more than one if-else/else-if) within another if-else.

POINTS TO REMEMBER

- For the problem having many cases, switch is more convenient than else-if ladder.
- In a switch block, if the code does not contain break in default, then, unlike C or C++, the code will not be compiled.
- case should have a constant along with it. It can be an integer, a string, or a character.
- If no case expression matches the switch value, then the control cannot be transferred to any of the cases in such case the code given in default is executed.
- We can also use goto instead of default. Therefore, the following code is valid, in spite of not having break.

```
switch(n)
{
    case 1:
        Console.WriteLine("Hi there!");
        break;
    case 2:
        Console.WriteLine("Hi there! Second time");
        goto case 1;
    default :
        Console.WriteLine("Hi there! I am default");
        break;
}
```

EXERCISES

I Debugging Exercise

A. Find the output of the following codes or the error if the codes are incorrect.

1.
```
namespace IfElseExer1
{
    class Program
    {
        static void Main(string[] args)
        {
            int number;
            if(number > 0)
            {
                Console.WriteLine("Hi");
            }
            else
            {
                Console.WriteLine("Bye");;
            }
        }
    }
}
```

2.
```
namespace IfElseExer1
{
        class Program
    {
        static void Main(string[] args)
        {
            int number = 5;
            if(number = 0)
            {
                Console.WriteLine("Hi");
            }
            else
            {
                Console.WriteLine("Bye");
            }
        }
    }
}
```

3.
```
namespace IfElseExer1
{
    class Program
    {
        static void Main(string[] args)
        {
            int number = 'a';
            if(number > 0)
            {
                Console.WriteLine("Hi");
            }
            else
            {
                Console.WriteLine("Bye");
            }
        }
    }
}
```

4. ```
namespace IfElseExer1
{
    class Program
    {
        static void Main(string[] args)
        {
            float number = 2;
            if(number == 2)
            {
                Console.WriteLine("Hi");
            }
            else
            {
                Console.WriteLine("Bye");
            }
            Console.ReadKey();
        }
    }
}
```

5. ```
namespace IfElseExer1
{
    class Program
    {
        static void Main(string[] args)
        {
            float number = 2 > 3;
            if(number == 0)
            {
                Console.WriteLine("Hi");
            }
            else
            {
                Console.WriteLine("Bye");
            }
            Console.ReadKey();
        }
    }
}
```

6. ```
namespace IfElseExer1
{
    class Program
    {
        static void Main(string[] args)
        {
            float number = float.Parse((2 > 3).ToString());
            if(number == 0)
            {
                Console.WriteLine("Hi");
            }
            else
            {
                Console.WriteLine("Bye");
            }
            Console.ReadKey();
        }
    }
}
```

7. ```
namespace IfElseExer1
{
    class Program
    {
        static void Main(string[] args)
        {
            int num = 34;
            float number = float.Parse(num.ToString());
            if(number == 0)
            {
                Console.WriteLine("Hi");
            }
            else
            {
                Console.WriteLine("Bye");
            }
            Console.ReadKey();
        }
    }
}
```

8. ```
namespace IfElseExer1
{
    class Program
    {
        static void Main(string[] args)
        {
            char c = (char) Console.Read();
            if(c)
            {
                Console.Writeline("It is a letter");
            }
        }
    }
}
```

9. ```
namespace IfElseExer1
{
    class Program
    {
        int n;
        static void Main(string[] args)
        {
            n = 2;
            switch(n)
            {
                case 1:
                    Console.WriteLine("Hi there! I am case 1");
```

```csharp
            break;
        case 2:
            Console.WriteLine("Hi
            there! I am case 2");
            break;
        case 3:
            Console.WriteLine("Hi
            there!I am case 3");
                break;
            default:
            Console.WriteLine("Hi
            there! I am default");
            break;
        }
     }
   }
}
```

10.
```csharp
namespace IfElseExer1
{
    class Program
    {
        int n;
        static void Main(string[] args)
        {
            n = 10;
            switch(n)
            {
                case 1:
                    Console.WriteLine("Hi
                    there! I am Case 1");
                    break;
                case 2:
                    Console.WriteLine("Hi
                    there! I am Case 2");
                    break;
                case 3:
                    Console.WriteLine("Hi
                    there! I am Case 3");
                    break;
                default:
                    Console.WriteLine("Hi
                    there! I am default");
                    break;
            }
        }
    }
}
```

B. State whether the following statements are true or false.

1. In Microsoft C#, the number of `case` values in a `switch` statement is limited.
2. An expression in a `switch` can be a class type.
3. We can write `default` without a `break` in C#.
4. Every `if` can have a corresponding `else`.
5. We can use an unassigned variable inside an expression of `if`.
6. If there are 20 cases, `if-else` is better than `switch`.
7. The conditional operator can substitute `switch`.
8. We can use `enums` in `switch`.
9. We can have an `if-else` statement inside another `if-else` statement.
10. C# does not allow unity type `case` values.

II. Review Questions

1. Compare `if-else` and `switch` constructs.
2. What can be the basic reasons for using an else-if ladder?
3. What are the various conditions that can be written inside an `if` condition?
4. Explain the concept of conditional statements.
5. Explain the importance of || and && operators. Also give an example using OR or AND.

III. Programming Exercise

1. Ask the user to enter a number and find whether it is even or odd.
2. Ask the user to enter the coefficients of two equations
   (a) $a_1x + b_1y + c_1 = 0$
   (b) $a_2x + b_2y + c_2 = 0$
   Find whether the lines are parallel or not.
3. Ask the user to enter a three digit number. Find the sum of the number and its reverse and also find if any of the digits of the sum is the same as that in the original number.
4. Ask the user to enter two numbers and find whether or not the first number is a factor of the second one.

5. Ask the user to enter a number and find whether or not it is divisible by 3 without using % operator.
6. Ask the user to enter a year and find whether it is a leap year or not.
7. Ask the user to enter a character and find whether it is uppercase or lowercase.
8. Ask the user to enter a character and find whether or not its ASCII value is greater than 80.
9. Ask the user to enter a number. If it is greater than π then subtract $\pi/2$ from it, else add $\pi/2$ to it.
10. Ask the user to enter 10 numbers. Find their mean. Now print the number of numbers greater than the mean.
11. Find the greatest of three numbers entered by the user without using `else-if`.
12. Ask the user to enter the day and date and find the day of the same date in the coming year.
13. Ask the user to enter the coefficients of a cubic equation $ax^3 + bx^2 + cx + d = 0$ and find whether or not the sum of the roots is equal to their product.
14. A function $f(x)$ is given by

$$f(x) = \begin{cases} x^2 + 5x + 3, & \text{when } x > 2 \\ x + 3, & \text{when } x \leq 2 \end{cases}$$

Ask the user to enter the value of x and find the value of $f(x)$.

15. The income tax slab is given as follows. Ask the user to enter the net salary and calculate the tax.

For men up to 60 years

Income tax		Rate
(a)	Up to 1,80,000	Nil
(b)	1,80,000 to 5,00,000	10 per cent of the amount exceeding 1,80,000
(c)	5,00,000 to 8,00,000	20 per cent of the amount exceeding 5,00,000 + 22,000
(d)	8,00,000 and above	30 per cent of the amount exceeding 8,00,000 + 82,000

16. In Question 15, if the educational cess is 2 per cent of the total tax, find the net tax by adding the educational cess to the total tax obtained.
17. The government of the day decides that if the net tax of a person exceeds 10,00,000, then he will be given an exception of 2,00,000 due to some strange reason. Implement the clause in your program.
18. The tax in Question 15 is of a fictitious country called Shangri-La1. The finance minister of that country is a corrupt person. He makes a policy that if the tax of a person exceeds 25,00,000, then the minister should be paid 25,00,000 in lieu of which the person in question will be shown as poor in the government papers. He will, therefore, get all the benefits provided to a poor person of that country. Write a program such that when a rich person enters his monthly profit, the commission given to the minister and the net profit are displayed.
19. Continuing from Question 18, the Comptroller and Auditor General (CAG) of that country decides that the net benefits given to a poor person costs 15,000 to the government. Now, write a program for the CAG of the country. It should calculate the presumptive losses incurred in Question 18 if the profits of the rich person are known.
20. Now, the son-in-law of the super prime minister of the country mentioned in Question 19 decides to refute the figure by saying that the net cost to the government is not what the CAG has calculated. A rich man provides job to 10,000 people. This people vote according to the wishes of his employer in which case the money of those in power would be saved. Assume that those in power pay 1000 Rs to each person to make him vote calculate the money saved in the election.

5 Loops

OBJECTIVES

After completing this chapter, the reader will be able to
Understand the importance of loops
Use the while, do, for, and for-each loops
Apply the break and continue statements
Appreciate why not to use the goto statement
Use goto statement to accomplish tasks
Compare the various looping constructs

5.1 INTRODUCTION

Looping is perhaps one of the most significant programming ideas in existence. There are many applications of loops. They allow us to execute a block of code over and over several times. It is assumed that readers are familiar with loops, irrespective of the kind of programming language they have already learnt. The different types of loops in C# are while, do-while, for, and for-each. In order to be able to write a program involving loops, we first need to understand the concept of a counter. A counter is a variable that is initialized and its value is incremented or decremented each time the loop is executed. When the counter reaches its terminal value, the loop ends. The control abstraction of a loop is given as follows:

Step 1 Initialize counter.
Step 2 Check if the value of counter is less than the terminal value; if yes then go to step 3, else go to step 5.
Step 3 Perform the requisite task.
Step 4 Increment the value of the counter (or decrement the value of counter if the condition in step 2 is of the form >=).
Step 5 End the loop.

If, for instance, the loop is to run 10 times, then the value of the counter can be initialized to 1. The condition for termination becomes 'counter <= 10'. It may be noted that the initial value, the initial condition, and the condition for termination depend on the problem. Every loop has the same control abstraction. The various loops in C# are discussed in Sections 5.2–5.6.

5.2 while LOOP

A while loop first checks a condition and then continues with the execution of the code inside the block until the condition remains true. As soon as the condition becomes false, the loop ends. Its syntax is as follows:

```
while(<Boolean expression>)
{
    <statements>
}
```

The statements can be any valid C# statements. First, the Boolean expression is evaluated. If it is *true*, then the statements inside the block are executed. Once the statements are executed, control returns to the commencement of the while loop to check the Boolean expression again. The process is repeated until the condition becomes *false*.

The procedure is depicted in Fig. 5.1.

When the expression changes to *false*, the statements inside the loop are skipped and execution begins after the closing brace of that block. The following code demonstrates the use of a while loop. It prints the multiplication table of five. It should be noted that three actions are needed to accomplish the task. The counter variable, which in this case is IntNum, must be initialized. Then, there must be a value up to which the value of the counter variable can reach. Inside the loop, the counter variable must be either incremented or decremented according to the situation. The detailed explanation of the code follows the code:

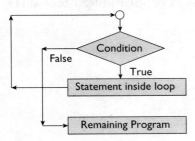

Fig. 5.1 while loop

```
using System;
class WhileLoopDemo
{
    public static void Main()
    {
        int IntNum = 1;
        while(IntNum < 10)
        {
            Console.Write("{0}", (IntNum*5));
            IntNum++;
        }
    }
}
```

This program generates the multiplication table of five. It illustrates a simple while loop. It begins with the keyword while, followed by a Boolean expression, which in this case is IntNum < 10, indicating that the loop is to run nine times. All control statements use Boolean expressions as their condition for entering the loop. This means that the expression must evaluate to either a true or a false value. In this case, we are checking the IntNum variable to see whether it is less

102 Programming in C#

than or equal to (<) 10. Since IntNum is initialized to 1, the Boolean expression will return true the first time it is evaluated. When the Boolean expression evaluates to true, the block immediately following the Boolean expression will be executed.

Within the while block, we print the number and a space to the console. Then we increment (++) IntNum to the next integer. Once the statements in the while block are executed, the Boolean expression is evaluated again. This sequence will continue until the Boolean expression evaluates to false. When the Boolean expression is evaluated as false, program control will jump to the first statement following the while block. In this case, we will see the numbers 5, 10, 15, 20, 25, 30, 35, 40, 45 in the output screen.

> **Note** The while loop executes a block of code as long as the condition is true.

5.3 do LOOP

A do loop is similar to the while loop, except that it checks its condition at the end of the loop. This means that the statements in the do loop will be certainly executed at least once. On the other hand, a while loop evaluates its Boolean expression at the beginning and there is no guarantee that the statements inside the loop will be executed. Hence, when the task is to be executed at least once, a do loop is to be used instead of a while loop. The syntax of the do loop is as follows:

```
do
{
    <Statements>
} while(<Boolean expression>);
```

The following listing demonstrates the use of a do loop.

```
using System;
class DoLoopDemo
{
    public static void Main()
    {
        string myChoice;
        do
        {
            Console.WriteLine("Calc\n");
            Console.WriteLine("1 - Add");
            Console.WriteLine("2 - Sub");
            Console.WriteLine("3 - Multiply");
            Console.WriteLine("4 - Quit\n");
            Console.WriteLine("Enter choice:\t");
            Ch = Console.ReadLine();
            switch(ch)
            {
                // Make a decision based on the user's choice
            }
            Console.Write("Press Enter key to continue...");
            Console.ReadLine();
```

```
            Console.WriteLine();
        } while(myChoice != "4");
            //Continue until the user wants to quit
    }
}
```

In the `Main` method, we declare the variable `myChoice` of type `string`. Then, we print a series of statements to the console. This is a menu of choices for the user. We must get input from the user; this is done using the `Console.ReadLine` method, which returns the user's value into the variable `myChoice`. We must take the user's input and process it. As discussed earlier, an efficient way to do this is with a `switch` statement. The statements can be any valid C# programming statements. The Boolean expression is the same as the ones we have discussed so far. It returns either true or false.

> **Note** The `do` loop evaluates the condition after the loop is executed, thus making sure that the block is executed at least once.

5.4 for LOOP

A `for` loop works like a `while` loop, except that the syntax of the `for` loop includes initialization and condition alteration. These loops are appropriate when we precisely know the number of times the statements within the loop are to be executed. The `for` loop has three parts, which are placed within parenthesis and are separated by semicolons.

```
for(<initializer list>; <Boolean expression>; <iterator list>)
{
    <statements>
}
```

The initializer list is a comma-separated list of expressions. These expressions are evaluated only once during the lifetime of the `for` loop. This one-time operation happens before loop execution. This section is commonly used to initialize an integer to be used as a counter.

Once the initializer list has been evaluated, the `for` loop gives control to its second section, the Boolean expression. There is only one Boolean expression. However, it can be complicated as the programmer wants, the only stipulation being that the result should evaluate to true or false. The Boolean expression is commonly used to verify the status of a counter variable.

When the Boolean expression evaluates to true, the statements within the curly braces of the `for` loop are executed. After executing the statements in the loop, control moves to the top of the loop and executes the iterator list, which is normally used to increment or decrement a counter. The iterator list can contain a comma-separated list of statements but is generally only one statement. The following listing shows the implementation of a `for` loop. The purpose of the program is to print the non-multiples of three that are less than 10.

```
using System;
class ForLoopDemo
{
    public static void Main()
    {
```

```
        for(int i = 0; i = 20; i++)
        {
            if(i == 10)
            break;

            if(i % 3 == 0)
            continue;

            Console.Write("{0}", i);
        }
        Console.WriteLine();
    }
}
```

Usually, `for` loop statements are executed from the opening curly brace to the closing curly brace without disruption. However, in the given program there are a squad of `if` statements disrupting the flow of control within the `for` block.

The first `if` statement checks whether *i* is equal to 10. If it is true, the `break` statement breaks out of the loop at that point and transfers control to the first statement following the end of the `for` block.

The second `if` statement uses the remainder operator to see if *i* is a multiple of 3. This will evaluate to true when *i* is divided by 3 with the remainder equal to zero (0). When true, the `continue` statement is executed compelling control to skip over the remaining statements in the loop and transfer back to the iterator list.

When program control reaches either a `continue` statement or the end of the block, control is transferred to the third section within the `for` loop parentheses, the iterator list. A `for` loop will continue as long as the Boolean expression is true. When the expression becomes false, control is transferred to the first statement following the `for` block.

5.5 foreach LOOP

Readers who have already learnt C or C++ must be familiar with the three loops discussed in Sections 5.2–5.4. C#, similar to JAVA, provides another loop, namely `foreach`. A `foreach` loop is used to iterate through the items in a list. It operates on arrays or collections. The syntax of a `foreach` loop is as follows:

```
foreach(<type> <variable name> in <list>)
{
    <statements>
}
```

The *type* is the type of item contained in the list. The *variable name* is a chosen identifier. The `in` is a required keyword. As mentioned earlier, the *list* could be either an array or a collection. It must be noted, though, that while iterating through the items of a list, the list is read-only. The use of `foreach` loop in arrays will become clear after going through Chapter 9, in which examples of array processing using `foreach` are explained. The following example, however, gives a basic idea of how to use a `foreach` loop.

```
using System;
class ForEachLoopDemo
{
```

```
public static void Main()
{
    string[] names = {"Hari", "Jish", "Naks", "Viru"};
    foreach(string name in names)
    {
        Console.WriteLine(" "+ name);
    }
}
}
```

In the `foreach` loop, we have used a string variable `name` to hold each element of the `names` array. As long as there are strings in the array, the `Console.WriteLine` method will print each value of the `name` variable on the screen.

> **Note** The `foreach` loop operates on collections of items, for instance arrays, hash table, or list.

5.6 LOOP WITHIN LOOP

A loop can be nested within another loop. The outer loop governs how many times the inner loop runs. For example, the following are the steps to print 10 times the multiplication table of five.

Step 1 Design an algorithm and implement the task that needs to be repeated. In this case, the multiplication table of five needs to run 10 times. So, the table of five is the task that is to be repeated. The following snippet accomplishes the task:

```
int i;
for(i = 1; i <= 10; i++)
{
    Console.WriteLine("{0} * 5 = {1}", i, (5 * i));
}
Console.ReadKey();
```

Step 2 Place the snippet given in Step 1 within another loop, which runs as many times as the task is to be repeated. The whole code now looks as follows:

```
int i,j;
for(j = 0; j < 10; j++)
{
    for(i = 1; i <= 10; i++)
    {
        Console.WriteLine("{0} * 5 = {1}", i, (5 * i));
    }
}
Console.ReadKey();
```

It may be noted that the nesting of loops is required even in the crafting of patterns. Section 5.7 serves two purposes—explaining the concept of nested loops and giving an idea of generation of patterns.

5.7 PATTERNS

Generating patterns can be one of the most fascinating tasks. It requires deep analysis and decision-making regarding what should be the initial value of the counter, what should be its final value, and what is to be written inside the loop. It is stongly recommended that the following examples should be attempted first, before looking at the solution. To help readers design the patterns themselves, the concepts have been explained along with each example.

Problem 5.1

Write a program to generate the following pattern:

```
*
**
***
****
*****
******
```

The number of rows will be entered by the user.

Concept

In the first row there is a single star, in the second row there are two stars, and as the row number increases the number of stars increases. So the outer loop (which represents the number of rows) should be from 0 upto n and the inner loop depends on the outer loop. So the value of the inner counter j should be from 0 to i.

Solution

```csharp
using System;
using System.Collections.Generic;
using System.Linq;
using System.Text;

namespace ConsoleApplication2
{
    class Program
    {
        static void Main(string[] args)
        {
            int i,j,n;
            Console.WriteLine("\nEnter the number of rows\t:");
            n = int.Parse(Console.ReadLine());
            for(i = 0; i < n; i++)
            {
                for(j = 0; j <= i; j++)
                {
                    Console.Write("*");
                }
                Console.WriteLine();
            }
            Console.ReadKey();
        }
    }
}
```

Output

```
Enter the number of rows:
10
*
* *
* * *
* * * *
* * * * *
* * * * * *
* * * * * * *
* * * * * * * *
* * * * * * * * *
* * * * * * * * * *
_
```

Problem 5.2

Write a program to generate the following pattern:

```
1
1 2
1 2 3
1 2 3 4
1 2 3 4 5
1 2 3 4 5 6
```

The number of rows will be entered by the user.

Concept

This problem is similar to Problem 5.1 exept for the fact that the output statement consists of '(j + 1)' instead of an astrerik.

Solution

```
using System;
using System.Collections.Generic;
using System.Linq;
using System.Text;

namespace Loops_2
{
    class Program
    {
        static void Main(string[] args)
        {
            int i,j,n;
            Console.WriteLine("\nEnter the number of rows\t:");
            n = int.Parse(Console.ReadLine());
            for(i = 0; i < n; i++)
            {
                for(j = 0; j <= i; j++)
                {
                    Console.Write(" "+(j+1));
                }
```

```
            Console.WriteLine();
        }
        Console.ReadKey();
    }
  }
}
```

Output

```
Enter the number of rows:
10
 1
 1 2
 1 2 3
 1 2 3 4
 1 2 3 4 5
 1 2 3 4 5 6
 1 2 3 4 5 6 7
 1 2 3 4 5 6 7 8
 1 2 3 4 5 6 7 8 9
 1 2 3 4 5 6 7 8 9 10
```

If the following pattern needs to be generated:

```
1
2 2
3 3 3
4 4 4 4
5 5 5 5 5
6 6 6 6 6 6
```

then just change $(j+1)$ to $(i+1)$. The following output would be generated:

```
Enter the number of rows:
10
 1
 2 2
 3 3 3
 4 4 4 4
 5 5 5 5 5
 6 6 6 6 6 6
 7 7 7 7 7 7 7
 8 8 8 8 8 8 8 8
 9 9 9 9 9 9 9 9 9
 10 10 10 10 10 10 10 10 10 10
```

Visual Studio also provides an easy way of inserting snippets. Section 5.8 throws some light on it.

5.8 WORKING IN INTEGRATED DEVELOPMENT ENVIRONMENT

Loops are a very important aspect of programming. The various types of loops and their applications have been discussed in Sections 5.2–5.7. It may be stated that loops can also be generated in an integrated development environment (IDE). This becomes essential as writing the basic construct can at times be tiresome (this is perhaps the only reason for providing 'insert snippet' feature in Visual Studio). In order to insert a snippet, go to File → New → Project. A screen will appear. In the name text box, insert LoopsDemo4 and proceed. The IDE is depicted in Fig. 5.2.

In the editor, define an integer type variable *i*. Right click anywhere and go to Insert → Snippet. The snapshot is shown in Fig. 5.3.

Select Visual C#.

Insert Snippet: Visual C# >

Select for loop. The snapshot is shown in Fig. 5.4.

The following code will be seen:

```
for(int i = 0; i < length; i++)
{

}
```

In the length part, fill the value up to which the loop is to be run. Let us take the value as 10. In addition, let us, for instance, take the example of factorial of a number. The factorial of a number is the continued product from 1 to that number. That is, $n! = 1 \times 2 \times \ldots \times n$.

Here we define a variable *f* of integer type and initialize it to 1. Run the loop *n* times and each time perform the following task:

```
f = f * i;
```

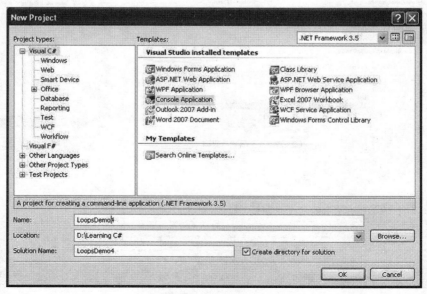

Fig. 5.2 Open screen

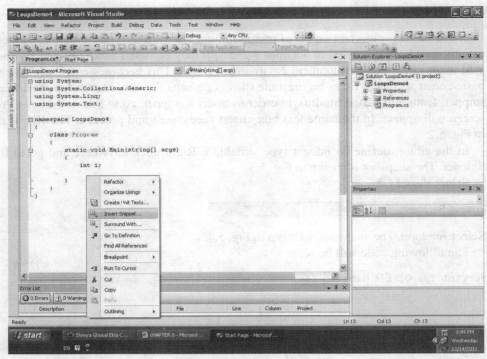

Fig. 5.3 Inserting a snippet

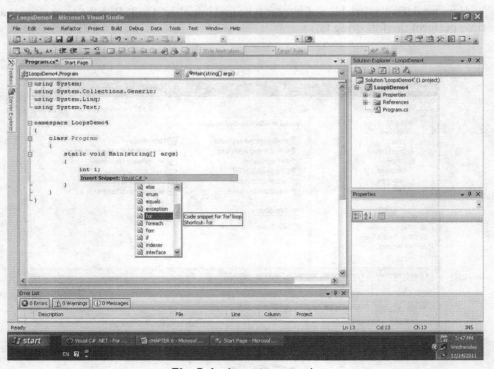

Fig. 5.4 Inserting a for loop

which makes the value of *f* as *n*!. The final program is as follows:

```
using System;
using System.Collections.Generic;
using System.Linq;
using System.Text;

namespace LoopsDemo4
{
    class Program
    {
        static void Main(string[] args)
        {
            int i,n,f = 1;
            Console.WriteLine("\nEnter a number\t:");
            n = int.Parse(Console.ReadLine());
            for(i = 1; i <= n; i++)
            {
                f = f * i;
            }
            Console.WriteLine("\nThe factorial of {0} is {1}", n, f);
            Console.ReadKey();
        }
    }
}
```

Output

```
Enter a number   :
5
The factorial of 5 is 120
```

5.9 break AND continue keywords

Keyword break helps us to come out of a loop when a particular condition is fulfilled. For example, let us assume that the user should enter a maximum of 10 numbers. The numbers can have any value but not 69. That is, if the user enters 69 then the loop ends. In this case, make a for loop that runs 10 times in the same way as any other loop and inside the loop ask the user to enter a number.

```
int j,number;
for(j = 0; j < 10; j++)
{
    Console.WriteLine("Enter a number");
    number = int.Parse(Console.ReadLine());
    Console.WriteLine("You have entered {0}", number);
}
Console.ReadKey();
```

Now the problem is to check whether the number entered by the user is 69 or not. This can be accomplished by using an 'if construct'. In the else part, a break is written making sure the loop ends immediately.

```csharp
int j,number;
for(j = 0; j < 10; j++)
{
    Console.WriteLine("Enter a number");
    number = int.Parse(Console.ReadLine());
    if(number != 69)
    {
        Console.WriteLine("You have entered {0}", number);
    }
    else
        break;
}
Console.ReadKey();
```

Output

```
Enter a number
2
You have entered 2
Enter a number
6
You have entered 6
Enter a number
9
You have entered 9
Enter a number
69
_
```

The position of control when break is encountered is shown here. In the first case there is just one loop and so the break takes the control to the end of the loop, whereas in the second case there is a loop within a loop and the break statement takes the control to the end of the inner loop.

```
for(i = 0; i < 10; i++)
{
    .
    .
    .
    break;
    .
    .}                These statements will not be executed.
}
```

Control comes here

In case of loop within a loop, the break statement takes the control outside the nearest closing block.

```
for(j = 0; j < 10; j++)
{
    for(i = 0; i < 10; i++)
```

```
    {
        .
        .
        .
        break;
        .
        .}
    }
```
→ These statements will not be executed.

```
Control comes here
}//End of the outer loop
```

On the other hand, the `continue` statement takes the control to the beginning of the loop and executes the next iteration. The statements following `continue` are skipped in the same way as those in `break`; however, the difference is that the `break` statement takes the control to the end of the loop whereas the `continue` statement takes it to the beginning. The position of control after the `continue` statement is encountered is shown here. In the first case there is just one loop and so the control goes to the beginning, whereas in the second case the control goes to the beginning of the inner loop.

```
for(i = 0; i < 10; i++) ← Control comes here
{
    .
    .
    .
    continue;
    .
    .}              → These statements will not be executed.
}
for(j = 0; j < 10; j++)
{
    for(i = 0; i < 10; i++) ← Control comes here
    {
        .
        .
        .
        continue;
        .
        .}          → These statements will not be executed,
    }
}
```

5.10 goto STATEMENT

The `goto` statement takes the control to the desired point specified by the label. The syntax of this statement is very simple. The keyword `goto` is to be written followed by the label. The label specifies the point where the control is to be taken. The following program demonstrates the use of goto:

...
...
...

```
goto a;
...
...
a: ...
...
...
```

Problem 5.3

Write a program to display 10 rows. The first row should have a '00' followed by '01'. The second row has '10', '11', '12'. The third row displays '20', '21', '22', '23' and so on.

Concept

Closely looking at the pattern gives us an idea about the way to decode it. The first number is the value of the outer loop counter and the second is the value of the inner loop counter. The value of the inner loop counter is at the maximum one more than the value of the outer loop counter. That is, if the counter of the outer loop is taken as i and that of inner loop is taken as j, then the condition for breaking the inner loop is '$j > i$'.

Solution

```
using System;
using System.Collections.Generic;
using System.Linq;
using System.Text;

namespace gotoDemo
{
    class Program
    {
        static void Main(string[] args)
        {
            int i, j;
            for(i = 0; i < 10; i++)
            {
                for(j = 0; j < 10; j++)
                {
                    Console.Write(i + " " + j+ ");
                    if(j > i)
                        goto a;
                }
                a:
                Console.WriteLine();
            }
            Console.ReadKey();
        }
    }
}
```

Output

```
0 0 0 1
1 0 1 1 1 2
2 0 2 1 2 2 2 3
3 0 3 1 3 2 3 3 3 4
4 0 4 1 4 2 4 3 4 4 4 5
5 0 5 1 5 2 5 3 5 4 5 5 5 6
6 0 6 1 6 2 6 3 6 4 6 5 6 6 6 7
7 0 7 1 7 2 7 3 7 4 7 5 7 6 7 7 7 8
8 0 8 1 8 2 8 3 8 4 8 5 8 6 8 7 8 8 8 9
9 0 9 1 9 2 9 3 9 4 9 5 9 6 9 7 9 8 9 9
```

The task in this program can also be accomplished without using goto. In fact, there is rarely a rightful reason for using goto. Though many tasks can be accomplished using the goto statement, most programmers avoid using it as much as possible as they are of the opinion that the use of goto violates the concept of structured programming.

Looping using goto statement

The subheading might appear presumptuous but is not entirely correct. Readers who have already learnt C might have read that goto should not be used. It was also stated in the last paragraph of Section 5.10 that there is seldom a good reason to use goto. These statements are, however, only partly correct as far as C# is concerned. In order to get an idea of the unexplored uses of goto, let us consider an example. Write a program to check whether a number entered by the user is prime or not. The concept is simple; we will divide the number by every number less than half of it (starting from two). If the number is divisible by any number except itself and one, then it is not considered a prime number. Intuitively anyone would use a for, while, or do-while loop for accomplishing the task. However, the following listing shows that the task can be done by using only if else and goto. Consider the following code:

```
using System;
using System.Collections.Generic;
using System.Linq;
using System.Text;

namespace LoopingGoto
{
    class Program
    {
        static void Main(string[] args)
        {
            int i, number,flag = 0;
            Console.WriteLine("Enter a number\t:");
            number = int.Parse(Console.ReadLine());
            i = 2;
            a:
            if(number % i == 0)
            {
```

```csharp
                flag = 1;
                goto b;
            }
            else
            {
            if(i < number / 2)
                {
                    i++;
                    goto a;
                }
            }
            Console.WriteLine("Number is prime");
            goto c;
            b:
            Console.WriteLine("Number is not prime");
            c:
            Console.ReadKey();
        }
    }
}
```

Output

In the first run, enter a prime number.

```
Enter a number   :
13
Number is prime
_
```

In the second run, enter a number that is not prime.

```
Enter a number   :
18
Number is prime
_
```

5.11 COMPARISON OF LOOPS

From the foregoing discussion, it is evident that a particular task can be accomplished using any of the three loops: `for`, `while`, or `do`. The only criterion of selection of a particular loop is the ease. The following points must be considered while selecting a loop to accomplish a task:

1. The easiest is the `for` loop.
2. If the number of iterations is not known, then use the `while` loop.
3. If the task is to be accomplished at least once, then use the `do` loop.
4. If the elements are to be read and not altered from a list or an array, then use the `foreach` loop.

However, as stated earlier any task can be accomplished by any of the three loops. This point can be reiterated with the help of an example. Consider the problem of calculating the value of one number raised to the power of another number. This can be performed using any of the three loops. The following programs ask the user to enter two numbers, store the numbers in

two variables—number1 and number2. They then calculate the first number raised to the power of the second number and store the answer in the variable power.
The first implementation is using for loop.

```
//To calculate number1 to the power of number2 using for loop

using System;
using System.Collections.Generic;
using System.Linq;
using System.Text;

namespace PowerUsingFor
{
    class Program
    {
        static void Main(string[] args)
        {
            int number1, number2, power = 1, i;
            Console.WriteLine("Enter the first number\t:");
            number1 = int.Parse(Console.ReadLine());
            Console.WriteLine("Enter the second number\t:");
            number2 = int.Parse(Console.ReadLine());
            for(i = 1; i <= number2; i++)
            {
                power = power * number1;
            }
            Console.WriteLine("{0} to the power of {1} is\t:{2}", number1, number2, power);
            Console.ReadKey();
        }
    }
}
```

Output

```
Enter the first number   :
3
Enter the second number  :
4
3 to the power of 4 is   :81
```

The second implementation uses a while loop. It should be noted that the procedure is the same but the counter variable is incremented inside the loop and initialized at its beginning.

```
//To calculate number1 to the power of number2 using while loop

        static void Main(string[] args)
        {
            int number1, number2, power = 1, i;
            Console.WriteLine("Enter the first number\t:");
            number1 = int.Parse(Console.ReadLine());
            Console.WriteLine("Enter the second number\t:");
            number2 = int.Parse(Console.ReadLine());
            i = 1;
            while(i <= number2)
```

```
        {
            power = power * number1;
            i++;
        }
        Console.WriteLine("{0} to the power of {1} is\t:{2}", number1, number2, power);
        Console.ReadKey();
    }
```

The third implementation uses a do-while loop. Here the condition is written at the end, thus making sure that the loop runs at least once.

```
//To calulate number1 to the power of number2 using do-while
    static void Main(string[] args)
    {
        int number1, number2, power = 1, i;
        Console.WriteLine("Enter the first number\t:");
        number1 = int.Parse(Console.ReadLine());
        Console.WriteLine("Enter the second number\t:");
        number2 = int.Parse(Console.ReadLine());
        i = 1;
        do
        {
            power = power * number1;
            i++;
        } while(i <= number2);
        Console.WriteLine("{0} to the power of {1} is\t:{2}", number1, number2, power);
        Console.ReadKey();
    }
```

It has to be noted that the output in all the three cases will be the same.

SUMMARY

Loops are an integral part of procedural programming. Any problem that requires certain task to be repeated involves loops. The chapter examines the three basic loops: while, for, and do-while. The foreach loop has also been discussed and exemplified. This loop is best suited for arrays. In general, the while loop is used when the number of iterations is not known, whereas the for loop is used when the number of iterations is known. However, it may be noted that both while and for loops can be used in any of the conditions; the only criterion is the ease. Moreover, it may also be stated that the section on patterns and a whole section of exercises dedicated to it are not provided because readers will be required to make a lot of patterns in course of their work. They are provided because learning how to make patterns will help in having a better understanding of loops.

GLOSSARY

Looping Looping helps in executing a block of code number of times.
Break break takes the control outside the present loop. The statements following the break keyword are not executed.
Continue continue takes the control at the beginning of the loop, to the next iteration. The statements following the continue statement are not executed.
goto The goto keyword takes the control to the location indicated by a label.

POINTS TO REMEMBER

- The different types of loops in C# are while, do-while, for, and foreach.
- A counter is a variable that is initialized and its value is incremented or decremented each time the loop is executed.
- A while loop first checks a condition and then continues with the execution of the code inside the block until the condition remains true.
- A do loop checks its condition at the end of the loop.
- for loops are appropriate when we precisely know the number of times the statements within the loop are to be executed.
- The foreach loop operates on collections of items, for instance arrays, hash table, or list.
- A loop can be nested within another loop; this is referred to as nesting.
- break is a keyword that helps us to come out of a loop when a particular condition is fulfilled.
- The continue statement takes the control to the beginning of the loop and executes the next iteration.
- The goto statement takes the control to the desired point specified by the label.

EXERCISES

I. Multiple-choice Questions

1. What will be the output of the following program?
    ```
    int i, j;
    for(i = 10, j = 0; i > 0, j < 10; i++, j--)
    {
       i =i * j;
    }
    Console.WriteLine(i);
    Console.ReadKey();
    ```
    (a) The code will not compile.
    (b) −986410
    (c) 0
    (d) None of these

2. What will be the output of the following program?
    ```
    int i, j;
    for(i = 10, j = 0; i > 0 || j < 10; i--, j++)
    {
       i = i * j;
    }
    Console.WriteLine(i);
    Console.ReadKey();
    ```
    (a) The code will not compile.
    (b) −986410
    (c) 0
    (d) None of these

3. What will be the output of the following program?
    ```
    int i, j;
    for(i = 10, j = 0; i > 0 || j < 10; i--, j++)
    {
       j = i * j;
    }
    Console.WriteLine(i);
    Console.ReadKey();
    ```
    (a) The code will not compile.
    (b) −986410
    (c) 0
    (d) None of these

4. What will be the output of the following program?
    ```
    int i, j;
    for(i = 10, j = 0; i > 0; i--)
    {
       i = i+++j++;
    }
    Console.WriteLine(i);
    Console.ReadKey();
    ```
    (a) The code will not compile.
    (b) 1
    (c) 0
    (d) None of these

5. What will be the output of the following program?
    ```
    int i, j, k;
    Console.WriteLine("Enter number\t:");
    i = int.Parse(Console.ReadLine());
    j = 1; k = 1;
    a:
    j = j * k;
    k++;
    if(k <= i)
       goto a;
    else goto b;
    b:
    Console.WriteLine(j);
    Console.ReadKey();
    ```
    (a) Factorial of *i* (b) *i* to the power of *j*
    (c) *k* * *i* (d) None of these

6. What will be the output of the following program?
   ```
   int i, j, k;
   Console.WriteLine("Enter number\t:");
   i = int.Parse(Console.ReadLine());
   j = 1; k = 1;
   a:
   j = j * i;
   k++;
   if(k <= i)
      goto a;
   else goto b;
   b:
   Console.WriteLine(j);
   Console.ReadKey();
   ```
   (a) Factorial of *i*
   (b) *i* to the power of *j*
   (c) *i* to the power of *i*
   (d) None of these

7. What will be the output of the following program?
   ```
   int i, j, k;
   Console.WriteLine("Enter number\t:");
   i = int.Parse(Console.ReadLine());
   j = 1; k = 1;
   a:
   j = j * j;
   k++;
   if(k <= i)
      goto a;
   else goto b;
   b:
   Console.WriteLine(j);
   Console.ReadKey();
   ```
   (a) Factorial of *i*
   (b) 0
   (c) 1
   (d) None of these

8. What will be the output of the following program?
   ```
   int i, j, k;
   Console.WriteLine("Enter number\t:");
   i = int.Parse(Console.ReadLine());
   j = 1; k = 1;
   a:
   j = j * k;
   k++;
   if(k <= i)
      goto b;
   else goto a;
   b:
   Console.WriteLine(j);
   Console.ReadKey();
   ```
   (a) Factorial of *i*
   (b) 0
   (c) 1
   (d) None of these

9. What will be the output of the following program?
   ```
   int i, j, k, n = 1;
   i = 4;
   for(k = 1; k < i; k++)
   {
      for(j = 1; j < k; j++)
      {
         n = n * (k + j);
      }
   }
   Console.WriteLine(n);
   Console.ReadKey();
   ```
   (a) 0   (b) 1   (c) 36   (d) 60

10. What will be the output of the following program?
    ```
    int i, j, k, n = 1;
    i = 4;
    for(k = 1; k < i; k++)
    {
       for(j = 1; j < k; j++)
       {
          n = n * (k * j);
       }
    }
    Console.WriteLine(n);
    Console.ReadKey();
    ```
    (a) 0   (b) 1   (c) 36   (d) 60

11. Only if the number of iterations are known can the for loop be used.
    (a) True
    (b) False
    (c) Can be true or false depending upon the situation
    (d) Data insufficient

12. for loop cannot initialize two variables.
    (a) True
    (b) False
    (c) Can be true or false depending upon the situation
    (d) Data insufficient

13. foreach is used for reading the values of a list or a vector.
    (a) True
    (b) False
    (c) Can be true or false depending upon the situation
    (d) Data insufficient

14. The counter variable in a `for` loop can be a string.
    (a) True
    (b) False
    (c) Can be true or false depending upon the situation
    (d) Data insufficient
15. `while` is sure to execute a statement at least once.
    (a) True
    (b) False
    (c) Can be true or false depending upon the situation
    (d) Data insufficient
16. It is possible that use of `do-while` may lead to a situation where the loop is executed not even once.
    (a) True
    (b) False
    (c) Can be true or false depending upon the situation
    (d) Data insufficient
17. Factorial of a number can be calculated only using `for`, `while`, or `do-while`.
    (a) True
    (b) False
18. Every task that is implemented using `goto` can be done using other statements such as `for`.
    (a) True
    (b) False
    (c) Can be true or false depending upon the situation
    (d) Data insufficient
19. Using loop within a loop increases the complexity of a program.
    (a) True
    (b) False
    (c) Can be true or false depending upon the situation
    (d) Data insufficient
20. Use of `goto` violates the principle of structured programming.
    (a) True
    (b) False
    (c) Can be true or false depending upon the situation
    (d) Data insufficient.

II. Review Questions

1. Differentiate between a `while` and a `do-while` loop.
2. Which loop is easy to use when the number of iterations is known?
3. Which loop is best adapted for arrays?
4. Explain the difference between a `while` and a `for` loop, if any.
5. What are the three basic things to be kept in mind while designing a program containing loops?

III. Programming Exercise

A. Patterns

Write a program to generate the following output. The number of rows is to be entered by the user.

1. a
   a b
   a b c
   a b c d
   a b c d e

2. 1
   2 3
   4 5 6
   7 8 9 10

3.   *
      ***
     *****
    ****

4. 1 2 3 4 5
   1 2 3 4
   1 2 3
   1 2
   1

5. a
   1 2
   b c d
   3 4 5 6 7
   e f g h i j

6. 1 1 1 1 1 1 1
   1 1 1 1 1 1
   1 1 1 1 1
   1 1 1 1
   1 1 1

```
    1 1
    1
    1 1
    1 1 1
    1 1 1 1
    1 1 1 1 1
    1 1 1 1 1 1
7.  *       *
     *     *
      *   *
      *****
      *   *
     *     *
    *       *
```

8. With the help of stars, craft 'M'.
9. With the help of stars, craft 'W'.
10. With the help of stars draw the following pattern:

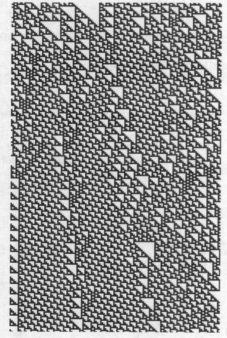

(Refer cellular automata literature and then try to create the above pattern. Arrays might also be required.)

B. Basic Programs

11. Ask the user to enter a number and calculate its factorial without using `for`, `while`, or `do-while`.
12. Ask the user to enter two numbers and calculate a^b using goto?

13. An arithmetic progression is a progression in which the difference between two terms is always the same. It can be depicted as

    $a, a + d, a + 2d, \ldots$

    where a is the first term and d is the common difference. Ask the user to enter the values of a, d, and n, n being the number of terms, and calculate the sum.

14. A geometric progression is a progression in which the ratio between two terms is always constant. It can be depicted as

    $a, ar, ar^2, ar^3, \ldots$

    where a is the first term and r is the common ratio. Ask the user to enter the values of a, r, and n, n being the number of terms, and calculate the sum.

15. A harmonic progression is a progression that is formed by taking reciprocals of an arithmetic progression. It can be depicted as

    $a, a/1 + d, a/1 + 2d, a/1 + 3d \ldots$

    where a is the first term and d is the common difference. Ask the user to enter the value of a, d, and n, n being the number of terms, and calculate the sum.

16. Ask the user to enter a number and check whether it is prime or not without using `for`, `while`, or `do-while`.
17. Ask the user to enter a number and print all the numbers that are relatively prime to it.
18. Ask the user to enter two numbers and find their highest common factor.
19. Ask the user to enter n numbers and find the maximum amongst them.
20. In Question 19, find the minimum number.
21. Generate the following sequences up to n terms, where n is to be entered by the user.
    (a) 1, 4, 9, 16, 25, ...
    (b) 1, 8, 27, ...
    (c) 1, 9, 17, 25, ...
    (d) 3, 5, 9, 15, 23, ...
    (e) 1, 3, 7, 13, 21, ...
    (f) 1, 4, 13, 40, 121, ...
    (g) Find the sum of $\sqrt{2}, \sqrt{8}, \sqrt{18}, \ldots$
22. Write a program to calculate the sum of first n natural numbers.
23. Calculate the sum of $1^2 + 2^2 + 3^2 + 4^2 + \ldots$
24. Calculate the sum of $1^2 + 3^2 + 5^2 + 7^2 + \ldots$

6 Collections

OBJECTIVES

After completing this chapter, the reader will be able to

Appreciate the importance of collections
Create a queue and a stack
Manage a directory
Use `HashSet`
Understand the importance and applications of Lazy

6.1 INTRODUCTION

At times, in a program we need to store many objects in one group. This can be done in two ways. One way is to make an array of objects. However, this can be done only when all the objects are of the same type and the maximum number of objects is known beforehand, this is not the case most of the times. Consider the case of a media player for which a developer is required to write a program for creating a playlist. The number of songs a user will include in the playlist cannot be known before creating the playlist. Moreover, one of the requirements of the project is that the user can add songs in the playlist in any format. This is only a sample scenario and in real-life situations there can be many such scenarios. The management of objects is, therefore, important. The group of objects in C# can be managed by `System.Collections` namespace.

Collections allow us to collect items in a list and iterate through those items. Collections in .NET include list and directories. A collection may contain references or values. Readers familiar with data structures must have an idea of linked lists. The motivation for using collections is the same as that of using linked lists. Collections are more flexible than arrays in more than one way. These concepts have been discussed in the later sections.

The various collection classes available in the .NET Framework are briefly explained in Table 6.1.

Table 6.1 Collections in C#

Name of the Collection	Explanation
Stack	It is a last in, first out data structure. We might use stack to evaluate a postfix expression or to track changes. A stack is just like a pile of books. The book that is kept at the topmost position will be picked first.
Queue	It is a first in, first out data structure. Queues are used in printer services, in the CPU scheduling, and in many more situations. The use and implementation of queues is explained in this chapter.
ArrayList	It is a collection that can store any type of objects. ArrayList is more flexible than an array. The concept has been discussed in Chapter 9.
StringCollections	It is an ArrayList in which the values are strongly typed as strings. Its use has been discussed later in the chapter.
BitArray	It is a collection of Boolean values.

6.2 STACK

Stack is a linear data structure that follows the principle of last in, first out or LIFO. Insertion or deletion of an element in a stack can be done only at the top position.

6.2.1 Static Implementation of Stack

The insertion of an element in a stack requires incrementing the value of the counter 'TOP' by one each time an insertion is done. Initially, the value of the variable 'TOP' is -1. Static implementation of stack is done using arrays. The algorithm of the static implementation of stack is as follows:

Specifications

1. Array : stack[], the first element is at 0
2. Maximum elements : Max
3. Initial value of TOP : -1

```
push(item)
    {
    if(TOP != Max-1)
        {
        TOP++;
        stack[TOP] = item;
        }
    else
        {
        print "OVERFLOW";
        }
    }
```

This algorithm inserts item at the topmost position if the array is not already full. If it is already full, then the algorithm prints 'OVERFLOW'. The problem with this algorithm is that we need to specify the maximum number of elements. In C#, this problem is handled by the stack class. The deletion of an element from the stack is called pop. The algorithm of the static implementation of the pop operation in a stack is as follows. The specifications of the pop algorithm are the same as that of the push algorithm. The following algorithm assumes that the elements in the stack are of `int` type. If there is no element in the stack, then the algorithm returns –1. Thus, it should be noted that if the value of TOP is –1, then the array is empty; in every other case, the value of the item at the TOP position is returned and TOP is decremented by –1.

```
int pop()
{
    if(TOP != -1)
    {
        return(stack[TOP--]);
    }
    else
    {
        print "UNDERFLOW";
        return -1;
    }
}
```

There are some problems with this implementation. These problems are handled by the collection provided by C#. Section 6.2.2 deals with the problems encountered in the given algorithms and their solutions.

6.2.2 System.Collections.Stack

The `Stack` class in the `System.Collections` namespace helps us to use a stack without implementing the algorithms in Section 6.2.1. Moreover, there is no practical restriction on the number of elements in the instance of the `Stack` class created. There is an added advantage; we can insert any type of element such as a string, a character, or an integer, to name a few. The following program depicts the use of this class:

```
using System;
using System.Collections.Generic;
using System.Linq;
using System.Text;
using System.Collections;

namespace StackDemo
{
    class Program
    {
        static void Main(string[] args)
        {
            Stack s = new Stack();
            s.Push("First Element");
            s.Push('S');
            s.Push(3);
            Console.WriteLine("Elements");
            for(int i = 0; i < 3; i++)
            {
                Console.WriteLine("Element\t:" + s.Pop().ToString());
            }

            Console.ReadKey();
        }
    }
}
```

```
Elements    : 3
Elements    : 5
Elements    : First Element
```

Having studied both the static and dynamic implementation of stack, let us move on to the next type of collection, that is, queue.

6.3 QUEUE

Queue is a linear data structure that follows the principle of first in, first out or FIFO. The insertion of an element in a queue can only be done at the end, called REAR. The deletion of an element from a queue can be done only at the first position, called FRONT. The static implementation of queue refers to the implementation of queue using arrays and is explained in Section 6.3.1

6.3.1 Static Implementation of Queue

In the static implementation of queue, the values of REAR and FRONT are −1 when there is no element in the queue. The insertion of an element requires incrementing the value of the counter REAR by 1, each time an insertion is done. Initially, the value of REAR is −1. If a queue is implemented as an array, then the algorithm for insertion is as follows:

Specifications

1. Array   : q[ ], the first element is at 0
2. Maximum elements   : Max
3. Initial value of REAR and FRONT   : −1

```
insert(item)
{
    if(REAR == -1)
    {
        REAR++;
        FRONT++;
        q[REAR] = item;
    }
    if(REAR != Max -1)
    {
        REAR++;
        q[REAR] = item;
    }
    else
    {
        print "OVERFLOW";
    }
}
```

This algorithm inserts item at the topmost position if the array is not already full. If it is already full, then 'OVERFLOW' is printed. Again, the problem with this algorithm is that we need to specify the maximum number of elements. The class that helps us to implement queue in C# is Queue. The deletion of an element from the stack is implemented as follows. The specifications of the deletion algorithm are the same as that of the insertion algorithm. The following algorithm assumes that the elements in the queue are of int type. The algorithm returns −1 if there is no element in the queue. Thus, it should be noted that if the value of REAR is −1, then the array is empty; in every other case, the value of the item at the FRONT position is returned and FRONT is incremented by −1.

```
int delete()
{
    if(REAR != -1)
    {
        return(q[REAR--]);
    }
    else
    {
        print "UNDERFLOW";
        return -1;
    }
}
```

Once again, the static implementation of queue suffers from inflexibility and the Queue class helps to overcome this situation. The implementation of a queue by the System.Collections.Queue class is depicted in Section 6.3.2.

6.3.2 System.Collections.Queue

The Queue class in the System.Collections namespace helps us to use a queue without implementing the algorithms given in Section 6.3.1. Again, there is no practical restriction on the number of elements in the instance of the Queue class created. We can also insert any type of element such as a string, a character, or an integer. The following program depicts the use of this class. In the following snippet, the Enqueue() function inserts an object in the queue and Dequeue() deletes an element:

```
using System;
using System.Collections.Generic;
using System.Linq;
using System.Text;
using System.Collections;

namespace QueueDemo
{
    class Program
    {
        static void Main(string[] args)
        {
            Queue q = new Queue();
            q.Enqueue("Hi");
            q.Enqueue('a');
            q.Enqueue(45);
            for(int i = 0; i < 3; i++)
            {
                Console.WriteLine("Element\t:" + q.Dequeue().ToString());
            }
            Console.ReadKey();
        }
    }
}
```

6.4 DIRECTORIES

Directories are sophisticated data types. They are also known as maps or hash tables. They are flexible in the sense that we can add, remove, or update an element as in an `ArrayList` but with minimal overhead.

Consider a situation in which we are asked to develop a management system of COMPUTERgrad, which is a computer training institute. The company stores the records of its students. The records are ordered on the basis of `StudentID`, which is not an integer. As per the Software Requirement Specifications, `StudentID` is alphanumeric, for example, CG2012BTECHVII52. In the software application, we need to have a variable called `student`, which can be treated as an array of `StudentRecord` object. The retrieval of the record should be as easy as an array. To handle this problem, a directory is made. Suppose `StudentID` is an object and `StudentRecord` contains `StudentID`, `name`, and `fees`. The `StudentID` object can be instantiated as follows:

```
StudentID id = new StudentID("CG2012BTECHVII53");
```

and `StudentRecord` can be instantiated as follows:

```
StudentRecord student1 = students[id];
```

Here `students` is a variable, which can be treated as an array. That is the advantage of directories. We do not need an integer to index into them; the indexing can also be done by, say, a string.

So, conceptually the directory has two parts: a key and the rest of the data. The part except for the key is decided on the basis of the problem at hand. The key, on the other hand, is any value on the basis of which you want to index the data. In case of employees it can be UID, in case of students it can be Student ID, and so on.

In a directory, both the key and the data are of the type object. It is represented by a `Hashtable`. The `Hashtable` can store any data type. The base class can be chosen depending upon the type of string. In most of the cases the base class will be the `Hashtable` but it may vary in some cases. For example, if the keys are all strings, as in the example of Student Management System of COMPUTERgrad, then you can use `System.Collections.Specialized.StringDirectory`. Section 6.4.1 depicts the use of directories.

6.4.1 Student Management by Directories

The following program depicts the use of directories. In, four classes have been created in three files. The Solution Explorer settings are depicted in Fig. 6.1.

Fig. 6.1 Solution Explorer

The first class to be crafted is the `StudentID` class. In order to create the class, right click on the name of the namespace in the right pane and add a new class. Write the following code in the class:

```csharp
using System;
using System.Collections.Generic;
using System.Linq;
using System.Text;

namespace DirectoriesDemo
{
    class StudentID
    {
        private string prefix;
        private int number;
```

```csharp
        public StudentID(string id)
        {
            prefix = id.Substring(0, 14);//The first part of ID contains the code, for
            example, CG (computer grad), 2012 (year), and BTECHVII (course and semester)
            Console.WriteLine("Prefix \t:" + prefix);
            number = int.Parse(id.Substring(14, 2));
            Console.WriteLine("Number\t:" + number);
        }
        public override string ToString()
        {
            return prefix.ToString() + number;
        }
        public override int GetHashCode()
        {
            return ToString().GetHashCode();
        }
        public override bool Equals(object obj)
        {
            StudentID std = obj as StudentID;
            if(std == null)
            {
                return false;
            }
            else if((prefix == std.prefix) && (number == std.number))
            {
                return true;
            }
            else
            {
                return false;
            }
        }
    }
}
```

The second class that needs to be created is the StudentRecord class. In order to create this class, right click on the name of the namespace in the right pane and add a new class. Write the following code in the class:

```csharp
using System;
using System.Collections.Generic;
using System.Linq;
using System.Text;

namespace DirectoriesDemo
{
    class StudentRecord
    {
        private String name;
        private double fees;
        private StudentID id;
        public StudentRecord(StudentID id, String name, double fees)
        {
            this.id = id;
            this.name = name;
            this.fees = fees;
```

```
            }
            public override string ToString()
            {
                StringBuilder strb = new StringBuilder(id.ToString(), 100);
                strb.Append(" ");
                strb.Append(name);
                strb.Append(" ");
                strb.Append(fees);
                return strb.ToString();
            }
        }
    }
```

The last step is to create a StudentManagementDirectory class, which has the Main() method. The listing of this class is given as follows.

```
using System;
using System.Collections.Generic;
using System.Linq;
using System.Text;
using System.Collections;
namespace DirectoriesDemo
{
    class StudentManagementDirectory
    {
        Hashtable students = new Hashtable(40);
        public void Run()
        {
            StudentID id1 = new StudentID("CO2012BTECHVII01");
            StudentRecord CGStudent1 = new StudentRecord(id1, "Harsh", 30500.00);
            StudentID id2 = new StudentID("CO2012BTECHVII02");
            StudentRecord CGStudent2 = new StudentRecord(id2, "Jish", 30501.00);
            StudentID id3 = new StudentID("CO2012BTECHVII03");
            StudentRecord CGStudent3 = new StudentRecord(id3, "Naks", 30500.00);
            students.Add(id1, CGStudent1);
            students.Add(id2, CGStudent2);
            students.Add(id3, CGStudent3);
            while(true)
            {
                try
                {
                    Console.WriteLine("Enter student ID (Q to Quit)\t:");
                    string inputString = Console.ReadLine();
                    inputString.ToUpper();
                    if(inputString == "Q")
                    {
                        return;
                    }
                    else
                    {
                        StudentID id = new StudentID(inputString);
                        ShowData(id);
                    }
                }
```

```
                catch(Exception e)
                {
                    Console.WriteLine("Error");
                }
            }
        }
        private void ShowData(StudentID id)
        {
            Object studentObject = students[id];
            if(studentObject != null)
            {
                StudentRecord student = (StudentRecord)studentObject;
                Console.WriteLine("Student" + student.ToString());
            }
            else
            {
                Console.WriteLine("Not found");
            }
        }
    }
    class StudentManagement
    {
        public static void Main(String[] args)
        {
            StudentmanagementDirectory dir = new StudentmanagementDirectory();
            dir.Run();
        }
    }
}
```

Output

```
Prefix      : CO2012BTECHVII
Number      : 1
Prefix      : CO2012BTECHVII
Number      : 2
Prefix      : CO2012BTECHVII
Number      : 3
Enter student ID <Q to quit> :
CO2012BTECHVII02
Prefix      : CO2012BTECHVII01
Number      : 2
Student CO2012BTECHVII02 Jish    30501
Enter student ID <Q to Quit>    :
Q
```

6.5 LAZY TYPE

The sleep method halts the execution of a program for some time. The Lazy instantiation also delays certain tasks. However, the two concepts are conceptually different. The sleep method has no relation to the Lazy instantiation. The Lazy type is used to perk up the start-up time. The constructor is invoked when the value property is accessed. The following program exemplifies the use of Lazy instantiation:

```csharp
using System;

class StringTest
{
    String str;
    public StringTest()
    {
        Console.WriteLine("Constructor of StringTest()");
        str = "Abide with me";
    }
    public int Length
    {
        get
        {
            return str.Length;
        }
    }
}
class Program
{
    static void Main()
    {
        Lazy<StringTest> lazyTest = new Lazy<StringTest>();
        Console.WriteLine("IsValueCreated = {0}", lazyTest.IsValueCreated);
        //Initially this value is false
        StringTest test1 = lazyTest.Value;
        //StringTest()is executed

        Console.WriteLine("IsValueCreated = {0}", lazyTest.IsValueCreated);
        //The IsValueCreated becomes true
        Console.WriteLine("Length = {0}", test1.Length);
    }
}
```

Output

```
IsValueCreated = False
Constructor of StringTest()
IsValueCreated = True
Length = 13
```

The code complexity internal to Lazy type is substantial. Therefore, it is advisable to use Lazy on slower computers. The Lazy type also allows specification of thread safety. Delayed objects, such as test1 in the earlier program, are referred to as trunks.

6.6 HashSet

C# provides us with many collections. At times we do not require duplicate items in a collection. In such cases HashSet is used. The union of two sets can also be easily taken using HashSet. The following program exemplifies the use of the HashSet constructor. First, the constructor eliminates the duplicate values. The array is then converted into the set data structure.

```
using System;
using System.Collections.Generic;

class Program
{
    static void Main()
    {
        string[] InputArray = {"testing", "testing", "testing", "intelligence",
        "genetic", "neural networks"};
        Console.WriteLine(string.Join(",", InputArray));
        var hash = new HashSet<string>(InputArray);
        string[] StringArray = hash.ToArray();
        Console.WriteLine(string.Join(",", StringArray));
    }
}
```

Output

```
testing, testing, testing, intelligence, genetic, neutral networks
testing, intelligence, genetic, neutral networks
```

Consider this output. Initially, testing was repeatedly given, but after removal of redundant values, it has become just one of the four values.

One of the very important methods in the HashSet is Overlaps(). It returns true or false depending upon whether any of the HashSet elements is contained in the IEnumerable argument's elements. For example, in the following program, the element 4 is in the HashSet. This means Overlaps returns true for array2 but false for array3.

```
using System;
using System.Collections.Generic;

class Program
{
    static void Main()
    {
        int[] SetArray1 = {4, 5, 6};
        int[] SetArray2 = {4, 7, 8};
        int[] SetArray3 = {9, 1, 2};

        HashSet<int> HSet = new HashSet<int>(SetArray1);
        bool x = HSet.Overlaps(SetArray2);
        bool y = HSet.Overlaps(SetArray3);
        Console.WriteLine(x);
        Console.WriteLine(y);
    }
}
```

Output

```
True
False
```

The Directory has a slightly better performance than the HashSet. It has been observed that in every test where the two collections had similar functionalities, the Directory is always faster.

SUMMARY

The chapter explains the importance and implementation of collections. The knowledge of collections is important both in data structures and in algorithm analysis and design. Collections are optimized, thus making the program more efficient. The chapter provides an introduction to the concept of collections. Their use will become clear once readers start writing programs regularly.

GLOSSARY

Stack It is a linear data structure that follows the principle of last in, first out. Items in a stack can be inserted and deleted only at the top.

Queue It is a linear data structure that follows the principle of first in, first out. Items in a queue can be added at the end and deleted from the beginning of the queue.

HashSet It is a type of collections, which removes duplicate elements and helps us to implement sets easily.

POINTS TO REMEMBER

- Collections allow us to collect items in a list and iterate through those items.
- Stack is a linear data structure that follows the principle of last in, first out or LIFO.
- The Stack class in the System.Collections namespace helps us to use a stack without implementing algorithms.
- Queue is a linear data structure that follows the principle of first in, first out or FIFO.
- Directories are also known as maps or hash tables. They are flexible in the sense that we can add, remove, or update an element as in an ArrayList but with minimal overhead.
- Lazy type is used to perk up the start-up time.

EXERCISES

I. Multiple-choice Questions

1. Which amongst the following is not a collection in C#?
   (a) List
   (b) Directory
   (c) Stack
   (d) Plex

2. Which of the following statements is true as regards ArrayList?
   (a) It contains the same type of elements.
   (b) It may contain different types of elements.
   (c) The number of elements in it is fixed.
   (d) None of these

3. Which of the following statements is true as regards stack?
   (a) It is a data structure that follows the principle of last in, first out.
   (b) It is a data structure that follows the principle of first in, first out.

(c) It is a 'neither in, neither out' data structure.
(d) It is an 'in out' data structure.

4. Which of the following can be used for the static implementation of stack?
   (a) Arrays
   (b) Strings
   (c) Int
   (d) None of these

5. Which of the following is true for Lazy types in C#?
   (a) It is the same as sleep.
   (b) It is used to perk up the start-up time.
   (c) It inspires the process not to run.
   (d) It makes the whole system dormant.

6. What happens when the value of Lazy type is accessed?
   (a) Constructors are invoked
   (b) Destructors are invoked
   (c) The value is not returned as it is Lazy
   (d) System crashes

7. Which of the following is used to eliminate duplicates?
   (a) HashSet
   (b) HarshSet
   (c) Stack
   (d) None of these

8. Which of the following helps to take union of two sets easily?
   (a) HashSet
   (b) Stack
   (c) Queue
   (d) None of these

9. Which amongst directory or HashSet has a better performance?
   (a) Directory
   (b) List
   (c) Both have equivalent performance
   (d) None of these

10. Directory is different from which of the following?
    (a) Maps
    (b) Hashtables
    (c) HashSets
    (d) None

II. Review Questions

1. What are stacks? Write a program to implement stacks using arrays.
2. Write a program to implement stacks using collections.
3. What are queues? Write a program to implement a queue using arrays.
4. Write a program to implement a queue using collections.
5. What is a HashSet? What are the advantages of using a HashSet?
6. Explain the concept of directory in C#.
7. What are the various types of collections in C#?
8. Discuss the advantages of static implemenation of queues.
9. Discuss the advantages of dynamic implemenation of stacks.
10. What is the difference between an array and an ArrayList?

III. Programming Exercises

1. Write a program to implement a stack via System.Collections.Stack.
2. Extend Question 1 to invert a string.
3. Use System.Collections.Stack to convert a postfix expression to an infix expression.
4. Use System.Collections.Stack to convert a prefix expression to an infix expression.
5. Use System.Collections.Stack to convert a prefix expression to an postfix expression.
6. Use System.Collections.Stack to convert an infix expression to a prefix expression.
7. Develop an employee management system using directories.
8. Create a class called arrayDemo, which has a method that displays the length of the array. Use Lazy type to call the constructor.
9. Use System.Collections.Queue to implement job sequencing.
10. Use queues to implement first in, first out scheduling.

PROJECT I
IP Addresses

You must have noticed that while filling a form you are generally asked to enter your email address. Have you ever wondered why? This is because every person has a unique email address (generally). The purpose of asking the email address is to uniquely identify the person. Like an email address that uniquely identifies a person, an IP address uniquely identifies a computer. IP stands for Internet Protocol. There are two types of IP addresses—classless and classful addresses.

An IP address is a 32-bit address. Two computers cannot have the same IP address. The address space of an IP address, that is, the total number of addresses, is 2^{32}. However, all the addresses have not been used. The type of addresses discussed in this Project is classful IP addresses. There are two ways of writing an IP address—binary and decimal. The address is divided into four quads. Each quad represents eight bits and hence the maximum decimal value of each quad is 255.

An example of a binary IP address is

$$11110000.11110101.10101010.00001111$$

An example of a decimal IP address is

$$127.23.90.11$$

In the decimal IP address, none of the quads can have a value more than 255.

The earlier conceptualization of IP addresses divided the address space into five classes. These classes are A, B, C, D, and E. Half the address space is allocated to class A. The rest is divided into four classes, of which 25 per cent space is allocated to class B, 12.5 per cent to class C, and 6.25 per cent each to classes D and E, as shown in Fig. PI.1 and Table PI.1.

The first quad of the address identifies the class of the address. In a binary address, if the first bit is 0, then the address belongs to class A. If the first two bits are 10, then it belongs to class B. The address belongs to class C if the first three bits are 110, and it belongs to class D if the first four bits are 1110. If, however, the first four bits are 1111, then the address belongs to class E.

As far as a decimal address is concerned, if the first quad is less than or equal to 127, then the address belongs to class A. If the first quad has a number between 128 and 191, then the address belongs to class B. If it has a number between 192 and 223, then the address belongs to class C. If it has a number between 224 and 239, then the address belongs to class D. If the first quad has a number between 240 and 255, then the address belongs to class E.

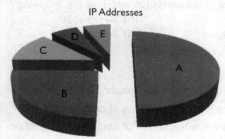

Fig. PI.1 Share of Classes A, B, C, and D in the IP address space

Table PI.1 Share of Class A, B, C and D in the IP address space

Class	Percentage
A	50
B	25
C	12.5
D	6.25
E	6.25

First quad
≤ 127 A
≤ 191 B
≤ 223 C
≤ 239 D
≤ 255 E

The following program asks the user to enter the address, checks it for correctness, and then identifies the class.

```csharp
//
using System;
using System.Collections.Generic;
using System.Linq;
using System.Text;

namespace IPAddressCaseStudy
{
    class Program
    {
        public static int isCorrectBinary(string address)
        {
            string[] part = new string[10];
            part = address.Split('.');
            if(part.Length != 4)
            {
                Console.WriteLine("IP address has four quads");
                return 1;
            }
            else if((part[0].Length != 8) || (part[1].Length != 8) || (part[2].Length != 8) || (part[3].Length != 8))
            {
                Console.WriteLine("Each part of an IP address has eight binary units");
                return 1;
            }
            else
            {
                int flag = 0;
                for(int i = 0; i < 4; i++)
                {
                    for(int j = 0; j < 8; j++)
                    {
                        if(part[i].ToCharArray()[j] != '0')
                        {
                            if(part[i].ToCharArray()[j] != '1')
                            {
                                //Console.WriteLine(part[i].ToCharArray()[j].ToString());
                                flag = 1;
                            }
                        }
                    }
                }
                if(flag == 1)
                {
                    Console.WriteLine("A binary IP address should have 0 or 1 at every place");
                    return 1;
                }
                else
                {
                    return 0;
                }
            }
        }
```

```csharp
public static int isCorrectDecimal(string address)
{
    string[] part = new string[10];
    part = address.Split('.');
    try
    {
        if(part.Length != 4)
        {
            Console.WriteLine("IP address has four quads");
            return 1;
        }
        else if(((int.Parse(part[0]) >= 0) && (int.Parse(part[0]) <= 255)) && ((int.
        Parse(part[1])) >= 0) && (int.Parse(part[1]) <= 255) && ((int.Parse(part[2]))
        >= 0) && (int.Parse(part[2]) <= 255) && (int.Parse(part[3]) >= 0) && (int.
        Parse(part[3]) <= 255))
        {
            return 0;
        }
        else
        {
            return 1;
        }
    }
    catch(Exception e1)
    {
        Console.WriteLine("Not an integer");
        return 1;
    }
}
static void Main(string[] args)
{
    char choice = '0';
    string address, part1;
    try
    {
        while(choice != '3')
        {
            Console.Clear();
            Console.WriteLine("\t\t\tIP ADDRESS CASE STUDY");
            Console.WriteLine("\n1\t:Binary");
            Console.WriteLine("\n2\t:Decimal");
            Console.WriteLine("\n3\t:Exit");
            Console.WriteLine("Enter your choice\t:");
            choice = char.Parse(Console.ReadLine());
            switch(choice)
            {
                case '1':
                Console.WriteLine("\nEnter Address");
                address = Console.ReadLine();
                if(isCorrectBinary(address) == 0)
                {
                    part1 = (address.Split('.'))[0];
                    if(part1.StartsWith("0"))
                    {
                        Console.WriteLine("Class A");
```

```csharp
                }
                else if(part1.StartsWith("10"))
                {
                    Console.WriteLine("Class B");
                }
                else if(part1.StartsWith("110"))
                {
                    Console.WriteLine("Class C");
                }
                else if(part1.StartsWith("1110"))
                {
                    Console.WriteLine("Class D");
                }
                else if(part1.StartsWith("1111"))
                {
                    Console.WriteLine("Class E");
                }
            }
            else
            {
                Console.WriteLine("Incorrect Address");
            }
            break;
            case '2':
            Console.WriteLine("\nEnter Address");
            address = Console.ReadLine();
            if(isCorrectDecimal(address) == 0)
            {
                part1 = (address.Split('.'))[0];
                if((int.Parse(part1) >= 0) && (int.Parse(part1) <= 127))
                {
                    Console.WriteLine("Class A");
                }
                else if((int.Parse(part1) >= 128) && (int.Parse(part1) <= 191))
                {
                    Console.WriteLine("Class B");
                }
                else if((int.Parse(part1) >= 192) && (int.Parse(part1) <= 223))
                {
                    Console.WriteLine("Class C");
                }
                else if((int.Parse(part1) >= 224) && (int.Parse(part1) <= 239))
                {
                    Console.WriteLine("Class D");
                }
                else if((int.Parse(part1) >= 240) && (int.Parse(part1) <= 255))
                {
                    Console.WriteLine("Class E");
                }
                else
                {
                    Console.WriteLine("Incorrect Result");
                }
            }
            else
```

```
                    {
                        Console.WriteLine("Incorrect Address");
                    }
                    break;
                    case '3':
                    Console.WriteLine("Ending program");
                    break;
                    default:
                    Console.WriteLine("Incorrect Choice");
                    break;
                }
                Console.ReadKey();
            }
        }
        catch(Exception e1)
        {
            Console.WriteLine("Error\n" + e1.ToString());
        }
    }
  }
}
```

Output

The output of this program is as follows. If you select binary address and enter an address belonging to class B, then the following output is displayed:

```
            IP ADDRESS CASE STUDY
1           :Binary
2           :Decimal
3           :Exit
Enter your choice    :
1
Enter Adress
10101010.11110000.00001111.10101010
Class B
```

If you select binary address and enter an address belonging to class E, then the following output is displayed:

```
            IP ADDRESS CASE STUDY
1           :Binary
2           :Decimal
3           :Exit
Enter your choice    :
1
Enter Adress
11111110.10101010.10101010.01010101
Class E
```

If you select binary address and enter an address belonging to class A, then the following output is displayed:

```
          IP ADDRESS CASE STUDY
1             :Binary
2             :Decimal
3             :Exit
Enter your choice    :
1
Enter Adress
00000101.10101010.00001111.10101010
Class A
```

If you select binary address and enter an address belonging to class C, then the following output is displayed:

```
          IP ADDRESS CASE STUDY
1             :Binary
2             :Decimal
3             :Exit
Enter your choice    :
1
Enter Adress
11000000.10101010.01010101.10101010
Class C
```

If you select decimal as the option and enter an address belonging to class A, then the following output is displayed:

```
          IP ADDRESS CASE STUDY
1             :Binary
2             :Decimal
3             :Exit
Enter your choice    :
2
Enter Adress
10.12.34.56
Class A
```

If you select decimal as the option and enter an address belonging to class B, then the following output is displayed:

```
        IP ADDRESS CASE STUDY

1              :Binary
2              :Decimal
3              :Exit
Enter your choice   :
2
Enter Adress
128.90.89.34
Class B
```

If you select decimal as the option and enter an address belonging to class C, then the following output is displayed:

```
        IP ADDRESS CASE STUDY

1              :Binary
2              :Decimal
3              :Exit
Enter your choice   :
2
Enter Adress
193.20.20.10
Class C
```

If you select decimal as the option and enter an incorrect address, then the following output is displayed:

```
        IP ADDRESS CASE STUDY

1              :Binary
2              :Decimal
3              :Exit
Enter your choice   :
2
Enter Adress
256.20.20.20
Incorrect Address
```

The reason for having this Project in the book is two-fold. It gives an idea of IP addresses as well as illustrates the implementation of the concepts studied in the previous chapters. However, it is also possible to determine the real IP address of a computer. The concept has been discussed in Chapter 23. It would be pointless to implement a program that finds the IP address of a DNS and determines the class of the IP address, as classful addressing is not used now.

7 Methods

OBJECTIVES

After completing this chapter, the reader will be able to
- # Appreciate the importance of methods
- # Understand the syntax and use of methods
- # Know the concept of variable parameters
- # Use the out keyword
- # Learn and use method overloading
- # Elucidate the crafting and use of methods with 'ref' parameters
- # Understand recursion and delegates

7.1 INTRODUCTION

The history of modern programming languages begins with the advent of C, the procedural language. Its shortcomings were handled by C++, which was the base of Visual C++. Gosling realized the importance of clubbing together object-oriented concepts and the syntax of C to produce what he called OAK, which later on evolved to become JAVA. The moral of the story is that it all started with C.

So, it must be understood that the concepts of C are important even now. The concepts of procedural programming are still of immense significance, in terms of both learning and implementation. The idea of C was to segregate a program into functions. The concept of functions gave rise to the concept of reusability. Reusability improved the performance of the programs and helped in controlling the size of the software.

The functions are disguised as methods in C#. The crux remains the same, but the name has been changed. It is important to understand the substance of such superficial changes in the socio-cultural context. Like in the United States of America, socialism is disguised as social security, in the same way functions are camouflaged as methods. Actually, in Visual Basic there is a difference between a method and a function, but there is hardly any difference between a method and a function in C#, except for the name. In general, object-oriented terminology uses the term method instead of function. Since C# is an object-oriented language, it will be better to use the name method.

A method is a block of statements that performs a particular task. It acts when it is invoked. It may return a value as well. A method can have parameters, which are of two types and are discussed in Section 7.8.

Though methods are being discussed only now, we have already been using them in our programs. For example, Main is a method, which is called by the common language runtime when a program is executed. In C#, methods are declared inside a class or a structure. If a method is declared outside the class, it results in an error. For example, in the following program, an error is displayed at the time of compilation:

```
namespace MethodsProg1
{
    public static void method1()
    {
        Console.WriteLine("Hi I am in method1");
    }
    class Program
    {
        static void Main(string[] args)
        {
        }
    }
}
```

On compilation, the following error is displayed:

```
Error:
Expected class, delegate, enum, interface, or struct
```

The reason for cropping up of this error is that the method 'method 1()' is not a member of any class. So, a function has to be a member of a class. The study of methods is taken up in detail in this chapter.

7.2 SIGNATURE: PARAMETERS, NAME, AND MODIFIERS

Every method has a signature. It includes the name of the method along with the parameters. While declaring a method, one may also specify the access level and modifiers. Figure 7.1 depicts the components of a method signature.

The access levels can be one of the access levels discussed later in Chapter 11. For example, the public access specifier is used when a method is to be called anywhere in the program. It is made private when it is to be used only within the class. After studying Chapters 11 and 12, readers will be able to appreciate the importance of two more access specifiers. However, a brief overview is presented in Table 7.1.

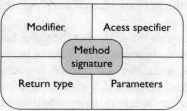

Fig. 7.1 Method signature

Table 7.1 Access specifiers

Access specifier	Meaning
Public	The method can be accessed anywhere in the program.
Private	The method can be accessed only within the class.
Protected	The method can be accessed in the class and in its derived classes.
Internal	The method can be accessed within the namespace.

A method name can also be preceded by a modifier. The modifier can be any of the valid modifiers such as abstract or sealed. The concept of abstract methods has been discussed in detail in Chapter 12. Table 7.2, however, gives a brief overview of the modifiers.

Table 7.2 Modifiers

Modifier	Meaning
abstract	A method that specifies what is to be done but not how it is to be done.
static	A method of which there can be only one copy and hence instance of a class need not be made.
virtual	A method that may be overridden (the concept has been discussed in Chapter 12).
sealed	A method that cannot be overridden.
extern	A method that has been externally implemented.

The return type of a method is the data type of the value returned by the method. It can be any of the valid data types discussed in Chapter 3.

A method can have any number of parameters. C# also provides a way of crafting methods that have variable number of arguments. Such methods are discussed in Section 7.7.

7.3 SYNTAX

The syntax of a method is as follows:

`<access specifier> <modifier> <return type> <name of the method>(<parameter(s)>)`

Let us consider an example. The following program has two classes in the namespace: abc and Program. A method method1() is made in the class abc. Therefore, in order to call the method we need to make an instance of the class abc. The concept of making an instance of a class, also called an object, has been discussed in Chapter 11. However, it may be noted here that the instance of a class is made by writing the name of the class followed by the name of the object that is to be crafted; this is equated to the keyword new followed by the constructor of the class. The keyword new allocates memory, and the constructor is a method of the same name as that of the class. The purpose of the constructor is to initialize the data members of the class. In the following program, abc is a class and abc() is its constructor. It may be noted here that a method is invoked by writing the name of the object formed followed by the dot operator and then the name of the method.

```csharp
using System;
using System.Collections.Generic;
using System.Linq;
using System.Text;

namespace MethodsProg1
{
    class abc
    {
        public static void method1()
        {
            Console.WriteLine("Hi I am in method1");
        }
    }
    class Program
    {
        static void Main(string[] args)
        {
            abc a = new abc();
            abc.method1();
            Console.ReadKey();
        }
    }
}
```

7.4 CALLING A METHOD

As explained in the program given here, a method is called by writing the name of the object followed by the dot operator and then the name of the method. It is done in the same way as accessing a data member of the class or structure. Figure 7.2 depicts the calling of a method by an object:

It may be noted that the method can be invoked only if the access specifier allows its invocation. For example, in the following program, the method cannot be invoked since it is private.

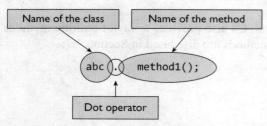

Fig. 7.2 Calling of a Method

```csharp
using System;
using System.Collections.Generic;
using System.Linq;
using System.Text;

namespace MethodProg2
{
    class abc
    {
        private void method1()
        {
            Console.WriteLine("Hi");
        }
    }
```

```
    class Program
    {
        static void Main(string[] args)
        {
            abc a = new abc();
            a.method1();
            Console.ReadKey();
        }
    }
}
```

The program results in an error.

Error

```
'MethodProg2.abc.method1()'is inaccessible due to its protection level.
```

However, if the access specifier of the method is changed to public and the program is then compiled, the program will be executed. The result of the execution would be: 'Hi'.

This section explained the invocation of a method. The return type of a method is discussed in Section 7.5.

7.5 RETURN TYPE OF A METHOD

A method may return the result of the task accomplished by it. The return type is, therefore, the data type of the value returned by the method. It may be noted that a method may also return a user-defined data type as in a class. The following program has a method called getHRA(), which calculates the house rent allowance (HRA) of an employee. The salary of the employee is taken through the method getdata(). The method putdata() displays the salary of the employee.

```
using System;
using System.Collections.Generic;
using System.Linq;
using System.Text;

namespace MethodProg3
{
    class employee
    {
        double salary, hra;
        public void getdata()
        {
            Console.WriteLine("Enter salary");
            try
            {
                salary = double.Parse(Console.ReadLine());
            }
            catch(Exception e)
            {
                Console.WriteLine("Exception " + e);
                salary = 0;
            }
        }
        public void putdata()
```

```csharp
        {
            Console.WriteLine("Salary is " + salary);
        }
        public double getHRA()
        {
            //hra is 20% of the salary entered
            hra = (20 * salary) / 100;
            return hra;
        }
    }
    class Program
    {
        static void Main(string[] args)
        {
            employee e = new employee();
            e.getdata();
            e.putdata();
            double Hra = e.getHRA();
            Console.WriteLine("HRA is " + Hra);
            Console.ReadKey();
        }
    }
}
```

As stated earlier, the concept of classes is discussed in Chapter 11. After reading the object-oriented section of the book, readers are requested to revisit the present chapter for a better understanding. The output of the given program is as follows:

Output

```
Enter salary
50000
Salary is 50000
HRA is 10000
```

7.6 PARAMETERS

The arguments given to a method are called parameters. As explained earlier, the definition of a method requires the type of the parameter followed by its name. The different parameters are separated by commas. The following example depicts the concept of parameters of a method. As given below, a, the instance of the class Aes, takes two arguments. The first argument is the value of an enumeration, whereas the second argument is a byte array. It should be noted that a method can take any data type as argument.

```
Aes a = new Aes(Aes.KeySize.Bits128, keyBytes);
```

The following program depicts the concept of parameters.

Problem 7.1

Write a program to find the prime divisors of a number.

Solution

The program should first find all the prime numbers up to half that number and then find which amongst them divides the number. The method should, therefore, return an array.

```csharp
using System;
using System.Collections.Generic;
using System.Linq;
using System.Text;
//A program to find the prime divisors of a number entered by the user

namespace MethodsExample1
{
    class Program
    {
        static int t = 0;
        static int[] primeDivisors(int number)
        {
            int[] result = new int[100];
            int[] prime = new int[100];
            int i, j, flag, k = 0;
            for(i = 2; i < number/2; i++)
            {
                flag = 0;
                for(j = 2; j < i/2; j++)
                {
                    if(i % j == 0)
                    {
                        flag = 1;
                    }
                }
                if(flag == 0)
                {
                    prime[k++] = i;
                }
            }
            Console.WriteLine("Prime numbers");
            for(i = 0; i < k; i++)
            {
                Console.Write(prime[i].ToString()+" ");
            }
            t = 0;
            for(i = 0; i < k; i++)
            {
                if(number % (prime[i]) == 0)
                {
                    result[t++] = prime[i];
                }
            }
            return result;
        }
        static void Main(string[] args)
        {
            int number1;
            int[] divisors = new int[100];
            try
            {
                Console.WriteLine("Enter the number");
                number1 = int.Parse(Console.ReadLine());
                divisors = primeDivisors(number1);
```

```
                    int k = 0;
                    Console.WriteLine("\nResult");
                    while(k < t)
                    {
                        Console.WriteLine(" " + divisors[k]);
                        k++;
                    }
                }
                catch(Exception e)
                {
                    Console.WriteLine("Exception " + e.ToString());
                }
                Console.ReadKey();
            }
        }
    }
```

Output

```
Enter the number
24
Prime numbers
2 3 5 7 11
Result
2
3
```

7.7 VARIABLE PARAMETERS

The examples given until now are based on the assumption that we already know the number of parameters. At times, this may not be true. So as to handle such situations, C# provides a way to craft methods accepting variable number of parameters. This is done by using the keyword params followed by the array of the type that is to be entered. The following program code depicts the concept:

```
using System;
using System.Collections.Generic;
using System.Linq;
using System.Text;

namespace MethodsExample2
{
    class Program
    {
        static void display(params int[] numbers)
        {
            Console.WriteLine("The arguments are");
            foreach(int y in numbers)
            {
                Console.WriteLine("Argument" + y);
            }
        }
        static void Main(string[] args)
        {
```

```
            int[] numbers = {1, 2, 3, 4};
            display(5);
            display();
            display(numbers);
            Console.ReadKey();
        }
    }
}
```

The function `display` is called three times in the Main function. In the first invocation a single number is passed in the function, in the second invocation nothing is passed, and in the third invocation an array is passed as an argument to the function. The output of the program is as follows:

Output

```
The arguments are
Argument    5
The arguments are
Argument    1
Argument    2
Argument    3
Argument    4
```

7.8 TYPES OF PARAMETERS

This section discusses two categories of parameters. The first category segregates the parameters as value and reference types. The second one gives an idea of out parameters. Both the concepts are conceptually important and, therefore, have been examined by taking appropriate examples.

7.8.1 Value and Reference Parameters

Parameters can be passed in two ways, by value and by reference. Call by value refers to passing a parameter in a method without any modifier. The value passed can be altered in the method, but the change is not reflected when the control comes back to the calling method.

If, however, one wants the change to be reflected in the calling method as well, then one can resort to using reference type parameters.

The following program implements a classic example of a swap method. When call by value is resorted to, then the parameters are swapped inside the swap method but the change is not reflected in the Main method. If, however, call by reference is used, then the change is reflected in the Main method as well.

```
using System;
using System.Collections.Generic;
using System.Linq;
using System.Text;

namespace MethodExample6
{
    class Program
    {
        public static void swap(int x, int y)
        {
```

```csharp
            int temp;
            temp = x;
            x = y;
            y = temp;
            Console.WriteLine("Inside the method x = "+ x.ToString() + " y = " +
            y.ToString());
        }
        public static void swap(ref int x, ref int y)
        {
            int temp;
            temp = x;
            x = y;
            y = temp;
            Console.WriteLine("Inside the method x = " + x.ToString() + " y = " +
            y.ToString());
        }
        static void Main(string[] args)
        {
            int x, y;
            try
            {
                Console.WriteLine("Enter first number");
                x = int.Parse(Console.ReadLine());
                Console.WriteLine("Enter second number");
                y = int.Parse(Console.ReadLine());
                Console.WriteLine("Before calling the method x = " + x.ToString() + " 
                y = " + y.ToString());
                swap(x, y);
                Console.WriteLine("Back in Main: x = " + x.ToString() + " y = " +
                y.ToString());
                swap(ref x, ref y);
                Console.WriteLine("Back in Main: x = " + x.ToString() + " y = " +
                y.ToString());
            }
            catch(Exception e)
            {
                Console.WriteLine("Exception " + e.ToString());
            }
        }
    }
}
```

Output

```
Enter the first number
5
Enter the second number
6
Before calling the method x = 5 y = 6
Inside the method x = 6 y = 5
Back in Main: x = 5 y = 6
Inside the method x = 6 y = 5
Back in Main: x = 6 y = 5
Press any key to continue …_
```

7.8.2 Out Parameters

The out parameters are the parameters that are passed as arguments of a method but are set by the methods themselves. They are, in fact, the outcome of the execution of a method. They pass the result back to the method that calls the method. The parameters are preceded by the keyword out.

The following example demonstrates the calling of a method, which takes two arguments a and b and sets the value of x and y, x being the product of two numbers and y being their sum. It may be noted that we cannot use the return type as an option, as only one value can be returned by a method. However, there is no practical limit to the number of out parameters a method can have.

```
using System;
using System.Collections.Generic;
using System.Linq;
using System.Text;
namespace MethodsExample5
{
    class Program
    {
        static void calc(int a, int b, out int x, out int y)
        {
            x = a * b;
            y = a + b;
        }
        static void Main(string[] args)
        {
            int number1, number2, result1, result2;
            try
            {
                Console.WriteLine("Enter a number\t:");
                number1 = int.Parse(Console.ReadLine());
                Console.WriteLine("Enter the second number\t:");
                number2 = int.Parse(Console.ReadLine());
                calc(number1, number2, out result1, out result2);
                Console.WriteLine("The product is " + result1);
                Console.WriteLine("The sum is " + result2);
            }
            catch(Exception e)
            {
                Console.WriteLine("Exception " + e.ToString());
            }
            Console.ReadKey();
        }
    }
}
```

Output

```
Enter a number :
23
Enter the second number :
12
The product is 276
The sum is 35
```

7.9 METHOD OVERLOADING

Having more than one method of the same name in the same class is referred to as method overloading. The concept assumes significance in the context of the object-oriented milieu of C#. The following program has three methods called set(). The first does not take any argument, the second takes a single argument, and the third takes two arguments. The concept has been discussed in Chapter 11 as well.

```
using System;
using System.Collections.Generic;
using System.Linq;
using System.Text;
namespace MethodsExample3
{
    class Program
    {
        class ABC
        {
            int x, y;
            public void set()
            {
                x = y = 0;
            }
            public void set(int number)
            {
                x = number;
                y = number;
            }
            public void set(int number1, int number2)
            {
                x = number1;
                y = number2;
            }
            public void dispay()
            {
                Console.WriteLine("x = " + x.ToString() + " " + " y = " + y.ToString());
            }
        }
        static void Main(string[] args)
        {
            ABC a = new ABC();
            a.set();
            a.dispay();
            a.set(5);
            a.dispay();
            a.set(3, 2);
            a.dispay();
            Console.ReadKey();
        }
    }
}
```

The first method sets both the variables of the class equal to zero. The second sets both the variables as five. The third sets the first variable equal to three and the second equal to two. The output of this program is as follows.

Output

```
x = 0 y = 0
x = 5 y = 5
x = 3 y = 2
```

It may be noted that a program can even have methods of the same name and different types of parameters. So, method overloading is having more than one method of the same name but different numbers of arguments or different types of arguments. Let us now have a look at another important aspect of functions, which is recursion.

7.10 RECURSION

When a function calls itself, then it is referred to as recursion. This concept is important in algorithms as well. The concept of divide and conquer can be easily implemented using recursion. It is helpful in implementing many other paradigms. However, many factors are to be taken care of while implementing a problem via recursion. The first point is that there must be a relation between the present and the previous instances of the function. The second point is that there must be a terminating condition, otherwise the execution of the program results in stack overflow. The concept can be understood with the help of the following program. Here, Main() calls itself, thus printing 'The Sufi Gospel Project' infinite times, which results in stack overflow (Fig. 7.2).

```
namespace Methods
{
    class Program
    {
        static void Main(string[] args)
        {
            Console.WriteLine("The sufi Gospel Project");
            //Console.ReadKey();
            Main(args);
        }
    }
}
```

Output

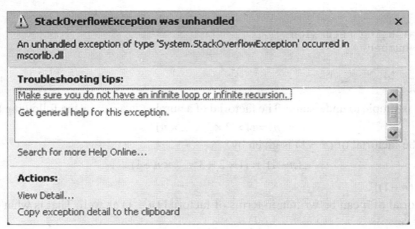

This example depicts one aspect of recursion, which may result in stack overflow. However, recursion can be useful as well. The following program shows how to calculate the factorial of a number using recursion:

```
namespace Methods
{
    class Program
    {
        static int factorial(int number)
        {
            if(number == 1)
            {
                return 1;
            }
            else
            {
                return(number * factorial(number - 1));
            }
        }
        static void Main(string[] args)
        {
            Console.WriteLine("Factorial using recursion");
            int number, fac;
            try
            {
                Console.WriteLine("Enter a number");
                number = Int16.Parse(Console.ReadLine());
                fac = factorial(number);
                Console.WriteLine("Answer " + fac);
            }
            catch(Exception e)
            {
                Console.WriteLine("Error " + e.ToString());
            }
            Console.ReadKey();
        }
    }
}
```

Output

```
Factorial using recursion
Enter a number
4
Answer    24
```

The concept is simple to understand. The factorial of a number is given by the following formula:
$$n! = (1 \times 2 \times 3 \times \ldots \times n)$$
Therefore, the factorial of $(n-1)$ is given by
$$(n-1)! = (1 \times 2 \times 3 \times \ldots \times n-1)$$
So, $n! = n \times (n-1)!$

That is, factorial of n can be written in terms of factorial $(n-1)$ as well. That is what the crux of recursion is.

Let us have a look at another example. The Fibonacci series is given by 1, 1, 2, 3, 5, …. In the series, every term is the sum of the previous two terms. So, the nth Fibonacci term is given by
$$T(n) = T(n-1) + T(n-2)$$
The following program gives the implementation of this concept:

```
namespace Methods2
{
    class Program
    {
        static int fib(int number)
        {
            if(number == 1)
            {
                return 1;
            }
            else if(number == 2)
            {
                return 1;
            }
            else
            {
                return(fib(number - 1) + fib(number - 2));
            }
        }
        static void Main(string[] args)
        {
            int number, fibNum;
            try
            {
                Console.WriteLine("Enter a number");
                number = int.Parse(Console.ReadLine());
                fibNum = fib(number);
                Console.WriteLine("The answer is " + fibNum);
            }
            catch(Exception e)
            {
                Console.WriteLine("Exception "+e);
            }
            Console.ReadKey();
        }
    }
}
```

Output

```
Enter a number
2
The answer is
1
```

Again, in the program, three points must be taken care of. The first is the recursion relation, which in this case is fib(n) = fib(n - 1) + fib(n - 2). The second is the terminating condition. In this case, if the value of number is one or two, then the function returns one, or else the recursion relation is used to calculate the answer. The third most important point is the calling of a static function inside a static function. It may be stated here that `fib` is called directly in `Main` owing to the fact that it is static.

7.11 DELEGATES

Delegates help us to use functions as objects. They perform the same task as was done by function pointers in C and C++. However, they also preserve type safety, thus removing the problems of function pointers. Readers familiar with functional languages such as F# must have found the functional relationship between delegates and lambda expressions as well. The following program depicts the use of delegates. The program asks the user to enter two numbers. The user is then asked to enter A or S depending upon whether he/she wants to add or subtract the two numbers. Once this has been done, the delegate is then associated with the requisite method. The example demonstrates the use and application of delegates and hence reinforces the fact that they are similar to 'pointers to functions' in C. There is a point to be noted, though, use of pointers is considered unsafe in C#, but the use of delegates is considered safe.

```
namespace DelegateDemo
{
    class Program
    {
        delegate int DelegateCal(int number1, int number2);
        static int add(int number1, int number2)
        {
            return(number1 + number2);
        }
        static int sub(int number1, int number2)
        {
            return(number1 - number2);
        }
        static void Main(string[] args)
        {
            int number1, number2;
            try
            {
                Console.WriteLine("Enter the first number");
                number1 = int.Parse(Console.ReadLine());
                Console.WriteLine("Enter the second number");
                number2 = int.Parse(Console.ReadLine());
                Console.WriteLine("A for add, S for subtract");
                string choice = Console.ReadLine();
                if(choice == "A")
                {
                    DelegateCal d = new DelegateCal(add);
                    Console.WriteLine("" + d.Invoke(number1, number2));
                }
                else
                {
                    DelegateCal d = new DelegateCal(sub);
                    Console.WriteLine("" + d.Invoke(number1, number2));
                }
            }
            catch(Exception e)
```

```
            {
        Console.WriteLine("Error " + e.ToString());
            }
        Console.ReadKey();
        }
    }
}
```
It may also be stated that delegates are used even in threads. `Delegate` is, in fact, a class in C#, which extends `MulticastDelegate` base class. The base class provides the invoke method.

SUMMARY

The importance of methods, as stated in the introduction, is immense. The knowledge of methods is a must for developing any kind of software. The chapter explains the theory and concepts of the topic along with examples. The crafting of a function requires the return type, parameters, name of the function, and body.

Calling a function in another function is referred to as invocation. Calling a function in itself is referred to as recursion. It should be noted that there must be a terminating condition in recursion. Delegates are similar to 'pointers to a function' in C. All these concepts have been described in detail in the chapter.

GLOSSARY

Method It is a block of statements that performs a particular task.
Signature of a function It includes the name of the method along with the parameters. While declaring a method, one may also specify the access level and modifiers.
Return type The return type of a method is the data type of the value returned by the method.
Parameters The arguments given in the body of a method are called parameters.

Out parameters These are the parameters that are passed as arguments of a method but are set by the methods themselves.
Method overloading Having more than one method of the same name in the same class is referred to as method overloading.
Recursion When a function calls itself, it is referred to as recursion.

POINTS TO REMEMBER

- Main is a method, which is called by the common language runtime when a program is executed.
- The public access specifier is used when a method is to be called anywhere in the program.
- The instance of a class is made by writing the name of the class followed by the name of the object that is to be crafted; this is equated to the new keyword followed by the constructor of the class.
- A method is called by writing the name of the object followed by the dot operator and then the name of the method.

- C# provides a way to craft methods accepting variable number of parameters.
- In the call by value type invocation, the value passed can be altered in the method, but the change is not reflected when the control comes back to the calling method.
- The use of delegates is considered safe in C#, whereas pointers are generally considered unsafe.

EXERCISES

I. Multiple-choice Questions

1. Which of the following is a type of parameter?
   (a) Out
   (b) Ref
   (c) Both (a) and (b)
   (d) None of these

2. Which of the following cannot be a return type of a method?
   (a) Int
   (b) Float
   (c) Char
   (d) Out

3. Which of the following is not valid in C#?
   (a) A class can have nested methods.
   (b) A class can have more than one method with the same name.
   (c) A class can have a method with no return type.
   (d) A class may have any number of methods.

4. What is a nested method?
   (a) A method within a method
   (b) A method outside a class
   (c) A method with no parameters
   (d) None of these

5. Which of the following statements is valid?
   (a) Methods are used only in procedural programming.
   (b) Methods must have parameters.
   (c) Methods must have return type.
   (d) All of these

6. Can we have a method outside a class?
   (a) Yes
   (b) No
   (c) Depends on the situation
   (d) Cannot say

7. Which of the following is a valid invocation of a method?
   (a) `<object name>.<method name>`
   (b) `<object name>.<method name>(<parameters>)`
   (c) `<return type>.<object name>.<method name>(<parameters>)`
   (d) None of these

8. How is a static method called?
   (a) By writing the name of the class followed by the dot operator and then the method
   (b) By writing the name of the object followed by the dot operator and then the method
   (c) Both (a) and (b)
   (d) None of these

9. How many `Main` methods can there be in a program?
   (a) 1
   (b) 2
   (c) 5
   (d) Any number

10. How many `Main` methods can there be in a class?
    (a) 1
    (b) 2
    (c) 5
    (d) Any number

II. Review Questions

1. Explain the concept of out parameters with the help of an example.
2. Explain the concept of call by reference with the help of an example.
3. Explain the concept of variable parameters with the help of an example.
4. What is the difference between call by value and call by reference?
5. Explain the concept of method overloading.
6. What is recursion? What are the essential conditions in order to implement recursion?
7. What can be the problems in implementing recursion?

III. Programming Exercises

1. Ask the user to enter *n* numbers and calculate the mean and standard deviation of the numbers using two methods, one for mean and one for standard deviation.
2. In Question 1, use just one method to accomplish the task. You may use 'out' parameters.
3. In Question 1, make changes so that the mean of any number of integers can be calculated.
4. Ask the user to enter *n* numbers and calculate the maximum from amongst the numbers using a method.
5. Ask the user to enter *n* numbers and calculate the minimum from amongst the numbers using a method.
6. Ask the user to enter three numbers and find the geometric mean of the numbers using a method.

7. Ask the user to enter two numbers and find the common factors of both the numbers.
8. Ask the user to enter two numbers and find the least common factor of the two numbers.
9. Ask the user to enter two numbers and find the greatest common divisor of the two numbers.
10. Ask the user to enter n numbers and find the second minimum number.
11. Ask the user to enter n numbers and find the second largest number.
12. Ask the user to enter n numbers and calculate the coefficient of correlation of the numbers.
13. Ask the user to enter 20 numbers and find whether the sum of the first 10 numbers is greater than that of the next 10 numbers.
14. Ask the user to enter five numbers and find the harmonic mean of the numbers.
15. Ask the user to enter 20 numbers and find the product of their arithmetic mean and harmonic mean.
16. Ask the user to enter two numbers and calculate their product using recursion.
17. Ask the user to enter two numbers and calculate their sum using recursion.
18. Ask the user to enter two numbers and calculate their difference using recursion.
19. Ask the user to enter two numbers and calculate the first number to the power of the second number using recursion.
20. Ask the user to enter a number and print Fibonacci series up to that number using recursion.

8 Strings

OBJECTIVES

After completing this chapter, the reader will be able to

\# Appreciate the importance of strings
\# Comprehend the use of strings
\# Understand the concept of mutable and non-mutable types
\# Create strings using `StringBuilder` class
\# Use various operators of `String` class
\# Explain the various methods of `String` class
\# Sort an array of strings

8.1 INTRODUCTION

A string is a sequence of characters at consecutive positions. A string is actually an instance of `System.String` class. It may be stated at this point that, as against the common perception, string is not a value type but is a reference type. However, it is immutable. This may be one of the reasons for perceiving it as a value type. The value of the string cannot be changed. This point is explained in Section 8.2.1. There are a few important factors that we need to consider with regard to strings. Strings also overload the == operator. They may also contain null values. This chapter discusses all these points and explains most of the methods provided by the string class. Let us, therefore, explore the fascinating world of strings.

Non-mutability

Strings are non-mutable. A non-mutable data type does not change. For example, if we define a string s, initialize it to 'Harsh', and then apply concatenation operator to add 'is' to the initial string, then the output will be 'Harshis'. However, the two strings will be different as far as memory is concerned. The latter string will be referenced and therefore will be visible to the user. The former string will be handled in the process of garbage collection.

```
string s ="Harsh";
s += "is";
using System;
using System.Collections.Generic;
using System.Linq;
using System.Text;

namespace StringHandling
{
    class Program
    {
        static void Main(string[] args)
        {
            string s1 = "Harsh";
            s1 += " is a";
            s1 += " good";
            s1 += " boy.";
            Console.WriteLine(s1);
            Console.ReadKey();
        }
    }
}
```

Output

```
Harsh is a good boy.
```

The final string will be 'Harsh is a good boy', but the latter and the former represent two different strings in the memory. As mentioned earlier, the latter string, `s1`, will be referenced. The former string, `s1`, will be handled in the garbage collection process. This, obviously, results in inefficiency.

8.2 CREATING STRINGS

Strings can be created by making an instance of `String` class or by using the `StringBuilder` class. However, using the latter is more efficient than using the former. This section explains and exemplifies the creation of strings by various methods. It may be stated here that any input or output in C# is done via strings. So, their creation and manipulation becomes all the more important. The section also explores the various constructors of the String class.

8.2.1 Using StringBuilder Class

As stated in Section 8.1, concatenation of a string results in the formation of a new string every time a change is made. The older strings are handled by garbage collection. This takes a lot of time, thus increasing the execution time and affecting the efficiency. However, the inefficiency can be tackled. This is done by making an instance of `StringBuilder` class and then using the `Append` method to accomplish the process of concatenation. The concept is depicted in the following program:

```
using System;
using System.Collections.Generic;
using System.Linq;
using System.Text;

namespace StringHandling2
```

```
{
    class Program
    {
        static void Main(string[] args)
        {
            StringBuilder b = new StringBuilder();
            b.Append("Harsh");
            b.Append("is");
            b.Append("a");
            b.Append("good");
            b.Append("boy.");
            string s = b.ToString();
            Console.WriteLine(s);
            Console.ReadKey();
        }
    }
}
```

Output

```
Harsh is a good boy.
```

8.2.2 Using String Class

It may be noted here that a string can also be created by making an instance of the class String. The instance is initialized by using one of the eight overloaded constructors of the class.

```
String s = new String();
s = "Harsh";
```

However, this task can also be performed by using a parameterized constructor. The following snippet illustrates the concept:

```
String s = new String("Harsh");
```

There is another way of creating a string, which is by making an instance of the String class and initializing it later. However, it is not possible to use a variable before initiating it.

```
String s;//Initialize it later
```

Strings can also be created and initialized using constructors of the String class. This is discussed in Section 8.3.

8.2.3 Verbatim Strings

At times we need strings that contain special meaning characters such as escape sequences. The task can be accomplished using a verbatim string. A verbatim string can be constructed by writing an @ followed by opening double quotes followed by whatever is to be included in the string and then closing double quotes. It may be stated that a verbatim string may span over many lines. The following strings depict verbatim strings:

```
@"hi there"         Output: hi there
@"hi \t there"      Output: hi \t there
@"hi ""there"       Output: hi "there"
```

8.3 CONSTRUCTORS OF String CLASS

Various methods are provided by the String class. The knowhow of these methods is important to carry out any programming task. The string methods make our task simpler. It may be stated at this point that the purpose of providing the explanation of these methods is not to discourage readers from trying to implement them via character arrays. The idea is to make it possible to accomplish a task well within time and with ease.

First, let us discuss the constructors of String class. The first constructor initializes the string by converting a char array to a string. As discussed earlier, a char array is different from a string in C#. However, it can be converted into a string, as depicted in the following program:

Syntax
```
public String(char[] value);
```

Program
```
using System;
using System.Collections.Generic;
using System.Linq;
using System.Text;

namespace StringHandling3
{
    class Program
    {
        static void Main(string[] args)
        {
            char[] charName = {'h', 'a', 'r', 's', 'h'};
            String s = new string(charName);
            Console.WriteLine("String" + s);
            Console.ReadKey();
        }
    }
}
```

Output
```
String harsh
```

Another constructor initializes the string by a character pointer. It may, however, be noted that use of pointers is not considered as safe programming in C#. The syntax of the method is as follows.

Syntax
```
public String(char* value);
```

It is also possible to initialize the string by a character and then specifying the number of times it is to be repeated. The use of this constructor has been depicted in the following program, which follows the syntax.

Syntax
```
public String(char c, int count);
```

Program
```
using System;
using System.Collections.Generic;
```

```
using System.Linq;
using System.Text;
namespace Stringhandling4
{
    class Program
    {
        static void Main(string[] args)
        {
            String s = new String('a', 5);
            Console.WriteLine(s);
            Console.ReadKey();
        }
    }
}
```

Output

```
aaaaa
```

Another way to initialize a string is by extracting a substring out of a character array. The concept is depicted in the following program.

Syntax
```
public String(char[] value, int startIndex, int length);
```

Program
```
static void Main(string[] args)
{
    char[] name = {'h', 'a', 'r', 's', 'h'};
    String s = new String(name, 1, 3);
    Console.WriteLine(s);
    Console.ReadKey();
}
```

Output

```
ars
```

The same task can also be performed via a character pointer.

```
public String(char* value, int startIndex, int length);
```

8.4 OPERATORS FOR Strings AND Compare METHOD

The String class has some overloaded operators for making the manipulation of strings easier. The meaning of overloading operators will become clear once we study classes in detail. However, it may be stated that overloading means giving another meaning to an existing thing. The existing things are associated with some meaning in a socio-cultural context. However, it may be given a new meaning as per the new needs. Aamir Khusro wrote 'Man Kunto Maula', thus giving a new meaning to passage and gate. Imam Sahib became the gate of the passage shown by Prophet Mohammed. This giving of a new meaning helped people to associate parascience with something they had always known.

8.4.1 != Operator

As we have already seen, the != operator returns true if the value on the left is not equal to the value on the right. The term 'value' should not be interpreted as 'value type'. The != operator has been overloaded in the String class for strings. The syntax of the operator is as follows.

Syntax

```
public static bool operator != (string a, string b);
```

8.4.2 == Operator

The == operator returns true if the value on the left is equal to the value on the right. Again, the term 'value' need not be interpreted as 'value type'. The != operator has been overloaded in the String class for strings. The syntax of the operator is as follows.

Syntax

```
public static bool operator == (string a, string b);
```

It may be stated here that this task can also be performed by the Compare method, which is also overloaded. The various overloads of the function and their meaning have been summarized in Table 8.1.

The combination of two strings is referred to as concatenation. For example, if the first string is str1 = "harsh" and the second string is str2 = "it", then the concatenenated string becomes "harshit".

Table 8.1 Compare method

Signature of the function	Details
`public static int Compare(string strA, string strB);`	If the value returned is less than zero, then the first string is less than the second string. If the value is greater than zero, then the first string is greater than the second string. Otherwise, the two strings are equal.
`public static int Compare(string strA, string strB, bool ignoreCase);`	If the value returned is less than zero, then the first string is less than the second string. If the value is greater than zero, then the first string is greater than the second string. Otherwise, the two strings are equal. However, this function ignores the case.
`public static int Compare(string strA, int indexA, string strB, int indexB, int length);`	If the value returned is less than zero, then the first substring is less than the second substring. If the value is greater than zero, then the first substring is greater than the second substring. Otherwise, the two substrings are equal. The substring is taken from the index specified. The last argument of the function gives the length of the substring to be compared.
`public static int Compare(string strA, int indexA, string strB, int indexB, int length, bool ignoreCase);`	If the value returned is less than zero, then the first substring is less than the second substring. If the value is greater than zero, then the first substring is greater than the second substring. Otherwise, the two substrings are equal. The substring is taken from the index specified. The last argument of the function gives the length of the substring to be compared. However, this function ignores the case of the two substrings.
`public int CompareTo(object value);`	The CompareTo function of a string instance returns a number indicating lexicographic relation between the two strings.
`public int CompareTo(string strB);`	This is similar to the previous function except for the fact that the second function is a string.

8.5 COMMON METHODS OF String CLASS

This section throws light on some of the common methods that help us to manipulate the strings. The Concat method concatenates two or more strings in order to generate a single string. The various overloads of the method are provided as follows:

```
public static string Concat(object arg0);
public static string Concat(params object[] args);
public static string Concat(params string[] values);
public static string Concat(object arg0, object arg1);
public static string Concat(string str0, string str1);
public static string Concat(object arg0, object arg1, object arg2);
public static string Concat(string str0, string str1, string str2);
public static string Concat(object arg0, object arg1, object arg2, object arg3);
public static string Concat(string str0, string str1, string str2, string str3);
```

The first method concatenates the string with the string passed in the argument. The second overload concatenates the various elements present in the array of objects with the string. The third overload performs the same task but with an array of strings. It may also be stated that the same methods may concatenate two objects or strings as well. The fourth and the fifth overloads depict the corresponding overloads. The next two methods demonstrate the overloads that concatenate three strings. The last two methods are for concatenating four strings.

Table 8.2 lists the various methods and the task performed by them.

Table 8.2 Common methods of String class

Method	Purpose
public bool Contains(string value);	The method returns a number signifying whether the given string occurs within the string.
public static string Copy(string str);	The method copies the value of str to a new string.
public bool EndsWith(string value);	The method determines whether the end of the string matches the argument.
public override int GetHashCode();	The method returns the hash code for this string.
public int IndexOf(char value);	The function gives a number indicating the index of the first occurrence of the specified character.
public string Insert(int startIndex, string value);	The function inserts the specified string at the specified index position.
public int LastIndexOf(char value);	The function returns the last index of character in the string.
public string PadLeft(int totalWidth);	The function right aligns the string by padding spaces on the left-hand side.
public string Remove(int startIndex);	The function deletes all the occurrences of the given character from the given string.
public string[] Split(params char[] separator);	The function splits the given string into an array of strings delimited by the character specified.

(Contd)

Table 8.2 (Contd)

Method	Purpose
`public string Substring(int startIndex);`	The function returns a substring starting from the specified position.
`public char[] ToCharArray();`	The function converts the string into a character array and returns the latter.
`public string ToLower();`	The function converts the characters of the given string to lower case.
`public override string ToString();`	The function returns this instance of the object.
`public string ToUpper();`	The function converts the characters of the given string to upper case.
`public string Trim();`	The function removes all the leading and trailing white spaces from the string.

8.6 MANIPULATION OF ARRAY OF STRINGS

This section explains the manipulation of array of strings by taking the example of sorting of a set of strings. Sorting of a set of strings refers to the process of arranging the given list in an order. This task requires dictionary-like sorting of the list. The list should first be ordered according to the first letter. The result needs to be sorted according to the second letter and so on. The task seems difficult, but the methods provided by the String class help us to accomplish the task easily. If the value returned by the Compare function is greater than zero, then the strings at the two positions need to be sorted. The list needs to be sorted in the following way.

The outer loop picks one string starting from the first position. The string is then compared with the rest of the strings; if the value returned by the Compare function is greater than zero, then the string should be swapped with the string that is compared. This implement sorts the list. The following listing depicts the implementation of this task.

```
namespace StringsComp
{
    class Program
    {
        static void Main(string[] args)
        {
            String[] names = new String[20];
            int number, counter, i, j;
            String temp;
            try
            {
                Console.WriteLine("Enter the number of elements");
                number = int.Parse(Console.ReadLine());
                for(counter = 0; counter < number; counter++)
                {
                    Console.WriteLine("Enter name\t:");
                    names[counter] = Console.ReadLine();
                }
                for(i = 0; i < number; i++)
                {
                    for(j = i + 1; j < number; j++)
```

```csharp
                    {
                        if(names[i].CompareTo(names[j]) > 0)
                        {
                            temp = names[i];
                            names[i] = names[j];
                            names[j] = temp;
                        }
                    }
                }
                Console.WriteLine("Sorted list");
                for(i = 0; i < number; i++)
                {
                    Console.WriteLine(names[i]);
                }
            }
            catch(Exception e)
            {
                Console.WriteLine("Error " + e.ToString());
            }
            Console.ReadKey();
        }
    }
}
```

Output

```
Enter the number of elements
5
Enter name:
Harsh
Enter name:
Murad
Enter name:
Sonam
Enter name:
Abida
Enter name:
Aamir
Sorted list
Aamir
Abida
Harsh
Murad
Sonam
```

8.7 USE OF ToCharArray()

The ToCharArray() method converts the string into a character array. This is required when manipulations have to be done at specific character positions. To exemplify the concept let us consider the following program. The problem requires us to swap the characters of a string at the even and odd positions. We are required to make a new string, which should have the characters. If the number of characters in the input string is even, then starting from the first position the characters at the even position should be appended to the resultant string followed by the characters at the odd position, taking two steps at a time. The following program implements this concept.

```csharp
namespace StringsSection4
{
    class Program
    {
        static void Main(string[] args)
        {
            String str, str1 = "";
            Console.WriteLine("Enter a string");
            str = Console.ReadLine();
            if(str.Length % 2 == 0)
            {
                for(int i = 0; i < (str.Length); i += 2)
                {
                    str1 += str.ToCharArray()[i + 1].ToString();
                    str1 += str.ToCharArray()[i].ToString();
                }
                Console.WriteLine("The resultant string is " + str1);
            }
            else
            {
                for(int i = 0; i < (str.Length - 1); i += 2)
                {
                    str1 += str.ToCharArray()[i + 1].ToString();
                    str1 += str.ToCharArray()[i].ToString();
                }
                Console.WriteLine("The resultant string is " + str1);
                Console.WriteLine("It is a string of odd length and therefore the last position cannot be swapped");
            }
            Console.ReadKey();
        }
    }
}
```

Output

```
Enter a string
acer
The resultant string is
care
Enter a string
sonam
The resultant string is
osan
It is a string of odd length and therefore the last position cannot be swapped.
```

8.8 BUILDING STRINGS EFFICIENTLY

In order to build a string whose length is not known or which needs to be appended a number of times, StringBuilder is used. An instance of StringBuilder is created and strings are added to it. This makes sense, as strings are non-mutable. So, if instead of StringBuilder we use strings, then every time we add something to a string a new string is created and the older one is handled by the garbage collection routine. StringBuilder, on the other hand, has the capability to append strings. The following program explains the concept. It asks the user to enter strings one by one and displays the final string. In order to accomplish the task, an instance of StringBuilder is made and the values added by the user are appended in the string.

```
namespace stringsDemo5
{
    class Program
    {
        static void Main(string[] args)
        {
            StringBuilder build = new StringBuilder();
            Console.WriteLine("Enter strings (\"end\" to quit)");
            String str = Console.ReadLine();
            while(str != "end")
            {
                build.Append(str);
                str = Console.ReadLine();
            }
            Console.WriteLine("The string is "+ build);
            Console.ReadKey();
        }
    }
}
```

8.9 REGULAR EXPRESSIONS

A powerful tool to incorporate pattern matching to the applications is regular expressions. These help us to find an expression from a large text. We can even find all the occurrences of that expression from the text. The pattern matching ability of regular expressions also helps us to accomplish naïve tasks such as finding the text that begins or ends with a particular subexpression. The examples that follow include a program to identify whether a string entered by the user is in the requisite format. It may be stated that a regular expression mainly consists of literals and metacharacters. The beginning or ending in a regular expression is denoted by \b. For example, the strings beginning with 'h' are denoted via regular expressions by '\bh' and those ending with 'h' are denoted by 'h\b', where \b is a metacharacter and h is a literal. The namespace that helps us to use the classes supporting regular expressions is System.Text.RegularExpression. The class that we will be using in the following examples is Regex.

As stated earlier, regular expressions are generally used in pattern matching. For example, if we intend to search a string from a set of sentences, then we may use regular expressions. It may also be noted that such searches can be both case sensitive and case insensitive. The IsMatch() method in Regex carries out the search of the given string. However, in order to use this method, the search pattern is also required. In the following program, a third argument is used to indicate that case should be ignored. The following program finds 'Ali' from the set of strings stored in the array lines. These lines are written by Hazrat Khusro. Though it will be difficult to find 'Ali', we can at least try to find his name.

```
using System;
using System.Collections.Generic;
using System.Linq;
using System.Text.RegularExpressions;
```

```
namespace Regular_Expressions
{
    class Program
    {
        public static void Main(String[] args)
        {
            string[] lines =
            {
                "Man Kunto Maula",
                "shaah-e-mardaan",
                "sher-e-yazdaan",
                "quvvat-e-parvardigaar",
                "laa fataa illaa Ali",
                "laa saif illaa zulfiqaar",
                "Ali imaam-e-manasto manam Ghulaam-e-Ali",
                "hazaar jaan-e-giraamii fidaa-e-naam-e-Ali"
            };
            string str = "Ali";
            Console.WriteLine("Man Kunto Maula: By Hazrat Khusro");
            foreach(string s1 in lines)
            {
                System.Console.Write("{0, 42}", s1);
                if(Regex.IsMatch(s1, str, RegexOptions.IgnoreCase))
                {
                    System.Console.WriteLine("   , {0} maula", str);
                }
                else
                {
                    System.Console.WriteLine(" ");
                }
            }
            Console.ReadKey();
        }
    }
}
```

Output

```
Man Kunto Maula: By Hazrat Khusro
                           Man Kunto Maula
                           shaah-e-mardaan
                            sher-e-yazdaan
                     quvvat-e-parvardigaar
                       laa fataa illaa Ali, Ali maula
                  laa saif illaa zulfiqaar
   Ali imaam-e-manasto manam Ghulaam-e-Ali, Ali maula
 hazaar jaan-e-giraamii fidaa-e-naam-e-Ali, Ali maula
```

The task of the next example is to determine whether or not the number entered by the user is in the correct format. The example uses a format string as the second argument of `IsMatch` method of the `Regex` class. It may be noted that the format string uses metacharacters such as d{4}, which depicts four characters followed by a '-' (hyphen). The number is in the format 0000-000-0000. The user is asked to enter a few numbers and the regular expression class finds out whether it is in the correct format or not.

```csharp
using System;
using System.Collections.Generic;
using System.Linq;
using System.Text;
using System.Text.RegularExpressions;

namespace RegularExp2
{
    class Program
    {
        static void Main(string[] args)
        {
            string[] LandLineNumbers = new string[100];
            int n;
            Console.WriteLine("Enter the number of times you want to enter the landline number");
            n = int.Parse(Console.ReadLine());
            for(int i = 0; i < n; i++)
            {
                Console.WriteLine("Enter number (first four digits of area code followed  by hyphen, then next three digits followed by hyphen, and then the next four digits): ");
                LandLineNumbers[i] = Console.ReadLine();
            }
            string sPattern = "^\\d{4}-\\d{3}-\\d{4}$";
            for(int i = 0; i < n; i++)
            {
                String s = LandLineNumbers[i];
                System.Console.Write("{0, 14}", s);
                if(Regex.IsMatch(s, sPattern))
                {
                    System.Console.WriteLine("It is a valid number");
                }
                else
                {
                    System.Console.WriteLine("An invalid number");
                }
            }
            Console.ReadKey();
        }
    }
}
```

SUMMARY

A string represents a sequence of characters. Unlike C and C++, string is a data type in C#. Strings are of many types. Verbatim strings help us to display special characters and escape sequences. Regular expressions are an influential device to integrate pattern matching. The Regex class has various methods to implement regular expressions. The inbuilt functions provided by C# help us to carry out many tasks that would otherwise be difficult to implement. The chapter provides some insight into these points and exemplifies the concepts.

GLOSSARY

String It is a sequence of characters at consecutive positions. It is different from a character array.

Regular expressions It is a powerful tool to incorporate pattern matching to the applications.

POINTS TO REMEMBER

- Strings can be created by making an instance of String class, by using `StringBuilder`, or by using verbatim strings.
- The overloaded operators of the String class help us to manipulate strings easily.
- The `ToCharArray()` method converts the string into a character array.
- StringBuilder class has the capability to append strings.
- Regular expressions are generally used in pattern matching.

EXERCISES

I. Multiple-choice Questions

1. What is the output of the following program?

    ```
    namespace StringsDemo1
    {
        class Program
        {
        static void Main(string[] args)
            {
            String str;
            str = 'computergrad';
            Console.WriteLine(str);
            Console.ReadKey();
            }
        }
    }
    ```

    (a) computergrad
    (b) Nothing is displayed.
    (c) Runtime error crops up.
    (d) The code does not compile.

2. What is the output of the following program?

    ```
    namespace StringsDemo1
    {
        class Program
        {
        static void Main(string[] args)
            {
            String str;
            str = "computergrad";
            Console.WriteLine(str);
            Console.ReadKey();
            }
        }
    }
    ```

    (a) computer
    (b) Nothing is displayed.
    (c) Runtime error crops up.
    (d) The code does not compile.

3. What is the output of the following program?

    ```
    namespace StringsDemo1
    {
        class Program
        {
        static void Main(string[] args)
            {
            String str;
            str = "computergrad";
            Console.WriteLine(str.
                    ToUpper());
            Console.ReadKey();
            }
        }
    }
    ```

    (a) COMPUTERGRAD
    (b) Nothing is displayed.
    (c) Runtime error crops up.
    (d) The code does not compile.

4. Which of the following functions converts string to double?
   (a) str.ToDouble();
   (b) Convert.ToDouble(str);
   (c) Convert.ToInt16(str);
   (d) None of these

5. What is the output of the following program?
   ```
   namespace ConsoleApplication1
   {
   class Program
       {
           static void Main(string[] args)
           {
           String str;
           Console.WriteLine(str);
           Console.ReadKey();
           }
       }
   }
   ```
   (a) Nothing is displayed.
   (b) Runtime error crops up.
   (c) The code does not compile.
   (d) None of these

6. What is the output of the following program?
   ```
   namespace ConsoleApplication1
   {
       class Program
       {
       static void Main(string[] args)
           {
           String str = (3-3).ToString();
           Console.WriteLine(str.
                       Length);
           Console.ReadKey();
           }
       }
   }
   ```
   (a) 0   (b) 1
   (c) 3   (d) 3-3

7. What is the output of the following program?
   ```
   namespace ConsoleApplication1
   {
   class Program
       {
       static void Main(string[] args)
           {
           String str = (313).ToString();
           String str1 = "";
           for(int i = 0; i < str.Length;
               i++)
               {
               str1 += (int.Parse(str) + 1);
               }
           Console.WriteLine(str1);
           Console.ReadKey();
           }
       }
   }
   ```
   (a) 314414514   (b) 314314314
   (c) 424   (d) None of these

8. What is the output of the following program?
   ```
   namespace ConsoleApplication1
   {
   class Program
       {
       static void Main(string[] args)
           {
           String str = (313).ToString();
           String str1 = "";
           for(int i = 0; i < str.Length;
               i++)
               {
               str1 += (int.Parse(str.
                       ToCharArray()[i].
                       ToString()) + 1);
               }
           Console.WriteLine(str1);
           Console.ReadKey();
           }
       }
   }
   ```
   (a) 314414514   (b) 314314314
   (c) 424   (d) None of these

9. What is the output of the following program?
   ```
   namespace ConsoleApplication1
   {
   class Program
       {
       static void Main(string[] args)
           {
           String str = (313).
                       ToString();
           String str1 = "";
           for(int i = 0; i < str.
               Length; i++)
               {
               str1 += (int.Parse(str.
                       ToCharArray()
                       [str.Length-i].
                       ToString())+1);
               }
   ```

```
            Console.WriteLine(str1);
            Console.ReadKey();
        }
    }
}
```
(a) 314414514 (b) 314314314
(c) 424 (d) None of these

10. What is the output of the following program?

```
namespace ConsoleApplication1
{
    class Program
    {
        static void Main(string[] args)
        {
            String str = (876).
                         ToString();
            String str1 = "";
            for(int i = 0; i < str.
                  Length; i++)
            {
                str1 += (str.ToCharArray()
                        [str.Length - i -
                         1]).ToString();
            }
            Console.WriteLine(str1);
            Console.ReadKey();
        }
    }
}
```
(a) 678
(b) 876
(c) None of these
(d) The program does not compile.

II. Review Questions

1. What are strings?
2. Explain various operations that can be performed on strings.
3. Explain various constructors of the String class.
4. Differentiate between a character array and a string.
5. How do you remove the leading and trailing spaces from a string?
6. What is meant by non-mutability of string instances?
7. Which is more efficient—appending string by + operator or using a StringBuilder class?
8. Examine the various overloads of Compare method.
9. How do you concatenate two strings?
10. Write a short note explaining the importance of strings.

III. Programming Exercises

You have been asked to develop an employee management system. In order to accomplish a task you make an array of strings.

1. Ask the user to enter the number of employees and their names.
2. Arrange the array in Question 1 in ascending order.
3. Find all the employee names that start with 'ab'.
4. Find all the employee names that end with 'ab'.
5. Find all the employee names that contain 'ab'.
6. Find all the employee names that do not contain 'ab'.
7. Display the names of all the employees whose names are palindrome.
8. Convert all the names to upper case.
9. Convert all the names to lower case.
10. Replace all the a's in the names with A's.
11. Ask the user to enter two numbers. Find whether the string at the first position is contained in the string at the second position.
12. If the answer to Question 11 is true, then remove the substring from the larger string.
13. Ask the user to enter a number. Now from that index in the array extract the name and swap the characters at the even positions with those at the odd positions.
14. Make a string by concatenating all the names.
15. Remove all the white spaces from the string formed in Question 14.
16. Now divide the string of Question 15 into different strings of equal lengths (except perhaps the last one).
17. Now arrange the array formed in Question 16 into ascending order.
18. From the array, find all the names that begin and end with the same character.
19. Check whether any two strings in the array in Question 18 have the same set of characters.
20. Find the total ASCII values of all the strings.

9 Arrays

OBJECTIVES

After completing this chapter, the reader will be able to

\# Declare and use an array in C#
\# Find the maximum or minimum value from amongst the elements of an array
\# Understand and implement linear search
\# Explain and use various sorting techniques
\# Employ two-dimensional and multidimensional arrays as well as understand and appreciate their uses
\# Recognize the utility of jagged arrays
\# Realize the importance of `System.Array` class

9.1 INTRODUCTION

An array is a linear data structure containing elements that are identified by an index. The elements of an array are of the same type. A one-dimensional (1D) matrix in mathematics is analogous to an array in computer science except for the fact that the index in a mathematical array starts from one whereas in computer science it starts from zero. As far as memory allocation is concerned, the elements of an array are consecutive. If we take the address of the first element as 2000H and the array in question is an `int16` array, then the address of the rest of the elements will be 2002H, 2004H, and so on.

This chapter does not only explain the functions and properties provided by C# for handling arrays, but it intends to teach how to implement some important programming concepts such as searching and sorting and finding the maximum and minimum numbers. The idea is to develop one's programming skills. If the developers of C# provided us with ready-to-use functions, then there is a plausibility that they do not want us to understand how things really work. So, let us defeat their purpose and try to understand what arrays are.

Consider a situation in which we are required to store the marks of five students and find the sum of the values. In order to accomplish the task, we create five variables, say marks1, marks2, marks3, marks4, and marks5. The variables will be assigned some memory locations, which may or may not be consecutive. In most of the cases the memory allocation will not be sequential. Such a situation results in more moment of the read–write head to access the data than otherwise. Therefore, the program will be inefficient.

Arrays are used to overcome this problem. An array is a linear data structure that stores the same type of elements.

In the present case, we create an array called marks after which consecutive memory locations will be assigned to the first, second, third, fourth, and fifth members. That is, marks[0], marks[1], marks[2], marks[3], and marks[4] will be assigned consecutive memory locations.

marks[0]	marks[1]	marks[2]	marks [3]	marks[4]

In order to create an array, first we need to declare the array. In C#, an array is declared as follows:

```
<data type>[] <name of the array> = new <data type>[size];
```

Here the type can be any one of the data types discussed in Chapter 2. The name of the array can be any name that follows the standard naming conventions discussed earlier. For example, if we intend to declare an array called marks containing a maximum of five elements, then the statement that we must write is as follows:

```
int[] marks = new int[5];
```

It must be noted that the index of the array starts from zero. Now let us see how to assign values to the elements of the array. There are three ways of accomplishing the task.

The first way is by assigning a value to every element. For example,

```
marks[0] = 23;
marks[1] = 27;
marks[2] = 80;
marks[3] = 90;
marks[4] = 78;
```

will make the array

23	27	80	90	78
marks[0]	marks[1]	marks[2]	marks[3]	marks[4]

The second way of assigning values to the elements is via loops. This can be done using a simple for loop in which the counter starts from zero, that is, the first index; the loop runs until the value of the counter reaches the number of elements we intend to enter (five in this case).

```
for(i = 0; i < 5; i++)
{
    marks[i] = i;
}
```

will convert the array to

0	1	2	3	4
marks[0]	marks[1]	marks[2]	marks[3]	marks[4]

The third way of entering values in the array is by asking the user to enter the values. For example,

```
for(i = 0; i < 5; i++)
{
    System.Console.WriteLine("\nEnter number\t:");
    marks[i] = int.Parse(Console.ReadLine());
}
```

This snippet will ask the user to enter the values five times and produce the requisite result. Suppose the values entered by the user are 45, 23, 22, 11, and 100, then the array becomes

45	23	22	11	100
marks[0]	marks[1]	marks[2]	marks[3]	marks[4]

This task is accomplished in Problem 9.1.

Problem 9.1

Write a program that asks the user to enter 10 numbers and then displays them.

Solution

```
using System;
using System.Collections.Generic;
using System.Linq;
using System.Text;

namespace ArraysDemo
{
    class Program
    {
        static void Main(string[] args)
        {
            int[] marks = new int[10];
            int i;
            for(i = 0; i < 10; i++)
            {
                Console.Write("\nEnter number\t:");
                marks[i] = int.Parse(Console.ReadLine());
            }
            for(i = 0; i < 10; i++)
            {
                Console.Write("\nNumber\t:{0}", marks[i]);
            }
            Console.ReadKey();
        }
    }
}
```

Output

```
Enter number: 2
Enter number: 3
Enter number: 1
Enter number: 6
Enter number: 4
Enter number: 9
Enter number: 8
```

```
Enter number: 7
Enter number: 5
Enter number: 10
Number: 2
Number: 3
Number: 1
Number: 6
Number: 4
Number: 9
Number: 8
Number: 7
Number: 5
Number: 10
```

Explanation

First we create an array called marks by writing

```
int[] marks = new int[10];
```

An array of type int is created and is allocated 10 int spaces in memory. Then we ask the user to enter the numbers.

```
for(i = 0; i < 10; i++)
{
    Console.Write("\nEnter number\t:");
    marks[i] = int.Parse(Console.ReadLine());
}
```

Since 10 numbers are to be added, a for loop is used. The values of the array are displayed with the help of another for loop as follows:

```
for(i = 0; i < 10; i++)
{
    Console.Write("\nNumber\t:{0}", marks[i]);
}
Console.ReadKey();
```

Problem 9.2

Write a program that asks the user to enter 10 numbers and then finds their sum.

Explanation

The program is similar to Problem 9.1 except for the fact that another variable called sum needs to be created whose value will be calculated as follows:

```
for(i = 0; i < 10; i++)
{
    sum = sum + marks[i];
}
```

Solution

```
using System;
using System.Collections.Generic;
```

```csharp
using System.Linq;
using System.Text;
namespace ArraysDemo
{
    class Program
    {
        static void Main(string[] args)
        {
            int[] marks = new int[10];
            int i, sum = 0;
            for(i = 0; i < 10; i++)
            {
                Console.Write("\nEnter number\t:");
                marks[i] = int.Parse(Console.ReadLine());
            }
            for(i = 0; i < 10; i++)
            {
                sum = sum + marks[i];
            }
            Console.WriteLine("The sum is \t:{0}", sum);
            Console.ReadKey();
        }
    }
}
```

Output

```
Enter number: 2
Enter number: 1
Enter number: 4
Enter number: 3
Enter number: 1
Enter number: 1
Enter number: 1
Enter number: 2
Enter number: 3
Enter number: 4
The sum is : 22
```

Problem 9.3

Write a program that asks the user to enter 10 elements and then finds the maximum element from amongst them.

Discussion

First we will declare a variable called max. We initialize max to marks[0]. Initially we assume the first element to be the maximum. Now we traverse through the array and check every element. If any element is greater than max, then we place the value of that element in the variable max. When we are done with the traversing, the variable max will have the maximum value.

Solution

```csharp
using System;
using System.Collections.Generic;
using System.Linq;
```

```csharp
using System.Text;

namespace ArraysDemo
{
    class Program
    {
        static void Main(string[] args)
        {
            int[] marks = new int[10];
            int i,max;
            for(i = 0; i < 10; i++)
            {
                Console.Write("\nEnter number\t:");
                marks[i] = int.Parse(Console.ReadLine());
            }
            max = marks[0];
            for(i = 1; i < 10; i++)
            {
                if(marks[i] > max)
                {
                    max = marks[i];
                }
            }
            Console.Write("\nThe maximum element is {0}", max);
            Console.ReadKey();
        }
    }
}
```

Output

```
Enter number: 2
Enter number: 10
Enter number: 20
Enter number: 3
Enter number: 5
Enter number: 90
Enter number: 100
Enter number: 1
Enter number: 7
Enter number: 2
The maximum element is 100
```

There is an alternate method to accomplish this task. It uses the Max() method of the Array class. By using this method, the element can be found easily.

```csharp
using System;
using System.Collections.Generic;
using System.Linq;
using System.Text;

namespace ArraysDemo
{
    class Program
    {
```

```csharp
        static void Main(string[] args)
        {
            int[] marks = new int[10];
            int i, max;
            for(i = 0; i < 10; i++)
            {
                Console.Write("\nEnter number\t:");
                marks[i] = int.Parse(Console.ReadLine());
            }
            max = marks.Max();
            Console.Write("\nThe maximum element is {0}", max);
            Console.ReadKey();
        }
    }
}
```

Output

```
Enter number: 2
Enter number: 10
Enter number: 20
Enter number: 3
Enter number: 5
Enter number: 90
Enter number: 100
Enter number: 1
Enter number: 7
Enter number: 2
The maximum element is 100
```

9.2 LINEAR SEARCH

Now that we have understood how to enter the elements in an array, let us move on to one of the most important processes in computer science theory, namely searching. Searching refers to the process of finding out an item in a given set of numbers. The set of numbers in our case will be stored in an array. One way of finding out the element from the array is to start from the first position and iterate through each and every element of the array. If the item is found, then its position is printed. If, on the other hand, the loop ends and we still do not find the element, then the message 'not found' is printed.

Algorithm for Linear Search

The following is the algorithm for linear search:
1. Ask the user to insert the value to be found.
2. Set i = 0, flag = 0;
3. Repeat
   while(i < n)
   {
       if(array[i] == item)
       {

```
            print : "found";
            flag = 1;
        }
        i++;
    }
4. if(flag == 0)
    {
        print : "Not found";
    }
```

Problem 9.4

Write a program that asks the user to enter the elements in an array and the item to be searched and then finds its position using linear search.

Solution
```
using System;
using System.Collections.Generic;
using System.Linq;
using System.Text;

namespace ArraysDemo
{
    class Program
    {
        static void Main(string[] args)
        {
            int[] marks = new int[10];
            int i, item, flag = 0;
            for(i = 0; i < 10; i++)
            {
                Console.Write("\nEnter number\t:");
                marks[i] = int.Parse(Console.ReadLine());
            }
            Console.Write("\nEnter item to be searched\t:");
            item = int.Parse(Console.ReadLine());
            for(i = 0; i < 10; i++)
            {
                if(item == marks[i])
                {
                    Console.WriteLine("\nFound at position\t:{0}", i);
                    flag = 1;
                }
            }
            if(flag == 0)
            {
                Console.Write("\nNot found");
            }
            Console.ReadKey();
        }
    }
}
```

Output

```
Enter number: 2
Enter number: 10
Enter number: 20
Enter number: 3
Enter number: 5
Enter number: 90
Enter number: 100
Enter number: 1
Enter number: 7
Enter number: 2
Enter item to be searched: 2
Found at position: 0
Found at position: 9
```

Output (Run 2)

```
Enter number: 2
Enter number: 10
Enter number: 20
Enter number: 3
Enter number: 5
Enter number: 90
Enter number: 100
Enter number: 1
Enter number: 7
Enter number: 2
Enter item to be searched : 9
Not found
```

Characteristics of Linear Search

Since every element needs to be traversed so as to find whether the item to be found exists in the array or not, the maximum number of comparisons will be n, n being the number of elements in the array. Therefore, the complexity of this program in the worst case becomes $O(n)$. The best-case complexity, however, will be $O(1)$ as the element might also be present at the first position itself. The advantage of linear search is that it does not require the array to be sorted as in other techniques like binary search.

9.3 SORTING

Sorting means the arrangement of a set of numbers in an order. In this section, we will be discussing the various sorting techniques.

Selection Sort

In selection sort, we take the element at the first position of the array and compare it with all other elements. If the element that is compared is smaller, then it is swapped with the element at the first position. The same procedure is repeated for the element at the second position and so on. For example, consider a set of numbers {3, 1, 4, 7, 5}. The first element, namely 3, is compared with all other elements starting from 1. Since 1 is smaller than 3, it is swapped with 3. The same process is repeated until the element at the first position is compared with all other elements. Similarly, the elements at the second, third, and fourth positions are compared with all other elements above them. The process is explained as follows:

First iteration

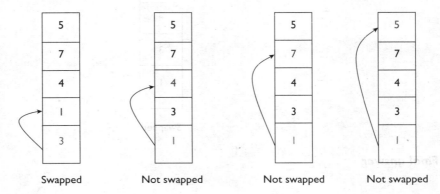

Second iteration

In the second iteration, we compare the element in the second position with those in the third, fourth, and fifth positions.

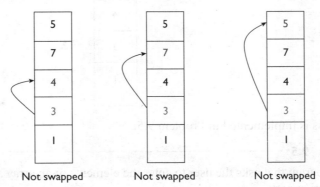

Third iteration

In the third iteration, we compare the third element with the rest of the elements above it.

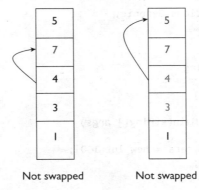

Fourth iteration

Swapped

Final answer

The process is implemented in Problem 9.5.

Problem 9.5

Write a program that asks the user to enter the elements of an array and then sorts the elements using selection sort.

Solution
```
using System;
using System.Collections.Generic;
using System.Linq;
using System.Text;

namespace ArraySorting
{
    class Program
    {
        static void Main(string[] args)
        {
            int[] numbers = new int[100];
            int i, n;
            try
```

```csharp
        {
            Console.WriteLine("Enter number of elements\t:");
            n = int.Parse(Console.ReadLine());
            for(i = 0; i < n; i++)
            {
                Console.WriteLine("Enter element\t:");
                numbers[i] = int.Parse(Console.ReadLine());
            }
            Console.WriteLine("Elements entered");
            for(i = 0; i < n; i++)
            {
                Console.WriteLine(numbers[i].ToString());
            }
            for(i = 0; i < n; i++)
            {
                for(int j = i + 1; j < n; j++)
                {
                    if(numbers[j] < numbers[i])
                    {
                        int temp = numbers[j];
                        numbers[j] = numbers[i];
                        numbers[i] = temp;
                    }
                }
            }
            Console.WriteLine("Sorted elements");
            for(i = 0; i < n; i++)
            {
                Console.WriteLine(numbers[i].ToString());
            }
        }
        catch(Exception e)
        {
            Console.WriteLine("Exception caught\t:" + e.ToString());
        }
        Console.ReadKey();
    }
  }
}
```

Output

```
Enter the number of elements:
5
Enter element:
4
Enter element:
1
Enter element:
5
Enter element:
3
Enter element:
4
```

```
Elements entered
4
1
5
2
3
Sorted elements
1
2
3
4
5
```

Now, let us move on to multidimensional arrays and jagged arrays.

9.4 TWO-DIMENSIONAL ARRAYS

A two-dimensional (2D) array is similar to a matrix in mathematics. It has rows and columns. A 2D array is declared in the following way:

```
<data type>[,] <name of the array> = new <data type>[index 1, index 2];
```

where data type can be any of the types discussed earlier, name of the array can be any valid identifier in C#, index 1 represents number of rows, and index 2 represents number of columns. For example, to declare a matrix having three rows and three columns the following declaration is written:

```
int[,] matrix = new int[3, 3];
```

This statement creates a 2D array called matrix, which has three rows, having indices 0, 1, and 2, and three columns. The individual elements have names of the form matrix $[i, j]$, where i is the row number and j is the column number. The array can be represented as follows:

matrix[0,0]	matrix[0,1]	matrix[0,2]
matrix[1,0]	matrix[1,1]	matrix[1,2]
matrix[2,0]	matrix[2,1]	matrix[2,2]

Assigning Values to Elements

The values to the elements of a matrix can be assigned using a `for` loop. For example, the following code initializes the elements of the earlier-mentioned matrix to $(i + j)^2$, where i is the row number and j is the column number.

```
for(i = 0; i < 3; i++)
{
    for(j = 0; j < 3; j++)
    {
        matrix[i, j] = (i + j) * (i + j);
    }
}
```

The listing of the task is as follows.

```
using System;
using System.Collections.Generic;
using System.Linq;
using System.Text;

namespace Matrix2
{
    class Program
    {
        static void Main(string[] args)
        {
            int[,] matrix = new int[3, 3];
            int i, j;
            for(i = 0; i < 3; i++)
            {
                for(j = 0; j < 3; j++)
                {
                    matrix[i, j] = (i + j) * (i + j);
                }
            }
            Console.WriteLine("\nThe matrix is\n");
            for(i = 0; i < 3; i++)
            {
                for(j = 0; j < 3; j++)
                {
                    Console.Write(matrix[i, j] + " ");
                }
                Console.WriteLine();
            }
            Console.ReadKey();
        }
    }
}
```

Output

```
The matrix is
0 1 4
1 4 9
4 9 16
```

In Problem 9.6, we will ask the user to input the elements of a 2D array. The task is simple and requires the use of Int16.Parse() discussed in Chapter 2.

Problem 9.6

Write a program that asks the user to enter the elements of a 3 × 3 matrix and then displays the matrix.

Solution

```
using System;
using System.Collections.Generic;
```

```csharp
using System.Linq;
using System.Text;

namespace Matrix1
{
    class Program
    {
        static void Main(string[] args)
        {
            int[,] matrix = new int[3, 3];
            int i, j;
            Console.WriteLine("\nEnter elements of the matrix");
            for(i = 0; i < 3; i++)
            {
                for(j = 0; j < 3; j++)
                {
                    Console.WriteLine("Enter element [{0}, {1}]\t:", i, j);
                    try
                    {
                        matrix[i, j] = Int16.Parse(Console.ReadLine());
                    }
                    catch(Exception e1)
                    {
                        Console.WriteLine("Error" + e1.ToString());
                    }
                }
            }
            Console.WriteLine("\nThe matrix is\n");
            for(i = 0; i < 3; i++)
            {
                for(j = 0; j < 3; j++)
                {
                    Console.Write(matrix[i, j] + " ");
                }
                Console.WriteLine();
            }
            Console.ReadKey();
        }
    }
}
```

Output

```
Enter elements of the matrix
Enter element [0, 0]:
1
Enter element [0, 1]:
2
Enter element [0, 2]:
3
Enter element [1, 0]:
4
Enter element [1, 1]:
5
```

```
Enter element [1, 2]:
6
Enter element [2, 0]:
7
Enter element [2, 1]:
8
Enter element [2, 2]:
9
The matrix is
1 2 3
4 5 6
7 8 9
```

In Problem 9.7, we will calculate the sum of two matrices entered by the user. Again, the declaration of the matrices will be the same as in Problem 9.6. The program has four parts. The first part asks the user to enter the elements of the first matrix and the second part asks to enter the elements of the second matrix. The third part calculates the sum and the fourth part displays the result.

Problem 9.7

Write a program that asks the user to enter two matrices and then displays their sum.

Solution

```
using System;
using System.Collections.Generic;
using System.Linq;
using System.Text;

namespace Matrices3
{
    class Program
    {
        static void Main(string[] args)
        {
            int[,] matrix1 = new int[3, 3];
            int[,] matrix2 = new int[3, 3];
            int[,] sum = new int[3, 3];
            int i, j;
            Console.WriteLine("\nEnter elements of the first matrix");
            for(i = 0; i < 3; i++)
            {
                for(j = 0; j < 3; j++)
                {
                    Console.WriteLine("Enter element [{0}, {1}]\t:", i, j);
                    try
                    {
                        matrix1[i, j] = Int16.Parse(Console.ReadLine());
                    }
                    catch(Exception e1)
                    {
                        Console.WriteLine("Error" + e1.ToString());
                    }
```

```
            }
        }
        Console.WriteLine("\nEnter elements of the second matrix");
        for(i = 0; i < 3; i++)
        {
            for(j = 0; j < 3; j++)
            {
                Console.WriteLine("Enter element [{0}, {1}]\t:", i, j);
                try
                {
                    matrix2[i, j] = Int16.Parse(Console.ReadLine());
                }
                catch(Exception e1)
                {
                    Console.WriteLine("Error" + e1.ToString());
                }
            }
        }
        for(i = 0; i < 3; i++)
        {
            for(j = 0; j < 3; j++)
            {
                sum[i, j] = matrix1[i, j] + matrix2[i, j];
            }
        }
        Console.WriteLine("\nThe sum is\n");
        for(i = 0; i < 3; i++)
        {
            for(j = 0; j < 3; j++)
            {
                Console.Write(sum[i, j] + " ");
            }
            Console.WriteLine();
        }
        Console.ReadKey();
    }
  }
}
```

Output

```
Enter elements of the first matrix
Enter element [0, 0]:
1
Enter element [0, 1]:
2
Enter element [0, 2]:
3
Enter element [1, 0]:
4
Enter element [1, 1]:
5
Enter element [1, 2]:
6
Enter element [2, 0]:
7
```

```
Enter element [2, 1]:
8
Enter element [2, 2]:
9
Enter elements of the second matrix
Enter element [0, 0]:
1
Enter element [0, 1]:
1
Enter element [0, 2]:
1
Enter element [1, 0]:
1
Enter element [1, 1]:
1
Enter element [1, 2]:
1
Enter element [2, 0]:
1
Enter element [2, 1]:
1
Enter element [2, 2]:
1
The sum is
2 3 4
5 6 7
8 9 10
```

In the programming exercises given at the end of the chapter, the concept of matrix multiplication and determinant is given. Moreover, matrices are also used in graphics and circuit solving.

9.5 MULTIDIMENSIONAL ARRAYS

Arrays can also have more than two dimensions. For example, a three-dimensional (3D) array is declared as follows:

```
// Three-dimensional array
    int[, ,] my3DArray = new int[, ,] { { { 1, 1, 1 }, { 2, 2, 2 } },
                                        { { 3, 3, 3 }, { 4, 4, 4 } } };
```

We can also specify the dimensions in the declaration. For example,

```
int[, ,] my3DArray = new int[2, 2, 3] { { { 1, 1, 1 }, { 2, 2, 2} },
                                        { { 3, 3, 3 }, { 4, 4, 4 } } };
```

Accessing Elements

The elements in a 3D array can be accessed in the same way as in a 2D array. For example,

```
System.Console.WriteLine(array3Da[1, 0, 1]);
```

In this statement, we are trying to display the value of the element at the second row (index 1), first column (index 0), and second 2D array (index 1).

```
                { { { 1, 1, 1 }, { 2, 2, 2} },
                { { 3, 3, 3 }, { 4, 4, 4 } } };
```

Output

```
3
```

In computer graphics, 3D transformation is a topic that makes use of 3D arrays extensively. 3D arrays also have many other applications.

Problem with Multidimensional Arrays

In C#, 2D and all other multidimensional arrays are slower than the 1D array. That is, it takes a longer time to access the elements of a 2D or a 3D array. The solution to this problem is jagged arrays, which are discussed in Section 9.6.

9.6 JAGGED ARRAYS

Imagine a situation requiring a 2D array, wherein each row is to have a different number of elements. For example, the first row in the required array should have one element, the second row two elements, the third row three elements, and so on. The situation is shown in Fig. 9.1.

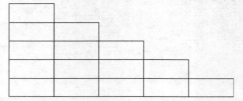

Fig. 9.1 Jagged array

C# has provided the answer to such kind of problems by introducing a concept called jagged array. A jagged array is an array whose elements are arrays. The elements of a jagged array can be of unequal sizes. Problem 9.8 shows how to declare, initialize, and access jagged arrays.

Problem 9.8

Write a program that asks the user to enter elements in a jagged array in which the first row has one element, second row has two, third row has three, and so on up to five rows. The program should also display the array.

Solution

```
using System;
using System.Collections.Generic;
using System.Linq;
using System.Text;

namespace JaggedDemo
{
    class Program
    {
        static void Main(string[] args)
        {
            int i, j;
            //Declaration
```

```csharp
            int[][] myJaggedArray = new int[5][];
            myJaggedArray[0] = new int[1];
            myJaggedArray[1] = new int[2];
            myJaggedArray[2] = new int[3];
            myJaggedArray[3] = new int[4];
            myJaggedArray[4] = new int[5];
            //Inserting values
            for(i = 0; i < 5; i++)
            {
                for(j = 0; j < myJaggedArray[i].Length; j++)
                {
                    Console.WriteLine("Enter element\t:");
                    try
                    {
                        myJaggedArray[i][j] = Int16.Parse(Console.ReadLine());
                    }
                    catch(Exception e1)
                    {
                        Console.WriteLine("Error\t:" + e1.ToString());
                    }
                }
            }
            Console.WriteLine("Jagged Array");
            for(i = 0; i < 5; i++)
            {
                for(j = 0; j < myJaggedArray[i].Length; j++)
                {
                    Console.Write(myJaggedArray[i][j]);
                }
                Console.WriteLine();
            }
            Console.ReadKey();
        }
    }
}
```

Output

```
Enter element:
1
Enter element:
2
Enter element:
3
Enter element:
4
Enter element:
5
Enter element:
6
Enter element:
7
Enter element:
8
Enter element:
9
```

```
Enter element:
0
Enter element:
1
Enter element:
2
Enter element:
3
Enter element:
4
Enter element:
5
Jagged array
1
23
456
7890
12345
```

9.7 System.Array CLASS

The `System.Array` class consists of predefined methods to manipulate the elements of an array. There are various methods to perform various tasks; for example, to sort an array we just have to write `Array.Sort(MyArray)`, where `MyArray` is the array to be sorted. There are many properties and methods in the class. The properties of the class are as follows:

`IsFixedSize`	: It tells us whether the given array is of fixed size or not.
`IsReadOnly`	: It tells us whether the array in question is read only (cannot be written) or not.
`IsSynchronized`	: It tells us whether the array is thread safe or not. Threads have been discussed in the chapter on threads.
`Length`	: It tells us the length of the array. It should be noted that the property returns a 32-bit number. For longer lengths, `LongLength` can be used.
`Rank`	: It returns the number of dimensions of the array. It should be noted that this does not refer to the (mathematical) rank of a matrix.

The important methods of the class are as follows:

`Sort(Array)`	: It sorts the elements in the array.
`Reverse(Array)`	: It reverses the sequence of the elements in the array.
`Copy(Array, Array, Int32)`	: It copies a range of elements from an array into another array starting at the first element. The length is specified as a 32-bit integer.
`Clear()`	: It sets the elements in the array to zero if it is an integer array.
`BinarySearch(Array, Object)`	: It searches the sorted array for a specific element and by the specified object.

There are many methods that we can use on as it is basis. The details of all such methods can be found in the documentation of the class (http://msdn.microsoft.com/en-us/library/system.array.aspx).

However, the following listing provides an idea of using the given methods. The listing asks the user to enter some numbers and then sorts them. The Sort method sorts the array in the increasing order. To get the array sorted in the decreasing order, reverse the order by using the Reverse method.

```
using System;
using System.Collections.Generic;
using System.Linq;
using System.Text;
namespace SystemArrayDemo
{
    class Program
    {
        static void Main(string[] args)
        {
            int i, n;
            int[] demoArray = new int[100];
            Console.WriteLine("Enter the number of elements");
            n = int.Parse(Console.ReadLine());
            for(i = 0; i < n; i++)
            {
                Console.WriteLine("Enter element");
                demoArray[i] = int.Parse(Console.ReadLine());
            }
            Array.Sort(demoArray);
            Array.Reverse(demoArray);
            Console.WriteLine("The sorted array is");
            for(i = 0; i < n; i++)
            {
                Console.WriteLine(demoArray[i].ToString());
            }
            Console.ReadKey();
        }
    }
}
```

Output

```
Enter the number of elements
5
Enter element
3
Enter element
6
Enter element
5
Enter element
2
Enter element
1
The sorted array is
6
5
3
2
1
```

9.8 System.ArrayList CLASS

The `System.ArrayList` class can prove handy for most of the tasks. Moreover, it is also good for persons who intend to use C# but do not have strong fundamentals. This can be done as long as the collection is not modified. All operations in an `ArrayList` must be done through the wrapper returned by the synchronized method. This is to provide thread safety. Enumerating throughout a collection is not a thread-safe process. In order to guarantee thread safety in case of enumeration, we can catch the exceptions resulting from changes made by other threads. The detailed examination is given in the chapter on threads.

SUMMARY

The chapter introduces the concept of arrays. It may be stated at this point that an array can have any type of element including an instance of a class or a structure. The concept is examined in Chapters 10 and 11. We may also have a 2D array, which is generally used in matrix multiplication and graphics. The chapter deals with the intricacies of such arrays. It also introduces 3D arrays and jagged arrays. The use of these arrays is not very common; however, graphics programming requires the knowhow of such arrays. The following must be noted about arrays in C#:
1. Arrays cannot be created on stacks.
2. There are predefined procedures for calculating length, copying, and so on. They can be found at http://msdn.microsoft.com/en-us/library/system.array%28v=vs.71%29.aspx.

GLOSSARY

Array It is a linear data structure that has elements identified by an index. The elements of an array are of the same type.

Linear search It is the process of searching for an element by examining each and every position of an array.

Jagged array It is an array whose elements are arrays. The elements of a jagged array can be of unequal sizes.

Sorting It is the process of arranging the elements in an order. A sorted array is called increasing if $\{a_i, a_i + 1, \ldots, a_i + j\}$ is such that for every value of i, $a_i + j > a_j$. It is decreasing if $\{a_i + j, a_i + (j - 1), \ldots, a_i + 1, a_i\}$ is such that for every value of i, $a_i + j < a_j$.

POINTS TO REMEMBER

- Searching in an array means finding an element in the given array.
- Sorting means arrangement of a set of numbers in an order.
- In C#, a 2D array is declared by [,] and not [][]; the latter represents a jagged array.
- In C#, 2D and all other multidimensional arrays are slower than the 1D array.
- A jagged array is an array whose elements are arrays.
- The System.Array class consists of predefined methods to manipulate the elements of an array.

EXERCISES

I. State True or False

1. The following assignment will be compiled:
   ```
   int[] array1 = new int [5];
   array1 = {1, 2, 3, 4, 5};
   ```
2. It is possible to make an array whose elements are arrays.
3. The following declaration is correct:

```
int [][] myArray = new int [][]
{
    new int[] {1, 2, 3, 4};
    new int[] {1, 2, 3};
    new int[] {1, 2};
    new int[] {1}
};
```

4. The elements of a jagged array can be 2D arrays.
5. C# arrays are zero indexed.
6. Array elements need not be initialized before being used.
7. Linear search can be performed on a sorted array.
8. The maximum dimension that an array can have is four.
9. Pascal's triangle can be created using jagged arrays.
10. We cannot create an array of a defined data type.

II. Multiple-choice Questions

1. Consider the following declaration:

   `newtype[] array1 = new newtype[100];`

   What will be the result of the above statements?
   (a) Creating an array of 10 instances of the type `newtype`
   (b) Creating an array of 100 elements each of which is initialized to null reference
   (c) Depends on whether `newtype` is value type or reference type
   (d) None of these

2. A student writes the following code and compiles it:

   ```
   int[] elements = new int[10];
   elements[10] = 5;
   ```

   What will be the output?
   (a) It will show a compilation error.
   (b) It will result in a runtime error.
   (c) Value 5 will be assigned to `elements[10]`.
   (d) None of these

3. Is it possible to declare an array without the rank specifier?
   (a) Yes
   (b) No
   (c) Depends on the type of array
   (d) Depends on other factors

4. Consider the following declaration:

   `int[][] myArray = new int[][];`

   (a) It will show a compilation error.
   (b) It requires the second rank to compile.
   (c) It is a jagged array.
   (d) None of these

5. Which of the following keywords is used to declare reference types?
   (a) `Interface`
   (b) `Delegate`
   (c) `Class`
   (d) All of these

6. An array is declared using the following code:

   `int[ , , ] myArray = new int[1, 2, 3];`

   State which of the following is correct?
   (a) It is an equivalent 2D array of one row and two columns.
   (b) The declaration is incorrect.
   (c) C# does not support 3D arrays.
   (d) None of these

7. Which of the following types of arrays is supported by C#?
   (a) 1D
   (b) Multidimensional
   (c) Jagged
   (d) All of these

8. Array types are reference type derived from _____.
   (a) `System.Array`
   (b) `System.Console`
   (c) Both (a) and (b)
   (d) None of these

9. In C#, an array can be created on stack.
   (a) True
   (b) False
   (c) Depends on the array
   (d) Depends on the number of elements

10. In C#, the length of an array can be directly found by `myArray.Length`.
    (a) True
    (b) False
    (c) Depends on the number of elements
    (d) Depends on the type of array

III. Review Questions

1. Define an array and enlist some of the scenarios wherein arrays are required.
2. Are array elements always stored in consecutive memory locations?
3. Is there any value type whose array cannot be made?
4. Explain the addressing of 2D arrays.
5. Explain how arrays can be passed in a function in spite of not being a basic data type.
6. Compare linear search and binary search techniques in terms of complexity.
7. What are the differences in the array implementation in C and C#?
8. Where can we use 3D arrays?
9. What is the difference between an array and a vector?
10. Can the elements of an array be arrays themselves?

IV. Programming Exercises

1. Write a program to implement a ternary search.
2. Write a program to reverse the elements of an array.
3. Write a program to pass an array in a function. The function should return the second largest element of the array.
4. Write a program to implement bubble sort.
5. Write a program to implement selection sort. The elements of the array are strings.
6. The transpose of a matrix is obtained by changing the rows of a matrix into columns. For example, if a matrix is

1	4	6
2	6	7
3	8	9

then the transpose of the matrix will be

1	2	3
4	6	8
6	7	9

Write a program that asks the user to enter a matrix and then finds its transpose.

7. A symmetric matrix is one in which every element of the matrix is equal to each element of its transpose. For example,

1	2	3
2	6	4
3	4	9

is a symmetric matrix. Write a program to check whether a given matrix is symmetric or not.

8. A skew symmetric matrix is one that satisfies the relation $A = -A'$, where A' is the transpose of A. Write a program that asks the user to enter a matrix and then checks whether it is skew symmetric or not.

9. Write a program that asks the user to enter two matrices and then frames a symmetric matrix from those matrices.
10. Write a program to multiply two matrices.
11. Write a program to find the determinant of a 3×3 matrix.
12. Write a program to find the inverse of a 2×2 matrix.
13. Write a program to swap the elements at the odd positions in an array with those at the even positions.
14. Write a program that asks the user to enter two arrays and then finds whether the second array is a part of the first array.
15. Write a program to find the second maximum number from amongst the elements of an array without sorting it.
16. Write a program to merge two arrays. Both the arrays should be sorted.
17. Write a program to create an array consisting of Fibonacci numbers.
18. Write a program that asks the user to enter a string. It should convert the string into a character array. It should then find the ASCII value of each character and add five to each value. Finally, the program should convert the set of numbers obtained into characters and then to a string.
19. Write a program to perform the tasks specified in Question 18 by not adding five but a random number and get the encrypted string.
20. Write a program that asks the user to enter a matrix. It should then find the maximum number from each row and construct an array of those numbers.

PROJECT II
Greedy Approach

1. INTRODUCTION

The intention of this book is not only to present the syntax of C# but also to make the reader a good programmer. Having learnt the basic procedural programming, let us now see how to use C# in solving problems. The present project and the others provided later intend to accomplish the task.

In order to solve a problem, an algorithmic approach is needed. The first approach that is being presented here is the greedy approach. As in economics, the main aim of a program is not just to solve a problem but to do it in a manner that optimizes the results. Greedy approach is one such approach. The project presents a brief overview of the greedy method. In order to help readers understand the concept better, two problems have been analysed, implemented, and tested.

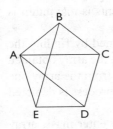

The project would help readers to tackle such problems in the future. It has to be remembered that a programmer is expected to have a problem-solving approach and not just acquire the knowledge of the syntax.

The greedy approach is one of the most commonly used approaches in solving optimization problems. In this approach, a decision is taken at every step so as to maximize the profit or minimize the cost. For example, a person needs to go from city A to city B, as per the map depicted in the following figure. The table gives the distances between the various cities; for example, the cell at row 2 and column 3 of the table gives the distance between city 2 (read B) and city 3 (read C).

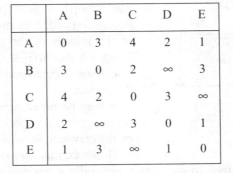

	A	B	C	D	E
A	0	3	4	2	1
B	3	0	2	∞	3
C	4	2	0	3	∞
D	2	∞	3	0	1
E	1	3	∞	1	0

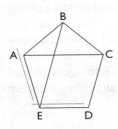

In order to go from A to E, first, the minimum cost path from A is selected. As per the table, it is A to E. Edge AE is therefore selected in the first iteration.

This is followed by selecting the minimum cost edge from E. Since we started from A, we must head to D, as the cost of going from E to D is one.

The only edge that we can next move along is DC. When we reach C, we must move to B, in order to cover all the vertices. The following figure depicts the final path.

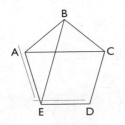

This approach is called the greedy approach, as the decision is taken considering the path that is the most promising at that point of time. The approach is very useful in designing algorithms. It is useful in many cases. The sections that follow give an introduction to two important problems that can be solved via the greedy approach. The first problem is knapsack and the second is job sequencing.

2. KNAPSACK PROBLEM

A person has to select a few items to put in his bag. The capacity of the bag is m units. There are n items in the room: $\{x_1, x_2, x_3, \ldots, x_n\}$. The weights of these items are given by the set $\{w_1, w_2, w_3, \ldots, w_n\}$ and the profits obtained by picking an item are $\{p_1, p_2, p_3, \ldots, p_n\}$. $x_n = 1$ denotes that the item has been picked and $x_n = 0$ means that the item has not been picked. The problem is to select items in such a way that the total weight of the selected items is less than or equal to the capacity of the bag. This constraint is depicted in Eq. (1).

$$x_1 \times w_1 + x_1 \times w_2 + x_3 \times w_1 \ldots \leq m \qquad (1)$$

In addition, we need to pick the items in such a way that the profit earned is maximum; that is, $x_1 \times p_1 + x_1 \times p_2 + x_3 \times p_1 \ldots$ is maximum. This problem is referred to as 0/1 knapsack problem.

Hence, the selection of items from a given set in such a way that the total weight is less than or equal to the given weight and also the profit earned by picking up the elements is maximum is referred to as the knapsack problem.

The solution to the problem can be determined by finding the profit per unit weight of the items and arranging the array obtained in decreasing order. Then, the items are picked from the array one by one as long as there is space in the bag. The process is depicted in the following diagram.

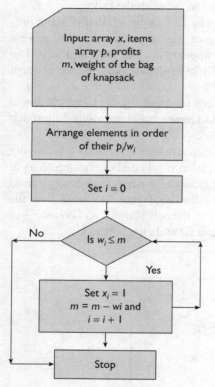

To implement this program, ask the user to enter mass, array profit [ ], and array weight [ ]. Make a new array ratio [ ] such that ratio[i] = profit[i]/weight[i]. Arrange the array ratio in decreasing order, in such a way that it is possible to keep track of the indices of the original array. Now, use a while loop to check whether $w[i] \leq m$; if yes, then make $m = m - 1$ and $i = 1 + 1$. The items selected and the total profit earned will be displayed as the answer.

It may be noted here that the knapsack problem is not just a simple greedy approach illustration. It can be used in data mining, by the crawlers, in networking, and so on.

However, this approach does not work properly when the number of items is too large. In such cases, generally, a randomization technique, or one based on artificial intelligence, is applied to solve the problem. Genetic algorithm is one such artificial intelligence-based technique, which may be used to solve it. The solution of the problem by genetic algorithm has been discussed in Project V.

Solution

The following program implements the knapsack problem:

```
using System;
using System.Collections.Generic;
using System.Linq;
using System.Text;
namespace CaseStudy2
{
        class Program
```

```csharp
{
    static void Main(string[] args)
    {
        double[] profits = new double[100];
        double[] weights = new double[100];
        double[] pbyw = new double[100];
        int[] items = new int[100];
        int[] result = new int[100];
        double temp, m, netProfit = 0;
        int temp1;
        int i, j, n, k = 0;
        try
        {
            Console.WriteLine("Enter number of elements\t:");
            n = int.Parse(Console.ReadLine());
            Console.WriteLine("Capacity of knapsack\t:");
            m = double.Parse(Console.ReadLine());
            for(i = 0; i < n; i++)
            {
                items[i] = i;
            }
            for(i = 0; i < n; i++)
            {
                Console.WriteLine("ITEM NUMBER " + i);
                Console.WriteLine("Enter profit\t:");
                profits[i] = double.Parse(Console.ReadLine());
                Console.WriteLine("Enter weight\t:");
                weights[i] = double.Parse(Console.ReadLine());
                pbyw[i] = profits[i]/weights[i];
            }
            for(i = 0; i < n; i++)
            {
                for(j = i + 1; j < n; j++)
                {
                    if(pbyw[j] > pbyw[i])
                    {
                        temp = pbyw[j];
                        pbyw[j] = pbyw[i];
                        pbyw[i] = temp;
                        temp1 = items[i];
                        items[i] = items[j];
                        items[j] = temp1;
                        temp = weights[i];
                        weights[i] = weights[j];
                        weights[j] = temp;
                        temp = profits[i];
                        profits[i] = profits[j];
                        profits[j] = temp;
                    }
                }
            }
            for(i = 0; i < n; i++)
            {
                Console.WriteLine("Item number " + items[i] + "Profit " + profits[i]
                    + " Weight " + weights[i] + "profit/Weight\t:" + pbyw[i]);
```

```csharp
            }
            Console.WriteLine("m = " + m.ToString());
            //Console.ReadKey();
            k = 0;
            while(weights[k] < m)
            {
                result[k] = items[k];
                m = m - weights[k];
                netProfit = netProfit + profits[k];
                k++;
            }
            netProfit = netProfit + ((m / weights[k]) * profits[k]);
            double fraction = (m / weights[k]);
            Console.WriteLine("Items selected");
            for(i = 0; i < k; i++)
            {
                Console.Write(result[i].ToString() + " ");
            }
            if(fraction != 0)
            {
                Console.WriteLine("The fraction of " + k + " item selected " +
                fraction);
            }
            Console.WriteLine("Profit " + netProfit);
        }
        catch(Exception e)
        {
            Console.WriteLine("Exception " + e.ToString());
        }
        Console.ReadKey();
    }
  }
}
```

Output

```
Capacity of knapsack "
20
ITEM NUMBER 0
Enter profit  :
25
Enter weight  :
18
ITEM NUMBER 1
Enter profit  :
24
Enter weight  :
15
ITEM NUMBER 2
Enter profit  :
15
Enter weight  :
10
```

```
Item number 1 Profit 24 Weight 15 Profit/Weight : 1.6
Item number 2 Profit 15 Weight 10 Profit/Weight : 1.5
Item number 0 Profit 25 Weight 18 Profit/Weight :1.38888888888889
m=20
Items selected
1 The fraction of item 1 selected 0.5
Profit 31.5
```

3. JOB SEQUENCING

Suppose your mother, father, brother, and sister ask you to perform a task each. For accomplishing the respective tasks, you will get different rewards from different people, say more from father than from sister. Moreover, you have to perform the tasks in such a way that the time limit mentioned by each person is not violated. Assume that each task takes a unit time to complete. For example, your father directs you to water the plants within three hours. You can, then, select the first, the second, or the third hour to accomplish the task. Formally, the problem is stated as follows.

There are n tasks: $\{x_1, x_2, x_3, \ldots, x_n\}$ having deadlines $\{d_1, d_2, d_3, \ldots, d_n\}$ and profits $\{p_1, p_2, p_3, \ldots, p_n\}$.

We have to select the jobs in such a way that the number of jobs finished is maximum and the profit earned by accomplishing the jobs is also maximum. The problem can be solved easily by employing the greedy approach. The procedure for solving the problem has been depicted with the help of the following:

Let $n = 5$, $\{p_1, p_2, p_3, \ldots, p_n\} = \{100, 200, 50, 40, 25\}$ and $\{d_1, d_2, d_3, \ldots, d_n\} = \{3, 2, 1, 2, 1\}$. The procedure for solving the problem is as follows.

In the first step, arrange the items in the order of their profits.

$\{p_2, p_1, p_3, p_4, p_5\} = \{200, 100, 50, 40, 25\}$ and the set d becomes $\{d_2, d_1, d_3, d_4, d_5\} = \{2, 3, 1, 2, 1\}$. Now, pick the task that results in the maximum profit. In this case, the second task should be included in the result set in the opening stride. Now, since you can do task 2 in either the first unit or the second unit of time, you must do it in the second slot since it will fetch you the profit earned by doing task 2 and still keep one of your slots free. The free slot can be used to carry out some other task, which will surely increase the net profit.

	Task 2 Profit 200		

The next job that can be selected is task 1, since it has the second-highest profit. However, the time slot allotted to the job should be slot 3 as it gives the advantage of doing some other tasks in the empty slots that precede slot 3.

	Task 2 Profit 200	Task 1 Profit 100	

The deadline for doing the next task is one. Therefore, it should be completed in slot 1.

Task 3 Profit 50	Task 2 Profit 200	Task 1 Profit 100		

Now, you cannot do tasks 4 and 5 as you have missed their deadlines. Therefore, the total profit earned is 350, which is the maximum possible amount that can be earned with the given time limits, leaving time slots 4 and 5 unused. The following program implements this task:

Program

```
using System;
using System.Collections.Generic;
using System.Linq;
using System.Text;

namespace CaseStudy2Program2
{
    class Program
    {
        static void Main(string[] args)
        {
            int[] jobs = new int[100];
            double[] profits = new double[100];
            int[] deadlines = new int[100];
            int i, j, k, n, temp;
            int[,] result = new int[100, 2];
            double temp1;
            // try
            //{
                Console.WriteLine("Enter the number of jobs");
                n = int.Parse(Console.ReadLine());
                for(i = 0; i < n; i++)
                {
                    jobs[i] = i;
                    Console.WriteLine("\nEnter profit\t:");
                    profits[i] = double.Parse(Console.ReadLine());
                    Console.WriteLine("\nEnter deadline\t:");
                    deadlines[i] = int.Parse(Console.ReadLine());
                    result[i, 1] = 0;
                }
                for(i = 0; i < n; i++)
                {
                    for(j = i + 1; j < n; j++)
                    {
                        if(profits[j] > profits[i])
                        {
                            temp1 = profits[i];
                            profits[i] = profits[j];
                            profits[j] = temp1;
                            temp = deadlines[i];
                            deadlines[i] = deadlines[j];
                            deadlines[j] = temp;
```

```csharp
                    temp = jobs[i];
                    jobs[i] = jobs[j];
                    jobs[j] = temp;
                }
            }
        }
        for(i = 0; i < n; i++)
        {
            Console.WriteLine("Job number\t:" + jobs[i].ToString() + " Profit :" +
            profits[i].ToString() + " Deadline :" + deadlines[i]);
        }
        i = 0;
        result[deadlines[0], 1] = 1;
        result[deadlines[0], 0] = jobs[0];
        i++;
        while(i < n)
        {
            int t = deadlines[i];
            if(result[t, 1] == 0)
            {
                result[t, 1] = 1;
                result[t, 0] = jobs[i];
            }
            else
            {
            while((t != -1) && (result[t, 1] != 0))
            {
                t--;
            }
            if(t != -1)
            {
                result[t, 1] = 1;
                result[t, 0] = jobs[i];
            }
            else
            {
                Console.WriteLine("Job " + i + " cannot be done");
                goto a;
            }
        }
            Console.WriteLine("Job " + i.ToString() + " slot " + result[i, 0] + " flag
            " + result[i, 1]);
            i++;
        }
        a:
        Console.WriteLine("Result");
        for(i = 0; i < n; i++)
        {
            if(result[i, 1] != 0)
            {
                Console.WriteLine(result[i, 0]);
```

```
                }
            }
    // }
        /*catch(Exception e)
        {
            Console.WriteLine("Exception " + e);
        }*/
        Console.ReadKey();
        }
    }
}
```

Output

The output of this program is as follows. It may be noted that the deadlines are one less than what you intend to insert, as they are to be stored in a zero-indexed array.

```
Enter the number of jobs5
Enter profit  :
100
Enter deadline    :
2
Enter profit  :
200
Enter deadline    :
1
Enter profit  :
50
Enter deadline    :
0
Enter profit  :
40
Enter deadline    :
1
Enter profit  :
25
Enter deadline    :
0
Job number      : 1 Profit : 200  Deadline   : 1
Job number      : 0 Profit : 100  Deadline   : 2
Job number      : 2 Profit : 50   Deadline   : 0
Job number      : 3 Profit : 40   Deadline   : 1
Job number      : 4 Profit : 25   Deadline   : 0
Job 1 slot 1 flag 1
Job 2 slot 0 flag 1
Job 3 cannot be done
Result
2
1
0
```

```
Enter the number of jobs
5
Enter profit       :
100
Enter deadline     :
2
Enter profit       :
200
Enter deadline     :
1
Enter profit       :
50
Enter deadline     :
0
Enter profit       :
40
Enter deadline     :
1
Enter profit       :
25
Enter deadline     :
0
Job number         :1 Profit :200 deadline :1
Job number         :0 Profit :100 deadline :2
Job number         :2 Profit :50  deadline :0
Job number         :3 Profit :40  deadline :1
Job number         :4 Profit :25  deadline :0
Job 1 slot 1 flag 1
Job 2 slot 0 flag 1
Job 3 cannot be done
Result
2
1
0
```

It may be noted that the problems given here can also be solved by other approaches. Moreover, there are many other approaches except greedy approach for solving problems. However, the project presents a way to attack the problem.

It may be stated that learning programming is not just understanding the syntax; it also involves developing the ability to solve complex problems. There is a difference between becoming a coder and becoming a programmer. Your target should be to become the latter and not the former. It is, therefore, advisable to value algorithm analysis and design along with C#.

10 Structures and Enumerations

OBJECTIVES

After completing this chapter, the reader will be able to
Appreciate the importance of structures
Understand the syntax and use of structures
Describe the concept of properties
Explain and use nested structures
Understand and apply array of structures
Declare and use enumerations

10.1 INTRODUCTION

Consider a situation in which we are required to create a software application for a school. In order to carry out the task, details such as name, age, and fees of every student are required. Assume that there are 500 students in the school. If we create different variables for each student, then we end up creating 1500 variables. This chapter explains how to accomplish the task in a more efficient manner. The concept that we will be studying here not only helps us to handle situations such as the one mentioned above but also acts as a theoretical base for the following chapters. A structure is the meeting point of procedural and object-oriented programming. Readers familiar with C or C++ must be aware of the importance of structures. However, there are some additional features in structures as far as C# is concerned. The concept of structures is elaborated in this chapter, which has been organized in such a way that even those readers who are not familiar with the concept will be able to understand and appreciate the importance and usage of structures.

We can make use of a structure when the entity in question is well defined. Structure is a collection of variables. It has the same significance in C# as a record in Pascal. In spite of being a collection of variables, a structure is patently different from an array. An array consists

> **Note** A structure may contain variables with different data types, but an array always has the same type of elements.

of homogeneous data types, whereas a structure may contain variables having different data types.

The chapter intends to explain the concept of structures via illustrations. This will be pivotal in understanding the rest of the chapters as well. The chapter discusses the creation, definition, instantiation, and applications of a structure along with other essential details. It will become clear that structure in itself is nothing more than a blueprint. Memory is allocated only when a structure is instantiated. The understanding of structures is important to become an accomplished programmer. Any management system will involve the concept of structures or classes. A class is a real or a conceptual entity just like a structure, but it supports many more features. The concept of classes will be dealt with in the next section of the book.

10.2 A SIMPLE STRUCTURE

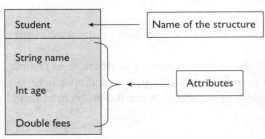

Fig. 10.1 Student structure

A program generally revolves around an entity. For example, a student management system revolves around the entity 'student', an invoicing system gyrates around an 'item', and an 'employee' is central to an employee management system. So, most of the times, there is a need to craft an entity. As stated earlier, a structure depicts an entity. An entity is defined by its attributes. Therefore, a structure also has attributes. We can also say that the group of attributes constitutes a structure (Fig. 10.1).

In order to understand the concept, consider an entity called student. Let the entity have name, age, and fees as its attributes. The entity can be implemented in C# as a structure, which is depicted as follows:

```
struct student
{
    public String name;
    public int age;
    public double fees;
}
```

So, a structure may contain many variables. The name of the structure is actually the entity of which the variables are ingredients. It is important to note that even methods can be a part of structures. We will be learning about the inclusion of methods in a structure in Section 10.8.

10.3 DEFINING A STRUCTURE

In order to define a structure, the keyword `struct` followed by the name of the structure is written. The definition of the structure is written in curly braces. Inside a structure, variables are defined. Such variables are referred to as the members of the structure. The keyword `public` is usually used before defining the variables, so that the variables can be accessed anywhere in the program. It may be noted that if a data member or a member function is public then it can be accessed anywhere in the program. A private member, however, can be accessed only within the structure. In general, data members are private and the member functions, or methods, are public. The reason for doing so is to prevent the accidental alteration of the values of the

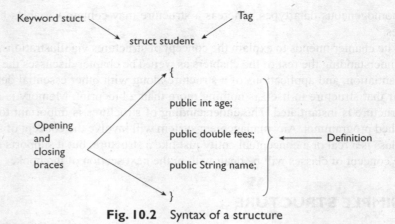

Fig. 10.2 Syntax of a structure

member variables. It may be stated that writing public or private does not, in any way, implement any security mechanism.

The declaration shown in Fig. 10.2 depicts a structure called student. The structure has name, age, and fees as its data members. All the data members in the structure depicted here are public. The data type of the members can be the same or different, as per the problem at hand. Figure 10.2 explains the syntax of a structure.

10.4 INSTANTIATION

Making instances of a structure is referred to as instantiation. It may be stated that the members of a structure are called by instances of the structure. Since a structure as such is only a blueprint, when we define a structure no memory is allocated to it. Memory is allocated only when instances are created, which is done by writing the name of the structure followed by the name of the instance. Figure 10.3 shows the instantiation of a structure called student. Two instances, s1 and s2, are created. The instances s1 and s2 will be created only after the following statement is executed:
    student s1, s2;

10.5 ACCESSING ELEMENTS OF A STRUCTURE

Once a structure is created, it is required to access the components of that structure. This can be done using the dot operator. The elements of a structure are accessed using the name of the instance of the structure followed by the dot operator and the member to be accessed. However, only those members that are accessible can be accessed. For example, consider a structure called student, having name, age, and fees as its attributes. In order to assign value 'Jisha' to the name attribute of an instance 's' of the structure, the following statement should be written:
s.name = "Jisha";

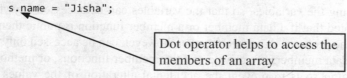

Structures and Enumerations 215

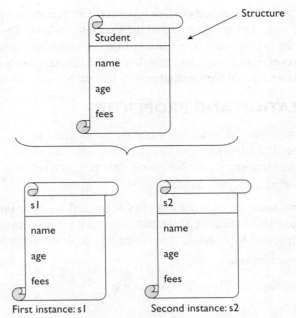

Fig. 10.3   Instances of a structure

The snippet shows this example in detail.

```
using System;
using System.Collections.Generic;
using System.Linq;
using System.Text;

namespace StructureDemo
{
    class Program
    {
        struct Student
        {
            public String name;
            public int age;
            public double fees;
        }
        static void Main(string[] args)
        {
            Student s;
            s.name = "Jisha";
            s.age = 28;
            s.fees = 5000.90;
            Console.WriteLine("Name\t:" + s.name + "\nAge\t:" + s.age + "\nFees\t:" + s.fees);
            Console.ReadKey();
        }
    }
}
```

In this listing, a structure called student has three data members—name, age, and fees. The statement Student s; makes an instance s of the structure student. The variables of the structure are accessed via the dot operator. The values of theses variables can be manipulated since they are 'public'. However, it may be noted that this would not have been possible if the variables were private. This is because of the fact that private members cannot be accessed outside the structure.

10.6 INITIALIZATION AND PROPERTIES

In C++, structures can be initialized equating the instance to
{<data member 1>, <data member 2>, …}.
For example, to initialize s1, the following statement is written:

```
s1 = {"Jisha", 28, 2430.25};
```

This procedure, however, does not work in C#; instead, we must instantiate the student structure via new operator. This is followed by initializing each variable inside curly braces, with the variables being separated by commas. The concept is depicted in the following program:

```
namespace StructureDemo
{
    class Program
    {
        struct Student
        {
            public String name;
            public int age;
            public double fees;
        }
        static void Main(string[] args)
        {
            Student s = new Student{name = "Jisha", age = 28, fees = 5000.90};
            Console.WriteLine("Name\t:" + s.name + "\nAge\t:" + s.age + "\nFees\t:" + s.fees);
            Console.ReadKey();
        }
    }
}
```

Output

```
Name : Jisha
Age  : 28
Fees : 5000.9
```

When this code is executed, s.name becomes Jisha, s.age becomes 28, and s.fees becomes 5000.9. A structure cannot inherit like a class, but it can have properties that simplify access to its data. The properties are get, which returns a value, and set, which inserts the value in the variable. The following program shows the use of these properties:

```
using System;
using System.Collections.Generic;
using System.Linq;
using System.Text;
```

```
namespace StructDemo2
{
    class Program
    {
        struct ABC
        {
            int x;
            public int a
            {
                get
                {
                    return this.x;
                }
                set
                {
                    this.x = value;
                }
            }
        }
        static void Main(string[] args)
        {
            ABC a1 = new ABC();
            a1.a = 5;
            Console.WriteLine("The number is" + a1.a);
            Console.ReadKey();
        }
    }
}
```

Output

```
The number is 5
```

10.7 NESTED STRUCTURES

At times we need a user defined data type which has many attributes, some of which can be complex. Theses complex attributes can also be conceptualized as structures. In such situations we need a user defined data type within a data type. C# provides solution to such problems by a concept called 'nested structures'. A structure may be nested within another structure. Such a structure is referred to as a nested structure. In order to understand the concept, consider a situation where the date of birth of a student is also required along with the name, age, and fees. The date of birth is a struct type, user-defined variable. In order to accomplish the task, a structure within a structure is used. We can define a structure called date and instantiate it inside the student structure.

```
using System;
using System.Collections.Generic;
using System.Linq;
using System.Text;

namespace StructureDemo
{
    class Program
    {
```

```csharp
struct date
{
    public int dd, mm, yy;
}
struct Student
{
    public String name;
    public int age;
    public double fees;
    public date dob;
}
static void Main(string[] args)
{
    Student s;
    try
    {
        Console.WriteLine("Enter name\t:");
        s.name = Console.ReadLine();
        Console.WriteLine("Enter age\t:");
        s.age = int.Parse(Console.ReadLine());
        Console.WriteLine("Enter fees\t:");
        s.fees = double.Parse(Console.ReadLine());
        Console.WriteLine("Enter date\t:");
        Console.WriteLine("Enter day\t:");
        s.dob.dd = int.Parse(Console.ReadLine());
        Console.WriteLine("Enter month\t:");
        s.dob.mm = int.Parse(Console.ReadLine());
        Console.WriteLine("Enter year\t:");
        s.dob.yy = int.Parse(Console.ReadLine());
        Console.WriteLine("Name\t:" + s.name + "\nAge\t:" + s.age + "\nFees\t:"
            + s.fees + "\nDate of birth\t:{0}\\{1}\\{2}", s.dob.dd, s.dob.mm,
            s.dob.yy);
    }
    catch(Exception e1)
    {
        Console.WriteLine("Error " + e1);
    }
    Console.ReadKey();
}
```

Output

```
Enter name      :Harsh
Enter age       :29
Enter fees      :5005.50
Enter date      :
Enter day       :03
Enter month     :12
Enter year      :00
Name            :Harsh
Age             :29
Fees            :5005.5
Date of birth   :3\12\0
```

10.8 METHODS INSIDE STRUCTURES

Now that we have studied the basics of structures, it will be interesting to know that, unlike in C, a structure in C# may also contain methods. A method inside a structure is made when a certain task is to be accomplished every time an instance is made. For example, consider a situation in which the details of a student are to be entered every time an instance is made. In order to do this, a method for getting the details from the user and displaying the details must be made inside the structure itself. The syntax is as follows:

```
struct <structure name>
{
    //Data members
    <return type> <method name>(argument list)
    {
        //Body of the method
    }
}
```

10.9 ARRAY OF STRUCTURES

An array is a homogeneous collection of elements having consecutive memory locations. It may be stated that these elements can also be structure instances. The need for having structure instances as the elements of an array arises when many user-defined elements are to be processed. The present section examines such situations and illustrates the concept.

An array of structure is declared as follows:

```
<name of the structure>[] <name of the array> = new <name of the structure>[number of elements];
```

In order to understand the concept, let us consider the following program. Here, we need to store the details of *n* students, *n* being entered by the user. The student structure contains name, age, and fees as its data members. It also has two functions, namely `getdata()` and `putdata()` for input and output, respectively.

```
using System;
using System.Collections.Generic;
using System.Linq;
using System.Text;

namespace StudentArray
{
    class Program
    {
        struct student
        {
            string name;
            int age;
            double fees;
            public void getdata()
            {
                Console.WriteLine("Enter name\t:");
                name = Console.ReadLine();
                Console.WriteLine("Enter age\t:");
                age = int.Parse(Console.ReadLine());
                Console.WriteLine("Enter fees\t:");
```

```csharp
            fees = double.Parse(Console.ReadLine());
        }
        public void putdata()
        {
            Console.WriteLine("\nThe details of the student are as follows\n");
            Console.WriteLine("Name\t:" + name + "\nAge\t:" + age + "\nFees\t:" + fees);
        }
    }
    static void Main(string[] args)
    {
        student[] s = new student[100];
        int n, i;
        Console.WriteLine("\nEnter the number of elements\t:");
        n = int.Parse(Console.ReadLine());
        for(i = 0; i < n; i++)
        {
            Console.WriteLine("Enter details of student number\t:" + i);
            s[i].getdata();
        }
        Console.WriteLine("\nThe details of the students are as follows");
        for(i = 0; i < n; i++)
        {
            s[i].putdata();
        }
        Console.ReadKey();
    }
}
```

Output

```
Enter the number of elements    : 5
Enter details of student number: 0
Enter name :Harsh
Enter age  :29
Enter fees :2003

Enter details of student number: 1
Enter name :Naks
Enter age  :22
Enter fees :3002

Enter details of student number: 2
Enter name :Jisha
Enter age  :27
Enter fees :4001

Enter details of student number: 3
Enter name :Yatin
Enter age  :25
Enter fees :4001

Enter details of student number: 4
Enter name :Pav
Enter age  :26
Enter fees :3002
```

```
The details of the students are as follows
Name        :Harsh
Age         :29
Fees        :2003

The details of the student are as follows
Name        :Naks
Age         :22
Fees        :3002

The details of the student are as follows
Name        :Jisha
Age         :27
Fees        :4001

The details of the student are as follows
Name        :Yatin
Age         :25
Fees        :4001

The details of the student are as follows
Name        :Pav
Age         :26
Fees        :3002
```

10.10 DIFFERENCES BETWEEN STRUCTURES AND CLASSES

A class is a real or a virtual object having importance to problem at hand. The concept of classes will be explained in Chapter 11. There are a few similarities between structures and classes as both are user-defined types. Both can be used when an entity is to be created and dealt with. Both can be used as the basic building blocks of any management system. However, there are a few differences too. Classes are reference types, whereas structures are value types. Structures do not store referenced data. Moreover, when the new operator is called on a class, it will be allocated on the heap, whereas if we instantiate a structure, it gets shaped on the stack.

In case the entity that we intend to design does not require inheritance or polymorphism, then we must opt for structures instead of classes. The differences between a class and a structure are shown in Table 10.1.

Table 10.1 Differences between a structure and a class

Class	Structure
Reference type	Value type
Allocated on stack	Allocated on heap
Supports inheritance	Does not support inheritance
Supports polymorphism	Does not support polymorphism

10.11 COMPLEX NUMBER CALCULATOR

Having studied the important concepts of structures, let us write a program that takes two complex numbers as input and shows a menu from which the user selects one of the options. The following is the menu to be displayed:

```
1 : Sum
2 : Difference
3 : Product
4 : Exit
Enter choice  :
```

A complex number contains two parts—real and imaginary. The sum of two complex numbers is a complex number whose real part is the sum of the real parts of the two complex numbers and the imaginary part is the sum of their imaginary parts. Similarly, the difference of two complex numbers is a complex number whose real part is the difference of the real parts of the two complex numbers and the imaginary part is the difference of their imaginary parts. So, if $z1$ and $z2$ are two complex numbers, then the sum, difference, and product of the two complex numbers are as follows.

First complex number   : $z1 = x1 + iy1$
Second complex number : $z2 = x2 + iy2$
Sum   : $(x1 + x2) + i(y1 + y2)$
Difference   : $(x1 - x2) + i(y1 - y2)$
Product   : $(x1 + iy1) \times (x2 + iy2) (x1 \times x2 - y1 \times y2) + i(x1 \times y2 + y1 \times x2)$

Here, $x1$ is the real part of the first complex number, $x2$ is the real part of the second complex number, $y1$ is the imaginary part of the first complex number, and $y2$ is the imaginary part of the second complex number.

```csharp
using System;
using System.Collections.Generic;
using System.Linq;
using System.Text;

namespace Complexnumbercalc
{
    class Program
    {
        struct complex
        {
            public int real;
            public int imaginary;
            public void getdata()
            {
                try
                {
                    Console.WriteLine("Enter the real part\t:");
                    real = int.Parse(Console.ReadLine());
                    Console.WriteLine("Enter the imaginary part\t:");
                    imaginary = int.Parse(Console.ReadLine());
                }
                catch(Exception e1)
                {
```

```csharp
                Console.WriteLine("Error\t:" + e1);
            }
        }
        public void putdata()
        {
            Console.WriteLine(real + " + i" + imaginary);
        }
    }
    static void Main(string[] args)
    {
        int choice;
        complex c1 = new complex();
        complex c2 = new complex();
        complex result = new complex();
        Console.WriteLine("Enter the first complex number");
        c1.getdata();
        c1.putdata();
        Console.WriteLine("Enter the second complex number");
        c2.getdata();
        Console.WriteLine("1\t:Sum\n2\t:Product\n3\t:Difference\t:\n4\t:Exit");
        Console.WriteLine("Enter your choice");
        try
        {
            choice = int.Parse(Console.ReadLine());
            switch(choice)
            {
                case 1:
                result.real = c1.real + c2.real;
                result.imaginary = c1.imaginary + c2.imaginary;
                result.putdata();
                break;
                case 2:
                result.real = c1.real - c2.real;
                result.imaginary = c1.imaginary + c2.imaginary;
                result.putdata();
                break;
                case 3:
                result.real = c1.real * c2.real - c1.imaginary * c2.imaginary;
                result.imaginary = c1.real * c2.imaginary + c1.imaginary * c2.real;
                result.putdata();
                break;
                case 4:
                Console.WriteLine("Exitting");
                break;
                default:
                Console.WriteLine("Wrong choice");
                break;
            }
        }
        catch (Exception e1)
        {
```

```
            Console.WriteLine("Error\t:" + e1);
        }
        Console.ReadKey();

    }
  }
}
```

Output

```
First run
Enter the first complex number
Enter the real part   :
2

Enter the imaginary part    :
3
2 + i3

Enter the second complex number
Enter the real part   :
1

Enter the imaginary part    :
2
1          :Sum
2          :Product
3          :Difference
4          :Exit

Enter your choice
1
3 + i5

Second run
Enter the first complex number
Enter the real part   :
2

Enter the imaginary part    :
3
2 + i3

Enter the second complex number
Enter the real part   :
1

Enter the imaginary part    :
1
1          :Sum
2          :Product
3          :Difference
4          :Exit
```

```
Enter your choice
2
1 + i4
```

Third run

```
Enter the first complex number
Enter the real part  :
2

Enter the imaginary part     :
3
2 + i3

Enter the second complex number
Enter the real part  :
1

Enter the imaginary part     :
1
1          :Sum
2          :Product
3          :Difference
4          :Exit

Enter your choice
3
-1 + i5
```

Fourth run

```
Enter the first complex number
Enter the real part  :
2

Enter the imaginary part     :
3
2 + i3

Enter the second complex number
Enter the real part  :
1

Enter the imaginary part     :
1
1          :Sum
2          :Product
3          :Difference
4          :Exit

Enter your choice
8
Wrong choice
```

10.12 ENUMERATIONS

While developing software applications, there might be situations wherein we need to create a variable that takes value from a set of predefined values. In such situations, enumerations are used. The concept of an enum (or enumeration) is the same as that of a drop-down list in a web page wherein we can select from amongst the values present in the list (Fig. 10.4).

An enumeration is declared using the enum keyword. It consists of a set of named constants. Every enumeration element has a type, which can be any integral type. The default type of the enumeration elements is int. The first enumerator has the value zero, and the value of every succeeding enumerator is increased by one.

The syntax for an enumeration is shown in Fig. 10.5.

```
enum <name of the enumeration>
{
<constant value>, <constant value>, … <constant value>
}
```

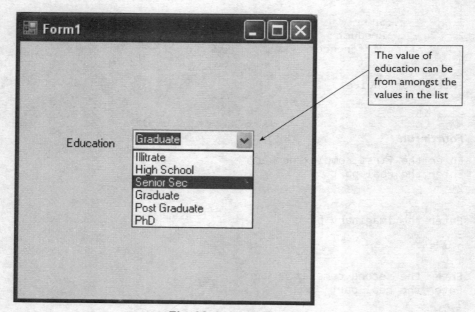

Fig. 10.4 List in a form

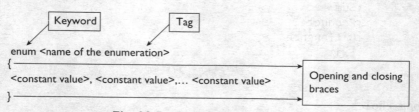

Fig. 10.5 Syntax for enumeration

For example, an enumeration months is defined as follows:

```
enum months
{
January, February, March, April, May, June, July, August, September, October, November, December
}
```

The following example shows the use of an enum and its conversion to int type and vice versa.

```
using System;
using System.Collections.Generic;
using System.Linq;
using System.Text;
namespace EnumDemo
{
    class Program
    {
        enum department
        {
            ComputerScience, Electronics, Electrical, Mech, Others
        }
        static void Main(string[] args)
        {
            department d;
            d = department.ComputerScience;
            Console.WriteLine(d);
            //Casting an enum to int
            int x = (int) d;
            Console.WriteLine(x);
            //Casting an int to enum
            int y = 3;
            d = (department)y;
            Console.WriteLine(d);
            Console.ReadKey();
        }
    }
}
```

Output

```
ComputerScience
0
Mech
```

We can change the type of enumeration by specifying the data type after a colon.

```
enum department:long
{
    ComputerScience = 67671, Electronics, Electrical, Mech, Others
}
static void Main(string[] args)
{
    department d;
    d = department.ComputerScience;
    Console.WriteLine(d);
    //Casting an enum to int
    int x = (int) d;
```

```
            Console.WriteLine(x);
            //Casting an int to enum
            int y = 67673;
            d = (department)y;
            Console.WriteLine(d);
            Console.ReadKey();
        }
```

Output

```
ComputerScience
67671
Electrical
```

SUMMARY

C# has provided us with many basic data types. However, there might be situations where the programmer needs custom data types. Structures help us to create our own data types, as per the need of the software. This helps us to achieve optimality and efficiency. This chapter examines the basics of structures and explains their crafting, use, and applications. Chapter 11 introduces the concept of classes, which are the starting point of object-oriented programming. So, from the next chapter onwards we will be studying an altogether new programming paradigm.

GLOSSARY

Structure It is a collection of variables. The data type of these variables can be either primary or user defined.
Array of structures An array whose elements are instances of a structure is referred to as an array of structures.
Enumeration An enumeration is a set of elements that may or may not have a data type, as against C++ in which it never has a data type.

POINTS TO REMEMBER

- A structure may contain variables with different data types but an array always has the same type of elements.
- A structure as such is only a blueprint; therefore, when we define a structure no memory is allocated to it.
- A structure inside another structure is referred to as a nested structure.
- A structure should have data members and it may have methods as well.
- Classes are reference types, whereas structures are value types.
- An enumeration consists of a set of named constants.

EXERCISES

I. Debugging Exercise

What is the error in the following, if any?

1.
```
struct ABC
{
    int x;
}
static void Main(string[] args)
{
    ABC a;
    a.x = 5;
```

```
        Console.WriteLine("Value\t:"    +
a.x);
    }
```

2. ```
struct ABC
   {
        internal int x;
   }
   static void Main(string[] args)
   {
        ABC a;
        a.x = 5;
        Console.WriteLine("Value\t:" +
a.x);
   }
```

3. ```
struct Chor
   {
        public string name;
        public int age;
        public float earning;
   }
   static void Main(string[] args)
   {
        Chor c;
        c.name = "Harsh";
        c.age = 29;
        Console.WriteLine("Name\t:"    +
                         c.name    +    "\
                         nAge\t:" + c.age
                         + "\nEarning\t:"
                         + c.earning);
   }
```

4. ```
struct Chor
   {
        public string name;
        public int age;
        public float earning;
   }
   static void Main(string[] args)
   {
        Chor c = {"Harsh", 29, 999999};
        Console.WriteLine("Name\t:"   +
                         c.name   +   "\
                         nAge\t:" + c.age
                         + "\nEarning\t:"
                         + c.earning);
   }
```

5. ```
struct Chor
   {
        public string name;
        public int age;
        public float earning;
   }
   static void Main(string[] args)
   {
        Chor c = new Chor {"Harsh", 29,
999999};
        Console.WriteLine("Name\t:"    +
                         c.name    +    "\
                         nAge\t:" + c.age
                         + "\nEarning\t:"
                         + c.earning);
   }
```

6. ```
struct Chor
   {
        public string name;
        public int age;
        public float earning;
   }
   static void Main(string[] args)
   {
        Chor c;
        c.name = "Harsh";
        c.age = 29;
        c.earning = 999999;
        Chor c1;
        c1 = c;
        Console.WriteLine("Name\t:"   +
                         c1.name   +   "\
                         nAge\t:" + c1.age
                         + "\nEarning\t:"
                         + c1.earning);
   }
```

7. ```
struct Chor
   {
        public string name;
        public int age;
        public float earning;
   }
   public void compare(Chor c1, Chor c2)
   {
        if(c1 == c2)
        {
             Console.WriteLine("Equal");
        }
        else
        {
             Console.WriteLine("\nNot
equal");
        }
   }
```

```csharp
        static void Main(string[] args)
        {
            Chor c;
            c.name = "Harsh";
            c.age = 29;
            c.earning = 999999;
            Chor c1;
            c1 = c;
            compare(c1, c);
            Console.WriteLine("Name\t:"   +
                              c1.name  +  "\
                              nAge\t:" + c1.age
                              + "\nEarning\t:"
                              + c1.earning);
        }

8.  struct Chor
    {
        public string name;
        public int age;
        public float earning;
    }
    static void Main(string[] args)
    {
        Chor* c1 ;
    }

9.  struct ABC
    {
        int a1;
    }
    struct XYZ
    {
        ABC a;
        public int x1;
    }
    static void Main(string[] args)
    {
        XYZ x = new XYZ();
        x.x1 = 5;
        x.a.a1 = x.x1;
    }

10. struct ABC
    {
        public int a1;
    }
    struct XYZ
    {
        ABC a;
        public int x1;
    }
    static void Main(string[] args)
    {
        XYZ x = new XYZ();
        x.x1 = 5;
        x.a.a1 = x.x1;
    }
```

II. Review Questions

1. When is memory allocated to a structure?
2. Which type of data type is a structure?
3. What is the difference between the structures in C++ and those in C#?
4. Compare structures and classes.
5. What is a nested structure?
6. Which operator helps us to access a data member of a structure?
7. What is the difference between a structure and an enumeration?
8. Explain the need for properties with respect to structures.
9. Can two identifiers in an enumeration have the same value?
10. Can the members of an enumeration be instances of a structure?

III. Programming Exercises

1. A company 'Computergrad.com' intends to computerize the management of employees. You are in the development team of the project. After studying the requirements of the company, the designers decide the following points.

A structure 'Employee' is to be created having the following members:

Variable	Data Type
Name	String
DateOfBirth	Struct Date1
DateOfJoining	Struct Date1
Salary	Double
Phone number	String
Department	Enumeration dept

Here, Date1 is another structure having dd, mm, and yy as its members. While designing the structure Date1, the following points must be noted:
(a) yy can be between 2011 and 2018 (both including).
(b) mm can be between 1 and 12.
(c) dd should depend on mm; for example if mm 2 and year 2012 then dd should be between 1 and 29.

Department is an enumeration having the following values:

Department
ComputerScience
Electronics
Mathematics
Physics
Chemistry
CognitiveSciences

The integer value of ComputerScience should be 10, that of Electronics should be 20, and so on.

It is also required to have the following methods inside the structure:

Method	Function
getdata()	Takes input from the user
putdata()	Displays the value
compare(Employee e)	Compares the salary of employee with that of e

Write a program to accomplish these tasks.

2. In the complex number example (Section 10.11), add the following functionalities:
   (a) A method called mod(), which calculates the modulus of the complex number. If a complex number is $z = x + iy$, then its mod is given by $\sqrt{x^2 + y^2}$.
   (b) A method called argument(), which calculates the argument of the complex number. The argument of a complex number is given by $\tan^{-1}\frac{x}{y}$.
   (c) A method called divide(complex z), which divides the complex number by z. If two complex numbers are $z1 = x1 + iy1$ and $z2 = x2 + iy2$, then $z1/z2 = \frac{x1+iy1}{x2+iy2} = \frac{(x1x2+y1y2)+i(x2y1-y1x2)}{x1^2+y1^2}$.
   (d) A method called compare(complex z), which compares the two complex numbers. Two complex numbers are equal if their real parts are equal and their imaginary parts are equal.

3. In Cartesian coordinate system, a point is depicted as (x, y), where x is the x-coordinate and y is the y-coordinate. Make a structure called point having x and y as its data members. In the Main function make two instances of point. Ask the user to enter two points and perform the following tasks:
   (a) Check whether any of the points lies on the x-axis.
   (b) Check whether any of the points lies on the y-axis.
   (c) Find the distance between the two points.
   (d) Find the midpoint of the line joining the two points.
   (e) Ask the user to enter m and n and find the point that divides the segment in the ratio of m:n.

4. A library needs to store the information of books. The following attributes are desired.

Book
Name of the book
Name(s) of author(s)
Name of the publisher
Price
Edition
Topic

Make a structure called book, which stores the given information. Now your program should display the following menu.
1. Add book
2. Search book
3. Delete book
4. Exit

On pressing 1, 3, or 4, the requisite tasks should be accomplished. When the user presses 2, the following menu should be displayed:

1. Author
2. Publisher
3. Topic
4. Back to the main menu

In this submenu, if the user enters 1 then your program should ask the user to enter author name and display all the books of that author. The same task is to be accomplished for the next two choices as well.

PART TWO
Object Oriented Programming

CHAPTER 11
Classes and Objects

CHAPTER 12
Inheritance

CHAPTER 13
Interfaces

CHAPTER 14
Operator Overloading

CHAPTER 15
Errors and Exceptions

CHAPTER 16
Generics

CHAPTER 17
Threads

> "The phrase "object-oriented" means a lot of things. Half are obvious, and the other half are mistakes."
>
> *Paul Graham*

11 Classes and Objects

OBJECTIVES

After completing this chapter, the reader will be able to
* Declare and use a class in C#
* Understand the concept of objects
* Declare and define methods in a class
* Draw a class diagram
* Create an array of objects
* Pass an object in a function
* Expound the types of constructors
* Appreciate the concept of private constructors
* Understand destructors
* Define and implement static members
* Use constant members
* Understand object-oriented terminology
* Define inheritance and elucidate its types
* Differentiate between inheritance and aggregation
* Explain specialization and generalization
* Use `Properties`
* Appreciate the concept of indexers

11.1 INTRODUCTION

This chapter provides an introduction to some of the very basic concepts of object-oriented programming. The importance of the concepts studied here can be gauged by the fact that object-oriented programming is used in almost every field—from operating system design to databases. This programming paradigm is used even in the set-top box that we connect to our TV sets. In fact, when Java, the language from which C# is 'inspired', was conceptualized, it was supposed to be a language for devices such as set-top boxes and coffee machines.

The chapter introduces the concept of a class. A class can be said to be a group of things that are considered to be at the same conceptual level. So, a class can be described as a set of things

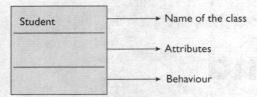

Fig. 11.1 Entity Student

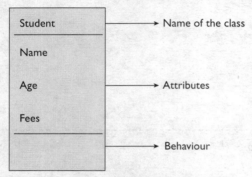

Fig. 11.2 Entity Student with attributes

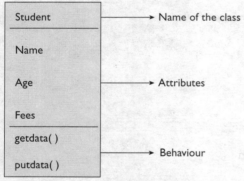

Fig. 11.3 Entity Student with attributes and behaviour

that share some common features. Some books define a class as a set of objects, which cannot be considered as a very thoughtful definition. It will be clear as we proceed that an object is an instance of a class and therefore we cannot define a class in terms of an object.

The concept of class is vital in software development as well. If we have to develop a software application for a college, then instead of thinking about the data structures to be used or the code, we start with the most significant entity, a 'Student'. We begin the design by conceptualizing the entity student. The entity will have some attributes and some behaviour, both of which will become clear as the design proceeds. The 'Student' class is depicted in Fig. 11.1. It may be noted that there is space for the attributes and behaviour as well. This space will be filled as we proceed. Only the name of the class has been decided as yet (Fig. 11.1).

After deciding the name, we need to determine the attributes of the class. In our example, let us consider the name, age, and fees of a student to be attributes. These attributes are shown in the second box of Fig. 11.2.

The next step in designing the entity is to surmise the behaviour of the entity, implemented as functions. In this case, the functions can be getdata() and putdata(). getdata() can be viewed as a function that takes input from the user and putdata() as a function that displays the attributes of the class (Fig. 11.3).

Now that the entity has been designed, we must write the code of the methods getdata() and putdata() and decide the access levels of the attributes. However, this can be done only if we know how to define a class in C#. Section 11.2 deals with the above task. Figures 11.1–11.3 are called class diagrams and will be dealt with in Section 11.2.

11.2 DEFINITION AND DESIGN OF A CLASS: ADDING VARIABLES AND METHODS

The concept of a class has been explained in Section 11.1. A class is a real or virtual entity having sharp boundaries and importance to the problem at hand.

11.2.1 Syntax

Classes are declared using the keyword class as follows:

```
class <name of the class>
{
// Methods, properties, fields, events, delegates
// and nested classes
}
```

The keyword `class` is followed by the name of the class. The opening and closing braces contain the definition of the class. The most important constituents of the definition are data members and member functions. The data members are generally implemented as variables and the member functions as methods.

As described earlier, class is the entity around which a problem gyrates. It has importance to the problem at hand. It consists of both the data and the functions that operate on that data. The data part is the same as the attributes described earlier. While implementing a class in C#, we need to think about the data type of the attributes as well. For example, name can be a string, age can be an integer, and fees can be a float. To explain this point, let us implement the class 'student'.

```
class student
{
    //Data members
    //Member functions
}
```

To understand this concept, we must take into account the fact that in a college there is no person called student but everyone is an instance of student. Therefore, student is not a real entity. Moreover, when obtaining the details of a student, the college asks only the relevant details and not the irrelevant ones. For example, a college does not ask for the number of cars a student has. This reinforces the point that a class has importance to the problem at hand and also has sharp boundaries. A class is depicted by what we call a class diagram. A class diagram has three parts. The first part is the name of the class, the second has the attributes, and the third has the functions of that class. Thus, a class has both data and the functions that operate on that data. This clubbing together of the data and the methods that operate on the data is called encapsulation.

Figure 11.4 represents a class called `student`. The attributes of the class are Name and Age and the behaviour of the class is implemented via the functions `getdata()` and `putdata()`. Hence, as mentioned earlier, a class may contain data as well as the functions that operate on that data and is depicted by a class diagram. The instance of a class is called an object. Thus, a class forms the basis of the object-oriented technology. As discussed earlier, defining a class as a group of objects is not very correct as an object itself is defined in terms of a class.

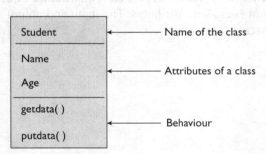

Fig. 11.4 Class Student

11.2.2 Instantiation

In Fig. 11.5, s1 and s2 are the instances of the class `Student`. In the `Main` function, creation of s1 and s2 requires the following code:

```
Student s1 = new Student();
Student s2 = new Student();
```

These statements ask the compiler to create two instances s1 and s2 of the class `Student`. In Problem 11.1, we will see how to give values to the respective variables of the class.

238 Programming in C#

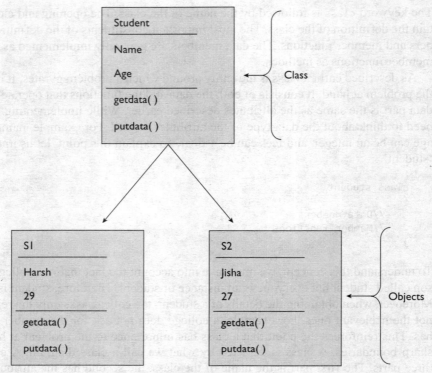

Fig. 11.5 Making objects from a class

Problem 11.1

Write a program that asks the user to enter the details of a student s1, which is an instance of a class Student. The Student class has name, age, and fees as its attributes. The input and output should be done via functions getdata() and putdata(), respectively.

Solution
```
using System;
using System.Collections.Generic;
using System.Linq;
using System.Text;
namespace ClassDemo1
{
    class Program
    {
        class Student
        {
            int age;
            string name;
            double fees;
            public void getdata()
            {
                try
                {
                    Console.WriteLine("Enter name\t:");
                    name = Console.ReadLine();
                    Console.WriteLine("Enter age\t:");
```

```csharp
            age = Int16.Parse(Console.ReadLine());
            Console.WriteLine("Enter fees\t:");
            fees = Double.Parse(Console.ReadLine());
        }
        catch(Exception e1)
        {
            Console.WriteLine("Error\t:" + e1.ToString());
        }
    }
    public void putdata()
    {
        Console.WriteLine("The data of the student are as follows");
        Console.WriteLine("\nName\t:" + name);
        Console.WriteLine("\nAge\t:" + age.ToString());
        Console.WriteLine("\nFees\t:" + fees.ToString());
    }
}
static void Main(string[] args)
{
    Student s1 = new Student();
    s1.getdata();
    s1.putdata();
    Console.ReadKey();
}
    }
}
```

Output

```
Enter name :
Harsh
Enter age :
29
Enter fees :
30000

The data of the student are as follows
Name    : Harsh
Age     : 29
Fees    : 30000
```

This listing creates a class called Student having data members name, age, and fees. The class has two functions, getdata() and putdata(). getdata() takes data from the user and putdata() displays that data. If two objects were to be made instead of one, then the following changes will have to be incorporated in this listing:

```csharp
using System;
using System.Collections.Generic;
using System.Linq;
using System.Text;
namespace ClassDemo2
```

```csharp
{
    class Program
    {
        class Student
        {
            int age;
            string name;
            double fees;
            public void getdata()
            {
                try
                {
                    Console.WriteLine("Enter name\t:");
                    name = Console.ReadLine();
                    Console.WriteLine("Enter age\t:");
                    age = Int16.Parse(Console.ReadLine());
                    Console.WriteLine("Enter fees\t:");
                    fees = Double.Parse(Console.ReadLine());
                }
                catch(Exception e1)
                {
                    Console.WriteLine("Error\t:" + e1.ToString());
                }
            }
            public void putdata()
            {
                Console.WriteLine("The data of the student are as follows");
                Console.WriteLine("\nName\t:" + name);
                Console.WriteLine("\nAge\t:" + age.ToString());
                Console.WriteLine("\nFees\t:" + fees.ToString());
            }
        }
        static void Main(string[] args)
        {
            Student s1 = new Student();
            Student s2 = new Student();      // Instantiation of the Student Class
            s1.getdata();
            s1.putdata();

            s2.getdata();                    // Calling functions of the student class
            s2.putdata();
            Console.ReadKey();

        }
    }
}
```

Output

```
Enter name :
Harsh
Enter age  :
29
Enter fees :
```

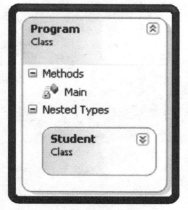

Fig. 11.6 Class diagram in Visual Studio

```
3002
The data of the student are as follows:
Name    : Harsh
Age     : 29
Fees    : 3002
Enter name :
Jisha
Enter age :
29
Enter fees :
2003
The data of the student are as follows:
Name    : Jisha
Age     : 29
Fees    : 2003
```

This listing can be depicted with the help of class diagram in Fig. 11.6.

The details of the Student class are depicted in the expanded class diagram shown in Fig. 11.7.

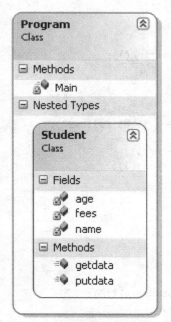

Fig. 11.7 Detailed class diagram

11.3 ARRAY OF OBJECTS

In Chapter 9, it was stated that it is possible to make an array of objects as well. The array of objects contains objects as its basic units. These arrays follow zero-based indexing, that is, the first element will have index zero. For example, in the following declaration, the names of the various elements in the array will be stu[0], stu[1], stu[2], stu[3], and stu[4] (Fig. 11.8).

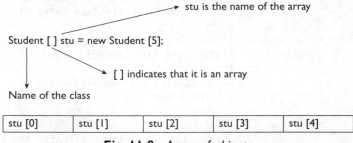

Fig. 11.8 Array of objects

Arrays of objects can be used for creating many software systems. However, in order to do that, it is essential that we learn the basic input–output first. Problem 11.2 demonstrates the concept.

Problem 11.2

Write a program to create an array of the Student class described in Problem 11.1. Ask the user to enter the number of students, say *n*. Enter the details of the *n* students and display them.

Solution

```csharp
using System;
using System.Collections.Generic;
using System.Linq;
using System.Text;
namespace ClassDemo3
{
    class Program
    {
        class Student
        {
            int age;
            string name;
            double fees;
            public void getdata()
            {
                try
                {
                    Console.WriteLine("Enter name\t:");
                    name = Console.ReadLine();
                    Console.WriteLine("Enter age\t:");
                    age = Int16.Parse(Console.ReadLine());
                    Console.WriteLine("Enter fees\t:");
                    fees = Double.Parse(Console.ReadLine());
                }
                catch(Exception e1)
                {
                    Console.WriteLine("Error\t:" + e1.ToString());
                }
            }
            public void putdata()
            {
                Console.WriteLine("The data of the student is as follows");
                Console.WriteLine("\nName\t:" + name);
                Console.WriteLine("\nAge\t:" + age.ToString());
                Console.WriteLine("\nFees\t:" + fees.ToString());
            }
        }
        static void Main(string[] args)
        {
            Student[] s = new Student[10];
            int number, i;
            try
            {
                Console.WriteLine("Enter the number of students\t:");
                number = Int16.Parse(Console.ReadLine());
                for(i = 0; i < number; i++)
                {
                    s[i] = new Student();
                    Console.WriteLine("Enter details");
                    s[i].getdata();
                }
                Console.WriteLine("The details of the students are as follows");
                for(i = 0; i < number; i++)
```

```
                    {
                        s[i].putdata();
                    }
                }
                catch(Exception e1)
                {
                    Console.WriteLine("Error\t:" + e1.ToString());
                }
            Console.ReadKey();
        }
    }
}
```

Output

```
Enter age      :
29
Enter fees     :
3002
Enter details
Enter Name     :
Jisha
Enter age      :
27
Enter fees     :
2003
Enter details
Enter Name     :
Nks
Enter age      :
23
Enter fees     :
2003
Enter details
Enter Name     :
Viru
Enter age      :
24
Enter fees     :
2003
Enter details
Enter Name     :
Sahil
Enter age      :
22
Enter fees     :
2003
The details of students are as follows
The data of the student is as follows
Name     :Harsh
```

```
Age        :29

Fees       :3002
The data of the student is as follows
Name       :Jisha
Age        :27

Fees       :2003
The data of the student is as follows
Name       :Nks
Age        :23

Fees       :2003
The data of the student is as follows
Name       :Viru
Age        :24

Fees       :2003
The data of the student is as follows
Name       :Sahil
Age        :22

Fees       :2003
```

The following listing is a modification of the first listing. The function getdata() is removed; it is left to the readers to guess the output.

```csharp
using System;
using System.Collections.Generic;
using System.Linq;
using System.Text;

namespace ClassDemo1
{
    class Program
    {
        class Student
        {
            int age;
            string name;
            double fees;
            public void putdata()

            {
                Console.WriteLine("The data of the student are as follows");
                Console.WriteLine("\nName\t:"+ name);
                Console.WriteLine("\nAge\t:"+ age.ToString());
                Console.WriteLine("\nFees\t:"+ fees.ToString());
            }
        }
        static void Main(string[] args)
        {
            Student s1 = new Student();
            s1.getdata();
```

```csharp
            s1.putdata();
            Console.ReadKey();
        }
    }
}
```

Output

```
The data of the student are as follows
Name  :
Age   : 0
Fees  : 0
```

Had the same program been in C++, the output would have been garbage values. The reason for not getting garbage values in this output is that the object was initialized by the default constructor of the class.

```
Student s1 = new Student();  ← Default constructor
```

Section 11.4 introduces and explains the concept of constructors.

11.4 CONSTRUCTORS

Constructors are the functions inside a class that initialize the members of the class. The name of a constructor is the same as that of its class. This section explains the types of constructors and their implementations.

11.4.1 Default Constructor

Default constructor is a constructor that has no arguments. It has no return type and has the same name as that of the class of which it is a constructor. Problem 11.3 shows the use of a default constructor in the Student class and the output. The difference in the output obtained when there was no constructor should be valued.

Problem 11.3

Write a program that makes use of a default constructor of the Student class (refer Problem 11.1).

Solution

```csharp
using System;
using System.Collections.Generic;
using System.Linq;
using System.Text;

namespace ClassDemo4
{
    class Program
    {
        class Student
        {
            int age;
            string name;
            double fees;
```

```csharp
            public Student()
            {
                name = "Harsh";
                age  = 29;
                fees = 3002;
            }
            public void putdata()
            {
                Console.WriteLine("The data of the student are as follows");
                Console.WriteLine("Name\t:"+ name);
                Console.WriteLine("Age\t:"+ age.ToString());
                Console.WriteLine("\nFees\t:"+ fees.ToString());
            }
        }
        static void Main(string[] args)
        {
            Student s1 = new Student();
            s1.putdata();
            Console.ReadKey();
        }
    }
}
```

Output

```
Name   : Harsh
Age    : 29
Fees   : 3002
```

11.4.2 Parameterized Constructor

Parameterized constructor is a constructor that has arguments. It has no return type and has the same name as that of the class of which it is a constructor. Problem 11.4 shows the use of a parameterized constructor in the Student class and the output. The instantiation of the parameterized constructor should be noted.

Problem 11.4

Write a program that makes use of a parameterized constructor of the Student class (refer Problem 11.1).

Solution

```csharp
using System;
using System.Collections.Generic;
using System.Linq;
using System.Text;

namespace ClassDemo5
{
    class Program
    {
```

```
class Student
{
    int age;
    string name;
    double fees;
    public Student(string s, int a, double f)
    {
        name = s;
        age = a;
        fees = f;
    }
    public void putdata()
    {
        Console.WriteLine("The data of the student are as follows");
        Console.WriteLine("\nName\t:" + name);
        Console.WriteLine("\nAge\t:" + age.ToString());
        Console.WriteLine("\nFees\t:" + fees.ToString());
    }
}
static void Main(string[] args)
{
    Student s1 = new Student("Jisha", 27, 3002.90);
    s1.putdata();
    Console.ReadKey();
}
}
}
```

Output

```
The data of the student are as follows:
Name    : Jisha
Age     : 27
Fees    : 3002.9
```

11.4.3 Copy Constructor

Copy constructor is a constructor that copies the attributes of an object to the object of which it is a constructor. It has no return type; it has the same name as that of the class of which it is a constructor. Problem 11.5 shows the use of a copy constructor in the Student class and the output. It should be noted that in order to call a copy constructor we must have an object that already has values. Therefore, Problem 11.5 has a parameterized constructor, which instantiates the first object, and a copy constructor, which copies the values of the first object to the second object.

Problem 11.5

Write a program that makes use of a copy constructor of the Student class (refer Problem 11.1).

Solution

```
using System;
using System.Collections.Generic;
```

```csharp
using System.Linq;
using System.Text;

namespace ClassDemo6
{
    class Program
    {
        class Student
        {
            int age;
            string name;
            double fees;
            public Student(string x, int y, double z)
            {
                name = x;
                age = y;
                fees = z;
            }
            public Student(Student s)
            {
                name = s.name;
                age = s.age;
                fees = s.fees;
            }
            public void putdata()
            {
                Console.WriteLine("The data of the student are as follows");
                Console.WriteLine("\nName\t:" + name);
                Console.WriteLine("\nAge\t:" + age.ToString());
                Console.WriteLine("\nFees\t:" + fees.ToString());
            }
        }
        static void Main(string[] args)
        {
            Student s1 = new Student("Sahil", 22, 4001);
            Student s2 = new Student(s1);
            s2.putdata();
            Console.ReadKey();
        }
    }
}
```

Output

```
The data of the student are as follows:
Name    : Sahil
Age     : 22
Fees    : 4001
```

11.4.4 Constructor Overloading

Constructor overloading refers to having more than one constructor in a class. Problem 11.6 shows the use of constructor overloading by taking an example of a class called `Employee`. The first object is instantiated via default constructor, the second one using a parameterized constructor, and the third one using a copy constructor.

Problem 11.6

Write a program to create a class called `Employee` having the details given in Fig. 11.9.

The class `Employee` should have more than one constructor; there should be at least one parameterized and one default constructor.

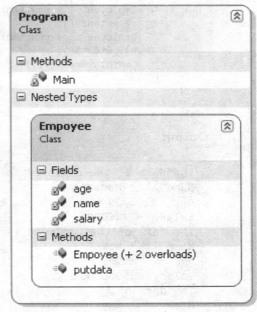

Fig. 11.9 Employee class

Solution

```
using System;
using System.Collections.Generic;
using System.Linq;
using System.Text;

namespace ClassDemo7
{
    class Program
    {
        class Employee
        {
            int age;
            string name;
            double salary;
            public Employee()//default constr
            {
                name = "Harsh";
                age = 29;
                salary = 480002.00;
            }
            public Employee(string x, int y, double z)//param constr
            {
                name = x;
                age = y;
                salary = z;
            }
            public Employee(Employee e)//copy constr
            {
                name = e.name;
                age = e.age;
                salary = e.salary;
            }

            public void putdata()
            {
                Console.WriteLine("The data of the employee is as follows");
                Console.WriteLine("Name\t:" + name);
```

```csharp
            Console.WriteLine("Age\t:" + age.ToString());
            Console.WriteLine("Salary\t:" + salary.ToString());
        }
    }
    static void Main(string[] args)
    {
        Employee e1 = new Employee();
        e1.putdata();
        Employee e2 = new Employee("Naks", 22, 360000.00);
        e2.putdata();
        Employee e3 = new Employee(e2);
        e3.putdata();
        Console.ReadKey();
    }
}
```

Output

```
The data of the employee is as follows
Name    : Harsh
Age     : 29
Salary  : 480002
The data of the employee is as follows
Name    : Naks
Age     : 22
Salary  : 360000
The data of the employee is as follows
Name    : Naks
Age     : 22
Salary  : 360000
```

11.4.5 Private Constructor

If the constructor of a class is private, then it will not be possible to create an object of that class. Hence, there is seldom a reason to create a private constructor. Compiling the following listing will make the concept clear to readers:

```csharp
class A
{
    private A()
    {
    }
}
class Program
{
    static void Main(string[] args)
    {
        A a1 = new A();
    }
}
```

On compilation, the following message appears.

```
Error   1   'ClassDemo8.A.A()' is inaccessible due to its protection level   D :
            Learning C#\Classes\ClassDemo8\Program.cs  19  20  ClassDemo8
```

This reiterates the point that if there is a private constructor in a class, then we will not be able to instantiate and hence use it:

11.4.6 Destructor

A destructor is the opposite of a constructor. It has the same name as that of its class but is preceded by a '~'. It has no arguments and no return type. Destructors are generally used for debugging purposes. Readers will be able to understand this better as we proceed further. The following code shows an example of a destructor:

```
~Student()
{
    //Print statements
}
```

C# calls a destructor when an object completes its life cycle. This process is called *finalization*.

11.5 this REFERENCE

Consider a situation wherein we are passing a variable in a function. The variable has the same name as one of the members of the class. For example, if in the earlier example of Student class, had there been a function called setdata() with name, age, and fees as its arguments, there would have been a problem in compiling the program. Such problems are handled by the this reference. this refers to the members of the class. The following snippet will make the concept clear:

```
setdata(string name, int age, double fees)
{
    this.name = name;
    this.age = age;
    this.fees = fees;
}
```

The function inserts the values of parameters in the members of the class.

11.6 STATIC MEMBERS

Static members are those members for which only one copy is created. If we have a static method, then it can use only those members that are static. Moreover, they are called by the name of the class and not by the object of the class. The following example demonstrates the use of a static function. The program has an interesting feature. When the program is run, it can be observed that the name of the car is not displayed. It is left to the readers to figure out the reason.

```
using System;
using System.Collections.Generic;
using System.Linq;
using System.Text;

namespace ClassDemo9
{
```

```
class car
{
    static string name;
    public car()
    {
        name = "Esteem";
    }
    public static void display()
    {
        Console.WriteLine("The car is" + name);
    }
}
class Program
{
    static void Main(string[] args)
    {
        car.display();
        Console.ReadKey();
    }
}
```

11.7 CONSTANT MEMBERS

The `const` keyword is used to adapt an avowal of a local variable. It spells out that the value of the local variable cannot be bespoken. The following code demonstrates the declaration:

```
public const int age = 29;
```

In the `Main` function, constant members are used in the same way as other variables.

11.8 PASSING OBJECTS TO A FUNCTION

An object is passed in the same way as a basic data type. However, care must be taken to ensure that the objects are initialized before passing them to a function. The following listing passes the object of the class ABC to a method method1(). It should be noted that method1() is deliberately declared as static, so that there is just one copy of method1() in the Program class and the function can be called without making an instance of Program.

```
namespace Passing Objetcs
{
    public class ABC
    {
        public void xyz()
        {
            Console.WriteLine("Hi");
        }
    }
    class Program
    {
        static void Main(string[] args)
        {
            ABC A1 = new ABC();
            Program.method1(A1);
```

```
            Console.ReadKey();
        }
        static public void method1(ABC A)
        {
            A.xyz();
        }
    }
}
```

Output

Hi

The process is depicted in Fig. 11.10.

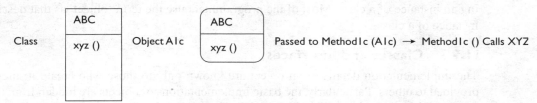

Fig. 11.10 Calling of a method

Now that we have seen the implementation part of classes and objects, let us revisit the concepts of an object-oriented programming system. Sections 11.9–11.13 concentrate more on concepts and less on coding. In order to understand C#, it is necessary to understand these concepts.

11.9 BASICS OF OBJECT-ORIENTED PROGRAMMING

Object-oriented technology is vast and extensive. It is used in many software applications and even in operating systems. The object-oriented concept is applied in almost all services such as banking, telecommunication, and software applications for appliances. An example is that of Java, which can be considered as the inspiration for C#. We can appreciate the importance of object-oriented programming in appliances by the fact that Gosling developed Java for his set-top box.

Object-oriented technology includes the following:
1. Object-oriented programming languages such as C# and Java.
2. Object-oriented development methodologies such as Booch, Rambugh, IBM, Martin and Odell, Shlaer and Mellor, and Wirfs-Brock.
3. Object-oriented computer hardware.

It is therefore important to understand the object-oriented terminology. Many of the terms commonly used in object-oriented technology have already been described in the chapter. However, it should be kept in mind that there is no one ultimate set of definitions for object-oriented terms and concepts.

11.9.1 Objects

Objects are the physical and conceptual things we find around us. They are the basic runtime entities in an object-oriented system. In a company, we can view employees and departments as objects. The state of an object is the stipulation of the object. We confine the possible states of the objects to only those that are appropriate to our models and hence implement the goal of containing a class within boundaries. Objects are static. That is, the state of an object will not change unless something outside the object requests the object to change its state.

11.9.2 Classes and Metaclasses

There are many views on the definition for a 'class'. One description of a class is that it contains the information needed to make instances. Some other definitions of a class are as follows:

1. A class is a set of all items created using a specific pattern. Therefore, the set of all instances of that pattern is termed as a class.
2. A class is a real or conceptual entity having importance to the problem at hand and having sharp boundaries.

It should be noted that it is possible for an instance of a class to be a class as well. For example, metaclass is a class whose instances themselves are classes. Instantiation is the process of creating an instance of a class. Most of the programmers use the term 'object' as that describing an instance of a class.

11.9.3 Classes and Interfaces

The implementation details of an object are known only to those who create it; they are not provided to others. Particularly, the basic implementations of objects are hidden from those that use the object; only the producer of an object knows the details about the internal construction of that object. The consumers of an object must, therefore, deal with an object via one of the following interfaces:

1. The *'public' interface:* This interface is open to everybody.
2. The *'parameter' interface:* This is used in the case of a parameterized class. The parameter interface characterizes the parameters that have to be supplied to create an instance of the class.

11.9.4 Aggregation

Aggregation is the process of creating a new object from two or more objects, as it is possible for objects to be composed of other objects. For example, a computer object contains the following objects—CPU, motherboard, and memory (Fig. 11.11).

The objects that include a composite object are referred to as component objects. Composite objects are those that have a definite structure. The structure can be tackled by means of a public interface.

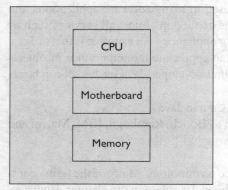

Fig. 11.11 Computer composed of CPU and memory

11.9.5 Specialization and Inheritance

Specialization is the process of defining a new object based on a more narrow definition of an existing object. For example, car is a specialization of vehicle and network security expert is a specialization of computer expert. Specializations can be considered as 'subclasses' and generalizations of the specializations can be considered as a 'superclasses'.

Inheritance can be defined as the process whereby one object obtains characteristics from one or more other objects. Many object-oriented systems allow for multiple inheritances in

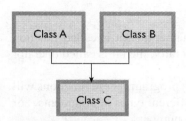

Fig. 11.12 Multiple inheritance—allowed in C++ but not in C#

which a class may obtain characteristics from two or more corresponding classes (Fig. 11.12). Languages such as C# and Java, however, do not allow multiple inheritance. Chapter 12 deals with the concept of inheritance. This section, however, provides an introduction to the concept.

Inheritance is allowed in C#, but a class can inherit implementation from only one base class. However, a class can implement more interfaces.

Types of Inheritances

A class can be derived from a class; this is called single inheritance. A derived class can also derive a class; this is called multilevel inheritance. A class can derive two classes, which is hierarchical inheritance. C# does not allow multiple inheritance. Figures 11.13–11.16 show examples of class inheritance and interface implementation. These types are discussed in detail in Chapter 12.

11.9.6 Polymorphism

Polymorphism is the ability to take more than one form. It is a Greek term, which might refer to a function or an operator. Polymorphism is of two types:
1. Compile time polymorphism
2. Runtime polymorphism

Suppose we have a function do() in the base class 'Base'. We make a derived class of Base; let us call it 'Derived'. In the Derived class, we again define a do() function with extended functionality. This function is expected to do whatever it was doing in the Base class as well as some new tasks. This concept is called overriding. This concept along with what we call a virtual function has been discussed in a Chapter 12. Function overloading and operator overloading are generally included in compile time polymorphism. These concepts are explained in Section 11.9.7.

Fig. 11.13 A simple class—no Inheritance

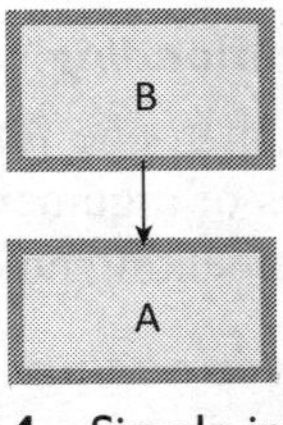

Fig. 11.14 Simple inheritance

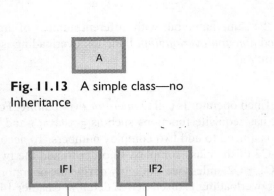

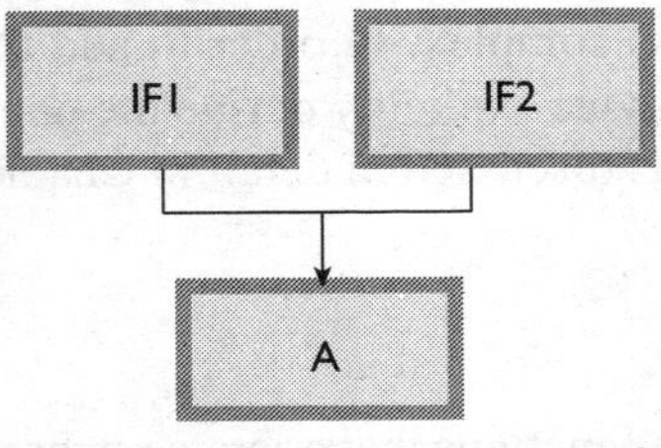

Fig. 11.15 Class A inherited from IF1 and IF2 (interfaces)

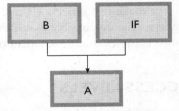

Fig. 11.16 Class A inherited from class B and interface IF

11.9.7 Overloading

If a program contains more than one function with the same name, then it is called function overloading. If we give a new meaning to an already defined operator, then it is called operator overloading.

There may be more than one function with the same name in a program. These functions will have different forms, as in different numbers of arguments or different types of arguments. For example, a sum() function might take two arguments to add two numbers.

```
public int sum(int x, int y)
{
    int s = 0;
    s = x + y;
    return s;
}
```

The function takes two aruguments x and y, both of which are integers. There is a local variable s inside the function, which is used to store the sum of the two numbers. The function returns s. In the same program, we may have another function having the same name but a different number of arguments.

```
public int sum(int x, int y, int z)
{
    int s;
    s = x + y + z;
    return s;
}
```

The function takes three aruguments x, y, and z, all of which are integers. There is a local variable s inside the function, which is used to store the sum of the three numbers. The function returns s. The first function calculates the sum of two numbers, whereas the second calculates the sum of three numbers. Hence, function overloading and operator overloading can be defined as follows:

Function Overloading

Having more than one function of the same name but with different number of arguments or different types of arguments is called *function overloading*. Function overloading is one of the ways of implementing polymorphism.

Operator Overloading

Giving a new name to an already defined operator is called *operator overloading*. For instance, consider a class called complex. It has requisite functions such as getdata() and putdata(). Suppose a situation in which there is a need to add two complex numbers. To accomplish the task, we make two objects C1 and C2 of the class complex. In order to add the two complex numbers, it is not possible to write C1 + C2, unless we explicitly define the operator + for adding two complex numbers. Operator overloading is discussed in detail in Chapter 14.

11.10 ACCESS LEVELS

Encapsulation is clubbing together the data and the functions that operate on that data. In a class, we specify both the attributes and the methods, which is encapsulation. Many languages support the concept of information hiding by means of access specifiers, which control access to class members. Their main intention is to separate the interface of a class from its implementation.

The following is a common set of access specifiers supported by many object-oriented languages:

1. *Private*: It confines the access to only within the class. Private members can be accessed by only those methods that are a part of the class. The intention is not to secure the data from intruders as perceived by many. The private specifier only helps in preventing erroneous change in the value of the variables by other programmers.
2. *Protected*: A protected member can be accessed by the methods of a class and its derived classes. The idea is to allow only the derived class, apart from the class itself, to be able to access the variables for well-intentioned changes. The point will become clear in Chapter 12.
3. *Public*: A public member can be accessed from anywhere in the program.

The difference between a private and a public data member can be better appreciated with help of the following program:

```
class ABC
{
    public int x;
    private int y;
}
class Program
{
    static void Main(string[] args)
    {
        ABC a1 = new ABC();
        a1.x = 5;
        Console.WriteLine("The value of x is " + a1.x.ToString());
        Console.ReadKey();
    }
}
```

Output

```
The value of x is 5
```

However, if we modify the code slightly and try to assign a value to the private variable, the program will not be compiled.

```
class ABC
{
    public int x;
    private int y;
}
class Program
{
    static void Main(string[] args)
    {
        ABC a1 = new ABC();
        a1.x = 5;
        Console.WriteLine("The value of x is " + a1.x.ToString());
```

```
            a1.y = 10;
            Console.WriteLine("The value of y is " + a1.y.ToString());
            Console.ReadKey();
        }
    }
```

In the error list window the following message is displayed, indicating that we cannot access a private variable outside a class.

```
Error   1   'Class_Acess_Prog.ABC.y' is inaccessible due to its protection level D:\
            Learning C#\Class Acess Prog\Program.cs    21  16  Class Acess Prog
Error   2   'Class_Acess_Prog.ABC.y' is inaccessible due to its protection level D:\
            Learning C#\Class Acess Prog\Program.cs    22  57  Class Acess Prog
```

C# has one more access specifier, namely internal. Internal members are accessible within the files of an assembly. At times, we need to have a variable that can be used in different files and still be confined to a particular section of our project. The internal specifier can be used in such situations. These variables can be customized by textual MSIL but not by C#. The summary of various access specifiers is provided in Table 11.1.

Some authors also call access specifiers as visibility controllers; this is not correct since even private members may be visible to the client code.

The policies of a language and other factors determine the access levels. Java does not allow client code to entrée the private data of a class to compile, whereas in languages such as Objective-C client code can do so. Access levels are also discussed in Chapter 12.

Table 11.1 Access specifiers

Can be accessed	Public	Internal	Protected	Private
Within class	Yes	Yes	Yes	Yes
In the derived class	Yes	Yes, provided it is in the same assembly	Yes	No
In the assembly	Yes	Yes	No, not in the classes that are not derived	No
Anywhere	Yes	No	No	No

11.11 COMPONENTS OF A CLASS

A class can include declarations of the following components:

1. Constructors
2. Destructors
3. Constants
4. Fields
5. Methods
6. Properties
7. Indexers
8. Operators
9. Events
10. Delegates
11. Classes
12. Interfaces
13. Structures

Some of these concepts have already been discussed in this chapter. Others have been dealt with in the following sections.

11.12 PROPERTIES

Properties are the mechanisms to read and write the values of objects. The data in a class should be private, but at times, it is required to access or change that private data. In such situations, the mutator and accessor methods come to our rescue. In addition, we can make use of the `get` and `set` properties as shown in the following snippet. In this snippet, the class `Student` has a property called `StudValue`. `get` returns the value of a private variable called `name`, whereas `set` sets the value of the name to `value`, which the user assigns.

```
namespace ClassProperties
{
    class Student
    {
        private String name;
        public String StudValue
        {
            get
            {
                return name;
            }
            set
            {
                name = value;
            }
        }
    }
    class Program
    {
        static void Main(string[] args)
        {
            Student s1 = new Student();
            s1.StudValue = "Harsh";
            Console.WriteLine("Name\t:" + s1.StudValue);
            Console.ReadKey();
        }
    }
}
```

Output

```
Name: Harsh
```

The task can also be accomplished using methods. The following example has a class called `Employee`, which has a private data member `name`. The `SetName(string s)` method is used to set the value of name and the `GetName()` method is used to read the value.

```
namespace PropertiesDemo
{
    class Employee
    {
        private string name;
        public void SetName(string s)
        {
```

```
                name = s;
            }
            public string GetName()
            {
                return name;
            }
    }
    class Program
    {
            static void Main(string[] args)
            {
                Employee e = new Employee();
                e.SetName("Harsh");
                string localVariable;
                localVariable = e.GetName();
                Console.WriteLine("The name is " + localVariable);
                Console.ReadKey();
            }
      }
}
```

Output

```
The name is Harsh.
```

The get() and set() methods help us to read and write the value of the variable name, while still keeping it private.

11.13 INDEXERS

An indexer is used to access the objects with the help of the index notation. It is written in the same way as a property. It is declared in the following way:

```
public type this [int index]
```

For example,

```
public string this [int index]
{
get
    {
    //Return the requisite data
    }
    set
    {
    //Put some value in the data member
    }
}
```

Moreover, it should be noted that indexers are the same as properties but take index as arguments just like an array. In addition, they are always declared using the keyword This.

SUMMARY

The chapter introduces the most important concept of object-oriented programming paradigm, namely classes. The concept of a class is important not just to understand the rest of the chapters in the book but also to develop a new perspective of programming. The idea of an object is the most important concept in modern software development. It may be stated at this point that if software engineering principles are to be implemented then the concept of a class must be thoroughly understood, both conceptually and in terms of development of programs. The knowledge of object-oriented programming is necessary even in the testing field. The ability to write programs is essential to test whether a program is being executed correctly or not.

The chapter introduces the concept of object-oriented paradigm and classes as well as explains the importance and implementation of constructors. This is the basic building block of the concepts discussed in the rest of the book.

GLOSSARY

Class It is a real or virtual entity having sharp boundaries and importance to the problem at hand.

Access specifiers The access specifiers govern the access of a member outside a class. C# offers four access specifiers—public, private, internal, and protected.

Object The instance of a class is called an object.

Constructor It is a function that initializes the data members of a class. It has same name as that of a class and has no return type.

Types of constructors The various types of constructors include default, parameterized, and copy constructors.

Constructor overloading Having more than one constructor in a class is called constructor overloading. The signatures of the various constructors must vary.

Destructor It frees the memory occupied by an object.

Specialization It is the process of defining a new object based on a more narrow definition of an existing object.

Aggregation It is the process of creating a new object from two or more other objects, as it is possible for objects to be composed of other objects.

Inheritance It can be defined as the process whereby one object obtains characteristics from one or more other objects.

Encapsulation It is the clubbing together of the data and the functions that operate on that data.

Polymorphism It is the ability to take more than one form. Operator overloading, functional overloading are the examples of polymorphism.

Function overloading Having more than one function of the same name but with different number of arguments or different types of arguments is called function overloading.

Properties These are the mechanisms to read and write the values of private members.

Indexers It is used to access the objects with the help of index notation.

POINTS TO REMEMBER

- In C++, class is defined in the following way:
  Class <class name>
  {
  //Data members
  //Member functions
  };
  However, in C#, a semicolon is not placed after the definition of a class.
- In C++ we instantiate a class as
  Student s1;
  and call the methods of Student as
  s1.getdata( );
  In C#, if the method is invoked as follows:
  Student s1;
  s1.getdata();
  an error will be displayed in the error window. The reason is C# does not allow the use of an object

without initiation. Therefore, the code should be written as follows:
```
Student s1 = new Student( );
s1.getdata( );
```
- C++ allows multiple inheritance, whereas C# does not allow it.
- C++ has three access specifiers, whereas C# has four.
- Visual Studio has the facility of depiction of classes via class diagrams.
- Indexers are not the same as properties. They always use the keyword This and take index as a parameter just like arrays.

EXERCISES

I. Multiple-choice Questions

1. Which of the following are object-oriented languages?
   (a) C#   (b) Java
   (c) Small Talk (d) All of these

2. Which of the following is a functional language?
   (a) C# (b) F#
   (c) J# (d) None of these

3. Which of the following is an access specifier?
   (a) Public   (b) Private
   (c) Protected (d) All of these

4. Which type of constructor hinders the instantiation of a class?
   (a) Public   (b) Private
   (c) Protected (d) None of these

5. What will be the result of the following code?
   Student s;
   (a) s is initialized to null.
   (b) We cannot use s, as of now, to call a function of Student.
   (c) Both (a) and (b)
   (d) Neither (a) nor (b)

6. Which type of constructor is not possible?
   (a) Public (b) Private
   (c) Static (d) All are possible

7. Consider the following code and choose the correct option.

   ```
   Class A
   {
       void A()
       {
           //
       }
   }
   ```
   (a) The code will result in a compile time error.
   (b) It will compile but will result in a runtime error.
   (c) The result depends on the rest of the class.
   (d) The result depends on how A is instantiated.

8. Which of the following is true with respect to a constructor?
   (a) There can be more than one constructor in a class.
   (b) A constructor cannot have a return type.
   (c) A constructor initializes the data members of a class.
   (d) All of these

9. Which of the following element in a class frees the memory of an object?
   (a) Constructor (b) Destructor
   (c) Interface   (d) Inline function

10. Which of the following element cannot be a part of a class?
    (a) Constructor (b) Destructor
    (c) Namespace   (d) Class

II. Review Questions

1. Differentiate between procedural and object-oriented programming.
2. Define a class. What are the components of a class?
3. What is a constructor? List the different types of constructors.
4. What is the purpose of making a destructor?

5. Differentiate between generalization and specialization.
6. Define aggregation.
7. What is an object? How does the conceptualization of a right object help in the development of software?
8. Explain the life cycle of an object.
9. What is a static function? What are the restrictions for the usage of a static function?
10. Explain the following terms:
    (a) Encapsulation   (b) Information hiding
    (c) Access levels   (d) Constant members
    (e) This reference   (f) Private constructor

III. Programming Exercises

1. Create a class called account having the following data members.

Data member	Type
Account name	String
Amount	Double

   Define two member functions inside the class: getdata(), which takes input from a user, and putdata(), which displays the data. In the main class, make two instances of the account class and call these two functions.

2. In the class account (Question 1), define a default constructor and depict its usage.

3. In the class account (Question 1), define a parameterized constructor and depict its usage.

4. Define and use a copy constructor in the class account (Question 1).

5. Make an array of account class (Question 1). Ask the user to input the data and display the details of the account having the maximum balance.

6. In Question 5, display the details of the account having the minimum balance.

7. In Question 5, arrange the objects in order of their increasing balances.

8. In Question 1, add a static variable called count and depict its usage.

9. Create a class called complex having two data members, real and imaginary. Define two functions getdata() and putdata() in the class. In Main make two instances, c1 and c2, of the complex class and fetch values into them using getdata() and putdata().

10. When we add two complex numbers, the real part of the resulting complex number is the sum of the real parts of the two complex numbers. The imaginary part of the sum (of two complex numbers) is the sum of the imaginary parts of the two complex numbers. Using this concept, modify Question 9 and make a function called sum, which calculates the sum of two complex numbers initialized in Main.

11. When we subtract two complex numbers, the real part of the resulting complex number is the difference of the real parts of the two complex numbers. The imaginary part of the difference (of two complex numbers) is the difference of the imaginary parts of the two complex numbers. Using this concept, modify Question 9 and make a function called difference, which calculates the difference of two complex numbers initialized in Main.

12. If we have two complex numbers $z1 = x1 + iy1$ and $z2 = x2 + iy2$, then the product of the two complex numbers is given by $z = (x1 \times x2 - y1 \times y2) + i(x1 \times y2 + y1 \times x2)$. Using this formula and the class made in Question 10, calculate the product of two complex numbers $z1$ and $z2$.

13. If we have a complex number $z = real + i*imag$, then the modulus of the complex number is given by the formula $m = |real^2 + imag^2|$. Using this formula make a new function in the class made in Question 10 to calculate the modulus of complex number z.

14. If we have a complex number $z = real + i*imag$, then the argument of the complex number is given by $arg(z) = tan^{-1}(imag/real)$. Using this formula make a new function in the class made in Question 10 to calculate the argument of complex number z.

15. If we have a complex number $z = real + i*imag$, then the polar form is given by the formula $p = re^{io}$, where r and o are the modulus and the argument of the complex number (defined in Questions 13 and 14). Using this formula make a new function in the class made in Question 10 to calculate the polar form of complex number z.

16. If we have two complex numbers $z_1 = x_1 + iy_1$ and $z_2 = x_2 + iy_2$, then the division of the two complex numbers is given by $z = ((x_1x_2 + y_1y_2) + i(-x_1y_2 + x_2y_1))/(x_2^2 + y_2^2)$. Using this formula and the class made in Question 10, calculate the division of two complex numbers z1 and z2.

17. If we have a complex number $z = x + iy$, then the conjugate of the complex number is $z = x - iy$. Ask the user to enter a complex number and display its conjugate.

18. If we have a complex number $z = x + iy$, then the logarithm of z is given by the formula $\log z = \log r + i\tan^{-1}(y/x)$, where r is the modulus of the complex number (Question 13). Using this formula and the class made in Question 10, calculate the logarithm of complex number z.

19. Using the concepts explained in Questions 9–18, create a program implementing a complex calculator.

20. Define a class called distance having data members m and cm. Define default, parameterized, and copy constructors in the class and make two functions `getdata()` and `putdata()` to insert and display the data. In addition, make a function called sum inside the class. In the Main function, make two instances of the class and display the sum of the two instances.

21. Consider a class Employee depicted in the following class diagram:

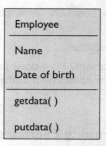

Implement this class

22. In the class given in Question 21, add all three types of constructors and depict their use.

23. In Question 21, create an array of employees and ask the user to enter the number of employees and the details of the employees.

24. In Question 23, find the details of the employee who is youngest.

25. In Question 23, what is the average age of the employees?

26. In Question 23, arrange the employees in the increasing order of their age.

27. In Question 23, what is the average difference between the ages of the employees?

28. In Question 23, which employee has the maximum salary?

29. In Question 23, what is the difference between the salary of the youngest and the oldest employees?

30. In Question 23, consider the data you have entered and find whether the salary and the age are correlated. Use coefficient of correlation.

12 Inheritance

OBJECTIVES

After completing this chapter, the reader will be able to
- Appreciate the importance of inheritance
- Understand the use of access specifiers
- Describe various types of inheritances
- Implement all type of inheritances
- Explain how to override functions
- Elucidate the importance of sealed methods
- Appreciate the concept of sealed classes and abstract classes
- Define and implement methods of subclass
- Understand runtime polymorphism
- Provide the meaning of hierarchical inheritance
- Explain multilevel inheritance
- Appreciate the use of the concept in real life scenarios

12.1 INTRODUCTION

The advent of C++ gave rise to a new concept called object-oriented programming. The concept of classes was central to the language. It changed the way programs were made. It showed a new path to the programming community, which was desperately looking for a messiah to guide them through the hollows of procedural paradigm. The most important concept in the language is classes, which, as discussed in Chapter 11, are real or conceptual entities that were central to the problem.

Inheritance is the second-most important feature in C++. It allows the programmers to use the features defined in the base class and thus helps in reusability of the code. The base class is the class from which other class(es), called derived class(es), are defined. The base class has some definitions and methods; the derived class can use those members and in addition can define their own methods and attributes as well. This concept helps us to implement real-life situations wherein a base class, say vehicle, has many subclasses, say car and bike. The situation is depicted in Fig. 12.1.

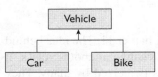

Fig. 12.1 Example of inheritance

Now let us analyse the advantage of this concept. Suppose vehicle has colour and number as its data members. The car class has an extra attribute `ac_type` and the bike class has an extra attribute called `bike_m`. Now, both the derived classes will be able to use the attributes of vehicle as well as their own attributes. This is true for methods as well. Suppose there are two methods `getdata()` and `putdata()` in the base class; the derived classes can also have their own `getdata()` and `putdata()`, which may enhance the capabilities of the base class methods and incorporate the input and output of their own attributes.

Figure 12.2 depicts the core attributes of the classes in normal font. The attributes that have been derived from the base class are depicted in bold. The methods `getdata()` and `putdata()` have been overridden in the derived classes and therefore have been shown in a italics. It may be noted that the arrow points towards the base class from the derived class. The arrow depicts the relationship of the type, that is, 'is derived from'.

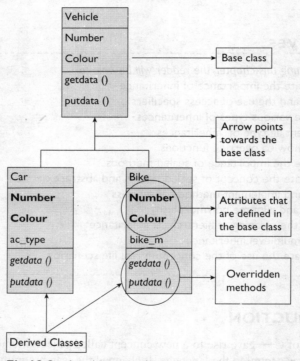

Fig.12.2 Attributes and methods of vehicle, car, and bike

The concepts of inheritance, overriding, and base class have been explained in detail in the following sections.

12.2 VISIBILITY CONTROL

The concept of visibility control was discussed in Section 11.10 of Chapter 11. The idea behind access specifiers is to contain the information flow and accidental change in another class. It may be noted that the access specifiers do not provide security as perceived by many. They are necessary to prevent any accidental change to values or objects by programmers. It is like restrictive use of an expensive tea set, which is meant to be used only for specific purposes.

Not everyone in the house is allowed to take it out and use it, not because they will intentionally break it but they might accidentally do so.

A class may be internal, public, or private. A public class can be accessed anywhere in the program. All the classes in the class library are, therefore, public. However, the default access specifier for a class is internal. The internal class specifier allows the class to be used anywhere within the namespace but not outside it. The point may be verified by the following snippet:

```
class ABC
{
}
    namespace Inheritance4
    {
        ABC a = new ABC();
        class Program
        {
            static void Main(string[] args)
            {
            }
        }
    }
```

The compiler will display the following error in the error pane:

```
A namespace does not directly contain members such as fields or methods.
```

As far as the members are concerned, visibility control is governed by the following access specifiers:
1. Public members can be accessed within a class, in a derived class, and in a class that is independent of the class in question. To summarize, writing public will make the member accessible anywhere in the program.
2. The protected members, however, can be accessed only within the class and in its derived classes. It is akin to a person's car, which can be used by the person and his/her family members but not by an outsider.
3. The private members, on the other hand, can be accessed only within the class.

C# has another access specifier called internal. This specifier has been discussed previously in Chapter 11. The summary of the access levels is also given in Section 11.10 of Chapter 11. The following are certain rules, as regards visibility control, that must be kept in mind while developing a program:
1. The base class should be at least as accessible as the derived class. For example, there cannot be a situation wherein the base class is private while the derived class is public.
2. It is not possible to have a class that is more accessible than the class it contains. Containment is discussed in Section 12.3.
3. Returning values via methods should be appropriate to the visibility control.

Section 12.3 discusses the various types of inheritance.

12.3 TYPES OF INHERITANCE

There are two types of inheritance; one is 'is a type of' relationship and the other is 'has a' relationship. The example mentioned in Section 12.1 belongs to 'is a type of' inheritance. The inheritance has a base class from which new classes called 'derived classes' are crafted.

The derived class or classes may use the attributes and methods of the base class, if allowed by the access specifier, as explained in Section 12.2. For example, if the data member or the member function is private, then the derived class will not be able to access it. However, in case of a public data member, the derived class can use the data member or the member function of the base class.

The class from which other classes are derived is called the base class, superclass, or parent class. The derived class is generally referred to as a child class. The derived class, as explained earlier, can use the members of the base class and at the same time can also have its own members. The `bike_m` member in the bike class and the `ac_type` member in the car class are such members. Thus, the example given in Section 12.1 may be summarized by the following statements:

1. Car is a type of vehicle.
2. Bike is a type of vehicle.

This chapter mainly focuses on this type of inheritance. As mentioned in Chapter 11, there are four inheritances, which are explained in Sections 12.4–12.6. However, there is another type of inheritance called containment. Containment is also considered as a type of inheritance in the literature. However, there are some reservations as regards this. Instantiating a class within another class is referred to as containment inheritance. For example, consider a class department and another class college. Suppose the department class is instantiated within the college class, then the type of inheritance is referred to as containment.

```
Class Department
{
    //Data members and member methods
}
Class College
{
    Department Computer_Department; //Computer_Department is an instance of the
    Department class
    //Data members and member functions of the class
}
College DCE; //DCE is an instance of the College class
```

The relationships in this snippet can be depicted by the following statements:
1. College 'has a' Department.
2. Computer_Department 'is a type of' Department.
3. DCE 'is a type of' College.

Try to decipher the part written in single quotes. The relationship therefore can be any one of the two types stated at the beginning of the section. Now that we are aware of the basic types, let us learn the syntax of inheritance and the types of 'is a type of' inheritance.

12.4 SIMPLE INHERITANCE: DEFINING SUBCLASS METHODS AND CONSTRUCTORS

A base class is defined in the same way as a normal class, which was explained in Chapter 11. The keyword `class` is written followed by the name of the class and then the definition. For more details, refer to Section 11.2 of Chapter 11.

After defining the base class, the derived class is defined. This definition is again similar to a normal class, followed by a colon and the name of the base class. The derived class may extend the functions defined in the base class. The concept has been discussed here.

```
Class base_class
{
}
Class derived_class : base_class
{
}
```

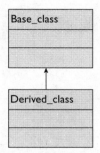

Fig. 12.3 Simple inheritance

This situation depicts a simple inheritance. The inheritance has a single base class and just one derived class. In the class diagram, the arrow points towards the base class, as stated earlier. Figure 12.3 depicts the situation.

The following program depicts an example of the implementation of simple inheritance. It has a class called `SoftwareTestingGuide` containing two data members, namely `number_rp` and `number_books`. The base class has a derived class called `ForcedScholar`, which has its own data member called `number_projects`. The base class has two methods called `getdata()` and `putdata()`. It may be noted that the constructors of the base class can be enhanced by the derived class as well. The constructor of the derived class when called will invoke the constructor of the base class. This can be done by placing a colon after the name of the constructor followed by writing the name of the base class constructor.

```
namespace ConsoleApplication1
{
    class SoftwareTestingGuide
    {
        int number_rp, number_books;
        public SoftwareTestingGuide()
        {
            number_books = 0;
            number_rp = 0;
        }
        public void getdata()
        {
            try
            {
                Console.WriteLine("Enter the number of research papers\t:");
                number_rp = int.Parse(Console.ReadLine());
                Console.WriteLine("Enter the number of books authored\t:");
                number_books = int.Parse(Console.ReadLine());
            }
            catch(Exception e)
            {
                Console.WriteLine("Exception " + e.ToString());
            }
        }
        public void putdata()
        {
            Console.WriteLine("Research papers " + number_rp);
            Console.WriteLine("Books authored " + number_books);
        }
```

```
        }
        class ForcedScholar : SoftwareTestingGuide
        {
            int number_projects;
            public ForcedScholar() : base()
            {
                number_projects = 0;
            }
            public void getdata()
            {
                try
                {
                    Console.WriteLine("Enter the number of projects\t:");
                    number_projects = int.Parse(Console.ReadLine());
                }
                catch(Exception e)
                {
                    Console.WriteLine("Exception " + e.ToString());
                }
            }
            public void putdata()
            {
                Console.WriteLine("Projects " + number_projects);
            }
        }
        class Program
        {
            static void Main(string[] args)
            {
                SoftwareTestingGuide r = new SoftwareTestingGuide();
                r.getdata();
                r.putdata();
                ForcedScholar h = new ForcedScholar();
                h.getdata();
                h.putdata();
                Console.ReadKey();
            }
        }
}
```

Output

It should be noted that when getdata() and putdata() of the derived class are called, the base class methods are not invoked.

```
Enter the number of research papers   :
45
Enter the number of books authored    :
1
Research papers 45
Books authored 2
Enter the number of projects          :
35
Projects 35
```

If, however we try to access the members of the base class in the derived class by making the members protected, then the value of the protected members initialized in the constructor is shown. This is coincidently correct analogically as well.

```
namespace ConsoleApplication1
{
    class SoftwareTestingGuide
    {
        protected int number_rp, number_books;
        public SoftwareTestingGuide()
        {
            number_books = 0;
            number_rp = 0;
        }
        public void getdata()
        {
            try
            {
                Console.WriteLine("Enter the number of research papers\t:");
                number_rp = int.Parse(Console.ReadLine());
                Console.WriteLine("Enter the number of books authored\t:");
                number_books = int.Parse(Console.ReadLine());
            }
            catch(Exception e)
            {
                Console.WriteLine("Exception " + e.ToString());
            }
        }
        public void putdata()
        {
            Console.WriteLine("Research papers " + number_rp);
            Console.WriteLine("Books authored " + number_books);
        }
    }
    class ForcedScholar : SoftwareTestingGuide
    {
        int number_projects;
        public ForcedScholar() : base()
        {
            number_projects = 0;
        }
        public void getdata()
        {
            try
            {
                Console.WriteLine("Enter the number of projects\t:");
                number_projects = int.Parse(Console.ReadLine());
            }
            catch(Exception e)
            {
                Console.WriteLine("Exception " + e.ToString());
            }
        }
        public void putdata()
```

```
            {
                Console.WriteLine("Projects " + number_projects + " papers " + number_rp +
                " books " + number_books);
            }
        }
        class Program
        {
            static void Main(string[] args)
            {
                SoftwareTestingGuide r = new SoftwareTestingGuide();
                r.getdata();
                r.putdata();
                ForcedScholar h = new ForcedScholar();
                h.getdata();
                h.putdata();
                Console.ReadKey();
            }
        }
    }
```

Output
The reason for this output is the initialization of the base class members when they are called in the derived class. It may also be noted that we can call the base class members in the derived class only by changing the default access level as discussed in Chapter 11.

```
Enter the number of research papers   :
45
Enter the number of books authored    :
1
Research papers 45
Books authored 1
Enter the number of projects          : 35
Projects 35 papers 0 books 0
```

In order to see the correct data of the base class members, we must add the following line to the getdata() method:

        base.getdata();

The inclusion of this line in the method will let us see the values of the base class data members as well.

12.5 MULTILEVEL INHERITANCE

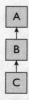

Fig. 12.4 Multilevel inheritance

When a class is derived from a derived class, the phenomenon is referred to as multilevel inheritance. For example, class B is derived from class A and class C is derived from class B. In such a situation, the parent class of a class may also have a parent class. There is no constraint on the level of inheritance, however. Figure 12.4 depicts this type of inheritance.

In order to explain the concept, the example given in Section 12.4 has been extended by deriving a class called 'YouCanChooseYrTopic' and creating in it a data member called 'number_jr'.

The class diagram of the following program is given in Fig. 12.5. It may be noted that the way of calling constructors and extending methods in the `YouCanChooseYrTopic` class is the same as that in `ForcedScholar` class. The point here is to learn how to extend the member functions in the derived class without having to actually change them. The invocation of the methods and the handling of constructors is the same as that in simple inheritance.

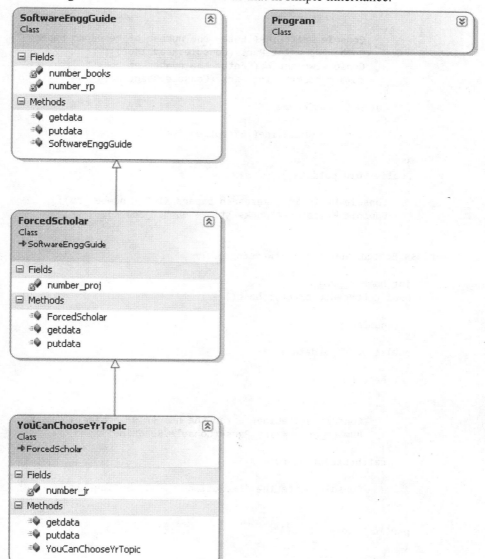

Fig. 12.5 Class diagram of an example for multilevel inheritance

```
namespace Inheritance2
{
    class SoftwareEnggGuide
    {
        int number_rp, number_books;
        public SoftwareEnggGuide()
```

```csharp
            {
                number_books = 0;
                number_rp = 0;
            }
            public void getdata()
            {
                try
                {
                    Console.WriteLine("Enter the number of research papers ");
                    number_rp = int.Parse(Console.ReadLine());
                    Console.WriteLine("Enter the number of books ");
                    number_books = int.Parse(Console.ReadLine());
                }
                catch(Exception e)
                {
                    Console.WriteLine("Exception " + e.ToString());
                }
            }
            public void putdata()
            {
                Console.WriteLine("Research papers \t:" + number_rp);
                Console.WriteLine("Books \t:" + number_books);
            }
        }
        class ForcedScholar : SoftwareEnggGuide
        {
            int number_proj;
            public ForcedScholar(): base()
            {
                number_proj = 0;
            }
            public void getdata()
            {
                base.getdata();
                try
                {
                    Console.WriteLine("Enter the number of projects ");
                    number_proj = int.Parse(Console.ReadLine());
                }
                catch(Exception e)
                {
                    Console.WriteLine("Exception " + e.ToString());
                }
            }
            public void putdata()
            {
                base.putdata();
                Console.WriteLine("Number of projects " + number_proj);
            }
        }
        class YouCanChooseYrTopic : ForcedScholar
        {
            int number_jr;
            public YouCanChooseYrTopic()
                : base()
```

```csharp
        {
            number_jr = 0;
        }
        public void getdata()
        {
            base.getdata();
            try
            {
                Console.WriteLine("Enter jr");
                number_jr = int.Parse(Console.ReadLine());
            }
            catch(Exception e)
            {
                Console.WriteLine("Exception " + e.ToString());
            }
        }
        public void putdata()
        {
            base.putdata();
            Console.WriteLine("Number of jr " + number_jr);
        }
    }
    class Program
    {
        static void Main(string[] args)
        {
            ForcedScholar h = new ForcedScholar();
            h.getdata();
            h.putdata();
            YouCanChooseYrTopic n = new YouCanChooseYrTopic();
            n.getdata();
            n.putdata();
            Console.ReadKey();
        }
    }
}
```

Output

```
Enter the number of research papers
25
Enter the number of books
2
Enter the number of projects
35
Research papers  : 25
Books            : 2
Number of projects 35
Enter the number of research papers
20
Enter the number of books
2
Enter the number of projects
10
```

```
Enter jr
2
Research papers  : 20
Books            : 2
Number of projects 10
Number of jr 2
```

12.6 HIERARCHICAL INHERITANCE

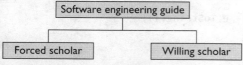

Fig. 12.6 Hierarchical inheritance

A class may have more than one derived class. For example, the `SoftwareEngineeringGuide` class in Section 12.5 has got a derived class `ForcedScholar`, which has its own data. Suppose the base class derives another class, say `WillingScholar`, having its own data members and probably own data. Such type of inheritance whereby a class has more than one derived class is called hierarchical inheritance. Figure 12.6 depicts the situation.

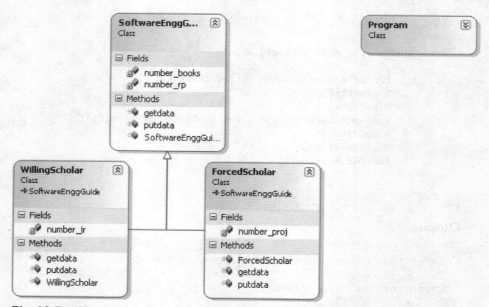

Fig. 12.7 Class diagram of an example for hierarchical inheritance

The following program demonstrates the implementation of hierarchical inheritance. It may be noted that the way of writing the program and the methodology of handling constructors and methods remains the same as in the previous two cases. The class diagram of the program is depicted in Fig. 12.7.

```
namespace Inheritance3
{
    class SoftwareEnggGuide
    {
        int number_rp, number_books;
```

```csharp
        public SoftwareEnggGuide()
        {
            number_books = 0;
            number_rp = 0;
        }
        public void getdata()
        {
            try
            {
                Console.WriteLine("Enter the number of research papers ");
                number_rp = int.Parse(Console.ReadLine());
                Console.WriteLine("Enter the number of books ");
                number_books = int.Parse(Console.ReadLine());
            }
            catch(Exception e)
            {
                Console.WriteLine("Exception " + e.ToString());
            }
        }
        public void putdata()
        {
            Console.WriteLine("Research papers \t:" + number_rp);
            Console.WriteLine("Books \t:" + number_books);
        }
    }
    class ForcedScholar : SoftwareEnggGuide
    {
        int number_proj;
        public ForcedScholar()
            : base()
        {
            number_proj = 0;
        }
        public void getdata()
        {
            base.getdata();
            try
            {
                Console.WriteLine("Enter the number of projects ");
                number_proj = int.Parse(Console.ReadLine());
            }
            catch(Exception e)
            {
                Console.WriteLine("Exception " + e.ToString());
            }
        }
        public void putdata()
        {
            base.putdata();
            Console.WriteLine("Number of projects " + number_proj);
        }
    }
    class WillingScholar : SoftwareEnggGuide
    {
        int number_jr;
        public WillingScholar()
            : base()
```

```csharp
        {
            number_jr = 0;
        }
        public void getdata()
        {
            base.getdata();
            try
            {
                Console.WriteLine("Enter jr");
                number_jr = int.Parse(Console.ReadLine());
            }
            catch(Exception e)
            {
                Console.WriteLine("Exception " + e.ToString());
            }
        }
        public void putdata()
        {
            base.putdata();
            Console.WriteLine("Number of jr " + number_jr);
        }
    }
    class Program
    {
        static void Main(string[] args)
        {
            ForcedScholar h = new ForcedScholar();
            h.getdata();
            h.putdata();
            WillingScholar a = new WillingScholar();
            a.getdata();
            a.putdata();
            Console.ReadKey();
        }
    }
}
```

Output

```
Enter the number of research papers
25
Enter the number of books
2
Enter the number of projects
35
Research papers : 25
Books           : 2
Number of projects 35
Enter the number of research papers
6
Enter the number of books
0
Enter jr
1
Research papers : 6
Books           : 0
Number of jr 1
```

This section explained the different types of inheritances and their implementation. Having gone through the basics, let us now move to more involved topics. Section 12.9 explains important concepts such as sealed classes. The concepts amalgamated with those already explained will help readers to write programs that use inheritance.

12.7 OVERRIDING METHODS

At times, we want the methods of the derived class to be invoked instead of those of the base class. In such cases, ideally, it will be required to specify the keyword `virtual` along with the method of the base class and override it with that in the derived class. Here, we want to create in the derived class a method with the same name and with the same arguments as that in the base class; however, we want this method in the derived class to behave differently from the method in the base class, when invoked.

In the example given in Section 12.6, the getdata() method of the ForcedScholar class can be invoked when called, instead of the method of the base class, by mentioning virtual with the base class method and overriding it with the method in the derived class. The change in the output in Listing 1 and Listing 2 must be noted.

Listing 1

```
namespace Inheritance5
{
    class SoftwareTestingGuide
    {
        public SoftwareTestingGuide()
        {
            //
        }
        public virtual void getdata()
        {
            Console.WriteLine("getdata of the base class\t:");
        }
    }
    class ForcedScholar : SoftwareTestingGuide
    {
        public ForcedScholar() : base()
        {
            //
        }
        public override void getdata()
        {
            Console.WriteLine("getdata of the derived class");
        }
    }
    class Program
    {
        static void Main(string[] args)
        {
            ForcedScholar h = new ForcedScholar();
            h.getdata();
            Console.ReadKey();
        }
    }
}
```

Output
It should be noted that the method of the derived class has been invoked and not that of the base class.

```
getdata of the derived class
```

In Listing 2, the `virtual` and `override` keywords have been deliberately removed.

Listing 2
```csharp
namespace Inheritance7
{
    class SoftwareTestingGuide
    {
        public SoftwareTestingGuide()
        {
            //
        }
        public void getdata()
        {
            Console.WriteLine("getdata of the base class\t:");
        }
    }
    class ForcedScholar : SoftwareTestingGuide
    {
        public ForcedScholar()
        : base()
        {
            //
        }
        public void getdata()
        {
            Console.WriteLine("getdata of the derived class");
        }
    }
    class Program
    {
        static void Main(string[] args)
        {
            ForcedScholar h = new ForcedScholar();
            h.getdata();
            Console.ReadKey();
        }
    }
}
```

Output
It must be surprising to see the following output of this listing:

```
getdata of the derived class
```

Readers familiar with C++ might find it strange or even weird. However, as and when we proceed further, the concept will become clear.

12.8 ABSTRACT CLASSES AND METHODS

Thought the method of the derived class should be called when it is invoked and that of the base class should be called when it is invoked, it has been explained in Section 12.7 that this may not always be the case. However, this can be achieved by making the base class abstract. That is, the base class will not be instantiated; rather it will be used only to make the derived classes. The derived classes will contain methods having the same signature as those in the base class. The base class will thus act as a patriarch who will do nothing but tell everyone else how to do things. The abstract base class is neither instantiated nor will it define any of its members, but it tells all its derived classes to implement the methods declared as abstract according to their own requirement. The following program depicts the pseudo use:

```csharp
namespace Inheritance7
{
    abstract  class SoftwareTestingGuide
    {
        public SoftwareTestingGuide()
        {
            //
        }
        public abstract void getdata();
    }
    class ForcedScholar : SoftwareTestingGuide
    {
        public ForcedScholar()
        : base()
        {
            //
        }
        public override void getdata()
        {
            Console.WriteLine("getdata of the derived class");
        }
    }
    class Program
    {
        static void Main(string[] args)
        {
            ForcedScholar h = new ForcedScholar();
            h.getdata();
            Console.ReadKey();
        }
    }
}
```

Output

It should be noted that there is no major difference in the output of the previous listings and the present one.

```
getdata of the derived class
```

The important points that may be noted as regards an abstract class are as follows:
1. It cannot be instantiated. It will have derived classes, which may be instantiated.
2. It can have only abstract methods. The abstract methods will have to be defined by the derived classes.

12.9 SEALED CLASSES AND METHODS

There are cases wherein we do not want a class to be the base class of any other class. In such cases, we mark the class as a sealed class. The `sealed` keyword hinders the derivation of the class and hence protects it from being the base class of any other class. However, there has to be a strong reason for doing it. In the following snippet class, XYZ tries to become a derived class of ABC.

```
sealed class ABC
{
    //
}
class XYZ : ABC
{
}
```

On compilation, an error will be generated.

```
'Inheritance8.XYZ': cannot derive from sealed type 'Inheritance8.ABC'.
```

Suppose in the class ABC, there is a method called method1(), and ABC is not sealed. Now we want to override method1() in such a way that the derived class of XYZ should not be able to use the method. In order to accomplish the task, we can mark the method method1() as sealed. The following snippet depicts the situation:

```
namespace Inheritance8
{
    class ABC
    {
        public virtual void method1()
        {
            //Something
        }
    }
    class XYZ : ABC
    {
        public sealed override void method1()
        {
            Console.WriteLine("Hi");
        }
    }
    class MNO : XYZ
    {
        public override void method1()
        {
            Console.WriteLine("Bye");
        }
    }
    class Program
    {
```

```
        static void Main(string[] args)
        {
        }
    }
}
```

On compilation, the following error will be generated:

```
'Inheritance8.MNO.method1()': cannot override inherited member 'Inheritance8.
XYZ.method1()' because it is sealed.
```

12.10 RUNTIME POLYMORPHISM

Now that we have gone through the basic concepts, let us revisit the concept of runtime polymorphism. This concept can be understood with the help of the following example. Consider a class called BaseClass and its two derived classes Derived1 and Derived2. Now there is a method called show() in the base class, which is virtual and the method is overridden in the derived classes. In the Main() method, an instance of BaseClass is created and is equated to the constructors of the derived classes one by one. Invoking the show() method will invoke the derived class methods. The situation has been depicted in the following snippet. In this program, method binding occurs at the runtime and not at the compile time, and therefore, the phenomenon is referred to as runtime polymorphism. Polymorphism as we understand is 'many forms of the same thing'. In the example too, the show() method has many forms, defined in the base and the derived classes. The association occurs at the runtime.

```
namespace Inheritance9
{
    class BaseClass
    {
        public virtual void show()
        {
            Console.WriteLine("From the Base");
        }
    }
    class Derived1 : BaseClass
    {
        public override void show()
        {
            Console.WriteLine("From Derived1");
        }
    }
    class Derived2 : BaseClass
    {
        public override void show()
        {
            Console.WriteLine("From Derived2");
        }
    }
    class Program
    {
        static void Main(string[] args)
        {
            BaseClass b = new BaseClass();
```

```
            b.show();
            b = new Derived1();
            b.show();
            b = new Derived2();
            b.show();
            Console.ReadKey();
        }
    }
}
```

Output

```
From the Base
From Derived1
From Derived2
```

SUMMARY

The concepts discussed in this chapter form the basis of object-oriented programming paradigm. The importance of inheritance can be understood by the fact that even after the advent of visual programming, the concept was not abandoned. It was refined and the concept of visual inheritance was introduced. Inheritance helps us in the reusability of the code, as a method defined in the base class need not be defined again in the derived class, as discussed in the chapter. Chapter 13 is the continuation of this chapter. It introduces the concept of interfaces. Since, multiple inheritance is not allowed in C#, interface helps us to implement the concept of multiple inheritance. It may be stated that readers can explore the advantages of inheritance only by writing numerous programs, as every management system requires at least some degree of inheritance.

GLOSSARY

Inheritance It is the process of creating new classes from the existing classes.
Overriding a function Having a function of the same name in the derived class as there is in the base class is called overriding.
Simple inheritance In simple inheritance, a single class is derived from a base class.
Hierarchical inheritance In hierarchical inheritance, more than one class(es) is/are derived from the base class.
Multilevel inheritance In multilevel inheritance, a derived class can also derive a class.
Containment When a class is instantiated within another class, it is referred to as containment.

POINTS TO REMEMBER

- A class may be internal, public, or private. However, the default access specifier for a class is internal.
- Inheritance can be classified as 'is a type of' and 'has a' relationships.
- Simple inheritance has a single base class and a single derived class.
- No class can inherit a sealed class.
- When method binding occurs at the runtime and not at the compile time, the phenomenon is referred to as runtime polymorphism.
- C# does not allow multiple inheritance.

EXERCISES

I. Multiple-choice Questions

1. What will be the output of the following program?
    ```
    namespace Inheritance9
    {
        class BaseClass
        {
            public void show()
            {
                Console.WriteLine("From the
                Base");
            }
        }
        class Derived1 : BaseClass
        {
            public override void show()
            {
                Console.WriteLine("From
                Derived1");
            }
        }
        class Derived2 : BaseClass
        {
            public override void show()
            {
                Console.WriteLine("From
                Derived2");
            }
        }
        class Program
        {
            static void Main(string[] args)
            {
                BaseClass b = new BaseClass();
                b.show();
                b = new Derived1();
                b.show();
                b = new Derived2();
                b.show();
                Console.ReadKey();
            }
        }
    }
    ```
    (a) An error will be generated as the base class function can be overridden only if it is virtual or abstract.
    (b) An error will be generated as the base class function can be overridden only if it is sealed.
    (c) From the Base, From Derived1, From Derived2
    (d) From the Base, From the Base, From the Base

2. What will be the output of the following program?
    ```
    namespace Inheritance9
    {
        class BaseClass
        {
            public virtual void show()
            {
                Console.WriteLine("From the
                Base");
            }
        }
        class Derived1 : BaseClass
        {
            public void show()
            {
                Console.WriteLine("From
                Derived1");
            }
        }
        class Derived2 : BaseClass
        {
            public override void show()
            {
                Console.WriteLine("From
                Derived2");
            }
        }
        class Program
        {
            static void Main(string[] args)
            {
                BaseClass b = new BaseClass();
                b.show();
                b = new Derived1();
                b.show();
                b = new Derived2();
                b.show();
                Console.ReadKey();
            }
        }
    }
    ```
    (a) An error will be generated as the base class function can be overridden only if it is virtual or abstract.
    (b) An error will be generated as the base class function can be overridden only if it is sealed.
    (c) From the Base, From Derived1, From Derived2
    (d) From the Base, From the Base, From Derived2

3. What will be the output of the program in Question 2, if the following statements are added in the Main() method?
   ```
   Derived1 d = new BaseClass();
   d.show();
   ```
   (a) An error will be generated, as implicit casting is needed.
   (b) An error will be generated, as the base class cannot be converted into a derived class.
   (c) From the Base, From Derived1, From Derived2
   (d) From the Base, From the Base, From Derived2

4. What will be the output of the following snippet?
   ```
   class ABC
   {
       public virtual void method1()
       {
           //Something
       }
   }
   class XYZ : ABC
   {
       public sealed override void method1()
       {
           Console.WriteLine("Hi");
       }
   }
   class MNO : XYZ
   {
       public override void method1()
       {
           Console.WriteLine("Bye");
       }
   }
   class Program
   {
       static void Main(string[] args)
       {
       }
   }
   ```
   (a) Error will be generated, as a sealed method cannot be overridden.
   (b) Error will be generated, as a sealed method cannot be public.
   (c) No error will be generated but no output is shown either.
   (d) None of these

5. What will be the output of the following snippet?
   ```
   abstract class ABC
   {
       public ABC()
       {
           //
       }
       public abstract void show();
   }
   class XYZ : ABC
   {
       public XYZ()
       : base()
       {
           //
       }
       public override void getdata()
       {
           Console.WriteLine("getdata of the derived class");
       }
   }
   class Program
   {
       static void Main(string[] args)
       {
           XYZ h = new XYZ();
           h.getdata();
           Console.ReadKey();
       }
   }
   ```
   (a) getdata of the derived class
   (b) getdata of the base class
   (c) None of these
   (d) The program does not compile.

6. What happens if the abstract keyword is removed from the snippet given in Question 5?
   (a) The output remains the same.
   (b) The base class method is invoked.
   (c) Output cannot be predicted.
   (d) None of these

7. Is the following snippet correct?
   ```
   class ABC
   {
   }
   namespace Inheritance4
   {
       ABC a = new ABC();
       class Program
       {
           static void Main(string[] args)
           {
           }
       }
   }
   ```
   (a) No
   (b) Yes
   (c) Cannot say
   (d) The names of the classes are not appropriate.

8. What change will have to be made to the snippet in Question 7 to make it run?
   (a) Place ABC in the namespace.
   (b) Place namespace in ABC.
   (c) Place XYZ in ABC.
   (d) None of these
9. Which type of inheritance is depicted in the below diagram?

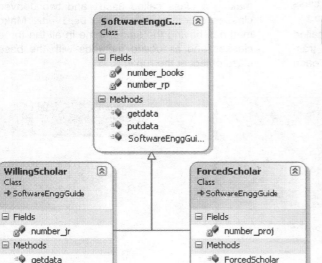

(a) Multiple   (b) Multilevel
(c) Hierarchical   (d) None of these

10. Which type of inheritance is not allowed in C#?
    (a) Multiple
    (b) Multilevel
    (c) Hierarchical
    (d) None of these

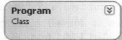

II. Review Questions

1. What is the importance of inheritance?
2. What are the different types of inheritance?
3. What is meant by containment?
4. What is the importance of sealed methods?
5. What is an abstract class? What can be the reason for having an abstract class in the program?
6. What is the significance of runtime polymorphism?
7. Which type of inheritance is not allowed in C#?
8. What is meant by overriding a method?
9. Explain the different access specifiers.
10. What is hierarchical inheritance?

III. Programming Exercises

1. Consider a class called student. It has two constructors: a default constructor and a parameterized constructor. There are two methods in the class: getdata(), which takes data from the user, and putdata(), which displays the data. Write a program to create this class and invoke the methods of the class via objects made in Main().

2. In Question 1, consider the class has two derived classes—regular_student and part_timer. The regular_student has a member called attendance. The part_timer has a member called material_charges. Create the two derived classes and make their objects in the Main class.

3. Override the corresponding constructors and methods in the derived classes.

4. Now, make a derived class of the regular_student class, namely very_regular. The regular_student class has a data member

called `numberOfClericalJobsDone`. Implement the two classes.

5. In Question 4, override the methods in the derived classes.

6. Create a class called train having `numberOfComp` and `speed` as its data members. Make two constructors, a default and a parameterized constructor. Make two methods `getdata()` and `putdata()` in the class. Now make an instance of the class and call `getdata()` and `putdata()` from Main.

7. In Question 6, create a derived class called metro and another called EMU from the train class. Make one extra data member in each class and override the methods.

8. In Question 6, make another class called vehicle, which has a data member called colour. Now change the framework to make vehicle the base class of train.

9. In Question 8, make the base class as abstract and depict the use of abstract keyword by calling methods.

10. Depict an example of runtime polymorphism by making a class called `Base1` and two derived classes called `Derived1` and `Derived2`. Make methods having the same name in all the three classes and associate methods with the base class object at the runtime.

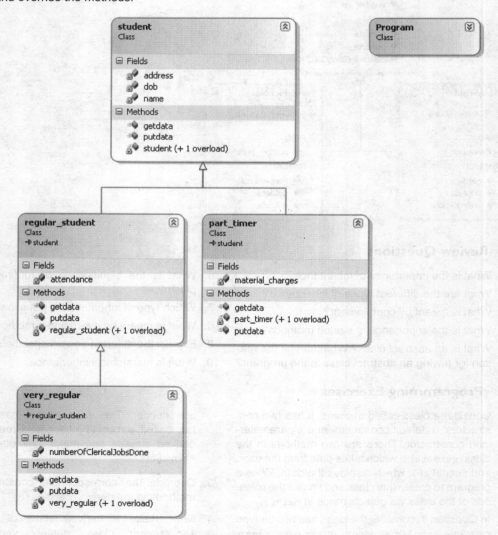

Class diagram for Questions 1–5

13 Interfaces

OBJECTIVES

After completing this chapter, the reader will be able to
- Appreciate the importance of an interface
- Understand the difference between `implement` and `extend`
- Implement an interface
- Describe how an interface extends another interface
- Handle ambiguity
- Appreciate the importance of `as` operator
- Explain the concept of explicit implementation

13.1 INTRODUCTION

The concept of inheritance was discussed in Chapter 12. Inheritance helps us to use the features of the base class, thus facilitating code reusability. At the same time, inheritance also helps us to extend the methods of the base class in the derived class. The concept is not hard to understand as it is inspired from a natural process. The question that comes to mind, therefore, is why multiple inheritance is not allowed in C#, though it is a phenomenon of common occurrence. All of us inherit characteristics from our father as well as our mother. The features in a child are the amalgamation of the features of both the parents. Then why did the developers of C# decided against the inclusion of multiple inheritance in the language?

The answer lies in the fact that, in programming, when a class is derived from more than one class there is a possibility of ambiguity. There might be a method, say A(), which is present in both the parent classes. If the derived class calls A(), then which of the two methods should be invoked? (Refer Fig. 13.1.).

This problem led to the non-inclusion of multiple inheritance in the language. This does not mean that multiple inheritance is not important. The developers of C# also understood this point and therefore chose the same solution to handle the problem as was chosen by the developers of Java. The problem is the same as that of a student who is allotted a particular teacher. Though the teacher might not be easy to handle, the student cannot afford to do away with him/her. Similarly, the developers

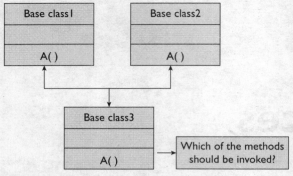

Fig. 13.1 Problem in multiple inheritance

could not do away with multiple inheritance, but at the same time, they could not include it on an as it is basis. The problem of the student cannot be solved, but the problem of multiple inheritance was partially solved by what we call interfaces. The word 'partially' has been used as interfaces declare a function but do not define them.

This chapter discusses the concept of interfaces and their crafting and use. The concept has been examined with the help of illustrations. The problems associated with interfaces have also been discussed. The chapter also discusses the use of the 'as' operator.

13.2 INTERFACES

An interface contains methods, properties, indexers, or events that a class can implement. It does not define anything at all. The components must be implemented by the class that implements the interface. The declaration of an interface is done using the keyword `interface`. This keyword should be followed by the name of the interface. As stated earlier, the body of an interface contains declarations but not definitions. An interface gives a free hand to the class that intends to implement it. It is just like an abstract class whose methods must be implemented by the class that implements it. Since the interface does not define any methods, it cannot be instantiated. A class that implements an interface can also extend a class and thus implement multiple inheritance.

13.2.1 Definition and Syntax

The syntax of an interface is as follows:

```
interface <name of the interface>
{
    //Methods, properties, indexers or events
}
```

For example, if an interface called shape is to have a method called `getdata()`, then the following code needs to be written in the editor:

```
interface shape
{
    void getdata()
    {
    }
}
```

In the same way, a properly defined interface should not define the `get` and `set` but should leave place for either or both as the case may be.

The interface in itself is not capable of being instantiated. It has to be implemented by a class to be able to do something. The following snippet presents the syntax of a class implementing an interface:

```
interface A
{
```

```
}
class B : A
{
    //Defines the methods declared by A
}
```

The following program defines an interface called shape, which has a property called numberOfSides. The interface is implemented in the class shape. The output of the program follows the snippet and reinforces the point that a class implements an interface and an interface cannot be directly instantiated.

```
namespace Interface1
{
    interface shape
    {
        int numberOfSides
        {
            get;
            set;
        }
        void putdata();
    }
    class triangle : shape
    {
        public int numberOfSides
        {
            get
            {
                return 3;
            }
            set
            {
                value = 3;
            }
        }
        public void putdata()
        {
            Console.WriteLine("The number of sides in a triangle is " + numberOfSides);
        }
    }
    class Program
    {
        static void Main(string[] args)
        {
            shape s = new triangle();
            s.putdata();
            Console.ReadKey();
        }
    }
}
```

Output

```
The number of sides in a triangle is 3
```

13.2.2 Abstract Classes and Interface

An abstract class can also use an interface. The methods of that interface are implemented as abstract methods. In order to understand this point let us consider the following program, which has an interface Soft, from which an abstract class Software is derived. The classes Har and Someone extend the Software class. The method publishPaper() is defined in the interface Soft and is implemented in the classes Har and Someone. The example demonstrates the use of interfaces in abstract classes.

```csharp
using System;
using System.Collections.Generic;
using System.Linq;
using System.Text;
namespace Interfaces
{
    class Program
    {
        public interface Soft
        {
            void publishPaper();
        }
        public abstract class SoftWare : Soft
        {
            public abstract void publishPaper();
        }
        public class Har : SoftWare
        {
            public override void publishPaper()
            {
                Console.WriteLine("ACM, Springer, IEEE Software Magazine, IEEE Computer Magazine");
                //throw new NotImplementedException();
            }
        }
        public class Someone : SoftWare
        {
            public override void publishPaper()
            {
                Console.WriteLine("ACM, grey literature");
                //throw new global::System.NotImplementedException();
            }
        }
        static void Main(string[] args)
        {
            Har h = new Har();
            h.publishPaper();
            Someone s = new Someone();
```

```
            s.publishPaper();
            Console.ReadKey();
        }
    }
}
```

Output

```
ACM, Springer, IEEE Software Magazine, IEEE Computer
Magazine
ACM, grey literature
```

Having seen the crafting, syntax, and use of an interface, we will now have a look at the extension and implantation of interfaces.

13.3 INTERFACE EXTENDING AN INTERFACE

An interface can extend an interface just like a class extends a class. Here is a catch; a class cannot extend two classes, but an interface can extend two interfaces. Multiple inheritance is implemented in this manner in C#. However, it may be stated that this type of implementation can also lead to some problems, which are discussed in Section 13.4. The following snippet depicts the syntax of extending an interface. Suppose there is an interface A and another interface B intends to extend it. Then the following code helps us in accomplishing the task:

```
interface A
{
}
interface B : A
{
}
```

As stated earlier, an interface can extend two interfaces as well.

```
interface A
{
}
interface B
{
}
interface C : A, B
{
}
```

The following program demonstrates the concept.

```
namespace Interface2
{
    interface shape
    {
        int numberOfSides
        {
            get;
            set;
        }
        void putdata();
    }
```

```csharp
        interface size
        {
            int level
            {
                get;
                set;
            }
        }
        class triangle : shape, size
        {
            public int numberOfSides
            {
                get
                {
                    return 3;
                }
                set
                {
                    value = 3;
                }
            }
            public int level
            {
                get
                {
                    return 2;
                }
                set
                {
                    value = 2;
                }
            }
            public void putdata()
            {
                Console.WriteLine("The number of sides in a triangle is " + numberOfSides + "
                and the size of the triangle is level " + level);
            }
        }
        class Program
        {
            static void Main(string[] args)
            {
                shape s = new triangle();
                s.putdata();
                Console.ReadKey();
            }
        }
    }
```

Output

```
The number of sides in a triangle is 3 and the size of the triangle
is level 2
```

13.4 EXPLICIT IMPLEMENTATION

As seen in Section 13.3, an interface can extend two interfaces. There might be a case, however, wherein both the interfaces have a method of the same name. Such a situation may lead to ambiguity. This section discusses this problem and its rectification.

Let us try to understand this kind of a situation by taking an example. An interface handles problems posed by multiple inheritance, but what if an interface, say A, extends two interfaces B and C both of which have methods called `method1( )`; then the problem discussed in Section 13.1 again crops up. This problem is handled by 'explicit interface' implementation. C# allows the name of the method to be qualified with the name of the interface to remove any sort of ambiguity.

For example, `method1` of A will be called by writing `A.method1( )` and `method1()` of B will be called by writing `B.method1( )`. The concept has been exemplified in the following program code.

Program

```
namespace Interface3
{
    interface shape
    {
        int numberOfSides
        {
            get;
            set;
        }
        void putdata();
    }
    interface size
    {
        int level
        {
            get;
            set;
        }
        void putdata();
    }
    class triangle : shape, size
    {
        public int numberOfSides
        {
            get
            {
                return 3;
            }
            set
            {
                value = 3;
            }
        }
        public int level
        {
            get
```

```
            {
                return 2;
            }
            set
            {
                value = 2;
            }
        }
        void shape.putdata()
        {
            Console.WriteLine("The number of sides in a triangle is " + numberOfSides);
        }
        void size.putdata()
        {
            Console.WriteLine("The size of the triangle is level " + level);
        }
    }
    class Program
    {
        static void Main(string[] args)
        {
            shape s = new triangle();
            s.putdata();
            Console.ReadKey();
        }
    }
}
```

Output

```
The number of sides in a triangle
is 3
```

13.5 as OPERATOR

The program code given in Section 13.4 demonstrated casting between a class and an interface. There is, however, another way of doing it. C# provides an 'as' operator, which helps us to cast an interface to a class. The casting is done by equating the name of the instance of the interface to the instance of the class followed by the 'as' operator followed by the name of the interface. The following example demonstrates the use of the 'as' operator. However, it may be noted that the 'as' operator offers no added advantage. Perhaps, it is just a matter of ease. The task can be accomplished in either of the two ways:

```
using System;
using System.Collections.Generic;
using System.Linq;
using System.Text;

namespace Interface5
{
    interface train
    {
```

```csharp
        void getdata();
        void putdata();
    }
    class metro : train
    {
        int numberOfComp;
        public void getdata()
        {
            numberOfComp = 4;
        }
        public void putdata()
        {
            Console.WriteLine("The number of compartments " + numberOfComp);
        }
    }
    class EMU : train
    {
        int numberOfCompartments;
        public void getdata()
        {
            numberOfCompartments = 10;
        }
        public void putdata()
        {
            Console.WriteLine("EMU : Number of compartments " + numberOfCompartments);
        }
    }
    class Program
    {
        static void Main(string[] args)
        {
            metro m = new metro(); ;
            EMU e = new EMU();
            train t;
            t =  m as train;
            t.getdata();
            t.putdata();
            t = e as train;
            e.getdata();
            e.putdata();
            Console.ReadLine();
        }
    }
}
```

SUMMARY

This chapter explains the concept of interface as well as its use and implementation. It may be noted that the importance of interface is mainly due to the non-availability of multiple inheritance in C#. The inclusion of interfaces becomes important owing to the fact that it helps to retain the positive aspects of multiple inheritance while at the same time allowing us to remove ambiguity that arises from it. However, there might be cases where use of interfaces may also lead to ambiguity, but the language provides a way to handle it. In order to make things clearer, it will be good if readers try to create a management system having a hierarchical structure and use interfaces and inheritance in it.

GLOSSARY

Interface An interface contains the declaration of properties and methods. It tells what is to be done and not how it is to be done.
Implementing an interface In order to implement an interface, a class is needed. The class must implement the methods declared in the interface.
as operator The as operator helps to cast an interface to a class.

POINTS TO REMEMBER

- Multiple inheritance is not allowed in C#.
- Interfaces solve the problem of non-inclusion of multiple inheritance in C#.
- Interfaces can have indexers, properties, methods, and/or events. However, these features cannot be defined by an interface.
- A class that implements the interface implements all the features in the interface.
- An interface cannot be directly instantiated.
- An abstract class can also extend an interface.
- An interface can extend two interfaces, whereas a class cannot extend two classes.
- The syntax of an interface extending an interface is the same as that of a class extending a class.
- When an interface extends two interfaces and both the interfaces have a method of the same name, explicit implementation is required.

EXERCISES

I. Multiple-choice Questions

1. Why does the following code not compile?

```
namespace InterfaceEx1
{
  interface student
  {
    int age;
    string name;
    void getdata()
    {
      Console.Write("Enter name");
      name = Console.ReadLine();
      Console.WriteLine("Enter age");
      age = int.Parse(Console.
      ReadLine());
    }
  }
  class studentClass : student
  {
    public void getdata()
    {
      //Something
    }
  }
  class Program
  {
    static void Main(string[] args)
    {
      studentClass s = new studentClass();
      student s = new studentClass();
      s.getdata();
    }
  }
}
```

(a) An interface cannot contain fields.
(b) It uses Write and writeLine methods.
(c) It uses the same name of instances of both class and interface.
(d) None of these.

2. What is the error in the following code?

```
interface student
{
    int age;
    string name;
    void getdata();
}
class studentClass : student
```

```csharp
    {
        public void getdata()
        {
            Console.Write("Enter name");
            name = Console.ReadLine();
            Console.WriteLine("Enter age");
            age = int.Parse(Console.ReadLine());
        }
    }
    class Program
    {
        static void Main(string[] args)
        {
            studentClass s = new studentClass();
            student s = new studentClass();
            s.getdata();
        }
    }
```

(a) An interface cannot contain fields.
(b) It uses Write and writeLine methods.
(c) It uses the same name of instances of both class and interface.
(d) None of these.

3. What is the error in the following code?

```csharp
namespace InterfaceEx1
{
    interface student
    {
        void getdata();
    }
    class studentClass : student
    {
        int age;
        string name;
        public void getdata()
        {
            Console.Write("Enter name");
            name = Console.ReadLine();
            Console.WriteLine("Enter age");
            age = int.Parse(Console.ReadLine());
        }
    }
    class Program
    {
        static void Main(string[] args)
        {
            studentClass s = newstudentClass();
            student s = new studentClass();
            s.getdata();
        }
    }
}
```

(a) An interface cannot contain fields.
(b) It uses Write and writeLine methods.
(c) It uses the same name of instances of both class and interface.
(d) None of these.

4. What is the error in the following code?

```csharp
namespace InterfaceEx1
{
    interface student
    {
        void getdata();
    }
    class studentClass : student
    {
        int age;
        string name;
        void getdata()
        {
            Console.Write("Enter name");
            name = Console.ReadLine();
            Console.WriteLine("Enter age");
            age = int.Parse(Console.ReadLine());
        }
    }
    class Program
    {
        static void Main(string[] args)
        {
            student s = new studentClass();
            s.getdata();
        }
    }
```

(a) The method in the class is not public.
(b) The interface does not have fields.
(c) A class instance cannot be casted to an interface.
(d) Both (a) and (b).

5. Which of the given options correctly depicts the compile time error?

```csharp
namespace InterfaceEx1
{
    interface student
    {
        void putdata();
```

```
      void getdata();
   }
   class studentClass : student
   {
     int age;
     string name;
     public void getdata()
     {
       {
         Console.Write("Enter name");
         name = Console.ReadLine();
         Console.WriteLine("Enter age");
         age = int.Parse(Console.
         ReadLine());
       }
     }
   }
   class Program
   {
     static void Main(string[] args)
     {
       student s = new studentClass();
       s.getdata();
     }
   }
}
```

(a) The code is correct and therefore will compile.
(b) All the interface members must be defined in the implementing class.
(c) Invalid cast.
(d) None of these.

6. Which of the following components can an interface not have?
   (a) Fields
   (b) Methods
   (c) Indexers
   (d) Properties

7. Which of the following concepts can be implemented by interfaces?
   (a) Multiple inheritance
   (b) Operator overloading
   (c) Both (a) and (b)
   (d) None of these.

8. Which of the following statements is incorrect?
   (a) An interface can extend an interface.
   (b) A class can extend an interface.
   (c) A class can implement an interface.
   (d) A class may implement two interfaces.

9. Which of the following statements is correct?
   (a) Interface is like an abstract class.
   (b) Interface is like a structure.
   (c) Interface and enumeration accomplish similar tasks.
   (d) None of these.

10. Which of the following is correct with respect to an interface?
    (a) All its methods must be implemented by the implementing class.
    (b) Some of the methods may be implemented, whereas some may not.
    (c) All the methods must be implemented but it is not necessary to implement all properties.
    (d) None of these.

II. Review Questions

1. What is the importance of the concept of interface?
2. What else can be used in place of an interface to realize multilevel inheritance?
3. What can be the components of an interface?
4. Which inheritance cannot be implemented without interfaces?
5. Explain the importance of multiple inheritance.
6. What is the problem with multiple inheritance?
7. Explain the problems with extending two interfaces.
8. With the help of an example, explain the implementation of an interface having some property.
9. Can a class define only selected methods of the interface it implements?
10. Can a class extend an interface?

III. Programming Exercises

1. Create two interfaces called employee and student having the following methods:
   Student
      getdata();
      putdata();
   Employee
      getSalary();
      putSalary();

Now create a class called empStudent. The class depicts a PhD scholar who is also teaching in the university. He is doing his PhD from the university; therefore, he is a student. Moreover, he is teaching in the university, say as a guest lecturer; therefore, he is also an employee of the university. The class should implement the interfaces. Write a program for this problem.

2. In Question 1, add `getdata()` to the employee interface and demonstrate ambiguity resolution.

3. In Question 2, create another class called programmer, which should have a property numberProjects. Define the property in the empStudent class by making the requisite changes.

4. In Question 3, insert a property called classesTaken in the employee interface and handle it in the implementing class.

5. Demonstrate the use of indexers in Question 4.

6. What changes will have to be made in Question 5 so that there is no ambiguity in the empStudent class?

7. In Question 6, derive another class called winner from the empStudent class. Create a method called `getAmount()` and the requisite variables in the method.

8. Create an interface called train and a class called metro, which implements the interface. Add the requisite methods and fields in the class to demonstrate the use of interfaces in putting multiple inheritance to action.

9. Create an interface called shape and a property called `numberOfSides` in it. Now create two classes named triangle and square, which implement the interface. The classes should have `getdata()` and `putdata()` methods.

10. In Question 9, add an interface called size having a property called level to depict the different relative sizes. A shape can have three sizes having the value of levels 0, 1, and 2.

14 Operator Overloading

OBJECTIVES

After completing this chapter, the reader will be able to
Appreciate the importance of operator overloading
Understand unary operator overloading
Use operator overloading for binary operators
Implement comparison operator overloading

14.1 INTRODUCTION

The chapter introduces an important concept of object-oriented programming, namely operator overloading. This concept is one of the essential language features of C#. In order to get a better understanding of the topic, let us consider a situation wherein a programmer intends to develop a complex number calculator. In order to do so, a class called `Complex` is created having two data members—real and imaginary. The class has a method each for getting the data from the user, say getdata(), and for displaying the data, say putdata(). The class is depicted in the class diagram shown in Fig. 14.1.

After designing the class, some operations are selected to be applied on the complex numbers, the first one being addition. In order to perform this operation, the programmer creates a function called sum. This function takes two arguments and returns the sum. The following program is developed to carry out the task:

Complex
real
imaginary
getdata()
putdata()

Fig. 14.1 Class diagram of `Complex` class

```
using System;
using System.Collections.Generic;
using System.Linq;
using System.Text;

namespace ComplexNumberAddition
{
```

```csharp
class Complex
{
    int real, imaginary;
    public void getdata()
    {
        try
        {
            Console.WriteLine("Enter the real part of the complex number");
            real = int.Parse(Console.ReadLine());
            Console.WriteLine("Enter the imaginary part of the complex number");
            imaginary = int.Parse(Console.ReadLine());
        }
        catch(Exception e)
        {
            Console.WriteLine("Exception " + e.ToString());
        }
    }
    public void putdata()
    {
        Console.WriteLine(real.ToString() + " + i" + imaginary.ToString());
    }
    public Complex sum(Complex c1)
    {
        Complex result = new Complex();
        result.real = c1.real + real;
        result.imaginary = c1.imaginary + imaginary;
        return result;
    }
}
class Program
{
    static void Main(string[] args)
    {
        Complex c1 = new Complex();
        Complex c2 = new Complex();
        Console.WriteLine("First complex number");
        c1.getdata();
        Console.WriteLine("Second complex number");
        c2.getdata();
        Complex s = new Complex();
        s = c2.sum(c1);
        Console.WriteLine("Sum");
        s.putdata();
        Console.ReadKey();
    }
}
```

Output

```
First complex number
Enter the real part of the complex number
2
Enter the imaginary part of the complex number
3
Second complex number
Enter the real part of the complex number
4
Enter the imaginary part of the complex number
5
sum
6 + i8
```

The program calculates the sum of two complex numbers by calling the sum method of the object c2, that is, c2.sum(c1). The sum method of c2 takes c1 as its arguments and returns the result, which is stored in s. In order to display s, the putdata() method of s has been called.

Writing c2.sum(c1) is unintelligible. We perceive the calculation of sum to be as simple as writing $s = c1 + c2$, but as we have discussed earlier, the operator + cannot be used for user-defined data types. In C#, there is, however, a provision for giving a new meaning to already-defined operators. The technique is referred to as operator overloading. The chapter introduces the concept and enlists its types, advantages, and disadvantages.

14.2 SYNTAX

Operator overloading presents a solution for the problem mentioned in Section 14.1. It lets us use the operators in the same manner as used for standard data types. The syntax of overloading is as follows:

```
public static <return type> operator <operator that can be overloaded>(argument list)
```

The various components of the definition have been described in Table 14.1.

Table 14.1 Components of declaration of operator overloading

public	This is written so that the operator can be accessed in the Main method.
static	This is to ensure that there is only one copy of the operator.
Return type	This is the type of the operand on the left side of the intended equation via which the operator is to be invoked.
List of operators that cannot be overloaded	These are given in Section 14.5.
Argument list	Unary operators should have one argument whereas binary operators should have two. The concept has been discussed in Sections 14.3 and 14.4.

For example, if we have to overload the * operator for complex numbers, then the following declaration should be used:

```
public static Complex operator *(Complex c1, Complex c2);
```

where c1 and c2 are the complex numbers to be multiplied.

14.3 UNARY OPERATOR OVERLOADING

As stated in Chapter 3, unary operators act on one variable. The increment and decrement operators explained in Chapter 3 are examples of unary operators. The operator ++, for example, is of two types—post-increment and pre-increment. The post-increment operator increments the variable after transferring its value, whereas the pre-increment operator does the task before incrementing the value.

Suppose a variable y has value five. If the value of x is y++, then the value of x becomes five and the value of y becomes six after the statement $x = y$++ has executed. However, had the value of x been ++y, then the value of y would have been incremented and then the new value would have been transferred to x. So, the value of x and y would have become six. Let us now see how the programmer mentioned in Section 14.1 implemented the complex number calculator.

The programmer, while developing the complex number calculator, decides to use the increment operator (++) in the program. The ++ operator will increment both the real and the imaginary parts. The programmer writes the following code to implement the operator. Now, the problem here is that we cannot simply overload the ++ operator like in C++, because in C#, user-defined operators cannot return null.

```
class Complex
{
    int real, imaginary;
    Complex()
    {
        real = 0;
        imaginary = 0;
    }
    public void getData()
    {
        Console.WriteLine("Enter the real part");
        real = int.Parse(Console.ReadLine());
        Console.WriteLine("Enter the imaginary part");
        imaginary = int.Parse(Console.ReadLine());
    }
    public void putData()
    {
        Console.WriteLine(real + " + i" + imaginary);
    }
    public void operator ++(Complex c)
    {
        c.real++;
        c.imaginary++;
    }
}
class Program
{
    static void Main(string[] args)
    {
        Complex c1 = new Complex();
        c1.getData();
        Console.WriteLine("You have entered ");
        c1.putData();
        c1++;
        Console.WriteLine("After increment ");
```

```
            c1.putData();
            Console.ReadKey();
        }
    }
```

When the program is compiled, the following errors will be displayed in the error pane:
- `The return type for ++ or -- operator must be the containing type or derived from the containing type.`
- `User-defined operators cannot return void.`
- `User-defined operator 'OperatorOverloading1.Complex.operator++ (OperatorOverloading1.Complex)' must be declared static and public.`

However, on making the following changes the code will be compiled:

```
class Complex
{
    int real, imaginary;
    public Complex()
    {
        real = 0;
        imaginary = 0;
    }
    public void getData()
    {
        Console.WriteLine("Enter the real part");
        real = int.Parse(Console.ReadLine());
        Console.WriteLine("Enter the imaginary part");
        imaginary = int.Parse(Console.ReadLine());
    }
    public void putData()
    {
        Console.WriteLine(real + " + i" + imaginary);
    }
    public static Complex  operator ++(Complex c)
    {
        c.real = ++c.real;
        c.imaginary = ++c.imaginary;
        return c;
    }
}
class Program
{
    static void Main(string[] args)
    {
        Complex c1 = new Complex();
        c1.getData();
        Console.WriteLine("You have entered ");
        c1.putData();
        c1 = ++c1;
        Console.WriteLine("After increment ");
        c1.putData();
        Console.ReadKey();
    }
}
```

Output

```
Enter the real part
2
Enter the imaginary part
3
You have entered
2 + i 3
After increment
3 + i 4
```

This program, therefore, brings out the following points:
1. The overloaded operators must be public access specifiers, so that they can be accessed outside the class as well.
2. The operator must be static, so that there is just one copy of the operator.
3. The unary operators must return a value, which is of the same type as that of the class.
4. The unary operators in C#, unlike C++, must have an argument, which is of same type as that of the class.

These points have been implemented in the given program to make it run. Not following any of these points will result in compile time errors.

14.4 OVERLOADING BINARY OPERATORS

Binary operators are those that operate on two operands and return the result, which can be stored in the variable on the left-hand side of the equation. This can be explained with the help of an example. Let $c1$ and $c2$ be the two instances of complex numbers. Writing $c3 = c1 - c2$ means that the difference of $c1$ and $c2$ will be stored in the variable $c3$. The operator, therefore, returns a value, which is of the same type as that of either of the classes. We assume that the type of the two operands is also the same, or at least implicitly castable. So, in the program given in Section 14.3, overloading '−' operator will be required to accomplish the task of subtraction. This is called binary operator overloading. The example of determining the difference of complex numbers has been implemented in the following program:

```
class Complex
{
    public int real, imaginary;
    public Complex()
    {
        real = 0;
        imaginary = 0;
    }
    public void getData()
    {
        Console.WriteLine("Enter the real part");
        real = int.Parse(Console.ReadLine());
        Console.WriteLine("Enter the imaginary part");
```

```csharp
            imaginary = int.Parse(Console.ReadLine());
        }
        public void putData()
        {
            Console.WriteLine(real + " + i" + imaginary);
        }
        public static Complex operator ++(Complex c)
        {
            c.real = ++c.real;
            c.imaginary = ++c.imaginary;
            return c;
        }
        public static Complex operator -(Complex c1, Complex c2)
        {
            Complex c3 = new Complex();
            c3.real = c1.real - c2.real;
            c3.imaginary = c1.imaginary - c2.imaginary;
            return c3;
        }
    }
    class Program
    {
        static void Main(string[] args)
        {
            Complex c1 = new Complex();
            Complex c2 = new Complex();
            c1.getData();
            Console.WriteLine("You have entered ");
            c1.putData();
            c2.getData();
            Console.WriteLine("You have entered ");
            c2.putData();
            Complex c3 = c1 - c2;
            Console.WriteLine("Result of subtraction ");
            c3.putData();
            Console.ReadKey();
        }
    }
```

Output

```
Enter the real Part
3
Enter the imaginary part
2
You have entered
3 + i2
Enter the real part
1
Enter the imaginary part
1
```

```
You have entered
1 + i1
Result of subtraction
2 + i1
```

From the implementation of the – operator, the following points may be noted about binary operator overloading:
1. The data type of either operand must be the same or implicitly convertible to each other.
2. The return type must be the same as that of either of the operators.
3. The operator must be public and static.
4. The meaning of the operator should not be changed. However, this is only a desirable property.

Some operators cannot be overloaded; the list of such operators is given in Section 14.5.

14.5 OPERATORS THAT CANNOT BE OVERLOADED

The developers of C# have decided not to allow the overloading of some of the operators. The reason for doing so may be to preserve the integrity of the operators. These operators, therefore, can be used only with the predefined types. The list of such operators is given in Fig. 14.2.

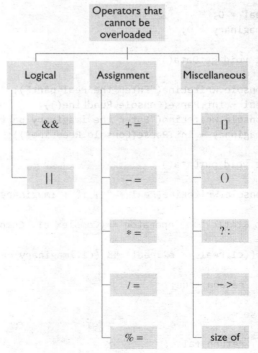

Fig. 14.2 Operators that cannot be overloaded

14.6 MISCELLANEOUS OPERATORS

Having gone through the earlier sections, readers might be tempted to use the == operator with complex numbers, since ++, ––. +, *, and – may now be easily defined. If the == operator can also be overloaded with the same ease as the other operators, then the development of the complex number calculator and many other such applications will become easy and efficient. In C#, overloading of the == operator is as uncomplicated as that of the other operators.

14.6.1 == Operator

The == operator has been explained by taking the example of complex number equality. The equality of two complex numbers is decided by determining whether their real parts as well as their imaginary parts are the same. Hence, if $c1$ and $c2$ are two complex numbers, then the following condition guarantees their equality:

$$c1.\text{real} == c2.\text{real} \text{ and } c1.\text{imaginary} == c2.\text{imaginary}$$

The program for overloading the == operator is as follows:

```
namespace OperatorOverloading2
{
    class Complex
    {
        public int real, imaginary;
        public Complex()
        {
            real = 0;
            imaginary = 0;
        }
        public void getData()
        {
            Console.WriteLine("Enter the real part");
            real = int.Parse(Console.ReadLine());
            Console.WriteLine("Enter the imaginary part");
            imaginary = int.Parse(Console.ReadLine());
        }
        public void putData()
        {
            Console.WriteLine(real + " + i" + imaginary);
        }
        public static bool operator ==(Complex c1, Complex c2)
        {
            if((c1.real == c2.real) && (c1.imaginary == c2.imaginary))
            {
                return true;
            }
            else
            {
                return false;
            }
        }
```

```csharp
            public static bool operator !=(Complex c1, Complex c2)
            {
                if((c1.real == c2.real) && (c1.imaginary == c2.imaginary))
                {
                    return false;
                }
                else
                {
                    return true;
                }
            }
        }
        class Program
        {
            static void Main(string[] args)
            {
                Complex c1 = new Complex();
                Complex c2 = new Complex();
                c1.getData();
                Console.WriteLine("You have entered ");
                c1.putData();
                c2.getData();
                Console.WriteLine("You have entered ");
                c2.putData();
                if(c1 == c2)
                {
                    Console.WriteLine("The complex numbers are equal ");
                }
                else
                {
                    Console.WriteLine("They are not equal");
                }
                Console.ReadKey();
            }
        }
    }
```

Output

```
Enter the real part
2
Enter the imaginary part
3
You have entered
2 + i3
Enter the real part
2
Enter the imaginary part
3
You have entered
2 + i3
The complex numbers are equal
```

In the second case, when the numbers entered are not equal, the following output is displayed:

```
Enter the real part
2
Enter the imaginary part
3
You have entered
2 + i3
Enter the real part
1
Enter the imaginary part
2
You have entered
1 + i2
They are not equal
```

14.6.2 >= and <= Operators

Overloading of the >= and <= operators requires clear definition of the greater and smaller operators. It may be noted that in case of most of the user-defined operators, the comparison will not be easy. However, in order to provide a clear understanding of the concept, the example of complex numbers has been explained here. The operator >= is defined as follows with respect to complex numbers:

If two complex numbers $c1$ and $c2$ are $x1 + iy1$ and $x2 + iy2$, then $c1 >= c2$ if $x1 >= x2$ and $y1 = y2 = 0$. Similarly, the <= operator can also be defined. The two operators have been overloaded in the following program:

```csharp
using System;
using System.Collections.Generic;
using System.Linq;
using System.Text;

namespace OperatorOverloading3
{
    class Program
    {
        class Complex
        {
            public int real, imaginary;
            public Complex()
            {
                real = 0;
                imaginary = 0;
            }
            public void getData()
            {
                Console.WriteLine("Enter the real part");
                real = int.Parse(Console.ReadLine());
                Console.WriteLine("Enter the imaginary part");
                imaginary = int.Parse(Console.ReadLine());
            }
```

```csharp
        public void putData()
        {
            Console.WriteLine(real + " + i" + imaginary);
        }
        public static bool operator >=(Complex c1, Complex c2)
        {
            if((c1.real >= c2.real) && (c1.imaginary == 0) && (c2.imaginary == 0))
            {
                return true;
            }
            else
            {
                return false;
            }
        }
        public static bool operator <=(Complex c1, Complex c2)
        {
            if((c1.real <= c2.real) && (c1.imaginary == 0) && (c2.imaginary == 0))
            {
                return true;
            }
            else
            {
                return false;
            }
        }
    }
    static void Main(string[] args)
    {
        Complex c1 = new Complex();
        Complex c2 = new Complex();
        c1.getData();
        Console.WriteLine("You have entered ");
        c1.putData();
        c2.getData();
        Console.WriteLine("You have entered ");
        c2.putData();
        if(c1 >= c2)
        {
            Console.WriteLine("The first complex number is greater");
        }
        else if(c1 <= c2)
        {
            Console.WriteLine("The first is smaller");
        }
        else
        {
            Console.WriteLine("The numbers cannot be compared");
        }
        Console.ReadKey();
    }
  }
}
```

Output

```
Enter the real Part
3
Enter the imaginary part
0
You have entered
3 +i0
Enter the real part
2
Enter the imaginary part
0
You have entered
2 + i0
The first complex number is greater
```

```
Enter the real part
2
Enter the imaginary part
0
You have entered
2 + i0
Enter the real part
3
Enter the imaginary part
0
You have entered
3 + i0
The first is smaller
```

The second output shown depicts the case when the second number is greater. In all other cases, however, the numbers cannot be compared.

```
Enter the real part
2
Enter the imaginary part
3
You have entered
2 + i3
Enter the real part
4
Enter the imaginary part
5
You have entered
4 + i5
The numbers cannot be compared
```

It may be noted that the comparison needs to be clearly defined before implementing it. In order to make our own class, we need to first conceptualize it, clearly define its operations, and then proceed towards the implementation.

SUMMARY

Operator overloading is essential when the operators of custom-made classes need to be defined. It is an important language feature of C#. Operator overloading was first introduced in ALGOL68. The language specification of ALGOL68 defined four overloaded operators. In the 1980s, ADA and C++ also used operator overloading. However, many restrictions were imposed on overloading in the later versions of ADA. The developers of Java decided not to include operator overloading in the language. It may be noted that operator overloading can also be considered as a type of polymorphism, owing to the fact that we give more than one meaning to an operator. It is also termed as ad hoc polymorphism by some. The analysis of Scala and Lua also brings out the fact that operator overloading is used by other names. Changing the name does not change the concept. The complete complex number calculator has been included in the web resources. The program puts together all what we have studied and therefore helps to see the concept in perspective. Let us conclude the chapter by acknowledging the importance of operator overloading in the modern software development process.

GLOSSARY

Operator overloading Assigning more than one meaning to an operator is referred to as operator overloading. This concept helps to apply predefined operators to user-defined classes.

Unary operator overloading When an operator is crafted in such a way that it can be applied only to a single operand, it is referred to as unary operator overloading.

Binary operator overloading An operator that can be applied on two operands (user-defined data types) is called binary operator and the phenomenon of giving new meaning to that operator is known as binary operator overloading.

POINTS TO REMEMBER

- User-defined operators cannot return void.
- The overloaded operators must be public access specifiers, so that they can be accessed outside the class as well.
- The unary operators must return a value, which is of the same type as that of the class.
- In operator overloading, the data type of either operand must be the same or implicitly convertible to each other.

EXERCISES

I. Multiple-choice Questions

1. What is the problem with the following declaration of the increment operator for a complex number having real and imaginary as its data members?

```
public static void  operator ++(Complex c)
{
```

```
        ++real;
        ++imaginary;
    }
```

(a) The removal of the keyword static will make the program run.
(b) Unary operators cannot have void return type.
(c) The ++ operator cannot be overloaded.
(d) The declaration is correct and the program will be compiled.

2. A hypothetical operator ++ increments only the real part of a complex number and leaves the imaginary part unchanged. Which of the following is the correct definition of the operator?

(a) public static void operator +(Complex c)
```
    {
        ++real;
    }
```
(b) public static Complex operator ++(Complex c)
```
    {
        ++real;
        ++imaginary;
        return this;
    }
```
(c) public static Complex operator ++(Complex c)
```
    {
        Complex c1;
        C1.real = ++c.real;
        C1.imaginary = imaginary;
        return c1;
    }
```
(d) None of these

3. Which of the following is the correct definition of the subtraction operator as regards complex numbers?

(a) static Complex operator –(Complex c1, Complex c2)
```
    {
        Complex c3 = new Complex();
        c3.real = c1.real - c2.real;
        c3.imaginary = c1.imaginary - c2.imaginary;
        return c3;
    }
```
(b) public Complex operator -(Complex c1, Complex c2)
```
    {
```

```
        Complex c3 = new Complex();
        c3.real = c1.real - c2.real;
        c3.imaginary = c1.imaginary - c2.imaginary;
        return c3;
    }
```
(c) public static Complex operator -(Complex c1, Complex c2)
```
    {
        Complex c3 = new Complex();
        c3.real = c1.real - c2.real;
        c3.imaginary = c1.imaginary - c2.imaginary;
        return c3;
    }
```
(d) public static void operator -(Complex c1, Complex c2)
```
    {
        real = c1.real - c2.real;
        imaginary = c1.imaginary - c2.imaginary;
    }
```

4. Which of the following is the correct definition of the multiplication operator as regards complex numbers?

(a) public static Complex operator *(Complex c1, Complex c2)
```
    {
        Complex c = new Complex();
        c.real = c1.real * c2.real - c1.imaginary * c2.imaginary;
        c.imaginary = c1.real * c2.imaginary + c2.real * c1.imaginary;
        return c;
    }
```
(b) public Complex operator *(Complex c1, Complex c2)
```
    {
        Complex c = new Complex();
        c.real = c1.real * c2.real - c1.imaginary * c2.imaginary;
        c.imaginary = c1.real * c2.imaginary + c2.real * c1.imaginary;
        return c;
    }
```
(c) public static Complex operator *(Complex c1, Complex c2)
```
    {
```

```
        Complex c = new Complex();
        c.real = c1.real * c2.real;
        c.imaginary = c2.imaginary *
            c2.imaginary;
        return c;
    }
(d) public    static    Complex    operator
    *(Complex c1, Complex c2)
    {
        Complex c = new Complex();
        c.real = c1.real * c2.real;
        c.imaginary = c2.imaginary *
            c2.imaginary;
        return c;
    }
```

5. Which of the following operators cannot be overloaded?
   (a) ==   (b) +   (c) –   (d) [ ]
6. Which of the following operators can be overloaded?
   (a) ?:   (b) [ ]   (c) ( )   (d) >=

7. Which of the following operators can be overloaded?
   (a) <=
   (b) >=
   (c) ==
   (d) All of these
8. Which type of polymorphism is operator overloading?
   (a) ad hoc polymorphism
   (b) Multiple inheritance
   (c) Both (a) and (b)
   (d) None of these
9. Which of the following statements about operator overloading is correct?
   (a) It is essential to implement sum, difference, and product of custom-made classes.
   (b) It is desirable since it helps to remove obscure syntax.
   (c) It is not supported in C#.
   (d) None of these.
10. Which of the following is not supported by C#?
    (a) Multiple inheritance
    (b) Operator overloading
    (c) Both (a) and (b)
    (d) None of these

II. Review Questions

1. What is the importance of operator overloading?
2. With the help of an example, explain the syntax of unary and binary operator overloading.
3. Which are the operators that cannot be overloaded?
4. Briefly explain the history of operator overloading.
5. Which object-oriented language does not support operator overloading?

III. Programming Exercises

Com-complex: The new number

The following questions are based on a hypothetical number called com-complex. The number has three parts—real, imaginary, and i_imaginary.

1. Create two constructors of the class. The first constructor should be a default constructor, which initializes the data members by zero each. The second constructor should be a parameterized constructor, which initializes the members with the arguments passed.
2. Create two functions—getData() and putData(). The former takes the values of the data members from the user, whereas the latter displays the number.
3. Now, overload the unary operator ++, which increments the real, imaginary, and i_imaginary parts. That is

   $com-complex++ = (real++) + (imaginary++) + (i\_imaginary++)$

4. The next task is to overload the unary operator --, which decrements the real, imaginary, and i_imaginary parts.

   $com-complex-- = (real--) + (imaginary--) + (i\_imaginary--)$

5. The addition of two com-complex numbers has been defined as follows:

   If c1 = real1 + i*imaginary1 + j*i_imaginary1,

   where $i = \sqrt{-1}$ and $j = \sqrt{\sqrt{-1}}$ and

   c2 = real2 + i*imaginary2 + j*i_imaginary2, then

$c1+c2 = (real1+real2)$
$\quad + i*(imaginary1+imaginary2)$
$\quad + j*(i\_imaginary1+i\_imaginary2)$

overload the + operator for the com-complex class.

6. The subtraction of two com-complex numbers has been defined as follows:

   If $c1 = real1 + i*imaginary1 + j*i\_imaginary1$, where $i = \sqrt{-1}$ and $j = \sqrt{\sqrt{-1}}$ and
   $c2 = real2 + i*imaginary2 + j*i\_imaginary2$, then

   $c1-c2 = (real1-real2)$
   $\quad + i*(imaginary1-imaginary2)$
   $\quad + j*(i\_imaginary1-i\_imaginary2).$

   Overload the − operator for the com-complex class.

7. The multiplication of two com-complex numbers is defined as follows:

   If $c1 = real1 + i*imaginary1 + j*i\_imaginary1$, where $i = \sqrt{-1}$ and $j = \sqrt{\sqrt{-1}}$ and
   $c2 = real2 + i*imaginary2 + j*i\_imaginary2$, then

   $c1*c2 = (real1*real2 - imaginary1*imaginary2)$
   $\quad + i*(imaginary1*real2 + real1*imaginary2$
   $\quad + i\_imaginary1*i\_imaginary2)$
   $\quad + j*(i\_imaginary1*real2 + i\_imaginary2*real1)$
   $\quad + i*j(imaginary1*i\_imaginary2$
   $\quad + imaginary2*i\_imaginary1)$

   Overload the * operator for the com-complex class.

8. Now work out the division of two com-complex numbers and overload the operator.

Time Class

The following questions are based on the class 'time' having three components hours, minutes, and seconds.

9. Create two constructors of the class. The first constructor should be a default constructor, which initializes the data members by zero each. The second constructor should be a parameterized constructor, which initializes the members with the arguments passed.

10. Create two functions `getData()` and `putData()`. The former takes the values of the data members from the user, whereas the latter displays the number.

11. Now, overload the unary operator ++, which increments the seconds, followed by minutes and then by hours. It may be noted that if the value of seconds is 59, then the next value should be 0, and the value of minutes should be incremented by 1. Similarly, when the value of minutes is 59, the next value should be 0, with the value of hours being incremented by 1. The maximum value of hours can be 23, after which each of the three components should become 0.

12. Create an operator − for this class.

15 Errors and Exceptions

OBJECTIVES

After completing this chapter, the reader will be able to

- # Appreciate the significance of exception handling
- # Use `try-catch` block
- # Explain the importance of nested `try-catch`
- # Use `finally` block
- # Describe the concept of multiple `catch`
- # Understand the `Exception` class
- # Create user-defined `Exception` class

15.1 ERRORS ARE GOOD

The best way to learn programming is to practise writing numerous programs. When one tries to implement a new algorithm for the first time, there is a high probability of multiple errors cropping up. However, the occurrence of so many errors should not unnerve a programmer. In fact, one learns from these errors and by making sure that such errors are not repeated one can become a good programmer.

There are two ways of looking at these errors. The first one is that in order to avoid errors in programming we must learn the syntax and language basics. The second is that we can learn the syntax and language basics from these errors. Errors tell us that we have not learned the language thoroughly yet, but they also teach the nuances at the same time. The process is much like the nagging of a teacher who always tells us that we have several shortcomings, which ultimately helps us to become better in the domain.

15.2 TYPES OF ERRORS

There are two types of errors. The first type of error occurs at compile time, that is, while converting the program to an object file. The second type occurs at runtime, that is, while executing the program. This section discusses both the types and provides ideas regarding the ways to handle them.

15.2.1 Compile Time Errors

The errors that are detected at the time of compilation are called compile time errors. These errors primarily occur due to incorrect syntax. However, there can be other reasons as well, as discussed later in the chapter. For example, consider the following snippet:

```
namespace Errors1
{
    class Program
    {
        static void Main(string[] args)
        {
            int number1;
            Console.WriteLine("Enter a number\t:");
            number1 = int.Parse(Console.ReadLine());
            Console.WriteLine("You have entered " + number1)
            Console.ReadKey();
        }
    }
}
```

Since there has to be a sentence terminator at the end of each line, an error will be displayed owing to a missing semicolon at the end of the last output statement. The error shown in Fig. 15.1 will be displayed in the error pane.

Such errors are detected at compile time. In fact, we do not even need to compile the program; the 'intellisense' detects these errors as and when we write them. Intellisence is one of the most powerful features of Visual C#. During automatic compilation, it also selects members that are most frequently used. Therefore, the probability of a programmer incorrectly writing a method decreases. However, readers must understand the reasons for the occurrence of compile time errors. The following list gives some of the reasons for such errors:

1. Missing semicolons
2. Misspelt keywords
3. Not having a matching closing brace for each opening brace
4. Use of undeclared or uninitialized variables
5. Incompatible assignments
6. Inappropriate references

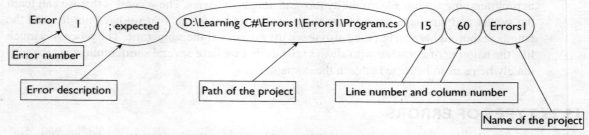

Fig. 15.1 Error shown in an error pane

15.2.2 Runtime Errors and Exceptions

The errors that crop up while a program is being executed are called runtime errors. The reason for such errors can be inappropriate input by the user, arithmetic exceptions, accessing an element of an array that does not exist, illegal conversion, and many more. In order to understand the concept, let us revisit the code given in Section 15.2.1 and insert a semicolon at the end of the last output statement. The program then compiles successfully, but at the runtime if we enter a string instead of a number, the program is halted.

```
using System;
using System.Collections.Generic;
using System.Linq;
using System.Text;

namespace Errors1
{
    class Program
    {
        static void Main(string[] args)
        {
            int number1;
            Console.WriteLine("Enter a number\t:");
            number1 = int.Parse(Console.ReadLine());
            Console.WriteLine("You have entered " + number1);
            Console.ReadKey();
        }
    }
}
```

Output

```
Enter a number :
harsh
```

Observe what happens. As soon as we enter 'harsh', the program is halted and the screen shown in Fig. 15.2 is displayed

This is called a runtime error. In this case, the error has occurred due to inappropriate input. Since the argument was not in the correct format, the program has halted and the programmer has been directed to the portion containing the source of the error. It may be noted here that the statements following the statement with error are never executed. Runtime error causes a condition called exception. Whenever a runtime error occurs, an exception is thrown, which halts the program. Therefore, all the exceptions must be properly thrown and handled. The steps of an effective exception handling mechanism are explained in Section 15.3.

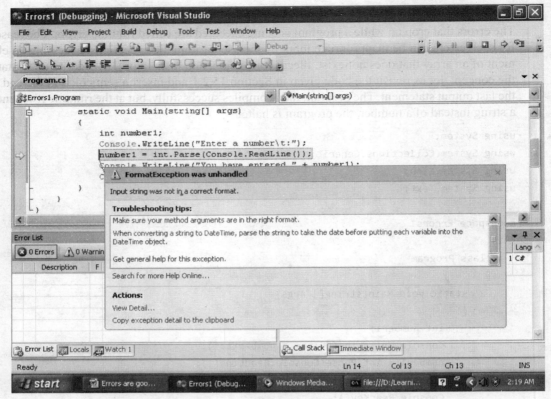

Fig. 15.2 Exception encountered on entering an illegal value

15.3 EFFECTIVE EXCEPTION HANDLING MECHANISM

In order to handle exceptions, we must first identify the portion of the code where an exception might occur. After identifying the portion, we must place that portion in a `try` block. For every `try` block, there has to be a corresponding `catch` block. Inside the `catch` block, any of the arguments shown in Table 15.1 may appear.

Table 15.1 Types of exceptions

Exception class	Meaning
Exception	For a general exception.
ArithmeticException	Overflow or underflow due to an arithmetic exception.
DivideByZeroException	When the denominator of an arithmetic exception becomes zero.
NotFiniteNumberException	Invalid number.
InvalidOperationException	The operation is not allowed between the operands.
SystemException	Failed runtime check.
CoreException	Base class of exception thrown at runtime.
NullReferenceException	Trying to utilize an exception that has not been dispensed.
StackOverflowException	When stack overflows.

(Contd)

Table 15.1 (Contd)

Exception class	Meaning
OutOfMemoryException	Memory allotted to the program not sufficient.
MissingMemberException	Inappropriate dll accessed.
InvalidCastException	Illegal cast attempted.
AccessException	Failure to access a type.
ArgumentException	Argument invalid.
ArgumentOutOfRangeException	Argument out of range.
ArgumentNullException	Null argument passed to a method that does not accept it.
ArrayTypeMismatchException	The element that one is trying to input is not of the type of the array in question.
FormatException	Illegal format of the argument.
IndexOutOfRangeException	Trying to access an element from an index exceeding the maximum capacity of the array defined at the runtime.

In the catch block, we can write the code to be executed when exception occurs.

```
try
{
    //The code that may result in a runtime error
}
catch(<Argument>)
{
    //The code that handles exception
}
```

It may be noted that we may also explicitly throw exceptions as discussed in the later sections. In order to understand the concept, in the earlier example, place the code that asks for the input in the try block and run the program. When the program is executed, give an incorrect input, say a string, and run the program. The exception will be displayed in the output screen.

```
namespace Errors1
{
    class Program
    {
        static void Main(string[] args)
        {
            int number1;
            try
            {
                Console.WriteLine("Enter a number\t:");
                number1 = int.Parse(Console.ReadLine());
                Console.WriteLine("You have entered " + number1);
            }
            catch(Exception e)
            {
                Console.WriteLine("Exception " + e.ToString());
            }
```

```
                    Console.ReadKey();
                }
            }
        }
```

Output

```
Enter a number :
harsh
Exception System.FormatException: Input string was not in a correct
format.
    at System.Number.StringToNumber<String str, NumberStyles options,
NumberBuffer & number, NumberFormatInfo info, Boolean parseDecimel>
    at System.Number.ParseInt32<String s, NumberStyles style,
NumberFormatInfo info>
    at System.Int32.Parse<String s>
    at Errors1.Program.Main<String[] args> in D:\Learning C#\Errors1\
Errors1\Program.cs:line 16
```

As readers must have observed, a `FormatException` has been displayed. The program was expecting an integer input, but what it has got is a string; therefore, an exception has been thrown. There are many more such exceptions. One of the most important exceptions is the `ArithmeticException`. It is thrown when an arithmetic error occurs at the runtime. The next example demonstrates the use of this exception.

The program asks the user to enter a number and calculates its square root. However, since the square root of a negative number is an imaginary number, exception is expected if one enters a negative number. However, this code does not result in an exception.

```
namespace Errors2
{
    class Program
    {
        static void Main(string[] args)
        {
            int number;
            double squareRoot;
            try
            {
                Console.WriteLine("Enter a number\t:");
                number = int.Parse(Console.ReadLine());
                squareRoot = Math.Sqrt(number);
                Console.WriteLine("The square root of "
                + number + " is " + squareRoot);
            }
            catch(ArithmeticException e)
            {
                Console.WriteLine("Exception " + e.ToString());
            }
            Console.ReadKey();
        }
    }
}
```

Output

When the appropriate number is given as input, the correct result is displayed.

```
Enter a number :
4
The square root of 4 is 2
```

It may be noted that as against general perception, ArithmeticException is not thrown when a negative number is given as an input. The square root of a negative number is NaN.

```
Enter a number :
-3
The square root of -3 is NaN
```

However, this is not the case when the denominator of an expression becomes zero. The following program calculates $(a + b)/(a - b)$, the values of a and b being entered by the user.

```
using System;
using System.Collections.Generic;
using System.Linq;
using System.Text;

namespace Errors3
{
    class Program
    {
        static void Main(string[] args)
        {
            int a, b;
            int x;
            try
            {
                Console.WriteLine("Enter the first number");
                a = int.Parse(Console.ReadLine());
                Console.WriteLine("Enter the second number");
                b = int.Parse(Console.ReadLine());
                x = (a + b) / (a - b);
                Console.WriteLine("The answer is " + x.ToString());
            }
            catch(ArithmeticException e)
            {
                Console.WriteLine("Exception " + e.ToString());
            }
            Console.ReadKey();
        }
    }
}
```

Output

Readers can run the program, enter the same number as a and b, and observe what happens. The DivideByZeroException is thrown and is displayed on the output screen.

```
Enter the first number
2
Enter the second number
2
Exception System.DivideByZeroException: Attempted to divide by zero.
    at Errors3.Program.Main<String[] args> in D:\Learning C#\Errors3\
Errors3\Program.cs:line 21
```

There is a catch here. On the face of it, something divided by zero is indeterminate, and hence giving the same value of *a* and *b* should result in an exception. However, we may also get infinity as the answer. The literature, especially Indian, gives an impression that something divided by zero always results in ArithmeticException, which is not the case. Try the following code and observe the result:

```
using System;
using System.Collections.Generic;
using System.Linq;
using System.Text;
namespace Errors3
{
    class Program
    {
        static void Main(string[] args)
        {
            int a, b;
            double x;
            try
            {
                Console.WriteLine("Enter the first number");
                a = int.Parse(Console.ReadLine());
                Console.WriteLine("Enter the second number");
                b = int.Parse(Console.ReadLine());
                x = (double) (a + b) / (a - b);
                Console.WriteLine("The answer is " + x.ToString());
            }
            catch(ArithmeticException e)
            {
                Console.WriteLine("Exception " + e.ToString());
            }
            Console.ReadKey();
        }
    }
}
```

Output

When we run the program and insert the same value for *a* and *b*, the following output is displayed:

```
Enter the first number
2
Enter the second number
2
The answer is Infinity
```

Thus, if the calculation is made via double, the answer obtained is infinity.

It may be noted that we may create more than one catch block for a try block. The different catch blocks must have different arguments. The exception that is encountered first is handled first. However, in case of more than one catch, the specific catch gets more priority as compared to a general one. For example, consider a slight change in the previous code.

```
namespace Errors3
{
    class Program
    {
        static void Main(string[] args)
        {
            int a, b;
            int x;
            try
            {
                Console.WriteLine("Enter the first number");
                a = int.Parse(Console.ReadLine());
                Console.WriteLine("Enter the second number");
                b = int.Parse(Console.ReadLine());
                x = (a + b) / (a - b);
                Console.WriteLine("The answer is " + x.ToString());
            }
            catch(ArithmeticException e)
            {
                Console.WriteLine("Arithmetic Exception caught");
            }
            catch(Exception e1)
            {
                Console.WriteLine("General Exception");
            }
            Console.ReadKey();
        }
    }
}
```

Output

When we enter the same value for both a and b, ArithmeticException is caught and not the general one, because of the reasons stated earlier.

```
Enter the first number
2
Enter the second number
2
Arithmetic Exception caught
```

It may also be noted that though we can have any number of catch blocks, we cannot have the super type catch along with its subclass. The following code will therefore result in an error:

```
namespace Errors3
{
    class Program
    {
        static void Main(string[] args)
```

```csharp
        {
            int a, b;
            int x;
            try
            {
                Console.WriteLine("Enter the first number");
                a = int.Parse(Console.ReadLine());
                Console.WriteLine("Enter the second number");
                b = int.Parse(Console.ReadLine());
                x = (a + b) / (a - b);
                Console.WriteLine("The answer is " + x.ToString());
            }
            catch(ArithmeticException e)
            {
                Console.WriteLine("Arithmetic Exception caught");
            }
            catch(Exception e1)
            {
                Console.WriteLine("General Exception");
            }
            catch(DivideByZeroException e3)
            {
                Console.WriteLine("Divide by Zero Exception caught");
            }
            Console.ReadKey();
        }
    }
}
```

Output
When this code is compiled, the following error is displayed in the pane:

```
A previous catch clause already catches all exceptions of this or of a super type
```

15.4 NESTED try–catch

There might be situations wherein we throw an exception in a function that is itself in a `try` block of the calling function. Exception handling within a `try` block is needed in a situation wherein the inner exception needs to be handled in one manner and the outer one in a different manner. Having a `try-catch` block within another `try-catch` block is called nested `try-catch`. The important point to be noted here is that a nested `try-catch` must be implemented only if it is necessary and not just for the sake of implementation. The following snippet gives a depiction of nested `try-catch`. If the input is inappropriate, then the `catch` block of the `Main` method comes into play. However, if *a* is equal to *b*, then the denominator becomes zero and exception is thrown and caught inside the method.

```csharp
using System;
using System.Collections.Generic;
using System.Linq;
using System.Text;

namespace Errors1
{
    class Program
    {
```

```
        static void Func(int a, int b)
        {
            double result;
            try
            {
                result = (a + b) / (a - b);
                Console.WriteLine("Result " + result);
            }
            catch(Exception e)
            {
                Console.WriteLine("Caught inside function");
            }
        }
        static void Main(string[] args)
        {
            int x, y;
            try
            {
                Console.WriteLine("Enter the first number");
                x = int.Parse(Console.ReadLine());
                Console.WriteLine("Enter the second number");
                y = int.Parse(Console.ReadLine());
                Func(x, y);
            }
            catch(Exception e)
            {
                Console.WriteLine("Caught inside main");
            }
            Console.ReadKey();
        }
    }
}
```

Output

The first output depicts the situation wherein the exception is caught inside the method.

```
Enter the first number
2
Enter the second number
2
Caught inside function
```

The second situation depicts the output when the exception is caught inside Main.

```
Enter the first number
1
Enter the second number
harsh
Caught inside main
```

However, if all the inputs are appropriate, the correct output is shown as follows:

```
Enter the first number
3
Enter the second number
2
Result 5
```

15.5 CREATING USER DEFINED EXCEPTIONS

The exception classes provided by C# are good and useful but not sufficient. A need may arise to craft new types of exceptions as per the requirement of the programmer. The situation and the complexity of the project in hand might force the programmer to create new exception classes. The conceptualization of the exception class will be guided by the needs as described earlier. Having our own exception class will give us the flexibility to incorporate appropriate error messages and decide on the premise of throwing exceptions. The throw keyword helps us to implement the concept. The syntax of the invocation of the exception class is as follows.

Syntax
```
        throw new <name of the exception subclass>;
```

The following example depicts a situation wherein the chlorine content of water is to be entered by the user. If the content is greater than the threshold value, then a custom exception is thrown. It may be noted that in this situation, another class called OwnException needs to be created. The class transfers the message to the predefined base class. When the the chlorine content of water is more than the threshold value, exception is thrown using the throw keyword. The message goes to the catch block from where it is passed on to the base class. The listing is given as follows:

```
namespace OwnException
{
    public class OwnException : Exception
    {
        public OwnException(string message)
        : base(message)
        {
        }
        public OwnException()
        {
        }
    }
    class Program
    {
        static void Main(string[] args)
        {
            double clContent, threshold = 0.1;
            try
            {
                Console.WriteLine("Enter the Cl content");
                clContent = double.Parse(Console.ReadLine());
                if(clContent > threshold)
                {
```

```
                    throw new OwnException("Content Harmful");
                }
                else
                {
                    Console.WriteLine("WATER SAFE");
                }
            }
            catch(Exception e)
            {
                Console.WriteLine("Exception " + e.Message);
            }
            Console.ReadKey();
        }
    }
}
```

Output

```
Enter the C1 content
0.3
Exception Content Harmful
```

15.6 finally STATEMENT

It is quite possible that even after having many catch statements we might miss the exact exception thrown by the program at runtime. The point is all the more relevant because the source of runtime errors is generally not known. If the anticipation of the problem is possible, then the corresponding catch block is crafted; if not, then a finally block is included at the end. This block is always executed. The advantage of having a finally block is that no exception will halt the program, and at the same time, actions such as freeing memory can also be included in the block. The following syntax depicts the use of finally statement:

```
try
{
    //Exception will be thrown here
}
catch(FormatException e)
{
    //This block is executed if format exception crops up
}
catch(ArithmeticException e1)
{
    //This block is executed if arithmetic exception occurs
}
catch(IndexOutOfRangeException e3)
{
    //This block is executed if IndexOutOfRangeException occurs
}
finally
{
    //This block is finally executed
}
```

SUMMARY

This chapter instructs us regarding the use of predefined exception classes. It also explains the concept of multiple `catch` blocks. Moreover, the chapter teaches techniques to craft and use our own exception class. The aim of this chapter is not just to give readers an idea of what exception handling is all about but also to enable them to create robust programs. The program should be able to cater to all possible situations, even those that are least expected. This can be accomplished with the help of predefined exception classes; what is equally important is being able to handle situations in which exceptions are not predefined.

GLOSSARY

Error Mistakes generally made by a programmer are referred to as errors. These are bugs in a program. Programs containing such errors may be halted when executed, thus resulting in a failure.

Compile time error Syntactic and semantic errors that crop up at the time of compilation of a program are referred to as compile time errors.

Runtime error While running a program, an error encountered due to situations such as array out of bound or inappropriate format is referred to as a runtime error.

POINTS TO REMEMBER

- A `DivideByZero` exception is thrown only when both the numerator and the denominator are integers and the result is stored in an integer.
- A `catch` block catches the exception thrown by the nearest `try` block.
- The exception class created by a user must be derived from the inbuilt `Exception` class.
- A program having the `finally` statement will always be executed.

EXERCISES

I. Multiple-choice Questions

1. What will be the output of the following snippet?
   ```
   static void Main(string[] args)
   {
       int x = -3, result;
       try
       {
           Console.WriteLine("Enter a number");
           x = int.Parse(Console.ReadLine());
           result = Math.Sqrt(x);
           Console.WriteLine("The result is " + result);
       }
       catch(Exception e)
       {
           Console.WriteLine("Error");
       }
       Console.ReadKey();
   }
   ```
   (a) NaN
   (b) Error
   (c) The code will not be compiled.
   (d) Incorrect exception class is used.

2. What will be the output of the following snippet?
   ```
   class Program
   {
       static void Main(string[] args)
       {
           int x = -3;
           double result;
           try
           {
   ```

```
        result = Math.Sqrt(x);
        Console.WriteLine("The result is " +
           result);
        }
        catch(Exception e)
        {
        Console.WriteLine("Error");
        }
        Console.ReadKey();
        }
    }
```
(a) NaN
(b) Error
(c) The code will not be compiled.
(d) Incorrect exception class is used.

3. What will be the output of the following code?
```
class Program
{
    static void Main(string[] args)
    {
        int x = -3;
        double result;
        try
        {
        result = Math.Sqrt(x);
        Console.WriteLine("The result is
           " + result);
        }
        catch(Exception e)
        {
        Console.WriteLine ("Exception");
        }
        catch(Exception e)
        {
        Console.WriteLine("Arithmetic
           exception");
        }
        Console.ReadKey();
        }
}
```
(a) NaN
(b) Error
(c) Arithmetic exception
(d) Will not compile because a previous catch clause already catches all exceptions of this or of a super type ('System.Exception')

4. What will be the output of the following?
```
class Program
{
    static void Main(string[] args)
```

```
    {
        int x = -3;
        double result;
        try
        {
        result = Math.Sqrt(x);
        Console.WriteLine("The result is "
           + result);
        }
        catch(Exception e)
        {
        Console.WriteLine ("Exception");
        }
        catch(ArithmeticException e)
        {
        Console.WriteLine("Arithmetic
           exception");
        }
        Console.ReadKey();
        }
}
```
(a) NaN
(b) Error
(c) Arithmetic exception
(d) Will not compile because a previous catch clause already catches all exceptions of this or of a super type ('System.Exception')

5. Which of the following depicts the correct output of the following snippet?
```
class Program
{
    static void Main(string[] args)
    {
        int x = -3;
        double result;
        try
        {
        result = Math.Sqrt(x);
        Console.WriteLine("The result
           is " + result);
        }
        catch(DivideByZeroException e)
        {
        Console.WriteLine
           ("Exception");
        }
        catch(ArithmeticException e)
        {
        Console.WriteLine("Arithmetic
           exception");
        }
        Console.ReadKey();
        }
}
```

(a) NaN
(b) Error
(c) Arithmetic exception
(d) Will not compile because a previous catch clause already catches all exceptions of this or of a super type ('System.Exception')

6. What will be the output of the following program?

```
class Program
{
    static void Main(string[] args)
    {
        string x = "Harsh";
        double result;
        try
        {
            result = Math.Sqrt(int.Parse(x));
            Console.WriteLine("The result is " + result);
        }
        catch(DivideByZeroException e)
        {
            Console.WriteLine ("Exception");
        }
        catch(ArithmeticException e)
        {
            Console.WriteLine("Arithmetic exception");
        }
        catch(FormatException e)
        {
            Console.WriteLine("Format exception");
        }
        Console.ReadKey();
    }
}
```

(a) NaN
(b) Error
(c) Arithmetic exception
(d) Format exception

7. What happens when you remove int.parse() from the Sqrt method?
   (a) The code will not be compiled.
   (b) The format exception is thrown.
   (c) Arithmetic exception occurs.
   (d) None of these

8. Which of the following is not an Exception class?
   (a) ArithmeticException
   (b) ProgramTooLongException
   (c) FormatException
   (d) All of these

9. Which of the following is not used in exception handling?
   (a) try
   (b) catch
   (c) finally
   (d) Crafting enumerations

10. Which of the following is correct?
    (a) Exception handling is used for the errors that crop up at the compile time.
    (b) Exception handling is used for polymorphism.
    (c) Exception handling is used for handling runtime errors.
    (d) None of these

II. Review Questions

1. What is the premise of using exception handling?
2. Explain the concept of nested try-catch.
3. Explain the concept of finally statement.
4. What is the difference between compile time and runtime errors?
5. What are the different compile time errors?
6. What is the difference between semantic and syntactic errors?
7. Explain the various errors handled by the different phases of a compiler.
8. Does division by zero always lead to an exception?
9. What is the relation between ArithmeticException and Exception classes? Can we have two catches having these exceptions in the same program?
10. How many catch statements can you have in your program? What happens if none of your catch handles the thrown exception?

III. Programming Exercises

Design the following programs using exception handling:

1. Ask the user to enter two numbers and find their quotient. Now divide the quotient with the root of the first number. Use ArithmeticException and/or DivideByZeroException.
2. Ask the user to enter a, b, and c of the quadratic equation $ax^2 + bx + c = 0$ and find the roots α and β given by the formula $\dfrac{-b \pm \sqrt{b^2 - 4ac}}{2a}$.
3. Ask the user to enter the values of a, b, and c of the cubic equation $ax^3 + bx^2 + c + d = 0$ and find the

sum and the product of the roots. The sum of the roots is given by the formula $\frac{-b}{a}$ and the product is given by the formula $\frac{c}{a}$.

4. Ask the user to enter the concentration of hydrogen ion in a strong acid and find the pH of the solution. It may be noted that the argument of log cannot be negative. You may use any of the appropriate error class.

5. Ask the user to enter the pH of a base and find its OH– ion concentration. The input should be according to the antilog function. Create your own error class to handle the exception.

6. Create your own error class to handle the chlorine content of water. If the chlorine content is greater than the critical value, an exception should be thrown. The critical value and the chlorine content are to be handled by the user.

7. Ask the user to enter the marks obtained by a student in five subjects. The marks are out of 100. If the average mark is less than 40, a fail exception should be thrown. Create your own exception class to handle the situation.

8. Design a program to gather the details of a student. The program should enquire the first name, the last name, and the middle name to start with. If the length of any of the three strings is less than two, then exception should be thrown.

9. Ask the user to enter 10 names. Store each name in a character array. Now, make an array of these arrays. If the length of any of the array is greater than 20, then the program must display an exception.

10. In the program given in Question 9, deliberately remove the appropriate exception. Now create a `finally` block, which handles the exception.

16 Generics

OBJECTIVES

After completing this chapter, the reader will be able to
- Appreciate and use `SortedList` with a custom class
- Use the `Queue` generic with a custom class
- Implement the `Stack` generic with a custom class
- Understand the working of the List and the use of the `sort` function

16.1 INTRODUCTION

Generics and collections are closely related. Both help us to implement data structures such as stacks and queues, among other things. Generics and collections can be used in operating system design and in distributed database handling as well. However, these tasks are beyond the scope of this book. The present chapter will focus on the basic applications of collections and generics. Collections in C# have already been covered in Chapter 6, wherein we have discussed the following:

1. Queue
2. Stack
3. Directory
4. HashSet
5. Lazy

In order to use these collections, we need to convert the data from one type to another. This may result in errors and hence may affect the quality of the software being developed. Moreover, at times we may want to create strongly typed collections for our own class. Since we have already studied classes in Chapter 11, it will be easy to comprehend the concept. However, it is advisable to go through Chapters 6 and 11 again before starting this chapter. This chapter presents the concept of collections for any class including user-defined classes.

The concept introduced in this chapter will give us the same amount of flexibility as is given by templates in C++. Collections like `ArrayList` help us to add any type of data in the collection. However, there are some collections that allow us to add only one type of data. Such collections are referred to as strongly typed collections. One example of a strongly typed collection is StringCollection, which adds only a string.

The problems of type casting and hence inefficiency of the code can be greatly reduced by using generics. For example, SortedList<t, U> is one of the generic collections that are analogous to a non-generic class SortedList. The present chapter discusses the SortedList, Queue, Stack, and List generic collections.

16.2 SORTED LIST

The sorted list, as the name suggests, sorts the items in a list. This can be used with custom classes as well. Since the definition and explanation of a class has already been provided in Chapter 11, it would not be difficult for readers to understand the making of a class. The values of a list are sorted on the basis of the key. The syntax of instantiation of SortedList is as follows:

```
SortedList<key, value> <instance name> = new SortedList<key, value>();
```

The key can be a string or any basic data type for that matter, whereas value can be any basic data type or a custom class. The following program explains this concept. It creates a class called employee. This class has two data members—firstName and lastName. The constructor of the class initializes the data members by the arguments passed therein. In SortedList, two values are passed—a string and an instance of the class employee. The Add function of the sorted list adds the elements in the list.

The elements of the list are retrieved using a for-each loop. The output of the program is given after the program. The second version of the program accomplishes the same task but in a more comprehensive way. It asks the user to enter the number of elements and the values of the data members as well.

Program

```
using System;
using System.Collections.Generic;
using System.Linq;
using System.Text;

namespace Generics_1
{
    class employee
    {
        private string firstName;
        private string lastName;
        public employee(string fName, string lName)
        {
            firstName = fName;
            lastName = lName;
        }
        override public string ToString()
        {
            return(firstName + " " + lastName);
        }
    }
```

```
class Program
{
    static void Main(string[] args)
    {
        SortedList<String, employee> sl = new SortedList<string, employee>();
        sl.Add("One", new employee("Harsh", "Bhasin"));
        sl.Add("Two", new employee("Naks", "Arora"));
        sl.Add("Three", new employee("Viru", "Sharma"));
        sl.Add("Four", new employee("S", "Kalra"));
        foreach(employee e in sl.Values)
        {
            Console.WriteLine("Name " + e.ToString());
        }
        Console.ReadKey();
    }
}
```

Output

```
Name S Kalra
Name Harsh Bhasin
Name Viru Sharma
Name Naks Arora
```

Program

```
using System;
using System.Collections.Generic;
using System.Linq;
using System.Text;

namespace Generics5
{
    class employee
    {
        private string firstName;
        private string lastName;
        public employee()
        {
            firstName = "";
            lastName = "";
        }
        public employee(string fName, string lName)
        {
            firstName = fName;
            lastName = lName;
        }
        public void getdata()
        {
            Console.WriteLine("Enter the first name");
            firstName = Console.ReadLine();
            Console.WriteLine("Enter the last name");
            lastName = Console.ReadLine();
        }
```

```csharp
        public void putdata()
        {
            Console.WriteLine("Name" + firstName + " " + lastName);
        }
        override public string ToString()
        {
            return(firstName + " " + lastName);
        }
    }
    class Program
    {
        static void Main(string[] args)
        {
            int n;
            SortedList<String, employee> sl = new SortedList<string, employee>();
            Console.WriteLine("Enter the number of employees whose details are to be entered");
            n = int.Parse(Console.ReadLine());
            char ch = 'a';
            for(int i = 0; i < n; i++)
            {
                employee e = new employee();
                e.getdata();
                sl.Add(ch.ToString(), e);
                ch++;
            }
            foreach(employee e in sl.Values)
            {
                e.putdata();
            }
            Console.ReadKey();
        }
    }
}
```

Output

```
Enter the number of employees whose details are
to be enter number
4
Enter the first name
Harsh
Enter the last name
Bhaisn
Enter the first name
Nakul
Enter the last name
Arora
Enter the first name
Rima
```

```
Enter the last name
Kalra
Enter the first name
Sonam
Enter the last name
Kalra
Name Harsh Bhaisn
Name Nakul Arora
Name Rima Kalra
Name Sonam Kalra
```

16.3 QUEUE

A queue is a linear data structure that follows the principle of first in, first out. The elements of the data structure are dequeued in the same order in which they are queued. The data structure has already been explained in Chapter 6. The use of queue has also been exemplified in that chapter. However, queues can also be used with custom classes. The definition and explanation of a class has already been provided in Chapter 11. As stated earlier, the values are sorted in the order in which the elements are entered. The syntax of instantiation of Queue is as follows:

```
Queue<data type> <instance name> = new Queue<data type>();
```

The value can be a basic data type or a custom class. The use of a queue with basic data types has been explained in Chapter 6. This chapter examines how a custom class uses a queue. The concept can be understood with the help of the following program. It creates a class called employee. The employee class has two data members—firstName and lastName. The constructor of the class initializes the data members by the arguments passed therein. In the queue, the data type (employee in this case) is passed. The Enqueue function of the queue adds the elements in the list.

The elements of the list are retrieved using a for-each loop. The output of the program is given after the program. The second version of the program accomplishes the same task but in a more comprehensive way. It asks the user to enter the number of elements and the values of the data members as well.

Program

```
using System;
using System.Collections.Generic;
using System.Linq;
using System.Text;

namespace Generics2
{
    class employee
    {
        private string firstName;
        private string lastName;
        public employee(string fName, string lName)
```

```
            {
                firstName = fName;
                lastName  = lName;
            }
            override public string ToString()
            {
                return(firstName + " " + lastName);
            }
        }
        class Program
        {
            static void Main(string[] args)
            {
                Queue<employee> q = new Queue<employee>();
                q.Enqueue(new employee("Harsh", "Bhasin"));
                q.Enqueue(new employee("Naks", "Arora"));
                q.Enqueue(new employee("Viru", "Sharma"));
                q.Enqueue(new employee("S", "Kalra"));
                for(int i = 1; i <= 4; i++)
                {
                    Console.WriteLine("Name" + q.Dequeue().ToString());
                }
                Console.ReadKey();
            }
        }
}
```

Output

```
Name Harsh Bhasin
Name Naks Arora
Name Viru Sharma
Name S Kalra
_
```

Program

```
using System;
using System.Collections.Generic;
using System.Linq;
using System.Text;

namespace Generics6
{
    class employee
    {
        private string firstName;
        private string lastName;
        public employee()
        {
            firstName = "";
            lastName = "";
        }
```

```csharp
            public employee(string fName, string lName)
            {
                firstName = fName;
                 lastName = lName;
            }
            public void getdata()
            {
                Console.WriteLine("Enter the first name");
                firstName = Console.ReadLine();
                Console.WriteLine("Enter the last name");
                lastName = Console.ReadLine();
            }
            public void putdata()
            {
                Console.WriteLine("Name" + firstName + " " + lastName);
            }
            override public string ToString()
            {
                return(firstName + " " + lastName);
            }
        }
        class Program
        {
            static void Main(string[] args)
            {
                int n;
                Queue<employee> q = new Queue<employee>();
                Console.WriteLine("Enter the number of employees whose details are to be entered");
                n = int.Parse(Console.ReadLine());
                for(int i = 0; i < n; i++)
                {
                    employee e = new employee();
                    e.getdata();
                    q.Enqueue(e);
                }
                for(int i = 0; i < n; i++)
                {
                    ((employee)(q.Dequeue())).putdata();
                }
                Console.ReadKey();
            }
        }
    }
```

Output

```
Enter the number of employees whose details are
to be entered
4
```

```
Enter the first name
Harsh
Enter the last name
Bhasin
Enter the first name
Nakul
Enter the last name
Arora
Enter the first name
Nikita
Enter the last name
Chandela
Enter the first name
Sonam
Enter the last name
Kalra
Name Harsh Bhasin
Name Nakul Arora
Name Nikita Chandela
Name Sonam Kalra
```

16.4 STACK

A stack is a linear data structure that follows the principle of last in, first out. The elements of the data structure are popped in the reverse order in which they are pushed. The data structure has been explained in Chapter 6. The use of stacks has also been elucidated in that chapter. However, stacks can also be used with custom classes. The syntax of the instantiation of Stack is as follows:

```
Stack<data type> <instance name> = new Stack<data type>();
```

The value can be a basic data type or a custom class. This section examines the use of stack with custom classes. The concept has been exemplified in the below program. It creates a class called employee. The class has two data members—firstName and lastName. The constructor of the class initializes the data members by the arguments passed therein. In the Stack, the data type (employee in this case) is passed. The Push function of the Stack adds the elements in the list.

The elements of the list are retrieved using a for-each loop. The output of the program is given after the program. The second version of the program accomplishes the same task but in a more comprehensive way. It asks the user to enter the number of elements and the values of the data members as well.

Program

```
using System;
using System.Collections.Generic;
using System.Linq;
using System.Text;
```

```csharp
namespace Generics3
{
    class employee
    {
        private string firstName;
        private string lastName;
        public employee(string fName, string lName)
        {
            firstName = fName;
            lastName = lName;
        }
        override public string ToString()
        {
            return(firstName + " " + lastName);
        }
    }
    class Program
    {
        static void Main(string[] args)
        {
            Stack<employee> s = new Stack<employee>();
            s.Push(new employee("Harsh", "Bhasin"));
            s.Push(new employee("Naks", "Arora"));
            s.Push(new employee("Viru", "Sharma"));
            s.Push(new employee("S", "Kalra"));
            for(int i = 1; i <= 4; i++)
            {
                Console.WriteLine("Name" + s.Pop().ToString());
            }
            Console.ReadKey();
        }
    }
}
```

Output

```
Name S Kalra
Name Viru Sharma
Name Naks Arora
Name Harsh Bhasin
-
```

Program

```csharp
using System;
using System.Collections.Generic;
using System.Linq;
using System.Text;
```

```csharp
namespace Generics7
{
    class employee
    {
        private string firstName;
        private string lastName;
        public employee()
        {
            firstName = "";
            lastName = "";
        }
        public employee(string fName, string lName)
        {
            firstName = fName;
            lastName = lName;
        }
        public void getdata()
        {
            Console.WriteLine("Enter the first name");
            firstName = Console.ReadLine();
            Console.WriteLine("Enter the last name");
            lastName = Console.ReadLine();
        }
        public void putdata()
        {
            Console.WriteLine("Name" + firstName + " " + lastName);
        }
        override public string ToString()
        {
            return(firstName + " " + lastName);
        }
    }
    class Program
    {
        static void Main(string[] args)
        {
            int n;
            Stack<employee> s = new Stack<employee>();
            Console.WriteLine("Enter the number of employees whose details are to be entered");
            n = int.Parse(Console.ReadLine());
            for(int i = 0; i < n; i++)
            {
                employee e = new employee();
                e.getdata();
                s.Push(e);
            }
            for(int i = 0; i < n; i++)
            {
                ((employee)(s.Pop())).putdata();
            }
            Console.ReadKey();
        }
    }
}
```

Output

```
Enter the number of employees whose details are
to be entered
4
Enter the first name
Harsh
Enter the last name
Bhasin
Enter the first name
Nakul
Enter the last name
Arora
Enter the first name
Sonam
Enter the last name
Kalra
Enter the first name
Nimit
Enter the last name
Soni
Name Nimit Soni
Name Sonam Kalra
Name Nakul Arora
Name Harsh Bhasin
-
```

16.5 USING sort FUNCTION WITH A LIST

A list adds elements with the help of Add method. The elements of the data structure are processed using a for-each loop. Similar to the other data structures, list can also be used with custom classes. However, in order to sort the list using the sort method, the following tasks must be accomplished:

1. Implement the IComparable interface.
2. Define the CompareTo() method as per the requirements.

In the below program, the CompareTo function compares the last name. If the last name is the same, then the first name is compared. Thus, the example sorts the list on the basis of the last name. However, if the last name is the same, then the first name is considered. It creates a class called employee. The employee class has two data members—firstName and lastName. The constructor of the class initializes the data members by the arguments passed therein. In the example that follows, the List has data type employee. The Sort function of the list sorts the elements in the list.

Program

```
using System;
using System.Collections.Generic;
using System.Linq;
using System.Text;
```

```csharp
namespace Generics4
{
    class employee : IComparable
    {
        private string firstName;
        private string lastName;
        public employee(string fName, string lName)
        {
            firstName = fName;
            lastName = lName;
        }
        override public string ToString()
        {
            return(firstName + " " + lastName);
        }
        public int CompareTo(object o)
        {
            if(lastName == ((employee)o).lastName)
            {
                return firstName.CompareTo(((employee)o).firstName);
            }
            else
            {
                return lastName.CompareTo(((employee)o).lastName);
            }
        }
    }
    class Program
    {
        static void Main(string[] args)
        {
            List<employee> l = new List<employee>();
            l.Add(new employee("Harsh", "Bhasin"));
            l.Add(new employee("Naks", "Arora"));
            l.Add(new employee("Viru", "Sharma"));
            l.Add(new employee("S", "Kalra"));
            foreach(employee e in l)
            {
                Console.WriteLine("Name" + e.ToString());
            }
            l.Sort();
            foreach(employee e in l)
            {
                Console.WriteLine("Name" + e.ToString());
            }
            Console.ReadKey();
        }
    }
}
```

Output

```
Name Harsh Bhasin
Name Naks Arora
Name Viru Sharma
Name S Kalra
Name Naks Arora
Name Harsh Bhasin
Name S Kalra
Name Viru Sharma
_
```

SUMMARY

The present chapter throws some light on the ways to use custom classes with generics. It discusses sorted list, queue, stack, and a general list. The concepts have been exemplified and implemented. The concept gains importance while developing a management system. For example, if we intend to develop an invoicing system, we develop a class called item. The different items can be sorted in accordance with the item ID of an Item. 'List' may be used to implement this concept. The Sort function of the list will be very helpful in sorting the list of items.

It may be noted that the programs in this chapter have been made in console; however, the same concept can be implemented in GUI as well. This concept amalgamated with form design concepts of Chapters 18 and 19 and will lead to the development of sound software.

GLOSSARY

Generic It helps to create strongly typed collections for any class.
Collection It is a class that helps us to collect items in a list and then iterate through them.
IComparable interface This interface allows the use of Sort method of the List class. The method sorts the items of the list on the basis of the specified field.

CompareTo() method This method needs to be defined in the class that overrides the IComparable interface in order to make the sort method compare the items.
Enqueue() This method adds items to the instance of a queue.
Dequeue() This method deletes items from the instance of a queue.

POINTS TO REMEMBER

- In order to use the Sort function of list, the IComparable interface needs to be implemented.
- The elements of a stack are popped in the reverse order in which they are pushed.
- The elements of a queue are dequeued in the same order in which they are queued.
- Generics reduce the problems of type casting and hence the inefficiency of the code.

EXERCISES

I. Multiple-choice Questions

Note: In the following questions, the `class student` should be taken as follows:

```
class student
{
    private string firstName;
    private string lastName;
    public student()
    {
        firstName = "";
        lastName = "";
    }
    public student(string fName,
    string lName)
    {
        firstName = fName;
        lastName = lName;
    }
    public void getdata()
    {
        Console.WriteLine("Enter the
        first name");
        firstName = Console.ReadLine();
        Console.WriteLine("Enter the
        last name");
        lastName = Console.ReadLine();
    }
    public void putdata()
    {
        Console.WriteLine("Name" +
        firstName + " " + lastName);
    }
    override public string ToString()
    {
        return(firstName + " " + last-
        Name);
    }
}
```

1. What will be the output of the following code?

   ```
   static void Main(string[] args)
   {
       int n;
       Stack<employee> s ;
       Console.WriteLine("Enter the num-
       ber of employees whose details are
       to be entered");
       n = int.Parse(Console.ReadLine());
       for(int i = 0; i < n; i++)
       {
           employee e = new employee();
           e.getdata();
           s.Push(e);
       }
       for(int i = 0; i < n; i++)
       {
           ((employee)(s.Pop())).put-
           data();
       }
       Console.ReadKey();
   }
   ```

   (a) The code will not be compiled.
   (b) A stack of student will be created and the concept of 'first in, last out' will be implemented.
   (c) While taking an integer input, try-catch is not used; therefore, the code may be compiled but runtime exceptions may occur.
   (d) The class declaration is incorrect.

2. What will be the output of the following code?

   ```
   static void Main(string[] args)
   {
       int n;
       Stack<employee> s = new
       Stack<employee> ("Harsh",
       "Bhasin");
       Console.WriteLine("Enter the num-
       ber of employees whose details are
       to be entered");
       n = int.Parse(Console.ReadLine());
       for(int i = 0; i < n; i++)
       {
           employee e = new employee();
           e.getdata();
           s.Push(e);
       }
       for(int i = 0; i < n; i++)
       {
           ((employee)(s.Pop())).put-
           data();
       }
       Console.ReadKey();
   }
   ```

   (a) The code will not be compiled as stacks cannot deal with a custom class.
   (b) A stack of student will be created and the concept of 'first in, last out' will be implemented.

(c) The code will not be compiled because there is no constructor of stack that takes two arguments.
(d) The code will not be compiled because there is no constructor of employee that takes two arguments.

3. What will be the output of the following code?

```
static void Main(string[] args)
{
    int n;
    Stack<employee> s = new Stack<employee>();
    Console.WriteLine("Enter the number of employees whose details are to be entered");
    n = int.Parse(Console.ReadLine());
    for(int i = 0; i < n; i++)
    {
        employee e = new employee();
        e.getdata();
        s.add(e);
    }
    for(int i = 0; i < n; i++)
    {
        ((employee)(s.delete())).putdata();
    }
    Console.ReadKey();
}
```

(a) The code will not be compiled as stacks cannot deal with a custom class.
(b) A stack of student will be created and the concept of 'first in, last out' will be implemented.
(c) The code will not be compiled because there is no method called add in a stack.
(d) The code will not be compiled because there is no method called add or delete in the stack class.

4. What will be the output of the following code?

```
static void Main(string[] args)
{
    int n;
    Stack<employee> s = new Stack<employee>();
    Console.WriteLine("Enter the number of employees whose details are to be entered");
    n = int.Parse(Console.ReadLine());
    for(int i = 0; i < n; i++)
    {
        employee e = new employee();
        e.getdata();
        s.EnQueue(e);
    }
    for(int i = 0; i < n; i++)
    {
        ((employee)(s.DeQueue())).putdata();
    }
    Console.ReadKey();
}
```

(a) The code will not be compiled as stacks cannot deal with a custom class.
(b) A stack of student will be created and the concept of 'first in, last out' will be implemented.
(c) The code will not be compiled because there is no method called add in a stack.
(d) The code will not be compiled because there is no method called EnQueue or DeQueue in the stack class.

5. Which of the following interfaces needs to be implemented in order to use the Sort method of List?
(a) IComparable   (b) Compare
(c) Sort   (d) None of these

6. Which of the following generics can deal with custom classes?
(a) SortedList   (b) Queue
(c) Stack   (d) All of these

7. Which of the following statements is correct?
(a) Generics in C# are the same as that in C++
(b) There is hardly any difference between a generic and a collection
(c) Collections are better than generics.
(d) None of these

8. Which of the following statements is correct?
(a) Generics are strongly typed collections.
(b) Generics are the same as an interface.
(c) For all generics, an interface needs to be implemented.
(d) None of these

9. Which of the following can be implemented via generics?
(a) Stack   (b) Queue
(c) Both (a) and (b)   (d) None of these

10. Which of the following statements is correct?
(a) Generics implement IComparable.
(b) Some of the generics may implement IComparable.
(c) No generic implements IComparable.
(d) None of these

II. Review Questions

1. Explain the concept of sorted list and write the syntax of its instantiation.
2. Explain the concept of queue and write the syntax of its instantiation.
3. Explain the concept of stack and write the syntax of its instantiation.
4. Explain the concept of list and write the syntax of its instantiation.
5. Explain how the sort method of the list can be used to sort the method of a custom class.

III. Programming Exercises

1. Consider a class called Book having the following data members and methods:

Book
BookId: Integer
Name: String
Book( );
Book(int, String);
Getdata ( );
Putdata ( );
ToString ( );
CompareTo (Book);

   (a) Implement this class by implementing the IComparable interface.
   (b) In the CompareTo() method, compare two books on the basis of ID (which is an integer).
   (c) Implement two constructors, one default and the other parameterized, having two arguments (an integer and a string).
   (d) The Getdata() method should ask the user to enter the ID and the name of the book.
   (e) The Putdata() method should display the details of the book.

2. Consider a class called Item having the following data members and methods:

Item
ItemId: Integer
Name: String
Item ( );
Item (int, String);
Getdata ( );
Putdata ( );
ToString ( );
CompareTo (Item);

   (a) Implement this class by implementing the IComparable Interface.
   (b) In the CompareTo() method, compare two items on the basis of ID (which is an integer).
   (c) Implement two constructors, one default and the other parameterized, having two arguments (an integer and a string).
   (d) The Getdata() method should ask the user to enter the ID and the name of the item.
   (e) The Putdata() method should display the details of the item.

17 Threads

OBJECTIVES

After completing this chapter, the reader will be able to
Appreciate the importance of threads
Use threads in a program
Understand the concept of thread pools
Recognize the intricacies of the class `System.Threading`
Use `Timer` class
Explain the concept of synchronization

17.1 INTRODUCTION

Initially, programs used to have only one thread of execution. When such a program runs, it forces other programs to wait until it terminates and hence consumes all the resources available. Doing one work at a time with concentration is good, but it may become an excuse for those not capable of doing multiple tasks at a time. However, this does not serve the purpose for which software applications are used, that is, increased efficiency in performance. Moreover, it also defeats the idea of time sharing, which has been the crux of modern operating systems.

For example, a task may be busy in reading from or writing to a disk. It may be noted at this point that while reading from or writing to the disk, the processor gives the control to the direct memory access controller or the DMA. After completing its task, the DMA gives the control back to the CPU. During the time that the control is with DMA, the CPU need not be idle; it can be used by another task, which is independent of the 'reading/writing task'. Thus, when two tasks do not share a common resource, there is a possibility of their getting executed simultaneously via time sharing. This example gives an idea of how two or more processes run simultaneously.

The execution of many processes simultaneously is referred to as multiprocessing. It may be noted that it is not necessary that the processor should implement multiprocessing whenever multiple tasks are required to run together. A better solution will be to divide a single task into many independent units called threads.

Thus, a thread is the basic unit of execution and multithreading is the phenomenon of running many threads at the same time. To understand the point, let us consider the example of Microsoft Word, in which many tasks run at the same time, from counting the number of words to spell check. In fact, nowadays almost all the applications rely on multithreading. For example, it is quite possible that the Antivirus running on our computer will download the updates and scan our computer simultaneously.

This chapter examines the concept of threads. The classes that help us to implement threads have been explained and the concepts have been exemplified. The chapter will be helpful for readers who decide to pursue a career in operating system design.

17.2 CLASSES IN System.Threading

Thread is perhaps the most important class in the System.Threading namespace and is needed in order to create a thread. The handling of a thread, as in setting its priority, is also controlled by this class. The class provides various methods and properties to create a program that implements multithreading. In order to understand the concept, consider an example of a street, which is a resource, and two cars coming from the opposite directions. Now, the two cars intend to use the same resource (read the street) at the same time, thus leading to a situation called deadlock. In order to handle the deadlock, synchronization is required. Here, street is a 'resource', which is needed by more than one 'thread' (cars).

As stated earlier, running many threads at the same time may lead to a crunch of resources. A particular resource may be needed by more than one thread. This may even lead to a deadlock. Readers who have studied operating systems must be aware of 'mutex'. In case of inter-thread or inter-process communication, 'mutex' can be used for synchronization. C# also provides the Mutex class to accomplish the task. Another class called Monitor also helps to synchronize the access to the critical resources.

If, however, we intend to curtail the thread that can access a resource or a pool of resources, then the Semaphore class needs to be used.

Many threads reading from the memory may not pose a problem but more than one process simultaneously trying to write to the memory can. That is to say, many reads may be allowed but only one write can be allowed at a time. The ReaderWriterLock class helps to achieve this target.

If the problem in hand requires more than one thread to be made, then the ThreadPool class can be used. The class is used to build a pool of threads and aids in their synchronization and handling.

At times, the tasks may need to be done at specified intervals of times. The Timer class helps us to set timings and hence accomplish the task in hand.

Table 17.1 summarizes the foregoing discussion.

Table 17.1 Important classes in the System.Threading namespace

Name of the class	Description
Thread	Creates thread, sets priority, and gets status.
Mutex	Helps achieve synchronization in the case of inter-process communication.
Semaphore	Restricts the number of threads that can entrée a resource.
Timer	Helps us to set timings.
ReaderWriterLock	Helps us to achieve the target of only one write at a time.
ThreadPool	Helps us to create a pool of threads and manipulate them.

17.3 BASIC THREADS

As per the discussion in Section 17.2, the creation of threads requires `System.Threading` namespace. The namespace has a class called `Thread`. The object of this class helps us to create a thread and handle it. Readers with Java background must be in the habit of creating a thread and associating it with an object. However, the strategy will not work in C#. The concept can be better understood with the help of the following program. When the following program is compiled, an error is displayed in the error pane stating that a thread cannot be initialized without an argument.

```csharp
using System;
using System.Collections.Generic;
using System.Linq;
using System.Text;
using System.Threading;   // Use this namespace for any program that implements threading

namespace Threading1
{
    class BookTicket
    {
        public void Display()
        {
            for(int i = 0; i < 5; i++)
            {
                Console.WriteLine("Ticket reserved ");
            }
        }
    }
    class Program
    {
        static void Main(string[] args)
        {
            BookTicket b = new BookTicket();
            Thread t = new Thread();
            t.Start(b.Display());
            Console.ReadKey();
        }
    }
}
```

Output

On compilation, the following error will be displayed in the error pane:

`'System.Threading.Thread' does not contain a constructor that takes '0' arguments`

However, a minor change will rectify the problem in this code. The `Thread` class is to be instantiated with a new instance of `ThreadStart`, in which the name of the method is to be given as an argument. It may be noted, though, that a method with parameters cannot be associated with a thread in this way. Such methods may use delegates to be associated with a thread. The following program demonstrates the correct use of threads:

```csharp
using System.Collections.Generic;
using System.Linq;
using System.Text;
```

```
using System.Threading;

namespace Threading1
{
    class BookTicket
    {
        public void Display()
        {
            for(int i = 0; i < 5; i++)
            {
                Console.WriteLine("From Object: " + (i + 1) + "Ticket reserved");
            }
        }
    }
    class Program
    {
        static void Main(string[] args)
        {
            BookTicket b = new BookTicket();
            Thread t1 = new Thread(new ThreadStart(b.Display));
            t1.Start();
            Console.ReadKey();
        }
    }
}
```

Output

```
From Object: 1Ticket reserved
From Object: 2Ticket reserved
From Object: 3Ticket reserved
From Object: 4Ticket reserved
From Object: 5Ticket reserved
```

17.4 Timer CLASS

As stated in Section 17.2, the class library provides the Timer class, which helps us to start and stop the timer, set the interval, and perform other such tasks. The class has two constructors: a default constructor and a parameterized constructor. The parameterized constructor takes a 'double' type argument, which is the interval property in milliseconds.

One of the most important properties of this class is Interval. It is set by using a dot operator with the object of the Timer class. The following code crafts an instance of the Timer class and sets the interval property to 1000 milliseconds. The AutoReset property of the class sets or gets a value, indicating whether the timer should invoke the elapsed event, at the point at which the interval elapses. The crafting of a thread will be in the following format:

```
Timer t = new Timer();
t.Interval = 1000;
```

The important methods of the Timer class have been briefly explained in Table 17.2.

Table 17.2 Methods of Timer class

Name of the method	Explanation
Start	Starts the thread
Stop	Stops the thread by setting Enabled to false by raising the elapsed event
Dispose	Releases all the resources being used by the thread
Close	Releases the resources being used by the timer

The Timer class also includes two events. The first is Dispose, which transpires at the invocation of the Dispose() method. The second is Elapse, which occurs when the Interval elapses. However, using these events may not be that easy, as depicted by the below mentioned program.

This program intends to use the Timer class to calculate the running time of an algorithm. The program implements linear search and calculates the time from the point the user enters the number to the point at which the result is displayed. The linear search method is called by invoking the method of the class. The timer starts as soon as the input is entered.

Program

```
using System;
using System.Collections.Generic;
using System.Linq;
using System.Text;
//Using System.Threading;
using System.Timers;

namespace Threading2
{
    class Search
    {
        public void linearSearch(int[] a, int n, int item)
        {
            int flag = 0;
            for(int i = 0; i < n; i++)
            {
                if(a[i] == item)
                {
                    flag = 1;
                    Console.WriteLine("Found at " + i);
                }
            }
            if(flag == 0)
            {
                Console.WriteLine("Not found");
            }
        }
    }
    class Program
    {
        static void Main(string[] args)
        {
```

```csharp
            int[] array = new int[100];
            int i, n, item;
            try
            {
                Console.WriteLine("Enter the number of elements ");
                n = int.Parse(Console.ReadLine());
                for(i = 0; i < n; i++)
                {
                    Console.WriteLine("Enter number");
                    array[i] = int.Parse(Console.ReadLine());
                }
                Console.WriteLine("Enter the item to be searched");
                item = int.Parse(Console.ReadLine());
                Timer t = new Timer();
                Search s = new Search();
                t.Interval = 1000;
                t.Start();
                s.linearSearch(array, n, item);
                t.Elapsed += time_Elapsed;
                //Console.WriteLine("Time elapsed " + t.Elapsed);
                t.Stop();
                t.Dispose();
            }
            catch(Exception e)
            {
                Console.WriteLine("Exception " + e.ToString());
            }
        }
        static public void time_Elapsed(Object sender, EventArgs e)
        {
            Console.WriteLine(DateTime.Now.ToString());
        }
    }
}
```

Output

The program seems fine, but when we compile the program, the following error is displayed in the message box.

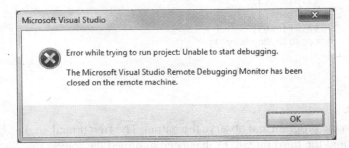

This happens due to running the application in the "no Authentication" mode. In order to solve the above problem run the Remote Debugging Monitor under the same user account. You need to select the "Allow any user to debug" option to be able to see the requisite output.

17.5 THREAD PRIORITY

In order to handle threads, the priority of threads needs to be set. In C#, a thread can have one of the five legal priorities, namely normal, lowest, highest, above normal, and below normal. However, the default priority of a thread is normal. The following snippet demonstrates the use of the property:

```
using System;
using System.Collections.Generic;
using System.Linq;
using System.Text;
using System.Threading;
namespace Threading3
{
    class WebServernegativeResponse
    {
        public void FileReqNegativeResponse()
        {
            Console.WriteLine("The request of the file cannot be catered");
        }
        public void ImageReqNegativeResponse()
        {
            Console.WriteLine("The request of the image cannot be catered");
        }
        public void DataReqNegativeResponse()
        {
            Console.WriteLine("The data cannot be found/Error in accessing data");
        }
    }
    class Program
    {
        static void Main(string[] args)
        {
            WebServernegativeResponse w = new WebServernegativeResponse();
            Thread t1 = new Thread(new ThreadStart(w.DataReqNegativeResponse));
            Thread t2 = new Thread(new ThreadStart(w.FileReqNegativeResponse));
            Thread t3 = new Thread(new ThreadStart(w.ImageReqNegativeResponse));
            t1.Priority = ThreadPriority.Highest;
            t3.Priority = ThreadPriority.Lowest;
            t1.Start();
            t2.Start();
            t3.Start();
            Console.ReadKey();
        }
    }
}
```

Output

Now, run the program and observe the output. The first thread, t1, has been assigned the highest priority and the third thread, t3, has been assigned the lowest priority. The second thread will have normal priority, as the default priority of a thread is normal. However, it will be interesting to compare the output with the case where in spite of assigning the same priority to the threads the calling sequence is tweaked specifically, when the thread of the lowest priority is invoked first and that of the highest priority is invoked at the end.

```
t3.Start( );
t2.Start( );
t1.Start( );
```
The output in the two cases is depicted as follows.

In this program, however, if the priority of the running thread needs to be checked, then `Thread.CurrentThread.Priority` should be used inside the method being called. For example, in the earlier snippet, the following change will let us see the current thread priority:

```
class WebServernegativeResponse
{
    public void FileReqNegativeResponse()
    {
        Console.WriteLine("The request of the
        file cannot be catered");
        Thread.CurrentThread.Priority;
    }
    public void ImageReqNegativeResponse()
    {
        Console.WriteLine("The request of the image cannot be fulfilled");
        Thread.CurrentThread.Priority;
    }
    public void DataReqNegativeResponse()
    {
        Console.WriteLine("The data cannot be found/Error in accessing data");
        Thread.CurrentThread.Priority;
    }
}
```

Writing `Thread.CurrentThread.Priority` will let us see the current priority of the running thread.

17.6 SYNCHRONIZATION

When more than one thread is running simultaneously, it may be possible that the threads will compete for the same resource. This may lead to a deadlock. In order to avoid this situation, the concepts used in the operating systems can be used to implement 'synchronization'.

Readers familiar with the fundamentals of an operating system will be able to appreciate the concept of locks. Locks are used to curtail the access to the resources. However, it is not a problem even if one is not familiar with operating system concepts; all that a programmer needs to do is to identify the code that can pose a problem if two threads simultaneously try to access it. The next step would be to place that code in the 'lock' block. The programmer need not do anything else; the developers of C# have taken care of all the difficult tasks involved in the synchronization process. In fact, 'lock' performs the same task as is done by 'synchronize' in Java.

In order to understand the concept, let us consider a simple example. Suppose that a program has two variables `NakulAcBalance`, which depicts the balance in Nakul's account, and `HariAcBalance`, which depicts the balance in Hari's account. A transaction is to be performed wherein $500 is to be deducted from Nakul's account and credited into Hari's account. The code is accessed by two different threads. Let us visualize the problems that can crop up while dealing with the situation when no synchronization is implemented (Table 17.3).

Table 17.3 Transaction problem

Time	Thread A	Thread B
1	*Read operation*: NakulAcBalance = 5000	*Read operation*: NakulAcBalance = 5000
2	*Read operation*: HariAcBalance = 8000	*Read operation*: HariAcBalance = 8000
3	*Write operation*: NakulAcBalance = 5000 – 500 = 4500	No task is performed.
4	No task is performed.	*Write operation*: NakulAcBalance = 4500 – 500 //Since the value in the variable has become 4500
5	*Write operation*: HariAcBalance = 8000 + 500 = 8500	...
6		Transaction abruptly ends.

It should be noted that in this example the two threads have not performed the write operation simultaneously; neither should they have done so. Now the problem is that if $500 is deducted from Nakul's account then $500 should have been credited to Hari's account as well. However, the discrepancy occurs due to abrupt termination of the second thread. Will it not be better if only one of the two threads accesses the variables at a particular time?

In order to make this happen, the code in which $500 is debited from the first account and credited to the second one must be placed in the 'lock' block.

17.7 THREAD POOL

The `QueueUserWorkItem` method queues the method, passed as an argument, for execution. The thread pool may have many methods in queue; when the required resources become available, the method is executed. In the following program, the `Main` method constitutes the main thread. It executes and then calls the child thread. The main thread then passes the control onto the child thread and sleeps for 1000 ms (1 s) when the control comes back to it.

```
using System;
using System.Collections.Generic;
using System.Linq;
using System.Text;
using System.Threading;
namespace Threading4
{
    class Program
    {
        static void Main(string[] args)
        {
            ThreadPool.QueueUserWorkItem(fun1);
            Console.WriteLine("The main thread, about to sleep");
            Thread.Sleep(1000);
            Console.WriteLine("End of the main thread");
            Console.ReadKey();
```

```
            }
            public static void fun1(object Information)
            {
                Console.WriteLine("From fun1");
            }
        }
    }
```

Output

Observe the delay in the appearance of the last statement during the execution of the program.

```
The main thread, about to sleep
From fun1
End of the main thread
```

This method may also be used to pass data from the main thread by creating a variable and assigning some value to it. The variable can be passed as the second argument of the method `QueueUserWorkItem`.

```
namespace Threading4
{
    class Program
    {
        static void Main(string[] args)
        {
            string Information = "Call from main";
            ThreadPool.QueueUserWorkItem(fun1, Information);
            Console.WriteLine("The main thread, about to sleep");
            Thread.Sleep(1000);
            Console.WriteLine("End of the main thread");
            Console.ReadKey();
        }
        public static void fun1(object Information)
        {
            Console.WriteLine("From fun1 " + Information);
        }
    }
}
```

Output

```
From fun1 Call from main
The main thread, about to sleep
End of the main thread
```

We can also check whether the thread running presently is the background thread or the foreground thread by using the property `Thread.CurrentThread.IsBackGround`. The property is true when the current thread is the background thread and is false when the current thread is the foreground one. A minor modification in the earlier code will let us see whether the child thread is a background thread or a foreground thread.

```
namespace Threading4
{
    class Program
    {
        static void Main(string[] args)
        {
            string Information = "Call from main";
            ThreadPool.QueueUserWorkItem(fun1, Information);
            Console.WriteLine("The main thread, about to sleep");
            Thread.Sleep(1000);
            Console.WriteLine("End of the main thread");
            Console.ReadKey();
        }
        public static void fun1(object Information)
        {
            if(Thread.CurrentThread.IsBackground)
            {
                Console.WriteLine("From fun1 running in background " +
                Information);
            }
            else
            {
                Console.WriteLine("From fun1 running in foreground " +
                Information);
            }
        }
    }
}
```

Output

```
The main thread, about to sleep
From fun1 running in background
Call from main
End of the main thread
```

It may be stated here that we can run many threads at the same time and not just two as shown in these examples. Moreover, the idea of this chapter is not just to teach how to run multiple threads at the same time but also to enable readers to appreciate their intricacies, the way of passing objects, and the way of checking whether the current thread is in the background or foreground.

SUMMARY

If only one process runs at a time, then this would lead to underutilization of the processor. One way of achieving optimization is by running simultaneously many processes, referred to as multiprocessing. Multiprocessing is expensive and requires different memory spaces for each process being executed. However, dividing a task into different units and executing each unit separately can be one of the ways of tackling underutilization of CPU, while saving memory space at the same time. This leads to the concept of threads. The use of threads, however, requires synchronization. Otherwise, trying to access the same resource at a particular instance may lead to what is referred to as deadlock. Synchronization may be achieved with the help of 'lock' block. 'Lock' in C# has the same importance as 'synchronize' in Java.

It may also be noted that at times there are many tasks to be performed. In such situations, the jobs are pooled. The concept of thread pooling has also been discussed in the chapter.

It may also be stated that the only thing certain while implementing threads is that nothing is certain. The priority given to the user threads, the request for a resource, invoking a thread all depend on the operating system used. It is advisable to go through the concept of threads in operating system in order to understand the concept in a better way.

This chapter helps in designing games, operating systems, and distributed databases. The chapter deals with the programming part of threads and the implementation of the requisite class.

GLOSSARY

Thread This is the fundamental element of execution. A process may have many threads and thus can perform many tasks at the same time.

Thread pool Creating multiple threads and placing them in a pool is referred to as a thread pool. The threads in a pool wait for the work while sitting idle.

Deadlock If a process requests for a resource and the resource is not available, then it enters the waiting state. It is possible that this process will never get a chance to use that resource, as the resource is currently being held by another waiting process. This is called deadlock.

Synchronization The handling of processes in such a way that the conditions mutual exclusion, progress, and bounded waiting are satisfied is referred to as synchronization.

POINTS TO REMEMBER

- A thread is the basic unit of execution and multithreading is the phenomenon of running many threads at the same time.
- If the problem in hand requires more than one thread to be made, then the `ThreadPool` class can be used.
- Timer class helps us to start and stop a timer and `Interval` is one of its most important properties.
- When more than one thread is running simultaneously and are competing for the same resource, it may lead to a deadlock.
- It is possible to check whether the thread running presently is the background thread or the foreground thread by using the property

  `Thread.CurrentThread.IsBackGround`

EXERCISES

I. Multiple-choice Questions

1. What will be the output of the following program?

   ```
   class Program
   {
       static void Main(string[] args)
       {
           string Information = "Call from main";
           ThreadPool.QueueUserWorkItem(fun1);
           Thread.Sleep(1000);
           Console.ReadKey();
       }
       public static void fun1(object Information)
       {
           if(Thread.CurrentThread.IsBackground)
           {
               Console.WriteLine("From fun1 running in background " + Information);
           }
           else
           {
               Console.WriteLine("From fun1 running in foreground " + Information);
           }
       }
   }
   ```

   (a) From fun1 running in background
   (b) From fun1 running in foreground
   (c) The output cannot be predicted.
   (d) The compilation will result in an error.

2. What will be the output of the following snippet?

   ```
   class Program
   {
       static void Main(string[] args)
       {
           string Information = "Call from main";
           ThreadPool.QueueUserWorkItem(fun1, Information);
           Thread.Sleep(1000);
           Console.ReadKey();
       }
       public static void fun1(object Information)
       {
           if(Thread.CurrentThread.IsBackground)
           {
               Console.WriteLine("From fun1 running in background " + Information);
           }
           else
           {
               Console.WriteLine("From fun1 running in foreground " + Information);
           }
       }
   }
   ```

   (a) From fun1 running in background Call from main
   (b) From fun1 running in background
   (c) Either (a) or (b)
   (d) None of these

3. What will be the output of the following code?

   ```
   namespace Threading4
   {
       class Program
       {
           static void Main(string[] args)
           {
               string Information = "Call from main";
               ThreadPool.QueueUserWorkItem(fun1, Information);
               Console.WriteLine("The main thread, about to sleep");
               Thread.Sleep(1000);
               Console.WriteLine("End of the main thread");
               Console.ReadKey();
           }
           public static void fun1(object Information)
           {
               if(Thread.CurrentThread.IsBackground)
               {
                   Thread.CurrentThread.Priority = ThreadPriority.Highest;
                   Console.WriteLine("From fun1 running in background " + Information);
               }
   ```

```
            else
            {
                Thread.CurrentThread.Priority
                = ThreadPriority.Lowest;
                Console.WriteLine("From fun1
                running in foreground " +
                Information);
            }
        }
    }
}
```

(a) From fun1 running in background Call from main
(b) From fun1 running in background
(c) Either (a) or (b)
(d) None of these

4. Which of the following statements is correct?
   (a) Threads share a common address space.
   (b) Threads have different memory spaces.
   (c) Processes have the same address space.
   (d) None of these

5. Which of the following is not a thread priority?
   (a) Highest   (b) Lowest
   (c) AboveAverage   (d) BelowHighest

6. Which of the following is the namespace used for making threads?
   (a) System.Threading
   (b) System.Thread
   (c) System.Process
   (d) None of these

7. In order to make more than one thread run at a time, which of the following classes may be used?
   (a) ThreadPool   (b) Pooling
   (c) ThreadStack   (d) ThreadQueue

8. In which of the following situations may threads be needed?
   (a) Calculating sum of two numbers
   (b) Calculating the square root of a number
   (c) Generating population of GA
   (d) Notepad

9. Which of the following is a method of a thread class?
   (a) Sleep   (b) WakeUp
   (c) DontSleep   (d) ScanDocuments

10. If two threads share a common code, which of the following can be used to handle the problem of synchronization?
    (a) Mutex
    (b) Synchronization Class
    (c) Semaphore class
    (d) All of these

II. Review Questions

1. Explain the concept of threads. How is multi-threading different from multiprocessing?
2. What is the need for synchronization? Explain with the help of an example.
3. What is meant by thread pool? Give an example with respect to operating system.
4. What is the importance of the Timer class? Is it present in just one namespace? If not, state the difference between the two classes.
5. What is the need for mutex? Explain with an example.
6. Examine the various thread priorities. What are the various states of a thread?
7. Differentiate between a process and a thread.
8. What is the need for using the Sleep method?
9. Can we have more than two threads associated with the same method? If yes, explain with an example.
10. What is the need for threads in the following?
    (a) Word processor
    (b) Databases

III. Programming Exercises

1. Create a class called Webserver. Create two methods downloadFile() and DownloadImage() in the class. Now, in the Main class create two threads T1 and T2. Associate T1 with downloadFile() and T2 with DownloadImage(). Now run the threads and also depict the use of the Sleep method.
2. In Question 1, set a highest priority for T1 and a lowest priority for T2.
3. Modify Question 2 to implement the concept of thread pool.
4. Now implement synchronization to make T1 and T2 share a common part.
5. Use Semaphore class to handle the synchronization problem. The example should depict the use of the class.

PART THREE

Component Object Model and Advanced Topics

CHAPTER 18
Windows Forms and Basic Controls

CHAPTER 19
Advanced Controls and Menus

CHAPTER 20
Common Dialogs
Project III: Notepad

CHAPTER 21
Data Connectivity

CHAPTER 22
Introduction to ASP.NET
Project IV: Online Voting System

CHAPTER 23
Networking

Chapter 24
Deployment

CHAPTER 25
Towards WPF and WCF
Project V: Genetic Algorithms

> "Programming today is a race between software engineers striving to build bigger and better idiot-proof programs, and the Universe trying to produce bigger and better idiots. So far, the Universe is winning."
>
> *Rich Cook*

18 Windows Forms and Basic Controls

OBJECTIVES

After completing this chapter, the reader will be able to

Appreciate the importance of Windows programming
Create Forms
Understand the significance of Anchor, Dock, and SnapLines
Add button at design time and run time
Add text box at design time and at run time
Add and use a Label
Use MaskedTextBox
Create a ListBox
Use a ComboBox
Add and manipulate NumericUpDown
Design a login form
Design a basic user interface

18.1 INTRODUCTION

A basic understanding of procedural and object-oriented programming is required to develop a robust software. These topics have already been covered in Parts I and II of the book. This chapter will help readers understand the basics of Windows programming. The concepts explained here together with database handling techniques discussed in later chapters will help readers to develop management systems and application software. These skills are essential for one's programming career. We begin our discussion with the development of front end which is the first thing that must be developed while developing software. If we are asked to develop a software for school to keep track of the details of the students, their marks, fees, and so on, then the first thing that we need to do is to design the front end. The front end will consist of forms. One of the forms can ask the user to enter the details of the student, another can ask for the fee details, and so on. This chapter introduces Windows forms and discusses some of the controls used to build the user interface.

The concept of forms was introduced by Microsoft Visual Basic. It helped the programmers to develop software easily and efficiently using prefabricated controls. As a result of this development, developers could spend more time concentrating on the business logic essential for application development rather than deliberating about how to make a button or a text box. This helped in what we call rapid application development (RAD).

RAD is a software development process. It was developed during the mid-1970s by the Systems Development Center of New York Telephone Co. As this process was successful, Gielan, who was heading the team, decided to formalize the methodology. RAD involves iterative development. Nowadays, the term is used in the sense of speeding application development.

'Speeding' can be done using software frameworks. .NET is one such framework and it provides many prefabricated controls. It may be stated at this point that the idea of RAD is not just limited to Microsoft Technologies but also available to the open source community. The idea gained importance during the 'IT boom' of the early twenty-first century. RAD is as relevant to web applications and websites as it is to desktop application development.

This chapter introduces Windows forms and the various controls that come with Visual Studio. The controls are very easy to use and simplify the whole development process. Developing user interface is essential; however, it is not the only factor to be learnt to develop an application software. The basics of databases and most importantly good business logic are needed to create high-quality software.

In this chapter, readers will learn about various types of controls such as text box, button, labels, and NumericUpDown. While learning about controls, it is important to understand the terms properties and events. Properties help to manipulate the behaviour of the control, whereas events are raised to call a function called event handler. The event handler functions are functions that have the same return type as required by the event.

In some controls, setting the values of the attribute accomplishes the required task, whereas some others require event handlers. For example, a button when pressed is expected to perform a task, thereby needing an event handler. We start our discussion with forms.

18.2 HOW TO ADD A FORM?

A form is the basic unit of a C# Windows Application project. A form in C# houses containers and controls. Most of the applications, which we work on, can be implemented using forms. For example, a word processor is nothing but a text box in a form. This section explains the creation of a basic form in a project.

When we start a new Windows project, a form called Form1 is automatically created. The name of the form can be changed if so desired. However, one can create any number of forms in a Windows Application project. In order to create a form in C#, the following steps must be carried out:

Step 1 Open Visual Studio. Go to File → New → Project (Fig. 18.1).
Step 2 Select Visual C# and write the name of the project at the required place. It is possible to change the location of the project by giving a new path in the Location text box (Fig. 18.2).
Step 3 On clicking OK, the screen shown in Fig. 18.3 appears. The solution contains a form called Form1.

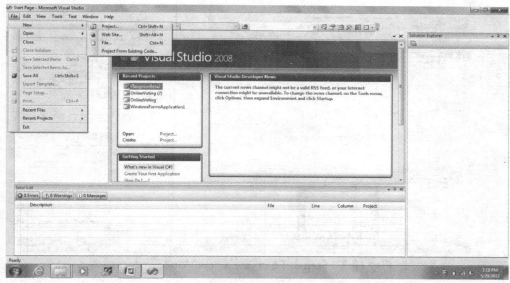

Fig. 18.1 Step 1: To create a new Windows form

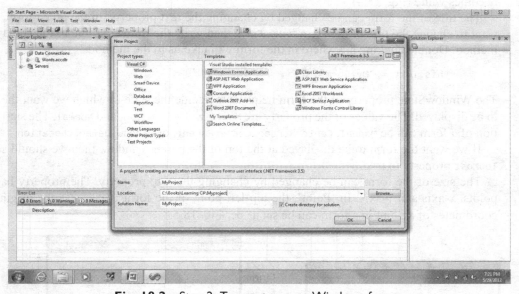

Fig. 18.2 Step 2: To create a new Windows form

18.3 BASIC PROPERTIES OF A FORM

The look and feel of a form can be changed by setting its properties. The `ForeColor` property sets the color of the fonts. The `BackColor` property sets the color of the background. A property can be set by changing the value in the property pallet provided on the lower right-hand side (refer to Section 1.5 of Chapter 1). Properties can also be changed at runtime by writing the following lines at the appropriate place:

```
this.ForeColor = Color.Blue;
this.BackColor = Color.White;
```

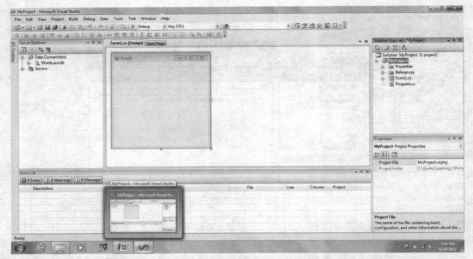

Fig. 18.3 Step 3: To create a new Windows form

These lines will make the fore colour as blue, and the colour of the background of the form becomes white (Fig. 18.4).

The title of the form can be changed by changing the text property. In the given form, if we want to change the title of the form to My Form, then write the following line to the Form1_Load method. Double clicking anywhere in the form will take us to the method.

```
this.Text = "My Form";
```

The WindowState property of the form helps us to decide the state in which we want the form to be displayed. The values of the property are Maximized, Minimized, and Normal. The start position of a form can be Manual, CenterScreen, CenterParent, or WindowsDefaultLocation.

If we want the form to be displayed at the top of the parent window, then we should set the TopMost property to true.

The size of the form can be changed by changing the size property. The property has two points, *x*-axis and *y*-axis. In 'Point', the top-left point of the form is taken as the origin. The coordinates of a point in a form can be set as per Fig. 18.5.

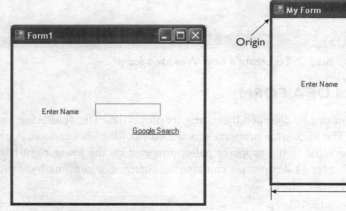

Fig. 18.4 A basic form

Fig. 18.5 The origin of a form

18.4 SNAP LINES

When a new control is added in a form, Snap lines appear. These lines give us visual support in locating the controls and in setting their relative alignment. Suppose we drag a text box in a form followed by another text box. We want the second text box to be vertically below the first one. In such a situation, snap lines can help us to align the controls. These lines divide the whole form into parts similar to a grid. There are three types of snap lines:

1. Horizontal
2. Vertical
3. Margin

They help us to align a control with respect to horizontal or vertical margins. Snap lines are shown in Fig. 18.6.

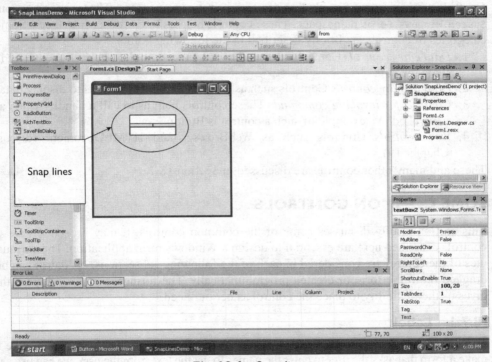

Fig. 18.6 Snap lines

18.5 ANCHOR AND DOCK

At times, we want the control to remain at a fixed distance from one of the edges. This is particularly helpful when the form is resized by the user. In such cases, the Anchor property helps us to keep the control at a fixed distance from the specified edge. This property has a special visual interface as shown in Fig. 18.7.

By default the control has fixed distance from the top and the left edge of a form. The value of the property can be any of the following:

Fig. 18.7 Anchor

1. Top, bottom, left, or right
2. A combination of any two, for example, top, left

Fig. 18.8 Dock

3. A combination of any three, for example, top, left, right
4. Top, bottom, left, right

The Dock property on the other hand helps us to stick the control to one of the edges. For example, in the case of a menu, the value of Dock can be top, and in case of the status bar, it can be bottom. The sidebars if required will be docked left or right. In case of applications such as notepad, where the whole form is to be covered by the control, the middle part can be selected from the visual interface of Dock. The graphical depiction of the Dock property is given in Fig. 18.8.

Now that we have seen the basics of forms, let us proceed to controls.

18.6 CONTROLS

Controls are instances of a subclass of Windows.Forms namespace. There are many controls in System.Windows.Forms namespace. These controls help us to craft user interfaces. Some of the categories of controls are briefly described in the following points:

1. *Data entry controls* Controls such as TextBox and ComboBox help us to enter and manipulate the data.
2. *Data display controls* Controls such as ListBox and Label help us to display data.
3. *Controls for invoking commands* These controls help us to call a handler when an event is invoked. An example of such a control is Button.
4. *Web controls* Controls such as WebBrowser and HTMLDocument (discussed in Chapter 19).

These and many other controls are discussed in Section 18.7.

18.7 SOME COMMON CONTROLS

This section briefly discusses some of the common controls. It may be stated here that the controls described here are essential to design a Windows form application. The various attributes of the control are considered in each of the following subsections. A control can be either dragged on to the form or created programmatically. The former is easier, whereas the latter gives us the flexibility to place the control as per our need.

18.7.1 Label

The Label control is generally used to display read-only text. For example, suppose we want to make a form that asks the user to enter the name. To get the text from the user, we can use a text box (described later in the chapter) but to display the text 'Enter name' we need a label. The text displayed in the label can be set by its text property. Figure 18.9 shows a label and a text box in a form.

18.7.2 Linklabel

Linklabel is a control used to display read-only text as in the case of a label, but it can also be used to access a link. It is similar to a hyperlink in a web page. It has properties such as LinkColor and VisitedLinkColor, which help us to specify the colours of the link and the visited link, respectively (Fig. 18.10).

18.7.3 Adding a Button at Design Time

Button is an important part of any form. All the tasks from clearing the form to submitting the data are generally done by pressing a button. Button in C# is a control present in the toolbox.

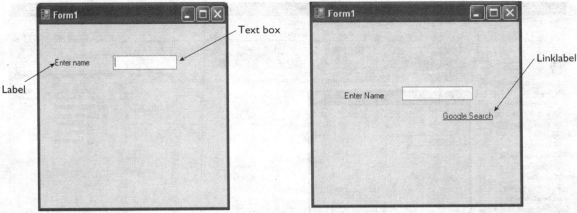

Fig. 18.9 A form with a label and a text box   **Fig. 18.10** A form with a Linklabel

We can drag and drop the button onto our form. We can also add a button at the runtime as discussed in Section 18.7.4. In order to add a button to the form, the following steps need to be performed:

Step 1 Go to File → New → Project.
Step 2 Select Visual C# → Windows Form Application.
Step 3 Write the name of the project in the text box along with the 'Name:' label.
Step 4 Change the location if required. Click OK (Fig. 18.11).
Step 5 From the toolbox, drag the button onto the form. If the toolbox is not visible, then go to View → ToolBox (Fig. 18.12).

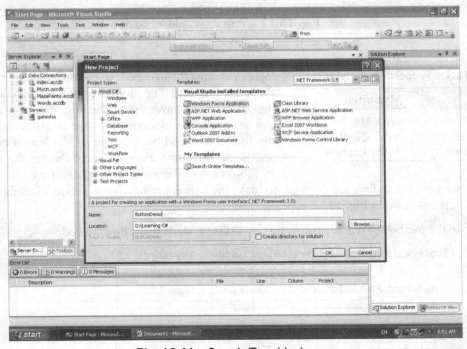

Fig. 18.11 Step 1: To add a button

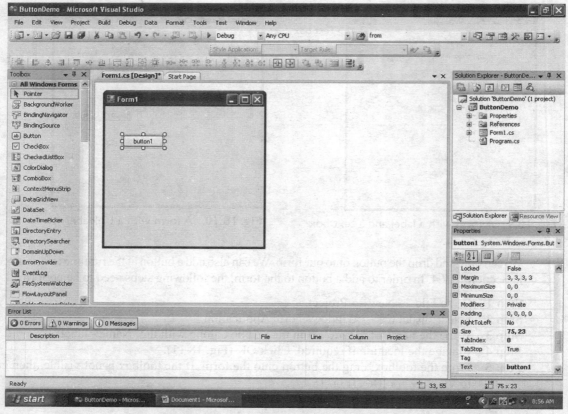

Fig. 18.12 Step 2: To add a button

Table 18.1 Properties of MyButton

Name	MyButton
Text	Click Me
ForeColor	ActiveCaptionText
BackColor	Active Caption

We can change the name of the button by changing the text of the name property. The properties of a button can be seen on the pallet on the lower right-hand side. The text on the button can be changed by changing the Text property. We can change the fore colour and back colour of the button by ForeColor and BackColor properties, respectively. Set the values given in Table 18.1 in the given properties. If we click the button, then event handlers are invoked. To make the button perform some action, click the button. The screen shown in Fig. 18.13 appears.

In the method private void MyButton_Click(), write the following code:

```
private void MyButton_Click(object sender, EventArgs e)
{
    MyButton.ForeColor = Color.Black;
    MyButton.BackColor = Color.White;
}
```

Now run the program by pressing F5. The following form will be displayed:

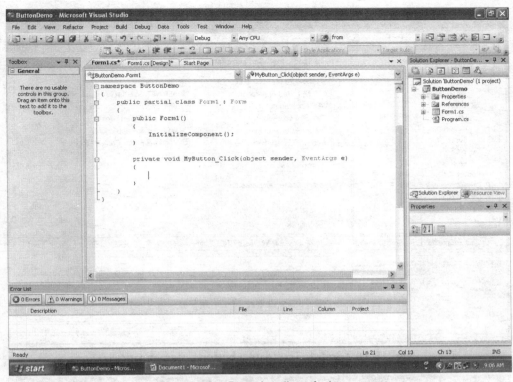

Fig. 18.13 Event handler of a button

Output

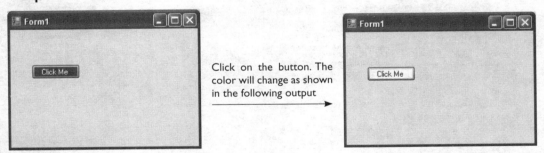

This example illustrates the ways to add a button to a form and to change its properties at design time. Section 18.7.4 describes the process to add a button at runtime.

18.7.4 Adding a Button at Runtime

A button can be added at runtime as well. In order to do so, the following steps need to be performed:

Step 1 Go to File → New → Project.
Step 2 Select Visual C# → Windows Form Application.
Step 3 Write the name of the project in the text box along with the 'Name:' label.
Step 4 Change the location if required. Click OK (Fig. 18.14).
Step 5 Double clicking anywhere on the form that appears (Form1 in this case) will take us to the Form1_Load method (Fig. 18.15).

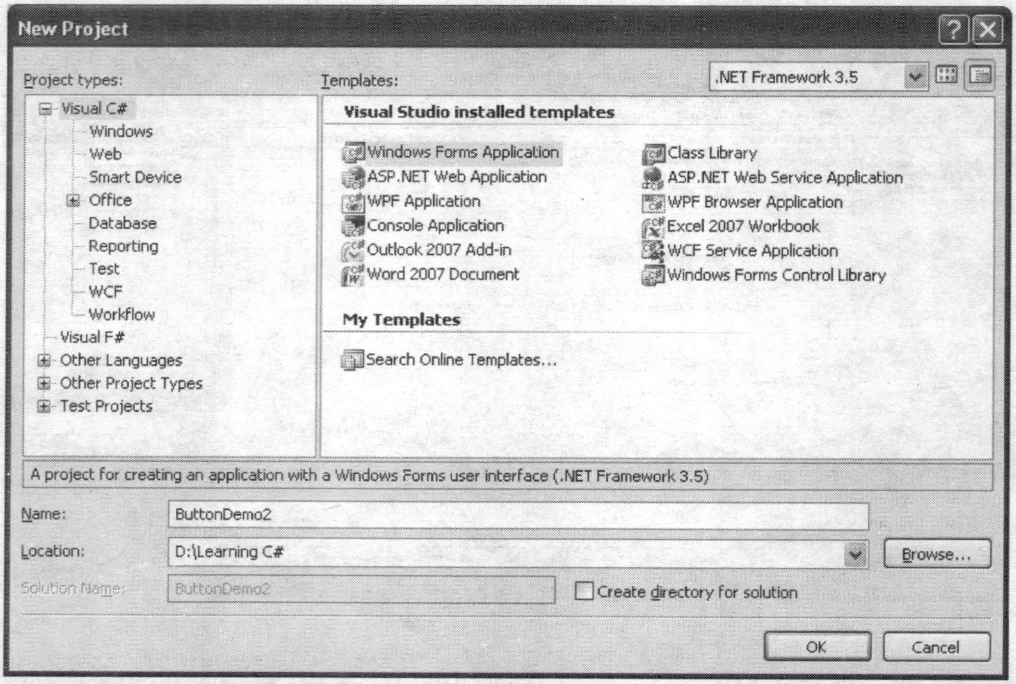

378 *Programming in C#*

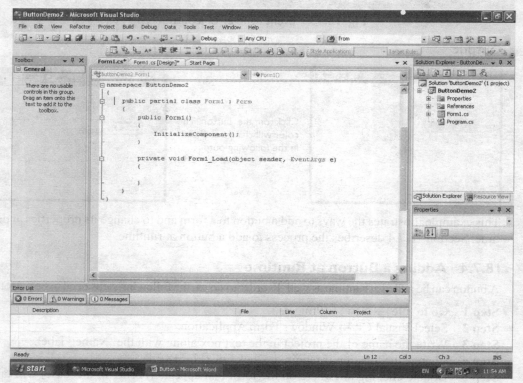

Fig. 18.14 Step 1: To create a button programmatically

Fig. 18.15 The Form_Load method

Inside this method, write the following code:

```
private void Form1_Load(object sender, EventArgs e)
{
    Button Button1 = new Button();
    Button1.Text = "Press Me";
    Point p = new Point(100, 100);
    Button1.Location = p;
    Button1.MouseClick += new MouseEventHandler(Button1_MouseClick);
    this.Controls.Add(Button1);
}
private void Button1_MouseClick(object sender, EventArgs e)
{
    MessageBox.Show("Hi");
}
```

It should be noted that Button is a predefined class. Button1 is an instance of Button. The second line sets the Text property of Button1 to 'Press Me'. In order to set the location at the runtime, the location property needs to have a value, which depicts a point; so an instance of point is made (p in this case) and Button1.Location is set to p. In order to make the button perform an action, a method called Button1.MouseClick is devised. It is just an ordinary method with arguments, which are instances of Object and EventArgs. When a user clicks the button, a message box saying 'Hi' should be displayed. Hence, in the Show method of the MessageBox class, the required text is given.

Press F5 to run the project. The following form will be displayed:

Output

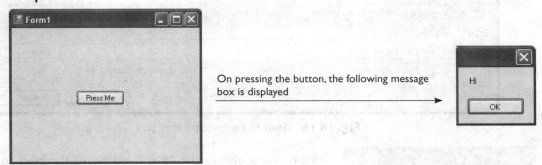

Section 18.7.5 describes the TextBox control. This control is as important as a button. It helps us to get the required data from the user.

18.7.5 Adding a Text Box at Design Time

Text box helps us to take data from the users. It can be added from the toolbox as described here or at the runtime as described in Section 18.7.6. The Text property of a text box is its most important property. We can make a string variable in the program and extract the text of the text box at the onset of some event such as pressing a button.

In order to restrain the amount of text entered by the user, set the MaxLength property to a specific number of characters. If the text box needs to be used as a password text box, then set the PasswordChar property to mask characters. The use of password text box has been explained in Problem 18.1.

If many lines are to be added in a text box, then `multiline` property of the text box needs to be true. The following steps describe the creation of a text box. The `multiline` text box will be dealt with in Problem 18.2:

Step 1 Go to File → New → Project.
Step 2 Select Visual C# → Windows Form Application.
Step 3 Write the name of the project in the text box along with the 'Name:' label.
Step 4 Change the location if required. Click OK (Fig. 18.16).
Step 5 From the toolbox drag text box and Label onto the form. If the toolbox is not visible, then go to View → Toolbox. The form now contains a label and a text box (Fig. 18.17).

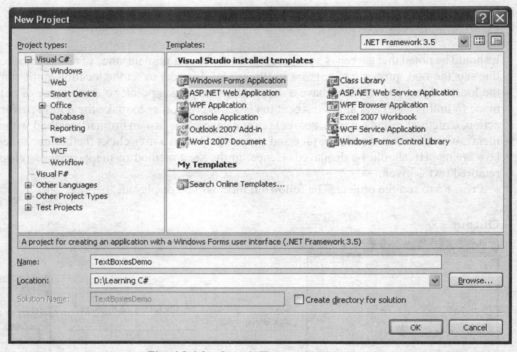

Fig. 18.16 Step 1: To create a text box

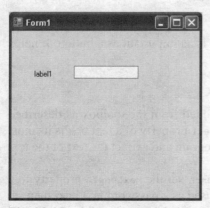

Fig. 18.17 A form with a label and a text box

Step 6 Now change the Text property of the label to 'Enter name' and the Name property of the text box to NameTextBox.

Step 7 In order to make the project work, add a button. Click the button and write the following code inside the method:

```
string name;
name = NameTextBox.Text;
MessageBox.Show("Hi " + name);
```

Here, we are declaring a string called name, which takes its value from TextBox. When we press F5, a form is displayed; enter a name in the text box. A message box containing the name of the person is finally displayed.

Output

Problem 18.1 makes use of the concepts studied so far and also shows the creation of a text box that can be used as a password text box.

Problem 18.1

Create a form containing two labels: Name and Password; there should be two text boxes in the form: NameTextBox and PassTextBox; make two buttons: ClearButton, which clears the text boxes, and SubmitButton, which displays a message box displaying whether the username/password combination is correct or not. Assume that the correct user name is jish and the correct password is jisha001.

Solution

In order to accomplish the task, carry out the following steps:

Step 1 Go to File → New → Project.
Step 2 Select Visual C# → Windows Form Application.
Step 3 Write the name of the project in the text box along with the 'Name:' label.
Step 4 Change the location if required. Click OK (Fig. 18.18).
Step 5 In the form that follows, add the following controls and set the requisite properties as shown in Table 18.2. The form should appear as shown in Fig. 18.19.
Step 6 Now, click on the ClearButton and write the following code:

```
namespace Example1
{
    public partial class Form1 : Form
    {
        public Form1()
        {
            InitializeComponent();
        }                                                code to be written
        private void ClearButton_Click(object sender, EventArgs e)
        {
            UserNameTextBox.Clear();
            PassTextBox.Clear();
        }
    }
}
```

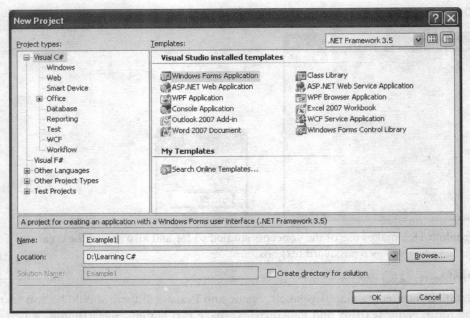

Fig. 18.18   Problem 18.1, Step 1

Table 18.2   Controls in Problem 18.1

Control	Control name	Property
Label	Label1	Text: User Name
Label	Label2	Text: Password
TextBox	NameTextBox	Name: NameTextBox
TextBox	PassTextBox	Name: PassTextBox, PasswordChar: *
Button	ClearButton	Name: ClearButton, Text: Clear
Button	SubmitButton	Name: SubmitButton, Text: Submit

Step 7   Click on the SubmitButton and write the following code:

```
using System;
using System.Collections.Generic;
using System.ComponentModel;
using System.Data;
using System.Drawing;
using System.Linq;
using System.Text;
using System.Windows.Forms;
namespace Example1
{
    public partial class Form1 : Form
    {
        public Form1()
        {
            InitializeComponent();
        }
```

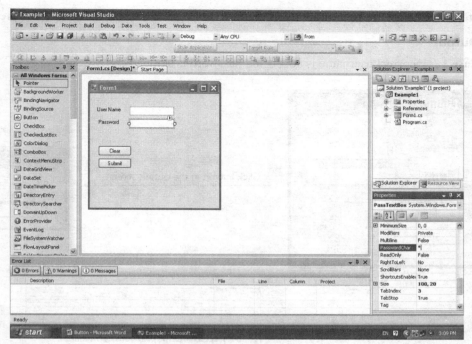

Fig. 18.19 Problem 18.1, Step 2

```
private void ClearButton_Click(object sender, EventArgs e)
{
    UserNameTextBox.Clear();
    PassTextBox.Clear();
}
private void SubmitButton_Click(object sender, EventArgs e)
{
    if(UserNameTextBox.Text == "")
    {
        MessageBox.Show("Enter the username");
    }
    else if(PassTextBox.Text == "")
    {
        MessageBox.Show("Enter the password");
    }
    else  if(!((UserNameTextBox.Text  ==  "jish") &&  (PassTextBox.Text  ==
    "jisha001")))
    {
        MessageBox.Show("Incorrect username/password combination");
    }
    else
    {
        MessageBox.Show("Welcome to the software");
    }
}
}
```

Step 8 Change the Text property of the form to Login and resize the form. Now press F5.

Output

Case 1 Incorrect username is added and password is skipped.

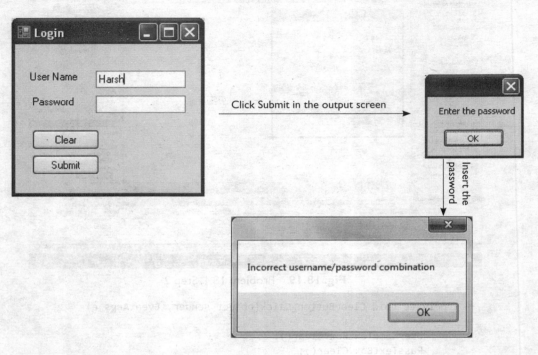

Case 2 Now, press the Clear button. The following output screen appears:

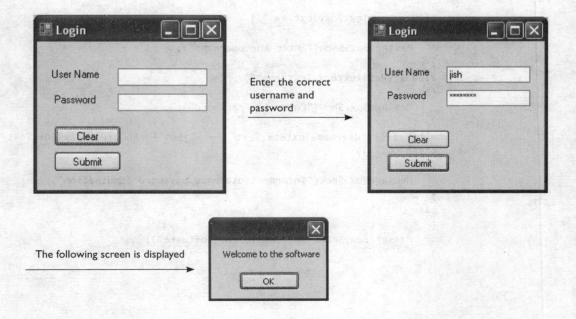

Some of the important methods of the text box control are explained in Table 18.3. These methods will be used in Project III, provided after Chapter 20. However, there are many more properties and methods associated with the text box control; the details can be found at www.microsoft.com/msdn.

18.7.6 Adding a Text Box at Runtime

In order to add a text box to the form at runtime, make an instance of the TextBox class. Set the name, location, and other details in the code and proceed as shown in the following steps:

Step 1 Go to File→ New → Project.
Step 2 Select Visual C# → Windows Form Application.
Step 3 Write the name of the project in the text box along with the 'Name:' label.
Step 4 Change the location if required. Click OK (Fig. 18.20).
Step 5 Double clicking anywhere on the form that appears (Form1 in this case) will take us to the Form1_Load method.
Step 6 Inside this method, write the following code:

```
using System;
using System.Collections.Generic;
using System.ComponentModel;
using System.Data;
using System.Drawing;
using System.Linq;
using System.Text;
using System.Windows.Forms;

namespace RunTimeTextBoxDemo
{
    public partial class Form1 : Form
    {
        public Form1()
        {
            InitializeComponent();
        }
        private void Form1_Load(object sender, EventArgs e)
        {
        TextBox TextBox1 = new TextBox();
        TextBox1.Location = new Point(100, 100);
        this.Controls.Add(TextBox1);
        }
    }
}
```

Table 18.3 Some methods associated with text box control

Method name	Function
AppendText	Appends text
Clear	Clears the text in the text box
Copy	Copy the selection to the clipboard
Cut	Moves the current selection to the clipboard
Paste	Replaces the selection with the text in the keyboard
Undo	Cancels or reverses the last operation

Fig. 18.20 Creating a text box at runtime

Step 7 Now press F5. The following form appears (Fig. 18.21).

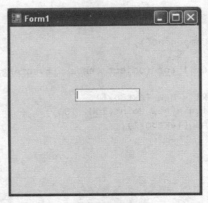

Fig. 18.21 Adding a text box at runtime

We have seen how to manipulate the text box control. Next, let us look at MaskedTextBox, which helps us to mask certain data such as phone number and social security number. Section 18.7.7 deals with various properties and some methods of MaskedTextBox.

18.7.7 MaskedTextBox

MaskedTextBox is a text box that allows one to define a pattern of the required input. The most important property of MaskedTextBox is the Mask property. In order to understand this property, we must understand the various masking elements (Table 18.4). These masking elements will help us to define masks, which will ultimately decide the user input.

For example, if the phone number of India needs to be entered, then the following mask must be set in the `Mask` property of the MaskedTextBox: 0000-0000000, that is, four required digits followed by a hyphen followed by seven required digits.

Table 18.4 Elements of a MaskedTextBox

Element	Meaning
0	Required digit
9	Optional digit
L	Required character
#	Optional digit, space, +, or −
?	Optional character capital or small
<	Changes all the following characters to lower case
>	Changes all the following characters to upper case
/	Date separator
\	Escape character

18.7.8 ListBox

ListBox control enables us to display a list of items. From a ListBox, we can select either a single item or a set of items. The most important properties of the control are provided in Table 18.5.

Apart from these properties, another important property is SelectionMode, which can be one of the following:

1. Single — Allows selection of single item
2. MultiSimple — Allows selection of multiple items
3. MultiExtended — Allows the use of Shift and Control keys during selection

A form with a ListBox is displayed in Fig. 18.22.

Table 18.5 Properties of ListBox control

Property	Explanation
DataSource	The data source can be a field of a table in database management system, an array, or a vector.
Items	This refers to the collection of items in the control.
MultiColumn	If this property is true, then more than one column appears at a time.
SelectedItem or SelectedItems	This returns the item or the collection of items as the case may be.
SelectedValue	This is useful in case of a data bound control.

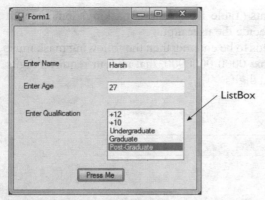

Fig. 18.22 Form having a ListBox

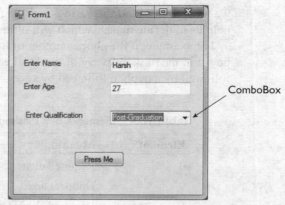

Fig. 18.23 Form having a ComboBox

18.7.9 ComboBox

If we want to select items from a list but at the same time want to type an element (if required), then ComboBox is used. For example, in a web browser, the address bar (location/URL bar) in which we write the address of a web page also shows us the list of the pages visited earlier. Figure 18.23 shows a form with a ComboBox.

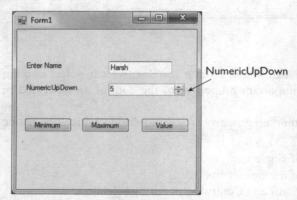

Fig. 18.24 Form having a NumericUpDown control

18.7.10 NumericUpDown

If we want some numbers to be selected from a particular range of numbers, then NumericUpDown can be used. It has the Minimum and Maximum properties to set the minimum and maximum numbers of that range. The Value property helps us to get the value selected, and the Increment property helps us to set the increment (or decrement). Figure 18.24 shows a NumericUpDown control.

Problem 18.2 makes use of most of the controls studied so far.

Problem 18.2

COMPUTERgrad is a company that provides IT training. You have been asked to develop the management system of the company. The first form is the registration form, which asks the name, address, stream, date of birth, and accomplishments from the students. The form has two buttons: Clear and Submit. The Clear button clears the text boxes and the Submit button displays the data entered. Design the form.

Solution

Step 1 Go to Project →New and Select Windows Forms Application. Now, Change the name of the project to Chapter18Ex2.
Set the size of the form Form1 to (500, 500) and the Text property to COMPUTERgrad Registration Form.
Add a panel and set its size to (290, 438) (Fig. 18.25).

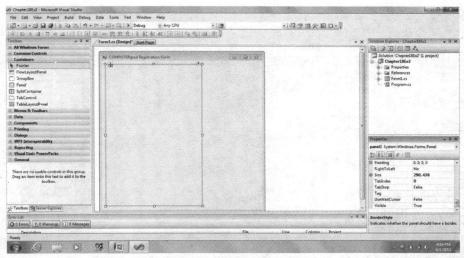

Fig. 18.25 Problem 18.2, Steps 1–3

Step 2 Add the labels shown in Table 18.6 to the form and set their Text property to the values shown in the table.

Table 18.6 Labels for Problem 18.2

Label	Text
Label1	Name
Label2	Date Of Birth
Label3	Stream
Label4	Phone Number
Label5	Address
Label6	Accomplishments

Step 3 Add the controls given in Table 18.7 to the form and set the property given in the second column to the value given in the third column of the table.

Table 18.7 Controls for Problem 18.2

Control	Property	Value
TextBox	Name	NameTextBox
DateTimePicker	Name	DOB
ListBox	Name	Stream
MaskedTextBox	Name	PhoneNumberTextBox
TextBox	Name	AddressTextBox
TextBox	Name	AccomplishmentsTextBox
	Multiline	True
Button	Name	ClearButton
Button	Name	SubmitButton

390 *Programming in C#*

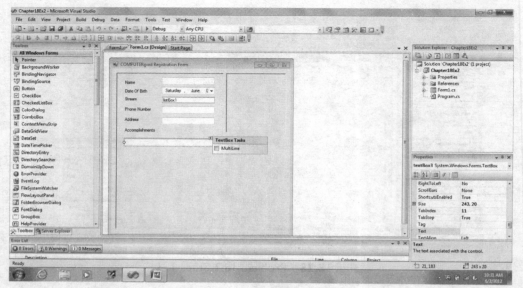

Fig. 18.26 Creating a form for Problem 18.2

Step 4 Set the AccomplishmentsTextBox's `Multiline` property as true (Fig. 18.26).

Step 5 In the Items property of the StreamListBox, write the following items:

1. Computer Science
2. IT
3. Electronics
4. Others

Step 6 In the Clear button handler, write the following code to clear every text box by using the clear method:

```
NameTextBox.Clear();
AddressTextBox.Clear();
PhoneNumberTextBox.Clear();
AccomplishmentsTextBox.Clear();
```

Step 7 In the SubmitButton handler, write the following code. In the snippet, each value is being extracted from the control and stored in variables. The variables are shown in the full program at the end of the section.

```
name = NameTextBox.Text;
dob = DOB.Value.ToString();
accomplishments = AccomplishmentsTextBox.Text;
phoneNumber = PhoneNumberTextBox.Text;
stream = Stream.Text;
address = AddressTextBox.Text;
MessageBox.Show("You have entered the following details" + Environment.
NewLine + "Name\t:" + name + Environment.NewLine + "Address\t:" + address +
Environment.NewLine + "Date of Birth\t:" + dob + Environment.NewLine + stream +
"Stream\t:" + Environment.NewLine + Environment.NewLine + "Accomplishments\t:" +
accomplishments);
```

Output

The overall form appears as shown in Fig. 18.27.
Insert some data in the form that appears (Fig. 18.28).
Press the Clear button. A form similar to that shown in Fig. 18.29 is displayed.
Now enter the correct data and press the Submit button. Figure 18.30 shows the snapshot of the output.

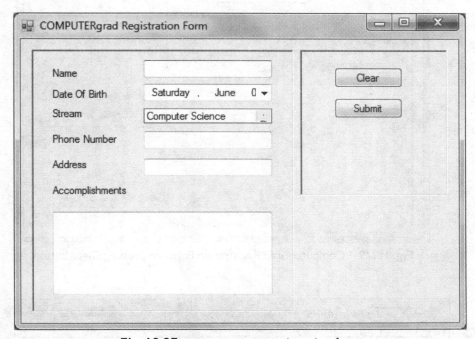

Fig. 18.27 ComputerGrad registration form

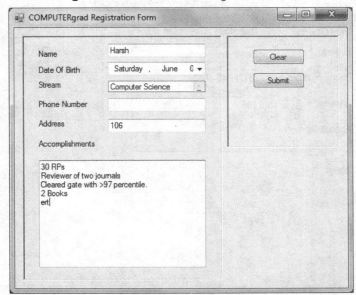

Fig. 18.28 Details entered in ComputerGrad registration form

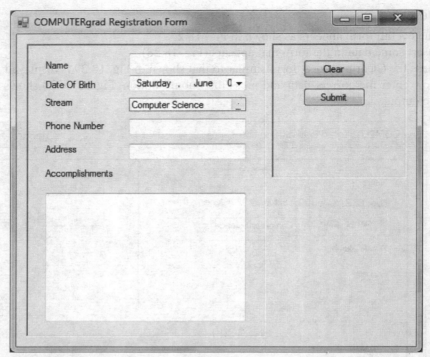

Fig. 18.29 ComputerGrad Registration Form on pressing Clear button

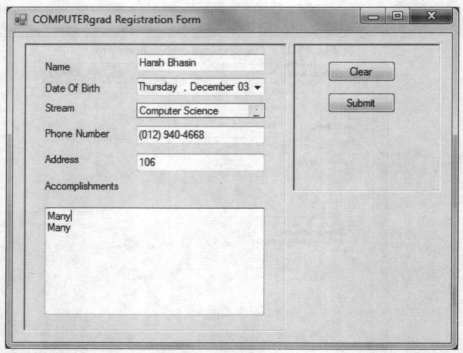

Fig. 18.30 ComputerGrad registration form on pressing Submit button

Once the Submit button is pressed, a message box appears, which displays the details entered by the user.

Program

```csharp
using System;
using System.Collections.Generic;
using System.ComponentModel;
using System.Data;
using System.Drawing;
using System.Linq;
using System.Text;
using System.Windows.Forms;

namespace Chapter18Ex2
{
    public partial class Form1 : Form
    {
        public Form1()
        {
            InitializeComponent();
        }
        string name, address, stream, dob, accomplishments, phoneNumber;
        private void ClearButton_Click(object sender, EventArgs e)
        {
            NameTextBox.Clear();
            AddressTextBox.Clear();
            PhoneNumberTextBox.Clear();
            AccomplishmentsTextBox.Clear();
        }
        private void SubmitButton_Click(object sender, EventArgs e)
        {
            name = NameTextBox.Text;
            dob = DOB.Value.ToString();
            accomplishments = AccomplishmentsTextBox.Text;
            phoneNumber = PhoneNumberTextBox.Text;
            stream = Stream.Text;
            address = AddressTextBox.Text;
            MessageBox.Show("You have entered the following details" + Environment.NewLine + "Name\t:" + name + Environment.NewLine + "Address\t:" + address + Environment.NewLine + "Date of Birth\t:" + dob + Environment.NewLine + stream + "Stream\t:" + Environment.NewLine + Environment.NewLine + "Accomplishments\t:" + accomplishments);
        }
    }
}
```

Notes

1. Always set the `Anchor` property; otherwise, the controls might not be rendered in the same manner when the form is maximized.
2. If many lines are to be added in a TextBox, then set `multiline` property to true.
3. When you are done with designing the form, then set the tab indices of controls in the order in which you want the user to traverse.
4. If there are multiple forms in a project, then make sure that the look and feel of each form is the same. It gives a professional appearance.
5. If you want to add a control on the onset of certain event, than add it at runtime and not at the design time (by making it invisible).
6. In order to keep all the buttons together, you can place them in a group box. Grouping makes the management of controls easy.
7. While designing a form, the name of the control should be similar to the work it is doing and not the name that ships along with it when we drag it onto our form. For example, a text box that takes the first name from the user can be called the FirstNameTextBox.
8. If there are many controls in a form, then TabControl can be used.
9. If the form is to be divided into two parts, then split container can be used.
10. The form should be readable and usable and must have a pleasant appearance.

SUMMARY

The chapter introduces Windows forms and some of the most common controls therein. The controls, along with the requisite attributes and their configurations, have been examined in the chapter. It is important to become familiar with these controls in order to become an accomplished client side developer. However, it may be noted that not all controls have been covered here. Chapter 19 deals with some of the remaining controls. The controls explained in these two chapters, along with database connectivity and knowledge of dialogs (Chapter 21), will help readers to develop a full-fledged management system.

This chapter forms the basis of RAD in C# and the .NET Framework. Readers are advised to design basic Windows forms and applications such as calculators to be able to understand the topic.

GLOSSARY

Windows forms These are containers that house controls and menus that allow an application to be created in a familiar manner.

Controls These are components that incorporate prefabricated functionality.

Text box This is used to get textual input from a user and to display data.

MaskedTextBox This is a text box that allows the user to define a pattern for accepting input.

Button This is a control that establishes interaction between the user and the application.

Label This is a control that displays read-only text to the user.

POINTS TO REMEMBER

- A form is the basic unit of a C# Windows Application project.
- The look and feel of a form can be changed by changing the settings of its properties.
- The Snap lines give us visual support in locating the controls and in setting their relative alignment.
- The Anchor property sets the distances from the edge of the control.
- The Dock property helps us to stick the control to one of the edges.
- Controls are instances of a subclass of Windows.Forms namespace.
- A Linklabel is a control used to display read-only text as in the case of a Label control, it but can also be used to access a link.
- The MaskedTextBox is a text box that allows one to define a pattern of the required input.
- ListBox control enables us to display a list of items.
- NumericUpDown helps us to select a value from a range of values.
- Any control can be configured either at compile time or at runtime

EXERCISES

I. Multiple-choice Questions

1. Which property is used to set the title of a Windows form (say Form1)?
   (a) Form1.Text (b) Form1.Title
   (c) Form1.FormTitle (d) Any of these

2. To set the startup form, which line needs to be modified in Program.cs?
   (a) `<summary>`
   (b) `Application.EnableVisualStyles();`
   (c) `Application.Run(new Form1());`
   (d) `Application.SetCompatibleTextRenderingDefault(false);`

3. What should be done to have a help button in a form?
   (a) A new button can be created and linked to help any form.
   (b) The help button property needs to be set.
   (c) BackColor must be set to red.
   (d) None of these

4. Which property defines constant distance between control and one or more edges of the form?
   (a) Anchor (b) Dock
   (c) Flat Style (d) Cursor

5. Which property enables us to attach the control to the edge of the parent control?
   (a) Dock (b) Anchor
   (c) Size (d) Position

6. Which control dynamically repositions the controls at the runtime?
   (a) TableLayoutPanel control
   (b) FlowLayoutPanel control
   (c) Tab control
   (d) None of these

7. The most important property of MaskedTextBox is
   (a) Font (b) ASCII only
   (c) Mask (d) ForeColor

8. A form needs to have a MaskedTextBox, which has Anti-social Security Number (ASSN). It is a number having four digits followed by hyphen followed by three digits. Which of the following mask will have to be set in the Mask property?
   (a) 9999-999 (b) 9999/999
   (c) 0000-000 (d) 0000/000

9. In Question 6 of Part I in Exercises, what would be the value of TextMask format?
   (a) Include prompt
   (b) Exclude literals
   (c) Include prompt and literals
   (d) Exclude prompt and literals

10. In a form, a user is asked to enter his research interest (maximum 100 words). Which of the following properties will help to accomplish this task?
    (a) Multiline = True
    (b) Max Length = 100
    (c) Scroll Bars = True
    (d) Multiline = False

II. State True or False

1. A windows form can be non-rectangular.
2. It is possible to change FormBorderStyle at runtime.
3. In order to make the form start at the centre of the screen, we can let either centre screen or centre parent be the Start position.
4. It is possible to have a scroll displayed on panel control.
5. There can be three panels in the SplitContainer control.
6. The phone number in India is of the form 0000-0000000. It is possible for the user to cut and paste the entire number including hyphen, but when the value is put into a variable, the hyphen does not appear.
7. To accomplish the task in Question 6, the CutCopyMark property id should include literals.
8. It is possible to have a scroll bar in a form (without panel).
9. If we set the Start position property of location to Manual, then the starting location is relative to upper left.
10. In order to set the MaximumSize to no upper limit, the value of the property size should be (100, 100).

III. Programming Exercises

1. Design a form in C# with a button called 'Click Me'. If the user presses the button, a message should be displayed and the program should dispose. The shape of the form should be as shown in the following figure.

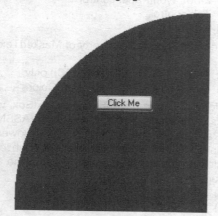

2. Design a form in C# that takes the details of a book from the user. Make two buttons Clear and Submit. On clicking the Clear button the text boxes should be cleared, and on clicking the Submit button a message box should be displayed. The message box should display the details of the books entered by the user.
3. The problem in Question 2 is to be extended to include the details of borrowers. The form should have the Clear and the Submit buttons as in Question 2.
4. Design a form with two buttons, Book and Borrower. On clicking the Book button the form in Question 2 should be displayed, and on clicking the Borrower button the form of Question 3 should be displayed.
5. Using Windows forms, make a calculator with the following functionalities:

   +   : Add
   –   : Subtract
   *   : Multiply
   /   : Divide
   %   : Remainder
   R   : Root
   C   : Clear
   +–   : For changing the sign
   =   : For displaying the result

   The calculator should use the Button control and the TextBox control and the coding should be done using Switch case.

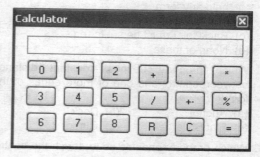

6. Extend the calculator of Question 5 to include the following functions:
   (a) Trigonometric functions
       (i) sin
       (ii) cos

    (iii) tan
    (iv) sec
    (v) cosec
 (b) Logarithm and antilog
    (i) log
    (ii) antilog
 (c) Complex number calculator
    (i) Addition
    (ii) Subtraction
    (iii) Multiplication
    (iv) Division
    (v) Mod
    (vi) Argument
 (d) Number system conversion
    (i) Binary to decimal
    (ii) Decimal to binary
    (iii) Hexadecimal to decimal
    (iv) Decimal to hexadecimal
    (v) Octal to decimal
    (vi) Decimal to octal
    (vii) Octal to binary
    (viii) Binary to octal
    (ix) Hexadecimal to binary
    (x) Binary to hexadecimal
 (e) Degree to radian and radian to degree conversion

7. COMPUTER grad Books is a books store. The outlet intends to develop management software. The software is expected to keep track of the customers along with many other details. The required details of the customers are as follows:
 (a) Name
    (i) First name
    (ii) Middle name
    (iii) Last name
 (b) Address
    (i) Street
    (ii) City
    (iii) State
    (iv) Country
 (c) Phone number
 (d) Email ID
 (e) Date of birth
 (f) Age (calculated field)

The company wants one more field called Customer ID in the form. The ID should be automatically generated when a new customer is added. Every customer should have a unique ID. Design the form keeping in view the aesthetics and usability in mind.

8. The form of Question 7 needs to be extended to include the details of the supplier having the same fields as in Question 7.

9. Explore ER diagrams (database management system). Draw the ER diagram of a school and create forms of all the entities.

10. Draw the ER diagram of an airlines reservation system and create the required management system.

19 Advanced Controls and Menus

OBJECTIVES

After completing this chapter, the reader will be able to

Use GroupBox
Appreciate the importance of Panel control, TableLayoutPanel control, and TabControl
Add and use SplitContainer control
Understand advanced list controls
Apply radio buttons
Set date and time using DateTimePicker control
Add and manipulate a MenuStrip and a ToolStrip
Design a web browser

19.1 INTRODUCTION

This chapter continues the task commenced in Chapter 18. The controls explained in this chapter, together with those learnt in Chapter 18, will help readers to develop applications such as a management system or a web browser. While creating a Windows application, the first act is to design the front end. The front end will consist of forms and controls placed therein. In general, an application will have a number of forms, each performing a specific task. For example, in a student management system, one form can ask the user to enter the details of the students, another can ask for the fee details, and so on. Similarly, an inventory control system or an invoicing system will contain many forms. This chapter gives an idea of tab controls and panels, which will help to provide a professional appearance to the application.

This chapter discusses menus and tool strips along with some container controls. As explained in Chapter 18, in some controls, setting the values of the attribute accomplishes the requisite tasks, whereas some controls require event handlers. In menus and tool strips, event handlers are essential to perform the requisite task.

19.2 ADVANCED CONTROLS

This chapter is a continuation of Chapter 18 and examines some more controls. Sections 19.2.1 –19.2.13 discuss container controls, namely GroupBox, Panel, SplitContainer, and TabControl, which can house various controls. While creating a form, we can place the labels and text boxes in the cells of a TableLayoutPanel control, as expounded here. In addition, controls such as MenuStrip and ToolStrip, which help in navigation, are also elucidated in this chapter. The usage of the controls has been illustrated with the help of the example of a web browser.

19.2.1 GroupBox Control

At times, we need to club together controls performing a similar task. The controls can be segregated into groups on the basis of the task performed or the design and aesthetics of the controls. GroupBox is a container control, which is used to group the controls. The caption of the GroupBox is set by its text property. We can drag and drop GroupBox from the toolbox. The use of the GroupBox will become clear in Section 19.2.9. In Section 19.2.5, the concept of segregation of controls has been examined again. Figure 19.1 shows a GroupBox and the way to set its caption.

19.2.2 Panel Control

Panel is a container that can house other controls. The idea for having a panel in the form is to make a subsection of the form. However, in order to make the subsection appear separate from the rest of the form, the BorderStyle property can be set to Fixed 3D. At times, we have many controls in the form. In such situations, the controls can be placed in the panel and the AutoScroll property of the panel can be set to true. This will make scroll bars appear in the panel. Section 19.2.3 of the chapter also makes use of the control. Figure 19.2 shows the Panel control.

19.2.3 TableLayoutPanel Control

The name TableLayoutPanel control suggests that the control is used for making a table, that is, only a table. However, it can be used for many other purposes and is especially used to organize the form. Snap lines help us to align the controls but only to a certain extent. When there are many

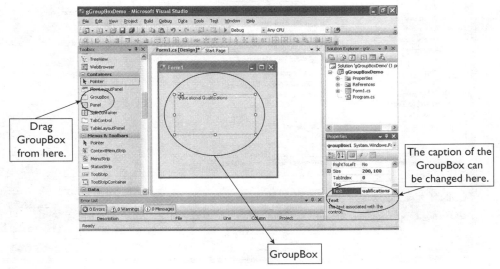

Fig. 19.1 GroupBox

400 *Programming in C#*

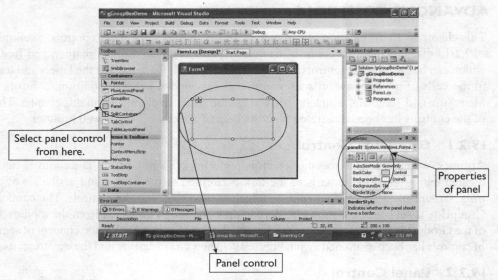

Fig. 19.2 Panel control

controls, even the snap lines are insufficient. In such a situation, we can drag a TableLayoutPanel control onto the form and place the controls one by one in the different cells. The borders of the table are not visible by default, so when we run the project the aligned controls will be seen but not the borders. The following steps depict how the task can be accomplished:

Go to Project → New. Select Windows Forms Application. Write the name of the project (Fig. 19.3).

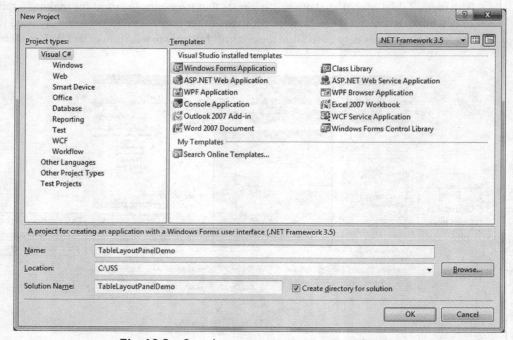

Fig. 19.3 Step 1: `TableLayoutPanel` control usage

Advanced Controls and Menus **401**

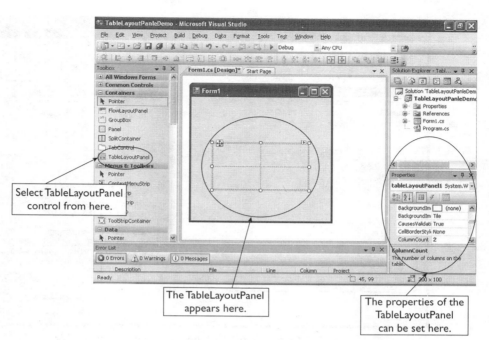

Fig. 19.4 Step 2: `TableLayoutPanel` control usage

1. The screen shown in Fig. 19.4 appears.
   From the toolbox, select the TableLayoutPanel control and set the number of rows and columns to the requisite values (Fig. 19.5).

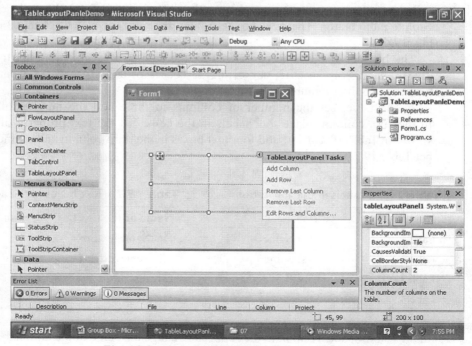

Fig. 19.5 Step 3: `TableLayoutPanel` control usage

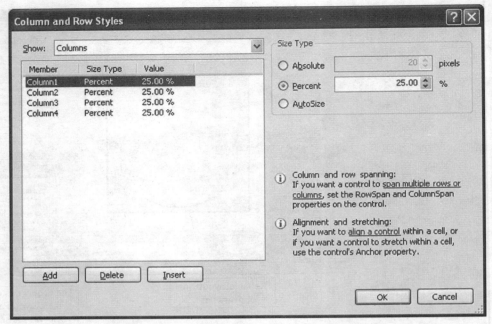

Fig. 19.6 Setting column and row style in a table

The styles of rows and columns can be changed by RowStyle and ColumnStyle, respectively. The screen depicting the column and row style is shown in Fig. 19.6. The width of columns can be set either as percentages and in pixels. The size in pixels can be set by clicking on the absolute radio button. The size and the style of the rows can also be changed in this manner (Fig. 19.6).

The borders of the table can be set by the `CellBorderStyle` property. It can be set to `Single`, `Inset`, `InsetDouble`, `Outset`, `OutsetDouble` or `OutsetPartial`, depending upon the type of the border required.

In the table, set the number of columns to three and the number of rows to six. In the first column, place four labels in the cells. Set the text property of the labels as shown in Table 19.1. Now, add four text boxes in the third column and set the properties as per Table 19.2.

Table 19.1 Labels in the application

Name	Text
Label1	First Name
Label2	Last Name
Lable3	City
Label4	State

Table 19.2 Text boxes in the application

Name of the text box	Tab index
FirstNameTextBox	1
LastNameTextBox	2
CityTextBox	3
StateTextBox	4

2. In the last row, add a button in the first cell. Change the name of the button to 'ClearButton' and its text to 'Clear'. Set the tab index of the button to 5. Set the text property of the form

Advanced Controls and Menus 403

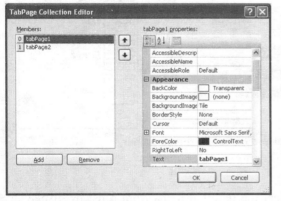

Fig. 19.7 Details of the form

Fig. 19.8 TabPage collection editor

as 'Details'. Now press F5. Figure 19.7 depicts the snapshot of the form. It may be noted that the controls are aligned and the relative position of the controls will remain the same even if the form is maximized (Fig. 19.7).

19.2.4 TabControl

If the number of controls is high such that even a scroll bar is of little help, then we can use Tab control. This control provides tabs, each of which can be treated as a separate container. The usability can be greatly enhanced using the tab control. In order to use this control, go to toolbox and drag TabControl onto your form. The most important property of the tab container is TabPage. If we click on the TabPage property, the screen shown in Fig. 19.8 appears.

We can add tab pages by clicking on the Add button. The title on the page can be set by setting the content of the text property of that page. We can also set the font, colour, back colour, and so on of each tab page separately by setting the requisite properties of the individual pages. If needed, we can add a scroll bar in the page by setting the AutoScroll property to true (Fig. 19.9).

19.2.5 SplitContainer Control

SplitContainer control divides a form into two parts. We can set the relative width of the two parts by setting the splitter distance property of the split container. We can also set the orientation of the panes to horizontal by changing the value in the orientation property to horizontal. The scroll bars can be shown

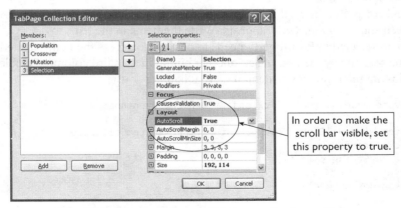

Fig. 19.9 Setting values in TabPage collection editor

by selecting the individual panels. It may be noted that the split container is used only to split the screen in exactly two parts. If further segregation of the form is required, we can add panels in any of the two panels provided by the split container (Fig. 19.10).

Font, Forecolor, BackColor, and BackGroundImage can be set to the desired values by setting the individual properties. An additional property of the split container is the cursor property, which can be used to select the type of the cursor.

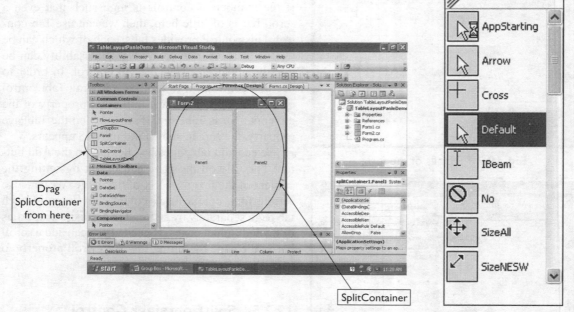

Fig. 19.10 SplitContainer control and cursor of the container

19.2.6 CheckedListBox Control

The CheckedListBox control allows us to select the required items from a list by displaying check boxes along with the items. However, only one value can be selected at a time, without shift. In order to understand this control, let us use it in the form created in Section 19.2.3. In the first column of the fourth row, insert a label and set the text property to Assets. Now, insert CheckedListBox in the third column of the row. Click on the Items property of the control. The screen shown in Fig. 19.11 appears. Write the items in the list.

The selected index property needs to be used to access the item selected. In order to see the value selected by the user, insert another button in the third column. Double click on the button and write the following code in the event handler:

```
private void button1_Click(object sender, EventArgs e)
{
System.Windows.Forms.CheckedListBox.CheckedItemCollection  c1  =  checkedListBox1.CheckedItems;
foreach(String c in c1)
{
MessageBox.Show(c);
}
}
```

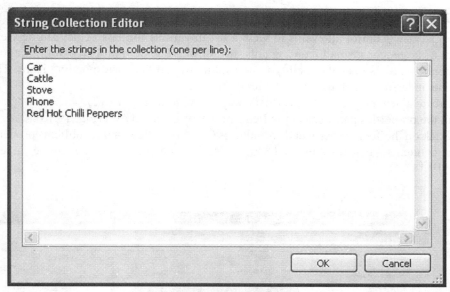

Fig. 19.11 CheckedListBox control

Run the project and select some of the items. The items selected will be displayed one by one in the message box.

Output

Press process and the assets will be displayed if you have selected them.

19.2.7 ListView Control

The ListView control allows us to view a list in various formats. A list can be viewed in the form of large icons, small icons, details, list, or tile. The item property of this control is more elaborate as it also has the facility to add subitems and the corresponding icons. This control can be understood with the help of a program.

Create a new project and add a ListView control to it (Fig. 19.12).

In the properties pane, select the Items property. Click on Add (Fig. 19.13).

Click on the Text property and set value as Car. Now, click on the SubItems property and add three subitems—Esteem, Alto, and Santro. Set the View property to one of the values shown in Fig. 19.14.

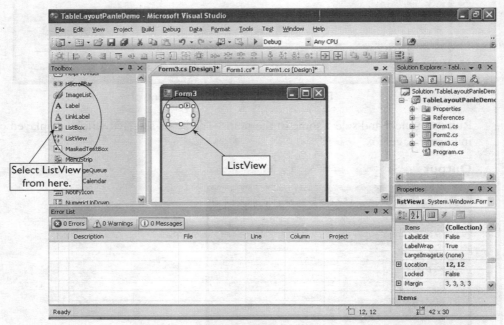

Fig. 19.12 Adding ListView to a form

19.2.8 CheckBox Control

One of the most common controls used when designing a web or Windows form is CheckBox. It contains a box, which can be checked or unchecked, for indicating acceptance or rejection of that item. The most important property of the control is checked, which can take the value true or false. It may be noted that as against common perception a check box can have three states. The states can be enabled by setting the state property to true. The three states are 'Checked', 'Unchecked', and 'Intermediate'.

In order to understand the control, let us consider a simple application.

Make a new Windows Application project. In the form that appears, add three check boxes—CheckBox1, CheckBox2, CheckBox3, a label—Label1, and a button—Button1. In the Text property of the label, set value as 'Select City'. The Text property of the check boxes should be

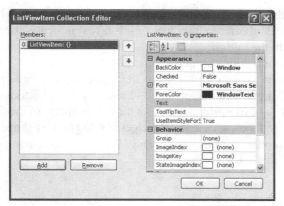

Fig. 19.13 ListViewItem collection editor

Fig. 19.14 A ListBox

set to 'Mumbai', 'Pune', and 'Navi Mumbai'. Now, go to the event handler of the button and write the following code:

```
String cities = "";
if(checkBox1.Checked == true)
{
    cities += "Mumbai";
}
if(checkBox2.Checked == true)
{
    cities += "Pune";
}
if(checkBox3.Checked == true)
{
    cities += "Navi Mumbai";
}
MessageBox.Show("Selected Cities " + cities);
```

Fig. 19.15 A form with a CheckBox

Now press F5. The form shown in Fig. 19.15 appears.

Select the cities and press the button. A screen as shown in Fig. 19.16 appears.

On pressing the Show button, the following message box appears.

Output

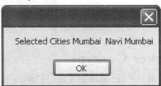

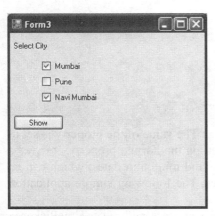

Fig. 19.16 Selecting values in a CheckBox

19.2.9 RadioButton Control

Radio button is similar to a check box except for the fact that only one option can be selected at a time from a group of radio buttons. The radio buttons are placed inside a GroupBox. One radio button will be selected from the group. The two important properties of a radio button are Text and Checked. The value of Checked can be either true or false. Text indicates the value that would appear in the label along with the button.

The control can be better understood with a simple application.

Make a new Windows Application project. In the form that appears, add three radio buttons—radioButton1, radioButton2, radioButton3, a label—Label1, and a button—Button1. Place the radio buttons in a GroupBox—GroupBox1—and set the text property of the GroupBox to 'Cities'. In the text property of the label, set value as 'Select City'. The text property of the radio buttons should be set to 'Mumbai', 'Pune', and 'Navi Mumbai'. Now, go to the event handler of the button and write the following code:

```
String cities = "";
if(radioButton1.Checked == true)
{
    cities += "Mumbai";
}
else if(radioButton2.Checked == true)
{
    cities += "Pune";
}
else if(radioButton3.Checked == true)
{
    cities += "Navi Mumbai";
}
MessageBox.Show("Selected City " + cities);
```

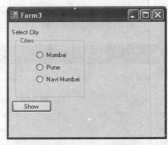

Fig. 19.17 A form with radio buttons

Now press F5. The form shown in Fig. 19.17 appears.

Select Mumbai and press the button. The following message box appears:

Output

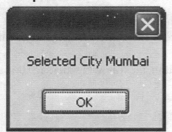

19.2.10 DateTimePicker Control

The date or time, or both, can be set using DateTimePicker. The value of the property is set to the chosen value. We can set the format of the date by setting the Format property. It may be noted that the control also allows us to set the maximum and minimum dates, which can be accomplished using the MinDate and MaxDate properties. The following simple application shows the use of DateTimePicker.

Make a new Windows Application project. In the form that appears, add a DateTimePicker—DateTimePicker1, a label—Label1, and a button—Button1. In the text property of the label,

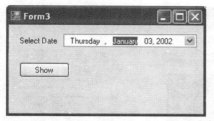

set value as 'Select Date'. The text property of the button should be set to 'Show'. Now, go to the event handler of the button and write the following code:

```
MessageBox.Show("Selected Date " + dateTimePicker1.Value.ToString());
```

Now press F5. The form shown in Fig. 19.18 appears.

Fig. 19.18 A form with DateTimePicker

Select date and press the Show button. The message box shown in the output appears.

Output

Thus, the task is accomplished.

19.2.11 MenuStrip Control

In almost all applications of Windows, we encounter a menu. The menu bar of the applications contains items called menu items. The menu items generally perform some task, which are set by the event handler of the item. We can add a menu bar in the form and perform the requisite tasks. The following illustration gives an idea about handling the menu bar:

Create a new project of the type Windows Application Form.

Set the text of the form to genetic algorithms (Fig. 19.19).

Drag a menu bar onto the form. MenuStrip is available in the Menus and Toolbars section of the Toolbox (Fig. 19.20).

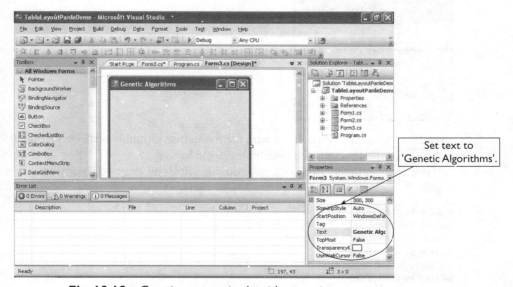

Fig. 19.19 Creating a genetic algorithms project

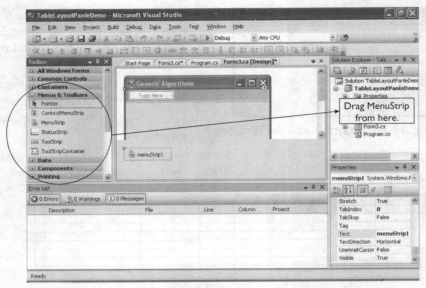

Fig. 19.20 Dragging MenuStrip onto the project

We can add the items in the MenuScript by placing an & (ampersand) before the letter, which helps us to access the menu item. For example, if we set the Text property of PopulationToolMenuStripItem to '&Population', then we will be able to access the population menu item by pressing Alt + P when the project runs. In order to see the effect, add two sub-menu items—Generate & Binary and Generate & Hexadecimal—to the MenuStrip. In order to display the result, add a label—Label1. Set the text property of the label to a null string. When the project runs, the following menu appears:

Output

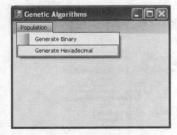

In order to associate some event with the menu items, double click on the menu items (or subitems) and write the requisite code in the event handler.

For instance, in the given example, double click on Generate Binary and write the following code:

```
using System;
using System.Collections.Generic;
using System.ComponentModel;
using System.Data;
using System.Drawing;
using System.Linq;
using System.Text;
```

```
using System.Windows.Forms;
namespace TableLayoutPanelDemo
{
    public partial class Form1 : Form
    {
        public Form1()
        {
            InitializeComponent();
        }
        int[,] population = new int[100, 25];
        int i, j;
        Random r = new Random();
        private void generateBinaryToolStripMenuItem_Click(object sender, EventArgs e)
        {
            for(i = 0; i < 100; i++)
            {
                for(j = 0; j < 25; j++)
                {
                    population[i, j] = ((r.Next() % 100) > 50) ? 1 : 0;
                }
            }
            for(i = 0; i < 100; i++)
            {
                for(j = 0; j < 25; j++)
                {
                    label1.Text += population[i, j] + " ";
                }
                label1.Text += Environment.NewLine;
            }
            MessageBox.Show("Task Accomplished");
        }
    }
}
```

Now, run the project and click on the Generate Binary menu item. The screen shown in the output appears.

Output

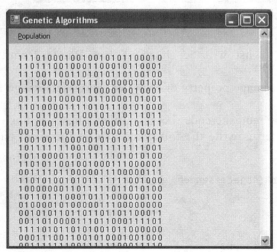

The concept and the algorithm of this task are given in Project V, in which the code will be examined. The aim here is to depict the format to associate a code with a menu or a submenu item. Another example on menus is given in Section 19.2.13.

19.2.12 ToolStrip Control

A ToolStrip is similar to a menu in the sense that every item is associated with some event. If an item is pressed in the ToolStrip, it triggers an event. However, instead of the name of the items, a ToolStrip has pictures. It works in a similar fashion to a menu. In order to understand the working of the ToolStrip control, let us add a ToolStrip in our project.

In the form, add a ToolStrip (Fig. 19.21).

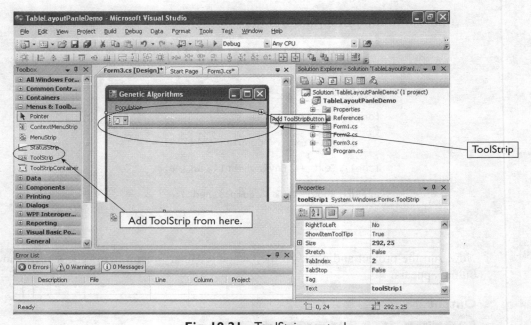

Fig. 19.21 ToolStrip control

When we click on the ToolStrip, a list will be shown. Select Button from that list (Fig. 19.22).

Add two such buttons. Now, go to image property of each item and select image from the local resources.

Click on each button and write the requisite code. Let us display a message box on clicking each ToolStrip menu item. So, let us write the following code in the event handler of ToolStripButton1:

```
private void toolStripButton1_Click(object sender, EventArgs e)
{
    MessageBox.Show("Book");
}
```

Run the application and click on the first icon.

Advanced Controls and Menus **413**

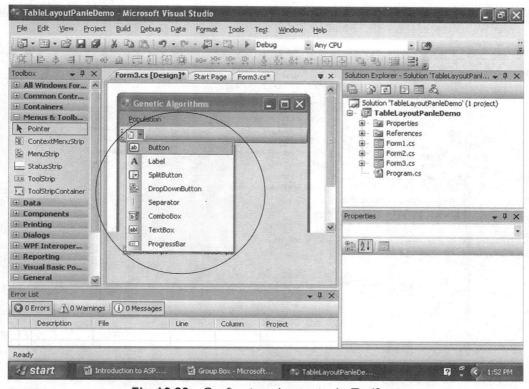

Fig. 19.22 Configuring a button in the ToolStrip

Output
The output depicted will be displayed on clicking the first image.

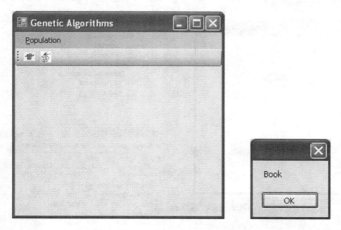

19.2.13 Browser Control
Browser control gives a ready-made web browser control, which can be used in any of the applications. The following steps explain the concept of a web browser and help us to craft our own web browser. Let the browser be called HBrowser.

Create a new project. Select Windows Forms Application and name the project as WebBrowser (Figs 19.23 and 19.24).

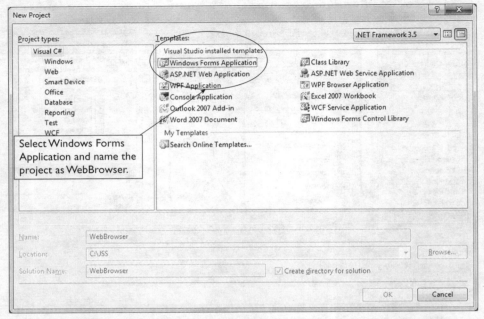

Fig. 19.23 Creating a browser project

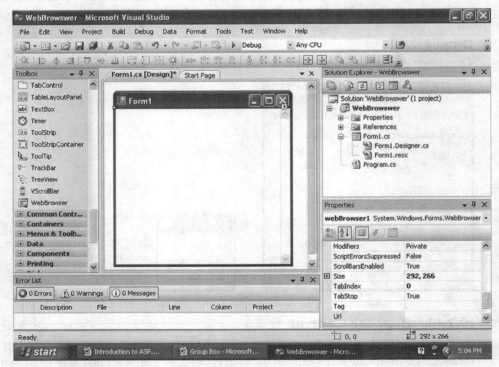

Fig. 19.24 Adding a form in the project

Figures 19.25 and 19.26 depict the next two steps of the application.

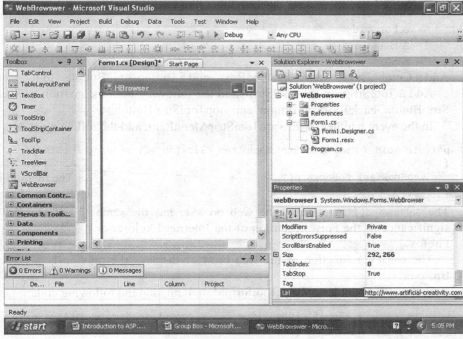

Fig. 19.25 Adding a browser in the form

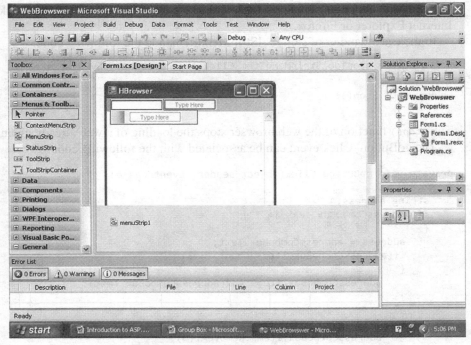

Fig. 19.26 Adding MenuStrip in the browser

To the MenuStrip, add the following:
- &Navigate
  - SubMenu
    - &Forward
    - &Backward
    - &Stop

Add a ComboBox—AddressComboBox—and a Button—GoButton—to the menu bar.

Add a ToolStrip. In the ToolStrip, add the following buttons: goToolStripButton, fwdToolStripButton, backToolStripButton, and stopToolStripButton.

In the event handler of forwardToolStripMenuItem, add the following code:

```
private void forwardToolStripMenuItem_Click(object sender, EventArgs e)
{
    webBrowser1.GoForward();
}
```

The method implements Forward functionality of a standard Web Browser.

The GoForward() function of the web browser has the same significance as the Forward button of the Internet Explorer or Firefox.

The GoBack() function of the web browser displays the previously accessed page in the Browser.

In the event handler of backToolStripMenuItem, add the following code:

```
private void backToolStripMenuItem_Click(object sender, EventArgs e)
{
webBrowser1.GoBack();
}
```

The GoBack() function of the web browser has the same significance as the Back button of the Internet Explorer or Firefox.

In the event handler of stopToolStripMenuItem, add the following code:

```
private void stopToolStripMenuItem_Click(object sender, EventArgs e)
{
webBrowser1.Stop();
}
```

The Stop() function of the web browser stops the loading of a web already given page.

The goButton_Click event can be associated with the following code:

```
private void goButton_Click(object sender, EventArgs e)
{
    string address;
    if(addressComboBox.Text != "")
    {
        address = addressComboBox.Text;
        if(addressComboBox.Items.Count != 3)
        {
            addressComboBox.Items.Add(addressComboBox.Text);
        }
        else
        {
            addressComboBox.Items.RemoveAt(0);
            addressComboBox.Items.Add(addressComboBox.Text);
```

```
            }
            webBrowser1.Navigate(address);
        }
        else
        {
            MessageBox.Show("\nEnter address in the address field", "Browser",
            MessageBoxButtons.OK, MessageBoxIcon.Error);
        }
    }
}
```

The final application is shown in the following output screen.

Output

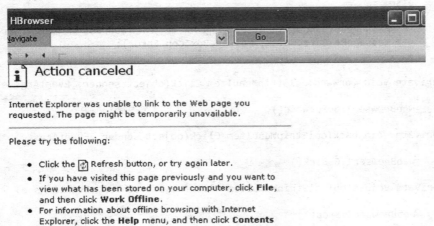

Output of web browser demo program

The complete code of the browser is as follows:

```
using System;
using System.Collections.Generic;
using System.ComponentModel;
using System.Data;
using System.Drawing;
using System.Linq;
using System.Text;
using System.Windows.Forms;

namespace Browser
{
    public partial class Form1 : Form
    {
        public Form1()
        {
            InitializeComponent();
        }
        private void goButton_Click(object sender, EventArgs e)
        {
            string address;
            if(addressComboBox.Text != "")
```

```csharp
        {
            address = addressComboBox.Text;
            if(addressComboBox.Items.Count != 3)
            {
                addressComboBox.Items.Add(addressComboBox.Text);
            }
            else
            {
                addressComboBox.Items.RemoveAt(0);
                addressComboBox.Items.Add(addressComboBox.Text);
            }
            webBrowser1.Navigate(address);
        }
        else
        {
            MessageBox.Show("\nEnter address in the address field", "Browser",
            MessageBoxButtons.OK, MessageBoxIcon.Error);
        }
    }
    private void forwardToolStripMenuItem_Click(object sender, EventArgs e)
    {
        webBrowser1.GoForward();
    }
    private void backToolStripMenuItem_Click(object sender, EventArgs e)
    {
        webBrowser1.GoBack();
    }
    private void stopToolStripMenuItem_Click(object sender, EventArgs e)
    {
        webBrowser1.Stop();
    }
}
}
```

SUMMARY

This chapter not only examines the various controls required to make a full-fledged Windows application but also paves way for the development of many minor projects. An example given is the Genetic algorithms tool. Genetic algorithms are heuristic search processes based on the theory of the survival of the fittest. The program code in Section 19.2.12 sets the stage for the development of a genetic tool. The tool has also been explained in Project V.

The above examples will help readers to develop minor projects. However, it is advisable to go through some of the research papers relating to genetic algorithms. After developing a genetic tool, readers are urged to select a problem, such as vertex cover or subset sum, and apply the tool to the selected problem. The upcoming chapters examine dialogs and database connectivity, thus covering all the concepts of a Windows application.

GLOSSARY

MenuStrip control This control is a ToolStrip control to display ToolStripMenuItems.

ToolStrip control This helps to facilitate the creation of a tool bar with the look and feel of Microsoft Office applications.

ListBox control This is a list-based control, which shows a list of items.

POINTS TO REMEMBER

- Each menu item can host submenus.
- Each menu item can have shortcut keys.
- TableLayoutPanel is used not just for drawing a table but also for configuring controls at specific positions.
- ToolStrip gives the application the look and feel of standard Microsoft Office applications.
- WebBrowser control helps to display web pages in the applications.
- For selection of items from amongst a list, the CheckBox and RadioButton controls can be used.
- NumericUpDown helps the user to select an integer from a particular range.

EXERCISES

I. Multiple-choice Questions

1. Which of the following properties is used to set the caption of a GroupBox?
   (a) Text
   (b) Caption
   (c) Title
   (d) None of these

2. Which of the following is used to align controls?
   (a) Snap lines
   (b) TableLayoutPanel control
   (c) FlowLayoutPanel control
   (d) All of these

3. Which is the most important property of TabControl?
   (a) TabPages   (b) BackColor
   (c) Font   (d) ForeColor

4. Which control helps in selecting multiple items at a time?
   (a) CheckedListBox   (b) TextBox
   (c) Label   (d) None of these

5. If you have to select only one item from a group of items, which control can be used?
   (a) RadioButton   (b) CheckBox
   (c) Both (a) and (b) (d) None of these

6. Which of the following controls helps you to select date as well as time?
   (a) Calendar
   (b) DateTimePicker
   (c) Both (a) and (b)
   (d) None of these

7. Which of the following controls is used to work according to the selected choice?
   (a) MenuStrip   (b) ToolStrip
   (c) Both (a) and (b) (d) None of these

8. How many panels can a split container have?
   (a) 1
   (b) 2
   (c) 3
   (d) Any number of panels

9. Which container is used to club like controls together?
   (a) GroupBox   (b) TextBox
   (c) Label   (d) All of these

10. Which control is used to display a web page?
    (a) WebBrowser control
    (b) Panel
    (c) SplitContainer
    (d) All of these

II. State True or False

1. TableLayoutPanel control is used to create only a data table.
2. TableLayoutPanel control can be added inside a TableLayoutPanel control.
3. TableLayoutPanel control helps in designing a form.
4. TabControl helps in saving space in an application.
5. A split container can have more than two panels.
6. There can be only one radio button in a form.
7. A panel can have many panels.
8. TabControl cannot have a button.
9. A menu can have any number of submenus.
10. ToolStrip is similar to MenuStrip in terms of functionality.

III. Review Questions

1. What is the utility of a Panel control?
2. Explain the use of a Panel control.
3. What is the importance of a GroupBox?
4. Explain the methods of WebBrowser control?
5. With the help of an illustration, explain the use of MenuStrip.
6. What is the difference between MenuStrip and ToolStrip?
7. Explain the difference between Button control and CheckBox control.
8. Apart from the TableLayoutPanel control, is there any other control that can help in managing the layout of a form?
9. Explain the use of DateTimePicker control.
10. Can a WebBrowser control be used to view word files?

IV. Programming Exercises

A page rank algorithm is to be developed. The project page ranking represents how important a page is on the web. Google figures it when one page links to another page. The importance of the page that is casting the vote determines how important the vote itself is. Google calculates a page's importance from the votes cast for it. The importance of each vote is taken into account when a page's page rank is calculated.

Page rank algorithm is used by Google to give importance metric to a page to be displayed as result of a query given by the user. It was first developed by Larry Page at Stanford University. Our idea is to implement it so as to see the working of page rank and its importance and to compare the ranks of web pages. We have to develop the algorithm in C#. The project will also help in creating a crawler as well. In developing the project, make use of the following controls:

1. GroupBox
2. Panel
3. TableLayoutPanel
4. SplitContainer
5. MenuStrip
6. WebBrowser

However, you can also make use of other controls.

20 Common Dialogs

OBJECTIVES

After completing this chapter, the reader will be able to
- # Appreciate the importance and use of `SaveFileDialog`
- # Realize the significance and use of `FontDialog`
- # Embed and use `ColorDialog`
- # Understand the working of the `OpenFileDialog`

20.1 INTRODUCTION

So far, we have seen how to develop various Windows applications. Now, we need to learn to use various dialogs in those applications. A dialog is a window that is opened in the context of another window. When we save a file in Microsoft Word, we are greeted with a 'Save As' or a 'Save' dialog box. When we open a file, an 'Open' dialog box crops up. Dialogs are present in almost all the applications currently in use. Hence, it would be better if we have dialogs in our applications as well in order to make them user friendly.

Dialogs help us to accomplish easily day-to-day tasks such as saving the document, printing it, and changing the font. These dialogs are a step towards genuine rapid application development (RAD). The application development time in RAD can be reduced by using pre-crafted components such as dialogs in the application. The following are the various dialogs provided by C#:

1. Save
2. Save As
3. Open
4. Font
5. Color
6. Print
7. Print Preview

These dialogs perform the tasks suggested by their names. For example, if we create a random population of Genetic Algorithms and accomplish a particular task, we might want our application to be able to save the initial population for analysis purposes. This is essential to compare the results of the present run with those generated by a different set. In order to accomplish this task, we can use the Save or Save As dialog box provided by C#.

If we are developing an application such as a notepad, we would like our application to be able to change the attributes such as size, color, and font of the text. This can be done with the aid of the `FontDialog`. Similarly, in order to print the document created in our application we can use the Print dialog, and in order to preview the application we can use the Print Preview dialog.

The present chapter explains and exemplifies various dialogs provided by C#. Dialogs such as Font, Print, Print Preview, and Save are illustrated via the notepad application and a menu-driven program. The chapter further discusses the Color and Open dialogs. The Print and Print Preview dialogs have been examined in Project III. However, once we understand the intricacies of these dialogs, we will be able to use them in any application.

20.2 SaveFileDialog

The `SaveFileDialog` helps us to save a document. In order to ask the user to save a particular file at a specific location in a specific format; the `SaveFileDialog` is used. This dialog requires an input file to be saved, the location at which the file is to be saved, and the format of the file. The `ShowDialog()` method of the instance of `SaveFileDialog` shows a standard `SaveFileDialog` box. It may be stated here that we can set the title of the dialog by setting the Title property to the requisite string. The Filter property allows us to restrict the types of files that can be saved. The description of the file followed by a '|' and type extension is written as depicted in the following example:

```
saveFileDialog1.Filter = "text|*.txt|All Files|*.*";
```

where `saveFileDialog1` is an instance of `SaveFileDialog`. The following illustration exemplifies the concept. The various steps to be followed to create the application are provided:

Step 1 Go to File → New → Project.

Step 2 Select Windows Forms Application and write the name of the project in the Name text box as shown in Fig. 20.1. If required, set the location of the application in the Location text box.

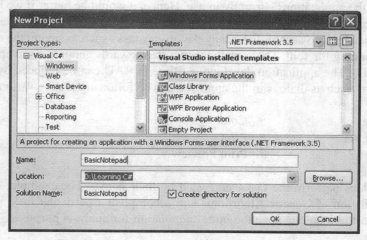

Fig. 20.1 Initial form design in Basic Notepad

Common Dialogs 423

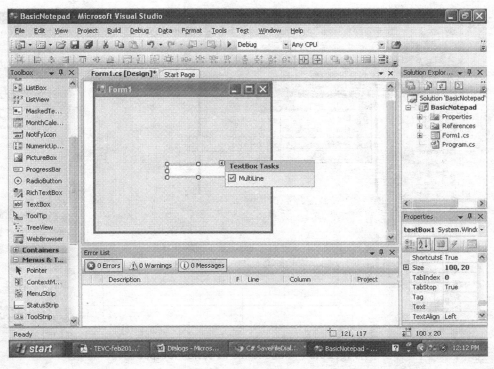

Fig. 20.2 Setting Multiline as true in Basic Notepad

Step 3 Now drag a text box onto the form and set the Multiline property of the text box to 'true' and set the text property of the form to 'Basic Notepad' as shown in Fig. 20.2.

Step 4 Now set the Dock property of the text box to 'Fill'. This makes the text box to occupy the whole text area. Drag a menu strip onto the form and create the various menu items listed in Table 20.1.

Step 5 The screen shown in Fig. 20.3 appears; it shows the various menu items. It should be noted that the basic framework of the application is ready. Now, the next step would be to drag SaveFileDialog onto the form.

Table 20.1 Menu items in basic notepad

Name of the item	Name	Text	Menu/Submenu
File	fileToolStripMenuItem	&File	Main menu
New	newToolStripMenuItem	&New	Submenu (Parent file)
Save	saveToolStripMenuItem	&Save	Submenu (Parent file)
Save As	saveAsToolStripMenuItem	Save &As	Submenu (Parent file)

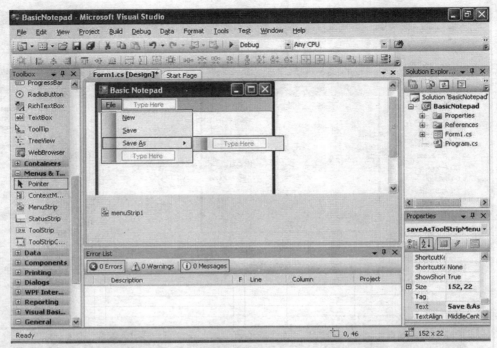

Fig. 20.3 Menu items in Basic Notepad

Step 6 Write the following code in the editor. It has to be noted that the System.IO namespace is used to implement the file operations. The WriteAllText() method is used to write the text in a file. The method takes two arguments, the first being the name and path of the file and the second being the source to be written in the file. It may be noted that the source in this case is the text of the text box.

```
using System;
using System.Collections.Generic;
using System.ComponentModel;
using System.Data;
using System.Drawing;
using System.Linq;
using System.Text;
using System.Windows.Forms;
using System.IO;

namespace BasicNotepad
{
    public partial class Form1 : Form
    {
        public Form1()
        {
            InitializeComponent();
        }
        private void saveToolStripMenuItem_Click(object sender, EventArgs e)
        {
            saveFileDialog1.Title = "Basic Notepad Save Dialog";
            saveFileDialog1.Filter = "text|*.txt|All Files|*.*";
            if(saveFileDialog1.ShowDialog() == DialogResult.OK)
```

```
            {
                try
                {
                    File.WriteAllText(saveFileDialog1.FileName, textBox1.Text);
                }
                catch(Exception e1)
                {
                    MessageBox.Show(e1.ToString());
                }
            }
        }
    }
}
```

Step 7 Execute the project and write some text in the notepad. If we save the file in a particular location, we will be able to retrieve it at a later stage, similar to the notepad in Windows. Figures 20.4 and 20.5 show the output when the program is executed.

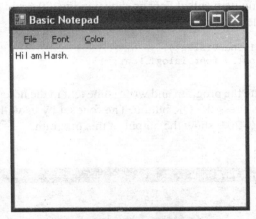

Fig. 20.4 Basic Notepad

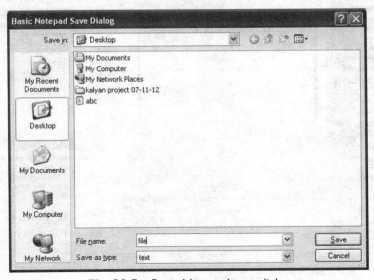

Fig. 20.5 Basic Notepad save dialog

The task is thus accomplished successfully. This is the first step towards creating a complete notepad. However, some more functionalities of notepad are implemented in Sections 20.3–20.5. Project III on Notepad gives the complete picture.

20.3 FontDialog

The `FontDialog` box helps us to set the font of the given text. The dialog is invoked using the `ShowDialog()` method of the `Font` class. The Font property of the instance gives the font once the OK button is pressed. In order to use the dialog, invoke the dialog, set the font, and set the text property of the text box to the Font property of the dialog. The `FontDialog` box has been explained using the basic notepad created in Section 20.2. The following steps are required to create an application that uses `FontDialog`:

Step 1 Drag and drop the `FontDialog` onto the form.

Step 2 Make a menu item called Font as shown in Fig. 20.6 and go to its event handler. In the event handler, write the following code:

```
fontDialog1.ShowDialog();
textBox1.Font = fontDialog1.Font;
```

Step 3 Now, execute the program and write some text in the notepad. Go to the Font menu and set the font. Press the OK button. The font set by us will be depicted in the Notepad. Figures 20.7–20.9 show the output of this program.

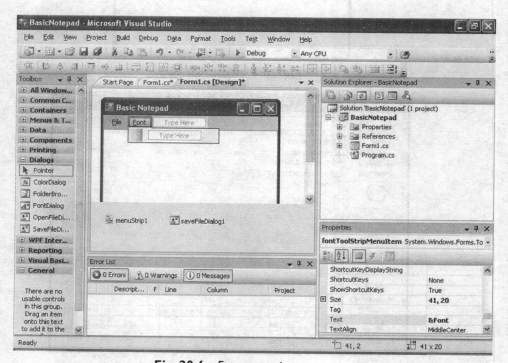

Fig. 20.6 Font menu item

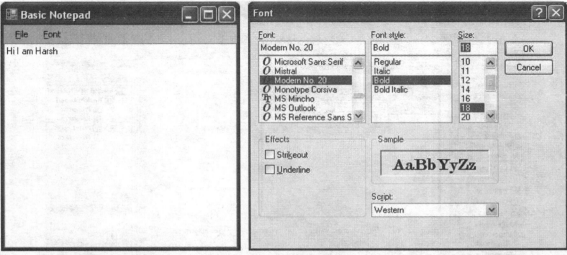

Fig. 20.7 Basic Notepad   **Fig. 20.8** Setting font in Basic Notepad

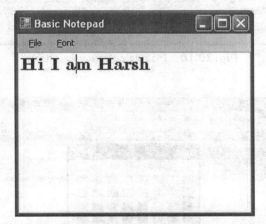

Fig. 20.9 Effect of setting font in Basic Notepad

20.4 ColorDialog

Let us now make our application colourful by using the `ColorDialog`. This dialog helps us to set the colour of the text. The dialog is invoked via the `ShowDialog()` method. The colour of the text can be set via setting the `ForeColor` property of the text box to the Color property of `ColorDialog`. The following steps are needed to develop an application using the `ColorDialog`:

```
textBox1.ForeColor = colorDialog1.Color;
```

Figure 20.10 shows the creation of the Color menu item. Figures 20.11 and 20.12 show the output of the program, which can be created by making requisite changes in the listing given in Section 20.1. However, the complete program is also given just after the snapshots.

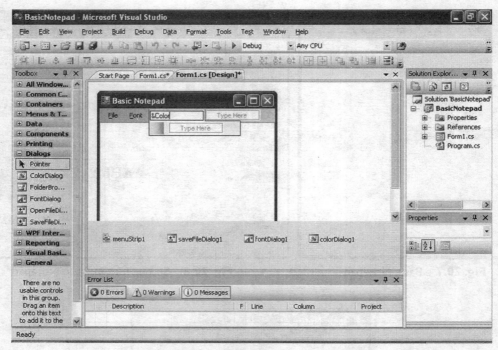

Fig. 20.10 Making colour menu item

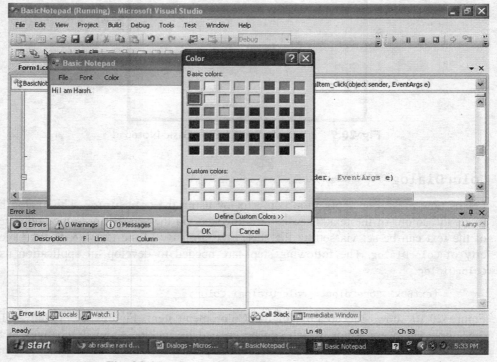

Fig. 20.11 Setting colour of text in Basic Notepad

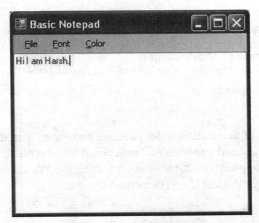

Fig. 20.12 Change in text colour

```
using System;
using System.Collections.Generic;
using System.ComponentModel;
using System.Data;
using System.Drawing;
using System.Linq;
using System.Text;
using System.Windows.Forms;
using System.IO;

namespace BasicNotepad
{
    public partial class Form1 : Form
    {
        public Form1()
        {
            InitializeComponent();
        }
        private void saveToolStripMenuItem_Click(object sender, EventArgs e)
        {
            saveFileDialog1.Title = "Basic Notepad Save Dialog";
            saveFileDialog1.Filter = "text|*.txt|All Files|*.*";
            if(saveFileDialog1.ShowDialog() == DialogResult.OK)
            {
                try
                {
                    File.WriteAllText(saveFileDialog1.FileName, textBox1.Text);
                }
                catch(Exception e1)
                {
                    MessageBox.Show(e1.ToString());
                }
            }
        }
        private void fontToolStripMenuItem_Click(object sender, EventArgs e)
        {
            fontDialog1.ShowDialog();
            textBox1.Font = fontDialog1.Font;
```

```
        }
        private void colorToolStripMenuItem_Click(object sender, EventArgs e)
        {
            colorDialog1.ShowDialog();
            textBox1.ForeColor = colorDialog1.Color;
        }
    }
}
```

Having seen the use of these dialogs, let us move on to the Open dialog. Section 20.5 will help us to create a basic notepad application. However, it may be noted that the dialogs are used not only in the notepad application but also in almost all the Windows applications. These dialogs have also been used in Project V on 'Genetic Algorithm'.

20.5 OpenFileDialog

The `OpenFileDialog` embeds a pre-crafted component with the capability of opening a file, displaying the existing files on the system, and selecting the type. The type selection is the same as that in `SaveFileDialog`. The filtering can be done via the Filter property of the class.

```
openFileDialog1.Filter = "Text|*.txt|All Files|*.*";
```

The dialog is invoked via the `ShowDialog()`. Moreover, the `ReadAllText` method can be used to read the text in the text file opened. In the basic notepad example, this text can be set as the text property of the text box. The event handler of the requisite menu item follows. Figure 20.13 shows the menu item creation of the dialog. The code that follows is to be written in the event handler of the menu item. Figure 20.14 shows the dialog and Fig. 20.15 shows the final basic notepad.

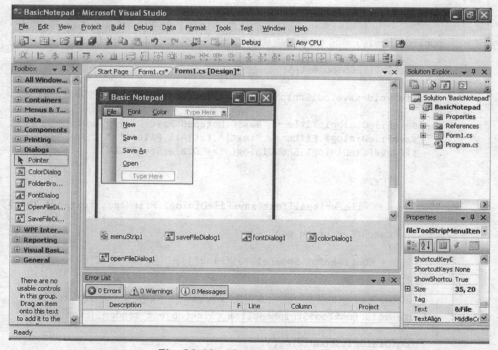

Fig. 20.13 Creating open menu

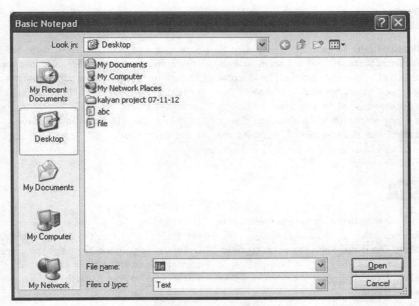

Fig. 20.14 OpenFileDialog

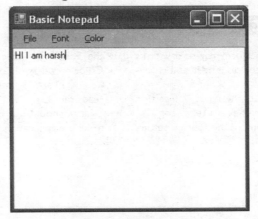

Fig. 20.15 Complete Basic Notepad

```
private void openToolStripMenuItem_Click(object sender, EventArgs e)
{
    openFileDialog1.Title = "Basic Notepad";
    openFileDialog1.Filter = "Text|*.txt|All Files|*.*";
    if(openFileDialog1.ShowDialog() == DialogResult.OK)
    {
        textBox1.Text = File.ReadAllText(openFileDialog1.FileName);
    }
}
```

This dialog can be used to open a file of any type. However, it may be noted that though text files can be opened in a text box, a sound file cannot be opened in it. It should be understood that when we open a file, our application should be able to support that file. Theoretically, we may open any file, but practically, the application's capabilities will decide which files can be opened at the invocation of a particular event.

SUMMARY

The dialogs discussed in this chapter are necessary to create a Windows application; they aid us in embedding the dialog boxes in our applications. The example of notepad has been taken because it is one of the most suitable applications to demonstrate the use of dialogs. These dialogs facilitate RAD. However, dialogs should not be used with the sole aim of improving the appearance of the application. There has to be a sound reason to use them, as they make the application bulky. Though the chapter covers the most important dialogs, `PrintDialog` and `PrintPreviewDialog` have been examined in Project III. To conclude, the dialogs help in making the application look good without having to exert much effort.

GLOSSARY

Dialog This is a window that is opened in the context of another window.
OpenFileDialog This dialog helps the users to select the file to be opened.
SaveFileDialog This dialog helps the users to save a file in the required format.
FontDialog This dialog helps the users to select and set the font of the text in the application.
ColorDialog This dialog helps the users to select and set the colour in the application.
Filter The file filter helps the user to select the type of file that can be opened.

POINTS TO REMEMBER

- The dialogs help us to perform day-to-day tasks such as saving the document, printing it, and changing the font.
- The Filter property restricts the types of files that can be saved while using the `SaveFileDialog`.
- The user can set the colour of the font by setting the ForeColor property of the text box to the Color property of `ColorDialog`.
- `ReadAllText()` method of `OpenFileDialog` reads the text.
- Dialogs should not be used unnecessarily, as they make the application bulky.

EXERCISES

I. Multiple-choice Questions

1. Which dialogs allow users to browse the file system and select the files to be saved?
    (a) SaveFile   (b) SaveAsFile
    (c) SavingFile   (d) None of these

2. Which dialog sets the colour of the text/selected text?
    (a) Color   (b) Font
    (c) Both (a) and (b) (d) None of these

3. Which dialog allows the size of the font to be changed?
    (a) Font   (b) Color
    (c) FontSize   (d) None of these

4. Which of the following dialogs helps you to open files?
    (a) FileOpen   (b) OpenFile
    (c) File   (d) FileOpenAs

5. Which property gets or sets a string containing the file name selected in the file dialog box?
    (a) FileName   (b) Name
    (c) NameOfFile   (d) None of these

6. Which property gets or sets the current file name filter string, which verifies the options that appear in the 'Save as file type' box?
    (a) Extension   (b) Filter
    (c) Type   (d) None of these

7. Which property gets or sets the index of the filter currently selected in the file dialog box?
   (a) Filter
   (b) Index
   (c) FilterIndex
   (d) None of these
8. Which property gets or sets the file dialog box title of the `SaveFileDialog`?
   (a) Caption
   (b) Title
   (c) Heading
   (d) All of these
9. Which method runs a common dialog box with a default owner in the `SaveFileDialog`?
   (a) `ShowDialog()`
   (b) `Show()`
   (c) `Display()`
   (d) `DisplayDialog()`
10. Which method runs a common dialog box with the specified owner?
    (a) `ShowDialog()`
    (b) `ShowDialog(IWin32Window)`
    (c) Both(a) and (b)
    (d) None of these
11. What is the purpose of the following?
    `saveFileDialog1.InitialDirectory = @"C:\";`
    (a) To set C drive as the initial directory for saving file
    (b) To set C drive as the only directory for saving file
    (c) Both (a) and (b)
    (d) None of these
12. Which of the following methods releases all resources used by the component?
    (a) `Reclaim()`
    (b) `Snach()`
    (c) `Dispose()`
    (d) `TakeBack()`

II. Review Questions

1. Explain the importance of dialogs in Windows Forms Application development.
2. Explain the various methods necessary to integrate the `SaveFileDialog` box in an application that implements notepad.
3. Explain the various methods necessary to integrate the `OpenFileDialog` box in an application that implements notepad.
4. Explain the various methods necessary to integrate the `ColorDialog` box in an application that implements notepad.
5. Explain the various methods necessary to integrate the `FontDialog` box in an application that implements notepad.

III. Programming Exercises

Natural language processing (NLP) is one of the most researched topics in the present scenario. The concept is used when one language is to be understood or converted into another language. Nakul was interested in NLP but he had little idea of the topic. He decided to work under a professor. Since he was good in programming, the professor asked him to implement his earlier research paper. He was required to make a Hindi to Marathi Translator. The various tasks assigned to him were as follows.

Design an interface that contains four buttons—Login, Admin, About Us, and Exit. The buttons should link to the various forms explained as follows.

The login form should lead to a login dialog box, which contains a text box for user name and a text box for password. On entering the user name and password, the user should be taken further.

The next form should show the corresponding Marathi word for the English word selected by the user.

At this point, Nakul made the following suggestions to the professor:

1. The form may contain a Save button, so that the word seen by the user on that day can be saved with data in a file.
2. This file may be used later in order to judge the person.
3. The person should be able to change the font and the colour of the form; in order to implement this, two dialog boxes must be used in the application.

Now, help Nakul to accomplish the task by designing these forms and make the requisite changes in the third form.

PROJECT III
Notepad

1. ABSTRACT

Notepad is one of the most commonly used applications. It is the first step towards the making of a full-fledged word processor. The basic idea was examined in Chapter 20. This project, however, takes a step forward and introduces the Print and Page Setup Dialogs. It may be noted that the notepad briefed in this project is a basic notepad. You can enhance the notepad as much as possible, and moreover, you can also connect the notepad to the database to restrict the access rights. However, the goal of this project is not to create a professional notepad but to make a student-level project to understand the uses of various dialogs.

2. PROCEDURE

The following steps must be carried out in order to make a notepad:

Step 1 Drag a text box onto the form and set the Multiline property of the text box to be true. The Dock property of the text box should be set to 'Fill'.

Step 2 Set the title of the form to be 'SSD Notepad' (or whatever you wish to name).

Step 3 Drag a menu onto the form and make four menu items: File, Edit, Format, and Help.

Step 4 Create the following submenus in the File menu: New, Open, Save, Save As, Page Setup, Print, and Exit. Figure PIII.1 shows the submenu items.

The event handlers of various submenus have been explained in the following section:

Step 5 In the Edit menu, create the following submenus: Cut, Copy, and Paste. Figure PIII.2 shows the submenu items.

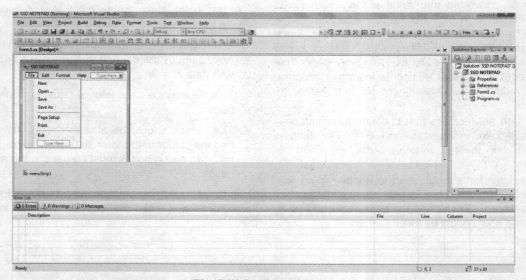

Fig. PIII.1 File submenu

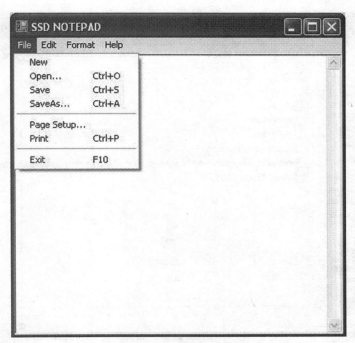

Fig. PIII.2 Edit submenu

Step 6 The Format menu can have Color and Font menus, as explained in Chapter 20. The Help menu, on the other hand, can have a custom form, having label indicating your name and your company's name followed by the instructions to use the software.

3. EXPLANATION OF THE SUBMENUS

3.1 Open File

Open File menu should open a file from your local file system. In order to accomplish the task, an `OpenFileDialog` box is dragged on from the toolbox to the form. The dialog box has already been explained in Chapter 20. It may be noted that as it is a notepad application, which is capable of opening just one application at a time, therefore, the `MultiSelect` property of the `OpenFileDialog` should be set to false. Moreover, the notepad should be able to open only the text documents; therefore, the filter is set to *.txt. The `ShowDialog()` method of the `OpenFileDialog` is then invoked and the file is read with the help of `ReadToEnd()` method of the `StreamReader` class. The following code shows the `OpenFile` menu event handler. Figure PIII.3 shows the `OpenFileDialog`.

```
openFileDialog1.MultiSelect = false;
openFileDialog1.Filter = "Text Files|*.txt";
openFileDialog1.ShowDialog();
if (File.Exists(openFileDialog1.FileName))
{
    fname = openFileDialog1.FileName;
    StreamReader sr = new StreamReader(fname);
    txt.Text = sr.ReadToEnd();
    sr.Close();
}
```

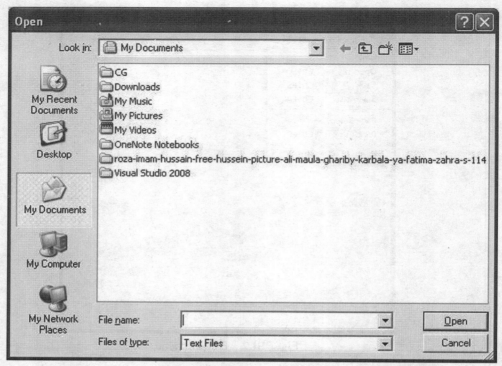

Fig. PIII.3 OpenFileDialog

3.2 Save Data

The next task is to save the text written in the text box to a .txt file. This task can be accomplished by dragging a SaveFileDialog from the toolbox to the form. The filter of the SaveFileDialog is set to .txt and the instance of the class DialogResult is set to ShowDialog(). This is done to check whether the user has pressed cancel. If it is not the case, then an instance of StreamWriter is made and the WriteLine() method of the class is invoked to write the text in the file. The following code shows the SaveFile menu event handler. Figure PIII.4 shows the SaveFileDialog.

```
if (fname == "")
{
    sfd.Filter = "Text Files|*.txt";
    DialogResult res = sfd.ShowDialog();
    if (res == DialogResult.Cancel)
    {
        return;
    }
    fname = sfd.FileName;
    MessageBox.Show(fname);
}
StreamWriter sw = new StreamWriter(fname);
sw.WriteLine(txt.Text);
sw.Flush();
sw.Close();
}
```

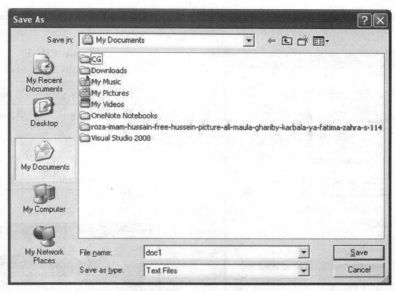

Fig. PIII.4 SaveFileDialog

3.3 Save As

The Save As dialog works in the same way as the Save dialog; the only difference is that the name can be set to the requisite name. The following code accomplishes the task:

```
sfd.Filter = "Text Files|*.txt";
            sfd.ShowDialog();
            fname = sfd.FileName;
            savedata();
```

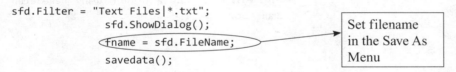

Set filename in the Save As Menu

Page Setup

The `PageSetup` dialog is dragged to the form. This is followed by assigning the document of the `PageSetup` dialog (psd in the following code) to the `PrintDocument` pd1. The `ShowDialog()` method of the class is then invoked to show the `PageSetup` Dialog when the user clicks the Page Setup Menu. Figure PIII.5 shows the `PageSetup` dialog.

```
PrintDocument pd1 = new PrintDocument();
pd1.DocumentName = fname;
psd.Document = pd1;
psd.ShowDialog();
```

The margins can be set using the margins text boxes in the `PageSetup` dialog. You can also set any of the following margins using the `PageSetup` dialog, as given in Table PIII.1.

The size in the `PageSetup` dialog can be any of the sizes as shown in Fig. PIII.6.

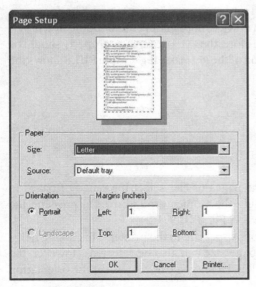

Fig. PIII.5 PageSetup dialog

It may also be noted that the printer can also be selected using the PageSetup dialog (Fig. PIII.7).

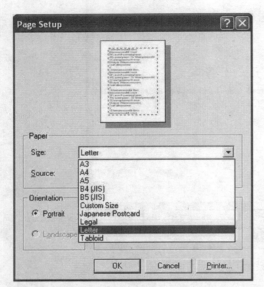

Fig. PIII.6 Different sizes in the PageSetup dialog

Table PIII.1 Setting margins in PageSetup dialog

Margin	Shortcut Key
Left	Alt + L
Right	Alt + R
Top	Alt + T
Bottom	Alt + B

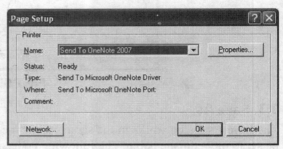

Fig. PIII.7 Setting a printer using PageSetup dialog box

3.4 PrintDialog

To print a document, the PrintDialog needs to be dragged to the form. This is followed by setting the DocumentName of the instance to the file name (set in the OpenFileDialog or saveFileDialog). The document of the instance is then set to the requisite print document. In a notepad application, there should be a provision to print few pages also (not just the whole document), therefore, the AllowSomePages property should be set to true. The last step would be call the ShowDialog() method of the PrintDialog. Figure PIII.8 shows the PrintDialog.

```
PrintDocument pd1 = new PrintDocument();
pd1.DocumentName = fname;
pd.Document = pd1;
pd.AllowSomePages = true;
pd.AllowPrintToFile = true;
pd.ShowDialog();
```

It is evident from Fig. PIII.8 that we can either print all the pages or can select the range of pages to be printed. The number of copies can also be selected using the Copies group box. On pressing the Properties button, the following dialog is displayed as shown in Fig. PIII.9.

The dialog that comes when pressing the Properties button is specific to the printer. This dialog helps you to set the height and the width of the page. Moreover, page size can also be selected. However, the options of Page Size are same as that in the Page Setup Dialog. Here, you can also select the orientation of the page to be printed.

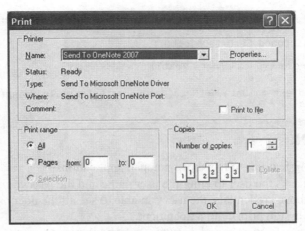

Fig. PIII.8 `PrintDialog`

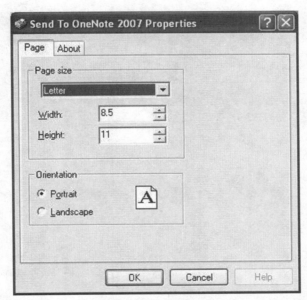

Fig. PIII.9 Properties of a printer in a print page dialog

3.5 Cut, Copy, and Paste

To move a selected section of the text to the clipboard, the cut method of the text box is invoked.

    txt.Cut();

However, to copy the text from the clipboard, the `SetDataObject` method of the `Clipboard` class is invoked and the `txt.SelectedText` is copied to the clipboard.

    Clipboard.SetDataObject(txt.SelectedText, true);

To paste the data to the text box from the clipboard, the following code is written:

```
IDataObject iData = Clipboard.GetDataObject();
   if (iData.GetDataPresent(DataFormats.Text))
      {
         txt.SelectedText = iData.GetData(DataFormats.Text).ToString();
      }
```

4. FUTURE SCOPE

You can add the following features to the above notepad applications:
1. A login form, which asks the user to enter the user name and the password, can be added.
2. On the basis of the above credentials, the user can able to see all the documents made by him.
3. The user can able to assign priority to a document.
4. There can be a provision to encrypt and decrypt a document by entering the password set by the user.
5. The Format menu can also have the provision of inserting tables.

21 Data Connectivity

OBJECTIVES

After completing this chapter, the reader will be able to
Appreciate the importance of data in application programs
Create a connection
Understand the significance of DataSet
Add a DataTable to a DataSet
Use command object
Develop an application that uses database
Explain data binding methods

21.1 INTRODUCTION

In the previous chapters, we have learnt the processes to create forms and to introduce the requisite features in them. However, the applications developed until now are not capable of storing data. Storage of data is essential in many applications, because at times, we need the data when the application runs the next time. Files are an excellent way to store and manipulate data. C# provides many classes that help to access and use a file. In order to understand files, we must understand what a stream is. The input and output in the .NET Framework takes place via streams. Data is accessed one byte at a time from a stream. Streams are of two types:

1. Input stream
2. Output stream

An input stream is used to read data from the variables or memory, whereas an output stream writes data to an external device. The `File` class in C# helps us to read, write, or delete a file. Many more classes help us in file handling. The `Path` class manipulates the path names; the `Directory` class helps to handle directories; and the `FileInfo` class and `DirectoryInfo` class are helpful in dealing with files and folders. The usage of these classes is given in Project III.

The data in an application can also be handled in another way, that is, using databases. This chapter introduces the database handling concepts and explains how to develop a full-fledged application using a database. However, it may be stated that a basic knowledge of database management system is required to understand the chapter. It is assumed that the reader is aware of the concepts of database management system. In addition, basic SQL expertise is desirable to understand the topic.

21.2 CREATING DATABASE IN MICROSOFT ACCESS

In order to create a project that uses a database, we must first make a database. As an example, a database called Student is created in Microsoft Access. The steps to create the database are as follows:

Step 1 Start Microsoft Access and enter the name of the database (Fig. 21.1).

Step 2 Now, create a new table and go to the design view. You will be asked to enter the name of the table (Fig. 21.2). Let the table be called Student. In the table, make three columns: ID, Name, and Fees. The ID will serve as the unique identification of the student; the Name field will contain the name of the student; and the Fees field stores the fees of the student (Fig. 21.3).

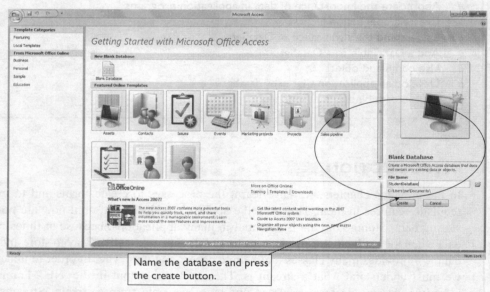

Fig. 21.1 Creating a database in Microsoft Access

Fig. 21.2 Saving Student Table

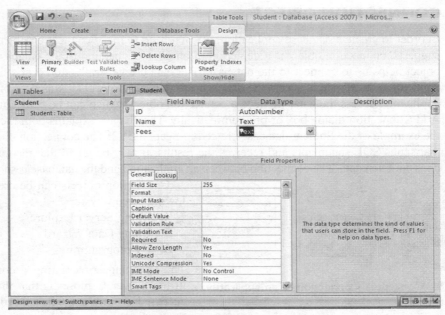

Fig. 21.3 Creating a table in Microsoft Access

Step 3 Now, save the table and enter some data by clicking on the table (Fig. 21.4). Since this is only a sample, only four rows are added. This database will be used in the examples that follow. The above table has been used throughout the chapter. So, it would be better to be familiar with the table. However, before we begin the project that accesses the data and manipulates them, here is a brief overview of the theoretical basics.

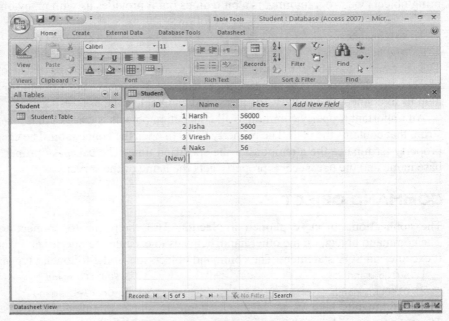

Fig. 21.4 Entering data in the table

21.3 CONNECTION OBJECT

In order to create a database application, we first need to make connection objects. As the name suggests, connection object is a depiction of an open connection to the database. A connection object helps us to connect to the database. The data are generally stored in a database, but the application developed to access the data is created in a high-level language. In order to make our application access the data, we need a connection object, which can be configured either by the Add Connection dialog box or programmatically. The chapter explains both the ways by taking the example of the Student database created in Section 21.2. The connection object is a channel that sends SQL statements and receives the results. It may be noted that the connection object does not fetch data. The connection between an application and the database is shown in Fig. 21.5.

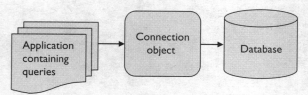

Fig. 21.5 Conceptual connection of an application and a database

Connection objects can be created in the following three ways:
1. Using Server Explorer
2. Using Data Wizard
3. By programming

The advantage of creating a connection object in the Server Explorer is that the object can be accessed in any project. In order to view the Server Explorer, go to the View menu and select Server Explorer. The purpose of the Server Explorer is to provide an easy-to-use location to handle all the data connections of the project.

The Data Source Configuration Wizard is easy to use. We just have to select the type of database and the database path to start the work. The process generates ready-to-use connection objects in our project.

These two methods are easy but provide limited flexibility. The third method, that is, configuring objects via programming, is a bit tedious but it provides us with many options.

The various connection objects are as follows:
1. SqlConnection
2. OleDbConnection
3. OdbcConnection
4. OracleConnection

The SqlConnection object helps us to connect to an SQL server database. The OleDbConnection object helps us to connect to an MS Office database. The OdbcConnection and OracleConnection help us to connect to an ODBC database and an Oracle database, respectively.

An important property common to all connection objects is ConnectionString. It is set to the string that contains the path. The property helps to open the connection. The ConnectionTimeOut property terminates the attempt after the specified time. The Database property sets the database name and the Datasource property gets the name of the server.

21.4 COMMAND OBJECT

The connection object, explained in Section 21.3, helps us to connect to the database. The command object, on the other hand, helps us to execute the queries and stored procedures. It executes an SQL statement. The command objects are of the following types:
1. SqlCommand
2. OleDbCommand
3. OdbcCommand
4. OracleCommand

These commands help us to execute statements and manipulate the respective databases. The SqlCommand helps us to execute statements in an SQL database. The OleDbCommand helps us to execute statements in an Office database. The `OracleCommand` and `OdbcCommand` help us to execute statements of Oracle and ODBC databases, respectively. The important properties of command objects are as follows:

1. `CommandText`, in which the SQL statement is written
2. `Connection`, which associates a command with a connection object
3. `CommandType`, which can be set to `'Text'` for an SQL statement or `'Stored Procedure'` for a stored procedure
4. `CommandTimeout`, which sets the time after which the attempt terminates

The following are the various methods that help us to execute statements:

1. `ExecuteNonQuery`
2. `ExecuteScalar`
3. `ExecuteReader`
4. `ExecuteXMLReader`

The `ExecuteNonQuery` method is used when the query does not return any record. An example is a select statement. `ExecuteScalar` is used when the query returns a single value. The `ExecuteReader` method is used when a table is returned, and the `ExecuteXMLReader` is used for the XML formatted data.

21.5 DATASET OBJECT AND DATATABLE OBJECT

The DataSet object contains the cache of the data. The DataTable object is a part of the DataSet object. The data that are used in the application need to be temporarily stored somewhere. DataSet objects are used to accomplish the task. There are two types of datasets:

1. Typed datasets
2. Untyped datasets

In order to create a dataset, we need to declare a DataSet object and create a DataTable. However, there is another way, in which the Data Source Configuration Wizard can be used to build a typed dataset.

If these ways appear tedious, then we can simply drag a DataSet object from the toolbox and use the Tables Collection editor to craft a schema. The syntax for creating a DataSet and a DataTable is given as follows:

Syntax: DataSet

```
DataSet <name of the DataSet> = new dataSet("<name>");
```

Syntax: DataTable

```
DataTable <name of the DataTable> = new DataTable();
```

The following program depicts the use of datasets:

Step 1 Create a new Windows Forms Application and drag a data grid onto the form.
Step 2 Now, write the following code in the constructor of the form:

```
using System;
using System.Collections.Generic;
using System.ComponentModel;
using System.Data;
using System.Drawing;
using System.Linq;
```

```csharp
using System.Text;
using System.Windows.Forms;
using System.Data.OleDb;
namespace WindowsFormsApplication5
{
    public partial class Form1 : Form
    {
        DataSet MarksDataSet = new DataSet();
        DataTable MarksTable = new DataTable();
        public Form1()
        {
            InitializeComponent();
            MarksDataSet.Tables.Add(MarksTable);
            DataColumn StudentIDCol = new DataColumn("StudentID", Type.GetType("System.Int16"));
            DataColumn MarksCol = new DataColumn("Marks", Type.GetType("System.Double"));
            MarksTable.Columns.Add(StudentIDCol);
            MarksTable.Columns.Add(MarksCol);
            dataGridView1.DataSource = MarksTable;
            DataColumn[] keyColumn = new DataColumn[1];
            MarksTable.PrimaryKey = keyColumn;
            DataRow MarksRow = MarksTable.NewRow();
            Object[] record = {1, 14.5};
            MarksRow.ItemArray = record;
            MarksTable.Rows.Add(MarksRow);
        }
        private void Form1_Load(object sender, EventArgs e)
        {
        }
        private void button1_Click(object sender, EventArgs e)
        {
        }
    }
}
```

Step 3 Run the application.

Output

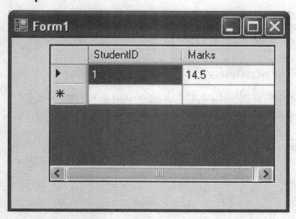

In order to associate the tables with the datasets, we can make an instance of the `DataRelation` class and initiate it with the constructor, giving the name of the relation, first table's column name, and second table's column name in that order.

21.6 CREATING A PRACTICAL APPLICATION

In order to create an application that uses a database, the following steps must be followed. The database taken is the one created in Section 21.2.

Step 1 Start a new Windows Forms Application project (Fig. 21.6).

Step 2 Create a form. In the form, drag the table layout panel. The panel should have three columns and five rows. Set the controls as specified in Table 21.1. Figure 21.7 shows the form in Visual Studio.

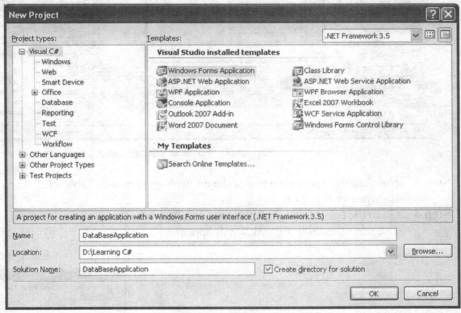

Fig. 21.6 Creating a new application

Table 21.1 Controls in the application

Control	Row	Column
Label1	1	1
Label2	2	1
Label3	3	1
TextBox1	1	3
TextBox2	2	3
TextBox4	3	3
Button1	4	1
Button2	4	3
Button3	5	1
Button4	5	3

448 *Programming in C#*

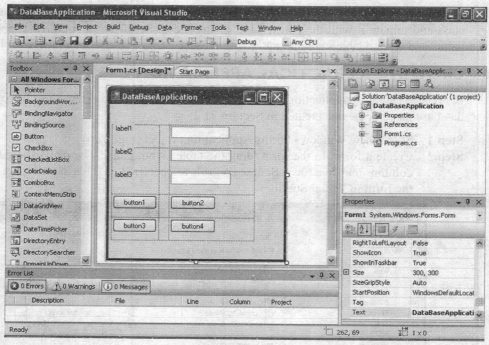

Fig. 21.7 Form in Visual Studio

Step 3 Now, change the properties of the controls as shown in Table 21.2. The properties grid is shown in Fig. 21.8.

Step 4 Go to the `DataBindings` property in the Properties pane and click on the `Text` property. The pane shown in Fig. 21.9 will appear.

Table 21.2 Properties of the controls in the form

Control	Text	Name
Label1	ID	
Label2	Name	
Label3	Fees	
TextBox1		IDTextBox
TextBox2		NameTextBox
TextBox3		FeesTextBox
Button1	First	FirstButton
Button2	Last	LastButton
Button3	Next	NextButton
Button4	Previous	PreviousButton

Fig. 21.8 Properties grid

Data Connectivity 449

Fig. 21.9 Binding data to the control

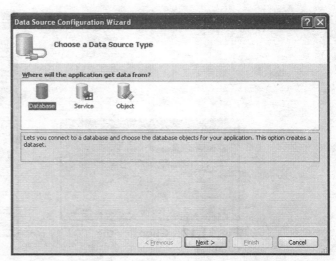

Fig. 21.10 Associating database with the control

Step 5 Click on Add Project Data Source to associate the text box controls with the corresponding fields of the table.
Step 6 This starts the Data Source Configuration Wizard. In the form that follows, select Database (Fig. 21.10).
Step 7 Click on Next. A screen as shown in Fig. 21.11 appears.
Step 8 Click on New Connection and select Microsoft ODBC Data Source, since our database is in Microsoft Access (Fig. 21.12).
Step 9 Press Continue. The screen shown in Fig. 21.13 appears, which asks you to add a connection.

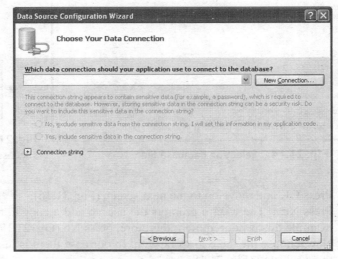

Fig. 21.11 Creating a new connection

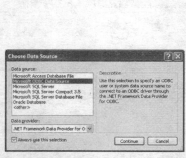

Fig. 21.12 Choosing the database

Fig. 21.13 Adding connection

Step 10 Choose the name of the database file. In our case, it is the Student database, created in Section 21.2 (Fig. 21.14).

Step 11 After accomplishing this task, press Test connection. In case the connection is fine, the following message box appears (Fig. 21.15).

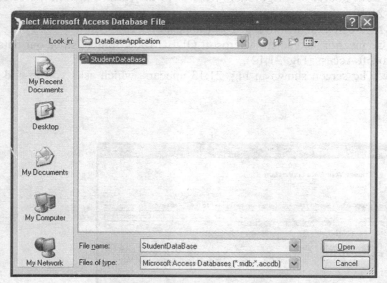

Fig. 21.14 Selecting database file

Fig. 21.15 Message indicating successful connection

Step 12 Press OK and move on to the next screen (Fig. 21.16).
Step 13 Press Next. The wizard prompts the user to add a copy to the project folder. In this example this is not required; therefore, press No (Fig. 21.17).
Step 14 Now, choose the table to work with. In our case there is just one table, which needs to be selected (Fig. 21.18).

Fig. 21.16 Adding connection

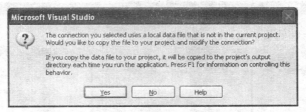

Fig. 21.17 Message prompt for creating a copy of the database in the project

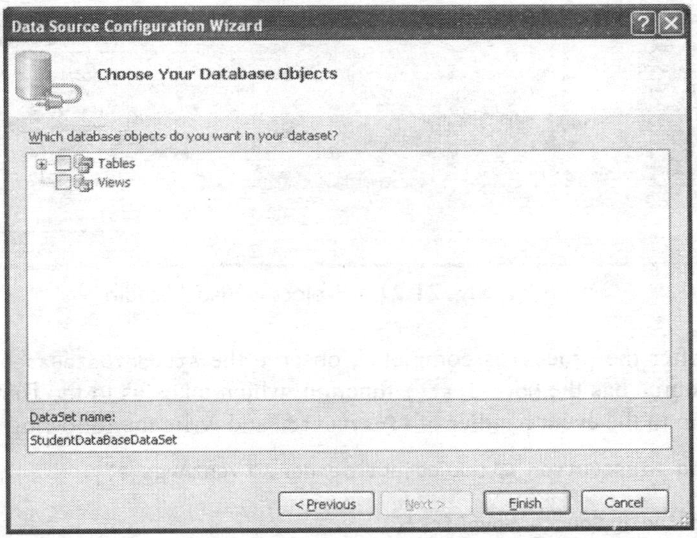

Fig. 21.18 Choosing database object

After the process is completed, the Data property of the IDTextBox will be binded with the ID field of the database (Figs 21.19 and 21.20).

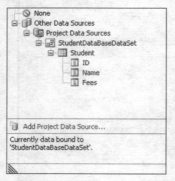

Fig. 21.19 Associating database field with the control

Fig. 21.20 Associating database field with the control: Selecting Column name

Step 15 Repeat the same process with the other two text boxes as well. Bind them with the Name and Fees fields of the table, respectively (Fig. 21.21).

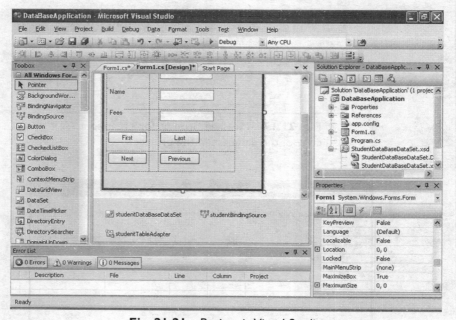

Fig. 21.21 Project in Visual Studio

Step 16 After the process is completed, observe the studentDataBaseDataSet. The binding source has the MoveFirst() function, which takes us to the first record of the table. Go to the event handler of FirstButton and write the following code:

```
private void FirstButton_Click(object sender, EventArgs e)
{
    studentBindingSource.MoveFirst()
}
```

Step 17 The binding source also has the MoveLast( ) function, which takes us to the last record of the table. Go to the event handler of LastButton and write the following code:

```
private void LastButton_Click(object sender, EventArgs e)
{
    studentBindingSource.MoveLast();
}
```

Step 18 The MoveNext() function of the binding source takes us to the next record of the table. Go to the event handler of NextButton and write the following code:

```
private void NextButton_Click(object sender, EventArgs e)
{
    studentBindingSource.MoveNext();
}
```

Step 19 Similarly, the MovePrevious() function of the binding source takes us to the previous record of the table. Go to the event handler of PreviousButton and write the following code:

```
private void PreviousButton_Click(object sender, EventArgs e)
{
    studentBindingSource.MovePrevious();
}
```

The complete code of the program is as follows:

```
using System;
using System.Collections.Generic;
using System.ComponentModel;
using System.Data;
using System.Drawing;
using System.Linq;
using System.Text;
using System.Windows.Forms;

namespace DataBaseApplication
{
    public partial class Form1 : Form
    {
        public Form1()
        {
            InitializeComponent();
        }
        private void Form1_Load(object sender, EventArgs e)
        {
            //TODO: This line of code loads data into the 'studentDataBaseDataSet.
            Student' table. You can move or remove it, as needed.
                this.studentTableAdapter.Fill(this.studentDataBaseDataSet.Student);
        }
        private void FirstButton_Click(object sender, EventArgs e)
        {
            studentBindingSource.MoveFirst()
        }
        private void LastButton_Click(object sender, EventArgs e)
```

```
        {
            studentBindingSource.MoveLast();
        }
        private void NextButton_Click(object sender, EventArgs e)
        {
            studentBindingSource.MoveNext();
        }
        private void PreviousButton_Click(object sender, EventArgs e)
        {
            studentBindingSource.MovePrevious();
        }
    }
}
```

Step 20 Now, run the project. The following output screen appears.

Output
Run 1

Press the Last button. The last record will be displayed.

Run 2

The Previous button takes us to the previous record.

Run 3

![DataBaseApplication form showing ID: 3, Name: Viresh, Fees: 560, with First, Last, Next, Previous buttons]

21.7 INSERTION OF ROWS AND UPDATING RECORDS

In order to make a form via which the user can add records in the database, perform the following steps.

Step 1 Go to Solution Explorer and add a new form (Fig. 21.22).

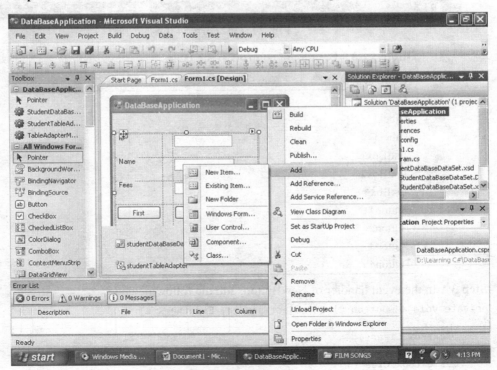

Fig. 21.22 Adding a new form

Step 2 In the form, drag table layout panel (Fig. 21.23). The panel should have three columns and five rows. Drag the specified controls in the cells given in Table 21.3.

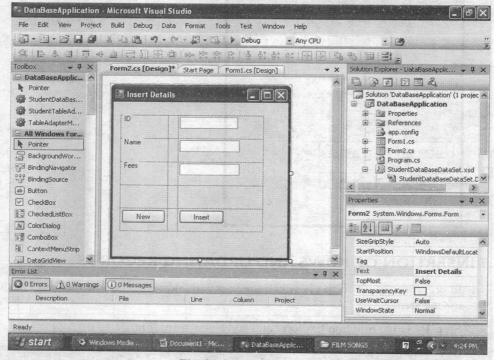

Fig. 21.23 Form in IDE

Table 21.3 Position of controls in the table

Control	Row	Column
Label1	1	1
Label2	2	1
Label3	3	1
TextBox1	1	3
TextBox2	2	3
TexBox4	3	3
Button1	4	1
Button2	4	3
Button3	5	1
Button4	5	3

Step 3 In the event handler of NewButton, add the following code:

```
private void NewButton_Click(object sender, EventArgs e)
{
    IDTextBox.Clear();
    NameTextBox.Clear();
    FeesTextBox.Clear();
}
```

Step 4 In the event handler of InsertButton, add the following code:

```csharp
private void InsertButton_Click(object sender, EventArgs e)
{
    OleDbCommand cmd = new OleDbCommand();
    cmd.CommandType = CommandType.Text;
    cmd.Connection = conn;
    cmd.CommandText = "INSERT INTO Student (Name, Fees) VALUES ('" + NameTextBox.Text +
"','" + FeesTextBox.Text + "');";
    conn.Open();
    if(cmd.ExecuteNonQuery() != 0)
    {
        MessageBox.Show("Insertion Successful");
    }
    else
    {
        MessageBox.Show("Failed");
    }
    conn.Close();
}
```

The complete program is as follows:

```csharp
using System;
using System.Collections.Generic;
using System.ComponentModel;
using System.Data;
using System.Drawing;
using System.Linq;
using System.Text;
using System.Windows.Forms;

using System.Data.OleDb;

namespace DataBaseApplication
{
    public partial class Form3 : Form
    {
        OleDbConnection conn = new OleDbConnection(@"Provider = Microsoft.ACE.OLEDB.
        12.0; Data Source = D:\\DataBaseApplication\\StudentDataBase.accdb");
        public Form3()
        {
            InitializeComponent();
        }
        private void NewButton_Click(object sender, EventArgs e)
        {
            IDTextBox.Clear();
            NameTextBox.Clear();
            FeesTextBox.Clear();
        }
        private void InsertButton_Click(object sender, EventArgs e)
        {
            OleDbCommand cmd = new OleDbCommand();
            cmd.CommandType = CommandType.Text;
            cmd.Connection = conn;
```

```
            cmd.CommandText = "UPDATE Student SET Name = '" + NameTextBox.Text + "', Fees
            = '" + FeesTextBox.Text + "' WHERE ID = " + int.Parse(IDTextBox.Text) + ";";
            conn.Open();
            if(cmd.ExecuteNonQuery() != 0)
            {
                MessageBox.Show("Updation Successful");
            }
            else
            {
                MessageBox.Show("Failed");
            }
            conn.Close();
        }
    }
}
```

Step 5 Now, run the project. Insert the data and press Insert (Fig. 21.24).

On the successful insertion of the data in the table, the following message box appears (Fig. 21.25):

Fig. 21.24 Insert details

Fig. 21.25 Message box that appears on successful update

In the same way, we can develop a program for updating the data. Change the Text property of this form to 'Update' and change the event handler of the Update button.

The complete program is as follows:

```
using System;
using System.Collections.Generic;
using System.ComponentModel;
using System.Data;
using System.Drawing;
using System.Linq;
using System.Text;
using System.Windows.Forms;
using System.Data.OleDb;

3namespace DataBaseApplication
{
    public partial class Form2 : Form
    {
        OleDbConnection conn = new OleDbConnection(@"Provider = Microsoft.ACE.OLEDB.
        12.0; Data Source = D:\\DataBaseApplication\\StudentDataBase.accdb");
        public Form2()
        {
            InitializeComponent();
        }
```

```
private void NewButton_Click(object sender, EventArgs e)
{
    IDTextBox.Clear();
    NameTextBox.Clear();
    FeesTextBox.Clear();
}
private void InsertButton_Click(object sender, EventArgs e)
{
    OleDbCommand cmd = new OleDbCommand();
    cmd.CommandType = CommandType.Text;
    cmd.Connection = conn;
    cmd.CommandText = "UPDATE Student SET Name = '" +
    NameTextBox.Text + "', Fees = '" + FeesTextBox.Text +
    "'WHERE ID = '"+IDTextBox.Text+"';";
    conn.Open();
    if(cmd.ExecuteNonQuery() != 0)
    {
        MessageBox.Show("Insertion Successful");
    }
    else
    {
        MessageBox.Show("Failed");
    }
    conn.Close();
}
```

Run the program. A screen similar to the one shown in Fig. 21.26 appears.

On successfully updating the data, the following message box appears (Fig. 21.27):
The data of the table change and the final table after the execution of this program is as follows (Table 21.4).

Fig. 21.26 Update form

Fig. 21.27 Message box that appears on successful update

Table 21.4 Table in the database after the execution of the program

1	Harsh	56000
2	Limka	6
3	Viresh	560
4	Naks	56
5	Kim	5
NULL	NULL	NULL

SUMMARY

The chapter examines database creation in Microsoft Access and explains the concepts of DataSet and DataTable. The chapter also provides an introduction to connection and command objects. Finally, it explains an application that makes use of all the concepts discussed here. The chapter will help readers to create projects that not only perform a task but also are capable of saving and manipulating the data. The project on 'Online Voting System (Project IV)' also deals with database connectivity. It can be used as a minor project in colleges. However, it is advisable to go through Chapters 18 and 19 before making the project.

GLOSSARY

Database management system This is a set of interrelated data and a collection of programs to manipulate the data.
Connection This is the representation of an open connection.
Command object This is used to execute SQL commands and stored procedures.
DataSet object This object stores the data temporarily.
DataTable object This object stores the tables of the database.
DataBinding This is the association between the field of a database and the control.

POINTS TO REMEMBER

- In order to connect to an Microsoft Access database, `OleDbConnection` object is used.
- In order to connect to an SQL Express database, the `SQLClientConnection` object is used.
- In order to execute a query, a command object is made.
- The command object needs to be associated with a connection.
- The command object has three important properties: connection, text, and type.
- In order to open a connection, `open()` method is invoked.
- In order to execute a query that does not return any data but returns only the number of rows affected, the `ExecuteNonQuery` method can be used.
- In order to execute a query that returns data, the `ExecuteReader` method can be used.

EXERCISES

I. Multiple-choice Questions

1. What is a stream?
   (a) An abstract representation of a serial device
   (b) Input file
   (c) Output file
   (d) None of these
2. Which class provides methods for moving, deleting, and manipulating files?
   (a) Directory (b) File
   (c) FileInfo (d) Path
3. Which of the following is not a type of connection object?
   (a) `SqlConnection` (b) `OdbcConnection`
   (c) `OracleConnection` (d) `MSWordConnection`
4. Which of the following is not a method common to all connection objects?
   (a) `Close` (b) `Open`
   (c) `Old` (d) `GetSchema`
5. Which of the following can be used to create a connection object?

(a) Server Explorer (b) Data Wizard
(c) Programming (d) All of these

6. Which method is not used in connection pooling?
   (a) `ClearPool` (b) `ReleaseObjectPool`
   (c) `ClearAllPool` (d) `UnclearPool`

7. In which of the following are command objects used?
   (a) Connected environment
   (b) Disconnected environment
   (c) Both (a) and (b)
   (d) None of these

8. Which of the following is defined by `System.Data.SqlDbType` enumeration?
   (a) Parameters (b) Blobs
   (c) Clobs (d) None of these

9. To which of the following is a parameter added?
   (a) Command object (b) Connection object
   (c) Dataset (d) None of these

10. Which of the following is used to access data in a disconnected environment?
    (a) Command (b) Connection
    (c) Dataset (d) Blob

II. State True or False

1. A connection object fetches data.
2. A connection object helps to update data.
3. A connection object helps to execute queries.
4. Data wizards can be used to create connection objects.
5. We can use a DataTable without creating a DataSet.
6. `OdbcConnection` is a type of dataset.
7. A connection string sets the string used to open connection.
8. The `Close` method closes the data connection.
9. We can use a command object without specifying the timeout.
10. We can use a command object without associating it with a connection.

III. Review Questions

1. What is a stream? What are the different kinds of streams?
2. What are the purposes of the following classes?
   (a) File (b) Directory
   (c) Path (d) FileInfo
3. What are the different ways of creating a connection?
4. What are the different types of connection objects?
5. Explain some of the important properties of connection objects.
6. What is a dataset?
7. Explain the steps to create a dataset.
8. Explain the steps to programmatically create a table via DataSet.
9. Explain command objects.
10. With the help of an example, illustrate the association of a command object with a connection object.

IV. Programming Exercises

A college decides to computerize its library. The library management system should store the details of the books and the students. It should store the time of issue of the book. When the student returns the book after due date, the software should display the fine to be paid.

The required details of the student are as follows:

Design a separate form for each of the following:

1. Displaying the details
2. Entering student data
3. Editing data
4. Deleting data

1.	Roll number
2.	First name
3.	Last name
4.	Father's name
5.	Mother's name
6.	Address
7.	Phone number
8.	Email

The system stores the following details of a book:

1.	Name
2.	Author
3.	Publisher
4.	Price
5.	Number of copies
6.	Genre

Design a form for each of the following:
1. Entering details
2. Showing details
3. Editing details
4. Deleting a book
5. Searching a book
   (a) By title
   (b) By author
   (c) By publisher

Develop a form to be used for the issue of a book and a form to be used when the student returns the book. Return of books beyond the allowed time incurs a fine of ₹2 per day of delay. The period for which a student can keep a book is given in the following table.

Student	Number of days
PhD	15
M.Tech	12
B.Tech	10
Others	7

Develop the system without using datasets. You can develop the database in any of the available database management systems.

22 Introduction to ASP.NET

OBJECTIVES

After completing this chapter, the reader will be able to

- # Differentiate between ASP and ASP.NET
- # List the advantages of ASP.NET
- # Explain the architecture of ASP.NET
- # Appreciate the importance of web forms
- # Describe the types of files in a website project
- # Create a basic website in ASP.NET
- # Explain user controls and server controls
- # Recollect basic HTML tags
- # Insert a table in a web page or a website
- # Create a form in a website
- # Understand the importance of SQL Express
- # View data of a table in grid view
- # Explain the concept of master page

22.1 INTRODUCTION

ASP.NET is generally perceived as an extension of ASP, which is a half-truth. It makes things simple for the developers who already know ASP; at the same time, it presents a whole new way of dealing with the web applications. ASP.NET provides a new model, a new infrastructure, and a new security model. Therefore, ASP.NET is much more than the next version of ASP. A short history of ASP.NET is discussed in the Exhibit. Some of the important features of ASP.NET are as follows:

1. It provides a combined web development model.
2. It is syntax compatible with ASP.
3. It provides a new programming model.
4. It introduces a new infrastructure for more scalable applications.
5. Applications can be created in any .NET compatible language, including Visual Basic.NET and C#.
6. It provides a graphic user interface (GUI), which developers can use to drop server controls onto a web page, and a fully integrated debugging support.
7. Developers can use web forms or XML web services when creating an ASP.NET application.

As stated earlier, there are many differences between ASP and ASP.NET. Section 22.2 briefly compares them.

ASP.NET—HISTORY

The code written in ASP (Active Server Pages) was not considered clean by some developers owing to the fact that the presentation and content were intermingled. The need for a better version of ASP, or a completely new technology, became a necessity with the release of Internet Information Services (IIS) 4.0. The task was assigned to Mark Anders and Scott Guthrie. They were assigned the responsibility of finding out the model for implementing this task. The initial design prepared to accomplish this task was called XPS, for no specific reason. Interestingly, the coding of XPS was done using Java and not Visual Basic or Visual C++. Perhaps a strange thing, as Scott had just joined Microsoft and Anders was working in the team that developed IIS. Probably in order to prove their loyalty to Microsoft, they decided to build the whole thing on top of CLR (common language runtime).

With the move to the CLR, XPS was reimplemented in C#. The name was changed to ASP+, thus granting the new platform to be the successor to ASP, which is perhaps a misnomer.

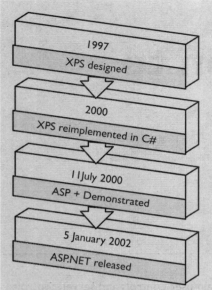

Fig. 22.1 Chronology of ASP.NET

Mark Anders first presented ASP+ at the ASP Connections conference in Phoenix, Arizona, in 2000. The initial beta release of ASP+ came in the middle of 2000. In the second half of 2000, it was decided to rename ASP+ to ASP.NET. ASP.NET 1.0 was released on 5 January 2002 as part of version 1.0 of the .NET Framework. Figure 22.1 depicts the chronology.

22.2 DIFFERENCES BETWEEN ASP.NET AND ASP

ASP.NET is the next generation ASP, but it is not an upgraded version of ASP. ASP.NET is an entirely new technology for server-side scripting. It is not completely backward compatible with ASP. Not all the projects made in ASP can run in ASP.NET. ASP.NET was developed because of the problems that developers had with ASP. Microsoft has made sure that the ASP scripts execute without modification on a machine with the .NET Framework. Therefore, IIS can house both ASP and ASP.NET scripts on the same machine.

22.3 SHORTCOMINGS OF TRADITIONAL ASP

The shortcomings of ASP when compared with ASP.NET are many, which are enumerated as follows:

Interpretation
ASP scripting code is usually written in languages such as JScript or VBScript. The script-execution engine that ASP relies on interprets the code line by line every time the page is called, thus making it harder to catch errors while writing a code.

Limited Tools
Many tools such as Microsoft Visual InterDev and Macromedia Visual UltraDev attempted to increase the productivity of ASP programmers by providing graphical development environments. However, these tools were not very successful.

No State Management

The concept of state management was not implemented in the way it should have been. Session state is maintained by the browser, which supports cookies. Session state information can be held only using the ASP session object.

Update When Server is Down

If the web application makes use of components, copying new files to the application should be done only when the web server is stopped.

Murky Configuration Settings

The configuration information for an ASP web application is stored in the IIS metabase in a proprietary format. Therefore, it can be modified only on the server machine with utilities such as the Internet Service Manager.

22.4 ADVANTAGES OF ASP.NET

ASP.NET was developed because of the problems present in ASP. Most of the problems in the traditional ASP were handled in ASP.NET. Following are the main advantages of ASP.NET:

Separation of Code

ASP.NET has the ability to separate layout and business logic. This increases efficiency. This also makes it easier for teams of programmers and designers to collaborate efficiently.

Compiled Languages

ASP.NET pages are precompiled to byte code and just in time (JIT) compiled when first requested. Successive requests are directed to the compiled code.

Use Services

The .NET Framework provides class libraries that can be used by an application.

Graphical Development Environment

Visual Studio.NET provides a very rich development environment for web developers. We can drag and drop controls and set properties.

State Management

State information can be kept in memory or stored in a database. It can also be shared across web forms.

Updating Files

Components of the application can be updated while the server is online and clients are connected. The framework will use the new files as soon as they are copied to the application.

Having seen the differences between ASP and ASP.NET and the advantages of ASP, let us now have a look at the architecture of ASP.NET.

22.5 ASP.NET ARCHITECTURE

ASP.NET is based on the elementary architecture of the .NET Framework. Visual Studio provides a way to combine a range of features of this architecture. Figure 22.2 depicts the architecture of ASP.NET.

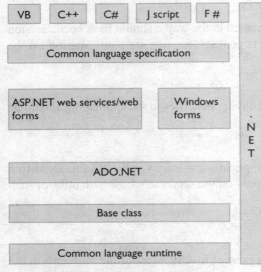

Fig. 22.2 ASP.NET architecture

The following points briefly explain the role of the various components of ASP.NET:

CLR
The CLR loads and executes code that targets the runtime. Chapter 1 explains the concept of managed code.

Base Classes
The concept has been explained in Chapter 1. All the classes are brought together by the Services Framework. They amass on top of the CLR.

ADO.NET
ADO.NET is the ADO model for the .NET Framework. Chapter 21 is dedicated to ADO.

The web application model includes web forms and web services. ASP.NET provides web form controls for crafting the user interface.

22.6 WEB FORMS

Web forms allow us to build powerful form-based web pages. ASP.NET server controls can be used to create common user interface elements. The controls allow us to rapidly build a web form out of reusable built-in or custom components.

We can access server functionality remotely via XML web service. It also helps businesses render programmatic interfaces to their data. The business logic can also be programmatically handled. This can be obtained and manipulated by client and server applications. It may be noted that XML web services are not attached to a specific technology, and therefore, programs written in any language can install XML web services.

The new ASP.NET programming model will appear familiar to an ASP developer. At the same time, many changes have been made to the old model, thus rendering complete backtracking impossible. ASP.NET provides much easier data access when compared to its predecessor. It even lets us manage the database from the code.

22.7 CREATING ASP WEBSITE

Creating a simple website in ASP.NET is as easy as updating the status on Facebook. Let us build a website in ASP.NET by performing the following steps:

Step 1 Go to File → New and select web site (not Project) (Fig. 22.3). When we select this option, a number of files will be created in the folder. Section 22.8 discusses the various file types.

Step 2 In the window that appears, select ASP.NET web site (Fig. 22.4). Change the location and language according to the preferences and proceed. It may be stated here that a web service is not the same as a website. The difference between the two has been explained in Section 25.2. We can also select a template from the web if we want to instantly create the framework without much programming. In this chapter, we will discuss only an empty website.

Step 3 The interface that appears is the door to a website (Fig. 22.5); it can be used to explore the world of ASP.NET, which has been created by the Microsoft Corp. to fight the

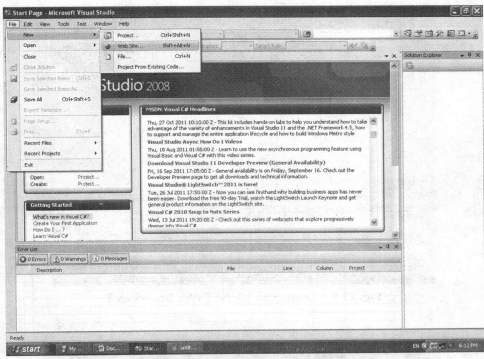

Fig. 22.3 Creating an ASP.NET Web Site—Step 1

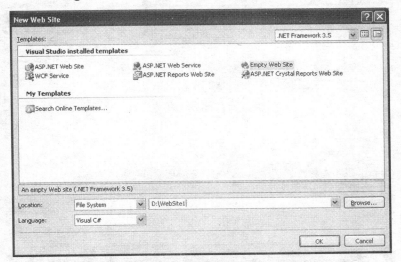

Fig. 22.4 Creating an ASP.NET Web Site—Step 2

advent of JSP. Figure 22.5 is a snapshot of the source. There are three different views of web forms: design, split, and source.

Design View

The view helps us to drag and drop various controls. It is best suited for a person who has some knowledge of creating a web page but wants to explore by dragging and dropping the controls. Figure 22.6 shows the design view of a page.

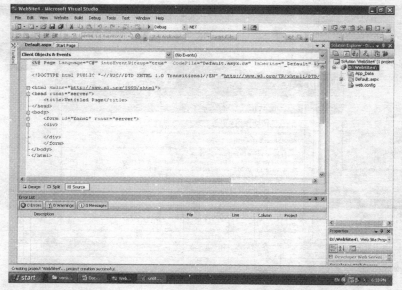

Fig. 22.5 Creating an ASP.NET Web Site—Step 3

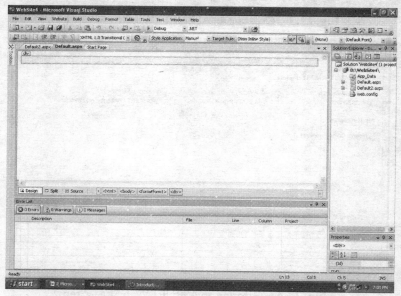

Fig. 22.6 Design view of a web page

Split View

The split view shows the design part as well as the source code at the same time, so that if changes are made in any one of them they are reflected in the other. Figure 22.7 shows the split view.

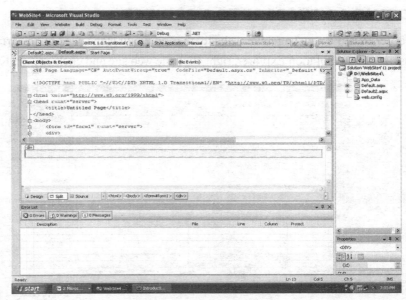

Fig. 22.7 Split view of a web page

Source View

The source view contains the coding of the page. It contains the scripts, references, and initialization of controls. Moreover, at times, it becomes difficult to manipulate a page using the design view. In such scenarios, the source view can be used.

22.8 FILE TYPES IN ASP.NET

Various file types are managed by ASP.NET; some are maintained and managed by ASP.NET and others by the IIS server. Table 22.1 briefly describes some of the file types.

Table 22.1 Types of files in ASP.NET

File type	Location	Description
.mdb	App_Data subdirectory	An access database file
Master	Application root	A master page that defines the layout for other web pages
.mdf	App_Data subdirectory	An SQL Server Express database file
.resources, .resx	App_GlobalResources or App_LocalResources subdirectory	A resource file that contains resource strings
.sitemap	Application root	A sitemap file that defines the logical structure of the web application
.sln	Visual Studio project directory	A solution file for a Visual Studio project
.soap	Application root or a subdirectory	A SOAP extension file

Section 22.9 discusses the way to add a new page to an existing website.

22.9 ADDING A NEW PAGE TO A PROJECT

In order to add a new page in a website, the following steps need to be carried out:

Step 1 In the Solution Explorer, right click the web site and click on Add New Item (Fig. 22.8).

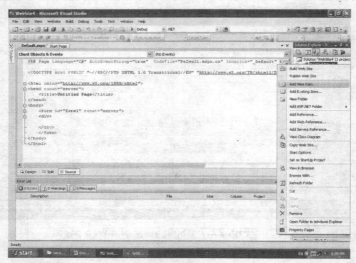

Fig. 22.8 Adding page to an existing Web Site—Step 1

Step 2 A window appears prompting you to select the item that you wish to add to your website. Select web form and click on Add (Fig. 22.9).

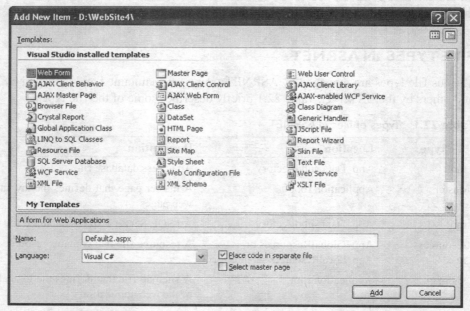

Fig. 22.9 Adding page to an existing Web Site—Step 2

Step 3 A web form would appear as shown in Fig. 22.10.

A new page is added to the website and is ready to be edited.

Introduction to ASP.NET   471

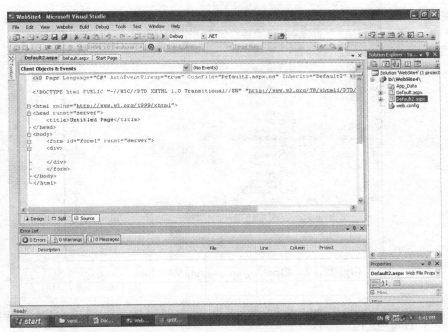

Fig. 22.10 Adding page to an existing Web Site—Step 3

22.10 OPENING AN EXISTING WEBSITE

In order to open an existing website, the following steps must be performed:

Step 1   Go to File → Open and select Web Site (Fig. 22.11).

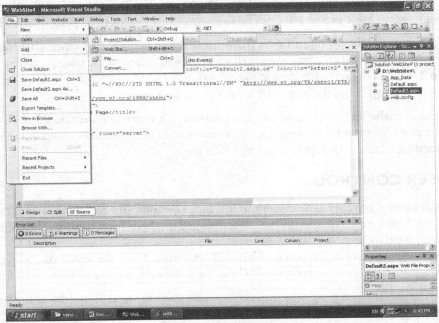

Fig. 22.11 Opening an existing Web Site—Step 1

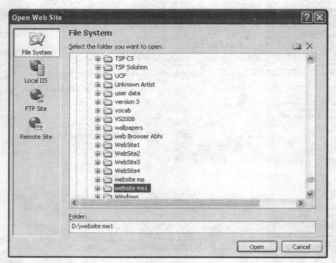

Fig. 22.12 Opening an existing Web Site—Step 2

Step 2 In the window that follows, select the website to be opened from the existing websites (Fig. 22.12).

Step 3 The website opens and is now ready to be edited.

22.11 INSERTING A TABLE IN A PAGE

We have seen the creation of a basic website and the addition of pages to an existing website. Let us now move on to creating tables onto the page. A table is necessary not only to display data but also to align control on a page. Visual Web Developer (VWD) or Visual Studio provides an easy way to insert a table in a web form. The following are the steps to be performed to insert a table:

Step 1 Go to Table → Insert Table. The window shown in Fig. 22.13 appears. Change the number of rows and columns, sizes, cell padding, and colour of the table according to the needs.

Step 2 Insert the requisite data in the cells (Fig. 22.14).

Step 3 Press F5 and the page will appear in the browser.

As stated earlier, a table is used to align controls in a web page. Section 22.12 discusses some of the most important user controls. The know-how of these controls along with the knowledge of creating a table will help in creating a web page.

22.12 USER CONTROL

A user control is a user-defined unit. It is a type of composite control that works much like an ASP.NET web page. We can define properties and methods for a control. The controls can also be implanted in ASP.NET web pages.

Suppose we have developed an ASP.NET web page. Now, we would like to access its functionality throughout the application. Then, the following steps will help us to make it a user control.

Step 1 Rename the control such that the file name extension is .ascx.

Step 2 Remove the html, body, and form elements.

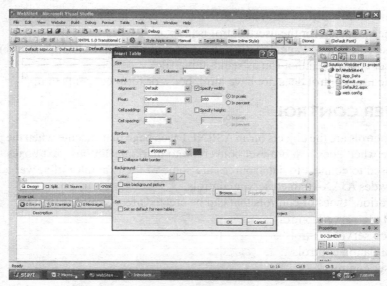

Fig. 22.13 Inserting table in a page—Step 1

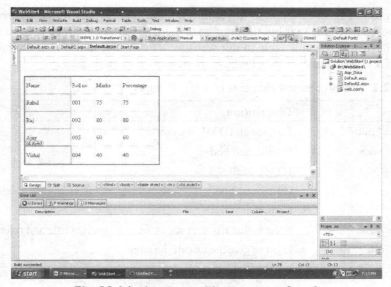

Fig. 22.14 Inserting table in a page—Step 2

Step 3 Change the @ Page directive to an @ Control directive.
Step 4 Remove all attributes of the @ Control directive except Language, AutoEventWireup CodeFile, and Inherits.
Step 5 Include a className attribute in the @ Control directive.

Custom Controls

A Custom Control is a class that is created by the user. It must derive from Control or WebControl. User controls are considerably easier to develop than custom controls. These controls help us to create controls with complex user interface elements.

A user controls differs from an ASP.NET web page in the following ways:
1. The extension for the user control is .ascx.
2. Instead of an @ Page directive, the user control contains an @ Control directive.
3. User controls cannot run as stand-alone files.
4. The user control does not have html, body, or form elements in it.

22.13 SERVER CONTROL

Server controls are the objects on an ASP.NET web page that execute when the page is requested. The page when goes to a browser converts into markup. Buttons, text boxes, and controls that can be used to connect to data sources are some of the examples of server controls. ASP.NET also provides AJAX-enabled server controls.

The various types of controls that can be created are as follows:
1. HTML server controls
2. Web server controls
3. Validation controls
4. User controls

22.14 COMMON HTML TAGS

The purpose of this section is to hover through the HTML tags we have already studied. The idea is not to teach the tags but to summarize them so that they can be used in a web page. Now that we have added a new table in our website, let us pause and revisit the most common elements of a HTML page, some of which are described in Table 22.2.

Table 22.2 Most common elements of a HTML page

Tag	Description
<html></html>	Defines an HTML document
<body><body>	Document's body
<h1> to <h6>	HTML headings
<hr />	Horizontal line
<!-->	Comment
<head></head>	Section that has data about the page such as title and references
<title></title>	Used to give the title of the page
<a>	Used to link one web page to another
<img>	Used to embed an image
<b>	Formatting tag used to make the text bold
<i>	Formatting tag for making the text italics
<u>	Formatting tag for underlining the text
<form></form>	Used for making forms
<table></table>	Used to create a table
<span>	Used for wrapping the influence of a set of elements

The following listing creates a basic web page using HTML. It is advisable to go through the complete HTML in order to understand ASP.NET in a better way.

```html
<HTML>
    <HEAD>
        <TITLE>
        Basic HTML Page
        </TITLE>
    </HEAD>
<BODY>
    <h1>How to become a popular researcher</h1>
<p>You can also become a popular researcher even if you don't understand your subject. Just follow these simple steps</p>
    <ul><li>Don't worry even if you have not done the requisite courses. You can pretend to understand the concepts by teaching the senior year. So, explore your contacts and get placed in a good college.</li>
    <li>Good English: It is required only for writing papers. Just don't speak, in your native language, in front of others.<br>You must ridicule anyone who speaks in your or his native language. This serves two purposes. It hides your inability to be able to converse in your own language. Hiding your ignorance is as important as showing off your achievements.</li>
        <li>Sycophancy:   A must.</li>
        <li>Read guidelines to prepare a good review, since it is the only thing you would be able to pull out.</li>
        <li>Become the editor of a journal and publish your own papers in every issue. Even if you are not able to come up with a new idea, ask your students to write a paper. It would
be advisable to select papers written by foreigners for your journal. The reason being you belong to this country and seem to believe that if a paper is written by a for-eigner, it must be good. </li>
        <li>If no one promotes you, then start promoting yourself. Make sure that your name is there in every news item and you are in every photo.</li></ul>
<p><i>Issued in public interest by "Save the real research society"</i></p>
</BODY>
</HTML>
```

Now, readers will be able to understand the source of their ASP page in a better way. See Fig. 22.15 here.

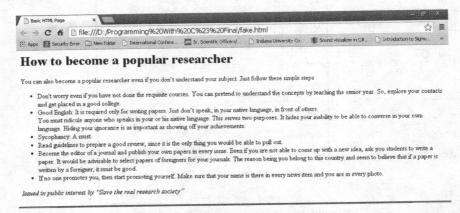

Fig. 22.15 Output

22.15 CREATING A USER FORM IN ASP

In order to create an ASP Form, the following steps must be performed:

Step 1 Create a new project called UserForm. Go to File → New → Web Site. Enter UserForm in the name field (Fig. 22.16).

Step 2 In the <head> element, change the text between <title> and </title> to UserForm.

```
<head runat = "server">
<title>User Form</title></head>
```

Step 3 Go to table menu and insert a table of seven rows and three columns (Fig. 22.17).

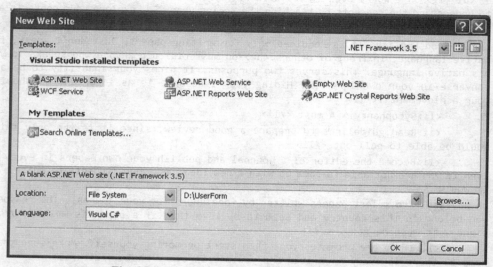

Fig. 22.16 Creating a UserForm in ASP—Step 1

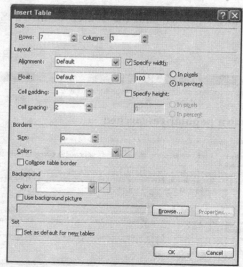

Fig. 22.17 Creating a UserForm in ASP—Step 3

Step 4 Go to the design view and drag three text boxes and three labels to the cells of the table as shown in Fig. 22.18.

Step 5 Right click on Label1. Go to properties and change the Text property to Name and ID to NameLabel (Fig. 22.19).

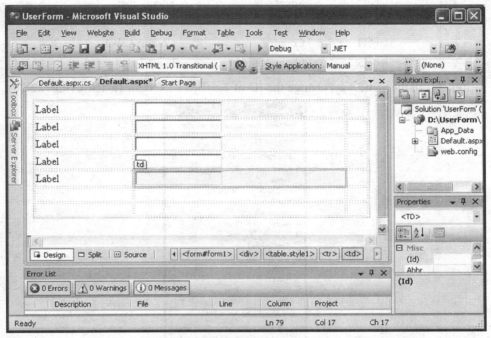

Fig. 22.18 Creating a UserForm in ASP—Step 4

Fig. 22.19 Creating a UserForm in ASP—Step 5

Step 6 Update the Text and ID properties for the next four labels (Table 22.3).

Table 22.3 Labels in the page

Label	Text	ID
label2	Street	StreetLabel
label3	City	CityLabel
label4	Country	CountryLabel
label5	Phone Number	PhoneLabel

Step 7 In the same way, change the ID of TextBox1 to NameTextBox (Fig. 22.20).

Fig. 22.20 Creating a UserForm in ASP—Step 7

Step 8 Change the ID of the rest of the text boxes as per Table 22.4.

Table 22.4 Textboxes in the page

Text box	ID
TextBox1	NameTextBox
TextBox2	StreetTextBox
TextBox3	CityTextBox
TextBox4	CountryTextBox
TextBox5	PhoneTextBox

Step 9 Now drag two buttons onto the web form. Change the Text property and ID property of the buttons as per Table 22.5.

Table 22.5 Buttons in the page

Property	Button1	Button2
Text	Clear	OK
ID	ClearButton	OKButton

Introduction to ASP.NET 479

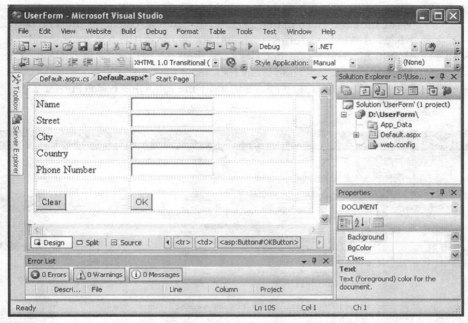

Fig. 22.21 Creating a UserForm in ASP—Step 9

The web page will look similar to the page given in Fig. 22.21.

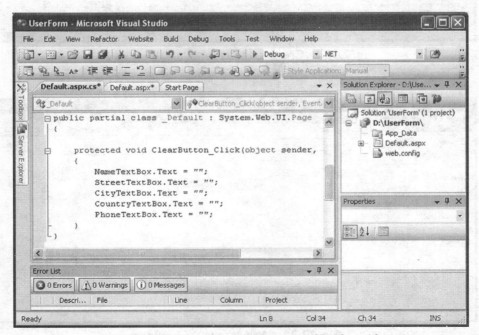

Fig. 22.22 Creating a UserForm in ASP—Step 10

480 Programming in C#

Step 10 Click on the Clear button; you will be taken to a C#-like editor called code behind. Write the code given in Fig. 22.22 in that editor. As readers must be familiar with the basics of Windows forms, it should not be too difficult to understand this.

Step 11 Before proceeding further, drag and drop a label below the buttons. Clear the Text property of the label and let its ID remain the same.

Step 12 Now click on the OK button and write the following code (Fig. 22.23):

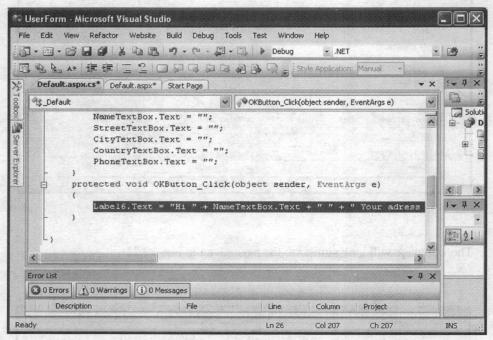

Fig. 22.23 Creating a UserForm in ASP—Step 12

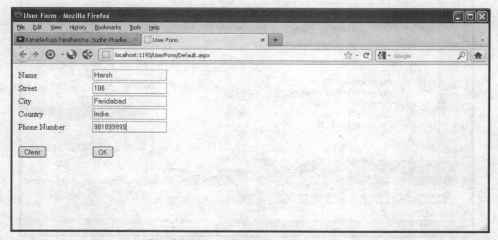

Fig. 22.24 Web page in the browser

```
Label6.Text = "Hi " + NameTextBox.Text + " " + " Your address is " +
StreetTextBox.Text + " " + CityTextBox.Text + " " + CountryTextBox.Text + "
" + "and phone number is " + PhoneTextBox.Text;
```

Step 13 Now press F5. The form shown in Fig. 22.24 will be displayed. Pressing the Clear button clears the fields (Fig. 22.25).

If you press the OK button, the form shown in Fig. 22.26 will be displayed.

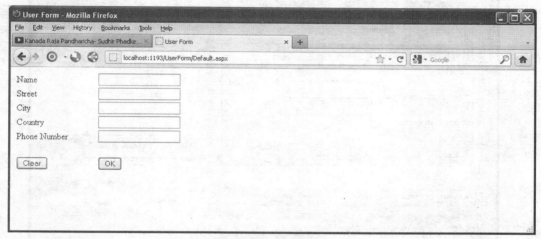

Fig. 22.25 Web page in the browser

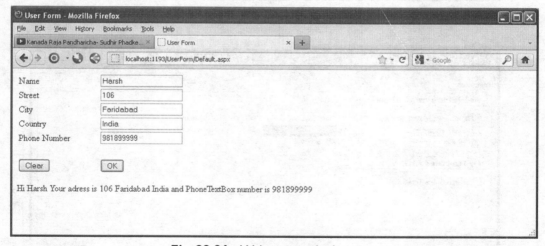

Fig. 22.26 Web page in the browser

22.16 DATABASE CREATION IN SQL EXPRESS

SQL Server Express is a free edition of SQL Server and is ideal for developing desktop, web, and small server applications. Some of the important features of SQL Server Express are as follows:
1. It allows 10 GB of storage per database.
2. It allows backup and restore with ease.

482 *Programming in C#*

3. It is compatible with all editions of SQL Server.
4. It is designed to work with Visual Studio and ASP.NET.
5. Its graphical management tool is available.

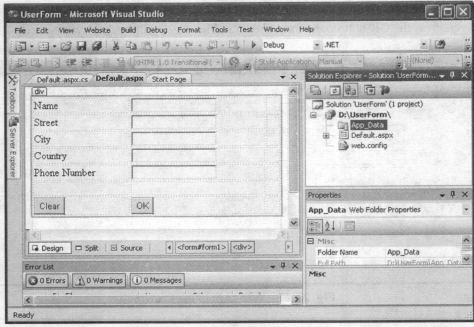

Fig. 22.27 Database connection—Step 1

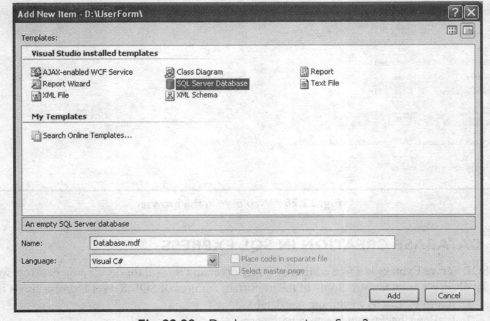

Fig. 22.28 Database connection—Step 2

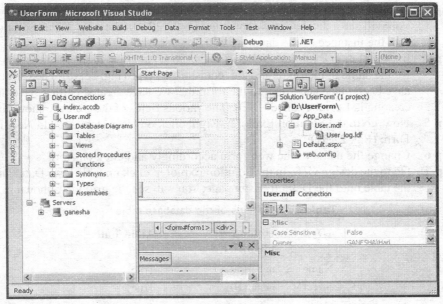

Fig. 22.29 Database connection—Step 3

In order to create a database in SQL Express, perform the following steps:

Step 1 Right click on App_Data and go to Add New Item (Fig. 22.27).
Step 2 Select SQL Server Database (Fig. 22.28).

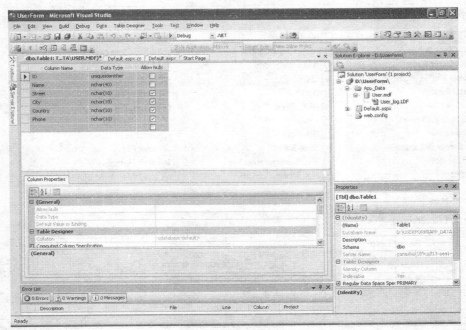

Fig. 22.30 Database connection—Step 4

Step 3 Change the name of the database to User.mdf and click on Add. In the Server Explorer, you will see a database (as shown in Fig. 22.29). In the App_Data (Solution Explorer) too, the instance of the database will be visible.

Step 4 In the Solution Explorer, click on Tables. Go to Add new Table. In the screen that follows, fill the name of the fields and the requisite data type (Fig. 22.30). The various data fields have been made according to the form that we have created earlier. Save the table after creating it. Let it be called USER. The various fields of the table are shown in Table 22.6.

Step 5 Now, go to the Solution Explorer. Right click on User Data → Add New Item → Web Form (Fig. 22.31).

Step 6 Change the name of the web form accordingly and click on Add.

Step 7 Go to the design view. In the Solution Explorer, click on table User Data. Drag and drop the table onto the Default2.aspx page. You will see the grid view shown in Fig. 22.32.

Table 22.6 Fields of the database table

ID	Unique identifier	Allow nulls: False
Name	nchar(40)	True
Street	nchar(10)	True
City	nchar(10)	True
Country	nchar(10)	True
Phone	nchar(10)	True

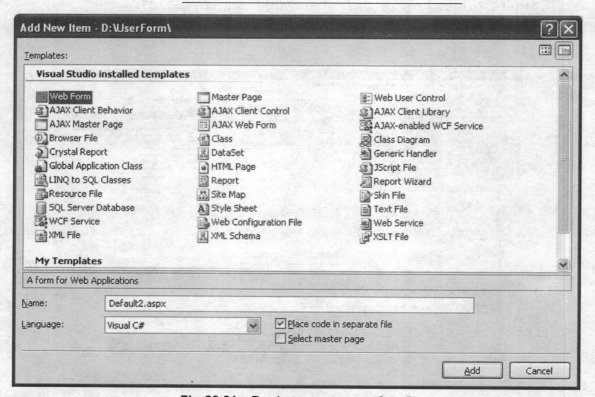

Fig. 22.31 Database connection—Step 5

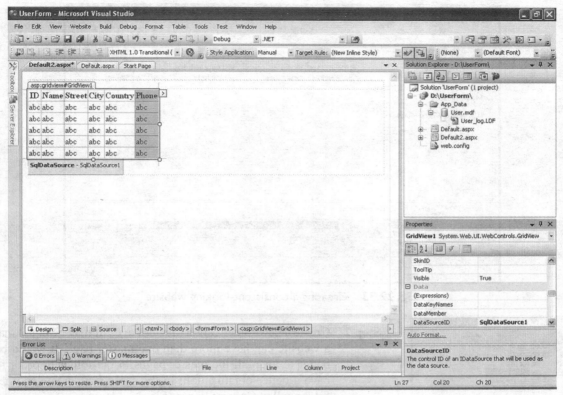

Fig. 22.32 Database connection—Step 7

Click on the grid view task to make the requisite changes. This is perhaps the easiest way of viewing data in an ASP.NET web form.

22.17 MASTER PAGE

It may be stated at this point that in a professional website each page has some common portion. Only a part of the page changes when you navigate. For instance, the header and the footer remain the same in a website while we navigate and only the content given at the centre changes. In order to make such consistent-looking websites, a master page is used.

Master pages were not always a part of ASP.NET; they were introduced in ASP 2.0. Master pages look like a normal ASP page. However, no content can be added in a master page; only the content that remains the same in all the pages is placed in the master page. A master page has a place where content can be added. The content pages are added in order to fill these places.

In order to create a consistent-looking website using a master page, the following steps must be followed:

Step 1 Open Visual Studio and go to New → Web Site → ASP.NET Web Site. Create a new empty website. In this program, the name of the website is 'Master Page Demo' (Fig. 22.33).

486 *Programming in C#*

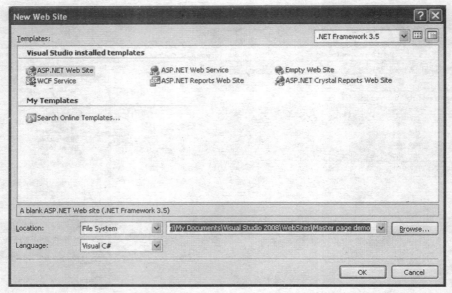

Fig. 22.33 Creating a consistent-looking website

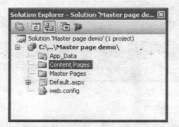

Fig. 22.34 Creating folders for master pages and content pages

Step 2 Create a new folder called Master Pages. It may be noted that a website can have more than one master page. It would be better to keep all the master pages in the folder in order to have a better organization. In the same way, create another folder called Content Pages (Fig. 22.34).

Step 3 In the Master Pages folder, add a new master page. In order to do it, right click on the Master Page folder. Go to Add New Item and select Master Page (Fig. 22.35).

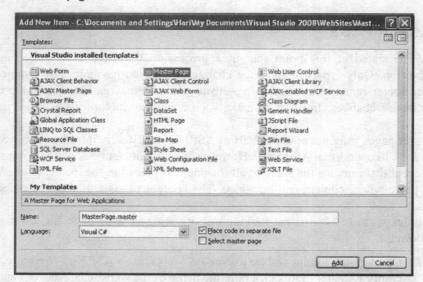

Fig. 22.35 Adding a master page

The source of the master page would be as follows. In the source, change the title of the master page. The content place holder is the housing for the content. This content would be rendered by the content page.

```
<%@ Master Language = "C#" AutoEventWireup = "true" CodeFile = "MasterPage.master.cs"
Inherits = "Master_Pages_MasterPage" %>
<!DOCTYPE html PUBLIC "-//W3C//DTD XHTML 1.0 Transitional//EN" "http://www.w3.org/TR/
xhtml1/DTD/xhtml1-transitional.dtd">
<html xmlns = "http://www.w3.org/1999/xhtml">
<head runat = "server">
    <title>Untitled Page</title>
    <asp:ContentPlaceHolder id = "head" runat = "server">
    </asp:ContentPlaceHolder>
</head>
<body>
    <form id = "form1" runat="server">
    <div>
    <asp:ContentPlaceHolder id = "ContentPlaceHolder1" runat = "server">
    </asp:ContentPlaceHolder>
    </div>
    </form>
</body>
</html>
```

Step 4 Go to the design view of the master page and design the page as per the requirement. In this program, the master page is created as per the design shown in Fig. 22.36.

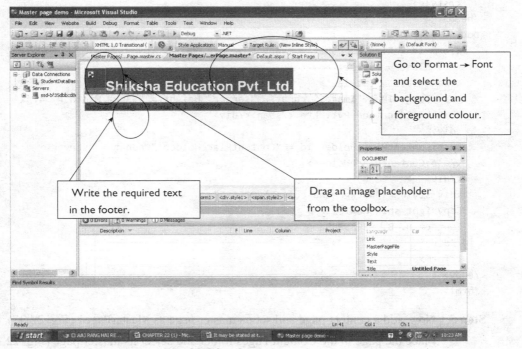

Fig. 22.36 Creating a master page

The final code of the master page would be as follows:

```
<%@ Master Language = "C#" AutoEventWireup = "true" CodeFile = "MasterPage.master.cs"
Inherits = "Master_Pages_MasterPage" %>

<!DOCTYPE html PUBLIC "-//W3C//DTD XHTML 1.0 Transitional//EN" "http://www.w3.org/TR/
xhtml1/DTD/xhtml1-transitional.dtd">

<html xmlns = "http://www.w3.org/1999/xhtml">
<head runat = "server">
    <title>Master page Demo</title>
    <asp:ContentPlaceHolder id = "head" runat = "server">
    </asp:ContentPlaceHolder>
    <style type = "text/css">
    .style1
    {
        font-family: Arial, Helvetica, sans-serif;
        font-size: large;
        color: #FFFFFF;
        font-weight: bold;
    }
    .style2
    {
        font-size: xx-large;
        background-color: #0066FF;
    }
    </style>
</head>
<body>
    <form id = "form1" runat = "server">
    <div class = "style1">
    <span class = "style2">
    <asp:Image ID = "Image1" runat = "server" Height = "53px" Width = "47px" />
    Shiksha Education Pvt. Ltd.</span></div>
    <div>
    <asp:ContentPlaceHolder id = "ContentPlaceHolder1" runat = "server">
    </asp:ContentPlaceHolder>
    </div>
    <div style = "background-color: #0066FF">
    Copyright shiksha@2013
    Contact H. B. 98989898
    </div>
    </form>
</body>
</html>
```

Step 5 Now, add a content page and set its master page as MasterPage1 (Fig. 22.37).

Place the page in the Content Pages folder and select its master page (Fig. 22.38).

Step 6 Write the required content in the content page (Fig. 22.39).

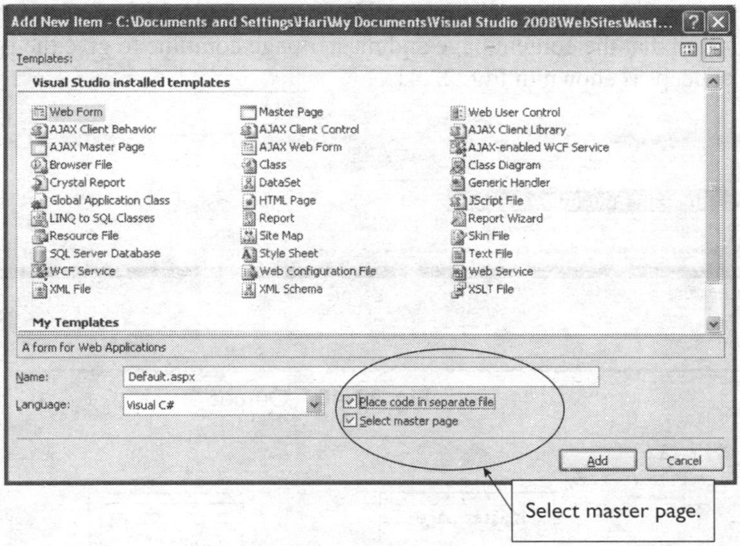

Introduction to ASP.NET **489**

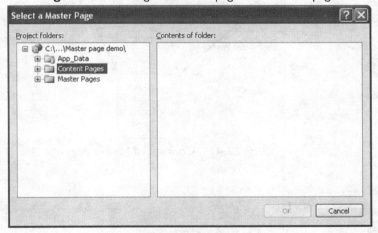

Fig. 22.37 Setting the master page of a content page

Fig. 22.38 Selecting master page

Fig. 22.39 Writing text in the content page

Step 7 Now, run the project. The output as shown in Fig. 22.40 will be displayed.

It may be stated that the content page and master page combine to give the final page at the run time. The concept is shown in Fig. 22.41.

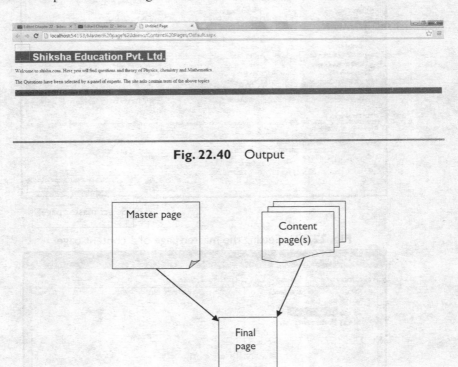

Fig. 22.40 Output

Fig. 22.41 Concept of Master page

SUMMARY

The chapter gives an introduction to ASP.NET. As stated earlier, ASP.NET is an enhancement of traditional ASP. It handles all the contentious issues of traditional ASP effectively and efficiently. Moreover, it is one of a kind. The point can be understood by the fact that the open source community appropriated many things from ASP.NET and incorporated them in JSP.

The technology helps to create dynamic, consistent-looking web pages. The advantage of ASP is that we can use our knowledge of C# to accomplish the tasks that otherwise would have been very difficult. The concept of master page helps us to create professional looking web pages. It may be stated at this point that the concepts of ADO are required to connect the web pages to a database. Hence, it is advisable to go through Chapter 21 before trying to create dynamic web pages.

A master page helps us in giving a consistent look and feel to a website. It also helps in the maintainability of a site. It may be stated at this point that the master page is not the only way to achieve this goal. It can also be achieved by using a centralized page. However, the concept is beyond the scope of the text.

The aim of this chapter is to enable readers to create web pages in ASP by using the concepts studied earlier. In no way should the chapter be considered a complete text in ASP.NET. However, it can be considered as a decent introduction.

GLOSSARY

Attribute It is the information associated with a control, which helps us to change the behaviour of that control.
Server controls These controls are used to build a web page in ASP.NET.
User control It is a user-defined unit. A user control is a type of composite control that works much like an ASP.NET web page.

Mater page It is the central page that defines the look and feel of every content page that is associated with it.
Content page It is a web form that uses the master page to build its appearance.
Data source controls These are the controls that serve as a bridge between the data source and data bound controls.

POINTS TO REMEMBER

- ASP.NET provides a new model, a new infrastructure, and a new security model. Hence, it is much more than the next version of ASP.
- In traditional ASP, session state is maintained by the browser, which supports cookies, whereas in ASP.NET, state information can be kept in memory or stored in a database.
- ASP.NET has the ability to separate layout and business logic.
- Web forms allow us to build powerful form-based web pages. ASP.NET server controls can be used to create common user interface elements.
- A web service is not the same as a website.

EXERCISES

I. Multiple-choice Questions

1. Who designed XPS?
   (a) Mark Anders and Scott Guthrie
   (b) Larry Page
   (c) Dennis Richie
   (d) None of these

2. Which of the following is true?
   (a) ASP+ is XPS reimplemented in C#.
   (b) ASP.NET is XPS reimplemented in C#.
   (c) XPS is ASP reimplemented in C#.
   (d) C# is XPS reimplemented in ASP.

3. Which of the following is true?
   (a) ASP.NET provides a combined web development model.
   (b) ASP.NET is syntax compatible with ASP.
   (c) In ASP.NET, applications can be created in any .NET compatible language, including Visual Basic.NET, C#, and JScript.NET.
   (d) All of these

4. Which of the following is not true?
   (a) Developers can use web forms or XML web services when creating an ASP.NET application.
   (b) ASP.NET provides a GUI that developers can use to drop server controls onto a web page.
   (c) ASP.NET is used for client-side programming.
   (d) None of these

5. Which of the following points depict the problems in classic ASP?
   (a) Interpretation
   (b) Limited tools
   (c) No state management
   (d) All of these

6. Which of the following is true with respect to classic ASP?
   (a) Update when server is down
   (b) Murky configuration settings
   (c) Supports C#
   (d) None of these

7. Which of the following depicts the features of ASP.NET?
   (a) Separation of code
   (b) Compiled languages
   (c) Use services
   (d) All of these

8. Which of the following is not supported by ASP.NET?
   (a) State management (b) Updating files
   (c) Windows forms   (d) All of these

9. Which of the following is not a part of ASP architecture?
   (a) CLR (b) Base classes
   (c) ADO.NET (d) VHDL

10. What are the different views of a web form in ASP?
    (a) Source (b) Design
    (c) Split (d) All of these

II. State True or False

1. In ASP, you can view the source and the design at the same time.
2. ASP.NET is just an extension of ASP.
3. ASP supports C#.
4. .pop is a file supported by ASP.
5. In ASP.NET, both .mdb and .mdf are database files.
6. Master page can be made using a web form.
7. We can add as many pages as we want in an ASP.NET website.
8. Web services and websites are the same.
9. We can use a table for managing the layout of our site.

III. Review Questions

1. What are the features of ASP.NET?
2. Differentiate between ASP and ASP.NET. Explain the architecture of ASP.NET.
3. What are the different files used in ASP.NET?
4. What are the different views in ASP.NET?
5. Differentiate between user controls and server controls.
6. What is the importance of ASP.NET application folders?
7. In the text, various HTML elements are given. Can you state the classes that control theses elements?
8. Can you apply styles to server controls?
9. What is a custom control?
10. Throw some light on the evolution of ASP.NET.

IV. Programming Exercises

1. Create a page in ASP.NET that has a text box, a label, and a button. Ask the user to enter his/her name in the text box and press the button. He/She should be greeted with the welcome message along with the date and time.

2. Create a web form called 'Employee Information'. The web form should have the following fields:
   (a) Name
   (b) Date of birth
   (c) City
   (d) State
   (e) Country
   (f) Phone number
   (g) E-mail ID

   There should be two buttons: Clear and Submit. On pressing the Clear button, the data in the text boxes should disappear. On pressing the Submit button, the data should be displayed in a label.

3. Craft a web form showing the data of the student table of a school database. The database should be made in MS Access.

4. Make a site that promotes Green Technology using HTML controls and server controls.

5. With the help of HTML controls and tags, design the following page:

V. Explore

1. Find the classes associated with HTML elements.
2. Find the meaning of page directives, for example, @Register.
3. Try finding out about the code behind a model.
4. Observe and elicit the compilation process of ASP.NET website.
5. What can be the motivation behind making a web application?
6. What are build providers?
7. The next part of the book deals with the page framework. Try finding out some details about it.
8. Explore the HTMLGenericControl class.
9. Are there any limitations on the file size in ASP.NET?
10. What is AJAX?

PROJECT IV
Online Voting System

1. INTRODUCTION

India is a democratic country and elections are the spine of a democracy. It is, therefore, important to device methods to encourage people to vote. This project aims at making the voting process easy in India. At present, voting is done using Electronic Voting Machines (EVMs). With liberalization and skewed economic policies, people are forced to go to other places in order to earn their living, and hence, a person who is away from his hometown finds it difficult to cast his vote. This, as a matter of fact, has become one of the causes of less voting percentage in any elections.

This project aims at tackling this problem. Moreover, it may be stated that this system should be used only by the people who are away from their constituency and have a valid reason of not being able to turn up on the Election Day. Such people can register their details on the website, and the details of the candidates too can be registered on the website. The complete project requires many concepts that have not been covered in this book. However, a scaled version of the project has been presented here.

2. FUNCTIONAL REQUIREMENTS

The project should have the following features:
1. A voter should be able to register.
2. The election officer should be able to enter the details of the candidates.
3. The application should be able to count the total number of votes.
4. The application should declare who won the election.

In order to accomplish the task, the following steps should be followed:

Step 1 Database Creation

To accomplish the task, a database called voting should be created. The database will have three tables. The first table stores the details of the candidates. The various fields of this table are shown in Table PIV.1.

Table PIV.2 shows the fields of the database table 'Party'. Table PIV.3 shows the fields of the database table 'Vote', and Table PIV.4 shows the fields of the 'Voter' table.

Table PIV.1 Fields in the candidate table

Name of the field	Data type	Checked/Unchecked
CandidateID	int	Unchecked
FirstName	nvarchar(50)	Checked
MiddleName	nvarchar(50)	Checked
LastName	nvarchar(50)	Checked
PhoneNumber	nvarchar(50)	Checked
Address	nvarchar(MAX)	Checked
FatherName	nvarchar(50)	Checked
Party	nvarchar(50)	Checked
DateOfBirth	nvarchar(50)	Checked
EducationLevel	nvarchar(50)	Checked
UID	nvarchar(50)	Checked

Table PIV.2 Fields in the party table

Name of the field	Data type	Checked/Unchecked
PartyID	int	Unchecked
PartyName	nvarchar(50)	Checked

Table PIV.3 Fields in the vote table

Name of the field	Data type	Checked/Unchecked
VoteID	int	Checked
CandidateID	int	Checked
VoterID	int	Checked

Table PIV.4 Fields in the voter table

Name of the field	Data type	Checked/Unchecked
VoterID	int	Checked
UserName	nvarchar(50)	Checked
Password	nvarchar(50)	Checked
EMail	nvarchar(50)	Checked

Another database created by configuring the registration page is shown in Fig. PIV.1. The Register New User control, the Forget Password control, and the Login control need a database, which can be created automatically by configuring the controls. The configuration of these controls can be found in the web resources.

Step 2 Style sheet creation

A style sheet is created with a header, a sidebar, a footer, and with the requisite containers. The code of the style sheet is as follows:

```
body
{
    color: Blue;
    font-family: Arial;
    font-size: medium;
}
a:link
{
    color:Green;
}
a:hover
{
    color:Orange;
}
a:visited
{
    color:Navy;
}
        RightAligned
        {
```

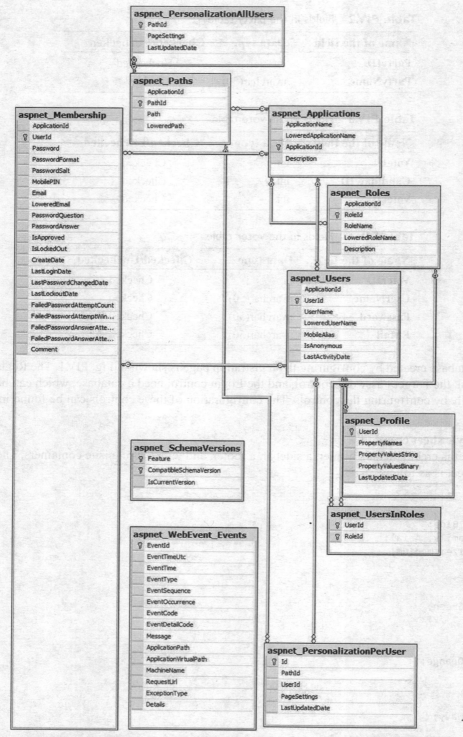

Fig. PIV.1 Database created by configuring the Register New User control

```css
    text-align:right;
}
LeftAligned
{
    text-align:left;
}
CentreAligned
{
    text-align:center;
}
#Intro
{
    font-size:large;
    font-family:Andalus;
    font-style:italic;
    background-color:Blue;
    color:White;
    border-bottom-style:groove;
}
#Sidebar
{
    width:140px;
    float:left;
    height:480px;
    background-color:Red;
    margin-left:0px;
}
#Header
{
    width:840px;
    height:120px;
    background:blue;
    color:White;
    font-weight:bold;
    font-family:Arial, Helvetica, sans-serif;
}
#Footer
{
    width:840px;
    height:80px;
    background-color:Red;
    color:White;
    font-weight:bold;
    clear:both;
}
#Menubar
{
    width:840;
    height:80;
}
#Maincontent
{
```

```
        width:644px;
        height:480px;
}
```

Step 3 Master page

A master page is created and saved in the Master Page folder created in the Solution Explorer. The code for the master page is as follows:

```
<%@    Master    Language="C#"    AutoEventWireup="true"    CodeFile="MasterPage.master.cs"
Inherits="MasterPages_MasterPage" %>

<!DOCTYPE html PUBLIC "-//W3C//DTD XHTML 1.0 Transitional//EN" "http://www.w3.org/TR/xhtml1/
DTD/xhtml1-transitional.dtd">

<html xmlns="http://www.w3.org/1999/xhtml">
<head runat="server">
    <title>Untitled Page</title>
    <asp:ContentPlaceHolder id="head" runat="server">
    </asp:ContentPlaceHolder>
    <link href="../Styles/StyleSheet1.css" rel="stylesheet" type="text/css" />
</head>
<body>
    <form id="form1" runat="server">
    <div id="Header"><asp:Image ID="Image1" runat="server" Height="116px"
          ImageUrl="~/Image.jpg" Width="118px" />       
                       &nb
          sp;             
                   India
</div>
<div id="Menubar"><asp:Menu ID="Menu1" runat="server" BackColor="#B5C7DE"
        DynamicHorizontalOffset="2" Font-Names="Verdana" Font-Size="0.8em"
        ForeColor="#284E98" Orientation="Horizontal" StaticSubMenuIndent="10px"
Width="841px">
    <StaticSelectedStyle BackColor="#507CD1" />
    <StaticMenuItemStyle HorizontalPadding="5px" VerticalPadding="2px" />
    <DynamicHoverStyle BackColor="#284E98" ForeColor="White" />
    <DynamicMenuStyle BackColor="#B5C7DE" />
    <DynamicSelectedStyle BackColor="#507CD1" />
    <DynamicMenuItemStyle HorizontalPadding="5px" VerticalPadding="2px" />
    <StaticHoverStyle BackColor="#284E98" ForeColor="White" />
    <Items>
    <asp:MenuItem NavigateUrl="~/Content pages/Registration.aspx"
          Text="User registration" Value="User registration"></asp:MenuItem>
        <asp:MenuItem NavigateUrl="~/Content pages/Login.aspx" Text="Password recovery"
          Value="Password recovery"></asp:MenuItem>
        <asp:MenuItem NavigateUrl="~/Content pages/Change Password.aspx"
          Text="Change Password" Value="Change Password"></asp:MenuItem>
        <asp:MenuItem NavigateUrl="~/Content pages/Login.aspx" Text="User login"
          Value="User login"></asp:MenuItem>
        <asp:MenuItem Text="Insert Candidate Details" Value="Candidate Details"
          NavigateUrl="~/Management/CandidateInsert.aspx"></asp:MenuItem>
        <asp:MenuItem Text="Candidate details" Value="Candidate details"
          NavigateUrl="~/Content pages/ViewCandidate.aspx"></asp:MenuItem>
        <asp:MenuItem Text="Cast Vote" Value="Cast Vote"
          NavigateUrl="~/VoterFolder/CastVote.aspx"></asp:MenuItem>
        <asp:MenuItem Text="About Us" Value="About Us"></asp:MenuItem>
```

```
        </Items>
        </asp:Menu></div>
<div id="Sidebar">This initiative intends to reduce the paper work in the process of elections.
Moreover, the details of the candidates can be seen anytime. The process will also help in the
speedy declaration of the results and encourage the youths to participate in the most important
process of strengthening the democracy. The site intends to include the criminal record, if
any, of the candidates soon.</div>
<div id="Maincontent">
    <asp:ContentPlaceHolder id="ContentPlaceHolder1" runat="server">

    </asp:ContentPlaceHolder>
    </div>
    <div id ="Footer">Maintained and Developed by SSD<br />For any queries contact 9999999999
        <br />
        <asp:LoginView ID="LoginView1" runat="server">
    <RoleGroups>
                                <asp:RoleGroup Roles="Managers">
                                <ContentTemplate>
    <asp:HyperLink ID="HyperLink1" runat="server"
    NavigateUrl="~/Management/CandidateInsert.aspx">Manage</asp:HyperLink>
</ContentTemplate>
                    </asp:RoleGroup>
                </RoleGroups>
        </asp:LoginView>
        </div>

    </form>
</body>
</html>
```

Step 4 Content pages

The following content pages are created:
1. **Change Password** This page helps the user to reset his password. The page is easy to create. Just drag and drop the Change Password control onto the content place holder (Fig. PIV.2).
2. **Login/Forget Password** This page helps the user to login to the system. The page also has a control that takes the user to the reset password page. This page is also easy to create. Just drag and drop the Forget Password control onto the content place holder. The same can be done with the Login control (Fig. PIV.3).
3. **Register page** This page helps the user to register. The page can be easily created by dragging the Create User Wizard from the Toolbox (Fig. PIV.4) onto the content place holder.
4. **Result page** This page displays the result of the election. The page can be easily created by creating a table with four columns displaying the Name of the candidate, Party name, Symbol, and the number of votes a candidate got (Fig. PIV.5).
5. **View Candidate Details page** This page displays the details of a candidate. The page can be easily made by creating a table and connecting it to the database as explained in Chapter 22 (Fig. PIV.6).
6. **Insert Candidate Details page** This page helps the election officer to insert the details of the candidates in the database. As the page is to be used only by the officer, it is placed in the Management folder (Fig. PIV.7).
7. **Default page** This page is the entry point of the system. You can create a basic page outside any folder and write the welcome message (Fig. PIV.8).

The following section gives the C# codes of the various forms created in this project.

500 Programming in C#

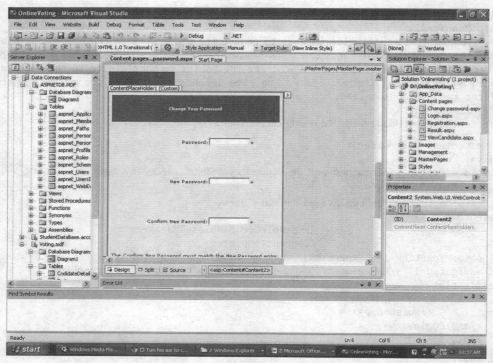

Fig. PIV.2 Change Password control

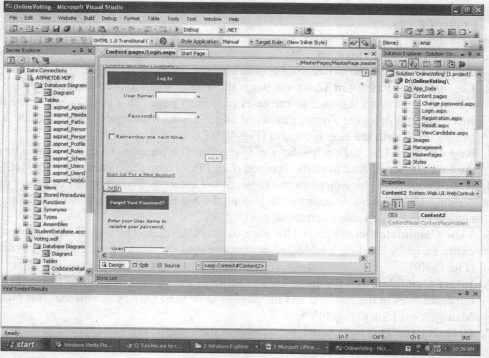

Fig. PIV.3 Login control

Fig. PIV.4 ToolBox

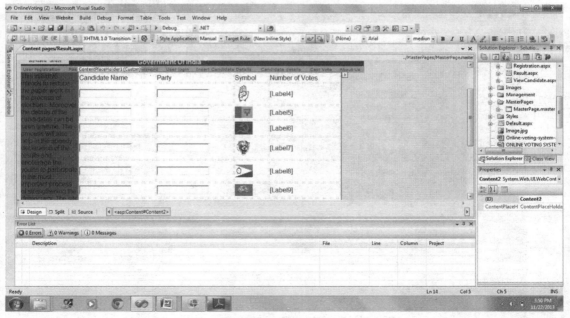

Fig. PIV.5 Result page

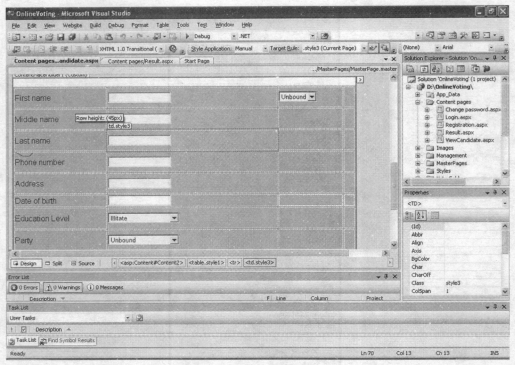

Fig. PIV.6 View Candidate Details page

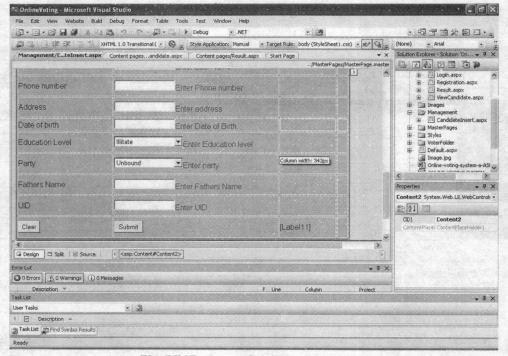

Fig. PIV.7 Insert Candidate Details page

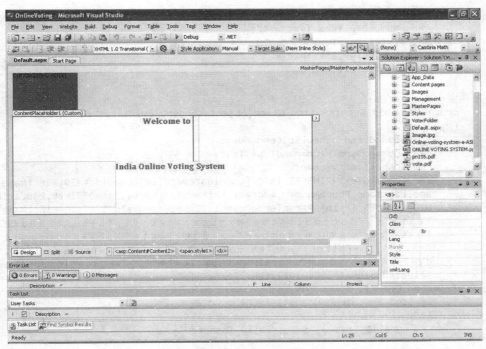

Fig. PIV.8 Welcome page

3. SOURCE CODES

1. The code of Insert Candidate Details page is as follows:

```
using System;
using System.Collections;
using System.Configuration;
using System.Data;
using System.Linq;
using System.Web;
using System.Web.Security;
using System.Web.UI;
using System.Web.UI.HtmlControls;
using System.Web.UI.WebControls;
using System.Web.UI.WebControls.WebParts;
using System.Xml.Linq;
using System.Data.SqlClient;
using System.Collections.Generic;
public partial class Content_pages_CandidateInsert : System.Web.UI.Page
{
    SqlConnection conn = new SqlConnection(@"Data Source=.\
                SQLEXPRESS;AttachDbFilename=D:\OnlineVoting\App_Data\Voting.
                mdf;Integrated Security=True;User Instance=True");
    protected void ClearButton_Click(object sender, EventArgs e)
    {
        FirstNameTextBox.Text = "";
        MiddleNameTextBox.Text = "";
        LastNameTextBox.Text = "";
```

```csharp
                DateOfBirthTextBox.Text = "";
                PhoneNumberTextBox.Text = "";
                AddressTextBox.Text = "";
                FathersNameTextBox.Text = "";
                UIDTextBox.Text = "";
        }

        protected void SubmitButton_Click(object sender, EventArgs e)
        {
            SqlCommand cmd = new SqlCommand();
            cmd.CommandType = CommandType.Text;
            cmd.Connection = conn;
            cmd.CommandText="INSERT INTO [CandidateDetails](CandidateID,FirstName,MiddleN
            ame,LastName,PhoneNumber,Address,FatherName,Party,DateOfBirth,EducationLevel,
            UID) VALUES ("+int.Parse(DropDownList1.SelectedValue) +",'"+FirstNameTextBox.
            Text+"','"+MiddleNameTextBox.Text+"','"+LastNameTextBox.
            Text+"','"+PhoneNumberTextBox.Text+"','"+AddressTextBox.
            Text+"','"+FathersNameTextBox.Text+"','"+PartyDropDownList.Selecte
            dValue+"','"+DateOfBirthTextBox.Text+"','"+EducationDropDownList.
            SelectedValue+"','"+UIDTextBox.Text+"');";
            conn.Open();
            if (cmd.ExecuteNonQuery() != 0)
            {
                Label11.Text = "Sucessfully Inserted";
            }
            conn.Close();
        }
        protected void Page_Load(object sender, EventArgs e)
        {
            SqlCommand cmd = new SqlCommand();
            cmd.CommandType = CommandType.Text;
            cmd.Connection = conn;
            cmd.CommandText = "SELECT PartyName FROM [Party]";
            SqlDataReader myReader;
            List<string> returnData = new List<string>();
            conn.Open();
            myReader = cmd.ExecuteReader(CommandBehavior.CloseConnection);
            while (myReader.Read())
            {
                returnData.Add(myReader["PartyName"].ToString());
            }
            PartyDropDownList.DataSource = returnData;
            PartyDropDownList.DataBind();

            conn.Close();
        }
}
```

2. The code of View Candidate Details page is as follows:

```csharp
using System;
using System.Collections;
using System.Configuration;
using System.Data;
using System.Linq;
using System.Web;
```

```csharp
using System.Web.Security;
using System.Web.UI;
using System.Web.UI.HtmlControls;
using System.Web.UI.WebControls;
using System.Web.UI.WebControls.WebParts;
using System.Xml.Linq;
using System.Data.SqlClient;
using System.Collections.Generic;

public partial class Content_pages_ViewCandidate : System.Web.UI.Page
{
    SqlConnection conn;
    protected void Page_Load(object sender, EventArgs e)
    {
        conn = new    SqlConnection(@"Data    Source=.\SQLEXPRESS;AttachDbFilename=D:\
            OnlineVoting\App_Data\Voting.mdf;Integrated         Security=True;User
            Instance=True");
        SqlCommand cmd = new SqlCommand();
        cmd.Connection = conn;
        cmd.CommandType = CommandType.Text;
        cmd.CommandText = "SELECT CandidateID FROM [CandidateDetails]";
        SqlDataReader myReader;
        List<string> returnData = new List<string>();
        conn.Open();
        myReader = cmd.ExecuteReader(CommandBehavior.CloseConnection);
        while (myReader.Read())
        {
            returnData.Add(myReader["CandidateID"].ToString());
        }
        CandidateIDDropDownList.DataSource = returnData;
        CandidateIDDropDownList.DataBind();
        conn.Close();
    }
    protected void CandidateIDDropDownList_SelectedIndexChanged(object sender, EventArgs e)
    {
        SqlCommand cmd = new SqlCommand();
        cmd.CommandType = CommandType.Text;
        cmd.Connection = conn;
        cmd.CommandText = "SELECT (FirstName,MiddleName,LastName,PhoneNumber,A
                          ddress,FatherName,Party,DateOfBirth,EducationLevel,
                          UID) FROM [CandidateDetails] WHERE CandidateID="+int.
                          Parse(CandidateIDDropDownList.SelectedValue);
        SqlDataReader myReader;
        conn.Open();
        myReader = cmd.ExecuteReader();
        if (myReader.Read())
        {
            FirstNameTextBox.Text = myReader[0].ToString();
            MiddleNameTextBox.Text = myReader[1].ToString();
            LastNameTextBox.Text = myReader[2].ToString();
            PhoneNumberTextBox.Text = myReader[3].ToString();
            AddressTextBox.Text = myReader[4].ToString();
            FathersNameTextBox.Text = myReader[5].ToString();
            PartyDropDownList.Text = myReader[6].ToString();
            DateOfBirthTextBox.Text = myReader[7].ToString();
```

```csharp
            EducationDropDownList.Text = myReader[8].ToString();
            UIDTextBox.Text = myReader[9].ToString();
        }
        while (myReader.Read())
        {
            FirstNameTextBox.Text = myReader[0].ToString();
            MiddleNameTextBox.Text = myReader[1].ToString();
            LastNameTextBox.Text = myReader[2].ToString();
            PhoneNumberTextBox.Text = myReader[3].ToString();
            AddressTextBox.Text = myReader[4].ToString();
            FathersNameTextBox.Text = myReader[5].ToString();
            PartyDropDownList.Text = myReader[6].ToString();
            DateOfBirthTextBox.Text = myReader[7].ToString();
            EducationDropDownList.Text = myReader[8].ToString();
            UIDTextBox.Text = myReader[9].ToString();
        }
            conn.Close();
        }
    }
```

3. The code of Results page is as follows:

```csharp
using System;
using System.Collections;
using System.Configuration;
using System.Data;
using System.Linq;
using System.Web;
using System.Web.Security;
using System.Web.UI;
using System.Web.UI.HtmlControls;
using System.Web.UI.WebControls;
using System.Web.UI.WebControls.WebParts;
using System.Xml.Linq;
using System.Data.SqlClient;
public partial class Content_pages_Result : System.Web.UI.Page
{
   SqlConnection conn = new SqlConnection(@"Data Source=.\
                    SQLEXPRESS;AttachDbFilename=D:\OnlineVoting\App_Data\Voting.
                    mdf;Integrated Security=True;User Instance=True");
   SqlConnection conn1 = new SqlConnection(@"Data Source=.\SQLEXPRESS;AttachDbFilename=D:\
                    OnlineVoting\App_Data\Voting.mdf;Integrated Security=True;User
                    Instance=True");
string[,] result = new string[100, 4];
protected void Page_Load(object sender, EventArgs e)
{
   for (int k = 0; k < 7; k++)
   {
    result[k, 2] = "0";
   }
   SqlCommand cmd = new SqlCommand();
   cmd.CommandType = CommandType.Text;
   cmd.Connection = conn;
   cmd.CommandText = "SELECT CandidateID,FirstName,LastName FROM CandidateDetails WHERE
                    Party='Congress'";
    conn.Open();
    SqlDataReader myReader;
```

```csharp
        myReader = cmd.ExecuteReader();
        if (myReader.Read())
        {
          TextBox1.Text = myReader[1].ToString() + " " + myReader[2].ToString();
          TextBox2.Text = "Congress";
          result[0, 0] = myReader[1].ToString();
          result[0, 1] = myReader[2].ToString();
          int number = int.Parse(myReader[0].ToString());
          int numberOfVotes = 0;
          SqlCommand cmd1 = new SqlCommand();
          cmd1.CommandType = CommandType.Text;
          cmd1.Connection = conn1;
          cmd1.CommandText = "SELECT VoterID FROM [Vote] WHERE CandidateID=" + number;
          conn1.Open();
          SqlDataReader myReader1;
          myReader1 = cmd1.ExecuteReader();
          if (myReader1.Read())
          {
            numberOfVotes++;
          }
          while (myReader1.Read())
          {
            numberOfVotes++;
          }
          result[0, 2] = numberofVotes.ToString();
          Label4.Text = result[0, 2];
          conn1.Close();
        }
        conn.Close();
        //
        cmd = new SqlCommand();
        cmd.CommandType = CommandType.Text;
        cmd.Connection = conn;
        cmd.CommandText = "SELECT CandidateID,FirstName,LastName FROM CandidateDetails WHERE
                          Party='BJP'";
        conn.Open();
        myReader = cmd.ExecuteReader();
        if (myReader.Read())
        {
          TextBox3.Text = myReader[1].ToString() + " " + myReader[2].ToString();
          //Label5.Text = myReader[0].ToString();
          TextBox4.Text = "BJP";
          result[1, 0] = myReader[1].ToString();
          result[1, 1] = myReader[2].ToString();
          int number = int.Parse(myReader[0].ToString());
          int numberOfVotes = 0;
          SqlCommand cmd1 = new SqlCommand();
          cmd1.CommandType = CommandType.Text;
          cmd1.Connection = conn1;
          cmd1.CommandText = "SELECT VoterID FROM [Vote] WHERE CandidateID=" + number;
          conn1.Open();
          SqlDataReader myReader1;
          myReader1 = cmd1.ExecuteReader();
          if (myReader1.Read())
          {
```

```csharp
      numberofVotes++;
    }
    while (myReader1.Read())
    {
      numberOfVotes++;
    }
    result[1, 2] = numberOfVotes.ToString();
    Label5.Text = result[1, 2];
    conn1.Close();
  }
  conn.Close();
  //
  cmd = new SqlCommand();
  cmd.CommandType = CommandType.Text;
  cmd.Connection = conn;
  cmd.CommandText = "SELECT CandidateID,FirstName,LastName FROM CandidateDetails WHERE 
                    Party='CPI'";
  conn.Open();

  myReader = cmd.ExecuteReader();
  if (myReader.Read())
  {
    TextBox5.Text = myReader[1].ToString() + " " + myReader[2].ToString();
    // Label6.Text = myReader[0].ToString();
    TextBox6.Text = "CPI";
    result[2, 0] = myReader[1].ToString();
    result[2, 1] = myReader[2].ToString();
    int number = int.Parse(myReader[0].ToString());
    int numberOfVotes = 0;
    SqlCommand cmd1 = new SqlCommand();
    cmd1.CommandType = CommandType.Text;
    cmd1.Connection = conn1;
    cmd1.CommandText = "SELECT VoterID FROM [Vote] WHERE CandidateID=" + number;
    conn1.Open();
    SqlDataReader myReader1;
    myReader1 = cmd1.ExecuteReader();
    if (myReader1.Read())
    {
      numberOfVotes++;
    }
    while (myReader1.Read())
    {
      numberOfVotes++;
    }
    result[2, 2] = numberOfVotes.ToString();
    Label6.Text = result[2, 2];
    conn1.Close();
  }
  conn.Close();
  //
  cmd = new SqlCommand();
  cmd.CommandType = CommandType.Text;
  cmd.Connection = conn;
  cmd.CommandText = "SELECT CandidateID,FirstName,LastName FROM CandidateDetails WHERE 
                    Party='Shiv Sena'";
```

```
conn.Open();

myReader = cmd.ExecuteReader();
if (myReader.Read())
{
 TextBox7.Text = myReader[1].ToString() + " " + myReader[2].ToString();
 //Label7.Text = myReader[0].ToString();
 TextBox8.Text = "Shiv Sena";
 result[3, 0] = myReader[1].ToString();
 result[3, 1] = myReader[2].ToString();
 int number = int.Parse(myReader[0].ToString());
 int numberOfVotes = 0;
 SqlCommand cmd1 = new SqlCommand();
 cmd1.CommandType = CommandType.Text;
 cmd1.Connection = conn1;
 cmd1.CommandText = "SELECT VoterID FROM [Vote] WHERE CandidateID=" + number;
 conn1.Open();
 SqlDataReader myReader1;
 myReader1 = cmd1.ExecuteReader();
 if (myReader1.Read())
 {
 numberOfVotes++;
 }
 while (myReader1.Read())
 {
   numberOfVotes++;
 }
 result[3, 2] = numberOfVotes.ToString();
 Label7.Text = result[3, 2];
 conn1.Close();
}
conn.Close();
//
cmd = new SqlCommand();
cmd.CommandType = CommandType.Text;
cmd.Connection = conn;
cmd.CommandText = "SELECT CandidateID,FirstName,LastName FROM CandidateDetails WHERE
                  Party='NCP'";
conn.Open();

myReader = cmd.ExecuteReader();
if (myReader.Read())
{
 TextBox9.Text = myReader[1].ToString() + " " + myReader[2].ToString();
 //Label8.Text = myReader[0].ToString();
 TextBox10.Text = "NCP";
 result[4, 0] = myReader[1].ToString();
 result[4, 1] = myReader[2].ToString();
 int number = int.Parse(myReader[0].ToString());
 int numberOfVotes = 0;
 SqlCommand cmd1 = new SqlCommand();
 cmd1.CommandType = CommandType.Text;
 cmd1.Connection = conn1;
 cmd1.CommandText = "SELECT VoterID FROM [Vote] WHERE CandidateID=" + number;
 conn1.Open();
```

```csharp
            SqlDataReader myReader1;
            myReader1 = cmd1.ExecuteReader();
            if (myReader1.Read())
            {
              numberOfVotes++;
            }
            while (myReader1.Read())
            {
              numberOfVotes++;
            }
            result[4, 2] = numberOfVotes.ToString();
            Label8.Text = result[4, 2];
            conn1.Close();
        }
        conn.Close();
        //
        cmd = new SqlCommand();
        cmd.CommandType = CommandType.Text;
        cmd.Connection = conn;
        cmd.CommandText = "SELECT CandidateID,FirstName,LastName FROM CandidateDetails WHERE
                           Party='Samajwadi Party'";
        conn.Open();

        myReader = cmd.ExecuteReader();
        if (myReader.Read())
        {
         TextBox11.Text = myReader[1].ToString() + " " + myReader[2].ToString();
         //Label9.Text = myReader[0].ToString();
         TextBox12.Text = "Samajwadi party";
         result[5, 0] = myReader[1].ToString();
         result[5, 1] = myReader[2].ToString();
         int number = int.Parse(myReader[0].ToString());
         int numberOfVotes = 0;
         SqlCommand cmd1 = new SqlCommand();
         cmd1.CommandType = CommandType.Text;
         cmd1.Connection = conn1;
         cmd1.CommandText = "SELECT VoterID FROM [Vote] WHERE CandidateID=" + number;
         conn1.Open();
         SqlDataReader myReader1;
         myReader1 = cmd1.ExecuteReader();
         if (myReader1.Read())
         {
         numberOfVotes++;
         }
         while (myReader1.Read())
         {
           numberOfVotes++;
         }
         result[5, 2] = numberOfVotes.ToString();
         Label9.Text = result[5, 2];
         conn1.Close();
        }
        conn.Close();
        //
```

```csharp
cmd = new SqlCommand();
cmd.CommandType = CommandType.Text;
cmd.Connection = conn;
cmd.CommandText = "SELECT CandidateID,FirstName,LastName FROM CandidateDetails WHERE
                 Party='SAD'";
conn.Open();

myReader = cmd.ExecuteReader();
if (myReader.Read())
{
 TextBox13.Text = myReader[1].ToString() + " " + myReader[2].ToString();
 //Label10.Text = myReader[0].ToString();
 TextBox14.Text = "SAD";
 result[6, 0] = myReader[1].ToString();
 result[6, 1] = myReader[2].ToString();
 int number = int.Parse(myReader[0].ToString());
 int numberOfVotes = 0;
 SqlCommand cmd1 = new SqlCommand();
 cmd1.CommandType = CommandType.Text;
 cmd1.Connection = conn1;
 cmd1.CommandText = "SELECT VoterID FROM [Vote] WHERE CandidateID=" + number;
 conn1.Open();
 SqlDataReader myReader1;
 myReader1 = cmd1.ExecuteReader();
 if (myReader1.Read())
 {
   numberOfVotes++;
 }
 while (myReader1.Read())
 {
   numberOfVotes++;
 }
 result[6, 2] = numberOfVotes.ToString();
 Label10.Text = result[6, 2];
 conn1.Close();
}
conn.Close();

int[] votes = new int[100];
try
{
 for (int i = 0; i < 7; i++)
 {
   votes[i] = int.Parse(result[i, 2]);
 }
 int max = votes[0];
 int index = 0;
 for (int j = 1; j < 7; j++)
 {
   if (votes[j] > max)
   {
       max = votes[j];
       index = j;
   }
```

```
      }
      VoteTextBox.Text = result[index,0] + " " + result[index,1];
      Label12.Text = result[index,0] + " " + result[index,1];
    }
    catch (Exception e1)
    {
      Label12.Text = "Error"+e1.ToString();
    }
  }
  protected void VoteButton_Click(object sender, EventArgs e)
    {
    }
}
```

4. CONCLUSION

It may be stated here that, although the above project gives an idea of how to accomplish the required task, there can be many enhancements in the project. Powered with your ability to be able to use C#, along with the amazing controls provided by ASP, you can take the project to the next level. The above implementation is just a beginning; it would be a good idea to create such a thing so that people living in remote areas can vote. It is good to learn, but more importantly, it is better to apply your knowledge for the upliftment of the society. It is, therefore, advisable to deliberate upon the given problem, propose a new design, and implement the above idea.

23 Networking

OBJECTIVES

After completing this chapter, the reader will be able to
- Understand the importance of networks
- Explain the different types of networks
- Distinguish between a switch and a router
- Understand the concept of IP address
- Describe the UDP and TCP protocols
- Create a server and a client
- Appreciate the importance of remoting

23.1 INTRODUCTION

Have you ever realized that the Internet you work on, the ATM which you use daily, your cable TV system, and so on are possible owing to the development of computer networks? This chapter introduces the concept of networking and discusses the application of C# to implement things like file sharing, finding out the Internet Protocol address (IP address) of a machine, creating client and server, and so on.

The realization of the need, of going beyond the proprietary solutions and sharing resources, has led to the development of computer networks. The development of personal computers and the problems in sharing data using floppies led to the development of the present-day networks from single-vendor integrated system. The scientists at Palo Alto Research Centre developed a local area network (LAN) called Ethernet, which became a prototype of the network models that followed. This was the starting point of the present-day open computing. This was later followed by the development of the DIX network.

There are many types of networks like LAN, metropolitan area network (MAN), and wide area network (WAN), and these networks help the users to communicate and share resources. However, this discipline reached its present status only after certain standards were developed.

The history of this discipline teaches us the need of standards. The standards are set by many bodies. The most prominent standard is the Open System Interconnect (OSI) reference model and Transmission Control Protocol (TCP) model. The OSI model has seven layers and the TCP model has five layers. Each layer supports particular functionalities. For example, the application layer of the TCP model helps in sharing files and support protocols for network management, mail transfer, and Domain Name System (DNS).

As is evident from the above discussion, networks support multi-vendor environment. In order to do so, functional modularity is needed. The OSI model was the first to incorporate this concept. The physical layer of this model is responsible for the transfer of bits. The bits are passed to the data link layer. The data link layer performs the task of framing. The physical layer handles issues like voltage levels, impedance, and the types of connectors used. It deals with the process of placing signal into transmission media. The data link layer forms frame, which is responsible for successful sending of data to its destination. Therefore, the order of delivery and integrity of frame's content are the main responsibilities of the layer.

The third layer is called network layer and is responsible for the establishment of route through which data can be transferred. It may be noted that some of the packets are lost in the delivery. The request for the retransmission of such packets is generated by the transport layer.

The session layer manages the flow of communication. The task of encryption and compression is handled by the presentation layer. The application layer provides interface between the application and the services provided by the network.

23.1.1 Definition

Networking is connecting computers or 'network-capable devices' in order to share resources and thus achieve optimization.

23.1.2 How are Computers Connected?

Networking is essentially connecting computers with each other. The computers are connected with the help of connecting devices such as routers and switches. Switches generally connect the computers within a building or a campus, whereas routers route the packets through a network. For example, if you want to connect your computer to the Internet, then you need a router, whereas if the computers of your workplace are to be connected with each other, then switches are used. The routers also find the optimal path for a packet. Earlier, switches provided faster transfer of packets, but now, even the routers, for example, those developed by CISCO, offer the same speed.

Switches can be broadly divided into two categories: managed and unmanaged. The unmanaged switches operate on their own, whereas the managed switches can be programmed and hence are much more flexible.

Routers use routing protocols to route a packet to another computer. The protocols are beyond the scope of this book. However, those of you who have studied networking as one of the courses must be familiar with the protocols.

According to CISCO, routers and switches are the unsung heroes that keep the business going. However, there are many more connecting devices such as brouters, gateways, bridges, and so on, which play an equally important role such as switches and routers. Some of the connecting devices are only capable of amplifying a signal. For example, hub is a repeater. It copies data to all ports for transmission. Figure 23.1 shows a simple network.

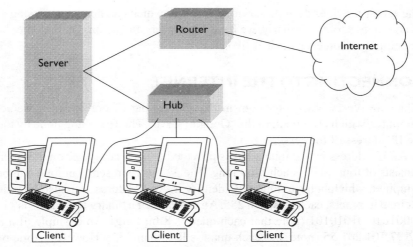

Fig. 23.1 A simple network

23.1.3 Types of Networks

You can connect computers at your workplace in two ways: peer-to-peer and client–server. In peer-to-peer network, the computers are connected to a hub. It is one of the simplest ways of connecting computers. However, it generally does not work with more than five computers. Moreover, peer-to-peer network is not very flexible. However, when the cost of setting up of a network is concerned, peer-to-peer network is a good option. It is depicted in Fig. 23.2.

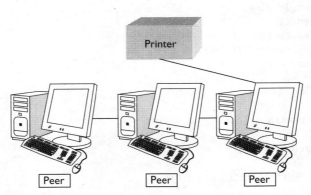

Fig. 23.2 Peer-to-peer network

The client–server network consists of many clients and a server. The clients make requests and the server cater them. The clients can be less powerful when compared with the server. This is generally done to contain the cost of the setup. It may be stated at this point that a client and a server can be set up in the same computer. Figure 23.1 depicts a client–server network.

The computer which stores the information and resources is referred to as the server. The computer is, in fact, loaded with a server software. This chapter deals with developing programs for clients and server, and running those programs in the machines and observing their functions.

The server provides definite services. A server which can help in accessing emails is referred to as an e-mail server. Similarly, we have file servers and so on. On the other hand, the clients can be computers and even devices like printers.

23.2 CONNECTING TO THE INTERNET

When we type www.google.com in the address bar of our browser, we actually connect our computer, which is a client, to the 'Google' server. The first thing done by the browser is to find the IP address of the server.

An IP address is a unique address provided to each computer on the Internet. An IP address consists of four quads, each 8-bit long. The 32 bits represent a unique number assigned to each computer, which helps to uniquely identify it. An IP address can also be written as a set of four decimal numbers, each less than 255. An example of a binary IP address is 11110000.10101010. 00001010.01010101 (note that each quad is 8-bit long). An example of a decimal IP address is 127.101.201.55 (note that each quad is less than 255). However, some of the addresses are reserved, so they cannot be used as IP addresses.

IP addresses can also be classful. Project I examines such addresses. However, this section explains how to find the IP address of a hostname. As IP addresses are difficult to remember, each server, therefore, has a hostname. However, each hostname is mapped to an IP address. DNS helps us to map an IP address to a hostname. In order to find out the IP address, the namespace System. Net is used. The following program finds out the IP addresses of the host name entered by the user.

Program
```
using System;
using System.Collections.Generic;
using System.ComponentModel;
using System.Data;
using System.Drawing;
using System.Linq;
using System.Text;
using System.Windows.Forms;
using System.Net;

namespace IP_address
{
    public partial class Form1 : Form
    {
        public Form1()
        {
            InitializeComponent();
        }
        private void ClearButton_Click(object sender, EventArgs e)
        {
            HostnameTextBox.Clear();
            IPTextBox.Clear();
        }
        private void FindButton_Click(object sender, EventArgs e)
        {
            if (HostnameTextBox.Text != "")
            {
                string hostString = HostnameTextBox.Text;
```

```
            IPHostEntry host = Dns.GetHostEntry(hostString);
            MessageBox.Show(host.HostName);
            if (host.Aliases.Length > 0)
            {
                MessageBox.Show("Hi");
                IPTextBox.Text = "Aliases" + Environment.NewLine;
                foreach (string s in host.Aliases)
                {
                    IPTextBox.AppendText(s);
                    IPTextBox.Text += Environment.NewLine;
                }
            }
            IPTextBox.Text += "Addresses" + Environment.NewLine;
            foreach (IPAddress add in host.AddressList)
            {
                IPTextBox.AppendText(add.ToString());
                IPTextBox.Text += Environment.NewLine;
            }
        }
        else
        {
            MessageBox.Show("Enter hostname", "DNS Lookup", MessageBoxButtons.OK,
            MessageBoxIcon.Error);
            HostnameTextBox.Focus();
        }
    }
}
```

Output

The DNS class provides the facility of domain name resolution. It has many methods to carry out different tasks. Some of them are, however, obsolete. Table 23.1 depicts some of the common methods and the tasks accomplished by them.

Table 23.1 Different methods of DNS class

Method	Function
GetHostAddresses	This method returns the IP addresses for the specific host.
GetHostEntry(IPAddress)	This method resolves an IP address to an IPHostEntry instance.
GetHostName	This method fetches the host name of the local computer.
BeginGetHostAddresses	This method asynchronously returns the IP addresses for the particular host.
EndGetHostAddresses	This method ends an asynchronous request for DNS information.

23.3 TRANSMISSION CONTROL PROTOCOL AND USER DATAGRAM PROTOCOL

A protocol is a set of rules. The Transmission Control Protocol (TCP) is a process to process a protocol. The communication happens through ports. The different protocols using TCP use different port numbers. To send a file, File Transfer Protocol (FTP) is used. It uses port number 21. Another protocol TELNET uses port number 23. TCP is a connection-oriented protocol and makes use of the error control mechanism at the transport layer. In TCP, the data are sent and received as a stream of bytes. The need of a buffer, both at the sender's end and at the receiver's end, therefore, arises. As soon as the read data are acknowledged, the space in the buffer becomes available for use. However, so as to make the flow of data smooth, the IP layer groups the bytes together to form packets.

The TCP, therefore, assigns a specific number to each byte in a segment and also to the segments. It may be stated that the acknowledgement number send by the TCP is the next byte it intends to receive.

The User Datagram Protocol (UDP) is an unreliable transfer protocol. The communication happens through ports. The different protocols using UDP use different port numbers. For Remote Procedure Call (RPC), port number 111 is used. The Simple Network Management Protocol (SNMP) uses port number 161. UDP is connectionless protocol and does not make use of the error control mechanism. The UDP packets are referred to as datagrams. The header of a datagram contains information about source port number, destination port number, and the length of the datagram.

It may be stated that UDP does not provide any flow control. The error control provided by UDP is also minimal. UDP provides only checksum. Therefore, UDP is suited for those applications that have the internal error control mechanism or else, TCP should be used.

23.4 SERVER

As stated in Section 23.1.2, a server serves client(s), and the requests from a client are catered by a server. For example, a server displays the files in a particular directory. The list of files is asked by a client. On getting the request, the server sends the data in bytes. The client, on the other hand, establishes the connection and requests the server to pass on the list of files.

In order to accomplish the above task, the following methods are needed. Table 23.2 gives the methods, their classes, and the functions accomplished by them.

Table 23.2 Methods and classes required to create a server

Name	Class or interface	Function
Directory	Class	The class has static methods. It helps to create and manipulate directories and subdirectories. It is a sealed class.
IEnumerable	Interface	It helps to iterate through a collection.
StringBuilder	Class	It helps to build a mutable string of characters.
TCPClient	Class	This class helps to create a TCP client.
NetworkStream	Class	This class gives underlying stream of data.
File	Class	This class helps in the Input/Output functionalities as per a file is concerned.
GetFileName(file)	Method	This method gets the name of the file; it is an element in the Directory.GetFiles.
TCPListener	Class	This class intercepts the connections from a TCP client. The arguments of the constructor of the class are IP address and Port number.
AcceptTcpClient()	Method	This method accepts the request of establishing a connection from a TCP client.

In order to create a server, the following steps must be carried out:

Step 1 Create a new project called Networking. Add a class in the project called Helper class. The class will have a GetFileList method. Figure 23.3 shows the snapshot of how to add a class.

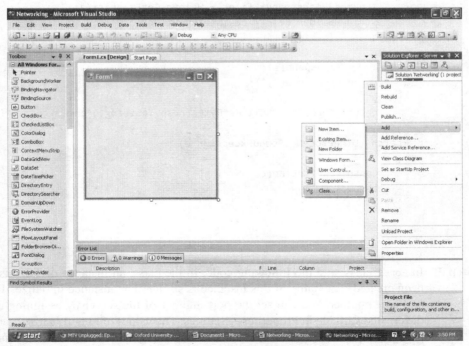

Fig. 23.3 How to add the helper class?

Step 2 In the class, insert the following code. The class helps to generate a list of files from 'C:\files' folder. The methods used by the class are explained in Table 23.2.

The `resp StringBuilder` generates response consisting of the list of files from the directory (C:\files). However, the output of the function is an array of bytes that needs to be converted into characters by the client. It may also be noted that ASCII ending has been used in the application.

```csharp
using System;
using System.Collections.Generic;
using System.Linq;
using System.Text;
using System.IO;

namespace Networking
{
    internal static class Helper
    {
        internal static IEnumerable<string> GetFileList()
        {
            return from file in Directory.GetFiles(
            Properties.Settings.Default.FileDirectory)
            select Path.GetFileName(file);
        }
        internal static byte[] GetFileListBytes()
        {
            try
            {
                IEnumerable<string> files = Helper.GetFileList();
                StringBuilder resp = new StringBuilder();
                oreach (string s in files)
                {
                    resp.Append(s);
                    resp.Append(";");
                }
                return Encoding.ASCII.GetBytes(resp.ToString());
            }
            catch (DirectoryNotFoundException e)
            {
                Console.WriteLine(e.ToString());
                throw;
            }
        }
    }
}
```

Step 3 In `Form1` class, add the following code. In the class, an instance of TCPListener has been created. The name of this instance is `server`. The instance initializes IP address and port number. You can set the port number of the server by assigning a value to the created variable in Properties→Settings. The values of `FileDirectory` variable and port (int type) can be set in the value column. Figure 23.4 shows the settings tab of the properties.

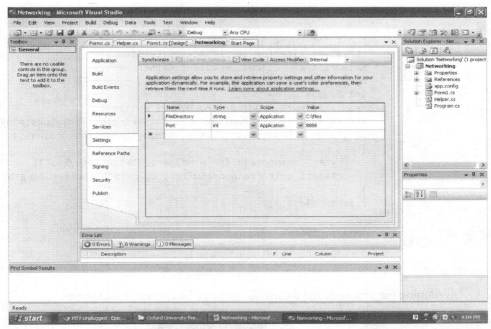

Fig. 23.4 Settings tab

The server can be started by the `Server.start` method. A client is created by making an instance of `TCPClient` class. The `AcceptTCPClient()` method helps to establish a connection to the client. An instance of `NetworkStream` class helps to call the `GetStream()` method. The `read` method of this instance would be used to read data from the stream. If request starts with the string 'List', then the `GetFileListBytes` of the `Helper` class is called. After the task has been accomplished, the `Close()` method is invoked.

```
using System;
using System.Collections.Generic;
using System.ComponentModel;
using System.Data;
using System.Drawing;
using System.Linq;
using System.Text;
using System.Windows.Forms;
using System.Net;
using System.Net.Sockets;
using System.IO;

namespace Networking
{
    public partial class Form1 : Form
    {
        TCPListener   server   =   new   TCPListener(IPAddress.Any, Properties.Settings.
        Default.Port);
        public Form1()
        {
            server.Start();
            MessageBox.Show("Server    Started",    "TCP",    MessageBoxButtons.OK,
            MessageBoxIcon.Asterisk);
```

```
            while (true)
            {
                const int bufferSize = 8192;
                TCPClient client = server.AcceptTCPClient();
                NetworkStream clientS = client.GetStream();
                byte[] buffer = new byte[bufferSize];
                int read = 0;
                read = clientS.Read(buffer, 0, bufferSize);
                string request = Encoding.ASCII.GetString(buffer).Substring(0, read);
                if (request.StartsWith("List", StringComparison.Ordinal))
                {
                    byte[] responseBuffer = Helper.GetFileListBytes();
                    clientS.Write(responseBuffer, 0, responseBuffer.Length);
                }
                clientS.Close();
            }
            InitializeComponent();
        }
    }
}
```

On running the program, the following message box would be displayed:

23.5 CLIENT

In order to create a client, add the using System.Net.Sockets and using System.IO. In order to create a TCP request, an instance of TCPClient and an instance of IPHostEntry needs to be created. This instance would be initialized by the GetHostEntry method of the DNS class. The client would then be connected and its address list would be fetched. The TCPClient would then be connected to the server and the results would be fetched through MemoryStream. The clientS.Read puts data in the byte array, thus generating the output.

In order to create a client, design a form in the WindowForm Projects. The form should have a text box with multiline attribute 'true'. The event handler of the button having the text 'Populate List' will contain the required code. Figure 23.5 shows the design of the form.

```
using System;
using System.Collections.Generic;
using System.ComponentModel;
using System.Data;
using System.Drawing;
using System.Linq;
using System.Text;
using System.Windows.Forms;
using System.Net;
using System.Net.Sockets;
using System.IO;
```

```
namespace Client
{
    public partial class Form1 : Form
    {
        public const int buffSize = 8192;
        public Form1()
        {
            InitializeComponent();
        }
        private TCPClient ConnectServer()
        {
            TCPClient client = new TCPClient();
            IPHostEntry host = DNS.GetHostEntry(Properties.Settings.Default.Server);
            var address = (from x in host.AddressList where x.AddressFamily
                == AddressFamily.InterNetwork select x).First();
            client.Connect(address.ToString(),
            Properties.Settings.Default.ServerPort);
            return client;
        }
        private void ListButton_Click(object sender, EventArgs e)
        {
            TCPClient client = ConnectServer();
            NetworkStream clientS = client.GetStream();
            string request = "List";
            byte[] reqBuffer = Encoding.ASCII.GetBytes(request);
            clientS.Write(reqBuffer, 0, reqBuffer.Length);
            byte[] responseBuffer = new byte[buffSize];
            MemoryStream memory = new MemoryStream();
            int byteread = 0;
            do
            {
                byteread = clientS.Read(responseBuffer, 0, buffSize);
                memory.Write(responseBuffer, 0, byteread);
                foreach(byte b in responseBuffer)
                {
                    if((char)b==';')
                    {
                        textBox1.AppendText(Environment.NewLine);
                    }
                    textBox1.AppendText(((char)b).ToString());
                }
            } while(byteread > 0);
        }
    }
}
```

Output

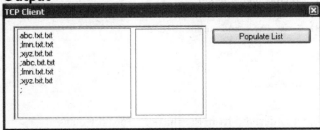

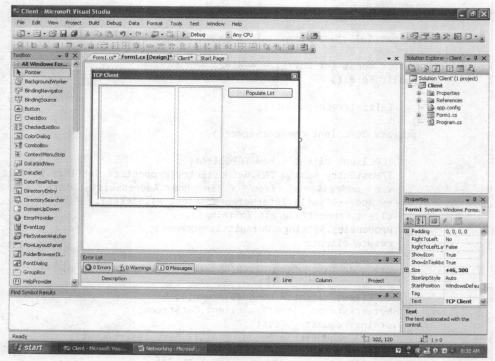

Fig. 23.5 Design of `Client`

23.6 REMOTING

Remoting helps us to use objects from different processes in the same computer or objects on different computers in order to build a client-side application. Therefore, with the help of remoting, we can use objects that are on different computers in our client application and can also implement inter-process communication.

Remoting helps us to build a distributed system and also comes with an added advantage of combining objects using different protocols. It gives your applications power to communicate with a client-side application or a web application. We need to have a server camouflaged as a host application that listens to the requests. A client camouflaged as an application that makes requests and a remotable object. It may be stated that in order to make the system work, one must configure the remoting system in each of the applications. The following snippet helps create a remotable object:

```
public class RemotableApp : MarshalByRefObject
{
    private string Str = "Hi I am from the RemotableApp";
    public string fun()
    {
        return str;
    }
}
```

Therefore, every remotable object is derived from `MarshalByRefObject` class.

SUMMARY

The chapter introduces the concept of networking. As most of you might not be familiar with the intricacies of a network, every effort, therefore, has been made to keep things as simple as possible. The chapter starts with the definition of a network and the basic introduction to connection devices. The difference between a switch and a router has been clearly explained. The chapter then gives an introduction to IP addresses and a program to find the IP addresses from DNS. In order to understand the concepts, the idea of TCP and UDP protocols is also needed. Creating a server and a client is the most important programming task in order to implement a network. The last section introduces the concept of remoting so that the creation of distributed system can be facilitated.

GLOSSARY

Networking Networking is connecting computers or 'network-capable devices' in order to share resources and thus achieve optimization.
Remoting Remoting helps us to use objects from different processes in the same computer or objects on different computers in order to build a client-side application.
Transmission Control Protocol It is a process to process a protocol and a connection-oriented reliable protocol.
UDP It is a connectionless, unreliable protocol.
DNS DNS is a naming system for computers and other devices that are connected to the Internet.
IP Address It is an address that uniquely identifies a connection on the Internet.
Routers They are the connecting devices that route the packets in accordance with a routing algorithm.

POINTS TO REMEMBER

- A network can be peer-to-peer or client–server type.
- A client–server network is more flexible.
- A server is loaded with server software. It is loaded with information or resources that can be accessed by the clients.
- There are many connecting devices like routers, switches, brouters, gateways, and so on.
- Routers forward packets to another computer and find the best possible path of a packet.
- Switches connect computers within a local area.
- Hub is a repeater. It copies data to all ports for transmission.
- IP address uniquely identifies a computer connected to the Internet.
- A binary IP address (IPV4) has 32 bits. It has four quads.
- A decimal IP address has 4 quads. Each quad is less than 255.
- Not all possible 2^{32} addresses can be used; some of them are used for special purposes.

EXERCISES

I. Multiple-choice Questions

1. Which of the following statements is not an advantage of networking?
   (a) Networking allows you to share data.
   (b) Network allows you to share devices like printers.
   (c) Networking increases productivity.
   (d) Networking promotes hacking.

2. Which of the following are the examples of connecting devices?
   (a) Switch (b) Router
   (c) Hub   (d) All of these

3. Which connecting device generally connects the computers within a building or a campus but cannot route the packets.

(a) Switch (b) Router
(c) Hub (d) None of these
4. Which of the following are the categories of switches?
(a) Managed (b) Unmanaged
(c) Both (d) None of these
5. What is the function of a hub?
(a) A hub is a repeater. It copies data to all ports for transmission.
(b) A hub finds optimal path of a packet.
(c) A hub connects two heterogeneous networks.
(d) None of these
6. In which of the following types of connection, computers are generally connected to a hub?
(a) Peer-to-peer (b) Client–Server
(c) Both (d) None of these
7. Which of the following generally does not work for more than five computers?
(a) Peer-to-peer (b) Client–Server
(c) Both (d) None of these
8. Which of the following is a correct IP address?
(a) 11110000.10101010.00001010.01010101
(b) 11110000.101010.000010.010101
(c) 1111000.1010101.0000101.0101010
(d) 111100000.101010100.000010100.010101010
9. Which of the following is a correct IP address?
(a) 127.401.201.55 (b) 300.101.0.50
(c) 127.101.201.55 (d) 255.256.257.258
10. Which of the following uniquely identifies a computer on the Internet?
(a) IP (b) PC (c) IC (d) II
11. Which of the following is not true as per IP addresses are concerned?
(a) A binary IP address has 32 bits. It has four quads.
(b) A decimal IP address has 4 quads. Each quad is less than 255.
(c) Not all possible 2^{32} addresses can be used; some of them are used for special purposes.
(d) IP acts as a firewall.
12. Which of the following is a process to process a protocol?
(a) TCP (b) UDP
(c) IPL (d) None of these
13. Which port is used by TCP to send a file?
(a) 21 (b) 20 (c) 420 (d) 240
14. Which port is used by TELNET?
(a) 23 (b) 32 (c) 420 (d) 240
15. Which of the following is not true as per TCP is concerned?
(a) TCP is a process to process a protocol.
(b) It does not use port numbers.
(c) It is connection oriented.
(d) Data are send and received as a stream of bytes.
16. Which port is used for remote procedure call?
(a) 21 (b) 23 (c) 111 (d) 420
17. The UDP packets are referred to as _____.
(a) Datagrams (b) Datarams
(c) Rams (d) Data
18. Which of the following are contained in the header of a datagram?
(a) Source port number
(b) Destination port number
(c) Length of the datagram
(d) All of these
19. Which of the following does not provide any flow control?
(a) UDP (b) TCP
(c) Both (a) and (b) (d) None of these
20. Which of the following is not true as per UDP is concerned?
(a) UDP is an unreliable transfer protocol.
(b) It does not use port numbers.
(c) It is connectionless.
(d) UDP only provides checksum.

II. Review Questions

1. What is a network? What are the different types of networks?
2. Differentiate between a switch and a router.
3. What is a hub?
4. Differentiate between a TCP and an UDP.
5. Differentiate between a peer-to-peer and a client–server networks.
6. What is an IP address?
7. What is a server? Implement a server in C#.
8. What is a client? Implement a client in C#.
9. What is meant by remoting?
10. Write a program that displays all the IP addresses of a domain entered by the user.

24 Deployment

OBJECTIVES

After completing this chapter, the reader will be able to
Understand the importance of an installer
Explain the different types of installers
Learn the concept of an installer project
Create an installer project
Understand the importance of `ClickOnce` Technology
Create an installer using `ClickOnce`

24.1 INTRODUCTION

When I was in the first year of B.Tech. and got my personal computer, I had to install many software in it. Windows 98 was the prevalent operating system at that point of time. When I was in the process of developing applications that could be installed, I started looking for something that could help me develop an installer. This was the requirement of many programming enthusiasts, and to ease the process, Microsoft created Windows Installer followed by the ClickOnce technology to help accomplishing the above target.

When we develop an application, then we would not probably give the executable file to our client. We would like to give a complete setup that would not only install the application but also help in updating it from time to time. ClickOnce is meant for this purpose only. It offers many advantages and hence makes the installation of our application fun. There is another good reason for making the setup file. It would package our application along with other dependencies in a presentable way.

To summarize, the setup file helps us achieve the following goals:

1. It helps engulf the dependencies in the package.
2. It helps the customer update the application as and when it is modified.
3. It helps specify the versions and hence implement software engineering.
4. It makes the software presentable.

From the above points, the third point is very important. You can become a software engineer if you are able to develop programs. The idea that the software is much more than a program is correct, but one has to know programming in order to develop a software or give his or her hypothesis on how they should be tested. So far, this book has helped you to develop programs, and this chapter will teach you how to create an installation file. There is an ancillary reason to learn making installation files. The reason of making an installation file is to make our application look good. People who do not understand programming would at least find the installer amusing.

24.2 SETUP PROJECT

The setup project helps to create an installer, which is flexible and even capable of modifying registries. With the help of a setup project, directories can also be created in the target computer. It also provides the opportunity of adding extra features in the installer application. The .msi file, which is created, launches the setup wizard when clicked.

The setup project has the following functionalities:
1. It helps create directories in the target computer.
2. It helps add extra features to the installer.
3. It helps modify the registry.
4. It helps copy files in the target computer.
5. It creates an .msi file, which starts the setup wizard.

It may also be stated that to clearly segregate the functionality, the setup project has many editors, and some of them are listed below:
1. File System Editor
2. Registry Editor
3. User Interface Editor
4. Custom Actions Editor
5. Launch Conditions Editor
6. File Types Editor

In order to configure the application in the file system of the target computer, the File System Editor may be used. The editor has two parts. The first part is the navigation pane, which has the list of folders. The folders depict the standard folders of the target computer. The right side of the pane displays the details when a folder in the left pane is selected.

The User Interface Editor, on the other hand, has just one pane. It contains a list of user interface dialog boxes. The options of a standard and an administrative installation are provided to the user. The stages of installation are given by the start progress and end node.

The Registry Editor helps to add the key value pairs in the registries of the target computer. It also contains the navigation and details panes. When a registry hive is selected, the details pane displays them.

The File Types Editor helps to map the applications with the type of files. In order to define custom actions, the Custom Actions Editor is used, and to set the launch conditions, the Launch Conditions Editor is used.

In order to make the installation file run only on computers having version greater than or equal to a particular version of windows, set the VersionNT property to the requisite value.

Some of the important properties of a setup project are given in Table 24.1.

Let us now move to the creation of a setup project. In order to create a setup project, the following steps must be carried out:

Step 1 Open any project that you have created in the previous chapters. The Genetic Phase 1 project has been taken as example.

Table 24.1 Properties of setup project

Property	Explanation
Author	Has information about the author.
Localization	Provides local information.
Manufacturer	We can enter our company name as the value of this property.
TargetPlatform	Specifies the target platform (e.g., x86).
Title	Contains the title of the program.
AddRemoveProgramIcon	We can specify the icon of our application here.
Version	Gives the version of the program.

Step 2 Go to File→Add→New Project in the visual studio. In the window that follows, select other projects and go to other project types→setup and deployment and select a setup project. The above steps have been depicted in Figs 24.1 and 24.2.

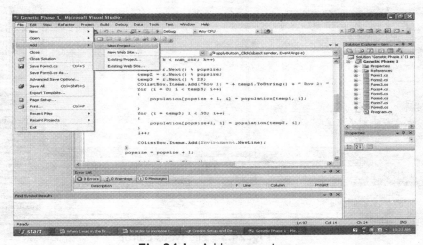

Fig. 24.1 Add new project

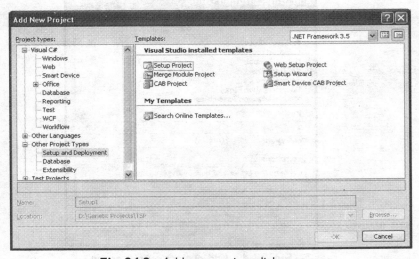

Fig. 24.2 Add new project dialog group

The screen that follows is shown in Fig. 24.3.

Step 3 Now go to the setup project in the Solution Explorer and right click on the setup1 project. Go to View→File System. In the File System Editor, Add project output. Figure 24.4 shows the Add Project Output Group.

Step 4 Create a shortcut to the primary output from Genetic Phase 1 by right clicking on the 'Primary output from the Genetic Phase 1 (Active)'.

Step 5 Now go to the User Interface Editor. The interface editor is shown in Fig. 24.5.

Step 6 Add a dialog by right clicking on Install→Start→Add Dialog. Figure 24.6 shows the Add Dialog.

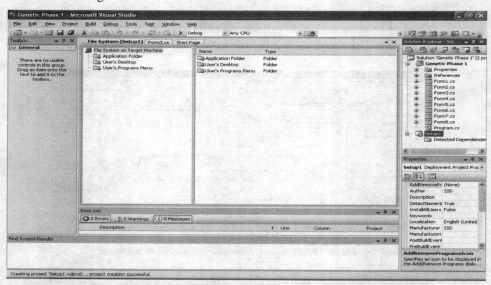

Fig. 24.3 File Types Editor

Fig. 24.4 Add project output group

Fig. 24.5 User Interface Editor

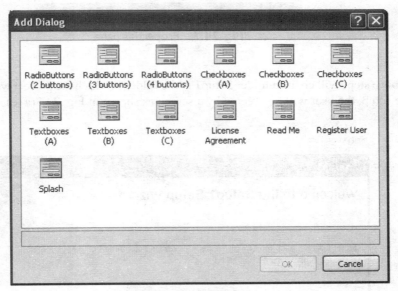

Fig. 24.6 Add dialog

In order to change the values of properties of the dialog, right click on the dialog and set the values of the properties. The properties pane is shown in Fig. 24.7.

Step 7 Prerequisites can also be installed. In order to do so, select the deployment project and right click. Go to properties→Expand the Configuration Properties→Build property page. Now, click the Prerequisites button.

Step 8 In the Prerequisites dialog box, the Create setup program to install prerequisite components box should be checked. If it not checked, then check it. Finally, in the Choose which prerequisites to install list, select the prerequisites that is to be installed.

Step 9 Click OK. Go to Build Application.

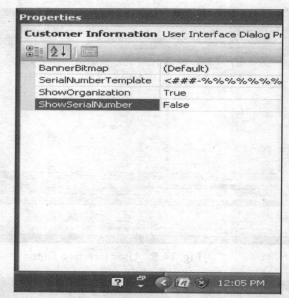

Fig. 24.7 Properties pane

The above steps will create a folder Setup1 in the folder in which the project was saved. Clicking on the setup, the user will be greeted by a screen as shown in Fig. 24.8(a–e).

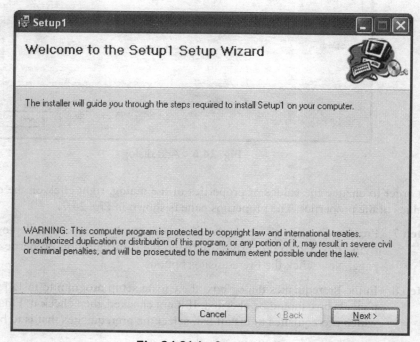

Fig. 24.8(a) Setup screen

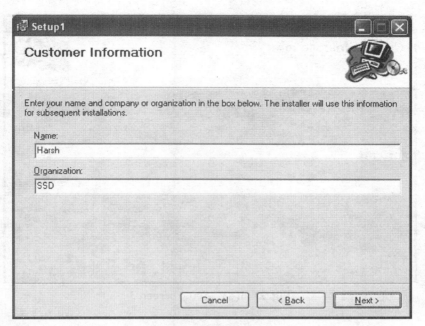

Fig. 24.8(b) Setup screen 1

Fig. 24.8(c) Setup screen 2

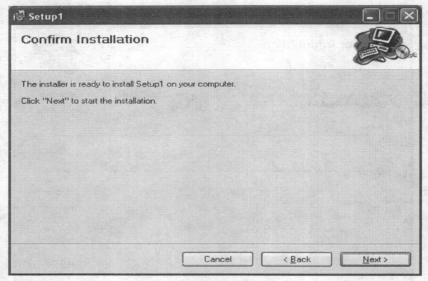

Fig. 24.8(d)   Setup screen 3

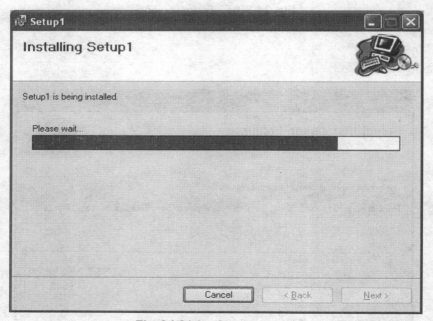

Fig. 24.8(e)   Setup screen 4

24.3 ClickOnce TECHNOLOGY

The ClickOnce technology addresses most of the problems in the previous installers and at the same time has excellent usability. It is very easy to use. A person who has never made an installer or the theorists who are not familiar with data link libraries and dependencies would find ClickOnce very useful. The making of an installation file is now just a click away. All the complexities and the requirements of in-depth knowledge for making an installation file are now a thing of past.

With the help of ClickOnce technology, the following task can be easily accomplished:

1. Self-updating applications can be created. Such applications will automatically check for the updates and hence will download the requisite files.
2. Installation can be done through a variety of sources such as Internet, CD, or file share.
3. ClickOnce applications are isolated from the system.
4. The applications can run on any security zones although the Internet or Intranet is the default security zone.

On completion of installation, the screen shown in Fig. 24.9 will be displayed.

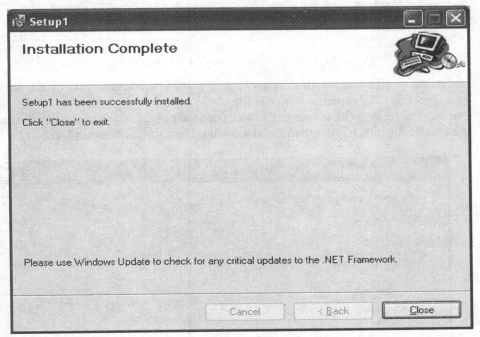

Fig. 24.9 End of setup screen

In order to create a ClickOnce application, go to the properties of the project and specify the publication location. The publication location can be a File Transfer Protocol (FTP) or Hyper Text Transfer Protocol (HTTP) address.

The install mode can also be specified in a ClickOnce application. The install mode can be either online or both online and offline. The online mode allows the application to be used only when the user is connected to the Internet. However, 'both online and offline' options allow the application to be used as and when desired. Figure 24.10 shows the Application tab.

The property window's Application tab has an Update button. Clicking on the button displays a screen wherein the minimum version of the application can be specified. This screen

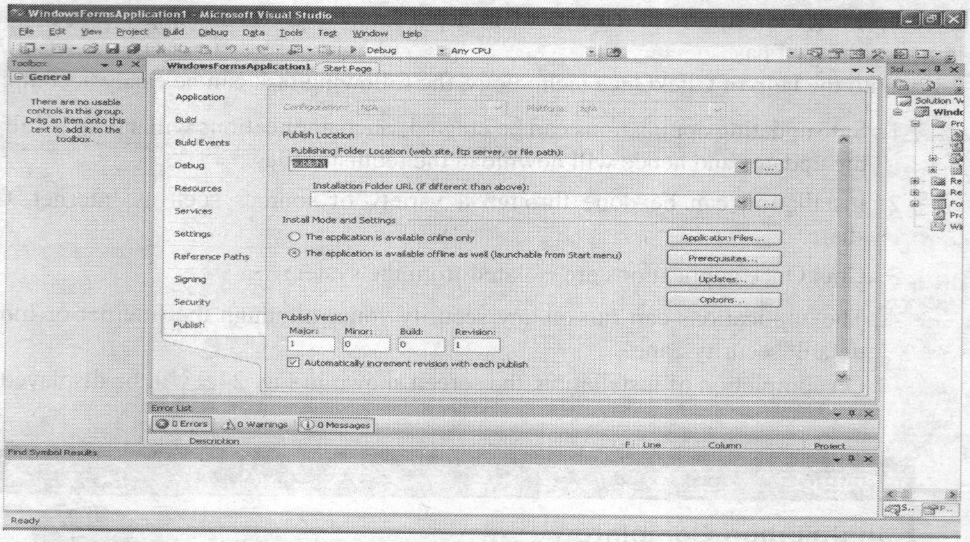

536 *Programming in C#*

Fig. 24.10 Application tab of properties

also lets the user choose whether the application should be updated every time it starts or after a specified time. The screen is shown in Fig. 24.11.

In order to create a ClickOnce application, open the project and right click on the name of the project in the Solution Explorer and go to properties. The screen as shown in Fig. 24.12 is displayed.

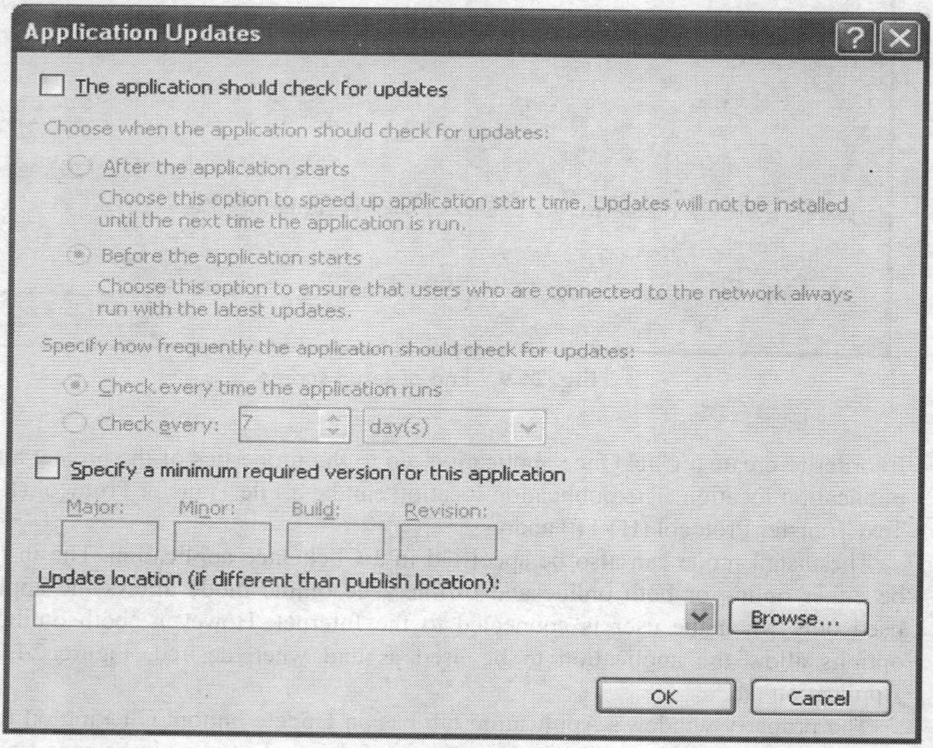

Fig. 24.11 Application update

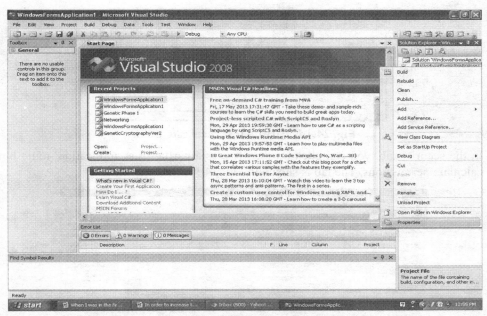

Fig. 24.12 Starting a ClickOnce application

The properties window of a project has been shown in Fig. 24.13.

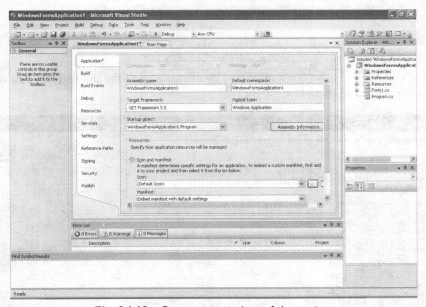

Fig. 24.13 Properties window of the project

You can also create a Test Certificate by going to the security tabs→Generate certificates. The test certificates will ensure the customer that the software has been created by you. The Create Test Certificate window is shown in Fig. 24.14.

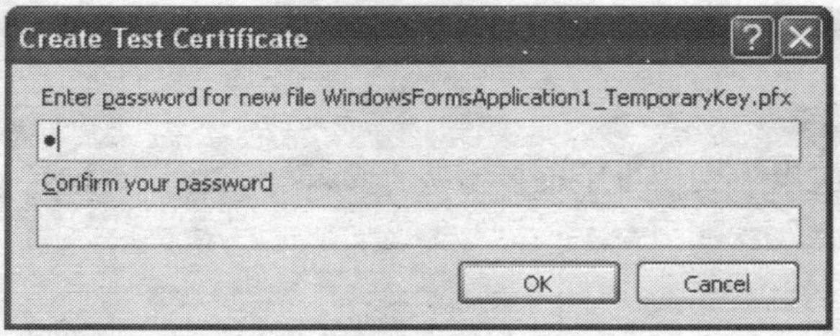

Fig. 24.14 Create test certificate dialog

In the security tab, you can click on the 'This is a partial trust application' radio button and calculate permissions. The tab is shown in Fig. 24.15.

Fig. 24.15 Security tab

Finally, you can publish your application by clicking on to the publish tab. You will be greeted with a screen as shown in Fig. 24.16(a–d).

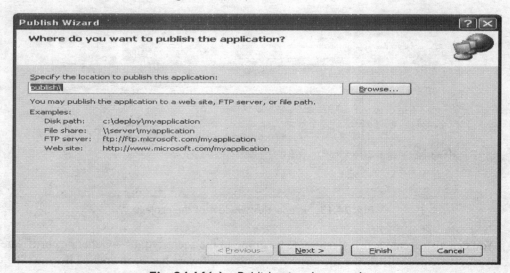

Fig. 24.16(a) Publish wizard screen 1

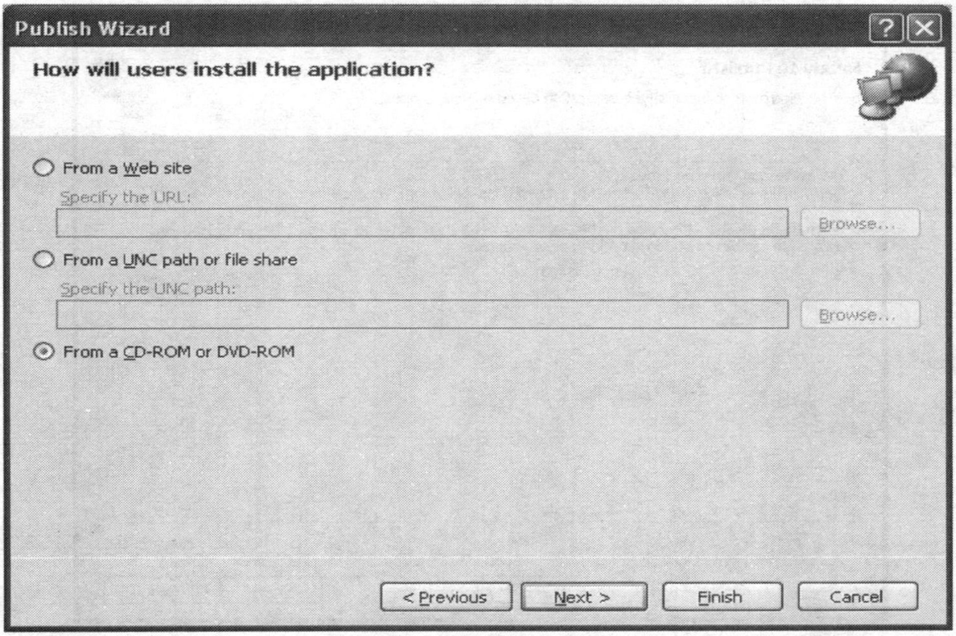

Fig. 24.16(b) Publish wizard screen 2

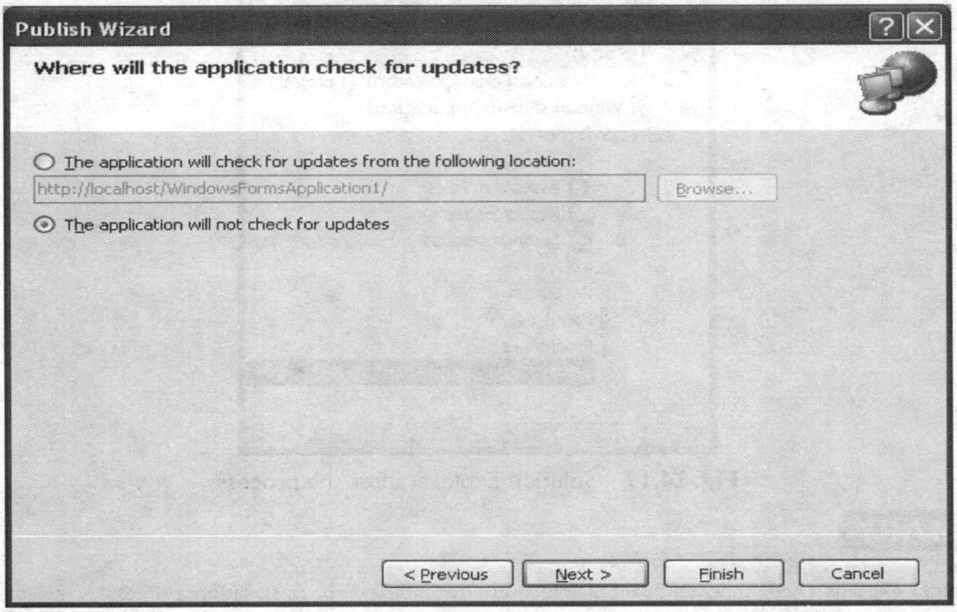

Fig. 24.16(c) Publish wizard screen 3

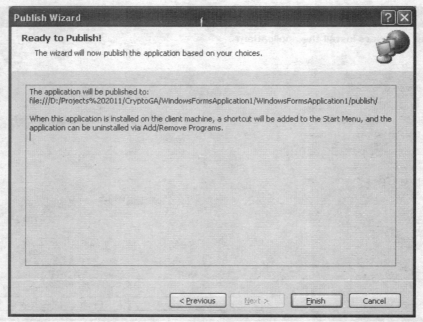

Fig. 24.16(d) Publish wizard screen 4

The process creates an .msi file that can be seen in the Solution Explorer. Figure 24.17 shows the screenshot of the Solution Explorer after the process.

Fig. 24.17 Solution Explorer after the process

SUMMARY

This chapter explains a very important part of software development, that is, deployment. Visual Studio provides two major ways of creating an installer. The first is the installation project and the second is the ClickOnce technology. The installation process is flexible, intricate, robust, and reliable. The ClickOnce, on the other hand, is for those who are technically not very sound. The ClickOnce technology, though simple, is not as flexible as Installer project. Depending on one's needs and the type of installer required, one can choose the type of installer that will be apt for the project. However, it may also be noted that it is not always required to create a setup with a program. However, if setup is required, then this chapter will be definitely helpful.

GLOSSARY

ClickOnce It is a deployment technology. It helps us to publish our work easily and reliably.

Installer Project It helps us to create directories in the target computer, add extra features to our installer, modify registry, and copy files in the target computer.

POINTS TO REMEMBER

- A setup file helps the customer to update the application as and when it is modified.
- A setup project has many editors like File System Editor, Registry Editor, User Interface Editor, Custom Actions Editor, Launch Conditions Editor, and File Types Editor.
- In a ClickOnce project, one can create a Test Certificate by going to the security tabs→Generate certificates.
- In ClickOnce, self-updating applications can be created, which will automatically check for the updates and hence will download the requisite files.

EXERCISES

I. Multiple-choice Questions

1. ClickOnce technology enables the user to publish work to _____.
   (a) Web sites   (b) File share
   (c) FTP sites   (d) All of these

2. ClickOnce technology can be configured to install updates _____.
   (a) every time an application starts
   (b) after a fixed time
   (c) Both (a) and (b)
   (d) None of these

3. What is the default security zone of ClickOnce applications?
   (a) Internet   (b) Fully trusted
   (c) Both (a) and (b)   (d) None of these

4. If additional permissions are required by an application whose installer is being created using ClickOnce, then which of the following tasks is to be performed?
   (a) Calculate permissions
   (b) Set permissions
   (c) Get permissions
   (d) None of these

5. Which of the following tasks is mandatory while building an application using ClickOnce technology?
   (a) Calculating permissions
   (b) Setting the frequency of updates
   (c) Clicking setup project
   (d) All of these

6. Which property page helps you to set the minimum version required for an application?
   (a) Publish   (b) Security
   (c) Signing   (d) Resources

7. Which property page helps you to set the frequency the application should check for updates?
   (a) Publish   (b) Security
   (c) Signing   (d) Resources

8. Which property page helps you to set when the application should check for updates?
   (a) Publish   (b) Security
   (c) Signing   (d) Resources

9. Which property page helps you to set whether the application should check for the updates or not?
   (a) Publish   (b) Security
   (c) Signing   (d) Resources

10. Which button on the property helps you to set properties of updates?
    (a) Updates   (b) Application Files
    (c) Prerequisites   (d) Options

11. Where do you specify the publish location?
    (a) Publish page→publish location
    (b) Security page→publish location
    (c) Any of these
    (d) Both (a) and (b)
12. Which of the following is more flexible?
    (a) ClickOnce
    (b) Setup project
    (c) Both are equally good
    (d) None of these
13. Which of the following is an editor in a setup project?
    (a) File System Editor (b) Registry Editor
    (c) File Types Editor   (d) All of these
14. Which of the following is an editor in setup project?
    (a) User Interface Editor
    (b) Custom Applications Editor
    (c) Launch Conditions Editor
    (d) All of these
15. Which of the following editors helps you to add the project output to the setup project?
    (a) File System Editor
    (b) Launch Conditions Editor
    (c) Both (a) and (b)
    (d) None of these
16. Which of the following helps you to associate an icon with your application in installation project?
    (a) File System Editor (b) File Types Editor
    (c) Both (a) and (b)   (d) None of these
17. Which property helps you to set the minimum version of the operating system in which your application needs to be installed?
    (a) VersionNT   (b) WindowVersion
    (c) Both (a) and (b)   (d) None of these
18. Which of the following applications provides local information for the application?
    (a) Localization   (b) Globalization
    (c) Communalism   (d) Communists
19. Which of the following specifies the command after the build ends?
    (a) Post-event   (b) Pre-event
    (c) Both (a) and (b)   (d) None of these
20. Which of the following specifies the command before the build begins?
    (a) Post-build   (b) Pre-build
    (c) Both (a) and (b)   (d) None of these
21. Custom action can be used to execute code upon which of the events?
    (a) Install   (b) Commit
    (c) Rollback   (d) All of these
22. How can you rollback the installation of a setup project?
    (a) By throwing InstallException
    (b) By throwing RollbackException
    (c) By throwing LaunchException
    (d) None of these
23. Where is the project that contains custom action specified?
    (a) Custom Actions Editor
    (b) File Types Editor
    (c) Both (a) and (b)
    (d) None of these
24. Which of the following provides an opportunity to run your own code at the time of setup?
    (a) Installer project   (b) BuildProject
    (c) CompileProject   (d) None of these
25. Which of the following helps you to create an installer?
    (a) ClickOnce   (b) Installer Project
    (c) Both (a) and (b)   (d) None of these

II. Review Questions

1. What is the importance of deployment? What are the various options available in Visual Studio to make a deployment project?
2. Explain the various features of ClickOnce technology. How is it better than Windows Installer?
3. Explain the advantages of installation project over ClickOnce?
4. What is the importance of File System Editor?
5. What is the importance of File Types Editor?
6. What is the importance of Custom Actions Editor?
7. What is the importance of Launch Conditions Editor?
8. What is the importance of pre-install and post-install?
9. How can you associate an icon with your application?
10. How can you rollback the installation project?

25 Towards WPF and WCF

OBJECTIVES

After completing this chapter, the reader will be able to
- # Draw a 2D figure in C# using GDI+
- # Explain the importance of WPF
- # Understand the architecture of WPF
- # Create a basic WPF project
- # Understand the concept of web services
- # Create a basic web service
- # Install a web service
- # Create a basic window service
- # Install a window service
- # Describe the concept of remoting
- # Appreciate the need and concept of WCF
- # Understand the architecture of WCF
- # Understand the classes required to implement messaging

25.1 INTRODUCTION

The previous chapters have already dealt with the basics of programming and COM. It is also important to make your project look good. In order to do that, dazzling graphics and fonts are needed. Moreover, one of the goals of .NET is to make projects whose components are created in different languages. So, there is a need to understand the basics of Windows Communication also. This chapter gives an introduction of Windows Presentation Foundation (WPF) and Windows Communication Foundation (WCF). WPF helps to create visually stunning user interfaces (UI). It is, therefore, necessary to understand graphics device interface classes (GDI+) before starting it. The WCF is an enhancement of remoting and web services. Therefore, these two topics have also been included.

25.2 GRAPHICS DEVICE INTERFACE CLASSES: GDI+

This section gives a brief overview of the graphics class in C#. The GDI+ in C# helps us to draw. To draw an image, you need 'Drawing Surface'. Drawing Surface is an area in which a drawing can be delivered. It can be of three types: the pages that are to be sent to a printer, the images, and Windows and controls. In C#, the graphics class encapsulates the Drawing Surface. In order to create a Graphics object, you can override the OnPaint(PaintEventArgs e) method. This method helps you to do many tasks including simple ones like drawing a drawing.

For example, to draw an ellipse, you can instantiate graphics and set the object to e.Graphics, where e is the argument of the method. After the task has been accomplished, you must call the Dispose() method of the graphics object. The coordinates x and y are referenced from the top left point of the window. The top left point of the window is (0, 0) or the origin. Figure 25.1 shows a basic form, and Fig. 25.2 shows an ellipse in GDI+.

To draw an image, you need to include the System.Drawing.Drawing2D namespace in the project. You also need to override the method OnPaint in the project. The method for ellipse takes five arguments. The first argument is a Pen object. The object of the Pen class takes two arguments: the color and the thickness. The second and the third arguments of the DrawEllipse method are the top left point of the ellipse. The next two arguments depict the width and the height of the ellipse.

```
using System;
using System.Collections.Generic;
using System.ComponentModel;
using System.Data;
using System.Drawing;
using System.Linq;
using System.Text;
using System.Windows.Forms;
using System.Drawing.Drawing2D;
namespace WindowsFormsApplication1
{
    public partial class Form1 : Form
    {
        public Form1()
```

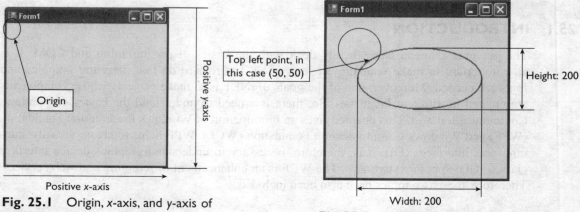

Fig. 25.1 Origin, x-axis, and y-axis of a form

Fig. 25.2 Ellipse using GDI+

```csharp
        {
            InitializeComponent();
        }

        private void Form1_Load(object sender, EventArgs e)
        {

        }
        protected override void OnPaint(PaintEventArgs e)
        {
            base.OnPaint(e);
            Graphics g = e.Graphics;
            Pen p = new Pen(Color.Red, 2);
            g.DrawEllipse(p, 50, 50, 200, 100);
            g.Dispose();
        }
    }
}
```

Having seen the creation of an ellipse, let us now see how to draw a face. To draw a smiling face, you can use the DrawArc method that takes initial *x*-coordinate, initial *y*-coordinate, width, height, start angle, and sweep angle as its parameters. The Brushes.Color fills the shape with the specified colour.

```csharp
using System;
using System.Collections.Generic;
using System.ComponentModel;
using System.Data;
using System.Drawing;
using System.Linq;
using System.Text;
using System.Windows.Forms;
using System.Drawing.Drawing2D;

namespace WindowsFormsApplication1
{
    public partial class Form1 : Form
    {
        public Form1()
        {
            InitializeComponent();
        }

        private void Form1_Load(object sender, EventArgs e)
        {

        }
        protected override void OnPaint(PaintEventArgs e)
        {
            base.OnPaint(e);
            Graphics g = e.Graphics;
            Pen p = new Pen(Color.Red, 2);
```

```
            g.DrawEllipse(p, 50, 50, 200, 200);
            g.FillEllipse(Brushes.Black, 100,75, 20,20);
            g.FillEllipse(Brushes.Black, 170, 75, 20, 20);
            p = new Pen(Color.Black, 2);
            g.DrawArc(p, 100, 85, 80, 70, 0, 180);
            g.Dispose();
        }
    }
}
```

Output

The presentation foundation takes the concept of graphics a step further.

25.3 WINDOWS PRESENTATION FOUNDATION

The idea of desktop applications being 'thick' and web application being 'thin' no longer holds. The richness of a desktop application now comes with their ability to connect to the Internet, to update automatically, and to access data from a web source. Similarly, a web application has features almost similar to a desktop application. The line between the two is becoming blurted day by day.

However, it may be stated that this was the dream we wanted to achieve. We wanted web applications to be as rich as a desktop application and a desktop application to be able to access data from any source anywhere. A technology was, therefore, needed to bridge the gap of desktop and web applications. WPF is one such technology.

As we have already studied creation of websites, it would not be difficult for us to understand the importance of a split between design and functionality. As in the case of an ASP.NET web site, we have a design and a .cs file that contains the 'code behind'; similarly, we have separate design and functionality in a WPF application. Although the similarities between ASP and WPF can be easily noticed, there are many differences between them.

A WPF application has the following features:
1. There is a complete separation between design and functionality.
2. It uses Extendible Application Markup language (XAML) for interface design. XAML is a complete declarative language and is much more powerful than ASP.
3. It supports vector graphics and floating point coordinates.

4. It supports advance font processing.
5. The tool used for designing the interface is Microsoft Expression Blend. However, Visual Studio can also be used.
6. The 3.0 version of WPF provides Bitmap effects. The 3.5 SP1 also has a class called `Effects`, which is an extendible class, thus promoting the specification of shader effects.
7. In WPF, the approach used for animations is time based rather than frame based.
8. The developer can bind the data with the application very easily in WPF.

Learning WPF is like learning a bike. You may read a book on how to ride a bike, but it will not be of any use until you really start riding it. Similarly, to learn WPF, you will have to dive into it and explore its features.

25.3.1 WPF Architecture

Architectures are generally of two types: monolayer and multiplayer. In a multilayer architecture, different layers are assigned different tasks and hence lead to efficient and effective hardware management. The WPF architecture is also a multilayer architecture. The architecture has been divided into managed code, unmanaged code, and operating system part.

The architecture can also be considered as being conceptually segregated into the presentation framework, core, and Media Integration Layer. The Media Interaction Layer is also referred to as `milCore`. As the `milCore` has to interact with the `DirectX`, it has been, therefore, written in unmanaged code. The task of software and hardware rendering is, therefore, handled by the `milCore`, thus making it the most important of all. There is a perception that `milCore` is in the unmanaged code because of the perceived gain in the performance.

The Application Programming Interface (API) is exposed through the managed layer. It may be stated that the majority of the code in WPF is managed. Here, it would be better to introduce the three dlls: `PresentationFramework.dll`, `PresentationCore.dll`, and `WindowsBase.dll`. The controls, styles, and so on are held by the `PresentationFramework.dll`. This is also responsible for animations, etc. The core services of WPF are implemented through `PresentationCore.dll`. The `Windowsbase.dll`, on the other hand, holds the reusable elements that can be even used outside the environment.

The unmanaged layer, on the other hand, includes `milCore.dll`, which has already been explained above, and `WindowsCodecs.dll`, which is responsible for imaging scaling.

As per the kernel is concerned, it contains DirectX and User32 components. The DirectX is responsible for rendering graphics, and the User32 manages the memory and the process segregation. The different layers have been depicted in Fig. 25.3.

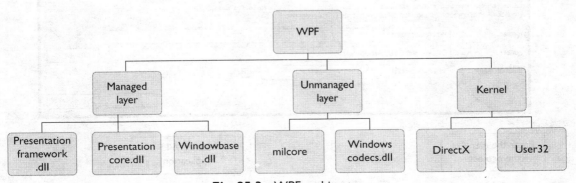

Fig. 25.3 WPF architecture

25.3.2 Creating a WPF Project

To create a WPF application, the following steps must be carried out:

Step 1 Start a new project and choose WPF in the 'project type' dialog. Figure 25.4 shows the dialog.

Step 2 After Step 1, you will be greeted with the screen shown in Fig. 25.5. Drag a label, a text box, and a button onto the screen. Set the properties of the controls to the values specified in Table 25.1.

Table 25.1 Attributes and their values

Control	Attribute	Value
Button	Content	Press
Button	Name	NameButton
Text Box	Name	NameTextBox
Label	Content	Enter
Window	Title	Name Application
Window	BitmapEffect	BevelBitmapEffect

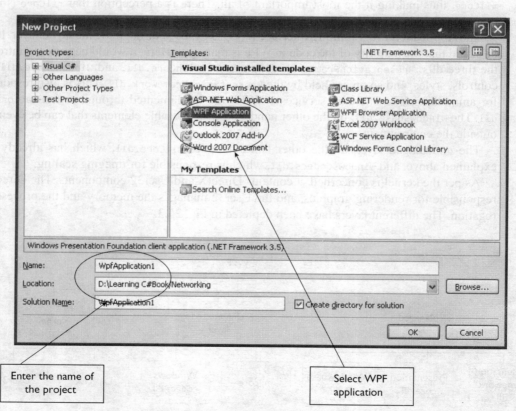

Fig. 25.4 Choose the project type

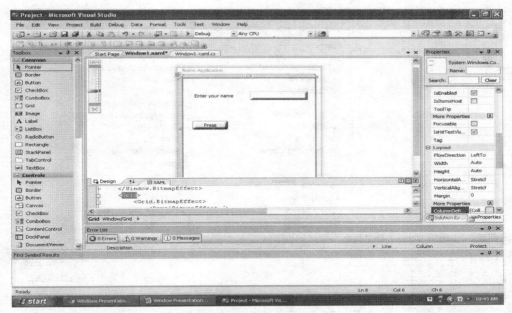

Fig. 25.5 Design view

Step 3 Press F5. On running the application, a window will be displayed as shown in Fig. 25.6, and on entering the name and pressing the button, a message box will be displayed as shown in Fig. 25.7.

The above example demonstrates a naive application, but it should be evident that the look and feel of this application is entirely different from a Windows form application. So, start making projects in WPF in order to learn it.

Fig. 25.6 Running application   **Fig. 25.7** Message box

25.4 WEB SERVICES

It is a communication between two applications over the Internet. The web service can be used via Internet or a Cloud. It may be stated that web service has helped in blurting the line between thin clients and thick clients. The functionalities that earlier considered apt to only websites, can now be used by a desktop client.

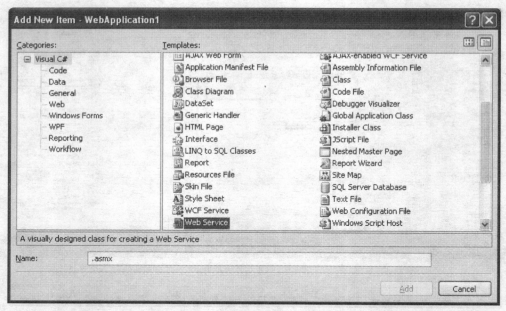

Fig. 25.8 Creating a web application

To create an application that uses web service, the following steps have to be followed:

Step 1 Create a new project. The project should be of 'ASP Web Application' project.

Step 2 Add a new web service to your project, Webservice1.asmx (Fig. 25.8). You can change the http to the page you like.

Program

```
using System;
using System.Collections;
using System.ComponentModel;
using System.Data;
using System.Linq;
using System.Web;
using System.Web.Services;
using System.Web.Services.Protocols;
using System.Xml.Linq;


namespace WebApplication1
{
    /// <summary>
    /// Summary description for WebService1
    /// </summary>
    [WebService(Namespace = "http://tempuri.org/")]
    [WebServiceBinding(ConformsTo = WsiProfiles.BasicProfile1_1)]
    [ToolboxItem(false)]
    // To allow this Web Service to be called from script, using ASP.NET AJAX, uncom-
    ment the following line.
    // [System.Web.Script.Services.ScriptService]
```

```
public class WebService1 : System.Web.Services.WebService
{

    [WebMethod]
    public string HelloWorld()
    {
        return "Hello World";
    }
}
}
```

> You need to create your own methods here:
>
> [WebMethod]
> public int sum(int a, int b)
> {
>   int c = a + b;
>   return c;
> }
>
> The above method adds two numbers and returns the sum.

Step 3 You can even add other projects to the above project. Add the following controls and set the properties of the controls to the values specified in Table 25.2.

On executing, the project view your web services in the browser (Fig. 25.9).

Choose the first web service and test it. The screenshot of the service is shown in Figs 25.10 and 25.11.

Table 25.2 Controls in Form 1

Control	Attribute	Property
Label1	Text	First Number
Label2	Text	Second Number
TextBox1	Name	FirstNumberTextBox
TextBox2	Name	SecondNumberTextBox
Button1	Name	EvaluateButton
Button1	Text	Evaluate

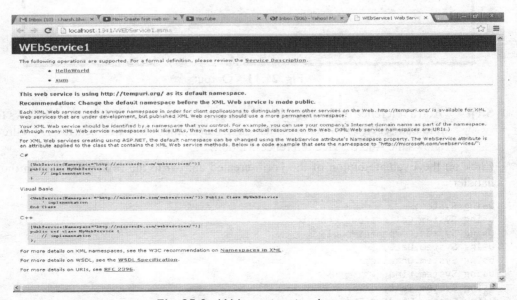

Fig. 25.9 Web services in a browser

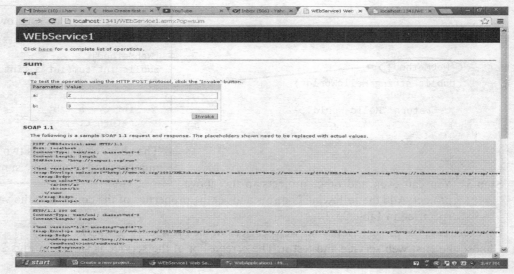

Fig. 25.10 Sum web service

When the invoke button is pressed, the screenshot shown in Fig. 25.11 appears:

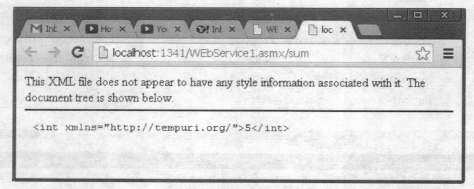

Fig. 25.11 Output

Step 4 Add a reference of the web service that was just created. Click on the Windows Project and add service Reference. Click on discover and select web service 1. Figure 25.12 shows the Add Service reference window.

Click on the Evaluate button of the Form created and write the following code in the event handler:

```
using System;
using System.Collections.Generic;
using System.ComponentModel;
using System.Data;
using System.Drawing;
using System.Linq;
using System.Text;
using System.Windows.Forms;
```

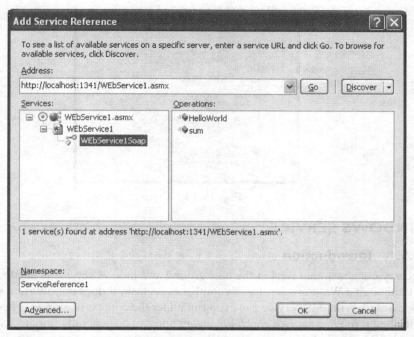

Fig. 25.12 Adding service reference

```
namespace WindowsFormsApplication2
{
    public partial class Form1 : Form
    {
        WebApplication1.WEbService1 ws = new WebApplication1.WEbService1();

        public Form1()
        {
            InitializeComponent();
        }

        private void EvaluateButton_Click(object sender, EventArgs e)
        {
            int c = ws.sum(int.Parse(FirstNumberTextBox.Text),
            int.Parse(SecondNumberTextBox.Text));
            label3.Text = c.ToString();
        }
    }
}
```

Step 5   To make the application work, add the reference System.Web.Services in the project.

Step 6   Make the project the startup project and press F5. The screen shown in Fig. 25.13 appears. Enter two numbers in the text boxes and press the evaluate button. The answer is displayed. However, the evaluation has been carried out by a web service and not just by invoking a method.

You might have found the way of adding two numbers strange, but the point was to tell you how to incorporate a web service to your application. Now, as you have learned making web services, it would be better to use them in you websites.

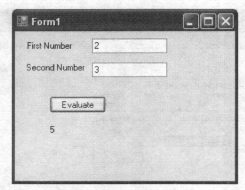

Fig. 25.13 Output

25.5 WINDOWS SERVICE

25.5.1 Introduction

To carry out a task that runs in the background, a Windows service is needed. It may be noted that although a Windows service accomplishes its task, it does not interfere with the front end processes. A Windows service can even run under the context of system. These services can be controlled through a service control manager and can be generally initiated, stopped, or paused as and when needed. However, the web services have become more popular as compared to Windows services. This section will give you an idea of how to create a Windows service.

25.5.2 Creating a Windows Service

In the File menu, go to 'New Project' and create a new project. Select Windows service and write the name of the project. Figure 25.14 shows the New Project Dialog.

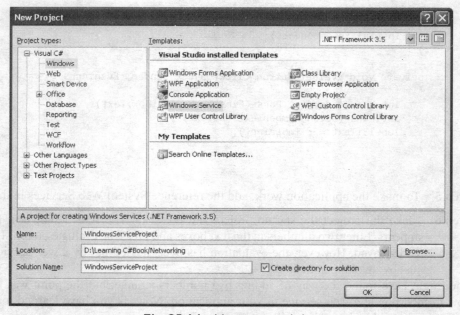

Fig. 25.14 New project dialog

Towards WPF and WCF 555

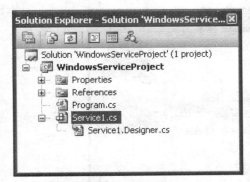

Fig. 25.15 Solution Explorer

Table 25.3 Properties of serviceInstaller

StartType	Automatic
ServiceName	NewService

Fig. 25.16 Properties of serviceInstaller

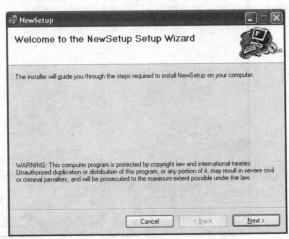

This will add a Service1 component to the project, and it can be done through Solution Explorer. Figure 25.15 shows the Solution Explorer.

Add an EventLog onto the designer of Service1.

Right click on the service and add an installer onto your application. This step adds a project installer class in the Solution Explorer. This class contains two installers: a serviceProcessInstaller and a serviceInstaller. The properties of serviceInstaller1 are to be set to the following values as given in Table 25.3. Figure 25.16 shows the properties of the serviceInstaller.

The properties of serviceInstaller1 are to be set to the values as given in Table 25.4. Figure 25.17 shows the properties of the serviceInstaller.

The next step is to add a setup project to the existing project. To do so, go to Solution Explorer and add a new project. Select a setup project from the project templates and set the name of the setup project to 'Mysetup'.

Now, right click on 'NewSetup' in the Solution Explorer and add Primary Output. In the custom action of the Mysetup project, select add custom action and add primary output.

Build MySetup project, right click on the Solution Explorer, and start the installation. Figures 25.18–25.21 show the screenshots of the setup.

Table 25.4 Properties of serviceInstaller

ServiceName	NewService
StartType	Automatic

Fig. 25.17 Properties of serviceInnstaller

Fig. 25.18 Setup Step 1

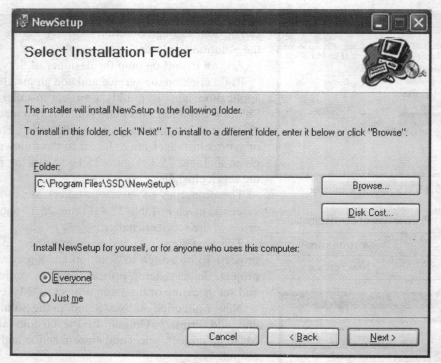

Fig. 25.19 Setup Step 2

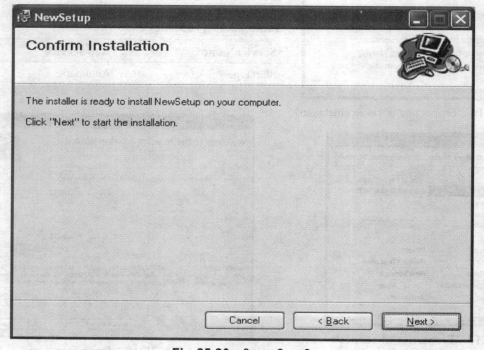

Fig. 25.20 Setup Step 3

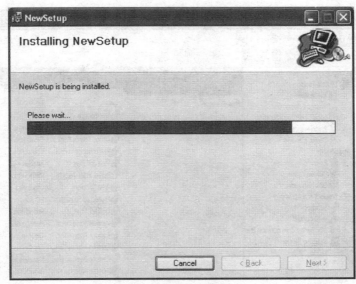

Fig. 25.21 Setup Step 4

To start the service, right click on My Computer and Go to manage. In the window that appears, select Services and Applications. Go to Service, you should see NewService. The Computer Management window is shown in Figs 25.22 and 25.23.

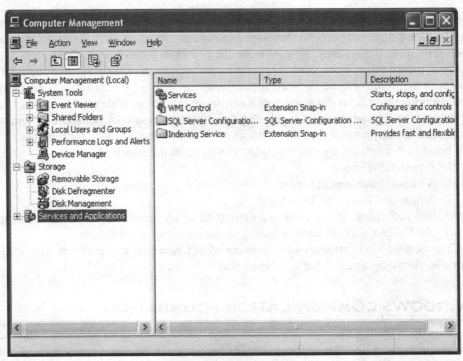

Fig. 25.22 Computer management

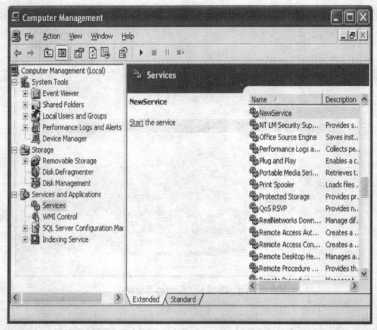

Fig. 25.23 Services in computer management

25.6 REMOTING REVISITED

To build larger projects, the task is divided into smaller subtasks. It might happen that the application's different parts are developed in different location, in different frameworks, and on different operating systems. Now, to make the complete project work, these parts are to be connected to each other. They need to communicate with each other in spite of the possible differences in their configurations. Such applications can be built via Remoting. An application can use an object that is on the same computer or on a different computer in some other location. It helps us to implement what is referred to as inter-process communication. Remoting allows substituting one protocol for other without recompiling the client or, for that matter, the server. To build such applications, the following components are required:

1. A remotable object
2. A client that can make request
3. A host that listens to the request

Remoting is flexible. It can work with any type of server. However, to make the applications work, configure the client and the host with the remoting infrastructure.

The next section introduces the concept of WCF, which can perform almost all the tasks done by remoting and that too in a better way.

25.7 WINDOWS COMMUNICATION FOUNDATION

As explained earlier, the applications nowadays are expected to be connected, to send data, and to communicate with other applications. The inability of a Windows application to communicate with other applications and to the servers is a thing of past. Similar to people forming society to fulfil their needs, the applications are expected to communicate with each other to form a society of applications that will enhance the capabilities of an application.

The modern applications need to send asynchronous data to another application and to be able to receive such data. Windows Communication Foundation helps achieving the task and also helps to build service-oriented applications. The application can gather data from an IIS server or, for that matter, from a service hosted by another application (as explained in the previous section).

The important question that comes to mind is what do the applications want? The answer is simple; it can be anything from a single character to a whole XML document. Depending on the need of an application, a communication is initiated. The communication can be a business transaction, a monitoring service's communication, a dashboard communication, or even a chat. The main features of WCF are as follows:

1. **Service oriented** It is a web service that helps you to send and receive data. The client on any machine can communicate with any service.
2. **Security** While communicating through WCF, the standard security algorithms like SSL can be used. The data of the sender and the receiver can be encrypted and decrypted easily, thus ensuring secured communication.
3. **Reliable messages** Communication, when initiated, is expected to be coherent and reliable, that is, the order in which messages are sent and received should be same. The WCF exchanges messages over WS-Reliable Messaging and using MSMQ.
4. **Durability** In WCF, the message is never lost in communication. Even if the communication gets disrupted, the message exchange resumes after the communication is established again.
5. **Transactions** Sometimes we want a set of instructions to be executed completely or not at all. For example, if we intend to transfer ₹500 to A's account, then the following steps must be followed:
   (a) Withdraw ₹500 from your account
   (b) Credit ₹500 to A's account
   Imagine that the communication is disrupted in between, resulting in the withdrawal of ₹500 from your account, but ₹500 is not credited to A's account. In order to avoid such scenarios, transactions are used. The set of command in a transaction is either executed completely or the system is restored to the initial point. WCF implements transaction through WS-Atomic Transactions.
6. **Ajax support** WCF also supports Ajax, thus making the communication efficient and effective.

The communication in a WCF application is carried out through communication protocols like HTTP, TCP, Named Pipe, and MSMQ. The Hypertext transfer protocol, or HTTP, helps us to communicate from anywhere including Internet. If, on the other hand, you want to communicate on your local network, then Transmission Control Protocol or TCP can be used. To communicate with the applications on the same machine, then Named Pipe can be used. As stated earlier, the communication needs to be durable. The MSMQ helps us to achieve this task.

It may be stated that WCF is flexible and hence can be used with many Microsoft products. It is also being used to build a cloud computing service called Microsoft.NET services. WCF has numerous capabilities; however, the implementation in intricacies of WCF projects is beyond the scope of this book. However, this section has given an idea of WCF so as to get you started.

25.7.1 WCF Architecture

Contracts and Descriptions

It is evident that WCF deals with communication and hence messages. There are many aspects in a message system, which are defined by Contracts. A service creates or consumes a message. In order to do so, the parameters of the methods need to be defined. This is done by the XML schema definition language. As interoperability is one of the goals of WCF, the specific message parts need to be defined precisely. To communicate with a service, policies and bindings need to be defined. The bindings specify the protocol as in HTTP and encoding.

Service Runtime

While a service is in operation, the behaviour is governed by this layer. The behaviour is to be displayed to the outside world. Hence, it is necessary to make sure that too much information is not leaked because such information can lead to attacks. This layer is also responsible for deciding how many instances of a method must run. The layer also provides a facility called message inspection. This facility inspects the parts of the message, thus making the task less prone to errors.

Messaging

The message send has to be processed. This processing is done by a component called channel. Channels are a part of the messaging layer. It may be noted that each task cannot be performed by a single channel. Therefore, a set of channels referred to as a channel stack operate on the messages. The channels can be segregated into two types: transport and protocol. The task of reading a message from a network, writing a message, encoding of a message, and so on is done by the transport channel. The message processing protocols, on the other hand, are implemented by the protocol channels.

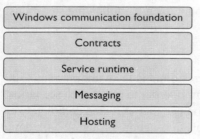

Fig. 25.24 WCF architecture

Hosting and Activation

Since a service is a program, it must be executable. However, an external agent can also host a service. This is referred to as hosting. The activation of a service can be manual or automatic. Figure 25.24 depicts the high level architecture of WCF.

25.8 MESSAGING

In C#, there is a Windows service that acts as a message router. Windows service has already been discussed in a separate section. This section does not intent to explain services rather it intends to touch the issue of messaging. It may be stated that the intricacies and complexities of messaging can be really overcome using some APIs. The aim should be implementing messaging.

To implement messaging in C#, you can use Qpid Messaging API. The beauty of Qpid Messaging API is its simplicity. It has only few classes that you need to understand. The message has standard field, properties, and content. The API is asynchronous messaging system. It may be noted that this API can also be used in other programming languages as well. Another advantage of this API is that it is supported on almost all the platforms. As per its documentation, Qpid also provides a WCF binding.

The terms connection, session, sender, and receiver have standard meanings in the API. In messaging, a remote computer or application is to be connected and hence a connection is to be established. The session helps to send message by ordering the context. The sender is the one who sends the message and the receiver receives the message. The send and fetch method helps us to send and receive the messages.

SUMMARY

The chapter introduces the concept of GDI+ and gives an idea of how to draw a 2D figure. GDI+ is the building block of animations. The concept can also be used to draw graphs and bar graphs also.

Windows Presentation Foundation helps us to create visually dazzling web and Windows-based projects. This chapter introduces WPF and explains its features and advantages.

The Chapter also explains WCF. The concept of web applications and Windows applications has been included in this chapter as they form the basis of WCF. A sample web and Windows service have also been included in the chapter.

The concept and importance of WCF have been covered in this chapter. The last section introduces the API that can be used to implement messaging. It may be stated that WCF and Windows Foundation are important topics as per industry is concerned and can be explored further.

GLOSSARY

Windows Presentation Foundation WPF offers developers with a combined programming mould for building rich Windows client experiences that incorporate UI, media, and documents.
Windows Communication Foundation WCF is a framework for building service-oriented applications.
Remoting .NET remoting helps you to create distributed applications.

GDI+ The Windows Graphics Device Interface (GDI) helps the applications to make use of graphics.
Web service It is a method of communication between two electronic devices over the Internet.
Windows service It is an application that may work in the background. However, it must adhere to the interface rules and protocols of the service control manager.

POINTS TO REMEMBER

- WPF helps the developer to build rich applications, which may integrate UI, media, and even documents.
- WPF supports vector graphics, floating point coordinates, and advance font processing.
- The tool used for designing the interface in WPF is Microsoft Expression Blend.
- A Windows service generally carries out a background task. It generally does not interfere with the front end processes.
- Remoting helps to build distributed applications. It is flexible and can work with any type of server.
- In order to build an application that implements remoting, you need to configure the client with the remoting infrastructure.
- WCF helps to build service-oriented applications. It provides security, reliability, and durability.
- The protocols used in WCF are HTTP, TCP, named pipe, and MSMQ.

EXERCISES

I. Multiple-choice Questions

1. Which of the following is used to draw an ellipse to your application form?
   (a) Remoting
   (b) WCF
   (c) GDI+
   (d) None of these

2. In order to draw an ellipse, you can instantiate graphics and set the object to e.Grahics. What is 'e' in e.Graphics?
   (a) e is the argument of the method
   (b) e is an instance of the ellipse class
   (c) e in an instance of the threading class
   (d) None of these

3. After your graphics task has been accomplished, you must call the Dispose() method. Why?
   (a) To display the Thank You Screen
   (b) To stop Web services
   (c) To stop Windows Service
   (d) None of these

4. The coordinates *x* and *y* in the DrawEllipse method are referenced from _____.
   (a) Centre of the Window
   (b) The top left point of the window
   (c) The bottom right point of the Window
   (d) None of these

5. Which namespace is needed in order to draw an image in C#?
   (a) System.Drawing.Drawing2D
   (b) System.Drawing.FakeTesting
   (c) System.Drawing.SoftwareEngineering
   (d) None of these

6. Which method needs to be overridden in order to draw an image in C# using GDI+?
   (a) OnPaint   (b) OnEllipseDraw
   (c) OnStop   (d) None of these

7. Which is the first argument in the DrawEllipse method of the Graphics class?
   (a) Pencil   (b) Shaper
   (c) Eraser   (d) Pen

8. How many arguments the object of the Pen class take?
   (a) Two   (b) Three
   (c) Four   (d) Five

9. What are the two arguments of the constructor of Pen class?
   (a) The colour and the thickness
   (b) The colour and the text
   (c) The colour and another colour
   (d) None of these

10. Generally, a client application is referred to as a _____ application and a Web Application as a _____ application.
    (a) Thick and thin   (b) Thin and Thick
    (c) Thick and Thick   (d) Thin and Thin

11. What is the major similarity between ASP and WPF?
    (a) There is a complete separation between design and functionality.
    (b) There is a no separation between design and functionality.
    (c) There is some separation between design and functionality.
    (d) None of these

12. Which language is used in WPF for interface design?
    (a) Extendible Application Markup language (XAML)
    (b) C
    (c) C++
    (d) Java

13. Which is more powerful ASP or XAML?
    (a) ASP
    (b) XAML
    (c) Both
    (d) None of them, C is the most powerful

14. Which of the following supports vector graphics and floating point coordinates?
    (a) Thread class   (b) Networking class
    (c) WPF   (d) None of these

15. Which of the following supports advance font processing?
    (a) WPF   (b) WMF
    (c) Both (a) and (b)   (d) None of these

16. Which tool can be used for designing the interface in WPF?
    (a) Microsoft Expression Blend
    (b) Microsoft Paint
    (c) Windows Media Player
    (d) None of these

17. Which version of WPF also has a class called Effects, which is an extendible class, thus promoting the specification of shader effects?
    (a) 3.5 SP1   (b) 2.0
    (c) 1.0   (d) None of these

18. In WPF, which approach is used for animations?
    (a) Time based   (b) Frame based
    (c) Both   (d) None of these

19. A Web service can be used via _____.
    (a) Internet   (b) Cloud
    (c) Both of (a) and (b) (d) None of these

20. What is needed in order to carry out a task that runs in the background?
    (a) A Windows service (b) Remoting
    (c) GDI+   (d) None of these

21. A Windows service can even run under the context of System. True/False?

(a) True
(b) False
(c) Cannot say
(d) Depends upon the operating system

22. These services are controlled via _____.
    (a) A service control manager
    (b) A control freak manger
    (c) A Freak manager
    (d) None of these

23. If the applications are at different places and they need to communicate with each other, which of the following can help?
    (a) Remoting   (b) Resorting
    (c) Reporting   (d) Retreating

24. In order to build applications that use remoting, which of following components are required?
    (a) A remotable object
    (b) A client that can make request
    (c) A host that listens to the request
    (d) All of these

25. What helps us to build distributed applications?
    (a) Remoting   (b) Reporting
    (c) Resorting   (d) Reprising

26. What helps the modern applications to send asynchronous data to another application?
    (a) Reporting
    (b) Windows Communication Foundation
    (c) Windows Media Foundation
    (d) Kedar Foundation

27. What helps us to build service-oriented applications?
    (a) WPF   (b) WCF
    (c) WWF   (d) WWE

28. WCF is _____.
    (a) Secure   (b) Not secure
    (c) Somewhat secure   (d) Cannot say

29. WCF messaging is _____.
    (a) Reliable   (b) Unreliable
    (c) Over reliable   (d) None of these

30. The communication initiated by WCF is _____.
    (a) Coherent   (b) Incoherent
    (c) Both (a) and (b) (d) None of these

31. The messaging in WCF is _____.
    (a) Durability and reliable
    (b) Not durable but reliable
    (c) Neither reliable nor durable
    (d) Durable but not reliable

32. Which of the following is supported in WCF?
    (a) Ajax   (b) Flash
    (c) Both   (d) None of these

33. The communication in a WCF application is carried out through communication protocols like _____.
    (a) HTTP
    (b) TCP
    (c) Named Pipe and MSMQ
    (d) All of these

34. Which of the following is supported in .NET Framework?
    (a) WCF   (b) WPF
    (c) Both of (a) and (b) (d) None of these

35. Which of the following is not a component of .NET?
    (a) WPF   (b) WCF
    (c) WWF   (d) All of these

II. Review Questions

1. Explain the features of WPF.
2. What are web services? How do you implement web services using C#?
3. What are Windows services? How do you implement Windows services using C#?
4. What is remoting?
5. Explain the features of WCF.
6. How can you implement messaging in C#?
7. Explain the steps of creating a Web service.
8. Explain the steps of creating a Windows service.
9. Explain the steps of creating a WPF project.
10. Explain the steps of creating a GDI+ application.

III. Programming Exercise

Design a form of 400 × 400. In the form, draw x- and y-axes and plot the origin. The upper right portion of the plane should depict the first quadrant, the left part of the upper portion should depict the second quadrant, the left portion of the lower plane should depict the third quadrant, and the right portion of the lower plane should depict the fourth quadrant (Fig. 25.25). With respect to this plane, draw the following figures (Questions 1–6).

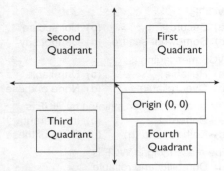

Fig. 25.25 Cartesian coordinates

1. Draw a circle with a centre at the origin and radius entered by the user.
2. Draw n concentric circles with radius r and centre (a, b). Ask the user to enter 'n', 'a', 'b', and 'r'.
3. Draw an ellipse having major axis twice the minor axis. The minor axis would be entered by the user.
4. Using the concept of loops, draw n circles having unit radius separated by 3 units. Ask the user to enter the value of n. The centre of the first circle is at the origin.
5. In the above question, draw a circle if the radius of the successive circles increase by a unit each.
6. In Question 4, draw the circles if the radius of the successive circles increases by unity and the coordinates of their centres by three units in each iteration.
7. Using rectangles and lines, draw the following figure (Fig. 25.26).

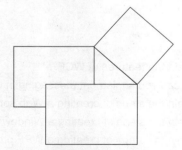

Fig. 25.26 Question number 7

8. Using rectangles and lines, draw the following figure (Fig. 25.27).

Fig. 25.27 Question number 8

9. Using rectangles and lines, draw the following figure (Fig. 25.28).

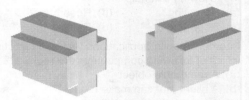

Fig. 25.28 Question number 9

10. Using rectangles, ellipses, and lines, draw the following figure (Fig. 25.29).

Fig. 25.29 Question number 10

PROJECT V
Genetic Algorithms

1. INTRODUCTION

Genetic algorithms (GAs) possess the capability to adapt according to the environment. The core idea behind these algorithms is to impersonate the unpredictability of the nature.

Genetic algorithms imitate nature. This process of natural selection can be used to solve optimization problem having huge population. However, it may be noted that the process imitates nature, and therefore, it may give the change of 'not so fit' chromosomes cropping up as the result. This is exactly what nature does at times.

The population of a GA is made up of chromosomes. Chromosomes can be binary, decimal, or hexadecimal depending on the problem. Each chromosome symbolizes a solution to the problem [3]. A chromosome is composed of cells of finite length. A binary chromosome contains 0 or 1 at each cell.

Genetic algorithms are heuristic search processes based on the theory of survival of the fittest. The search process is used in solving many problems like the following:
1. Test data generation [1, 2]
2. Subset sum problem [3]
3. Maximum clique problem [4]
4. Vertex cover problem [5]
5. Travelling salesman problem [6]
6. Post correspondence problem [7]
7. Regression testing [8]
8. Cryptography [9, 10]

2. POPULATION GENERATION AND THRESHOLD CHECK

This implements the following basic steps of GAs:

Step 1 A population having *n* chromosomes is randomly generated. This task is accomplished by the pseudorandom generator of C#. The random class helps us to generate a number. The cells of each chromosome may depict a feasible solution.

Step 2 Individual members of the population are evaluated to find the objective function value. In this project, a chromosome is deemed to be fit if the decimal equivalent of the chromosome is greater than the threshold value entered by the user.

The first two steps have been implemented in Form 1. It may be stated that the implementation extensively use the concepts that were elaborated in Chapter 20.

3. POPULATION GENERATION

The form has a group box having two radio buttons. The first radio button, when selected, produces a binary population, whereas the second button produces a hexadecimal population. The Generate button generates the population. The clear button clears the form. The Save button invokes a Save Dialog box. The Open button helps to open a saved population. The Help button presents a form with instructions written on a label. The Next button takes us to the next form. Figures PV.1–PV.5 show the various operations of Form 1.

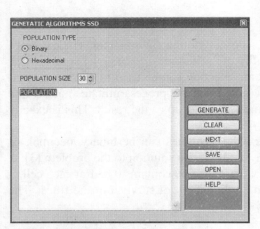

Fig. PV.1 Population generation form

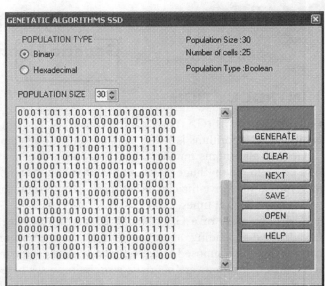

Fig. PV.2 Population generated on pressing Generate button

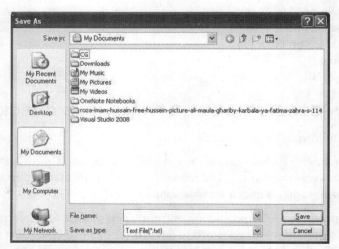

Fig. PV.3 Save As Dialog of the application

The following code implements the above functions.

Form 1: Code

```
using System;
using System.Collections.Generic;
using System.ComponentModel;
using System.Data;
using System.Drawing;
using System.Linq;
using System.Text;
```

Project V: Genetic Algorithms

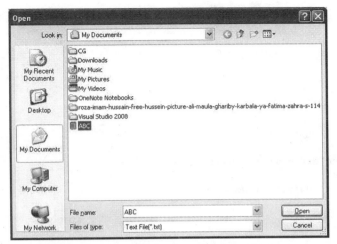

Fig. PV.4 Open Dialog of the application

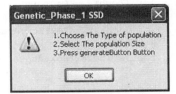

Fig. PV.5 Help form of the application

```
using System.Windows.Forms;
using System.IO;

namespace Genetic_Phase_1
{
public partial class Form1 : Form
{
    public Form1()
    {
        InitializeComponent();
    }
    int populationSize,random,count1,count2;
    int[,] population = new int[150,30];
    char[,] population1 = new char[150, 30];
    String filename,buffer;
    string[] buffer1 = new string[150];
    Random r = new Random(20);
    private void generateButton_Click(object sender, EventArgs e)
    {
        populationTextBox.AppendText(Environment.NewLine);
        populationSize = (int)populationSizeUpDown.Value;
        label2.Text = "Population Size :" + populationSize.ToString();
        label3.Text = "Number of cells :25";
        if (binaryRadioButton.Checked == true)
        {
            label4.Text = "Population Type :Boolean";
            for (count1 = 0; count1 < populationSize; count1++)
            {
                for (count2 = 0; count2 < 25; count2++)
                {
                    random = r.Next()%100;
                    if (random > 50)
                    {
                        population[count1, count2] = 1;
```

```csharp
                    }
                    else
                    {
                        population[count1, count2] = 0;
                    }
                }
            }
            for (count1 = 0; count1 < populationSize; count1++)
            {
                for (count2 = 0; count2<25; count2++)
                {
                    populationTextBox.AppendText(population[count1, count2] + " ");
                }
                populationTextBox.AppendText(Environment.NewLine);
            }

        }
        else
        {
            label4.Text = "Population Type :Hexadecimal";

            for (count1 = 0; count1 < populationSize; count1++)
            {
                for (count2 = 0; count2 < 25; count2++)
                {
                    random = (r.Next())%16;
                    switch (random)
                        {
                            case 1: population1[count1, count2] = '1';
                                break;
                            case 2: population1[count1, count2] = '2';
                                break;
                            case 3: population1[count1, count2] = '3';
                                break;
                            case 4: population1[count1, count2] = '4';
                                break;
                            case 5: population1[count1, count2] = '5';
                                break;
                            case 6: population1[count1, count2] = '6';
                                break;
                            case 7: population1[count1, count2] = '7';
                                break;
                            case 8: population1[count1, count2] = '8';
                                break;
                            case 9: population1[count1, count2] = '9';
                                break;
                            case 10: population1[count1, count2] = 'A';
                                break;
                            case 11: population1[count1, count2] = 'B';
                                break;
                            case 12: population1[count1, count2] = 'C';
                                break;
                            case 13: population1[count1, count2] = 'D';
                                break;
                            case 14: population1[count1, count2] = 'E';
```

```csharp
                        break;
                    default: population1[count1, count2] = 'F';
                        break;
                }
            }
        }
        for (count1 = 0; count1 < populationSize; count1++)
        {
            for (count2 = 0; count2 < 25; count2++)
            {
                    populationTextBox.AppendText(population1[count1, count2] + " ");
            }
                populationTextBox.AppendText(Environment.NewLine);
            }
        }
    }
    private void button1_Click(object sender, EventArgs e)
    {
        label2.Text = "";
        label3.Text = "";
        label4.Text = "";
        populationTextBox.ResetText();
    }

    private void helpButton_Click(object sender, EventArgs e)
    {
        MessageBox.Show("1.Choose The Type of population" + Environment.NewLine + "2.Select The
        population Size" + Environment.NewLine + "3.Press generateButton Button", "Genetic_Phase_1
        SSD", MessageBoxButtons.OK, MessageBoxIcon.Exclamation);
    }

    private void saveButton_Click(object sender, EventArgs e)
    {
        saveFileDialog1.Filter = "Text File(*.txt)|*.txt|Population File(*.pop)|*.pop";
        if (saveFileDialog1.ShowDialog() == DialogResult.OK)
        {
            //saveFileDialog1.FileName = "Untitled";
            try
            {
                filename = saveFileDialog1.FileName;
                File.WriteAllText(filename, populationTextBox.Text);
                buffer = populationTextBox.Text;
            }
            catch (Exception e1)
            {
                MessageBox.Show("Error" +e1.ToString(),"SSD",MessageBoxButtons.OK,MessageBoxIcon.
                Error);
            }
        }
    }

    private void button1_Click_1(object sender, EventArgs e)
    {
        openFileDialog1.Filter = "Text File(*.txt)|*.txt|Population File(*.pop)|*.pop";
        if (openFileDialog1.ShowDialog() == DialogResult.OK)
```

```csharp
        {
            try
            {
                MessageBox.Show("You      Have      Opened" +  openFileDialog1.FileName,  "SSD",
                MessageBoxButtons.OK, MessageBoxIcon.Exclamation);
                this.Text = "You have opened"+openFileDialog1.FileName;
                populationTextBox.Text = File.ReadAllText(openFileDialog1.FileName);
                buffer = populationTextBox.Text;
                /*int count_new = 0;
                while(buffer.Length! = 0)
                {
                buffer.CopyTo(buffer.IndexOf('\n'),buffer1[count_new].ToCharArray(),0,25);
                buffer1[count_new].ToString();
                buffer.Remove(count_new * 25, 25);
                count_new++;
                }
                for (int i = 0; i < count_new ; i++)
                {
                    populationTextBox.AppendText(buffer1[i]);
                }*/
            }
            catch (IOException e2)
            {
                MessageBox.Show("Error " + e2,"SSD", MessageBoxButtons.OK, MessageBoxIcon.Error);
            }
        }
    }

    private void nextButton_Click(object sender, EventArgs e)
        {
            Form2 f2 = new Form2(population, populationSize);
            f2.Show();
            //this.Close();
            //this.Dispose();
        }
    }
}
```

Form 2 implements the concept of threshold. The value of threshold is entered by the user, and the application selects the chromosomes that have value higher than the threshold value.

Form 2: Code

```csharp
using System;
using System.Collections.Generic;
using System.ComponentModel;
using System.Data;
using System.Drawing;
using System.Linq;
using System.Text;
```

```csharp
using System.Windows.Forms;
using System.IO;

namespace Genetic_Phase_1
{
    public partial class Form2 : Form
    {
        double[] values = new double[150];
        double[] values1 = new double[150];
        int threshold, i, j,k, populationSize, popsize1;
        int[,] population = new int[150, 25];
        int[,] population1 = new int[150, 25];

        string filename;
        public Form2(int[,] initialPopulation, int populationSize)
        {
            InitializeComponent();
            this.populationSize = populationSize;
            for (i = 0; i < populationSize; i++)
            {
                for (j = 0; j < 25; j++)
                {
                    population[i, j] = initialPopulation[i, j];
                }
            }
        }

        private void Form2_Load(object sender, EventArgs e)
        {

        }

        private void getValuesButton_Click(object sender, EventArgs e)
        {
            try
            {
                for (i = 0; i < populationSize; i++)
                {
                    values[i] = 0;
                    for (j = 0; j < 25; j++)
                    {
                        values[i] = values[i] + Math.Pow(2, j - 12) * population[i, j];
                    }
                }
                for (i = 0; i < populationSize; i++)
                {
```

```csharp
                populationTextBox.AppendText("Value Number " + i + " :" + values[i]);
                populationTextBox.AppendText(Environment.NewLine);
                // MessageBox.Show("Value :" + values[i]);
            }
            MessageBox.Show("Done");
        }
        catch (Exception e1)
        {
            MessageBox.Show(e1.ToString());
        }
    }

    private void clearButton_Click(object sender, EventArgs e)
    {
        populationTextBox.Clear();
    }

    private void saveButton_Click(object sender, EventArgs e)
    {
        saveFileDialog1.Filter = "Population File Phase 2(*.pop2)|*.pop2";
        if (saveFileDialog1.ShowDialog() == DialogResult.OK)
        {
            //saveFileDialog1.FileName = "Untitled";
            try
            {
                filename = saveFileDialog1.FileName;
                File.WriteAllText(filename, populationTextBox.Text);
                //buffer = populationTextBox.Text;
            }
            catch (Exception e1)
            {
                MessageBox.Show("Error" + e1.ToString(), "SSD", MessageBoxButtons.OK,
                MessageBoxIcon.Error);
            }
        }
    }

    private void button1_Click(object sender, EventArgs e)
    {
        openFileDialog1.Filter = "Population File Phase 2(*.pop2)|*.pop2";
        if (openFileDialog1.ShowDialog() == DialogResult.OK)
        {
            try
            {
                MessageBox.Show(" You Have Opened " + openFileDialog1.FileName, "SSD",
                MessageBoxButtons.OK, MessageBoxIcon.Exclamation);
                this.Text = "You have opened" + openFileDialog1.FileName;
```

```csharp
            populationTextBox.Text = File.ReadAllText(openFileDialog1.FileName);
            //buffer = populationTextBox.Text;
            /*int count_new = 0;
            while(buffer.Length! = 0)
            {
                buffer.CopyTo(buffer.IndexOf('\n'),buffer1[count_new].
                ToCharArray(),0,25);
                buffer1[count_new].ToString();
                buffer.Remove(count_new * 25, 25);
                count_new++;
            }
            for (int i = 0; i < count_new ; i++)
            {
                populationTextBox.AppendText(buffer1[i]);
            }*/
        }
        catch (IOException e2)
        {
            MessageBox.Show("Error " + e2, "SSD", MessageBoxButtons.OK, MessageBoxIcon.
            Error);
        }
    }
}

private void helpButton_Click(object sender, EventArgs e)
{
    MessageBox.Show("1.Choose The Type of population( already selected)" + Environment.
    NewLine + "2.Insert the population Threshold" + Environment.NewLine + "3.Press 
    Get Values Button", "Genetic_Phase_2 SSD", MessageBoxButtons.OK, MessageBoxIcon.
    Exclamation);
}

private void applyButton_Click(object sender, EventArgs e)
{
    threshold = (int)ThresholdNNUD.Value;
    k = 0;
    for (i = 0; i < populationSize; i++)
    {
        if (values[i] > threshold)
        {
            for (j = 0; j < 25; j++)
            {
            }
            population1[k, j] = population[i, j];
        }
        values1[k] = values[i];
        k++;
```

```csharp
        }
        popsize1 = k;
        populationTextBox.Clear();
        for (i = 0; i < popsize1; i++)
        {
            populationTextBox.AppendText("Value [" + i + " ]\t:" + values1[i] + Environment.
            NewLine);
            for (j = 0; j < 25; j++)
            {
                populationTextBox.AppendText(population1[i, j].ToString());
            }
            populationTextBox.AppendText(Environment.NewLine);
            populationTextBox.AppendText(Environment.NewLine);
        }
        label6.Text = "Population Left " + popsize1;
    }

    private void nextButton_Click(object sender, EventArgs e)
    {
        Form3 f3 = new Form3(population1, popsize1, values1,threshold);
        f3.Show();
        //this.Close();
        //this.Dispose();
    }
  }
}
```

Figures PV.6–PV.8 show the output of Form 2, which implements the threshold concept explained above.

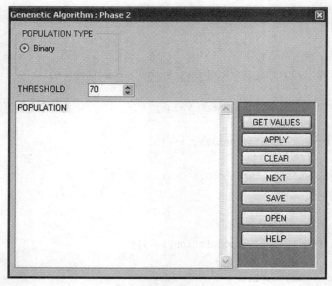

Fig. PV.6 Form 2

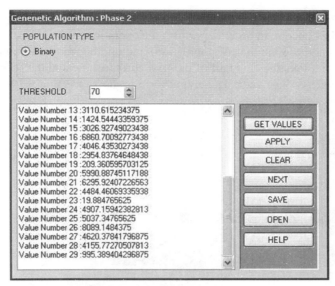

Fig. PV.7 Fetching values from form 1

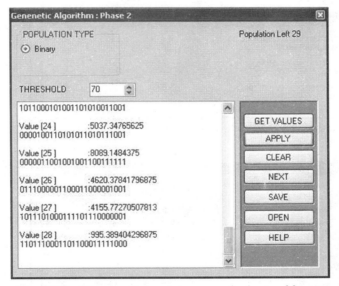

Fig. PV.8 Filtering chromosomes on the basis of fitness

4. CROSSOVER

Form 3 implements the concept of crossover. It may be stated that the crossover operator amalgamates the features of two randomly selected chromosomes. It is like a baby having some features of the father and some of the mother. It may be stated that the rate of crossover should not be too high. It is never the case that if the population of a country is 100 crores, it will become 150 crores next year and 225 crores the year following it. Nature has a fascinating mechanism to check this. The growth rate of a population should not be even 10%. As GAs replicate nature, the crossover rate should not be too high. The following code implements the concept. In order to perform the operation, two random numbers are generated. One random number (mod the number of population) and another random number (mod the number of cells in a chromosome) take the first half of the first chromosome and the second half of the second chromosome, respectively, or vice versa. The output form is shown in Figures PV.9–PV.11.

Form 3: Code

```
using System;
using System.Collections.Generic;
using System.ComponentModel;
using System.Data;
using System.Drawing;
```

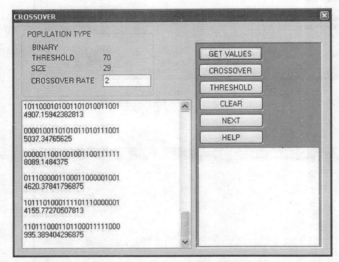

Fig. PV.9 Crossover—fetching values from the previous form

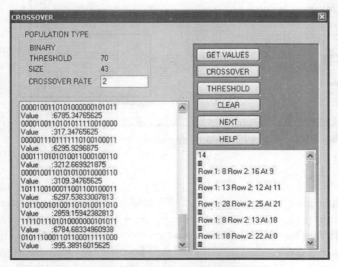

Fig. PV.10 Performing crossover

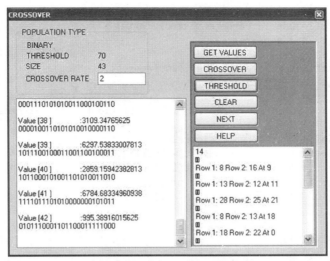

Fig. PV.11 Filtering the crossovered population

```
using System.Linq;
using System.Text;
using System.Windows.Forms;

namespace Genetic_Phase_1
{
    public partial class Form3 : Form
    {
        int[,] population = new int[150, 25];
        int popsize, popsize1,threshold, i, j, k, num_cor, temp1, temp2, temp3, l;
        double[] values = new double[150];
        double[] values1 = new double[150];
        int[] temp = new int[25];
        double cor = 2;
        Random r = new Random();
        public Form3(int[,] population, int popsize, double[] values, int threshold)
        {
            InitializeComponent();
            this.popsize = popsize;
            this.threshold = threshold;
            for (i = 0; i < popsize; i++)
            {
                for (j = 0; j < 25; j++)
                {
                    this.population[i, j] = population[i, j];
                }
                this.values[i] = values[i];
            }
        }

        private void getValuesButton_Click(object sender, EventArgs e)
        {
            populationTextBox.Clear();
            try
```

```csharp
        {
            cor = (double)Double.Parse(MRtextBox.Text);
            for (i = 0; i < popsize; i++)
            {
                populationTextBox.AppendText(Environment.NewLine);
                for (j = 0; j < 25; j++)
                {
                    populationTextBox.AppendText(population[i, j].ToString());
                }
                populationTextBox.AppendText(Environment.NewLine);
                populationTextBox.AppendText(values[i].ToString());
                populationTextBox.AppendText(Environment.NewLine);
                label8.Text = threshold.ToString();
                label10.Text = popsize.ToString();
            }
        }
        catch (Exception e1)
        {
            MessageBox.Show("Please enter a float Number", "SSD GENETIC", MessageBoxButtons.
            OK, MessageBoxIcon.Error);
        }
    }

    private void clearButton_Click(object sender, EventArgs e)
    {
        populationTextBox.Clear();
    }

    private void helpButton_Click(object sender, EventArgs e)
    {
        MessageBox.Show("1.PRESS GET VALUES" + Environment.NewLine + "2.PRESS CROSS OVER" +
        Environment.NewLine + "3.PRESS NEXT", "Genetic_Phase_1 SSD", MessageBoxButtons.OK,
        MessageBoxIcon.Exclamation);
    }

    private void applyButton_Click(object sender, EventArgs e)
    {
        l = 0;
        num_cor = (int) ((cor * 25 * popsize) / 100);
        COlistBox.Items.Add(num_cor.ToString());
        COlistBox.Items.Add(Environment.NewLine);
        for (k = 0; k < num_cor; k++)
        {
            temp1 = r.Next() % popsize;
            temp2 = r.Next() % popsize;
            temp3 = r.Next() % 25;
            COlistBox.Items.Add("Row 1: " + temp1.ToString() + " Row 2: " + temp2.ToString()
            + " At " + temp3);
            for (i = 0; i < temp3; i++)
            {
                population[popsize + l, i] = population[temp1, i];
            }
            for (i = temp3; i < 25; i++)
```

```csharp
            {
                population[popsize+1, i] = population[temp2, i];
            }
            l++;
            COlistBox.Items.Add(Environment.NewLine);
        }
        popsize = popsize + 1;
        populationTextBox.Clear();
        for (i = 0; i < popsize; i++)
        {
            populationTextBox.AppendText(Environment.NewLine);
            values[i] = 0;
            for (j = 0; j < 25; j++)
            {
                populationTextBox.AppendText(population[i, j].ToString());
                values[i] += (population[i,j] * Math.Pow(2, j - 12));
            }
            populationTextBox.AppendText(Environment.NewLine + "Value\t:");
            populationTextBox.AppendText(values[i].ToString());
        }
        label10.Text = popsize.ToString();
    }

    private void thresholdButton_Click(object sender, EventArgs e)
    {
        k = 0;
        for (i = 0; i < popsize; i++)
        {
            if (values[i] > threshold)
            {
                for (j = 0; j < 25; j++)
                {
                    population[k, j] = population[i, j];
                }
                values1[k] = values[i];
                k++;
            }
        }
        popsize1 = k;
        populationTextBox.Clear();
        for (i = 0; i < popsize1; i++)
        {
            populationTextBox.AppendText("Value [" + i + " ]\t:" + values1[i] + Environment.NewLine);
            for (j = 0; j < 25; j++)
            {
                populationTextBox.AppendText(population[i, j].ToString());
            }
            populationTextBox.AppendText(Environment.NewLine);
            populationTextBox.AppendText(Environment.NewLine);
        }
        label10.Text = popsize1.ToString();
    }
```

```
    private void nextButton_Click(object sender, EventArgs e)
    {
        Form4 f4 = new Form4(population, popsize1, values, threshold);
        f4.Show();
        //this.Close();
        //this.Dispose();
    }
  }
}
```

5. MUTATION

Form 4 implements the concept of mutation. It may be stated that mutation breaks the local maxima. It is like a mutant in the society which is altogether different from the rest of the community but may have a very high fitness value. The mutant appears once or may be twice in many generations. The society follows the mutant, and ultimately, the fitness of the whole society increases due to him. In order to implement mutation, a chromosome is randomly selected and one of its bits is flipped. Figures PV.12 and PV.13 show the output of Form 4, which implements the concept of mutation.

Form 4: Code

```
using System;
using System.Collections.Generic;
using System.ComponentModel;
using System.Data;
using System.Drawing;
using System.Linq;
using System.Text;
using System.Windows.Forms;
```

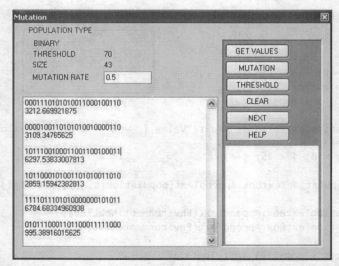

Fig. PV.12 Mutation form—fetching population from the previous form

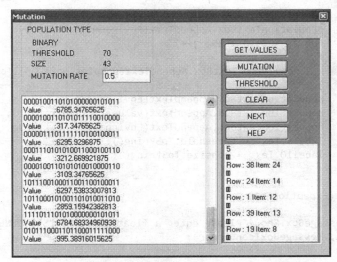

Fig. PV.13 Mutation form—on pressing the mutation button

```csharp
namespace Genetic_Phase_1
{
    public partial class Form4 : Form
    {
        int[,] population = new int[150, 25];
        int popsize, popsize1,threshold, i, j, k, num_m, temp1, temp2, temp3, l;
        double[] values = new double[150];
        double[] values1 = new double[150];
        int[] temp = new int[25];
        double mr = 2;
        Random r = new Random();
        String finalKey = "";
        public Form4(int[,] population, int popsize, double[] values, int threshold)
        {
            InitializeComponent();
            this.popsize = popsize;
            this.threshold = threshold;
            for (i = 0; i < popsize; i++)
            {
                for (j = 0; j < 25; j++)
                {
                    this.population[i, j] = population[i, j];
                }
                this.values[i] = values[i];
            }
        }

        private void getValuesButton_Click(object sender, EventArgs e)
        {
            populationTextBox.Clear();
            try
            {
                mr = (double)Double.Parse(MRtextBox.Text);
                for (i = 0; i < popsize; i++)
```

```csharp
        {
            populationTextBox.AppendText(Environment.NewLine);
            for (j = 0; j < 25; j++)
            {
                populationTextBox.AppendText(population[i, j].ToString());
            }
            populationTextBox.AppendText(Environment.NewLine);
            populationTextBox.AppendText(values[i].ToString());
            populationTextBox.AppendText(Environment.NewLine);
            label8.Text = threshold.ToString();
            label10.Text = popsize.ToString();
        }
    }
    catch (Exception e1)
    {
        MessageBox.Show("Please enter a float Number", "SSD GENETIC", MessageBoxButtons.
        OK, MessageBoxIcon.Error);
    }
}

private void clearButton_Click(object sender, EventArgs e)
{
    populationTextBox.Clear();
}

private void helpButton_Click(object sender, EventArgs e)
{
    MessageBox.Show("1.PRESS GET VALUES" + Environment.NewLine + "2.PRESS CROSS OVER" +
    Environment.NewLine + "3.PRESS NEXT", "Genetic_Phase_1 SSD", MessageBoxButtons.OK,
    MessageBoxIcon.Exclamation);
}

private void applyButton_Click(object sender, EventArgs e)
{
    l = 0;
    num_m = (int) ((mr * 25 * popsize) / 100);
    COlistBox.Items.Add(num_m.ToString());
    COlistBox.Items.Add(Environment.NewLine);
    for (k = 0; k < num_m; k++)
    {
        temp1 = r.Next() % popsize;
        temp3 = r.Next() % 25;
        COlistBox.Items.Add("Row : " + temp1.ToString() + " Item: " + temp3);
        if (population[temp1, temp3] == 1)
        {
            population[temp1, temp3] = 0;
        }
        else
        {
            population[temp1, temp3] = 0;
        }
        COlistBox.Items.Add(Environment.NewLine);
    }

    populationTextBox.Clear();
```

```csharp
        for (i = 0; i < popsize; i++)
        {
            populationTextBox.AppendText(Environment.NewLine);
            values[i] = 0;
            for (j = 0; j < 25; j++)
            {
                populationTextBox.AppendText(population[i, j].ToString());
                values[i] += (population[i,j] * Math.Pow(2, j - 12));
            }
            populationTextBox.AppendText(Environment.NewLine + "Value\t:");
            populationTextBox.AppendText(values[i].ToString());
        }
        label10.Text = popsize.ToString();
    }

    private void thresholdButton_Click(object sender, EventArgs e)
    {
        k = 0;
        for (i = 0; i < popsize; i++)
        {
            if (values[i] > threshold)
            {
                for (j = 0; j < 25; j++)
                {
                    population[k, j] = population[i, j];
                }
                values1[k] = values[i];
                k++;
            }
        }
        popsize1 = k;
        populationTextBox.Clear();
        for (i = 0; i < popsize1; i++)
        {
            populationTextBox.AppendText("Value [" + i + " ]\t:" + values1[i] + Environment.NewLine);
            for (j = 0; j < 25; j++)
            {
                populationTextBox.AppendText(population[i, j].ToString());
            }
            populationTextBox.AppendText(Environment.NewLine);
            populationTextBox.AppendText(Environment.NewLine);
        }
        label10.Text = popsize1.ToString();
    }

    private void nextButton_Click(object sender, EventArgs e)
    {
        int random_num = r.Next(popsize1);
        for (j = 0; j < 25; j++)
        {
```

```
        finalKey += population[random_num, j].ToString();
    }
    MessageBox.Show("The Final Key is " + finalKey, "SSD GENETIC CRYPTOGRAPHY",
    MessageBoxButtons.OK, MessageBoxIcon.Asterisk);
    Form5 f5 = new Form5(finalKey);
    f5.Show();
    }
}
```

6. FUTURE SCOPE

Form 4 leaves the place for Form 5. You are advised to go through various research papers given in the Reference section on the project and implement selection and diploid genetic as well.

It may also be stated that the task of making computers creative is also been done using this amazing concept of GAs. The concept is dealt with in artificial creativity, which is an interdisciplinary endeavour.

REFERENCES

The use of GAs and cellular automata can be found in the paper.

[1] H. Bhasin and N. Singla, 'Cellular Genetic Test Data Generation', *ACM Sigsoft Software Engineering Notes*, September 2013.

[2] Although the paper uses cellular automata, the continuation of the paper amalgamates GAs with the process.
H. Bhasin et al., 'Test Data Generation Using Cellular Automata', *ACM Sigsoft Software Engineering Notes*, July 2013.

[3] The use of GAs in subset sum problem can be found in the following paper.
H. Bhasin and N. Singla, 'Modified Genetic Algorithms Based Solution to Subset Sum Problem, *IJARAI*, Vol. 1, Issue 1, April 2012.

[4] The paper examines the use of GAs in maximum clique problem.
H. Bhasin and R. Mahajan, 'Genetic Algorithms Based Solution to Maximum Clique Problem', *IJCSE*, Vol. 4, Issue 8, pp. 1444–1448, e-ISSN: 0975-3397, Print ISSN: 2229-5631.

[5] Vertex cover problem has been dealt with in the paper. In order to find the solution, GAs have been applied.
H. Bhasin and G. Ahuja, 'Harnessing Genetic Algorithm for Vertex Cover Problem', *IJCSE*, Vol. 4, Issue 2, January 2012, e-ISSN: 0975-3397, Print ISSN: 2229-5631.

[6] Travelling salesman problem has been solved using a technique that uses cellular automata and GAs.
H. Bhasin and N. Singla, 'Harnessing Cellular Automata and Genetic Algorithms to Solve Travelling Salesman Problem', ICICT-2012, April 2012.

[7] Post-correspondence problem is an important problem in theory of computation. The problem has been solved by GAs in the following paper.
H. Bhasin and N. Gupta, 'Randomized Algorithm Approach for Solving PCP', *IJCSE*, Vol. 4, Issue 1, 2012, e-ISSN: 0975-3397, Print ISSN: 2229-5631.

[8] The papers deal with regression testing. As the search space is generally too large, GAs, therefore, have been used to accomplish the task.
The details of eight papers on regression testing via genetic algorithms can be found on Google Scholar or www.academia.edu.

[9] Both cryptography and cryptanalysis have been done using GAs.
H. Bhasin and S. Bhatia, 'Breaking AES Using GA', *IEEE Sponsored 2012 4th International Conference on Electronics Computer Technology* (ICECT 2012).

[10] H. Bhasin and V. Dhankar, 'DNA Cryptography Using Finite Field Arithmetic', *IEEE Sponsored 2012 4th International Conference on Electronics Computer Technology* (ICECT 2012).

Appendix
Answers to Objective Type Questions

Chapter 1

1. (a)   2. (a)   3. (a)   4. (b)   5. (e)
6. (d)   7. (d)   8. (a)   9. (d)   10. (c)
11. (a)   12. (b)   13. (a)   14. (a)   15. (a)
16. (a)   17. (a)   18. (a)   19. (a)   20. (a)

Chapter 2

1. (b)   2. (a)   3. (b)   4. (b)   5. (a)
6. (a)   7. (a)   8. (a)   9. (d)   10. (a)

Chapter 3

1. (c)   2. (d)   3. (c)   4. (d)   5. (a)
6. (d)   7. (a)   8. (a)   9. (d)   10. (c)
11. (d)   12. (d)   13. (d)   14. (d)   15. (c)
16. (a)   17. (a)   18. (b)   19. (a)   20. (d)
21. (b)   22. (a)   23. (a)   24. (b)   25. (d)
26. (b)   27. (d)   28. (d)   29. (d)   30. (d)

Chapter 4

A. 1. Use of unassigned local variable 'number', since 'number' has not been assigned any value.
2. Cannot implicitly convert type 'int' to 'bool'. Since number = 0 is an assignment statement and is inside the opening and closing parentheses, a Boolean condition is expected.
3. No error; the output is 'Hi'.
4. Output: Hi. But in C, the same output will not be obtained.
5. Cannot implicitly convert type 'bool' to 'float'.
6. Runtime error.
7. Output: Bye.
8. Error: Cannot implicitly convert type 'char' to 'bool'.
9. Error: Object reference is required.
10. Output: Hi there! I am default.

B. 1. True   2. True (if there is integer conversion)
3. False   4. False
5. False   6. False
7. False   8. True
9. True (Nested if-else)
10. False

Chapter 5

1. (a)   2. (b)   3. (c)   4. (d)   5. (a)
6. (c)   7. (c)   8. (c)   9. (d)   10. (c)
11. (b)   12. (b)   13. (a)   14. (b)   15. (b)
16. (b)   17. (b)   18. (a)   19. (a)   20. (a)

Chapter 6

1. (d)   2. (b)   3. (b)   4. (a)   5. (b)
6. (a)   7. (a)   8. (a)   9. (a)   10. (c)

Chapter 7

1. (c)   2. (d)   3. (c)   4. (a)   5. (c)
6. (b)   7. (c)   8. (a)   9. (d)   10. (a)

Chapter 8

1. (d)   2. (a)   3. (a)   4. (b)   5. (c)
6. (b)   7. (b)   8. (c)   9. (d)   10. (a)

Chapter 9

I. 1. False   2. True
3. True   4. True
5. True   6. False
7. True   8. False
9. True   10. False

II. 1. (c)   2. (a)   3. (a)   4. (c)   5. (d)
6. (a)   7. (d)   8. (a)   9. (b)   10. (d)

Answers to Objective Type Questions

Chapter 10

I. 1. `ABC.x` is inaccessible due to its protection level.
2. No error.
3. Use of possibly unassigned field `earning`.
4. Can use only array initializer expressions to assign to array types.
5. Cannot initialize type `StructEx.Program.Chor` with a collection initializer because it does not implement `System.Collections.IEnumerable`.
6. No error.
7. Inconsistent accessibility: parameter type `StructEx.Program.Chor` is less accessible than method `StructEx.Program.compare(StructEx.Program.Chor, StructEx.Program.Chor)`.
8. Cannot declare pointer to managed type.
9. `StructEx.Program.XYZ.a` is inaccessible due to its protection level.
10. `StructEx.Program.XYZ.a` is inaccessible due to its protection level.

Chapter 11

1. (a) 2. (b) 3. (d) 4. (b) 5. (b)
6. (d) 7. (a) 8. (d) 9. (b) 10. (c)

Chapter 12

1. (a) 2. (d) 3. (a) 4. (a) 5. (a)
6. (a) 7. (a) 8. (a) 9. (b) 10. (a)

Chapter 13

1. (a) 2. (a) 3. (c) 4. (a) 5. (b)
6. (a) 7. (a) 8. (b) 9. (a) 10. (a)

Chapter 14

1. (b) 2. (c) 3. (c) 4. (a) 5. (d)
6. (d) 7. (d) 8. (a) 9. (b) 10. (a)

Chapter 15

1. (c) 2. (a) 3. (d) 4. (d) 5. (a)
6. (d) 7. (a) 8. (b) 9. (d) 10. (c)

Chapter 16

1. (a) 2. (c) 3. (c) 4. (d) 5. (a)
6. (d) 7. (d) 8. (a) 9. (c) 10. (b)

Chapter 17

1. (a) 2. (a) 3. (d) 4. (a) 5. (d)
6. (a) 7. (a) 8. (d) 9. (c) 10. (d)

Chapter 18

I. 1. (a) 2. (c) 3. (b) 4. (a) 5. (b)
6. (b) 7. (c) 8. (c) 9. (d) 10. (b)

II. 1. True   2. True
3. False   4. True
5. False   6. True
7. True   8. True
9. True   10. False

Chapter 19

I. 1. (a) 2. (d) 3. (a) 4. (a) 5. (a)
6. (b) 7. (c) 8. (b) 9. (a) 10. (a)

II. 1. False   2. True
3. True   4. True
5. False   6. False
7. True   8. False
9. True   10. True

Chapter 20

1. (a), (b) 2. (a) 3. (a) 4. (b) 5. (a)
6. (b)   7. (c) 8. (b) 9. (a) 10. (b)
11. (a) 12. (c)

Chapter 21

I. 1. (a) 2. (b) 3. (d) 4. (c) 5. (d)
6. (d) 7. (a) 8. (a) 9. (a) 10. (c)

II. 1. False   2. False
3. False   4. True
5. False   6. False
7. True   8. True
9. True   10. False

Chapter 22

I. 1. (a)   2. (a)   3. (d)   4. (c)   5. (d)
    6. (c)   7. (d)   8. (c)   9. (d)   10. (d)

II. 1. True   2. False
    3. False   4. False
    5. True   6. False
    7. True   8. False
    9. True

Chapter 23

1. (d)   2. (d)   3. (a)   4. (c)   5. (c)
6. (a)   7. (a)   8. (a)   9. (c)   10. (a)
11. (d) 12. (a) 13. (a) 14. (a) 15. (b)
16. (c) 17. (a) 18. (d) 19. (a) 20. (b)

Chapter 24

1. (d)   2. (c)   3. (a)   4. (a)   5. (c)
6. (a)   7. (a)   8. (a)   9. (a)   10. (a)
11. (a) 12. (b) 13. (d) 14. (d) 15. (a)
16. (a) 17. (a) 18. (a) 19. (a) 20. (b)
21. (d) 22. (a) 23. (a) 24. (a) 25. (c)

Chapter 25

I. 1. (c)   2. (a)   3. (d)   4. (b)   5. (a)
    6. (a)   7. (d)   8. (a)   9. (a)   10. (a)
    11. (a) 12. (a) 13. (b) 14. (c) 15. (a)
    16. (a) 17. (a) 18. (a) 19. (c) 20. (a)
    21. (a) 22. (a) 23. (a) 24. (d) 25. (a)
    26. (b) 27. (b) 28. (a) 29. (a) 30. (a)
    31. (a) 32. (a) 33. (d) 34. (c) 35. (c)

Index

.NET
  Architecture 4, 7
  Benefits 16
  Tools 6, 7

Abstract 43, 145, 281, 282, 290
  Class 282, 290, 292, 298, 300
AcceptTCPClient 519, 521, 522
Access levels 144, 236, 256, 258, 263, 272
Access specifiers 17, 46, 58, 144, 145, 257, 258, 261, 262, 265, 266
Accessing elements 195, 214
Active server pages (ASP) 2, 8, 464
Add connection 444
ADO.NET 9, 466, 492
Aggregation 235, 254, 261
Ajax support 474, 559
Anchor 369, 373, 394
Application layer 514
Arithmetic expression 65, 67, 68
Arithmetic operators 52, 68
Array 6, 17, 32, 35, 47, 104, 105, 116, 118, 119
  of objects 123, 168, 235, 241
  of strings 162, 168, 169, 177
  of structures 212, 219, 228
ASP.NET 8–10, 17, 18, 463–9, 472, 474, 475, 482, 485
Assemblies 5, 17, 18

BackColor 371, 376, 404
Binary operator overloading 307, 309, 315, 317
Boxing 45, 68
Break 17, 43, 94, 96, 97, 100, 104, 111–4, 118
Browser control 413, 419
Brushes.Color 545

Button 14, 15, 369, 370, 374–9, 388, 389, 390–4, 398, 402–4, 406–9, 412
Bytecode 4

C# 5–7, 10, 17, 18, 20–3, 25, 26, 30
Cells 399, 400, 402, 456, 472, 477, 565, 567, 576
Ceiling 62
CheckBox 406, 407, 419
CheckedListBox 404, 405, 419
Class 4–6, 9, 16–8, 22–9, 31, 32, 36, 38, 39, 41–6
  definition 25
  diagram 16, 235–7, 241, 262, 264, 269, 273, 276, 288, 302
  System.Array 178, 198, 200
Classful addressing 142
ClickOnce Technology 527, 534, 540, 541
Client 8, 42, 61, 258, 394, 465, 466, 513, 515, 516
Client-server 515, 525
Close() 356, 521
Code blot 3
Codesmith 7
ColorDialog 421, 427, 430, 432, 433
Collections 104, 105, 119, 123, 124, 133, 134, 336, 337, 348
ComboBox 369, 374, 388, 416
Command line arguments 20, 32, 33, 35
Command object 441, 444, 445, 460
CommandText 445, 457
CommandTimeOut 445
CommandType 445
Comments 20, 30, 31, 35, 36
Common Type System (CTS) 6, 18

Common intermediate language (CIL) 4
Common language runtime (CLR) 4, 6, 7, 9, 144, 159, 464, 466
Common language specification (CLS) 6, 9, 18, 466
Compilation process 33, 34
Compile time errors 37, 44, 307, 320, 332
Complex number calculator 222, 302, 305, 310, 315
Compression 514
Conditional statement 53, 68, 76–8, 80, 83, 91, 92, 95
Connection 3, 8, 11, 12, 22, 441, 444, 445, 449, 450
Connection objects 444, 460
Console application 14–16, 21
const keyword 43, 58, 59, 68, 252
Constant members 252
Constant variables 38, 44, 58, 68
Constructor overloading 249, 261
Constructors 48, 163–5, 235, 245, 258, 261, 268, 269, 273, 276
Contextual keywords 43
Continue statement 100, 104, 113, 118, 119
ColorDialog 421, 427, 430, 432
Controls 8, 369, 373, 374, 381, 388, 389, 394, 395, 398
CommandText 445, 457
Copy constructor 247, 249, 261
Core 266, 547, 565
Cross language interoperability 8
Crossover 575, 576
Custom control 473
Custom Actions Editor 528, 541

Dangling else 76, 88, 93, 95
Data display controls 374

Data entry controls 374
Data link layer 514
Data source configuration 444, 445, 449
Data types 1, 16, 19, 38, 42, 44, 58, 60, 68, 145
Data Wizard 444
Database 3–6, 8, 9, 11, 12, 16, 22, 235, 336, 363
DataSet 441, 445, 447, 460
DataTable 441, 445, 446, 460
DateTimePicker 389, 398, 408, 409
Default constructor 40, 48, 245, 249, 355
Default value 40, 58, 72
Defining a structure 213
Delegates 42, 68, 72, 143, 158, 159, 236, 258, 354
Design view 442, 467–469
Destructor 135, 235, 251, 258, 261, 262
Dialogs 367, 394, 418, 421–3, 430, 432–4
Directory 78, 80, 81, 123, 128, 134, 135, 336, 433, 441, 460, 461, 518–20
DirectoryInfo 441
DirectX 547
Dispose() 356, 357, 433, 544–6, 562, 570, 574, 580
DIX network 513
DivRem function 62
Dock 369, 373, 374, 395, 423, 434
Documentation 7, 22, 30, 35, 37, 198, 560
Domain Name System 514
DrawArc 545, 546
Drawing2D 545, 546
Drawing surface 544
Durability 559, 561, 563

Encryption 514
Effects 547
Enumerations 39, 212, 213, 226, 334
Evaluation of an expression 67
Event log 555
Encapsulation 237, 256, 261, 263
Environment specific optimization 5
Error list 11, 12, 35, 258

Errors 5, 8, 12, 20, 34, 35, 37, 44, 261, 306, 307, 319–321, 323, 325, 327
Event handlers 370, 376, 398, 434
Eventlog 555
Events 24, 36, 42, 68, 236, 258, 290, 298, 356, 370, 542
Exceptions 6, 7, 25, 200, 321–4, 328, 330, 3–4, 349
Exception handling mechanism 321
ExecuteNonQuery 445, 457–60, 504
ExecuteReader 445, 460, 504, 505, 507–11
ExecuteScalar 445
ExecuteXMLReader 445
Explicit implementation 289, 295, 298
Extends 10, 159, 289, 293, 295, 298
Extern 43, 145

F# 10, 18, 158, 262
FileInfo 441, 460, 461
Filedirectory 520
File System Editor 528, 530, 541, 542
File Types Editor 528, 530, 541, 542
File transfer protocol 518, 535
Finally 43, 319, 331, 332
Finalization process 251
Floating point type 39, 40
Floor functions 62
FontDialog 421, 422, 426, 432, 433
ForeColor 371, 376, 395, 419, 427, 430, 432
Framework class library (FCL) 6, 18 19, 42
Framing 514
Function
  Abs 61
  Overloading 255, 256, 261

Garbage collection 6, 17–19, 45, 162, 163, 172
GDI+ 543, 544, 561–3
Generics 233, 336–8
Genetic algorithms 367, 409, 418, 421, 565–85
GetFileList 519, 520

GetFileList method 519
GetFileListBytes 520–2
GetHostEntry 517, 518, 522, 523
GetStream 521–3
Goto 43, 96, 100, 113–16, 118–22, 209, 416
Graphics 4, 8, 195, 196, 200, 543–7, 561, 562
Greedy approach 203, 204, 207, 211
GroupBox 398, 399, 407, 408, 419, 420

'Has a' relationship 267, 284
Hosting and activation 560
HashSet 123, 133, 134, 336
Hierarchical inheritance 255, 265, 276, 284, 287
HTML 8, 374, 463, 472, 474, 475, 487, 488, 498, 499, 503, 505, 506
Hub 514, 515, 525
Hyperbolic sine 62
HTTP 535, 559–61, 563

if statement 76–8, 95, 104
if-else ladder 76, 78, 85, 86, 92
if-else statement 78, 80, 95, 98
Implements 24, 42, 151, 171, 204, 208, 290, 291, 298, 300
Indexer 52, 59, 235, 258, 260–2, 290, 298, 300, 301
Integrated development environment (IDE) 4, 109
Increment 45, 47, 48, 51, 52, 100–3, 117
Inheritances 254, 255, 265, 268, 279
  Multilevel 255, 265, 272, 273, 284
Input 6, 20, 25, 26, 30, 33–5, 38, 63, 67
InputStream 441
Installer 527, 528, 534, 540–2, 555
Instantiation 131, 132, 213, 214, 237, 240, 246, 254, 262, 337
  of a class 262
  of a structure 214
Inverse sine 61
Integral types 39–41, 50
Internal 43, 132, 145, 229, 254, 258, 261, 267, 284, 518, 520

Interval 355–7, 363
Interface 4–6, 8, 10, 11, 17, 24, 35, 39, 42
Internet Information Services (IIS) 464
Internet Protocol address 513
Interpretation 19, 464, 491
IP address 78, 136–8, 140–2, 513, 516, 517
IPHostEntry 517, 518, 522, 523

Jagged array 178, 190, 196–8
Job sequencing 135, 203, 207
Just-in-Time (JIT) 5, 18, 465

Knapsack problem 204
Keywords 42, 43, 48, 68, 111, 201, 213, 214, 280, 290, 316, 320

Label 113, 118, 319, 369, 370, 374, 375, 377, 380
Launch Conditions Editor 528, 541
Lazy type 131, 132
Library assemblies (DLL) 5
Linear search 178, 184–6, 200, 356
   characteristics 186
Linking 14
LinkLabel 374, 375, 395
ListBox 369, 374, 387, 389
ListView 406, 407
Local Area Network (LAN) 513
Local variable 40, 60, 252, 256
Loops 68, 100–105, 107–109, 111, 113, 115–9
   Comparison 116
   do-loop 102, 103, 116, 119
   do-while loop 100, 115, 118
   for-each loop 100, 337, 340, 343, 346
   for loop 32, 103, 104, 109, 111, 116–21, 179, 181
   while loop 101, 115–9, 121, 204
Looping 100, 115, 118

Main method 16, 20, 21, 26, 27, 35, 36, 42, 67

Managed code 5, 17, 49, 466, 547
Math class 29, 61–64, 68
MaskedTextBox 369, 387, 389, 394
Master pages 485–8
Mathematical functions 29, 38, 61
Metropolitan Area Network (MAN) 513
MaxLength 379
Max function 63
Media Integration Layer 547
MemoryStream 522, 523
MenuStrip Control 409
Messaging 543, 559–61
Meta classes 254
Metadata 5, 6, 17, 18
Method 1, 5, 8, 16, 20, 21, 23, 24–7, 29
   Compare 98, 100, 166, 167, 169, 170, 177, 202
Method overloading 143, 154, 155, 159, 160
Methods of string class 162, 168
Microsoft Access 442, 443, 449, 460
Microsoft intermediate language (MSIL) 4
milCore 547
milCore.dll 547
Min function 63
Modifier 58, 144, 145, 151, 159
Monitor 353, 357, 559
MSMQ 559, 561
Multidimensional arrays 178, 190, 195, 196, 200
MultiLine 380, 389, 390, 394, 423, 434, 522
Mutation 580, 581
Mutex 353, 365
MVC 8

Named pipe 559, 561, 563
Namespace 6, 7, 16, 22, 23, 25–7, 29, 31, 32
Nested if-else 83–5, 95
NumericUpDown 369, 370, 388, 395, 419
Nested loops 105
Nested structures 212, 217
Nested try-catch 319, 328
Network layer 514

New operator 40, 48, 216, 221
Non-mutable 162, 171
NumericUpDown 369, 370, 388

Objects 6, 7, 9, 10, 18, 42, 45, 48, 68, 72, 123, 124, 132, 158
Object-oriented technology 237, 253
ODBCCommand 444, 445
OdbcConnection 444
OleDbCommand 444, 457, 459
OleDbConnection 22, 23, 444, 457, 458
OnPaint 544, 545
Open System Interconnect (OSI) 514
OpenFileDialog 421, 430–6, 438, 569, 570, 572, 573
Operator overloading 48, 233, 255, 256, 302–7
Operators 34, 38, 40, 43–8, 49–57, 59, 63, 65, 67–69
   && 45, 54–6, 76, 77, 89
   || 45, 54, 76, 77, 89, 90
   (/) divides 51
   () Operator 47
   [] Operator 47
   ++ Operator 47, 305
   – – Operator 306
   → Operator 49
   + Operator 49
   – Operator 49, 67, 68, 309
   ~ Operator 50
   & Operator 50
   as Operator 289, 290, 296, 298, 304, 315
   Assignment 57
   Binary 51, 68, 302, 304, 307
   Bitwise 54, 56
   Dot 46, 68, 145, 146, 159, 160, 214, 216
   Logical 54
   Multiplication 50, 316
   for strings 166
   Relational 52, 68
   Ternary 51, 52
Optimization problems 203
OracleCommand 444, 445
OracleConnection 444
Out parameters 151, 153
Output stream 441

Overloading 48, 143, 154, 155, 166, 233, 249, 255, 256
Overriding 255, 266, 279

Page Setup 434, 437, 438
  Dialogs 434
Panel control 398, 399, 400
Parameters 42, 143–5, 148, 150, 151, 153
Parameter interface 254
Parameterized constructor 164, 246, 247, 249
Patterns 105, 106
Peer-to-peer 515
Pen 544–6
Physical layer 514
Polymorphism 221, 255, 256, 261, 265, 283, 284
Population 410, 411, 421, 565–9
Power function 63
Precedence of operators 67
Presentation framework 547
Presentation layer 514
PresentationCore.dll 547
Presentation framework 547
PrintDialog 432, 438, 439
Private 446, 452–4, 456, 457, 459, 516, 523
Private constructor 235, 250, 251
Process assemblies (EXE) 5
Project installer 555
Protected 43, 145, 257, 258, 261, 262, 267, 271, 503
Properties 520, 521, 523, 528, 529, 531, 532, 535, 536
Properties window 11, 13, 537
Public 36, 42, 43, 46, 59, 61–4, 80, 101–03
Public interface 254, 292
Pseudorandom generator 565

Qpid Messaging API 560
Quadratic equation 81
Queue 123, 124, 126, 127, 134, 340

RadioButton 407, 419
Rapid Application Development 370, 421

ReaderWriterLock 353
Read 115, 116, 198, 259–61, 353, 360
Recursion 143, 155–7
Reference parameter 151
Reliable messages 559
Reference types 38, 39, 42, 68, 72, 151, 201, 221, 228
Reflection 5
Registry editor 528
Registries 528
Regular expressions 172–5
Remote procedure call (RPC) 518
Remoting 513, 543, 558, 561
Return type of a method 26, 145, 147, 159
Routers 514, 525
Round function 63
Runtime 4–7, 9, 17, 26, 144, 159, 253, 255, 283
  Errors 5, 321, 331, 334
  Hosts 9
  Polymorphism 255, 265, 283, 284, 287, 288
  Safety 5

Save 14, 15, 421–3
SaveFileDialog 430, 432, 436–8, 421, 422
Scope of variable 59
Sealed 145, 265, 279, 282–5, 519
  classes 265, 279, 282
Selection sort 186
Semaphore 353
Searching 178, 184, 200, 462
Server 444, 461, 463, 465, 474, 475, 481–3, 491
Server controls 463, 466, 474, 491
Session layer 514
Server Explorer 11, 12, 444, 461, 484
Service Oriented 559, 561
Security 6, 7, 9, 17, 19, 143, 214, 254, 266, 387, 395, 463, 491, 541, 542, 559, 561
Service runtime 560
ServiceInstaller 555
ServiceProcessInstaller 555
Setup 434, 437, 438, 515, 527–31

Setup project 528–30, 541, 542, 555
Signature 42, 62–4, 68, 144, 159, 167, 261, 281
Signatures of a function 63, 64, 167
Simple inheritance 255, 268, 269, 273, 284
Simple Network Management Protocol (SMNP) 518
Sign function 64
Sizeof 3, 18, 50, 143, 294, 296, 309, 372, 388, 432
SnapLines 369
Software framework 3, 4, 17, 18, 370
Solution Explorer 11, 12, 32, 128, 455, 470, 484, 498, 530, 536, 540, 555
Sort 36, 151, 162, 186, 188, 198, 199
  function 336, 346
Sorted list 337
Sorting 169, 178, 186, 200
Source view 469
Specifications 124, 126, 128
Specialization 235, 254, 261
Split View 468, 469
SplitContainer Control 396, 398, 403, 404
SQL Server Express 469, 481
SqlCommand 444, 504, 505
SqlConnection 444, 503, 505, 506
Square root 30, 64, 66, 67, 324
Stack 6, 7, 9, 43, 123–6, 134, 155, 156, 200, 201, 221, 322, 336, 337, 343–5, 348, 560
Static 66, 67, 69–71, 78, 80, 81, 84, 86, 88
State Management 3, 465
Static implementation of queue 126, 127
Static implementation of stack 124, 135
Static members 235, 251
Stream 388–90, 393, 441, 518, 519, 521, 526
String type 41, 49
String class 41, 162–9, 175
StringBuilder 130, 162–4, 171, 172, 175, 177, 519, 520

Structures 76, 78, 123, 134, 212, 213, 216, 217, 219
Student 5, 6, 24, 25, 42, 46–9, 93, 128
Switch statement 17, 76, 92, 98, 103
Switches 514, 525
Synchronization 352, 353, 359, 363
System.Array 178, 198, 200, 201
System.ArrayList 200
System.Collections namespace 7, 123, 125, 127, 134
System.Collection.Queue 127, 135
System.Collection.Stack 125, 135
System.Drawing 382, 385, 393, 410, 417, 424, 429, 445, 453, 457
System.Threading 6, 352–6, 358, 360, 365

TabControl 394, 398, 399, 403, 419
TableLayoutPanel 395, 398–01
TCP 522, 523, 525, 526, 559, 561, 563
TCPClient 519, 521–3
TCPListener 519–21
Test certificate 537, 538, 541
Text Box 109, 369, 370, 373–5, 377, 379–81
this reference 251
Thread pool 352, 360, 363
Thread priority 358, 365
ThreadStart 354, 355, 358
Threshold check 565
Threads 159, 198, 200, 233, 352–4, 358–60
Timer class 352, 353, 355, 356, 363, 365

ToCharArray() 169–71, 175–7, 570, 573
Tool box 11
ToolStrip 398, 399, 412, 413, 416, 418, 419
Transactions 559
Transmission Control Protocol (TCP) 514, 518, 525, 559
Transport layer 514, 518
try-catch 319, 328
Two dimensional (2D) array 190
Type casting 38, 60, 61, 65, 68, 337, 348
Type conversion 5, 38, 44
Truncate function 64

Unary operators 51, 68, 304, 305, 307
  Overloading 305, 315
Unboxing 45, 68
Unmanaged 5, 19, 49, 514, 526
  Code 5, 19, 49, 547
Update 14, 15, 128, 134, 353, 458, 470
User control 463, 472–4, 491, 495, 496
User interface editor 528, 530, 531, 541
User Datagram Protocol (UDP) 518
User defined exceptions 330
User 4, 8, 25, 26, 38–40, 42, 44, 45, 48, 49, 51
User Interface Editor 528, 530, 531, 541, 542

Value 6, 26, 37–41, 43–53, 58–65, 67–9

Value types 6, 39, 40, 45, 48, 68, 72, 221, 228
Variables 18, 38, 39, 40, 42–4, 51, 52, 58, 59, 61, 63, 68
Variable parameters 143, 150, 160
Verbatim string 164, 174, 175
Visibility control 258, 266, 267
Virtual 43, 145, 221, 236, 255, 261, 279, 280, 282, 283, 285, 286
Visual Basic.NET 2, 10, 463, 491
Visual Web developer (VWD) 472

Web controls 374
Web Forms 8, 9, 16, 463, 465, 466, 467, 491
Web pages 8, 16, 17, 419, 420, 466, 469, 472, 490, 491
Web services 9, 10, 14, 463, 466, 491, 492, 543, 549, 550
Wide area network (WAN) 513
Windows application 370, 558, 561
Windows Form 466, 522
Window Communication Foundation 543, 560, 561, 563
Window Presentation Foundation (WPF) 543, 546, 561
Windows service 9, 543, 554, 560
Windows forms 369, 370–372, 374, 382, 385, 393, 395, 404, 411, 417, 424, 429
Window Base.dll 547
Window Codecs.dll 547
WindowState 372
Writing a program 20, 21, 35

XPS 464

Related Titles

Software Testing [9780198061847]

Naresh Chauhan, *Professor & Chairman, Deptt. of Computer Engg, YMCA University of Science & Technology, Faridabad*

Software Testing focuses on software testing as not just being a phase of software development life cycle (SDLC) but a complete process to fulfill the demands of quality software.

Key Features
- Comprises separate chapters on regression testing, software quality assurance, and test maturity model and debugging for better understanding of software testing process
- Covers testing techniques for two specialized environments: object-oriented software and web-based software
- Includes a large number of examples, multiple-choice questions, and unsolved problems for practice

Digital Image Processing
[9780198070788]

S. Sridhar, *Associate Professor, Dept. of Information Technology and Science, College of Engineering Guindy, Anna University, Chennai*

Digital Image Processing is a basic textbook designed to cater to the needs of undergraduate engineering students of computer science, information technology, electronics and communication, and electrical engineering. The book aims to provide an understanding of the principles and processing techniques of digital images.

Key Features
- Adopts algorithmic approach to illustrate image processing
- Provides simple explanations to topics such as Shannon-Fano coding, morphological gradient, polygonal approximations, shape number, and component labelling
- Includes a laboratory manual with simple examples illustrated through MATLAB and augmented through ImageJ, a GUI-based public domain software

In the CD
- MATLAB programs discussed in the lab manual, with representative input and output images
- Select images from Chapters 1, 2, 8, 9, 10, and 12 of the book reproduced in colour
- Additional test images for performing laboratory exercises

Distributed Computing
[9780198093480]

Sunita Mahajan, *Principal, Institute of Computer Science, MET League of Colleges, Mumbai*

Seema Shah, *Acting Principal, Vidyalankar Institute of Technology, Mumbai University*

The second edition of *Distributed Computing* is specially designed for students of computer science engineering, information technology, and computer applications. It provides a clear understanding of the computing aspects of distributed systems.

Key Features
- Includes new topics on API for Internet Protocol in Java and formal model for simulation
- Includes objective and review questions at the end of each chapter, which will help students review the basic concepts discussed
- Contains several relevant case studies including two new case studies on CORBA and Mach

Professional Ethics
[9780198086345]

R. Subramanian, *retired Professor and Head, Civil Engineering Department, National Institute of Technical Teachers Training and Research, Chandigarh*

Professional Ethics is a textbook designed for budding engineers, managers, and other professionals. It will aid them in understanding concepts that will enable them to effectively resolve the ethical issues they will face in their professional lives.

Key Features
- An 'Ethically Speaking' section at the beginning of each chapter with hypothetical situations and questions that require students to think out of the box
- Sample codes of ethics in engineering of organizations such as ASME, ASCE, CSI, NSPE, and IEEE
- A 'What do you think' section at the end of the chapter presents a case related to a recent incident
- A chapter on 'Ethical Living' discussing the basic human needs based on Maslow's and ERG theories

Other Related Titles

9780195686289 Pudi & Radha Krishna: *Data Mining*
9780195699616 Thareja: *Data Warehousing*
9780195692327 Tiwary: *Natural Language Processing and Information Retrieval*
9780198066224 Roy: *Web Technologies*
9780195671544 Padhy: *Artificial Intelligence & Intelligent Systems*